CHEMISTRY:

GENERAL, MEDICAL, AND PHARMACEUTICAL,

INCLUDING

THE CHEMISTRY OF THE U. S. PHARMACOPŒIA.

A MANUAL

ON THE GENERAL PRINCIPLES OF THE SCIENCE, AND THEIR APPLICATIONS TO MEDICINE AND PHARMACY.

BY

JOHN ATTFIELD, PH.D., F.C.S.,

PROFESSOR OF PRACTICAL CHEMISTRY TO THE PHARMACEUTICAL SOCIETY OF GREAT BRITAIN;
FORMERLY DEMONSTRATOR OF CHEMISTRY AT ST. BARTHOLOMEW'S HOSPITAL, LONDON;
HONORARY MEMBER OF THE COLLEGES OF PHARMACY OF PHILADELPHIA,
NEW YORK, AND CHICAGO;
HONORARY CORRESPONDING MEMBER OF THE SOCIETY OF PHARMACY OF PARIS;
HONORARY MEMBER OF THE PHARMACEUTICAL ASSOCIATIONS OF MANCHESTER, SHEFFIELD,
AND LIVERPOOL;
SECRETARY OF THE BRITISH PHARMACEUTICAL CONFERENCE.

FROM THE SECOND AND ENLARGED ENGLISH EDITION.

REVISED BY THE AUTHOR.

PHILADELPHIA:
HENRY C. LEA.
1871.

"But the greatest error of all is, mistaking the ultimate end of knowledge; for some men covet knowledge out of a natural curiosity and inquisitive temper; some to entertain the mind with variety and delight; some for ornament and reputation; some for victory and contention; many for lucre and a livelihood; and but few for employing the Divine gift of reason to the use and benefit of mankind. Thus some appear to seek in knowledge a couch for a searching spirit; others, a walk for a wandering mind; others, a tower of state; others, a fort, or commanding ground; and others, a shop for profit or sale, instead of a storehouse for the glory of the Creator and the endowment of human life."—LORD BACON.

PREFACE.

THIS manual is intended as a systematic exponent of the general truths of Chemistry. It is written solely for the pupils, assistants, and principals engaged in medicine and pharmacy. The volume will be found equally useful as a reading-book for gentlemen having no opportunities of attending lectures or performing experiments, and as a handbook for college pupils; while its comprehensive Index, containing five thousand references, will fit the work for consultation in the course of business or professional practice.

From other text-books it differs in three particulars: first, in the exclusion of matter relating to compounds which at present are only of interest to the scientific chemist; secondly, in containing the chemistry of every substance recognized officially, or in general practice, as a remedial agent; thirdly, in the paragraphs being so cast that the volume may be used as a guide in studying the science experimentally.

The order of subjects is that which, in the author's opinion, best meets the requirements of medical and pharmaceutical students in Great Britain and America. Introductory pages are devoted to a few leading properties of the elements. A review of the facts thus unfolded affords opportunity for stating the views of philosophers respecting the manner in which these elements influence each other. The consideration in detail of the relations of the elementary and compound radicals follows; synthetical and analytical bearings being pointed out, and attention frequently directed to connecting or underlying truths or general principles. The chemistry of substances naturally associated in vegetables and animals is next considered. Practical toxicology and the chemical as well as microscopical characters of morbid urine, urinary sediments, and calculi are then given. The concluding sections form a laboratory-guide to the chemical and physical study of quantitative analysis. The appendix includes a long table of tests for impurities in medicinal preparations; also a short one of the saturating powers of acids and alkalies, designed for use in prescribing and dispensing.

In the course of the treatment outlined in the preceding paragraph, it will be observed that the whole of the elements are first noticed superficially, and that the chemistry of the common metallic radicals precedes that of the rarer; while the sections on the acidulous radicals are similarly divided. The basylous radicals will be found to be arranged according to analytical relations, the common acidulous according to saturating-power or quantivalence, and the rarer acidulous radicals alphabetically. It will be apparent, also, that in certain cases the same classes of facts and principles are brought three or four times under consideration, the points of view, however, differing according as interest is concentrated on physical, synthetical, analytical, or quantitative properties. This arrangement of matter was adopted partly from the belief that the separate and general truths of chemistry never enter the mind in the order of any scientific classification at present possible. In the current state of chemical knowledge consistency in the methodical arrangement even of elements can only be carried out in one direction, and is necessarily accompanied by inconsistencies in other directions, a result most perplexing to learners, and hence totally subversive of the chief advantage of classification. For this reason the writer has preferred to lead up to, rather than follow, scientific classification—has allowed analogies and affinities to suggest, rather than be suggested by, classification.

Among the acidulous radicals, especially, any known system of classification would have given undue prominence to one set of relations and undeserved obscurity to others. Then, by separating more important from less important matter, instruction is adapted to the wants of gentlemen whose opportunities of studying chemistry vary greatly, and are unavoidably insufficient to enable them to gain a thorough knowledge of the science. One great advantage of the mode of treatment is that difficulties of nomenclature, notation, chemical constitution, and even those arising from conventionality of language, are explained as they arise, instead of being massed under the head of "Introductory Chapters," "Preliminary Considerations," or "General Remarks," which are commonly too difficult to be understood by a beginner, and too voluminous to be remembered except by the aid of subsequent lessons.

The chemical notation of the work is in accordance with modern theories. Equations illustrative of pharmacopœial processes have a name attached to each formula.

Chemical nomenclature has been modernized to the extent of defining the alkali-metal and earthy salts as those of potassium, sodium, ammonium, barium, calcium, magnesium, and aluminium, instead of potash, soda, ammonia, baryta, lime, magnesia, and alumina. The author confidently believes that this change, now adopted by all prominent writers on chemistry, will be accepted and become popular with pharmacists, as it is a step in the direction of simplicity and consistency, and involves far less hypothesis than is contained in the old system. The name nitrate of potash, for example, was based on the pure assumption that nitre contained oxide of potassium or potash and nitric anhydride, then erroneously termed acid. By the modern name, nitrate of potassium, all that is intended to be conveyed is that nitre contains the element common to all potassium compounds, and the group of elements common to all nitrates. Under the old method, students always experienced difficulty in distinguishing salts of the metal from salts of its oxide—salts of potassium, for instance, from salts of potash; under the new view no such difficulty arises. Names such as potassium nitrate or potassic nitrate are also consistent with modern views, but for general adoption are too unlike the original. The contractions in Latin for names like "nitrate of potassium" are identical with those names resembling "nitrate of potash;" an accidental circumstance that will much facilitate the general introduction of the former among medical practitioners and pharmacists, and a practical advantage that must determine the choice over the other chemically equivalent names just mentioned. It is not too much to expect that these slight modifications of the old names will be adopted in the next editions of the Pharmacopœias of the United States and Great Britain, and those works thus be made to reflect the present state of chemical science.

The Metric System of Weights and Measures—that which, doubtless, is destined to supersede all others—is alone used in the sections on Quantitative Analysis. In other parts of the manual avoirdupois weights and imperial measures are employed.

It is hoped that the numerous etymological references scattered throughout the following pages will be found useful. Words in Greek have been rendered in English characters, letter for letter.

Students are strongly recommended to test their progress by frequent examination. To this end appropriate questions are appended to each subject.

In response to a call from professional friends in the United States, I have carefully revised the work for the American student, introducing the Chemistry of the Preparations and Materia Medica of the United States Pharmacopœia, and making such other additions and corrections as seemed necessary to present the science in its latest development.

LONDON, December, 1870.

APPARATUS.

List of apparatus suitable for a short course of practical chemistry, including the preparation of elementary gases, analytical reactions of common metals and acidulous radicals, analysis of single salts, chemical toxicology, and the examination of urine, urinary sediments, and calculi:—

One dozen test-tubes.
Test-tube stand.
Test-tube cleaning-brush.
A few pieces of glass tubing, 8 to 16 in. long, with a few inches of India-rubber tubing to fit.
Small flask.
Two small beakers.
Two small funnels.
Two watch-glasses.
Two or three glass rods.
Wash-bottle.
Small pestle and mortar.
A 2-pint basin.
A 2-inch and a 3-inch evap. basin.
Two porcelain crucibles.
Blowpipe.
Crucible-tongs.
Round file.
Triangular file.
Small retort-stand.
Sand-tray.
Wire triangles.
Platinum wire and foil.
Test-papers.
Filter-paper.
Towel.
Two dozen corks.

(*This set can be obtained of any chemical-apparatus maker for about seven dollars.*)

A larger set, suitable for the performance of nearly all the experiments described in this manual:—

A set of evaporating-basins, of the following sizes:—
One 8½-inch. One 4-inch.
One 7¼-inch. Two 3-inch.
One 6½ inch.
One retort-stand and three rings.
Two test-glasses.
One half-pint flask.
One half-quire filter-paper.
Two porcelain crucibles.
One measure-glass, 5 oz.
Blowpipe, 8-inch, Black's.
Two glass funnels.
One dozen test-tubes (German glass).
One test-tube brush.
One pair of 8-inch brass crucible-tongs.
Two soup-plates.
One flat plate.
Two spatula knives.
One pair of scissors.
One round file.
One triangular file.
One half-pound of glass rods.
One half-pound of glass tubing.
One foot of small India-rubber tubing.
Three doz. corks of various sizes.
Platinum wire and foil.
Test-papers.
A nest of three beakers.

(*This set can be obtained of any chemical-apparatus maker for about twelve dollars.*)

A sponge, towels, and note-book may be included.

The following apparatus should be ready to the hand of students following an extended course of practical chemistry, in a room set apart for the purpose:—

A bench or table and stool.
Water-supply and waste-pipe.
A cupboard attached to a chimney with an outward draught.
A furnace fed with coke; tongs, hot-plate or sand-bath, &c.
A waste box.
Shelves for chemicals and other materials in jars or bottles.
Gas-supply and lamp with flexible tube.
Test-tube rack, two dozen holes.
Iron stand or cylinder for supporting large dishes.
Iron adaptors for fitting dishes to cylinder.
Pestle and mortar, 5 or 6 inches.
One 6-inch funnel.
Brown pan, 1 or 2-gallon.
White jug, 1-gallon.
Water-bottle, quart.
Twenty-eight test-bottles, 6-oz.

Other articles, such as flasks, retorts, receivers, condensers, large evaporating-dishes, may be obtained as wanted. In Quantitative Analysis the apparatus described in the sections on that subject will be required.

REAGENTS.

Certain chemicals are used so frequently in analytical processes that it is desirable to have small quantities placed in bottles in front of the operator. As these reagents or "tests" are generally employed in a state of solution, nearly all the solid salts may at once be dissolved in distilled water. The bottles should not be more than about three-quarters full; single drops, if required, can then be poured out with ease and precision. The following list is recommended:—

Sulphuric Acid, strong.
Nitric Acid, strong.
Hydrochloric Acid, strong.
Acetic Acid, strong.
Sol. of Potash, 5 per ct. or U.S.P.
" Soda, 5 to 15 per cent.
" Ammon. 10 p. ct. or U.S.P.
Lime Water, saturated.

The next nine may contain about 10 per cent. of solid salt:—

Carbonate of Ammonium (p. 67).
Chloride of Ammonium.
Oxalate of Ammonium.
Phosphate (p. 68) or Arseniate (p. 130) of Ammonium.
Sulphydrate of Ammon. (p. 68).
Chloride of Barium.
Chloride of Calcium (p. 78).
Phosphate of sodium.
Neutral Chromate (p. 76).

The succeeding six may have a strength of 5 per cent.:—

Ferrocyanide of Potassium.
Ferridcyanide of Potassium.
Iodide of Potassium.
Perchloride of iron (p. 110).
Nitrate of Silver.
Perchloride of Platinum (p. 201).

SOLID SALTS.

Tartaric Acid, in powder.
Copper, in borings or turnings.
Borax, in powder.
Sulphate of Iron, in crystals.

CONTENTS.

CHEMISTRY:

GENERAL, MEDICAL, AND PHARMACEUTICAL.

INTRODUCTION.*

THE numerous solid, liquid, and gaseous substances of which our earth and atmosphere, and, apparently, the sun, moon, and other celestial bodies are composed, may be resolved into sixty-three distinct forms of matter, appropriately termed Elements. Of these elements only a few (such as gold) occur naturally in the uncombined state, the greater number being disguised by a kind of union so close as to conceal them from ordinary methods of observation. Thus none of the common properties of water indicate that it is composed of two elements, both gases, but differing much from each other: nor can the senses of sight, touch, and taste, or other common means of examination, detect in their concealment the three elements of which sugar is composed. The art by which these and all other compound substances are resolved into their elements, is termed Chemistry, derived possibly from the Arabic word *kamai*, to conceal, whence *al kimia*, or alchemy, an art which at the time the name alchemy was given had but little more for its object than the transmutation of the baser metals into gold. The *art* of chemistry also includes the construction of compounds from elements, and the conversion of substances of one character into those of another. The general principles or leading truths relating to the elements, to the manner in which they severally combine, and to the properties of the compound substances formed by their union, constitute the *science* of chemistry.†

* After reading the first three pages, the laboratory-student may commence practical work by preparing oxygen.

† Persons who practise the art and science of Chemistry are known as Chemists, though conventionally the latter name includes those

From these few words concerning the nature of the art and science of chemistry, it will be seen that in most of the occupations that engage the attention of man it plays an important part—in few more so than in the practice of Therapeutics* and Pharmacy.†

Air, water, food, drugs, and chemicals, in short all material substances, are composed of a few elements. An intimate knowledge of the properties of these, and of the various substances they form by combining with each other, a knowledge of the power or force (the chemical force or chemical affinity) by which the elements contained in those compounds are held together, and an application of such knowledge to Pharmacy and Medicine, must be the objects sought to be attained by the learner, for whom this work has been especially written.

The Elements.—Of the sixty-three elements only thirty-nine are of medical or pharmaceutical interest; of these, about two-thirds are metals, and one-third non-metals: the remainder are so seldom met with in nature as to have received no practical application either in medicine, art, or

who simply deal in chemicals. Hence have risen the distinguishing appellations of Analytical, Pharmaceutical, and Manufacturing Chemists. The compounder of medicine is by common consent a chemist only because he is constantly engaged in operations with chemical substances used as remedial agents, his moral right to the name depending on the amount of chemical knowledge he possesses concerning those substances. If he keeps an open shop, he is in Great Britain known as a *Chemist and Druggist*, his higher title being *Pharmaceutical Chemist;* these respective designations he legally assumes on passing the minor and major Examinations, conducted by the Pharmaceutical Society of Great Britain in accordance with the provisions of the Pharmacy Acts of 1852 and 1868. These classes are frequently spoken of collectively as *Pharmacists*, a term also used in the United States.

* Therapeutics (θεραπευτικος *therapeutikos*, from θεραπευω, *therapeuo*, to nurse, serve, or cure) is that branch of medicine which treats of the application of remedies for diseases: it includes dietetics. The therapeutist also takes cognizance of hygiene, that department of medicine which respects the preservation of health.

† Pharmacy (from φάρμακον, *pharmakon*, a drug) is the generic name for the operations of preparing or compounding medicines, whether performed by the Medical Practitioner or by the Chemist and Druggist. It is also sometimes applied, like the corresponding term in Surgery, to the apartment in which the operations are conducted.

manufacture. Before intimately studying the elements,* it is desirable to have some general notions concerning them: such a procedure will also serve to introduce the practical student to his apparatus, and make him better acquainted with the various methods of manipulation.†

Metallic Elements.—With regard to the metallic elements, it may be safely assumed that the reader has sufficient knowledge for present purposes; but little, therefore, need now be said respecting them. He has an idea of the appearance, relative weight, hardness, &c., of such metals as gold, silver, copper, lead, tin, zinc, and iron. If he has not a similar knowledge of mercury, antimony, arsenic, platinum, nickel, aluminium, magnesium, potassium, and sodium, he should commence his studies by seeing and handling specimens of each of these metals.

Non-metallic Elements.‡—With regard to the non-metallic elements, it is here supposed that the student has no general knowledge. He should commence his studies therefore by a series of operations as follows, on eight out of their number.

OXYGEN.

Preparation.—As oxygen is the most abundant element in nature, forming, though in a combined state, about one-half of the whole weight of our globe, it may safely be assumed that this element can readily be obtained in the free condition in a state of purity. In fact, the air itself contains about one-fifth of its bulk of oxygen, though that element cannot be separated sufficiently easily and readily for experimental purposes. It is preferable to apply heat—that force which will often be noticed as antagonistic, so to speak, to chemical union, heat generally separating particles of matter further from

* Possibly some of these bodies may, hereafter, be proved to be *compounds;* at present they cannot be resolved into simpler forms of matter, hence must be considered to be *elements.*

† This allusion to apparatus need not discourage the youngest pupil. With the aid of a few phials, wine-glasses, or other similar vessels always at hand, he may, by studying the following pages, learn the chemical reactions which are constantly occurring in the course of making up medicines, understand the processes by which medicinal preparations are manufactured, and detect adulterations, impurities, or faults of manufacture. Among the substances used in medicine, will be found nearly all the chemicals required. If, in addition, a dozen test-tubes, and a few feet of glass tubing be procured, most of the experiments described may be performed. For lists of apparatus and chemicals see Appendix.

‡ These bodies are sometimes termed *metalloids* (from μέταλλον, *metallon,* a metal, and εἶδος, *eidos,* likeness); but the name is not appropriate, for the non-metallic elements have no likeness to metals.

each other, while chemical attraction tends to bind them closer together: it is better to heat certain compounds containing oxygen; the latter is then evolved in its normal, natural condition of gas. Several substances, when heated, yield oxygen; but, for convenience and economy, the crystalline body known as chlorate of potassium is best fitted for the experiment. The size and form of the vessel in which to heat it will mainly depend on the quantity required; but for the purposes of the student the best is a *test-tube*, an instrument in constant requisition in studying practical chemistry. It is simply a thin tube of glass, a few inches in length, and half or three-quarters of an inch in diameter, closed by fusion at one end. It is made of thin glass, in order that it may be rapidly heated or cooled without risk of fracture.

Process.—Heat chlorate of potassium (say, as much as will lie on a shilling) in a test-tube, by means of a spirit- or gas-flame; gaseous oxygen is quickly evolved. Before applying heat, however, provision should be made for collecting the gas.

Collection of Gases.—Procure a piece of glass tubing about the thickness of a quill pen, and a foot or eighteen inches long, and fit it accurately to the test-tube by means of a cork. (Longer tubes may be neatly cut to any size by smartly drawing the edge of a triangular file across the glass at the required point, then clasping the tube, the scratch being between the hands, and pulling the portions asunder, force being exerted in a *slightly* curved direction so as to open out the crack which the file has commenced.) The tube is fixed in the cork through a round hole made by the aid of a red-hot wire, or, better, a rat-tail file, or, best of all, by one of a set of cork-borers—pieces of brass tubing sharpened at one end and having a flat head at the other. Setting aside the test-tube for a few minutes, proceed to bend the long piece of tubing to the most convenient shape for collecting the gas.

To bend Glass Tubes.—Hold the part of the tube required to be bent in any gas- or spirit-flame (a fish-tail gas-jet answers very well), constantly rotating it, so that about an inch of the glass becomes heated. It will soon be felt to soften, and will now, yielding to the *gentle* pressure of the fingers, assume any required angle. In the present case, the tube should be heated at about four inches from the extremity to which the cork is attached, and bent to an angle of about 90 degrees.

Source of Heat.—The source of heat for the test-tube may be the flame of an ordinary spirit-lamp, or, still better where coal-gas is procurable, a mixture of the latter with air. The simple flame of a common argand gas-burner is preferred by some operators, especially when the usual gas chimney is replaced by a metal one about four or five inches long. If a piece, or cap, of wire gauze be fixed on to the top of the metal chimney, then the unlit gas which issues from the jets of the argand burner become mixed with air inside the chimney, and the mixture, when lit on the outer side of the gauze, burns with a flame as smokeless and as little colored as that of a spirit-lamp. Gas-lamps especially constructed to burn a mixture of coal-gas and air are sold by chemical-apparatus manufacturers.

Collection, etc. (continued).—Fit the cork and bent tube into the test-tube; the apparatus will then be ready for delivering gas at a convenient distance from the heated portion of the arrangement. To collect it, have ready three or four test-tubes filled with water, and inverted in a basin, or other similar vessel, also containing water, taking care to keep the mouths of the tubes a little below the surface. Now apply heat to the chlorate contained in the test-tube, and so arrange the open end of the bent tube under the water that the gas which presently issues may bubble into and gradually fill the inverted test-tubes. The first tubeful may be rejected, as it probably consists of little more than the air originally in the apparatus, and which has been displaced by the oxygen. That which comes afterwards will be pure oxygen.

On the large scale, oxygen may be made in the same way, larger vessels (glass flasks or iron bottles) being employed. Less heat also will be necessary if the chlorate of potassium be previously mixed with very fine sand, or, still better, with about a fourth of its weight of common black oxide of manganese.

Note on the Collection and Storage of Gases.—It may be as well to state that nearly all gases, whether for experimental or practical purposes, are collected and stored in a similar manner. Even coal-gas is generated at gas-works in iron retorts very much the shape of test-tubes, only they are as many feet long as a test-tube is inches; and the well-known gigantic gas-holders may be viewed as inverted iron test-tubes of great diameter.

Properties.—One characteristic of this non-metallic element is invisibility. Again, it obviously is not very soluble in water, or it could not be collected by the aid of that liquid.

Oxygen is soluble to a certain extent, however (about 3 volumes in 100, at common temperatures), or fishes could not breathe.

Other noticeable features are its want of taste and smell. Next, to show the relation of oxygen to combustion, remove one of the tubes from the water by placing the thumb over its mouth, apply for a second a lighted wood match to the orifice; the gas will be found to be incombustible. Extinguish the flame of the match, and then quickly introduce the still incandescent carbonaceous extremity of the wood halfway down the test tube; the wood will at once burst into flame, owing to the extreme violence with which oxygen supports combustion. These tests of the presence of oxygen may also be applied at the extremity of the delivery-tube whilst the gas is being evolved. (It is desirable to retain two tubes of the gas for use in subsequent experiments.)

Relation of Oxygen to Animal and Vegetable Life.—Not only the carbon at the end of a piece of charred wood, but any other substance that will burn in air (which, as will be seen presently, is diluted oxygen) will burn more brilliantly in pure oxygen. The warmth of the body of animals is kept up by the continuous burning of the carbonaceous matter of the blood in the oxygen of the air drawn into the lungs. The product of this combustion is a gaseous compound of carbon and oxygen termed carbonic acid gas, a gas which, in sunlight, is decomposed in the cells of plants with fixation of the carbon and liberation of the oxygen; hence the atmosphere is kept constant in composition.

Memorandum.—At present it is not advisable that the reader should trouble himself with the consideration of the chemical action which occurs either in the elimination of oxygen from its compounds, or in the separation of any of the following non-metallic elements from their combinations. It is to the properties of the elements themselves that he should restrict his attention. Working thus from simple to more complex facts, he will in due time find that the comprehension of such actions as occur in the preparation of these few elements will be easier than if he attempted their full study now.

HYDROGEN.*

Preparation and Collection.—The element of hydrogen is also a gas, and is obtainable from its commonest compound, water (one-ninth of which is hydrogen), by the agency of hot zinc or iron, or by the action of either of those metals on cold diluted sulphuric acid. The appa-

* Within the past year Graham has obtained alloys of hydrogen with palladium and other metals, compounds in which several hundred times its bulk of gas is retained by the metal in vacuo or even at a red heat. This is physical confirmation of the opinion long held by chemists, that hydrogen is a metal. Graham already terms it hydrogenium, and considers its relative weight in the solid state to be nearly three-fourths that of water.

ratus used for making oxygen may be employed for this experiment; but no lamp is required. Place several pieces of thin zinc* in the generating-tube, and cover them with water. The collecting-tubes being ready, add strong sulphuric acid (oil of vitriol) to the zinc and water, in the proportion of about 1 volume of acid to 5 of water, and fit on the delivery-tube; the hydrogen is at once evolved. Having rejected the first portions, collect four or five tubes of the gas in the manner described under Oxygen.

In making larger quantities, bottles may be used instead of test-tubes.

Other metals, notably potassium and sodium, liberate hydrogen the moment they come into contact with water; but the processes are not economical.

Properties.—Like oxygen, hydrogen is invisible, inodorous, and tasteless. If made with iron it has a strong smell, but this is due to impurities contained in the metal. Apply a flame to the mouth of the delivery tube; ignition of the hydrogen ensues, showing that, unlike oxygen, it is combustible. Immerse a lighted match into a tube containing hydrogen; the gas is ignited, but the match becomes extinguished. This shows that hydrogen is not a supporter of combustion. Hydrogen in burning unites with the oxygen of the air and forms water, which may be condensed on a cool glass or other surface. Prove this by holding a glass vessel a few inches above a hydrogen-flame. In burning the hydrogen contained in one of the tubes, the flame is best seen when the tube is held mouth upwards, and water poured in so as to force out the gas gradually. If, instead of this gradual combination of the two elements oxygen and hydrogen, they be mixed together in the right proportions and then ignited, explosion results. Prepare a mixture of this kind by filling up with hydrogen a test-tube from which one-third of the water has been expelled by oxygen. Remove the tube from the water, placing a finger over the mouth, and, having a lighted match ready, apply the flame; a slight explosion

* The best form is *granulated zinc* (*Zincum Granulatum*, B. P.) made by heating scraps of common sheet zinc in a ladle over a fire, and as soon as melted pouring, in a slow stream, into a pail of water from a height of 8 or 10 feet. Each drop of zinc thus yields a thin little bell, which, for its weight, presents a large surface to the action of the acid water. If the zinc is allowed to become hotter than necessary, the little bells will not be formed.

will result, owing to the instantaneous combination of the two elements, and the expansive force of the steam produced.

These two gases thus unite at a temperature considerably above that of boiling-water, two volumes of hydrogen and one of oxygen yielding two volumes of gaseous water (true steam).

The noise of such explosions is caused by concussion between the particles of the gaseous body and those of air.

The force of the explosion, or, in other words, the expansive force of the steam produced, is exceedingly slight, certainly very far below that necessary to break the test-tube. Some force, however, is exerted, and hence the necessity of the precaution previously suggested of allowing all the air which may be in a hydrogen-apparatus to escape before proceeding with the experiments. If a flame be applied to the delivery-tube before all the air is expelled, the probable result will be ignition of the mixture of hydrogen and oxygen (of the air) and consequent explosion. But even in this case the generating-vessel is not often fractured unless it be large and of thin glass, the ordinary effect being that the cork is blown out, and the delivery-tube broken on falling to the ground.

Hydrogen is a prominent constituent of all the substances used for producing artificial light, such as tallow, oil, and coal-gas. The explosive force of large quantities, such as a roomful, of coal-gas and air, though vastly below that of an equal weight of gunpowder, is well known to be sufficient at least to blow out that side of the room which offers least resistance.

The composition of water can be proved analytically as well as synthetically, a current of electricity decomposing it into its constituent gases, twice as much hydrogen as oxygen, by volume, being produced.

Combustion (from *comburo*, to burn).—The experiments with hydrogen and oxygen illustrate the true character of combustion. Whenever chemical combination is sufficiently intense to be accompanied by heat and light, the materials are said to undergo combustion. Combustion only occurs at the line of contact of the combining bodies; a jet of oxygen will burn in an atmosphere of hydrogen quite as easily as a jet of hydrogen in oxygen. A jet of air (diluted oxygen) will burn as readily in a jar of coal-gas as a jet of coal-gas burns in air; each is combustible, each supports the combustion of the other. Hence the terms *combustible* and *supporter of combustion* are purely conventional, and only applicable so long as the circumstances under which they are applied remain the same. In the case of substances burning in air, the conditions are, practically, always the same; hence no confusion arises from regarding air as the great supporter of combustion, and bodies which burn in it as being combustible.

Structure of Flame.—A candle or oil-flame is a jet of gas intensely heated; the central portion consists of unburnt gas, the next envelope is formed of partially burnt and very dense gaseous particles heated sufficiently high to give light, and the outer cone of completely burnt gases. Air made, by any mechanical contrivance of burner, to mix with the interior of a flame at once burns up, or perhaps prevents the formation of dense gases, giving a hotter, but non-luminous, jet. The "Bunsen" gas-burners commonly used in chemical laboratories are constructed on this principle: their flame has the additional advantage of not yielding a deposition of soot.

In the Bunsen gas-burner a mixture of gas and air passes along a pipe. It only burns at the end, and not within the pipe, because the metal of the burner, by conducting heat away, cools the mixture below the temperature at which it can ignite. The *Davy safety-lamp* acts on the same principle: a wire-gauze cage surrounds an oil-flame; an inflammable mixture of gas (fire-damp) and air can pass through the gauze and catch fire and burn inside; but the flame cannot be communicated to the mixture outside, because the metal of the gauze cools down the gas below the temperature at which it can burn.

Properties (continued).—Hydrogen is the lightest substance known. It was formerly used for filling balloons, but was soon superseded by coal-gas. Coal-gas is not so light as hydrogen, but is cheaper and more easily obtained. The lightness of hydrogen may be rendered evident by the following experiment: Fill two test-tubes with the gas, and hold one with its mouth downwards and the other with its mouth upwards. The hydrogen will have escaped from the latter in a few seconds, whereas the former will still contain the gas after the lapse of some minutes. This may be proved by applying a lighted match to the mouths of the respective tubes.

The relative weight or specific gravity of oxygen is sixteen times that of hydrogen. A tube holding one grain of hydrogen will hold sixteen grains of oxygen. The relation of the weight of hydrogen to air is as 0.0693 to 1.0.

Mem.—It is desirable to retain two tubes of hydrogen for use in subsequent experiments.

Diffusion of Gases.—Hydrogen cannot be kept in such vessels as the inverted test-tube; for, though much lighter than air, it *diffuses* downwards into the air, while the air, though much heavier, diffuses upwards into the hydrogen. This power of *diffusion* is characteristic of all gases, and proceeds according to a fixed law, namely, "in inverse proportion to the square root of the specific gravity of the gas" (Graham). Thus hydrogen diffuses four times faster than oxygen.

PHOSPHORUS.

Appearance and Source.—Phosphorus (*Phosphorus*, B. P. and U. S. P.) is a solid element, in appearance and consistence resembling white wax; but it gradually becomes yellow by exposure to light. It is a characteristic constituent of bones, and is always prepared from that source by a process which will be subsequently described.

Caution.—Phosphorus takes fire very readily, and should therefore be kept under water. When wanted for use it must be cut under water. It is employed in tipping lucifers, though *red* or *amorphous phosphorus* (*vide* Index) is least objectionable for this purpose.

Properties.—Dry a piece about one-fourth the size of a pea by quickly and carefully pressing it between the folds of porous (filter or blotting) paper; place it on a plate, and ignite by touching it with a piece of warm wire or wood. Observe that the product of combustion is a dense white smoke, which must be confined at once by placing an inverted tumbler, test-glass, or other similar vessel over the phosphorus. The fumes rapidly aggregate, and fall in white flakes on the plate. When this has taken place, and the phosphorus is no longer burning, moisten the powder with a few drops of water, and observe that some of the water is converted into steam, an effect due to the intense affinity with which the two combine.

The powder produced by the combustion of phosphorus is phosphoric anhydride; the combination of the latter with the elements of water produces phosphoric acid, which dissolves in the water, forming a dilute solution of phosphoric acid. The Diluted Phosphoric Acid of the British and United States Pharmacopœias is a somewhat similar solution, made, however, in a different way, and of a definite strength.

NITROGEN.

Source.—The chief source of this gaseous element is the atmosphere, nearly four-fifths of which consists of nitrogen (the remaining fifth being almost entirely oxygen).

Preparation.—Burn a piece of dried phosphorus, the size of a pea, in a confined portion of air. The oxygen is thus removed, and nitrogen alone remains. The readiest mode of performing this experiment is to fix a piece of earthenware (the lid of a small porcelain crucible answers very well) on a piece of cork, so that it may float in a dish of water. Place the phosphorus on the lid, ignite by a warm rod, and then invert a tumbler, or any glass vessel of about a half-pint capacity, over the burning phosphorus, so that the mouth of the glass may dip into the water. Let the arrangement rest for a short time for the fumes of phosphoric anhydride to subside and dissolve in the water, and then decant the gas into test-tubes in the manner already indicated.

Larger quantities are made in the same way. Other combustibles, such as sulphur or a candle, might be used to burn out the oxygen from a given quantity of air, but none answer so quickly and completely as phosphorus; added to which, the product of their combustion would not always be dissolved by water, but would remain with and contaminate the nitrogen.

Mem.—The statement concerning the composition of the air is roughly confirmed in preparing nitrogen, about one-fifth of the volume of the air originally in the glass vessel having disappeared, its place being occupied by water from the dish.

Properties.—Like oxygen and hydrogen, nitrogen is invisible, tasteless, and inodorous. It is only slightly soluble in water. It is distinguished from all other gases by the absence of any characteristic or positive properties. Apply a flame to some contained in a tube; it will be found to be incombustible. Immerse a lighted match in the gas; the flame is extinguished, showing that nitrogen is a non-supporter of combustion.

The chief office of nitrogen in the air is to dilute the energetic oxygen, a mere *mechanical* mixture resulting. The *chemical* compounds of nitrogen and oxygen are numerous (*vide* Index). The compound formed by the union of nitrogen with hydrogen is gaseous ammonia.

Nitrogen is fourteen times as heavy as hydrogen.

The air is nearly fourteen and a half (14.44) times as heavy as hydrogen. Its average composition, including minor constituents, which will be referred to subsequently, is as follows:—

Composition of the Atmosphere.

	In 100 volumes.
Oxygen	20.61
Nitrogen	77.95
Carbonic acid gas	.04
Aqueous vapor	1.40
Nitric acid	traces.
Ammonia	traces.
Carburetted hydrogen	traces.
Sulphuretted hydrogen	traces in towns.
Sulphurous acid	traces in towns.

The above proportions are by volume. By weight there will be nearly 23 parts of oxygen to nearly 77 of nitrogen, oxygen being the heavier in the ratio of 16 to 14. Ozone (*vide* Index) is also said to be a normal constituent of air.

CHLORINE.

Source.—This element is a gas. Its chief source is common salt, more than half of which is chlorine.

Preparation.—About a quarter of an ounce of salt and the same amount of black oxide of manganese are placed in a test-tube with sufficient water to cover them; on adding a small quantity of sulphuric acid, the evolution of chlorine commences.

As the action of the sulphuric acid on the salt in the above process is mainly to give hydrochloric acid, the latter acid and the black oxide of manganese may be used in making the gas, instead of salt, sulphuric acid, and black oxide of manganese. This is the process of the British and United States Pharmacopœias.

Larger quantities may be made from hydrochloric acid and black oxide of manganese (about 4 parts to 1) in a Florence flask, fitted with a delivery-tube, the flask being supported over a flame by the ring of a retort-stand or any similar mechanical contrivance.

Mem.—Flasks and similar glass vessels are less liable to fracture if protected from the direct action of the flame by being placed on a piece of wire gauze 2 to 4 inches square, or on a *sand-bath*, that is, a saucer-shaped tray of sheet iron, on which a thin layer of sand is placed.

Collection and Properties.—Chlorine is a most suffocating gas. Great care must consequently be observed in experimenting with this element. As soon as its penetrating odor indicates that it is escaping from the test-tube, the cork and delivery-tube should be fitted on, and the gas allowed to pass to the bottom of another test-tube half filled with water. When thirty or forty small bubbles have passed, their evolution being assisted by slightly heating the generating-tube, the latter should be removed to the cupboard usually provided in laboratories for performing operations with noxious gases, or dismounted, and the contents washed away. The water in the collecting-tube will now be found to smell of the gas, chlorine being, in fact, soluble in about half its bulk of water. Chlorine-water is official* in the British and United

* The Pharmacopœia and all in it are official (*office*, Fr. from L. *officium*, an office). There are many things which in pharmacy are officinal. (Fr. from L. *officina*, a shop) but not official. To restrict the word *officinal*, first, to the contents of a pharmacist's shop, and, second, to that portion of the contents which is Pharmacopœial, is radically wrong, and should be avoided.

States Pharmacopœias (*Liquor Chlori*, B. P., *Aqua Chlorinii*, U. S. P.).

The *Vapor Chlori*, B. P., or Inhalation of Chlorine, is simply moist chlorinated lime so placed that some of the chlorine given off may be inhaled.

During these manipulations the operator will have noticed that chlorine is of a light green color. That tint is readily observed when the gas is collected in large vessels. As it is soluble in water ($2\frac{1}{3}$ vols. in 1 vol. at 60° F.), it cannot be economically stored over that liquid. Being, however, nearly twice and a half as heavy as air, it may be collected by simply allowing the delivery-tube to pass to the bottom of the test-tube or dry bottle.

The distinctive property of chlorine is its bleaching-power. Prepare some colored liquid by placing a few chips of logwood or other dyeing material in a test-tube half full of hot water. Pour off some of this red decoction into another tube, add a few drops of the chlorine-water, and note how rapidly the color is destroyed.

Chlorine readily decomposes noxious gases, and hence is one of the most powerful of the *deodorizers*. Used in excess it arrests and prevents putrefaction, hence it is one of the best of *disinfectants*.

Combination of Hydrogen with Chlorine, forming Hydrochloric Acid.—If an opportunity occurs of generating the gas in a closed chamber or in the open air, a test-tube of the same size as one of those in which hydrogen has been retained from a previous operation, is filled with the gas. The hydrogen-tube is then inverted over that containing the chlorine, the mouths being kept together by encircling them with a finger. After the gases have mixed, the mouths of the tubes are quickly in succession brought near a flame, when explosion occurs, and fumes of hydrochloric acid gas are formed. The hydrochloric acid of pharmacy (*Acidum Hydrochloricum*, B. P., *Acidum Muriaticum*, U. S. P.) is a solution of this gas (made in a more economical way) in water.

The foregoing experiment affords evidence of the powerful affinity of chlorine and hydrogen for each other. Chlorine dissolved in water will, in sunlight, slowly remove hydrogen from some of the water and liberate oxygen. The bleaching-power of chlorine is generally referred to this indirect oxidizing effect it produces in presence of water; for dry chlorine does not bleach.

Density.—Chlorine is thirty-five and a half times as heavy as hydrogen.

SULPHUR, CARBON, IODINE.

The physical properties of those elements are probably familiar. Their leading chemical characters will also be understood when a few facts concerning each are made the subject of experiment.

SULPHUR.—Burn a small piece of sulphur; a penetrating odor is produced, due to the formation of a colorless gas, the same as that formed on igniting a common sulphur-tipped lucifer match.

This product is a perfectly definite chemical compound of the oxygen of the air with the sulphur. It is termed sulphurous acid gas.

Carbon is familiar in the forms of soot, coke, charcoal, graphite (plumbago, wrongly termed blacklead), and diamond. The presence of carbon in wood, and in other vegetable and animal matter, is at once rendered evident by heat. Place a little tartaric acid on the end of a knife in a flame; the blackening that occurs is due to the separation of carbon. The black matter at the extremity of a piece of half-burned wood is also carbon.

Carbon, like hydrogen, phosphorus, and sulphur, has a great affinity for oxygen at high temperatures. A striking evidence of that affinity is the evolution of sufficient heat to make the materials concerned red or even white-hot. When ignited in the dilute oxygen of the air, carbon simply burns with a moderate glow, as seen in an ordinary coke or charcoal fire, but when ignited in pure oxygen, the intensity of its combination is greatly exalted. The product of the combination of the two elements, if the oxygen be in excess, is an invisible gaseous body termed carbonic acid gas; if the carbon be in excess, another invisible gas termed carbonic oxide results.

IODINE.—The main chemical characteristic of iodine is its great affinity for metals. Place a piece of iodine, about the size of a pea, in a test-tube with a small quantity of water, and add a few iron-filings or small nails. On gently warming this *mechanical* mixture, or even shaking if longer time be allowed, the color and odor of the iodine disappear; it has *chemically* combined with the iron; a *chemical compound* has been produced. If the solution be filtered, a clear aqueous solution of the compound of the two elements is obtained.

This compound is an iodide of iron. Its solution, made as above, and mixed with sugar, forms, when of a certain strength, the ordinary Syrup of Iodide of Iron of pharmacy (*Syrupus Ferri Iodidi*, B. P.

and U. S. P.). A strong solution mixed with sugar and liquorice-root (sugar, marshmallow, gum Arabic, and reduced iron, U. S. P.) constitutes the corresponding Pill (*Pilula Ferri Iodidi*, B. P. and U. S. P.). The solid iodide (*Ferri Iodidum*, B. P.) is obtained on removing the water of the above solution by evaporation.

THE ELEMENTS, THEIR SYMBOLS, ETC.

From the foregoing statements a general idea will have been obtained of the nature of several of the more frequently occurring elements. Some additional facts concerning them may be gathered from the following Table, which gives the name in full, the symbol (or short-hand character*) of the name, and its origin.

For the purposes of study the elements may be divided into three classes, viz., those frequently used in pharmacy, those seldom, and those never used.

Name.	Symbol.	Derivation of name.
Oxygen.............	O	From ὀξὺς (oxūs) *acid*, and γένεσις (genesis) *generation*, i. e., generator of acids. It was supposed to enter into the composition of all acids when first discovered.
Hydrogen..........	H	From ὕδωρ (hudōr) *water*, and γένεσις (genesis) *generation*, in allusion to the product of its combustion in air.
Nitrogen...........	N	From νίτρον (nitron), and γένεσις (genesis), *generator of nitre.*
Carbon.............	C	From *carbo*, *coal*, which is chiefly carbon.
Chlorine...........	Cl	From χλωρὸς (chlōros) *green*, the color of this element.
Iodine..............	I	From ἴον (ion) *a violet*, and εἶδος (eidos) *likeness*, in reference to the color of its vapor.
Sulphur...........	S	From *sal* a *salt*, and πῦρ (pūr) *fire*, indicating its combustible qualities. Its common name, *brimstone*, has the same meaning, being the slightly altered Saxon word *brynstone*, i. e., burnstone.
Phosphorus.......	P	φῶς (phōs) *light*, and φέρειν (pherein) *to bear*. The light it emits may be seen on exposing it in a dark room.
Potassium........ (Kalium.)	K	*Kalium*, from *kali*, Arabic for *ashes*. Manufactories in which certain compounds of potassium and allied sodium salts are made are called alkali-works to this day. *Potassium*, from *pot-ash;* so called because obtained by evaporating the lixivium of wood-ashes in pots. From such ashes the element was first obtained, hence the name.

* The symbol is also much more than the short-hand character, as will be presently apparent.

Name.	Symbol.	Derivation of name.
Sodium............ (Natrium.)	Na	*Natrium*, from *natron*, the old name for certain natural deposits of carbonate of sodium. *Sodium*, from *soda-ash* or *sod-ash*, the residue of the combustion of masses or *sods* of marine plants. These were the sources of the metal.
Ammonium	Am (NH_4)	This body is not an element; but its components exist in all ammoniacal salts, and apparently play the part of such elements as potassium and sodium. Sal ammoniac (chloride of ammonium) was first obtained from near the temple of Jupiter Ammon in Libya; hence the name.
Barium............	Ba	From βαρὺς (barūs) *heavy*, in allusion to the high specific gravity of "heavy spar," the most common of the barium minerals.
Calcium............	Ca	*Calx*, *lime*, the oxide of calcium.
Magnesium	Mg	From *Magnesia*, the name of the town (in Asia Minor) near which the substance now called "native carbonate of magnesia" was first discovered.
Iron .... (Ferrum.)	Fe	The spelling is from the Saxon *iren*, the pronunciation probably from the kindred Gothic "*iarn;*" the derivation is unknown to the author.
Aluminium.......	Al	The metallic basis of alum was at first confounded with that of sulphate of iron, which was the alum of the Romans, and was so called in allusion to its tonic properties, from *alo*, *to nourish*.
Zinc	Zn	The derivation of this word is unknown to the author.
Arsenicum........	As	Ἀρσενικὸν (arsenikon), the Greek name for orpiment, a sulphide of arsenicum. Common white arsenic is an oxide of arsenicum.
Antimony......... (Stibium.).....	Sb	Στίβι (stibi), or στίμμι (stimmi) was the Greek name for the native sulphide of antimony. The word *antimony* is said to be derived from ἀντὶ (anti) *against*, and *moine*, French for *monk*, from the fact that certain monks were poisoned by it.
Copper............ (Cuprum)......	Cu	From *Cyprus*, the name of the Mediterranean island where this metal was first worked.
Lead............... (Plumbum.)	Pb	The Latin word is expressive of "something heavy," and the Saxon *læd* has a similar signification.

Name.	Symbol.	Derivation of name.
Mercury............ (Hydrargyrum.)	Hg	*Hydrargyrum*, from ὕδωρ (hudōr) *water*, and ἄργυρος (arguros) *silver*, in allusion to its liquid and lustrous characters. *Mercury*, after the messenger of the gods, on account of its susceptibility of motion. The old name *quicksilver* also indicates its ready mobility and argentine appearance.
Silver .... (Argentum.)	Ag	Ἄργυρος (arguros) *silver*, from ἀργὸς (argos) *white*. Words resembling the term *silver* occur in several languages, and indicate a white appearance.

The following are names of some of the less frequently occurring elements, compounds of which, however, are alluded to in the British and U. S. Pharmacopœias, or met with in pharmacy.

Name.	Symbol.	Derivation of name.
Bromine	Br	From βρῶμος (brōmos), a *stink*. It has an intolerable odor.
Fluorine	Fl	Fluo *to flow*. Fluoride of calcium, its source, is commonly used as a flux in metallurgic operations.
Boron	Bo	From *borak* or *baurak*, the Arabic name of *borax*, the substance from which the element was first obtained.
Silicon..............	Si	From *silex*, Latin for *flint*, which is nearly all silica (an oxide of silicon).
Lithium............	L	From λίθειος (litheios) *stony*, in allusion to its supposed existence in the mineral kingdom only.
Strontium	Sr	This name is commemorative of *Strontian*, a mining village in Argyleshire, Scotland, in the neighborhood of which the mineral known as *strontianite* or carbonate of strontium was first found.
Cerium	Ce	Discovered in 1803, and named after the planet *Ceres*, which was discovered on Jan. 1, 1801. The oxalate, $CeC_2O_4,3H_2O$, is official, but seldom used.

Name.	Symbol.	Derivation of name.
Chromium........	Cr	From χρῶμα (chrōma) *color*, in allusion to the characteristic appearance of its salts.
Manganese........	Mn	Probably a mere transposition and repetition of most of the letters of the word magnesia, with whose compounds those of manganese were confounded till the year 1740.
Cobalt..............	Co	*Cobalus* or *Kobold* was the name of a demon supposed to inhabit the mines of Germany. The ores of cobalt were formerly troublesome to the German miners, and hence received the name their metallic radical now bears.
Nickel..............	Ni	*Nickel*, from *nil*, is a popular German term for *worthless*. The mineral now known as nickel ore was formerly called by the Germans *Kupfernickel*, *false copper*, on account of its resemblance to copper (*Kupfer*) ore. When a new metallic element was found in the ore, the name nickel was retained.
Tin (Stannum)..	Sn	Both words are possibly corruptions of the old British word *staen*, or the Saxon word *stan*, a stone. Tin was first discovered in Cornwall, and the ore (an oxide) is called *tinstone* to the present day.
Gold (Aurum)...	Au	*Aurum* (Latin) from a Hebrew word signifying the color of fire. *Gold*, an old Saxon word expressive of *yellow*, the color of this metal.
Platinum..........	Pt	From *platina* (Spanish), diminutive of *plata*, *silver*, in allusion to its inferiority in lustre, but otherwise general resemblance to silver.
Bismuth...........	Bi	Slightly altered from the German *Wismuth*, derived from *Wiesematte* "a beautiful meadow," a name given to it originally by the old miners in allusion to the prettily variegated tints presented by the freshly exposed surface of this crystalline metal.
Cadmium..........	Ca	Καδμεία (Kadmeia) was the ancient name of calamine (carbonate of zinc), with which carbonate of cadmium was long confounded, the two often occurring together.

Gold, Platinum, Tin, and Silicon are here classed with the less important elements, because their compounds are seldom used in pharmacy.

It will be noticed that the symbol of an element is simply the first letter of its Latin name, which is generally the same as in the English. Where two names begin with the same letter, the less important has an additional letter added.

QUESTIONS AND EXERCISES.

1. Of how many elements is terrestrial matter composed?
2. In what state do the elements occur in nature?
3. State the difference between the *art* and the *science* of chemistry.
4. What is the difference between an element and a compound?
5. Enumerate the chief non-metallic elements.
6. Describe a process for the preparation of oxygen.
7. How are gases usually stored?
8. Mention the chief properties of oxygen.
9. What is the source of animal warmth?
10. State the proportion of oxygen in air.
11. Is the proportion constant, and why?
12. Give a method for the elimination of hydrogen from water.
13. State the properties of hydrogen.
14. Why is a mixture of hydrogen and air explosive?
15. Explain the effects producible by the ignition of large quantities of coal-gas and air.
16. What is the nature of combustion?
17. Give the conventional meanings of the terms *combustible* and *supporter of combustion.*
18. Describe the structure of flame.
19. State the principle of the Davy safety-lamp.
20. To what extent is hydrogen lighter than oxygen?
21. What do you mean by *diffusion* of gases?
22. State Graham's law concerning diffusion.
23. Name the source of phosphorus, and describe its appearance.
24. Why does phosphorus burn in air?
25. What remains when ignited phosphorus has removed all the oxygen from a confined portion of air?
26. Mention the properties of nitrogen.
27. What office is fulfilled by the nitrogen of air?
28. State the centesimal proportions of the chief constituents of air, by volume.
29. Mention the minor or occasional constituents of air.
30. What is the proportion by weight of nitrogen to oxygen in the atmosphere?
31. Give the specific gravity of nitrogen.
32. How is chlorine prepared?
33. Enumerate the properties of chlorine.
34. Define the terms *deodorizer* and *disinfectant.*
35. Explain the bleaching effect of chlorine.
36. What proportion of hydrogen to chlorine is necessary for the formation of hydrochloric acid gas?
37. State the prominent characters of sulphur.
38. State the prominent characters of carbon.

39. State the prominent characters of iodine.
40. Give the derivations of the names of some of the elements.
41. What are the symbols of oxygen, hydrogen, nitrogen, carbon, chlorine, iodine, sulphur, phosphorus?

THE GENERAL PRINCIPLES OF CHEMICAL PHILOSOPHY.

The learner may now proceed to study the manner in which substances react chemically with each other.

That this tendency to act, when the bodies are brought into contact under favorable circumstances, exists, is obvious from the preceding experiments, and indeed from the operations of every-day life. In a common fire, coal needs only to have its temperature slightly raised to afford it an opportunity of showing the liking or affinity which it and the oxygen of the air have for each other. The evolution of heat in this instance is only one of the incidents of the action. The presence of chimneys and the means of ventilation are adjuncts to a fire, which should at once suggest that there are still more deeply hidden incidents of the mutual action of coal and air. Such a formation of complex bodies from simple ones, and the resolution of complex into simple bodies, is constantly occurring in nature. From the air and the earth vegetables construct complex matters, which are resolved into their original simple forms after having served as food for animals. To discover and remember the laws which govern these transformations, the general student of Chemistry educes elements from compounds, and builds up compounds from elements—the student of Pharmaceutical Chemistry restricting his attention to those with which he is more immediately concerned.

This tendency to combination being a prominent feature in everything material, the mind naturally assumes the existence of some sort of power or energy in matter by which its particles are bound together, a sort of force or affinity which only needs opportunity to manifest itself. In order to distinguish this force from those of gravitation, heat, light, electricity, and magnetism, it is called chemical force or chemical affinity. It is a peculiar and distinctive function of the chemical force that it confers on bodies joined by its means properties entirely different from their constituents: for example, a mere mixture of hydrogen and oxygen has all the characters, or the mean of the characters, of those gases, but a chemical combination of hydrogen and oxygen (water) has the qualities of neither element, but fresh properties altogether.

Chemical Force.

Having thus acquired a knowledge of certain facts concerning each element, the experiments already performed may be reviewed in order to obtain a clear idea of the manner in which chemical substances are believed by philosophers to unite, or influence each other, and to learn how memoranda concerning those actions are best recorded on paper and in the mind.

The student must look upon every particle of matter, solid, liquid, or gaseous, as being absolutely *indestructible*, and as being the seat of a certain amount of a peculiar attractive energy or force, commonly termed chemical affinity. This affinity is so natural that probably separate or single particles cannot exist alone for an instant, and, if liberated from their combinations, immediately reunite in pairs or groups. Apparently the natural affinity of any particle is for a particle of another element, but, if the latter is not at hand, the particle instantly combines with a particle of the same element as itself; hence, doubtless, the greater frequency in nature of compounds (wood, stone, water, etc.) than of elements (hydrogen, sulphur, gold, etc.*). The exertion of chemical affinity (the force or power by which this indestructible matter suffers change of form or condition) is only possible when the substances in question are in close contact. Thus, it was necessary to bring the oxygen, hydrogen, phosphorus, chlorine, sulphur, carbon, iodine, and iron into intimate

* The grounds for the statement that elements never exist in single particles, but that, if the particle (the most minute volume imaginable) of an element has not the opportunity of combining with a particle of another element, it will combine with another particle of like nature to itself, are shortly as follows: Equal volumes of elementary or compound gases, under similar pressure, expand equally when heated, and contract equally when cooled; equal volumes must, therefore, be similarly constituted, must contain an equal number of molecules (the diminutive of mole or mass—literally, little masses), all of the same size. For example, in a previous experiment (p. 25) a test-tubeful of chlorine gas and one of hydrogen gave on mixture and explosion two test-tubefuls of hydrochloric acid gas. Now it could be easily demonstrated that these three gases expand equally on the addition of heat, and contract equally on its abstraction. Hence the inference that the number and size of the molecules of each volume are similar. We have no conception of the actual number of molecules of a gas that a test-tube, or any other vessel, is capable of containing; but whatever it be, that number is constant for all gases. Imagine that it is 1000; then 1000 of hydrogen and 1000 of chlorine have given 2000 of hydrochloric acid. But each of these 2000 molecules of hydrochloric acid contains a particle of hydrogen and a particle of chlorine. Therefore the 1000 *molecules* of hydrogen must have contained 2000 *particles*, and the 1000 molecules of chlorine, 2000 particles of chlorine. In other words, every molecule of an elementary gas consists of two particles, or, as they will be termed on a subsequent page, atoms (ἄτομος, indivisible, from the privative α, *a*, and τέμνω, *temno*, to cut). See also Hofmann's 'Modern Chemistry,' pp. 136–162.)

Additional evidence of the existence of molecules of elements is found in the fact that at the moment certain elements are liberated from their combination, they are far more active than afterwards, when the atoms have probably united to form molecules. This highly active condition is often spoken of as the *nascent* state.

contact before reaction occurred. The exact nature of these actions, as indeed of all in which substances act chemically (*i.e.*, with obvious alteration of properties in the product), would seem to be an interchange, most generally a mutual one, of the particles of which the bodies consist.

Chemical Force and Chemical Notation.

As an example of chemical action and the best and simplest way of expressing it by notation, take the experiment in which two volumes of hydrogen and one of oxygen were caused to combine. The production of flame and noise proved that chemical action of some kind had taken place; had the experiment been performed in dry vessels, evidence of the precise action would have been found in the bedewment or moisture produced by the condensation of the water on the sides of the tube. Similar evidence was afforded on holding a cool glass surface over the hydrogen-flame. The action is expressed in the following way, the symbols or short-hand characters previously referred to (p. 27) being now invested with a second function, namely, that of indicating quantity by measure or volume; single letters indicate single and equal volumes of the respective gaseous elements.

$$H_2 + O = H_2O.$$

Or more correctly, because exhibiting the natural occurrence of *pairs* of particles,

$$2H_2 + O_2 = 2H_2O.$$

Here the symbol H_2 and O, or rather $2H_2$ and O_2, standing alone indicate the state of things prior to the experiment: in juxtaposition thus, H_2O, they indicate the result. Two molecules of hydrogen ($2H_2$) and one of oxygen (O_2) give two of water ($2H_2O$).

A small figure multiplies symbols only, a large figure multiplies any symbols, small figures, or formulæ before which it may be placed. H is a *symbol*, H_2O is a *formula*.

The sign *plus* (+) between the symbols H_2 and O indicates that the one element is simply mixed with or added to the other.

The sign (=), or *equal*, has the usual signification given to it in arithmetic.

Instead of an equation, a diagram may be employed for expressing the above and similar actions on paper. Thus:—

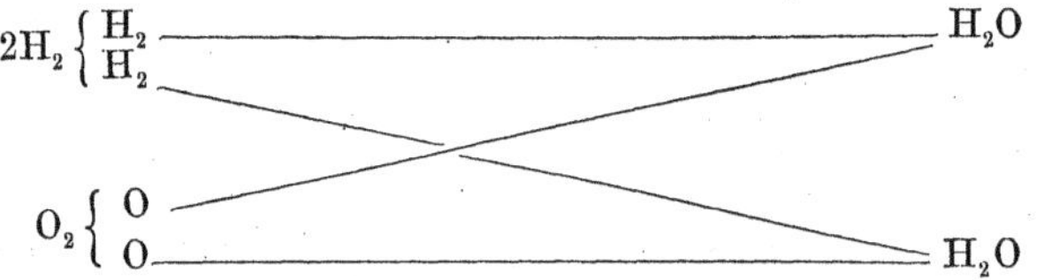

Here lines indicate the paths taken by the respective substances.

The foregoing aggregation of symbols or short-hand characters, viz., H_2O, is, then, a convenient picture of the facts that have already come before us, viz., that water is formed of the elements hydrogen,

H, and oxygen, O, and, moreover, that it is formed of two measures or volumes of hydrogen, H_2, and one of oxygen, O.* These symbols so arranged have a deeper signification still, as will soon be apparent.

Another experiment already performed, illustrating the character of the manifestations of chemical force and its symbolic expression, was that in which the red-hot carbon of wood was plunged into oxygen. The evidence of chemical action in that case was the sudden inflammation of the carbonaceous extremity of the wood. The particles of carbon and oxygen having intense attraction or affinity for each other at that temperature, rushed together so impetuously as suddenly to produce a large additional quantity of heat, an amount sufficient to cause the particles to emit an intense white light. Here it may be again remarked that this attraction, distinguished from all others by the term chemical, is *the only form of attraction by which the properties of the product are rendered totally different from those of its constituents.* The action between carbon and oxygen is expressed on paper in either of the following ways:—

$$C_2 + 2O_2 = 2CO_2.$$

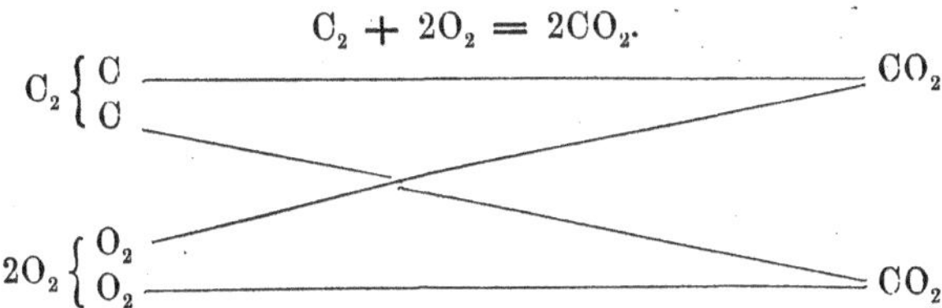

CO_2† is the formula of the well-known gaseous body commonly termed carbonic acid gas.

The reader should here draw for himself similar equations or diagrams, showing the formation of the four other bodies produced—namely, hydrochloric acid (HCl), phosphoric anhydride (P_2O_5), sulphurous acid gas (SO_2), and iodide of iron (FeI_2), submitting the same, if possible, to a tutor or other authority to assure himself of their correctness.

Note.—In the foregoing experiments several illustrations occur of the formations of compounds having the gaseous, liquid, and solid conditions, in one of which three forms all matter in the universe exists.

* Further, the formula H_2O represents two volumes of water in the state of gas; indeed all such formulæ represent *two* gaseous volumes of the respective vaporizable compounds. This subject will be again alluded to in connection with the specific gravity of gases.

† The formula CO_2 indicates that two volumes of carbonic acid gas contain one volume of carbon gas and two volumes oxygen gas, the three volumes being condensed to two. But we have only indirect evidence of the relation of the volume of carbon gas to oxygen gas in carbonic acid gas, free carbon never having been obtained in the gaseous condition; still, the evidence, though indirect, is sufficiently good to warrant chemists in according to these single letters or short-hand characters the function of representing equal gaseous volumes of elements at any given temperature.

Laws of Chemical Combination and the Atomic Theory.

Chemistry, as a science, is little more than one hundred years old. Very many of the facts and operations we now term chemical have been known as isolated items of knowledge for centuries. The ancient Egyptians made glass, vitriol, soap, and vinegar; and the Greeks started the idea that matter was composed of elements (earth, air, fire, and water). But the great general principles which interlace and bind together separate facts, those which, from their extensive application and importance, are denominated *laws*, have all been brought to light since the year 1770. Between 1785 and 1800, Bryan Higgins, William Higgins, Richter, and Proust, traced with more or less accuracy the following truths:—

1st. A definite compound always contains the same elements in the same proportions (by weight as well as by volume)—the law of Constant Proportions.

2d. Two elements uniting in more than one proportion (either by weight or volume) do so in simple multiples—the law of Multiple Proportions.

3d. The proportions (weight or volume) in which two different bodies unite with a third are the proportions in which they unite with each other—the law of Reciprocal Proportions.

In 1803–8 Dalton offered an explanation of these laws, gave a probable reason why they should be as stated, and indeed was the first to set them forth in a clear and definite manner.

Dalton suggested that matter was not infinitely divisible, but composed of minute particles or atoms having an invariable character. This hypothesis ("atomic theory," as it is generally termed) being accepted, the comprehension of the three laws becomes extremely simple. A compound (water, for example,) being invariably composed of invariable atoms, it follows that it itself must be invariable. One atom of a given element, *a*, and groups of two or more atoms of the same element, each atom invariable in weight, uniting with a single invariable atom of another element, *b*, and forming one, two, or more distinct compounds (*e.g.*, carbonic oxide gas, 12 parts carbon and 16 oxygen; and carbonic acid gas, 12 parts carbon and 32 oxygen), it follows that these compounds will contain a common proportion of one element, *b*, and simple multiple proportions of the other, *a*. Single atoms of different elements, *a*, *b*, *c*, uniting consecutively with a single atom of any common element, *d*, (*ad*, *bd*, *cd*,) and being capable of union amongst themselves, it follows that resulting compounds, *ab*, *ac*, *bc*, will contain proportions of each constituent, *a*, *b*, *c*, identical with the proportions in which those constituents united with the common element, *d*. Since Dalton's time the tendency of speculation has been towards the unity of matter—the identity of all elements; to regard the so-called *atoms* of different elements as being composed of identical *ultimates* in a state of vibration, the rate of vibration of groups of ultimates alone causing the different properties of the so-called elements. Prout's hypothesis that all atomic weights are multiples of that of hydrogen, and Dumas's modification that every atomic weight is a multiple of that of an unknown body whose atomic weight is .25, would have strongly supported this idea of chemical force being but a mode of motion, had not the researches of chemists, especially those of Stas, demonstrated that neither hypothesis has any shadow of foundation in fact. At present therefore, so far as chemistry is concerned, the matter-and-motion theory of the constitution of the world is unsupported by experimental proof—belongs to the region of pure speculation. Hence we may continue to believe in atoms, regarding them perhaps rather as "particles of matter which undergo no other division in chemical metamorphoses" (Kekule) than as absolutely indivisible. The study of these atoms is the object of *chemistry*,—the natural properties of substances in mass and their relations to heat, light, electricity, magnetism and gravitation, constituting the subject of *physics* (from φύσις, *phusis*, nature). Possibly some grand simple truth underlies and connects chemical and physical facts, but at present there is no indication of such a law or laws.

An *atom* is the smallest portion of matter which can exist in a state of combination; a *molecule*, the smallest portion which can exist in the free state. *The symbol* of an element is intended, as a third function (*c*), to indicate this *atom;* thus H and Cl respectively indicate one atom of hydrogen and one atom of chlorine. A symbol also indicates, as we have seen, (*a*) the name of an element and (*b*) one volume of that element in the state of gas, supposing it to be capable of existing in that form. Two symbolical letters indicate two atoms or volumes—that is, one molecule—thus OO, or rather O_2. *The formula of a compound always indicates* (*a*) *the molecule,* (*b*) *two volumes of the compound in the gaseous state, and* (*c*) *the number of atoms and* (*d*) *gaseous volumes concerned in the formation of the molecule.* Thus HCl is the *formula* of the molecule of a compound containing one atom each of the elements hydrogen and chlorine. Further, like the formulæ of all molecules, it is the picture of two volumes of hydrochloric acid, one volume being chlorine, and the other hydrogen. It shows, therefore, that the volume of chlorine and the volume of hydrogen suffered no condensation on combining to form a molecule compounded of both. Similarly H_2O indicates the existence of a body (water) containing hydrogen and oxygen, the molecule containing two atoms of H to one of O (H_2O), two volumes of which body in the gaseous state (*i. e.* steam) were formed from two volumes of hydrogen and one volume of oxygen, the three volumes therefore suffering condensation to two-thirds their bulk.

Atomic Weights.

If there be such things as atoms (and the mind necessarily assumes their existence), they must have weight. What are these weights? First, they are represented by the smallest proportion (relative to 1 part of hydrogen) in which they migrate from compound to compound. Thus 1 part by weight of hydrogen can be eliminated from 18 similar parts of water by action of certain metals, leaving 1 of hydrogen and 16 of oxygen combined with the metal. From the latter compound 1 more of hydrogen is eliminated by a second experiment with more metal, leaving 16 of oxygen combined with the metal. In these and other well-known reactions 16 parts of oxygen take part in the various operations; 16, therefore, is the probable atomic weight of oxygen. And so with other elements and radicals. Secondly, the weights of the atoms, or the atomic weights of the gaseous elements already studied, must differ from each other to the extent that equal volumes of those elements differ in weight. For equal volumes contain an equal number of molecules equal in size, and each molecule is composed of two atoms; so that equal volumes contain an equal number of atoms. Now, bulk for bulk, chlorine is thirty-five and a half (35.5) times as heavy as hydrogen; so that the molecule of chlorine must be 35.5 times the weight of the molecule of hydrogen; for molecules are equal in bulk. And as the molecules of chlorine and hydrogen contain two atoms each, the atom of chlorine must be 35.5 times as heavy as that of hydrogen. The actual weight of atoms can never be ascertained, but that is of little consequence if we can only determine, with exactitude, their comparative weights. Comparing, then, all atomic weights, sometimes obscurely termed equivalents, with each other and selecting hydrogen as the standard of comparison (because it is the lightest body known, and therefore, probably, will have the smallest atomic weight), and assigning to it the number 1, we see that the atomic weight of chlorine will be represented by the number 35.5. By parity of reasoning the atomic weight of oxygen is 16; for oxygen is found, by experiment, to be 16 times as heavy as hydrogen. Similarly the atomic weight of nitrogen is found to be 14. The atomic weight of carbon is 12,—not because its vapor has been proved to be 12 times as heavy as hydrogen, for it has never yet been converted into the gaseous state, but because no gaseous compound of carbon, which has been analyzed, has been found to contain in 2 volumes (one of which, if hydrogen, would weigh 1 part) less than 12 parts of carbon.

By thus weighing equal volumes of gaseous elements, or equal volumes of gaseous compounds of non-volatile elements, and ascertaining by analysis the proportion of the non-volatile element, whose atomic weight is being sought, to the volatile element, whose atomic weight is known, the atomic weights of a large number of the elements have been determined. Some of the elements, however, do not form volatile compounds of any kind; the stated atomic weights of these elements, therefore, are at present simply the proportions by weight in which they combine with or displace elements whose atomic weights have been determined, the proportion being in most cases checked by isomorphic considerations and the relation of the element to other forces, especially heat.*

* *Isomorphous* bodies (from ἴσος, *isos*, equal, and μορφὴ, *morphē*, form) are those which are similar in the shape of their crystals. The identity in crystalline form is so commonly associated with similarity of constitution that non-crystalline substances resembling each other in structure are often regarded as isomorphous. When one element unites with another in more than one proportion, and consequently its atomic weight is uncertain, the isomorphism of either of its compounds with some other compound of known constitution is usually accepted as decisive evidence as to which proportion is atomic.

The weight of the molecule (molecular weight) is simply the sum of the weights of its atoms; thus

$$O_2=32, Cl_2=71, H_2O=18, HCl=36.5.$$

Memoranda.—Though the symbols of the common elements should be committed to memory, their atomic weight need be sought out only as occasion may arise. A complete Table will be found at the end of the volume.

Construction of Formulæ.—The composition of hydrochloric acid (HCl), water (H_2O), ammonia (NH_3), carbonic acid gas (CO_2), or any other compound, as well as the weight of an element that may be concerned in its formation, cannot be ascertained by actual experiment until the student is far advanced in practical chemistry—until he is able to *analyze* not only *qualitatively*, but, by help of a balance, *quantitatively*. The percentage composition of a substance having been determined by quantitative analysis, its formula is constructed by help of the foregoing and other theoretical considerations. The correctness of such formulæ can be verified by expert analysts, but must be taken for granted by learners.

QUANTIVALENCE.

Turning from the *weights* of atoms, their *value* may now be considered; their *quantivalence* (from *quantitas*, quantity, and *valens*, being worth) may be stated. Here again hydrogen is conventionally adopted as the standard of comparison. Oxygen in its relations to hydrogen is bivalent (pronounced thus, biv′-a-lent; of double worth, from *bis*, twice, and *valens*); an atom of it will displace two atoms of hydrogen, or combine with the same number; nitrogen is usually trivalent (triv′-a-lent; from *tres*, three, and *valens*); and carbon quad-riv′-a-lent (from *quatuor*, four, or *quater*, four times, and *valens*). Chlorine, iodine, and bromine, as well as potassium, sodium, and silver among the metals, are, like hydrogen, univalent (u-niv′-a-lent; from *unus*, one, and *valens*). Barium, strontium, calcium, magnesium, zinc, cadmium, mercury, and copper, like oxygen, are bivalent. Phosphorus, arsenicum, antimony, and bismuth, like nitrogen, usually exhibit trivalent properties; but the composition of certain compounds of these elements shows that the several atoms are sometimes quinquivalent (quin-quiv′-a-lent; *quinquies*, five times, and *valens*). Gold and boron are trivalent. Silicon (the characteristic element of flint and sand), tin, aluminium, platinum, and lead resemble carbon in being quadrivalent. Sulphur, chromium, manganese, iron, cobalt, and nickel are sexivalent (sex-iv′-a-lent; from *sex*, six, or *sexies*, six times, and *valens*), but frequently exert only bivalent, trivalent, or quadrivalent activity. This *quantivalence* (quant-iv′-a-lence; from *quantitas*, quantity, and *valens*), also somewhat obscurely termed *atomicity*, *dynamicity*, and *equivalence* of elements, may be ascertained at any time on referring to the Table of the Elements at the end of this volume, where Roman numerals, I, II, III, IV, V, VI, are attached to the symbols of each element to indicate atomic univalence, bivalence, trivalence, quadrivalence, quinquivalence, or sexivalence. Dashes (H', O'', N''') similar to those used in accentuating words are often used instead of figures in expressing quantivalence. The quantivalence of elements, as they one after another come under notice, should be carefully committed to memory; for the composition of compounds can often be thereby predicated with accuracy and remembered with ease. For instance, the hydrogen compounds of chlorine, Cl′, oxygen, O″, nitrogen, N‴, and carbon, C⁗, will be respectively $H'Cl'$, H'_2O'', H'_3N''', and H'_4C'''',—one univalent atom, H′, balancing or saturating one univalent atom Cl′; two univalent atoms, H'_2, and one bivalent atom O″, saturating each other; three univalent atoms, H'_3, and one atom having trivalent activity, N‴, saturating each other; and four univalent atoms, H_4, and one quadrivalent atom, C⁗, saturating each other. Carbonic acid gas, $C^{IV}O^{II}_2$, again, is a saturated molecule containing one quadrivalent and two bivalent atoms.

The doctrine of quantivalence will again be mentioned after the first six metals have been studied, when abundant illustrations of its applications will have occurred.

QUESTIONS AND EXERCISES.

42. Adduce familiar examples of the manifestation of chemical action.

43. What are the characteristics of the chemical force? how is it distinguished from those of gravitation, heat, light, electricity, and magnetism?

44. How may the results of chemical reactions be briefly expressed on paper?

45. Illustrate the difference between chemical symbols and formulæ.

46. Give an equation expressive of the formation of water from its elements.

47. Draw a diagram showing the reaction that ensues when red-hot charcoal is plunged into oxygen gas.

48. Describe, by diagrams, the formation of HCl, P_2O_5, SO_2, and FeI_2.

49. How many chief laws regulate chemical combination?

50. State the law of constant proportions.

51. State the law of multiple proportions.

52. State the law of reciprocal proportions.

53. Describe the origin and uses of the atomic theory.

54. Define the terms *atom* and *molecule.*

55. In what does an atom of oxygen differ from a molecule?

56. Describe the method of producing ammoniacal gas.

57. How many pints of their constituents are represented by one quart of hydrochloric acid gas, steam, and ammoniacal gas respectively?

58. What is *atomic weight?*

59. Admitting the existence of atoms, and assigning the weight 1 to that of hydrogen, what are the atomic weights of oxygen,

chlorine, nitrogen, and carbon? Give reasons for considering the stated weights to be correct.

60. Define isomorphism.

61. Explain the value of isomorphism as evidence of atomic weight.

62. What is to be understood by quantivalence? Give examples of univalent, bivalent, trivalent, and quadrivalent atoms.

63. How may the quantivalence of an element be expressed in its atomic symbol?

64. Give the formulæ of two or three compounds in which the quantivalence of one atom is saturated by the combined quantivalence of others.

THE ELEMENTS AND THEIR COMPOUNDS.

Having thus obtained a general idea of the nature of such elements as have especial interest for the medical and pharmaceutical student, and which indeed are all with which any student of chemistry should at present occupy his attention, we may pass on to consider in detail the relations of the elements to each other. The elements themselves, in the free condition, are seldom used in medicine, being nearly always associated, bound together by the chemical force; in this combined condition, therefore, they must be studied. Each combination of elements or chemical compound will, in the following pages, be regarded as containing two parts or roots, two radicals: the one usually metallic, or, to speak more generally, basylous; the other commonly a non-metallic, simple or complex, acidulous radical. The basylous radicals, or metals, will be considered first, the acidulous radicals afterwards. Each radical will be studied from two points of view, the synthetical and the analytical: that is to say, the properties of an element on which the preparation of its compounds depends will be illustrated by descriptions of actual experiments (usually performed on a small scale), and thus the chemistry of the Pharmacopœia be systematically learnt; then the reactions by which the element is detected, though combined with other substances, will be performed, and so the student be instructed in qualitative analysis. Synthetical and analytical reactions are, in truth, frequently identical, the object with which they are performed giving them synthetical interest on the one hand, or analytical interest on the other.

A good knowledge of chemistry may be acquired synthetically by manufacturing specimens of the salts of the different metals, or analytically by going through a course of pure qualitative analysis. But the former demands a larger expenditure of time than most students have to spare, while under the latter system they generally lose sight of the synthetical interest which attaches to analytical reactions. Hence the more useful system, now offered, of studying each metal, &c., from both points of view, time being economized by omitting the preparation of large specimens of all compounds.

Chemical synthesis and analysis, thoughtfully and conscientiously followed, will insensibly carry the principles of chemistry into the mind and fix them there indelibly.

POTASSIUM.

Symbol K. Atomic weight 39.

Memoranda.—The chief sources of the potassium salts* are the nitrate, found in soils, especially in warm countries, and the compounds of potassium existing in plants. The latter, vegetable salts of potassium, are converted into carbonate with some sulphate, etc., when the wood is burned to ashes. The ashes lixiviated with water, the solution evaporated to dryness, and the residue fused, constitute *crude potashes.* If the residue be calcined on the hearth of a reverberatory furnace till white, the product is termed *pearlash* (*Potassæ Carbonas Impura,* U. S. P.). Large quantities of carbonate are thus produced in North America and Russia; and it is from this salt, purified "by treating the pearlash with its own weight of distilled water, filtering, and evaporating the solution so formed to dryness, while it is kept briskly agitated" (*Potassæ Carbonas,* B. P., K_2CO_3, "with about 16 per cent. of crystallization"), that nearly all other compounds of potassium are made. An exception occurs in cream of tartar (*Potassæ Tartras Acida,* B. P.; *Potassæ Bitartras,* U. S. P.), which is simply the purified natural potassium salt of the grape-vine. Potassium is a constituent of between forty and fifty chemical or Galenical preparations of the British Pharmacopœia.

Carbonate of potassium is a white crystalline or granular powder, insoluble in alcohol, very soluble in water, rapidly liquefying in the air through absorption of moisture, alkaline and caustic to the taste. It loses all water at a red heat. *Potassæ Carbonas Pura,* U. S. P., is obtained by heating the bicarbonate to redness: the resulting white anhydrous carbonate is converted into hydrous granular carbonate by solution in water and evaporation until a dry semi-crystalline salt remains.

Preparation.—Potassium itself is isolated with some difficulty by distilling a mixture of its carbonate and charcoal. It rapidly oxidizes in the air, and hence is always kept below the surface of mineral naphtha, a liquid containing no oxygen.

Quantivalence.—The atom of potassium is univalent, K′.

REACTIONS HAVING (*a*) SYNTHETICAL AND (*b*) ANALYTICAL INTEREST.

(*a*) *Synthetical Reactions.*

These are actions utilized in manufacturing preparations of potassium. The word *synthesis* is from σύνθεσις (*sŭnthĕsis*), a putting together, as opposed to analysis, from ἀναλύω (*analuo*), I resolve.

* The term *salt* includes any definite solid chemical substance, but more especially those which assume a crystalline form.

Hydrate of Potassium.—Caustic Potash.

First Synthetical Reaction.—Boil together, for a few minutes, in a test-tube, five or six grains of carbonate of potassium (K_2CO_3) and a like quantity of slaked lime ($Ca2HO$) with a small quantity of water. Set the mixture aside in the test-tube rack till all solid matter has subsided.

This liquid is a solution of caustic potash, or hydrate of potassium (KHO). Made of a prescribed strength, it forms the *Liquor Potassæ*, B. P. (5.84 per cent.), and U. S. P. (5.8 per cent.).

The mixture is known to be boiled long enough when a little of the clear liquid, poured into another test-tube and warmed, gives no effervescence on the addition of an acid (sulphuric, hydrochloric, or acetic)—a test whose mode of action will be explained hereafter.

Best method of expressing decompositions.—This will be easy of comprehension if what has already been stated concerning symbols and formulæ on pages 27 to 36, has been carefully and thoughtfully considered. The best means of showing on paper the action which occurs when chemical substances attack each other is by the employment either of equations or diagrams. In an *equation* the formulæ of the salts used are written on one line, the sign of addition (+) intervening; the sign of equality (=) follows, and then the formulæ of the salts produced also separated by a plus sign (+). Thus:—

$$K_2CO_3 + Ca2HO = 2KHO + CaCO_3.$$

In this reaction (the operation just performed) the metals of the two salts change places: from K_2CO_3 and $Ca2HO$ there are produced $CaCO_3$ and KHO (two molecules); from carbonate of potassium and hydrate of calcium there result carbonate of calcium (the insoluble portion) and hydrate of potassium (in solution).

In constructing a *diagram*, or pictorial illustration of a chemical reaction, firstly, the formulæ of the salts used are written under each other on the left side of a leaf of a note-book; secondly, on the right are written the formulæ of the salts produced; thirdly, the paths which may be supposed to be taken by the respective elements are indicated by the use of brackets and lines, as follows:—

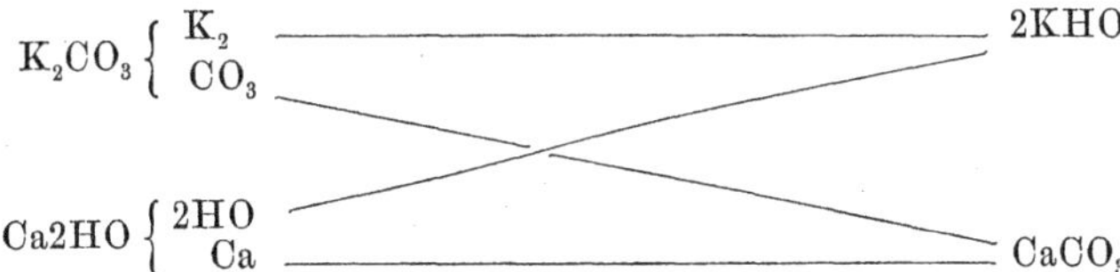

It will be noticed that the only important data required in making either equationary or diagrammatic notes of decompositions are the symbolic formulæ of the various compounds employed or produced. These formulæ are, in this manual, given whenever necessary. (Chemists obtain them in the first instance by the help of quantitative analysis.)

Note on Nomenclature.—*Hydrates* are bodies indirectly or directly derived from water by one-half of its hydrogen becoming displaced by an equivalent quantity of another radical. Thus, a piece of potassium thrown on to water (HHO) instantly liberates hydrogen, hydrate of potassium (KHO) being formed. The temperature produced at the same time is sufficiently high to cause ignition of the hydrogen, which burns with a purple flame (owing to the presence of a little vapor of potassium), while the hydrate of potassium remains dissolved in the bulk of the water.

Explanation.—With regard to the groups of atoms represented by the symbols CO_3 and HO, only a few words need be said here. The former (CO_3) is the grouping (root or radical) found in all carbonates; it is termed the carbonic radical, and is as characteristic of carbonates as potassium (K) is of potassium salts. HO is characteristic of all hydrates. CO_3 is a bivalent grouping or root, HO univalent; hence CO_3 is found united with two equivalent atoms, as in carbonate of potassium, K_2CO_3, or with one bivalent atom, as in carbonate of calcium, $CaCO_3$; and HO is found united in singl proportion with univalent atoms as in hydrate of potassium, KHO or in double proportion with bivalent atoms as in hydrate of calcium, Ca2HO. The quantivalence of a metal has only to be learnt, and the formulæ of its carbonate and hydrate are ascertained without seeing the formula of either. The formulæ of all other metallic salts are constructed on the same principle. But, beyond committing to memory the formulæ and quantivalence of the various groupings characteristic of carbonates, hydrates, nitrates, sulphates, acetates, etc. (see the following Table), special attention should not at present be devoted to the subject of the constitution of salts, but restricted to what may be called the metallic or basylous side of salts. The formulæ and quantivalence of the chief acidulous groupings referred to and the symbols and quantivalence of allied elementary bodies are included in the following Table:—

Formulæ and Quantivalence of Acidulous Radicals.

All chlorides contain	Cl	Univalent radicals.
" bromides "	Br	
" iodides "	I	
" cyanides "	NC	
" hydrates "	HO	
" nitrates "	NO_3	
" chlorates "	ClO_3	
" acetates "	$C_2H_3O_2$	
" sulphides "	S	Bivalent radicals.
" sulphites "	SO_3	
" sulphates "	SO_4	
" carbonates "	CO_3	
" oxalates "	C_2O_4	
" tartrates "	$C_4H_4O_6$	

All citrates contain	. . . . .	$C_6H_5O_7$	Trivalent radicals.
" phosphates "	. . . . .	PO_4	
" borates "	. . . . .	BO_3	

Radicals.—The above elements and compounds are termed *radicals*, each being the common *root* (*radix*) in a series of salts. A compound radical loses its peculiar power when, by superior force, it is broken up into its constituent elements; and an element apparently loses its power as a radical when it is forced to join with other elements in forming a compound radical. Some of the compound radicals are obtainable in the free state, others have yet to be proved capable of isolated existence.*

Pure solution of potash.—Solution of potash generally contains a trace of alumina dissolved from the lime by the hot alkali, but not enough to interfere with the use of the liquid in medicine. If the solution is required for analytical purposes, it may be obtained free from alumina by avoiding the employment of heat, in the manner suggested by Redwood. Half a gallon is made by mixing half a pound of slaked lime with about three pints of water, placing the mixture in a half-gallon bottle (Winchester quart), and adding to it, in small quantities at a time, a solution of half a pound of carbonate of potassium dissolved in the other pint of water, shaking the mixture well for several minutes after each addition. The whole is now set on one side till clear; and then, if a small quantity poured into a test-tube and warmed does not effervesce on the addition of hydro chloric acid, the solution is fit for use. If effervescence (carbonic acid gas) occurs, the mixture must be again well shaken. If the lime be good and recently slaked, and the bottle violently shaken once every half-hour, the decomposition will be complete in about ten or twelve hours.

Liquor Potassæ is officially directed to be made as follows:—

Dissolve 1 pound of carbonate of potassium in 1 gallon of water; heat the solution to the boiling-point in a clean iron vessel, gradually mix with it 12 ounces of slaked lime, and continue the ebullition for ten minutes with constant stirring. Then remove the vessel from the fire; and when by the subsidence of the insoluble matter the supernatant liquor has become perfectly clear, transfer it by means of a siphon or by decantation to a green-glass bottle furnished with an air-tight stopper, and add distilled water, if necessary, to make it correspond with the tests of *specific gravity* and *neutralizing-power*. The method of applying these tests will be explained in subsequent sections.

Solid potash.—Solution of potash evaporated to dryness in a silver or clean iron vessel and the residue fused and poured into moulds constitutes *Potassa Caustica*, B. P.; *Potassa*, U. S. P. It often contains chloride and sulphates, detected by nitrate of silver and a barium salt, as described subsequently in connection with hydrochloric and sulphuric acids. *Potassa cum Calce*, U. S. P., is a

* A few modern authors term these roots *radicles*, a form of the word more usefully expressive of little roots or rootlets.

grayish-white powder, made by rubbing together equal weights of solid potash and quicklime.

Sulphurated Potash.

Second Synthetical Reaction.—Into a test-tube put a few grains of carbonate of potassium previously mixed with half its weight of sulphur. Heat the mixture gradually until it ceases to effervesce. The resulting fused mass poured on a slab and quickly bottled is the *Potassa Sulphurata*, Sulphurated Potash, of B. P., or the *Potassii Sulphuretum*, U. S. P.

This salt is not a definite chemical compound, but a mixture of several substances, among which are sulphate of potassium (K_2SO_4), and one or more of the sulphides of potassium. In short, the chemical character of this compound is well indicated by its vague name. It is of the color of liver when freshly prepared (whence the old name "liver of sulphur"); but from absorption of oxygen it soon changes to green and yellow, and ultimately becomes white and useless. Recently made, "about three-fourths of its weight are dissolved by rectified spirit." It is occasionally employed in the form of ointment.

In preparing large quantities of sulphurated potash, the test-tube is replaced by an earthenware vessel termed a *crucible* (from *crux*, a cross, for originally a cross was impressed upon the melting-pot as used by alchemists and goldsmiths; others derive the word from crux, an instrument of torture, the sense here being symbolical).

Heating crucibles.—Crucibles of a few ounces' capacity may be heated in an ordinary grate-fire. Larger ones require a stove with a good draught—that is, a *furnace*. Even the smaller ones are more conveniently and quickly heated in a furnace. Half-ounce or one ounce experimental porcelain crucibles may be heated in a spirit- or gas-flame; the air gas-flame already described being generally the most suitable.

Acetate of Potassium.

Third Synthetical Reaction.—Place ten, twenty grains, or more of carbonate of potassium in a small dish, and *saturate* (*satur*, full) with acetic acid; that is, add acetic acid so long as effervescence is thereby produced; the resulting liquid is a strong solution of acetate of potassium.

Evaporate most of the water, stirring with a glass rod* to promote the evolution of vapor; a white salt remains which fuses on the further application of heat: this is the

* Glass rod is usually purchased in the form of long sticks. The pieces may be cut to convenient lengths of from 6 to 12 inches (*vide* p. 16), sharp ends being rounded off by holding in a flame for a few minutes.

official Acetate of Potash (*Potassæ Acetas*, B. P. and U. S. P.), or Acetate of Potassium as it is more correctly called. It forms a white deliquescent foliaceous satiny mass, neutral to test-paper, and wholly soluble in spirit. A ten per cent. solution in water forms the "Solution of Acetate of Potash," B. P.

K_2CO_3	+	$2HC_2H_3O_2$	=	$2KC_2H_3O_2$	+	H_2O	+	CO_2
Carbonate of potassium.		Acetic acid.		Acetate of potassium.		Water.		Carbonic acid gas.

Explanation of formulæ.—The formula for acetic acid (the acetate of hydrogen) is $HC_2H_3O_2$, and of acetate of potassium $KC_2H_3O_2$. The grouping, $C_2H_3O_2$, is characteristic of all acetates; it is univalent, and may be shortly, though less instructively, written $\overline{A}$.

Explanation of process.—When two molecules of acetic acid ($2HC_2H_3O_2$) and one of carbonate of potassium (K_2CO_3) react, two molecules of acetate of potassium ($2KC_2H_3O_2$) and one of carbonic acid (H_2CO_3) are produced, the latter at once splitting up into water (H_2O) and carbonic acid gas (CO_2), as already shown in the equation.

Diagram of the Reaction.—The nature of the above operation is indicated by an equation; it (and all succeeding reactions) should be expressed in the student's note-book as a diagram, similar to that just given in connection with the first synthetical reaction. In constructing a diagram, a little reflection concerning the formulæ of the bodies produced will show how the symbols in the formulæ of the bodies employed are to be arranged on the right-hand side of the brackets.

Evaporation of water from a liquid is best conducted in wide shallow vessels rather than in narrow deep ones, as the steam can thus quickly diffuse into the air and be rapidly conveyed away; hence a small round-bottomed basin is far more suitable than a test-tube for such operations. On the manufacturing scale, iron, or iron lined with enamel or semiporcelain, copper, tinned copper, or solid tin pans are used. Up to 12 or 18 inches diameter, pans, basins, or dishes, made of Wedgwood ware or porcelain composition, may be employed.

Note.—The above reaction has a general as well as a special synthetical interest. It represents one of the commonest methods of forming salts, namely, the saturation of an acid with a carbonate. Carbonates added to acetic acid yield acetates, to nitric acid, nitrates, to sulphuric acid, sulphates. Many illustrations of this general process occur in pharmacy.

Bicarbonate of Potassium.

Fourth Synthetical Reaction.—Make a strong solution of carbonate of potassium by heating in a test-tube a mixture of several grains of the salt with rather less than an equal weight of water. Through the cooled solution pass carbonic acid gas, slowly but continuously; after a time a white crystalline precipitate of Acid Carbonate or Bicarbonate of Potassium ($KHCO_3$), the Bicarbonate of Potash of the Pharmacopœias (*Potassæ Bicarbonas*, B. P. and U. S. P.), will be formed. The more economical official arrangements of the apparatus employed in this process will be described under the corresponding sodium salt (p. 61).

$$\underset{\text{Carbonate of potassium.}}{K_2CO_3} + \underset{\text{Water.}}{H_2O} + \underset{\text{Carbonic acid gas.}}{CO_2} = \underset{\text{Bicarbonate of potassium.}}{2KHCO_3}$$

The carbonic acid gas necessary for this operation is to be prepared from marble, though it might be obtained from any carbonate. Thus the previous synthetical reaction could be made available for this purpose, the carbonic gas evolved on the addition of the acetic acid to the carbonate of potassium being conducted into a strong solution of more carbonate of potassium by a glass tube bent and fitted as described when treating of oxygen gas. But motives of economy induce the use of carbonate of calcium, the form known as marble being always employed. Economy and convenience also cause hydrochloric acid to be used in preference to acetic or any other.

Generate the carbonic acid gas by adding common hydrochloric acid, diluted with twice its bulk of water, to a few fragments of marble contained in a test-tube or small flask, and conduct the gas into the solution of carbonate of potassium by a glass tube bent to a convenient angle or angles, and fitted to the test-tube by a cord in the usual way.

Deposition of the bicarbonate explained.—Bicarbonate of potassium is to a certain extent soluble in water; but as it is less so than the carbonate of potassium, and as a *saturated* solution of the latter has been used, the precipitation of a part of the bicarbonate inevitably occurs. In other words, the quantity of water present is sufficient to keep the carbonate, but insufficient to retain the equivalent quantity of bicarbonate in solution.

Properties.—Prepared on the large scale, bicarbonate of potassium occurs in colorless, non-deliquescent, right rhombic prisms; it has a saline, feebly alkaline, non-corrosive taste.

Effervescing solution of potash.—A solution of 30 grains of bicarbonate of potassium in one pint of water, charged with 7 times its bulk (often less) of carbonic acid gas by pressure, constitutes the ordinary "potash-water," the so called *Liquor Potassæ Effervescens*, B. P.

Notes on Nomenclature.—The prefix *bi-* in the name "bicarbonate of potassium," serves to recall the fact that to a given amount of potassium this salt contains *twice* as much carbonic radical as the carbonate. The salt is really a "carbonate of potassium and hydrogen" ($KHCO_3$); it is intermediate between carbonate of potassium (K_2CO_3) and carbonate of hydrogen, or true carbonic acid (H_2CO_3); it is "acid carbonate of potassium" or "hydric potassium carbonate;" chemically, though not physically, it is an acid salt.

Salts whose specific names end in the syllable "*ate*" (carbon*ate*, sulph*ate*, etc.) are in general conventionally so termed when they contain an acidulous radical, or the characteristic elements of an acid, whose name ends in "*ic*," and from which acid they have been or may be formed. Thus the syllable "*ate*," in the words sulph*ate*, nitr*ate*, acet*ate*, carbon*ate*, etc., indicates that the respective salts contain a radical whose name ended in *ic*, the previous syllables, sulph-, nitr-, acet-, carbon-, indicating what that radical was—the sulphuric, nitric, acetic, or carbonic. Occasionally a letter or syllable is dropped from or added to a word to render the name more euphonious; thus the sulphuric radical forms sulphates, not sulphurates.

Citrate of Potassium.

Fifth Synthetical Reaction.—Dissolve a few grains or more of citric acid ($H_3C_6H_5O_7$) in water, and add carbonate (bicarbonate, U. S. P.) of potassium until it no longer causes effervescence, and the solution after well stirring is neutral or faintly acid to test paper. The resulting liquid is a solution of citrate of potassium ($K_3C_6H_5O_7$) (*Liquor Potassæ Citratis*, U. S. P.). Evaporated to dryness, in an open dish, a pulverulent or granular residue is obtained, which is the official *Potassæ Citras*, B. P. and U. S. P., a white deliquescent powder.

$$3K_2CO_3 + 2H_3C_6H_5O_7 = 2K_3C_6H_5O_7 + 3H_2O + 3CO_2$$

$3K_2CO_3$	$2H_3C_6H_5O_7$	$2K_3C_6H_5O_7$	$3H_2O$	$3CO_2$
Carbonate of potassium.	Citric acid.	Citrate of potassium.	Water.	Carbonic acid gas.

Citrates.—The citric radical or group of elements, which with three atoms of hydrogen forms citric acid, and with three of potassium citrate of potassium, is a trivalent grouping; hence the three atoms of potassium in a molecule of the citrate. The full chemistry of citric acid and other citrates will be subsequently described.

Nitrate of potassium (KNO_3) (*Potassæ Nitras*, B. P. and U. S. P.) and *Sulphate of potassium* (K_2SO_4) (*Potassæ Sulphas*, B. P. and U. S. P.) could obviously also be made by saturating nitric acid (HNO_3), and sulphuric acid (H_2SO_4), respectively, by carbonate of potassium. Practically they are not made in that way—the nitrate occurring, as already stated, in nature, and the sulphate as a by-product in many operations. Both salts will be hereafter alluded to in connection with nitric acid.

Tartrate of Potassium.

Sixth Synthetical Reaction.—Place a few grains of carbonate of potassium in a test-tube with a little water, heat to the boiling-point, and then add acid tartrate of potassium ($KHC_4H_4O_6$ or $KH\bar{T}$) till there is no more effervescence, and the solution is neutral to test-paper; a solution of neutral tartrate of potassium ($K_2\bar{T}$) results, the *Potassæ Tartras* of the British and United States Pharmacopœias. Crystals (4- or 6-sided prisms) may be obtained on concentrating the solution by evaporation and setting the hot liquid aside. Larger quantities are made in the same way, 20 of acid tartrate and 9 of carbonate (with 50 of water) being about the proportions necessary for neutrality.

$$2KHC_4H_4O_6 + K_2CO_3 = 2K_2C_4H_4O_6 + H_2O + CO_2$$

Acid tartrate of potassium. Carbonate of potassium. Neutral tartrate of potassium. Water. Carbonic acid gas.

Tartrates.—$C_4H_4O_6$ are the elements characteristic of all tartrates; they form a bivalent grouping; hence the formula of the hydrogen tartrate, or tartaric acid, is $H_2C_4H_4O_6$; that of the potassium tartrate $K_2C_4H_4O_6$; of the intermediate salt, the acid potassium tartrate (cream of tartar), $KHC_4H_4O_6$. If the acid tartrate of one metal and the carbonate of another react, a neutral dimetallic tartrate results, as seen in Rochelle salt ($KNaC_4H_4O_6$).

Acid salts (*e. g.* $KHC_4H_4O_6$), that is, salts intermediate in composition between a normal or neutral salt (*e. g.* $K_2C_4H_4O_6$) and an acid (*e. g.* $H_2C_4H_4O_6$) will frequently be met with. All acidulous radicals, except those which are univalent, may be concerned in the formation of acid salts.

Iodide of Potassium.

Seventh Synthetical Reaction.—To a solution of potash, heated in a test-tube, flask, or evaporating-basin, according to quantity, add a small quantity of solid iodine. The deep color of the iodine disappears entirely. This is due to the formation of the colorless salts, iodide of potassium (KI) and iodate of potassium (KIO_3), which remain dissolved in the liquid. Continue the addition of iodine so long as its color, after a few minutes' warming and stirring, disappears; when this point is reached, the whole of the potash in the solution of potash has been converted into the salts mentioned.

$$6KHO + 3I_2 = 5KI + KIO_3 + 3H_2O$$

Hydrate of potassium. Iodine. Iodide of potassium. Iodate of potassium. Water.

Separation of the iodide from the iodate.—Evaporate the above solution to dryness. If both salts were required, the solid mixture might be digested in spirits of wine, which dissolves the iodide, but not the iodate. But the iodide only is used in medicine. Mix the residue, therefore (reserving a grain or two for a subsequent experiment), with about a twelfth of its weight of charcoal, and gently heat in a test-tube or crucible until slight deflagration ensues.*

$2KIO_3$	+	$3C_2$	=	$2KI$	+	$6CO$
Iodate of potassium.		Carbon.		Iodide of potassium.		Carbonic oxide.

Under these circumstances the iodide remains unaffected, but the iodate loses all its oxygen, and is thus also reduced to the state of iodide. Treat the mass with a little water, and filter to separate excess of charcoal; a solution of pure iodide of potassium results. It may be used as a reagent or evaporated to a small bulk, and set aside to crystallize.

This is the process mentioned in the British and United States Pharmacopœias (*Potassii Iodidum*). "Solution of Iodate of Potassium" is also official as a test-liquid.

Properties.—Iodide of potassium crystallizes in small cubical crystals, very soluble in water, less so in spirit. One part in ten of water forms "Solution of Iodide of Potassium," B. P.

The addition of charcoal in the above process is simply to facilitate the removal of the oxygen of the iodate of potassium. Iodate of potassium (KIO_3) is analogous in constitution, and in composition, so far as the atoms of oxygen are concerned, to chlorate of potassium ($KClO_3$), which has already been stated to be more useful than any other salt for the actual preparation of oxygen gas itself. Hence the removal of the oxygen of the iodate might be accomplished by heating the residue without charcoal. In that case the liberated oxygen would be detected on inserting the incandescent extremity of a strip of wood into the mouth of the test-tube in which the mixture of iodide and iodate had been heated. The charcoal, however, burns out the oxygen more quickly, and thus economizes heat.

* Deflagration means violent burning, from *flagratus*, burnt (*flagro*, I burn), and *de*, a prefix augmenting the sense of the word to which it may be attached. Paper thrown into a fire simply burns, nitre deflagrates. *De*-tonate (*detono*) is a precisely similar word, meaning to explode with violent noise.

If, in the operation of heating iodate of potassium with charcoal, excess of the latter be employed, slight incandescence rather than deflagration occurs; if the charcoal be largely in excess, the reduction of the iodate to iodide of potassium is effected without visible deflagration or even incandescence.

Detection of iodate in iodide of potassium.—Iodate of potassium remaining as an impurity in iodide of potassium may be detected by adding to a solution of the latter salt some tartaric acid, shaking, and then adding mucilage of starch; blue "iodide of starch" is formed if a trace of iodate be present, but not otherwise. The tartaric acid liberates iodic acid (HIO_3) from the iodate of potassium and hydriodic acid (HI) from the iodide of potassium; neither acid alone attacks starch, but by reaction on each other the two give rise to free iodine which then forms the blue color. This experiment should be tried on a sample of pure iodide of potassium and on a grain or two of the impure iodide reserved from the previous experiment.

$$HIO_3 + 5HI = 3H_2O + 3I_2.$$

Note on Nomenclature.—The syllable *ide* attached to the syllable *iod* in the name "iodide of potassium," indicates that the element *iodine* is combined with the potassium. An iod*ate*, as already explained, is a salt containing the characteristic elements of iod*ic* acid and all iodic compounds. Salts, one of whose names ends in *ide*, are those which are, or may be, formed from elements. The names of salts which are, or may be, formed from compounds include other syllables, *ate* being one (see page 49). The only other syllable is *ite*, which is included in the names of salts which are, or may be, formed from acids and radicals whose names end in *ous:* thus hyposulph*ite* of sodium, &c. To recapitulate: A salt whose name ends in *ate* contains a compound acidulous radical whose name ends in *ic;* a salt whose name ends in *ite* contains a compound acidulous radical whose name ends in *ous;* a salt whose name ends in *ide* contains an element for its acidulous radical. Thus, sulph*ide* relates to sulphur, sulph*ite* to the sulphurous radical, sulph*ate* to the sulphuric radical, and so on with all other "ides," "ites," or "ates."

Bromide of Potassium (*Potassii Bromidum*, B. P.).—This salt is identical in constitution with iodide of potassium, and may be made in exactly the same way, bromine being substituted for iodine. The formula of bromic acid is $HBrO_3$. It will be noticed that the following equations are similar in character to those showing the preparation of iodide of potassium.

$6KHO$	+	$3Br_2$	=	$5KBr$	+	$KBrO_3$	+	$3H_2O$
Hydrate of potassium.		Bromine.		Bromide of potassium.		Bromate of potassium.		Water.

$2KBrO_3$	+	$3C_2$	=	$2KBr$	+	$6CO$
Bromate of potassium.		Carbon.		Bromide of potassium.		Carbonic oxide.

Potassii Bromidum, U. S. P., is made by decomposing solution of bromide of iron (FeI_2) by solution of pure carbonate of potassium (K_2CO_3), evaporating and crystallizing.

Manganates of Potassium.

Eighth Synthetical Reaction.—Place a fragment of solid caustic potash (KHO), with about the same quantity of chlorate of potassium ($KClO_3$), and of black oxide of manganese (MnO_2), on a piece of platinum foil.* Hold the foil by a small pair of forceps or tongs in the flame of a blowpipe for a few minutes until the fused mixture has become dark green. This color is that of *manganate of potassium* (K_2MnO_4).

$$6KHO + KClO_3 + 3MnO_2 = 3K_2MnO_4 + KCl + 3H_2O$$

Hydrate of potassium. Chlorate of potassium. Black oxide of manganese. Manganate of potassium. Chloride of potassium. Water.

Ninth Synthetical Reaction.—Permanganate of Potassium ($K_2Mn_2O_8$) (*Potassæ Permanganas*, B. P. and U.S.P.), which is purple, is obtained, or rather a solution of it, on placing the foil and its adherent mass in water, and boiling for a short time.

$$3K_2MnO_4 + 2H_2O = K_2Mn_2O_8 + 4KHO + MnO_2$$

Manganate of potassium. Water. Permanganate of potassium. Hydrate of potassium. Black oxide of manganese.

On the large scale, the potash set free in the reaction is neutralized by sulphuric or carbonic acid, and the solution evaporated to the crystallizing point. Further details will be given in connection with manganese.

Solutions of manganate or permanganate of potassium so readily yield their oxygen to organic matter, that they are used on the large scale as disinfectants, under the name of "Condy's Disinfecting Fluids."

Synthetical Reactions bringing under consideration the remaining official compounds (namely, bichromate, arsenite, chlorate, cyanide, ferrocyanide, and ferridcyanide of potassium) are deferred at present.

(*b*) *Reactions having Analytical Interest* (Tests).

Note.—These are reactions utilized in searching for small quantities of a substance (in the present instance of potassium) in a solution. They are best performed in test-tubes or other small vessels. Each should be expressed, in the form of an equation or diagram, in the student's note-book. *All previous or future equations given in this*

* The foil may be 1 inch broad by 2 long. No ordinary flame will melt, or common chemical substance attack platinum; hence the same piece may be used in experiments over and over again. Metals form a fusible alloy with platinum, and phosphorus rapidly attacks it, hence such substances, as well as mixtures likely to yield them, should be heated in a small porcelain crucible.

volume should be transferred to the note-book in the form of diagrams similar to that given on page 43.

First Analytical Reaction.—To a solution of any salt of potassium (chloride,* for example) add solution of perchloride of platinum ($PtCl_4$), and stir the mixture with a glass rod; yellow double chloride of platinum and potassium ($PtCl_42KCl$) will be precipitated.†

Explanation.—The precipitate is, practically, insoluble in water. It is for this reason that a very small quantity of any soluble potassium salt (or, rather, of the potassium in that salt) is thrown out of solution by perchloride of platinum.

Precaution.—Only chloride of potassium forms this characteristic compound; hence, if the potassium salt in the solution is known not to be a chloride, or if its composition is unknown, a few drops of hydrochloric acid must be added, otherwise some of the perchloride of platinum will be utilized for its chlorine only, the platinum being wasted. Thus, if nitrate of potassium (KNO_3) be present, a few drops of hydrochloric acid enable the potassium to assume the form of chloride when the perchloride of platinum is added, nitric acid (HNO_3) being set free.

Memoranda.—Experiments with such expensive reagents as perchloride of platinum are economically performed in watch-glasses, drops of the liquids being operated on. When the precipitate is long in forming, it is sometimes of an orange-yellow tint. If iodide of potassium happen to be the potassium salt under examination, some iodide of platinum (PtI_4) will also be formed, giving a red color to the solution, and a larger quantity of the *precipitant* (that is, the precipitating agent) be required.

Note on Nomenclature.—When distinct molecules of salts unite and form a single crystalline compound, the product is termed a *double* salt. The double chloride of potassium and platinum is such a body.

Acid Tartrate of Potassium.

Second Analytical Reaction.—To a solution of any salt of potassium add some strong solution of tartaric acid ($H_2C_4H_4O_6$), and shake or well stir the mixture; a white granular precipitate of acid tartrate of potassium ($KHC_4H_4O_6$) will be formed.

Limits of the Test.—Acid tartrate of potassium is soluble in about 180 parts of cold and in 6 parts of boiling water. Hence, in applying the tartaric test for potassium, the solutions must not be hot. Even if

* A few fragments of carbonate of potassium, two or three drops of hydrochloric acid, and a small quantity of water, give a solution of chloride of potassium at once, $K_2CO_3+2HCl=2KCl+H_2O+CO_2$.

† By *precipitation* (from *præcipito*, to throw down suddenly) is simply meant the formation of particles of solid in a liquid, no matter whether the solid, the *precipitate*, subsides or floats.

cold, no precipitate will be obtained if the solutions are very dilute. This test, therefore, is of far less value than the first mentioned. The acid tartrate of potassium is less soluble in diluted alcohol than in water; so that the addition of spirit of wine renders the reaction somewhat more delicate.

Cream of Tartar.—The precipitate is the *Bitartrate or Acid Tartrate of Potassium,* though the official preparation is not formed in the above manner; on the contrary, the acid is derived from the salt, which occurs naturally in the juice of many plants.

Memorandum.—When the tartaric acid is added to the salt of potassium, and the acid tartrate formed, the acid whose chief elements were previously with the potassium is set free; and in such acid solutions the acid tartrate is somewhat soluble. To prevent loss on this account, acid tartrate of sodium, a salt tolerably soluble in water, may be used as a test instead of tartaric acid (Plunkett). The sodium uniting with the acidulous radical, thus gives a neutral instead of an acid solution. But this advantage is of less importance from the fact that more water is introduced by the saturated solution of acid tartrate of sodium than by a saturated solution of tartaric acid.

Third Analytical Reaction.—The *flame-test.* Dip the looped end of a platinum wire into a solution containing a potassium salt, and introduce the loop into a spirit-flame, the flame of a mixture of gas and air, a blowpipe flame, or other slightly colored flame. A violet tint will be produced highly characteristic of salts of potassium.

Fourth Analytical Fact.—Salts of potassium are not volatile. Place a fragment of carbonate, nitrate, or any other potassium salt, on a piece of platinum foil, and heat the latter in the flame of a lamp; the salt may fuse to a transparent liquid and flow freely over the foil, water also if present will escape as steam, and black carbon be set free if the salt happen to be of vegetable origin; but the potassium compound itself will not be vaporized. This is a valuable negative property, as will be evident when the analytical reactions of ammonium come under notice.

QUESTIONS AND EXERCISES.

65. Name the sources of potassium.
66. Give the source, formula, and characters of Carbonate of Potassium.
67. Distinguish between synthetical and analytical reactions.
68. How is the official *Liquor Potassæ* prepared?
69. What is the systematic name of Caustic Potash?
70. State the chemical formula of Caustic Potash.

71. Construct an equation or diagram expressive of the reaction between carbonate of potassium and slaked lime.
72. Define a *hydrate*.
73. What group of atoms is characteristic of all carbonates?
74. Define the term *radical*.
75. How is "Sulphurated Potash" made, and of what salts is it a mixture?
76. What is the formula of the acetic radical—the radical of all acetates?
77. Draw a diagram showing the formation of Acetate of Potassium.
78. Give a general process for the conversion of carbonates into other salts.
79. What is the difference between Carbonate and Bicarbonate of Potassium? How is the latter prepared?
80. What is the relation between salts whose specific names end in the syllable "*ate*," and acids ending in "*ic*"?
81. Draw out diagrams descriptive of the formation of Tartrate of Potassium from the Acid Tartrate, and Citrate from the Carbonate of Potassium.
82. Distinguish between a normal and an acid salt.
83. How is Iodide of Potassium made? Illustrate the process by either diagrams or equations.
84. Describe the appearance and chemical properties of iodide of potassium.
85. Give a method for the detection of iodate in iodide of potassium. Explain the reaction,
86. Has the syllable "*ide*" any general signification in chemical nomenclature?
87. What is the difference between sulphides, sulphites, and sulphates?
88. Mention the chemical relations of Bromide to Iodide of Potassium.
89. Describe the formation of Permanganate of Potassium, giving equations or diagrams.
90. How do manganate and permanganate of potassium act as disinfectants?
91. Enumerate the tests for potassium, explaining by diagrams the various reactions which occur.

SODIUM.

Symbol Na. Atomic weight 23.

Memoranda.—Most of the sodium salts met with in Pharmacy are directly obtained from carbonate of sodium, which is now manufactured on an enormous scale from chloride of sodium (common salt, sea-salt, or rock-salt), the natural source of the sodium salts. When pure, salt (*Sodii Chloridum*, B. P. and U. S. P.) occurs "in small white crystalline grains, or transparent cubic crystals, free from moisture." Besides the direct and indirect use of carbonate of sodium, or carbonate of soda, as it is commonly called in medicine, it is largely used for household cleansing-purposes under the name of "soda," and in the manufacture of soap. Nitrate of sodium also occurs in nature, but is valuable for its nitric constituents rather than its sodium. Sodium is a constituent of about forty chemical or Galenical preparations of the Pharmacopœias.

Sodium is prepared by a process similar to that for potassium, but with less difficulty. Its atom is univalent, Na′.

REACTIONS HAVING (*a*) SYNTHETICAL AND (*b*) ANALYTICAL INTEREST.

(*a*) *Reactions having Synthetical Interest.*

Hydrate of Sodium. Caustic Soda.

First Synthetical Reaction.—The formation of solution of hydrate of sodium or caustic soda, NaHO (*Liquor Sodæ*, B. P. and U. S. P.). This operation resembles that of making solution of potash.

The practical student should refer to the remarks made concerning solution of potash, applying them to solution of soda. He may perform the corresponding experiments or omit them, as he considers he does or does not clearly comprehend all they are designed to teach.

$$\underset{\text{Carbonate of sodium.}}{Na_2CO_3} + \underset{\text{Hydrate of calcium.}}{Ca2HO} = \underset{\text{Hydrate of sodium.}}{2NaHO} + \underset{\text{Carbonate of calcium.}}{CaCO_3}$$

Pure Solution of Soda, free from any trace of alumina, may be prepared by shaking in a Winchester quart, once every 20 or 30 minutes for 5 or 6 hours, 14 ozs. of crystals of carbonate of sodium and 8 ozs. of good recently slaked lime. The official *Liquor Sodæ* is made from 28 ounces of crystals of carbonate of sodium, 12 of slaked lime, and 1 gallon of water, under precisely similar circumstances to those detailed for *Liquor Potassæ* (p. 45). If the solution be evaporated to dryness, and the residue fused and poured into moulds, solid hydrate of sodium (*Soda Caustica*, B. P.) is obtained.

Action of Sodium on Water.—Sodium, like potassium, decomposes water (HHO or H_2O) with production of hydrate of sodium (NaHO) and hydrogen (H); but unless the sodium is confined to one spot by placing it on a small floating piece of filter-paper, the action is not sufficiently intense to cause ignition of the escaping hydrogen. When the latter does ignite, it burns with a yellow flame, due to the presence of a little vapor of sodium.

Second Synthetical Reaction.—The reaction of sulphur and carbonate of sodium at a high temperature resembles that of sulphur and carbonate of potassium; but as the product is not used in medicine, nor otherwise interesting, the experiment may be omitted. It is mentioned here to draw attention to the close resemblance of the potassium salts to those of sodium.

Acetate of Sodium.

Third Synthetical Reaction.—Add the powder or fragments of carbonate of sodium (Na_2CO_3) to some strong acetic acid in a test-tube or evaporating-basin as long as effervescence occurs, and then evaporate some of the water.* When the solution is cold, crystals of acetate of sodium ($NaC_2H_3O_2 3H_2O$) (*Sodæ Acetas*, B. P. and U. S. P.) will be deposited. A ten per cent. solution in distilled water forms the "Solution of Acetate of Soda," B. P.

$$\underset{\text{Carbonate of sodium.}}{Na_2CO_3} + \underset{\text{Acetic acid.}}{2HC_2H_3O_2} = \underset{\text{Acetate of sodium.}}{2NaC_2H_3O_2} + \underset{\text{Water.}}{H_2O} + \underset{\text{Carbonic acid gas.}}{CO_2}$$

Bicarbonate of Sodium.

Fourth Synthetical Reaction.—The action of carbonic acid (H_2CO_3), or carbonic acid gas (CO_2) and water (H_2O), on carbonate of sodium (Na_2CO_3). This resembles that of carbonic acid on carbonate of potassium, but is applied in a different manner. The result is bicarbonate of sodium ($NaHCO_3$) (*Sodæ Bicarbonas*, B. P. and U. S. P.).

$$\underset{\text{Carbonate of sodium.}}{Na_2CO_3} + \underset{\text{Water.}}{H_2O} + \underset{\text{Carbonic acid gas.}}{CO_2} = \underset{\text{Bicarbonate of sodium.}}{2NaHCO_3}$$

Process.—Heat crystals of carbonate of sodium in a porcelain crucible until no more steam escapes. Mix the product, in a mortar, with two-thirds its weight of crystals, and place the powder in a test-tube or small bottle into which carbonic acid gas may be conveyed by a tube passing through a cork and terminating at the bottom of the vessel. To generate the carbonic acid gas fill a test-tube having a small hole in the bottom (or a similar piece of glass tubing, of which one end is plugged by a grooved cork) with fragments of marble, insert a cork and delivery-tube, and connect the latter with the similar tube of the vessel containing the carbonate of sodium by a piece of India-rubber tubing. Now plunge the tube of marble into a test-glass, or other vessel, containing a mixture of one

* The "water" alluded to occurs in the acid, which, though commonly termed "acetic acid," is really a solution of that acid in water.

part hydrochloric acid and two parts water, and loosen the cork of the carbonate-of-sodium tube until carbonic acid gas, generated in the marble tube, may be considered to fill the whole arrangement; then replace the cork tightly and set the apparatus aside. As the gas is absorbed by the carbonate of sodium, hydrochloric acid rises into the marble tube, generates fresh gas, which, in its turn, drives back the acid liquid, and thus prevents the production of any more gas until further absorption has occurred. When the salt is wholly converted into bicarbonate ($NaHCO_3$), it will be found to have become damp through the liberation of water from the crystallized carbonate (Na_2CO_3, $10H_2O$). (It would be inconveniently moist, even semi-fluid, if a part of the carbonate had not previously been rendered anhydrous.) To purify the resulting bicarbonate from any carbonate or traces of other salts, add half its bulk of cold distilled water, set aside for about half an hour, shaking occasionally, drain the undissolved portion, and dry it by exposure on filtering paper.

This is the official process for *Sodæ Bicarbonas*, B. P.: that of the U. S. P. is similar. The arrangement of apparatus is also that adopted in the Pharmacopœias for *Potassæ Bicarbonas*, one part of carbonate dissolved in two-and-a-half parts of water being subjected to the action of the gas, and not the solid carbonate as in the case of the sodium salt.

A *crystal* of carbonate of sodium is carbonate of sodium plus water; on heating it, more or less of the water is evolved, and *anhydrous* carbonate of sodium is partially or wholly produced (*Sodæ Carbonas Exsiccata*, B. P. and U. S. P.).

$Na_2CO_3,10H_2O$	—	$10H_2O$	=	Na_2CO_3
Crystallized carbonate of sodium.		Water.		Dried carbonate of sodium.

Note on Nomenclature.—Anhydrous bodies (from α, *a*, and ὕδωρ, *udōr*, i. e. without water) are compounds from which water has been taken, but whose essential chemical properties are unaltered. Salts containing water are *hydrous* bodies; of these the larger portion are crystalline, and their water is then termed *water of crystallization*. Non-crystalline *hydrous* compounds were formerly spoken of as *hydrated* substances; *hydrates* are, however, a distinct class of bodies, salts derived from water by one-half of its hydrogen becoming displaced by an equivalent quantity of another radical. *Anhydrides* are compounds from which the elements of water have been removed, their essential chemical (acid) properties being thereby greatly altered. (For illustrations, see Index, "Anhydrides.")

Water of Crystallization.—The water in crystallized carbonate of sodium is in the solid condition, and, like ice and other fusible substances, requires heat for its liquefaction. Many salts (freezing-mixtures), when dissolved in water, give a very cold solution. This is because they and their solid water, if they have any, are then converted into liquids which absorb heat from surrounding media. Take away from water some of its heat, the result is ice. Give to ice (at 32° F.) more heat than it contains already, the result is water (still at 32° F.). (Heat thus taken into a substance without increasing its temperature is said to become *latent*—from *latens*, hiding; it is no longer discoverable by the sense of touch or the thermometer. The term *latent* now gives a somewhat incorrect idea, however, of the process; for our knowledge of the extent and readiness with which one form of force is convertible into another renders highly probable the assumption that heat is in these cases converted into motion, the latter enabling the particles of a solid to take up the new positions demanded by their liquid condition.) The only apparent difference between ice and the water in such crystals as carbonate of sodium is that ice is solid water in the free, and water of crystallization solid water in the combined state. The former can only exist at and below freezing, the latter at ordinary temperatures. In chemical formulæ, the symbols representing water are usually separated by a comma from those representing salts. The crystals of acetate of sodium (of the third reaction) contain water in this loose state of combination—water of crystallization ($NaC_2H_3O_2$, $3H_2O$).

"*Soda-water.*"—A solution of bicarbonate of sodium in water charged with carbonic acid gas under pressure constitutes the official *Liquor Sodæ Effervescens*, B. P., and, like the "potash-water" of the shops, is a true medicine, an antacid. Ordinary "soda-water," however, is in many cases simply a solution of carbonic acid gas in water, and would be more appropriately termed "aërated water": any medicinal effect it may possess is due to the sedative influence of its carbonic acid gas on the coats of the stomach. At common temperatures water dissolves about its own volume of carbonic acid gas, both being under equal pressure. One pint of the official soda-water contains 30 grains of bicarbonate of sodium and a pint of carbonic acid gas; but the solution is under a pressure of seven atmospheres, so that seven pints of the gas at ordinary atmospheric pressure are required for the quantity mentioned.

Solubility of gases in water.—Whatever the weight and volume of a gas dissolved by a liquid at ordinary atmospheric pressure, that weight is doubled by double pressure, the two volumes of gas thereby being reduced to one, trebled at treble pressure, the three volumes of gas being reduced to one, quadrupled at quadruple pressure, the four volumes of gas being reduced to one, and so on. This is a general law regarding the solubility of gases in liquids under given temperatures. An average bottle of "soda-water" contains about four times the weight of carbonic acid gas which can exist in it without artificial pressure, so that on removing its cork three times its bulk escape, its own bulk remaining dissolved.

Bicarbonate of sodium may also be medicinally administered in the form of lozenge (*Trochisci Sodæ Bicarbonatis*, B. P. and U. S. P.).

Tartrate of Potassium and Sodium.

Fifth Synthetical Reaction.—To some hot strong solution of carbonate of sodium in a test-tube or larger vessel add acid tartrate of potassium till no more effervescence occurs (about three parts to four will be required); when the solution is cold, crystals of double tartrate of potassium and sodium (*Soda Tartarata*, B. P., *Potassæ et Sodæ Tartras*, U. S. P.), the old *Rochelle Salt*, will be deposited.

Na_2CO_3	+	$2KHC_4H_4O_6$	=	$2KNaC_4H_4O_6$	+	H_2O	+	CO_2
Carbonate of sodium.		Acid tartrate of potassium.		Double tartrate of potassium and sodium.		Water.		Carbonic acid gas

FORMULÆ OF TARTRATES.

Tartaric acid	$HH\ C_4H_4O_6$
Acid tartrate of potassium	$KH\ C_4H_4O_6$
Tartrate of potassium and sodium . .	$KNaC_4H_4O_6$

Very close analogy will be noticed in the constitution of these salts. When the other tartrates come under notice it will be found they also have a similar constitution. The crystals of the above double tartrate contain water ($KNaC_4H_4O_6,4H_2O$).

Hypochlorite of Sodium.

Sixth Synthetical Reaction.—Pass chlorine (*vide* page 24) into a solution of carbonate of sodium. The result is a bleaching and disinfecting liquid, which, when made of prescribed strength (12 ounces of carbonate in 36 of water, charged by the washed chlorine from 15 fluid ounces of hydrochloric acid and 4 ounces of black oxide of manganese), is the Solution of Chlorinated Soda (*Liquor Sodæ Chloratæ*) of the British Pharmacopœia. It is said to contain chloride of sodium (NaCl) and hypochlorite of sodium (NaClO), with some undecomposed acid carbonate of sodium.

MnO_2	+	$4HCl$	=	$MnCl_2$	+	$2H_2O$	+	Cl_2
Blk. oxide of manganese.		Hydrochloric acid.		Chloride of manganese.		Water.		Chlorine.

Na_2CO_3	+	Cl_2	=	$NaCl,NaClO$	+	CO_2
Carbonate of sodium.		Chlorine.		Chlorinated soda.		Carbonic acid gas.

Liquor Sodæ Chlorinatæ, U. S. P., is made by decomposing solution of carbonate of sodium by solution of chlorinated lime, sp. gr. 1.045.

$2Na_2CO_3$	+	$CaCl_2,Ca2ClO$	=	$2(NaCl,NaClO)$	+	$2CaCO_3$
Carbonate of sodium.		Chlorinated lime.		Chlorinated soda.		Carbonate of calcium.

Other Sodium Compounds.

Synthetical Reactions portraying the chemistry of the remaining official compounds (namely, nitrate, sulphate, hyposulphite, borate, arseniate, and valerianate of sodium are deferred until the several acidulous radicals of these salts have been described. For phosphate of sodium see page 83.

The official Citro-Tartrate (*Sodæ Citro-tartras Effervescens*, B. P.), is a mixture of bicarbonate of sodium (17 parts), citric acid (6), and tartaric acid (8), heated (to 200° or 220°) until the particles aggregate to a granular condition. When required for medicinal use, a dose of the mixture is placed in water; escape of carbonic acid gas at once occurs, and an effervescing liquid results.

Soda Powders (*Pulveres Effervescentes*, U. S. P.) are formed of 30 grains of bicarbonate of sodium and 25 of tartaric acid, wrapped separately in papers of different color. When mixed with water, tartrate of sodium results, a little bicarbonate also remaining.

In the manufacture of Carbonate of Sodium from chloride, the latter is first converted into sulphate, the sulphate is then roasted with coal and limestone, and the resulting *black-ash* lixiviated (*lixivia*, from *lix*, lye—water impregnated with alkaline salts: hence *lixiviation*, the operation of washing a mixture with the view of dissolving out salts). The lye, evaporated to dryness, yields crude carbonate of sodium (soda-ash). This process will be further described in connection with Carbonates.

Deliquescence and Efflorescence.—The carbonates of sodium and potassium, chemically closely allied, are readily distinguished physically. Carbonate of potassium quickly absorbs moisture from the air and becomes damp, wet, and finally fluid—it is *deliquescent* (*deliquescens*, melting away). Carbonate of sodium, on the other hand, yields some of its water of crystallization to the air, the crystals becoming white, opaque, and pulverulent—it is *efflorescent* (*efflorescent*, blowing as a flower.

Analogy of Sodium salts to Potassium salts.—Other synthetical reactions might be described similar to those given under potassium, and thus citrate, iodide, bromide, iodate, bromate, chlorate, manganate, and permanganate of sodium, and many other salts be formed. But enough has been stated to show how chemically analogous sodium is to potassium. Such analogies will constantly present themselves. In few departments of knowledge are order and method more perceptible; in few is there as much natural law, as much *science*, as in chemistry.

Substitution of Potassium and Sodium salts for each other.—Sodium salts being cheaper than potassium salts, the former may sometimes be economically substiuted. That one is employed rather than the other, is often merely a result due to accident or fashion. But it must be borne in mind that in some cases a potassium salt will crystallize more readily than its sodium analogue, or that a sodium salt is stable when the corresponding potassium salt has a tendency to absorb moisture, or one may be more soluble than the other, or the two may have different medicinal effects. For these or similar reasons, a potassium salt has come to be used in medicine or trade, instead of the corresponding sodium salt, and *vice versâ*. Whenever the acidulous portion only is to be utilized, the least expensive salt of the class would nearly always be selected.

(b) *Reactions having Analytical Interest.*

1. *The chief analytical reaction* for sodium is the *flame-test*. When brought into contact with a flame in the manner described under potassium (page 55), an intensely yellow color is communicated to the flame by any salt of sodium. This is highly characteristic—indeed, almost too delicate a test; for if the point of the wire be touched by the fingers, enough salt (which is contained in the moisture of the hand) adheres to the wire to communiate a very distinct sodium reaction. These statements should be experimentally verified, the chloride, sulphate, or any other salt of sodium being employed.

2. *Precipitant of sodium.*—Sodium is the only metal whose common salts are all soluble in water. Hence no ordinary reagent can be added to a solution containing a sodium salt which shall give a precipitate containing the sodium. A neutral or alkaline solution of a sodium salt gives, however, a granular precipitate of antimoniate of sodium ($Na_2H_2Sb_2O_7$, $6H_2O$) if well stirred or shaken with a solution of *antimoniate of potassium* ($K_2H_2Sb_2O_7$), but the reagent precipitates other metals, and is liable to decompose and become useless, and hence is seldom employed.

Antimoniate of potassium is made by adding, gradually, finely powdered metallic antimony to nitrate of potassium fused in a crucible so long as deflagration continues. The resulting mass is boiled with a large quantity of water, the solution filtered and preserved in a well-stoppered bottle; for the carbonic gas in the air is rapidly absorbed by the solution, antimonic acid being deposited.

3. Sodium salts, like those of potassium, are not volatile. Prove this fact by the means described when treating of the effect of heat on potassium salts (p. 56).

QUESTIONS AND EXERCISES.

92. How is the official solution of soda prepared? Give a diagram.

93. Explain the action of sodium or potassium on water. What colors do these elements respectively communicate to flame?

94. Acetate of sodium: give formula, process, and diagram.

95. Give a diagram showing the formation of bicarbonate of sodium.

96. Why is a mixture of dried and undried carbonate of sodium employed in the preparation of the bicarbonate?

97. State the difference between anhydrous and crystallized carbonate of sodium.

98. Define the terms *anhydrous*, *hydrous*, *hydrate*, *anhydride*.

99. What do you understand by *water of crystallization?*

100. What is the nature of "Soda-water?"

101. How many volumes of gas (reckoned as at ordinary atmospheric pressure) are contained in any given volume of the British official "Soda-water?"

102. What is the general law regarding the solubility of gases in liquids under pressure?

103. What is the systematic name of Rochelle salt, and how is the salt prepared?

104. What is the relation of Rochelle salt to cream of tartar and tartaric acid?

105. Give the mode of preparation and composition of solution of chlorinated soda, and express the process by a diagram.

106. How is the granular effervescing Citro-tartrate of Sodium prepared?

107. Define *Deliquescence*, *Efflorescence*, and *Lixiviation*.

108. What is the general relation of potassium salts to those of sodium?

109. How are sodium salts analytically distinguished from those of potassium?

AMMONIUM.

Symbol NH_4 or Am. Atomic weight 18.

Memoranda.—The elements nitrogen and hydrogen, in the proportion of one atom to four (NH_4) are those characteristics of all the compounds about to be studied, just as potassium (K) and sodium (Na) are the characteristic elements of the potassium and sodium compounds. Ammonium is a univalent nucleus, root, or radical, like potassium or sodium; and the ammonium compounds closely resemble those of potassium or sodium. In short, if, for an instant, potassium or sodium be imagined to be compounds, the analogy between these three series of salts is complete. Yet ammonium never having been isolated, its existence remains a matter of assumption.

Source.—The source of nearly all the ammoniacal salts met with in commerce is ammonia-gas (NH_3) obtained in distilling coals in the manufacture of ordinary illuminating gas. It is doubtless derived from the nitrogen of the plants from which the coal has been produced.

Ammonia.—When this gas (NH_3) comes into contact with water (H_2O), in the process of washing and cooling coal-gas, hydrate of ammonium (NH_4HO, or AmHO) is believed to be formed, the analogue of hydrate of potassium (KHO) or sodium (NaHO). The grounds for this belief are the observed analogy of the well-known ammoniacal salts to those of potassium and sodium, the similarity of action of solution of potash, soda, and ammonia on salts of metals, and the existence of crystals of an analogous sulphur salt (NH_4HS).

Chloride of Ammonium.—The "ammoniacal liquor" of the gas-works is usually neutralized by hydrochloric acid, by which *chloride of ammonium* (sal-ammoniac) is produced,

$$NH_4HO+HCl=NH_4Cl+H_2O;$$

and from this salt, purified, the others used in pharmacy are directly or indirectly made. Chloride of ammonia (*Ammonii Chloridum*, B. P., *Ammoniæ Murias*, U. S. P., occurs "in colorless, inodorous, translucent fibrous masses, tough, and difficult to powder, soluble in water [1 in 10 is the 'Solution of Chloride of Ammonium,' B. P.] and in rectified spirits."

Sulphate of Ammonium $(NH_4)_2, SO_4$, results when "ammoniacal liquor" is neutralized by oil of vitrol. It is largely used as a constituent of artificial manure in England, and when purified by re-crystallization is employed in pharmacy (*Ammoniæ Sulphas*, U. S. P.)

Volcanic Ammonia.—The purest form of ammonia is that met with in volcanic districts, and obtained as a by-product in the manufacture of borax; the crude boracic acid as imported contains about 10 per cent. of ammonium salts, chiefly sulphate, and double sulphates of ammonium with magnesium, sodium, and manganese (Howard).

Reactions having (*a*) General, (*b*) Synthetical, and (*c*) Analytical Interest.

Amalgam of Ammonium and Mercury.

(*a*) *General Reaction.*—To forty or fifty grains of dry mercury in a *dry* test-tube, add one or two small pieces of sodium (freed from adhering naphtha by gentle pressure with a piece of filter-paper), and amalgamate by gently warming the tube. To this amalgam, when cold, add some fragments of chloride of ammonium and a strong solution of the same salt. The sodium amalgam soon begins to swell and rapidly increase in bulk, probably overflowing the tube. The light spongy mass produced is the so-called ammonium amalgam, and the reaction is usually adduced as evidence of the existence of ammonium; the sodium of the amalgam unites with the chlorine of the chloride of ammonium, while the ammonium is supposed to form an amalgam with the mercury.

Hydrate of Ammonium. Ammonia.

(*b*) *Reactions having Synthetical interest.*

First Synthetical Reaction.—Heat a few grains of sal-ammoniac with about an equal weight of hydrate of calcium (slaked lime) damped with a little water in a test-tube ammonia gas is given off, and may be recognized by its well-known odor. It is very soluble in water. Pass a delivery tube, fitted to the test-tube as described for the preparation of oxygen and hydrogen, into a second test-tube, at the bottom of which is a little water; solution of ammonia will be thus formed.

$$\underset{\text{Chloride of ammonium.}}{2NH_4Cl} + \underset{\text{Hydrate of calcium.}}{Ca2HO} = \underset{\text{Chloride of calcium.}}{CaCl_2} + \underset{\text{Water.}}{2H_2O} + \underset{\text{Ammonia gas.}}{2NH_3}$$

Ammonia gas is composed of one atom of nitrogen with three atoms of hydrogen; its formula is NH_3; two volumes of it contain one volume of nitrogen combined with three atoms or volumes of hydrogen. Its constituents have therefore in combining suffered condensation to one-half their normal bulk. Its conversion into hydrate of ammonium may be thus shown:—

$$\underset{\text{Ammonia gas.}}{NH_3} + \underset{\text{Water.}}{H_2O} = \underset{\text{Hydrate of ammonium (ammonia).}}{NH_4HO \text{ or } AmHO}$$

Solutions of Ammonia, prepared by this process on a large scale and in suitable apparatus, are met with in pharmacy—the one (sp. gr. 0.891) containing 32.5 per cent., the other (sp. gr. 0.959), 10 per cent. by weight of ammonia gas, NH_3, or 66.9 and 20.6 of ammonia, NH_4HO (*Liquor Ammoniæ Fortior* and *Liquor Ammoniæ*, B. P. One part, *by measure*, of the former, and two of water form the latter). On the large scale, bottles are so arranged in a series as to condense all the ammonia evolved during the operation. *Aqua Ammoniæ Fortior*, U. S. P., sp. gr. 0.900, contains 26 per cent. of ammonia gas. *Aqua Ammoniæ*, U. S. P., has a sp. gr. of 0.960.

Acetate of Ammonium.

Second Synthetical Reaction.—To acetic acid and water in a test-tub add powdered commercial carbonate (acid carbonate and carbamate) of ammonium until effervescence ceases; the resulting liquid, made of prescribed strength, is the official solution of Acetate of Ammonium ($NH_4C_2H_3O_2$) (*Liquor Ammoniæ Acetatis*, B. P. and U. S. P.).

$$\underset{\text{Acid carbonate and carbamate of ammonium.}}{(NH_4HCO_3)_2NH_4NH_2CO_2} + \underset{\text{Acetic acid.}}{4HC_2H_3O_2} = \underset{\text{Acetate of ammonium.}}{4NH_4C_2H_3O_2}$$

$$+ \underset{\text{Water.}}{2H_2O} + \underset{\text{Carbonic acid gas.}}{3CO_2}.$$

Carbonates of Ammonium.

Commercial carbonate of ammonium is made by heating a mixture of chalk and sal-ammoniac; chloride of calcium ($CaCl_2$) is produced, ammonia gas (NH_3) and water (H_2O) escape, and the ammoniacal carbonate sublimes* in cakes (*Ammoniæ Carbonas*, B. P. and U. S. P.). This salt, the empirical formula of which is $N_4H_{16}C_3O_8$, is probably a mixture of two molecules of acid carbonate or bicarbonate of ammonium ($2NH_4HCO_3$) and one of a salt termed carbamate of ammonium ($NH_4NH_2CO_2$). The latter belongs to an important class of salts known as carbamates, but is the only one of interest to the pharmacist. Cold water extracts it from the commercial carbonate of ammonium, leaving the acid carbonate of ammonium undissolved, if the amount of liquid used be very small. In water carbamate soon changes into neutral carbonate of ammonium,

$$NH_4NH_2CO_2 + H_2O = (NH_4)_2CO_3 \text{ or } Am_2CO_3;$$

so that an aqueous solution of commercial carbonate of ammonium contains both acid carbonate and neutral carbonate of ammonium. If to such a solution some ordinary solution of ammonia be added, a solution of *neutral carbonate of ammonium* is obtained; and this is the common reagent always found on the shelves of the analytical laboratory.

$$AmHCO_3 + AmHO = Am_2CO_3 + H_2O.$$

Neutral carbonate of ammonium is the salt formed on adding strong solution of ammonia to the commercial carbonate in preparing a pungent mixture for toilet smelling-bottles; but it is unstable, and on continued exposure to air is reduced to a mass of crystals of the acid carbonate or bicarbonate of ammonium. Bicarbonate of ammonium (NH_4HCO_3) is also produced on passing carbonic acid gas into an aqueous solution of commercial carbonate.

Sal Volatile (*Spiritus Ammoniæ Aromaticus*, B. P. and U. S .P.) is a spirituous solution of ammonia (AmHO), neutral carbonate of ammonium (Am_2CO_3), and the oils of nutmeg and lemon (and lavender, U. S. P.). Fetid spirit of ammonia (*Spiritus Ammoniæ Fœtidus*, B. P.) is an alcoholic solution of the volatile oil of assafœtida mixed with solution of ammonia. "Solution of Carbonate of Ammonia," B. P., is formed by dissolving half an ounce of the salt in ten ounces of water. *Spiritus Ammoniæ*, U. S. P., is an alcoholic solution of ammonia.

Citrate, Phosphate, and Benzoate of Ammonium.

Third Synthetical Reaction.—To solution of citric acid ($H_3C_6H_5O_7$ or $H_3\overline{Ci}$) add solution of ammonia (AmHO) until the liquid is neutral to test-paper; the product is So-

* *Sublimation* (from *sublimis*, high). Vaporization of a solid substance by heat, and its condensation on an upper and cooler part of the vessel or apparatus in which the operation is performed.

lution of Citrate of Ammonium ($Am_3\overline{Ci}$) *Liquor Ammoniæ Citratis*, B. P.).

Phosphate of Ammonium (Am_2HPO_4) (*Ammoniæ Phosphas*, B. P.), and *Benzoate of Ammonium* ($AmC_7H_5O_2$) *Ammoniæ Benzoas*, B. P.), are also made by adding solution of ammonia to phosphoric acid (H_3PO_4) and benzoic acid ($HC_7H_5O_2$) respectively, evaporating (keeping the ammonia in slight excess by adding more of its solution), and setting aside for crystals to form.

$H_3C_6H_5O_7$ Citric acid.	+	$3AmHO$ Ammonia	=	$Am_3C_6H_5O_7$ Citrate of ammonium.	+	$3H_2O$ Water.
H_3PO_4 Phosphoric acid.	+	$2AmHO$ Ammonia.	=	Am_2HPO_4 Phosphate of ammonium.	+	$2H_2O$ Water.
$HC_7H_5O_2$ Benzoic. acid.	+	$AmHO$ Ammonia.	=	$AmC_7H_5O_2$ Benzoate of ammonium.	+	H_2O Water.

Phosphate of ammonium occurs in transparent colorless prisms, soluble in water, insoluble in spirit; benzoate in crystalline plates, soluble in water and in spirit.

Bromide of Ammonium (*Ammonii Bromidum*, B. P.) will be noticed in connection with Hydrobromic Acid and other Bromides.

Oxalate of Ammonium.

Fourth Synthetical Reaction.—To a nearly boiling solution of 1 part of oxalic acid in about 8 of water add carbonate of ammonium until the liquid is neutral to test-paper, filter while hot, and set aside for crystals ($(NH_4)_2C_2O_4, H_2O$) to form. The mother-liquor is useful as a reagent in analysis: 1 of the salt in 40 of water constitutes "Solution of Oxalate of Ammonia," B. P.

$2H_2C_2O_4$ Oxalic acid.	+	$N_4H_{16}C_3O_8$ Carbonate of ammonium.	=	$2(NH_4)_2C_2O_4$ Oxalate of ammonium.	+	$3CO_2$ Carbonic acid gas.	+	$2H_2O$ Water.

Sulphydrate of Ammonium.

Fifth Synthetical Reaction.—Pass sulphuretted hydrogen gas (H_2S) through a small quantity of solution of ammonia in a test-tube, until a portion of the liquid no longer causes a white precipitate in solution of sulphate of magnesium (Epsom salt); the product is solution of sulphydrate (or sulphide) of ammonium (NH_4HS), a most valuable chemical reagent, as will presently be apparent.

$$NH_4HO + H_2S = NH_4HS + H_2O.$$

"*Solution of Sulphide of Ammonium*," B. P., is made by passing the gas prepared in the apparatus described below, into 3 fluidounces of solution of ammonia (*Liquor Ammoniæ*) so long as the gas continues to be absorbed, then adding 2 more ounces of solution of ammonia, and preserving the solution in a well-stoppered green-glass bottle.

Sulphuretted hydrogen is a compound of noxious odor; hence the above operation, and many others, described further on, in which this gas is indispensable, can only be performed in the open air, or in a fume-cupboard, a chamber so contrived that deleterous gases and vapors shall escape into a chimney in connection with the external air. In the above experiment, the small quantity of gas required can be made in a test-tube, after the manner of hydrogen itself. To two or three fragments of sulphide of iron (FeS), add water and then sulphuric acid; the gas is at once evolved, and may be conducted by a tube into the solution of ammonia.

$$FeS + H_2SO_4 = H_2S + FeSO_4.$$

The iron remains dissolved in the water in the state of sulphate of iron.

Crystals of sulphydrate of ammonium (NH_4HS) may be obtained on bringing ammonia gas (NH_3) and sulphuretted hydrogen (H_2S) together at a low temperature. They are soluble in water without decomposition.

Sulphuretted-hydrogen Apparatus.—As no heat is necessary in making sulphuretted hydrogen, the test-tube of the foregoing operation may be advantageously replaced by a bottle, especially when larger quantities of the gas are required. In analytical operations, the gas should be purified by passing it through water contained in a second bottle.

The most convenient arrangement for experimental use is prepared as follows: Two common wide-mouth bottles are selected, the one having a capacity of about half a pint, the other a quarter pint; the former may be called the generating-bottle, the latter the wash-bottle. Fit two corks to the bottles. Through each cork bore two holes by a round file or other instrument, of such a size that glass tubing of about the diameter of a quill pen shall fit them tightly. Through one of the holes in the cork of the generating-bottle pass a funnel-tube, so that its extremity may nearly reach the bottom of the bottle. Such "funnel-tubes" may be purchased at the usual shops; or, if the student has access to a table-blowpipe, and the advantage of a tutor to direct his operations, they may be made by himself. To the other hole adapt a piece of tubing, 6 inches long, and bent in the middle to a right angle. A similar "elbow-tube" is fitted to one of the holes in the cork of the wash-bottle, and another elbow-tube, one arm of which is long enough to reach to near the bottom of the wash-bottle, fitted to the other hole. Removing the corks, two or three ounces of water are now poured into each bottle, an ounce or two of sulphide of iron put into the generating-bottle, and the corks replaced. The elbow-tube of the generating-bottle is now attached by a short piece of India-rubber tubing to the long-armed elbow-tube of the wash-bottle, so that gas coming from the generator may pass through the water in the wash-bottle. The delivery-tube of the wash-bottle is then lengthened by attaching to it, by India-rubber tubing, a straight piece of glass tubing, three or four inches long. The apparatus is now ready for use. Strong sulphuric acid is poured down the funnel-tube in small quantities at a time, until brisk effervescence is established, and more added from time to time as the evolution of gas becomes slow. The gas passes through the tubes into the wash-bottle, where, as it bubbles up through the water, any trace of sulphuric acid, or other matter mechanically carried over, is arrested, and thence flows out at the delivery-tube into any vessel or liquid that may be placed there to receive it. The generator must be occasionally dismounted, and the sulphate of iron washed out.

Luting (*latum*, mud). If the corks of the above apparatus are sound, and tube-holes well made, no escape of gas will occur. If rough corks have been employed, or the holes are not cylindrical, linseed-meal lute may be rubbed over the defective parts. The lute is prepared by mixing linseed-meal with water to the consistence of stiff paste. A neat appearance may be given to the lute by gently rubbing a well-wetted finger over its surface.

(c) *Reactions having Analytical Interest* (*Tests.*)

First Analytical Reaction.—To a solution of any salt of ammonium (the chloride, for example) in a test-tube add solution of caustic soda (or solution of potash, or a little slaked lime); ammonia gas is at once evolved, recognized by its well-known odor.

$$NH_4Cl + NaHO = NH_3 + H_2O + NaCl.$$

Though ammonium itself cannot exist in the free state, its compounds are stable. Ammonia is easily expelled from those compounds by action of the stronger alkalies, caustic potash, soda, or lime. As a matter of exercise, the student should here draw out equations in which acetate ($NH_4C_2H_3O_2$), sulphate (Am_2SO_4), nitrate (NH_4NO_3), or any other ammoniacal salt not already having the odor of ammonia, is supposed to be under examination; also representing the use of the other hydrates, potash (KHO) or slaked lime (Ca2HO).

The *odor* of ammonia gas is perhaps the best means of recognizing its presence; but the following tests are also occasionally useful. Into the test-tube in which the ammonia gas is evolved insert a glass rod moistened with hydrochloric acid (that is, with the solution of hydrochloric acid gas, conventionally termed hydrochloric acid, the *Acidum Hydrochloricum* of the Pharmacopæias); white fumes of chloride of ammonium will be produced.

$$NH_3 + HCl = NH_4Cl.$$

Hold a piece of moistened red litmus paper in a tube in which ammonia gas is present; the red color will be changed to blue.

Test-papers.—*Litmus* (B. P.) is a blue vegetable pigment, prepared from various species of *Roccella* lichen, exceedingly sensitive to the action of acids, which turn it red. When thus reddened, alkalies (potash, soda, and ammonia) and other soluble hydrates readily turn it blue. The student should here test for himself the delicacy of this action by experiments with paper soaked in solutions of litmus and dipped into very dilute solutions of acids, acid salts ($KHC_4H_4O_6$ *e. g.*), alkalies, and such neutral salts as nitrate of potassium, sulphate of sodium, or chloride of ammonium.

Tincture of Litmus.—1 ounce of litmus is macerated for two days in 10 fl. ounces of proof spirit, and the solution poured off from insoluble matter.

Blue litmus paper is unsized white paper steeped in tincture of litmus and dried by exposure to the air. *Red litmus paper* is unsized white paper steeped in tincture of litmus which has been previously reddened by the addition of a very minute quantity of sulphuric acid, and dried by exposure to the air.

Turmeric paper, similarly prepared from tincture of turmeric (1 of turmeric root or rhizome to 6 of rectified spirit macerated for seven days), is occasionally useful as a test for alkalies, which turn its yellow to brown; acids do not affect it.

Second Analytical Reaction.—To a few drops of a solution of an ammonium salt add a drop or two of hydrochloric acid and a like small quantity of solution of perchloride of platinum ($PtCl_4$); a yellow crystalline precipitate of the double chloride of platinum and ammonium ($PtCl_4 2NH_4Cl$)

will be produced, similar in appearance to the corresponding salt of potassium, the remarks concerning which (p. 54) are equally applicable to the precipitate under notice.

Third Analytical Reaction.—To a moderately strong solution of an ammonium salt add a strong solution of tartaric acid, and shake or well stir the mixture; a white granular precipitate of acid tartrate of ammonium will be formed.

For data from which to draw out an equation representing this action, see the remarks and formulæ under the analogous salt of potassium (p. 55).

Fourth Analytical Fact.—Evaporate a few drops of a solution of an ammonium salt to dryness, or place a fragment of a salt in the solid state on a piece of platinum foil, and heat in a flame; the salt is readily *volatilized.* As already noticed, the salts of potassium and sodium are *fixed* under these circumstances, a point of difference of which advantage will frequently be taken in analysis. A porcelain crucible may often be advantageously substituted for platinum foil in experiments on volatilization.

A wire triangle may be used in supporting crucibles. It is made by placing three (5 or 6 inch) pieces of wire in the form of a triangle and then twisting each pair of ends together through half the length of the wires. A piece of tobacco-pipe stem (about 2 inches) is sometimes placed in the centre of each wire before twisting, the transference of any metallic matter to the sides of the crucible being thus prevented.

Practical Analysis.

With regard to those experiments which are useful rather as means of detecting the presence of potassium, sodium, and ammonium, than as illustrating the preparation of salts, the student should proceed to apply them to certain solutions of any of the salts of potassium, sodium, and ammonium, with the view of ascertaining which metal is present; that is, proceed to practical analysis.* A

* Such solutions are prepared in educational laboratories by a tutor. They should, under other circumstances, be mixed by a friend, as it is not desirable to know previously what is contained in the substance about to be analyzed.

The analysis of solutions containing only one salt serves to impress the memory with the characteristic tests for the various metals and other radicals, and familiarize the mind with chemical principles. Medical students seldom have time to go further than this. More thorough analytical and general chemical knowledge is only acquired little thought will enable him to apply these reactions in the most suitable order and to the best advantage for the contemplated purpose; but the following arrangements are perhaps as good as can be devised:—

DIRECTIONS FOR APPLYING THE FOREGOING ANALYTICAL REACTIONS TO THE ANALYSIS OF AN AQUEOUS SOLUTION OF A SALT OF ONE OF THE METALS, POTASSIUM, SODIUM, AMMONIUM.

Add caustic soda to a small portion of the solution to be examined, and warm the mixture in a test-tube; the odor of ammonia gas at once reveals the presence of an ammonium salt.

If ammonium be not present, apply the perchloride-of-platinum test; a yellow precipitate proves the presence of potassium.

(It will be observed that potassium can only be detected in the absence of ammonium, salts of the latter radical giving similar precipitates.)

The flame-test is sufficient for the recognition of sodium.

DIRECTIONS FOR APPLYING THE FOREGOING ANALYTICAL REACTIONS TO THE ANALYSIS OF AN AQUEOUS SOLUTION OF SALTS OF ONE, TWO, OR ALL THREE OF THE ALKALI METALS.

Commence by testing a small portion of the solution for an ammonium salt. If present, make a memorandum to that effect, and then proceed to get rid of the ammoniacal compound to make way for the detection of potassium: advantage is here taken of the volatility of ammonium salts and the fixity of those of potassium and sodium. Evaporate the original solution to dryness in a small basin, transfer the solid residue to a porcelain crucible, and heat the latter to low redness, or until dense white fumes (of ammoniacal salts) cease to escape. This operation should be conducted in a fume-cupboard, to avoid

by working on such mixtures of bodies as are met with in actual practice, beginning with solutions which may contain any or all the members of a group. Hence in this manual, two Tables of short directions for analyzing are given under each group. Pharmaceutical students should follow the second Table.

contamination of the air of the apartment. When the crucible is cold, dissolve out the solid residue with a small quantity of water, and test the solution for potassium by the perchloride-of-platinum test, and for sodium by the flame-test.

If ammonium is proved to be absent, the original solution may, of course, be at once tested for potassium and sodium.

Flame-test.—The violet tint imparted to flame by potassium salts may be seen when masked by the intense yellow color due to sodium, if the flame be observed through a piece of dark-blue glass, a medium which absorbs the yellow rays of light.

Note on Nomenclature.—The operations of *evaporation* and heating to redness, or *ignition*, are frequently necessary in analysis, and are usually conducted in the above manner. If vegetable or animal matter be also present, carbon is set free, and ignition is accompanied by *carbonization;* the material is said to *char.* When all carbonaceous matter is burnt off, the crucible being slightly inclined and its cover removed to facilitate combustion, and mineral matter, or *ash,* alone remains, the operation of *incineration* has been effected.

Note on the Classification of Elements.—The compounds of potassium, sodium, and ammonium have many analogies. Their carbonates, phosphates, and most other salts are soluble in water. The atoms of the radicals themselves are univalent—that is, replace or are replaced by one atom of hydrogen. In fact, they constitute by their similarity in properties a distinct group or family. All the elements thus naturally fall into classes—a fact that should constantly be borne in mind, and evidence of which should always be sought. It would be impossible for the memory to retain the details of chemistry without a system of classification and leading principles. Classification is also an important feature in the art as well as in the science of chemistry; for without it practical analysis could not be undertaken. The classification adopted in this volume is founded, as far as possible, on the quantivalence of the elements, but chiefly on their analytical relations.

QUESTIONS AND EXERCISES.

110. Why are ammoniacal salts classed with those of potassium and sodium?

111. Mention the sources of the ammonium salts.

112. Describe the appearance and other characters of Chloride of Ammonium.

113. Adduce evidence of the existence of ammonium.

114. How are the official Solutions of Ammonia prepared? Give diagrams.

115. How is the official Solution of Acetate of Ammonium prepared?

116. What is the composition of commercial Carbonate of Ammonium?

117. Define *sublimation*.

118. What ammoniacal salts are contained in *Spiritus Ammoniæ Aromaticus?*

119. Give diagrams illustrating the formation of Citrate, Phosphate, and Benzoate of Ammonium.

120. Give the formula of Oxalate of Ammonium.

121. Show how hydrate of ammonium may be converted into sulphydrate.

122. Describe the preparation of Sulphuretted Hydrogen gas.

123. Enumerate and explain the tests for ammonium.

124. How is potassium detected in a solution in which ammonium has been found?

125. Draw diagrams illustrating the action of hydrate of sodium on acetate of ammonium; hydrate of potassium on sulphate of ammonium; and hydrate of calcium on nitrate of ammonium.

126. What are the effects of acids and alkalies on litmus and turmeric?

127. Describe the analysis of an aqueous liquid containing salts of potassium, sodium, and ammonium.

128. What meanings are commonly assigned to the terms *evaporation, ignition, carbonization,* and *incineration?*

129. Write a short article descriptive of the analogies of potassium, sodium, and ammonium, and their compounds.

BARIUM, CALCIUM, MAGNESIUM.

These three elements have many analogies. Their atoms are bivalent.

BARIUM.

Symbol Ba. Atomic weight 137.

The analytical reactions only of this metal are of interest to the general student of pharmacy. The chloride ($BaCl_2$) (Chloride of Barium, B. P. and U. S. P., and "Solution of Chloride of Barium," 1 in 10 of water, B. P.) and nitrate ($Ba2NO_3$) are the soluble salts in common use in analysis; and these and others are made by dissolving the native carbonate ($BaCO_3$), *Barytæ Carbonas*, U. S. P., the mineral *witherite*, in acids, or by heating the other common natural compound of barium, the sulphate, *heavy white* or *heavy spar* ($BaSO_4$), with coal—

$$BaSO_4 + C_4 = 4CO + BaS,$$

and dissolving the resulting sulphide in acids. When the nitrate is strongly heated it is decomposed, the oxide of barium or *baryta* (BaO) remaining. Baryta, on being moistened, assimilates the elements of water with great avidity, and yields hydrate of barium ($Ba2HO$). The latter is tolerably soluble, giving *baryta-water;* and from this solution crystals of hydrate of barium are obtained on evaporation.

The operations above described may all be performed in test-tubes and small porcelain crucibles heated by the gas-flame. Quantities of 1 oz. to 1 lb. require a coke-furnace.

Peroxide of barium (BaO_2) is formed on passing air over heated baryta. By the action of dilute hydrochloric acid it yields solution of *peroxide of hydrogen* (H_2O_2) or *oxygenated water.*

Quantivalence.—The atom of barium is bivalent, Ba″.

Reactions having Analytical Interest (Tests).

First Analytical Reaction.—To the solution of any soluble salt of barium (nitrate or chloride, for example) add dilute sulphuric acid; a white precipitate is obtained. Set the test-tube aside for two or three minutes, and when some of the precipitate has fallen to the bottom pour away most of the supernatant liquid, add strong nitric acid, and boil; the precipitate is insoluble.

The production of a white precipitate by sulphuric acid, insoluble even in hot nitric acid, is highly characteristic of barium. The name of this precipitate is sulphate of barium; its formula is $BaSO_4$.

Antidotes.—In cases of poisoning by soluble barium salts, any sulphates, such as those of magnesium and sodium (Epsom salt, Glauber's salt, alum), would be obvious antidotes.

Second Analytical Reaction.—To a barium solution add solution of the yellow chromate of potassium (K_2CrO_4); a pale yellow precipitate ($BaCrO_4$) falls. Add acetic acid to a portion of the chromate of barium; it is insoluble. Add hydrochloric or nitric acid to another portion; it is soluble.

"*Neutral Chromate.*"—The red chromate (or bichromate) of potassium (K_2CrO_4,CrO_3) must not be used in this reaction, or the barium will be only imperfectly precipitated; for the red salt gives rise to the formation of free acid, in which chromate of barium is to some extent soluble:—

$$K_2CrO_4, CrO_3 + 2BaCl_2 + H_2O = 2BaCrO_4 + 2KCl + 2HCl.$$

Yellow chromate is obtained on adding carbonate of potassium, in small quantities at a time, to a hot solution of the red chromate until effervescence ceases; a little more red chromate is then added to insure decomposition of any slight excess of carbonate of potassium.

$$K_2CrO_4, CrO_3 + K_2CO_3 = 2K_2CrO_4 + CO_2.$$

For analytical purposes solution of a neutral chromate is still more readily prepared by simply adding solution of ammonia to solution of red chromate of potassium, until the liquid turns yellow, and, after stirring, smells of ammonia.

$$K_2CrO_4, CrO_3 + 2NH_4HO = 2KNH_4CrO_4 + H_2O.$$

Other Analytical Reactions.—To a barium solution add a soluble carbonate (carbonate of ammonium (Am_2CO_3) will generally be rather more useful than others); a white precipitate of carbonate of barium ($BaCO_3$) results.——To more of the solution add an alkaline phosphate or arseniate (phosphate of sodium (Na_2HPO_4) is the most common of these chemically analogous salts, but phosphate of ammonium (Am_2HPO_4) or arseniate (Am_2HAsO_4) will subsequently have the preference); white phosphate of barium ($BaHPO_4$) insoluble in pure water, but slightly soluble in aqueous solutions of some salts, or arseniate of barium ($BaHAsO_4$), both soluble even in acetic and other weak acids, are precipitated.——To another portion add oxalate of ammonium ($Am_2C_2O_4$); white oxalate of barium (BaC_2O_4) is precipitated, soluble in strong acids, and sparingly so in acetic acid.——The silico-fluoride of barium ($BaSiF_6$) is insoluble, and falls readily if an equal volume of spirit of wine be added to the solution under examination after the addition of hydrofluosilicic acid (H_2SiF_6).

——Barium salts, moistened with hydrochloric acid, impart a greenish color to flame.

Mem.—Good practice will be found in writing out equations descriptive of each of the foregoing reactions.

QUESTIONS AND EXERCISES.

130. What are the quantivalent relations of barium to other radicals?

131. Write down the formulæ of oxide, hydrate, chloride, nitrate, carbonate, and sulphate of barium; and state how these salts are prepared.

132. Describe the preparation of peroxide of hydrogen.

133. Which of the tests for barium are most characteristic? Give an equation of the reactions.

134. Name the antidote in cases of poisoning by soluble barium salts, and explain its action.

CALCIUM.

Symbol Ca. Atomic weight 40.

Calcium compounds form a large proportion of the crust of our earth. Carbonate of calcium is met with as chalk, marble, limestone, calc-spar, &c., the sulphate, as gypsum or plaster of Paris ("Plaster of Paris, native sulphate of calcium—$CaSO_4$, $2H_2O$—deprived of water by heat."—B. P.), and alabaster, the silicate in many minerals, the fluoride of calcium as fluor-spar. The phosphate is also a common mineral. The element itself is only isolated with great difficulty. The atom of calcium is bivalent, Ca''.

REACTIONS HAVING SYNTHETICAL INTEREST.

Chloride of Calcium.

First Synthetical Reaction.—To some hydrochloric acid add carbonate of calcium (chalk, or, the purer form, white marble, *Marmor Album*, B. P. and U. S. P.) ($CaCO_3$) until effervescence ceases, filter; solution of chloride of calcium ($CaCl_2$), the most common soluble salt of calcium, is formed.

$$\underset{\text{Carbonate of calcium.}}{CaCO_3} + \underset{\text{Hydrochloric acid.}}{2HCl} = \underset{\text{Chloride of calcium.}}{CaCl_2} + \underset{\text{Water.}}{H_2O} + \underset{\text{Carbonic acid gas.}}{CO_2}$$

This solution contains carbonic acid, and will give a precipitate of carbonate of calcium on the addition of lime-water. It may be obtained quite neutral by well boiling before filtering off the excess of marble. It is a serviceable test-liquid in analytical operations.

Solution of chloride of calcium evaporated to a syrupy consistence readily yields crystals. These are extremely deliquescent. The solution, evaporated to dryness, and the white residue strongly heated, gives solid anhydrous chloride of calcium in a porous form. The resulting agglutinated lumps (*Calcii Chloridum*, B. P. and U. S. P.) are much used for drying gases, and for freezing certain liquids from water. The salt is soluble in alcohol. One part in ten of water constitutes "Solution of Chloride of Calcium," B. P. Four parts in five of water forms the "Solution (saturated) of Chloride of Calcium," B. P.

Marble often contains ferrous carbonate ($FeCO_2$), which in the above process becomes converted into ferrous chloride, rendering the chloride of calcium impure:—

$$\underset{\text{Ferrous carbonate.}}{FeCO_3} + \underset{\text{Hydrochloric acid.}}{2HCl} = \underset{\text{Ferrous chloride.}}{FeCl_2} + \underset{\text{Water.}}{H_2O} + \underset{\text{Carbonic acid gas.}}{CO_2}$$

If absolutely pure chloride of calcium be required, a few drops of the solution should be poured into a test-tube or test-glass, diluted with water, and examined for iron (by adding sulphydrate of ammonium, which gives a black precipitate with salts of iron), and, if the latter is present, hypochlorite of calcium (in the form of chlorinated lime) and slaked lime be added to the remaining bulk of the liquid, and the whole boiled for a few minutes, whereby iron is precipitated; on filtering, a pure solution of chloride of calcium is obtained:—

$$\underset{\text{Ferrous chloride.}}{4FeCl_2} + \underset{\text{Hypochlorite of calcium.}}{Ca2ClO} + \underset{\text{Hydrate of calcium.}}{4CaH_2O_2} + \underset{\text{Water.}}{2H_2O}$$

$$= \underset{\text{Ferric hydrate.}}{2(Fe_26HO)} + \underset{\text{Chloride of calcium.}}{5CaCl_2}$$

This is the official process, and may be imitated on the small scale by adding a minute piece of iron to a fragment of the marble before dissolving in acid.

The names, formulæ, and reactions of these compounds of iron will be best understood when that metal comes under treatment.

Oxide of Calcium (Quick Lime).

Second Synthetical Reaction.—Place a small piece of chalk in a strong grate-fire or furnace and heat until a trial fragment, chipped off from time to time and cooled, no longer effervesces on the addition of acid; caustic lime, CaO (*Calx*, B. P. and U. S. P.), remains.

$$\underset{\text{Carbonate of calcium (chalk).}}{CaCO_3} = \underset{\text{Oxide of calcium (lime).}}{CaO} + \underset{\text{Carbonic acid gas.}}{CO_2}$$

Note.—Etymologically considered, this action is analytical (ἀναλύω, *analuo*, I resolve) and not synthetical (σύνθεσις, *sūnthesis*, a putting together); but conventionally it is synthetical, and not analytical; for in this, the usual sense, and the sense in which the words are used throughout this book, synthesis is the application of chemical action with the view of producing something, analysis the application of chemical action with the view of finding out the composition of a substance. In the etymological view of the matter there is scarcely an operation performed either by the analyst or by the manufacturer but includes both analysis and synthesis.

Lime-kilns.—On the large scale the above operation is carried on in what are termed *lime-kilns* (*Kiln*, Saxon, *cyln*, from *cylene*, a furnace).

Hydrate of Calcium (Slaked Lime).

Slaked Lime.—When cold, add to the lime about half its weight of water, and notice the evolution of steam and other evidence of strong action; the product is *slaked* lime or hydrate of calcium (Ca2HO) (*Calcis hydras*, B. P.), with whatever slight natural impurities the lime might contain.

$$\underset{\text{Lime.}}{CaO} + \underset{\text{Water.}}{H_2O} = \underset{\text{Hydrate of calcium (slaked lime).}}{Ca2HO}$$

Lime-water.—Place the hydrate of calcium in about a hundred times its weight of water: in a short time a saturated solution, known as *lime-water* (*Liquor Calcis*, B. P. and U. S. P.), results. It contains about 16 grains of hydrate of calcium (Ca2HO), equivalent to about 11 or 12 grains of lime (CaO), in one pint.

Strong Solution of Lime.—Slaked lime is much more soluble in aqueous solution of sugar than in pure water. The *Liquor Calcis Saccharatus*, B. P., is such a solution, containing 2 ounces of sugar and 188 grains of hydrate of calcium (Ca2HO), equivalent to 142 grains of lime (CaO), in 1 pint. It is a more efficient precipitant of hydrates and carbonates than lime-water. The official process is as follows: Mix 1 ounce of lime and 2 of sugar by trituration in a mortar. Transfer the mixture to a bottle containing 1 pint of water, and, having closed this with a cork, shake it occasionally for a few hours. Finally separate the clear solution with a siphon and keep it in a stoppered bottle.

Carbonate of Calcium.

Third Synthetical Reaction.—To a solution of chloride of calcium add excess of carbonate of sodium, or about 5 parts of dry chloride to 13 of carbonate; a white precipitate of carbonate of calcium (*Calcis Carbonas Præcipitata*, B. P. and U. S. P.), ($CaCO_3$) results. If the solutions of the salts be made hot before admixture, and the whole set aside for a short time, the particles aggregate to a greater extent than when cold water is used, and the product is finely granular or slightly crystalline. The official variety is thus prepared.

$$\underset{\text{Chloride of calcium.}}{CaCl_2} + \underset{\text{Carbonate of sodium.}}{Na_2CO_3} = \underset{\text{Carbonate of calcium.}}{CaCO_3} + \underset{\text{Chloride of sodium.}}{2NaCl}$$

Collect and purify this *Precipitated Chalk* by pouring the mixture into a paper cone supported by a funnel, and, when the liquid has passed through the filter, pour water over the precipitate three or four times until the whole of the chloride of sodium is washed away. This operation is termed *washing a precipitate.* When dry (*vide* Index, "drying precipitates") the precipitate is fit for use.

Filtering-paper or *bibulous-paper* (from *bibo*, to drink), is simply good unsized paper made from the best white rags—white blotting-paper, in fact, of unusually good quality. Students' or analysts' filters, on which to collect precipitates, are round pieces of this paper, from three to six inches in diameter, twice folded, and then opened out so as to form a hollow cone. Square pieces are rounded by scissors *after* folding. The cone is supported by a glass or earthenware funnel.

Washing-bottle.—Precipitates are best washed by a fine jet of water directed on to the different parts of the filter. A common narrow-necked bottle of about half-pint capacity is fitted with a cork; two holes are bored through the cork, the one for a glass tube reaching to the bottom of the bottle within, and externally bent to a slightly acute angle, the other for a tube bent to a slightly obtuse angle, the inner arm terminating just within the bottle. The outer arms may be about 3 inches in length. The extremity of the outer arm continuous with the long tube should be previously drawn out to a fine capillary opening by holding the original tube, before cutting, in a flame, and, when soft, gently pulling the halves away from each other until the heated portion is reduced to the thinness of a knitting-needle. The tube is now cut at the thin part by a file, and the sharp edges rounded off by placing in a flame for a second or two. The outer extremity of the shorter tube should also be made smooth in the flame. The apparatus being put together, and the bottle nearly filled with water, air blown through the short tube by the lungs, forces water out in a fine stream at the capillary orifice.

Decantation.—Precipitates may also be washed by allowing them to settle, pouring off the supernatant liquid, agitating with water, again allowing to settle, and so on. This is washing by *decantation* (*de*, from, *canthus*, a brim). If a stream of liquid flowing from a basin or other vessel exhibits any tendency to run down the outer side of the vessel, it should be guided by a glass rod placed against the point whence the stream emerges.

If the vessel be too large to handle with convenience, the wash-water may be drawn off by a *siphon*. A siphon is a tube of glass, metal, gutta percha, or India-rubber, bent into the form of a V or U, filled with water, and inverted; one end immersed in the wash-water, and the other allowed to hang over the side of the vessel: so long as the outer orifice of the instrument is below the level of the liquid in the vessel, so long will that liquid flow from within outwards until the vessel be empty.*

* *The nature of the action of a siphon* is simple. The column of water in the outer limb is longer, and therefore heavier, than the column of similar area in the inner limb. (The length of the inner limb must be reckoned from the surface of the liquid, the portion below the surface playing no part in the operation.) Being heavier, it naturally falls by gravitation, the liquid in the shorter limb instantly following, because pressed upwards by the air. The air, be it observed, exerts a similar amount of pressure on the liquid in the outer limb: in short, atmospheric pressure causes the retention of liquid in the instrument, while gravitation determines the direction of the flow.

Prepared carbonate of calcium (*Creta Præparata*, B. P. and U. S. P.) is merely washed chalk (*Creta*, B. P. and U. S. P.) or *whiting*, only that in Pharmacy fashion demands that the chalk be in little conical lumps, about the size of thimbles, instead of in the larger rolls characteristic of "whiting." Wet whiting pushed, portion by portion, through a funnel, and each separately dried, gives the conventional *Creta Præparata*. Its powder is amorphous.

Testa Præparata, U. S. P., is powdered oyster-shell, similarly treated. It is an inferior kind of prepared chalk.

Phosphate of Calcium.

Fourth Synthetical Reaction.—Digest bone-ash (bones burnt in an open crucible with free access of air till all animal and carbonaceous matter has been removed—impure phosphate of calcium (*Os Ustum*, B. P.)) with nearly twice its weight of hydrochloric acid (diluted with three or four times its bulk of water) in a test-tub or larger vessel; the phosphate is dissolved.

$$\underset{\text{Phosphate of calcium (impure).}}{Ca_32PO_4} + \underset{\text{Hydrochloric acid.}}{4HCl} = \underset{\text{Acid phosphate of calcium.}}{CaH_42PO_4} + \underset{\text{Chloride of calcium.}}{2CaCl_2}$$

Dilute with water, filter, boil, and when cold add excess of solution of ammonia; the phosphate of calcium, now pure (*Calcis Phosphas*, B. P.; *Calcis Phosphas Precipitata*, U. S. P.), is reprecipitated as a light white amorphous powder. After well washing, the precipitate should be dried over *a water-bath* (*vide* Index), or at a temperature not exceeding 512°, to prevent undue aggregation of the particles.

$$\underset{\text{Acid phosphate of calcium.}}{CaH_42PO_4} + \underset{\text{Chloride of calcium.}}{2CaCl_2} + \underset{\text{Ammonia.}}{4AmHO} = \underset{\text{Phosphate of calcium (pure).}}{Ca_32PO_4} + \underset{\text{Chloride of ammonium.}}{4AmCl} + \underset{\text{Water.}}{4H_2O}$$

Bone-black, or *Animal Charcoal* (*Carbo Animalis*, B. P. and U. S. P.), is the residue obtained on subjecting dried bones (*Os*, U. S. P.) to a red heat without access of air. The operation may be imitated by heating a few fragments of bone in a covered porcelain crucible in a fume-chamber until smoke and vapor cease to be evolved. Purified Animal Charcoal (*Carbo Animalis Purificatus*, B. P. and U. S. P.) is obtained by digesting animal charcoal (16 parts) in hydrochloric acid (10 parts) and water (20 parts) in a warm place for a day or two, filtering, thoroughly washing, drying over a water-bath, and igniting the product in a closely covered crucible. The acid dissolves out phosphate of calcium, according to the previous reaction, decomposes and dissolves carbonate of calcium and sulphide of calcium, the carbon remaining unaltered.

Wood Charcoal (*Carbo Ligni*, B. P. and U. S. P.) is wood similarly ignited without access of air.

Decolorizing power of Animal Charcoal.—Animal charcoal, in small fragments, is the material employed in decolorizing solutions of common brown sugar with the view of producing white lump sugar. Its power and the nearly equal power of an equivalent quantity of the purified variety may be demonstrated on solution of litmus or logwood.

Phosphate of Sodium.—Phosphate of calcium is converted into phosphate of sodium (*Sodæ Phosphas*, B. P. and U. S. P.) ($Na_2HPO_4,12H_2O$) as follows: Mix, in a mortar, 3 ounces of ground bone-earth with 1 fluidounce of sulphuric acid; set aside for twenty-four hours to promote reaction; mix in about 3 ounces of water, and put in a warm place for two days, a little water being added to make up for that lost by evaporation; stir in another 3 ounces of water, warm the whole for a short time, filter, and wash the residual sulphate of calcium on the filter to remove adhering acid phosphate of calcium; concentrate the filtrate (solution of acid phosphate of calcium) to about 3 ounces, filter again if necessary, add solution of (about 4½ ounces of crystals of) carbonate of sodium to the hot filtrate until a precipitate (phosphate of calcium, Ca_32PO_4) ceases to form, and the fluid is faintly alkaline; filter, evaporate, and set aside to crystallize.

Phosphate of sodium occurs "in transparent colorless rhombic prisms, terminated by four converging planes, efflorescent, tasting like common salt." One part in ten of water constitutes "Solution of Phosphate of Soda," B. P. This is an official as well as the ordinary process. The following equations show the two decompositions which occur during the operations:—

$$\underset{\substack{\text{Phosphate}\\\text{of calcium.}}}{3(Ca_32PO_4)} + \underset{\substack{\text{Sulphuric}\\\text{acid.}}}{6H_2SO_4} = \underset{\substack{\text{Acid phosphate}\\\text{of calcium.}}}{3(CaH_42PO_4)} + \underset{\substack{\text{Sulphate of}\\\text{calcium.}}}{6CaSO_4}$$

$$\underset{\substack{\text{Acid phosphate}\\\text{of calcium.}}}{3(CaH_42PO_4)} + \underset{\substack{\text{Carbonate}\\\text{of sodium.}}}{4Na_2CO_3} = \underset{\substack{\text{Phosphate of}\\\text{sodium.}}}{4Na_2HPO_4} + \underset{\text{Water.}}{4H_2O} + \underset{\substack{\text{Carbonic}\\\text{acid gas.}}}{4CO_2} + \underset{\substack{\text{Phosphate}\\\text{of calcium.}}}{Ca_32PO_4}$$

Hypochlorite of Calcium.

Fifth Synthetical Reaction.—Pass chlorine, generated as already described, into damp slaked line contained in a piece of wide tubing, open at the opposite end to that in which the delivery-tube is fixed. (A test-tube, the bottom of which has been accidentally broken, is very convenient for such operations.) The product is ordinary *bleaching-powder*, said to be a mixture of hypochlorite and chloride of calcium, commonly called *chloride of lime*, *Calx chlorata*, B. P. (*Calx Chlorinata*, U. S. P.)

$$\underset{\text{Black oxide of manganese.}}{MnO_2} + \underset{\text{Hydrochloric acid.}}{4HCl} = \underset{\text{Chloride of manganese.}}{MnCl_2} + \underset{\text{Water.}}{2H_2O} + \underset{\text{Chlorine.}}{Cl_2}$$

$$\underset{\text{Hydrate of calcium.}}{2CaH_2O_2} + \underset{\text{Chlorine.}}{2Cl_2} = \underset{\text{Water.}}{2H_2O} + \underset{\text{Hypochlorite of calcium.}}{CaCl_2O_2}\ ,\ \underset{\text{Chloride of calcium.}}{CaCl_2}$$

Chlorinated lime, exposed to air and moisture, as in disinfecting the air of sick rooms, slowly yields hypochlorous acid ($HClO$). Free hypochlorous acid soon breaks up into water, chloric acid ($HClO_3$), and free chlorine. Chloric acid is also unstable, decomposing into oxygen, water, chlorine, and perchloric acid ($HClO_4$). The small quantity of hypochlorous acid diffused through an apartment when bleaching-powder is exposed thus, yields fourteen-fifteenths of its chlorine in the form of chlorine gas—one of the most efficient of known disinfectants.

Bleaching-liquor.—Digest chlorinated lime in water, in which the bleaching compound is soluble, filter from the undissolved lime, and test the bleaching-powers of the clear liquid by adding a few drops to a decoction of logwood slightly acidulated. One pound of this bleaching-powder, shaken several times during three hours, with 1 gallon of water, forms Solution of Chlorinated Lime (*Liquor Calcis Chloratæ*, B. P.).

Gummate of Calcium.

Gummate of Calcium is the only official calcium salt that remains to be noticed. This compound is, in short, *arabin*, the ordinary Gum-Acacia or Gum-Arabic (*Acaciæ Gummi*, B. P. and U. S. P.), a substance too well known to need description. A solution of gum-arabic in water (*Mucilago Acaciæ*, B. P. and U. S. P.) yields a white precipitate of oxalate of calcium on the addition of solution of oxalate of ammonium. Or a piece of gum burnt to an ash in a porcelain crucible yields a calcareous residue, which, dissolved in dilute acids, affords characteristic reactions with any of the following analytical reagents for calcium. The gummic radical may be precipitated as opaque gelatinous gummate of lead by the addition of solution of oxyacetate of lead (*Liquor Plumbi Subacetatis*, B. P.) to an aqueous solution of gum. These statements may be experimentally verified by the practical student.

Tragacanth (*Tragacantha*, B. P. and U. S. P.) is usually considered to be a mixture of soluble gum or arabin and a variety of calcium gum insoluble in water, termed *bassorin:* Guibourt thought it to be gelatinoid. With water a gelatinous mucilage is formed (*Mucilago Tragacanthæ*, B. P. and U. S. P.).

Reactions having Analytical Interest (Tests).

First Analytical Reaction.—Add sulphuric acid, highly diluted, to a calcium solution contained in a test-tube or small test-glass; sulphate of calcium ($CaSO_4$, $2H_2O$) is formed, but is *not* precipitated, it being, unlike sulphate of barium, slightly soluble in water.

Solution of Sulphate of Calcium.—A quarter of an ounce of that (dried) form of sulphate of calcium known as plaster of Paris ($CaSO_4$) digested in one pint of water for a short time, with occasional shaking, and the mixture filtered, yields the official test-liquid termed "Solution of Sulphate of Lime," B. P. About 400 parts of the solution contain 1 of sulphate of calcium.

Second Analytical Reaction.—Add yellow chromate of potassium (K_2CrO_4) to a calcium solution slightly acidified with acetic acid; chromate of calcium ($CaCrO_4$) is probably formed, but is *not* precipitated.

These two negative reactions are most valuable in analysis, as every precipitant of calcium is also a precipitant of barium; but the above two reagents are precipitants of barium only. Hence calcium, which when alone can be readily detected by the following reactions, cannot by any reaction be detected in the presence of barium. But by the sulphuric or chromic test barium is easily removed, and then either of the following reagents will throw down the calcium.

Other Analytical Reactions.—Add carbonate of ammonium, phosphate of sodium, arseniate of ammonium, and oxalate of ammonium to calcium solutions as described under the analytical reactions of barium, and write out descriptive equations. The precipitates correspond in appearance to those of barium; their constitution is also identical, hence their correct formulæ can easily be deduced. Of these precipitants oxalate of ammonium is that most commonly used as a reagent for calcium salts, barium being absent. The oxalate of calcium is insoluble in acetic, but soluble in hydrochloric or nitric acids.——Calcium compounds impart a reddish color to flame.

QUESTIONS AND EXERCISES.

135. Enumerate some of the common natural compounds of calcium.

136. Explain, by an equation, the action of hydrochloric acid on marble. What official compounds result?

137. Why is chloride of calcium used as a desiccator for gases?

138. How would you purify Chloride of Calcium which has been made from ferruginous marble? Give diagrams.

139. Write a few lines on the chemistry of the lime-kiln.

140. In what sense is the conversion of chalk into lime an analytical action?

141. What occurs when lime is slaked?

142. To what extent is lime soluble in water? to what in syrup?

143. Describe the preparation of the official Precipitated Carbonate of Calcium; in what does it differ from Prepared Chalk?

144. In what does filtering-paper differ from other kinds of paper?

145. Explain the construction of "a washing-bottle" for cleansing precipitates by water.

146. Define *decantation.*

147. Describe the construction and manner of employment of a siphon.

148. Explain the mode of action of a siphon.

149. What is the difference between Bone, Bone-earth, and Precipitated Phosphate of Calcium?

150. How is "Bone-earth" purified for use in medicine?

151. Explain the action of hydrochloric acid on Animal Charcoal in the conversion of *Carbo Animalis* into *Carbo Animalis Purificatus.*

152. What is the chemical difference between *Carbo Animalis* and *Carbo Ligni?*

153. Give equations showing the conversion of Phosphate of Calcium into Phosphate of Sodium.

154. Write a short article on the manufacture, composition, and uses of "bleaching-powder."

155. How may calcium be detected in Gum-Arabic?

156. State the chemical nature of Tragacanth.

157. To what extent is sulphate of calcium soluble in water?

158. Can calcium be precipitated from an aqueous solution containing barium?

159. Barium being absent, what reagents may be used for the detection of calcium? Which is the chief test?

MAGNESIUM.

Symbol Mg. Atomic weight 24.

Source.—Magnesium is abundant in nature in the form of magnesian or mountain limestone, or *dolomite,* a double carbonate of magnesium and calcium in common use as a building-stone (*e. g.* the Houses of Parliament, and the School of Mines in London), and *magnesite,* a tolerably pure carbonate of magnesium, though too "stony" for direct use in medicine, even if very finely powdered. Chloride of magnesium and sulphate of magnesium (Epsom salt) also occur in sea-water and the water of many springs. Metallic magnesium may be obtained from the chloride by the action of sodium. It burns readily in the air, emitting a dazzling light due to the white heat to which the resulting particles of magnesia (MgO) are exposed.

Quantivalence.—The atom of magnesium is bivalent, Mg''.

Reactions having Synthetical Interest.

Sulphate of Magnesium.

First Synthetical Reaction.—To a few drops of sulphuric acid and a little water in a test-tube (or to larger quantities in larger vessels), add carbonate of magnesium (preferably the native carbonate *magnesite,* $MgCO_3$) until effervescence ceases, subsequently boiling to aid in the expulsion of the carbonic acid gas. The filtered liquid is a solution of sulphate of magnesium ($MgSO_4$), crystals of which, *Epsom salt* ($MgSO_4$, $7H_2O$) (*Magnesiæ Sulphas,* B. P. and U. S. P.), may be obtained on evaporating most of the water, and setting the concentrated solution aside to cool. This is an ordinary manufacturing process. Instead of magnesite, *dolomite,* the common magnesian limestone ($CaCO_3$, $MgCO_3$) may be employed, any iron being removed by evaporating the solution (filtered from the sulphate of calcium produced) to dryness, gently igniting to decompose sulphate of iron, dissolving in water, filtering from oxide of iron, and crystallizing.

Sulphate of magnesium readily crystallizes in large, colorless, transparent, rhombic prisms; but, from concentrated solutions, the crystals are deposited in short thin needles, a form more convenient for manipulation, solution, and general use in medicine.

Iron may be detected in sulphate of magnesium by adding the common alkaline solution of chlorinated lime or chlorinated soda to an aqueous solution of the salt; brown hydrate of iron ($Fe_2 6HO$) being precipitated.

Carbonates of Magnesium.

Second Synthetical Reaction.—To solution of sulphate of magnesium add solution of carbonate of sodium and boil; the resulting precipitate is *light* carbonate of magnesium (*Magnesiæ Carbonas Levis*, B. P.), a white, partly amorphous, partly minutely crystalline mixture of carbonate and hydrate of magnesium ($3MgCO_3$, $Mg2HO$, $4H_2O$). A denser, slightly granular precipitate of similar chemical composition (*Magnesiæ Carbonas*, B. P. and U. S. P.) is obtained on mixing strong solutions of the above salts, evaporating to dryness, then removing the sulphate of sodium by digesting the residue in hot water, filtering, washing, and drying the precipitate.

$$\underset{\text{Sulphate of magnesium.}}{4MgSO_4} + \underset{\text{Carbonate of sodium.}}{4Na_2CO_3} + \underset{\text{Water.}}{H_2O} = \underset{\text{Official carbonate of magnesium.}}{3MgCO_3, Mg2HO} + \underset{\text{Sulphate of sodium.}}{4Na_2SO_4} + \underset{\text{Carbonic acid gas.}}{CO_2}$$

The official proportions for the light carbonate are 10 of sulphate of magnesium and 12 of crystals of carbonate of sodium, each dissolved in 80 of cold water, the solutions mixed, boiled for 15 minutes, the precipitate collected on a filter, well washed, drained, and dried over a water-bath. The heavier carbonate is made with the same proportions of salts, each dissolved in 20 instead of 80 of water, the mixture evaporated quite to dryness, and the residue washed by decantation or filtration until all sulphate of sodium is removed (shown by a white precipitate—sulphate of barium—ceasing to form on the addition of solution of chloride or nitrate of barium to a little of the filtrate).

Third Synthetical Reaction.—Pass carbonic acid gas, generated as described on page 48, into a mixture of water and carbonate of magnesium contained in a test-tube. After some time, separate undissolved carbonate by filtration; the filtrate contains carbonate of magnesium dissolved by carbonic acid. When of a strength of about 13 grains in one ounce, the solution constitutes "*Fluid Magnesia*" (*Liquor Magnesiæ Carbonatis*, B. P.).

Officially, 1 pint is directed to be made from freshly prepared carbonate. The latter is obtained by adding a hot solution of 2 ounces of sulphate of magnesium in half a pint of water to one of 2½ ounces of crystals of carbonate of sodium in another half pint of water, boiling the mixture for a short time (to complete decomposition), filtering, thoroughly washing the precipitate, placing the latter in 1 pint of distilled water, and transmitting carbonic acid gas through the liquid (say, at the rate of three or four bubbles per second) for an hour or two, then leaving the solution in contact with the gas under slight pressure for twenty-four hours, and, finally, filtering from undissolved carbonate, and, after passing in a little more gas, keeping in a well-corked bottle. Slight pressure is best created by placing the carbonate and water in a bottle fitted with a cork and tubes as for a wash-bottle (p. 69 or 81), conveying the gas by a tube which reaches to the bottom, and allowing excess of gas to flow out by the upper tube, the external end of which is continued to the bottom of a common phial containing about an inch of mercury. The phial should be loosely plugged with cotton wool, to prevent loss of metal by spurting during the flow of the gas through it. (Each inch in depth of mercury through which the gas escapes corresponds to about half-a-pound pressure on every square inch of surface within the apparatus.)

Heat a portion of the solution; true carbonate of magnesium containing combined water ($MgCO_3$, $3H_2O$) is precipitated. The water in this compound is probably in the state of water of crystallization, for a salt having the same composition is deposited in crystals by the spontaneous evaporation of the solution of carbonate of magnesium. The official "carbonate" ($3MgCO_3$, $Mg2HO$, $4H_2O$) is another of these very common *hydrous* compounds.

Exposed to cold, the solution of "fluid magnesia" sometimes affords large thick crystals ($MgCO_3$, $5H_2O$), which, in contact with the air, lose water, become opaque, and then have the composition of those deposited by evaporation ($MgCO_3$, $3H_2O$).

Oxide of Magnesium (Magnesia).

Fourth Synthetical Reaction.—Heat some of the above light dry carbonate in a porcelain crucible over a lamp (or in a larger earthen crucible in a furnace) till it ceases to effervesce on adding, to a small portion, water and acid; the residue is light magnesia (MgO) (*Magnesia Levis*, B. P.). The same operation on the heavy carbonate yields heavy magnesia (MgO) (*Magnesia*, B. P.). Both are sometimes spoken of as "calcined magnesia" (*Magnesia*, U. S. P.). A given weight of the official light magnesia occupies three and a half times the bulk of the weight of heavy magnesia.

$$\underset{\text{Official carbonate of magnesium.}}{3MgCO_3, Mg2HO} = \underset{\text{Oxide of magnesium.}}{4MgO} + \underset{\text{Water.}}{H_2O} + \underset{\text{Carbonic acid gas}}{3CO_2}$$

A trace only of magnesia is dissolved by pure water. Moisten a grain or two of magnesia with water, and place the paste on a piece of red litmus-paper; the wet spot, after a time, becomes blue, showing that the magnesia is slightly soluble.

Reactions having Analytical Interest (Tests).

First Analytical Reaction.—Add solution of hydrate or carbonate of ammonium to a magnesian solution (sulphate for example) and boil the mixture in a test-tube; the precipitation of part only of the magnesium as hydrate ($Mg2HO$) or carbonate ($MgCO_3$) occurs. Add now to a small portion of the mixture of precipitate and liquid a considerable access of solution of chloride of ammonium; the precipitate is dissolved.

This is an important reaction, especially as regards carbonate of magnesium, the presence of chloride of ammonium enabling the analyst to throw out from a solution barium and calcium by an alkaline carbonate, magnesium being retained. The cause of this reaction is the tendency of magnesium to form soluble double salts with potassium, sodium, or ammonium. In analysis, the chloride of ammonium should be added before the carbonate, as it is easier to prevent precipitation than to redissolve a precipitate once formed.

Second Analytical Reaction.—To some of the solution resulting from the last reaction, add solution of phosphate of sodium or ammonium; phosphate of magnesium and ammonium ($MgNH_4PO_4$) is precipitated.——*3d.* To another portion add arseniate of ammonium; arseniate of magnesium and ammonium ($MgNH_4AsO_4$) is precipitated.

Note.—Barium and calcium are also precipitated by alkaline phosphates and arseniates. The other precipitants of magnesium are also precipitants of barium and calcium. In other words, there is no *direct* test for magnesium. Hence the analyst always removes any barium or calcium by an alkaline carbonate, as above indicated; the phosphate of sodium or arseniate, or phosphate of ammonium, then become very delicate tests of the presence of magnesium. In speaking of magnesium tests, the absence of barium and calcium salts is to be understood.

QUESTIONS AND EXERCISES.

160. Name the natural sources of the various salts of magnesium.

161. Give a process for the preparation of Epsom salt.

162. Draw diagrams illustrative of the formation of sulphate of magnesium from *magnesite* and from *dolomite*.

163. Show by an equation the process for the preparation of the official Carbonate of Magnesium.

164. What circumstances determine the two different states of aggregation of the *Magnesiæ Carbonas* and *Magnesiæ Carbonas Levis?*

165. What are the relations of *Magnesia* and *Magnesia Levis* to the official Carbonates of Magnesium?
166. How much denser is the one than the other?
167. Is magnesia soluble in water?
168. How is "Fluid Magnesia" prepared?
169. Mention the effects of heat and cold on "Fluid Magnesia."
170. Can magnesium be detected in presence of barium and calcium?
171. Describe the analysis of an aqueous liquid containing salts of barium, calcium, and magnesium.
172. How may magnesium be precipitated from solutions containing ammoniacal salts?

Quantivalence.

On reviewing the foregoing statements regarding compounds of the three univalent radicals, potassium, sodium, and ammonium, and the three bivalent elements, barium, calcium, and magnesium, the doctrine of quantivalence will be more clearly understood, and its usefulness more apparent. Quantivalence, or the value of atoms, is, in short, in chemistry, closely allied to value in commercial barter. A number of articles, differing much in weight, appearance, and general characters, may be of equal money value; and if these be regarded, for convenience, as having a sort of unit of value, others worth double as much might be termed bivalent, three times as much trivalent, and so on. In like manner, chemical radicals, no matter whether elementary, like potassium (K), iodine (I), or sulphur (S), or compound, like those of nitrates (NO_3), sulphates (SO_4), or acetates ($C_2H_3O_2$), have a given chemical power or value in relation to each other, and are exchangeable for, or will unite with each other to an extent exactly determined by that value.

Most chemical salts apparently, though probably not really, have two parts, a basylous and an acidulous, the one quantivalently balancing the other. The formulæ of the chief of these radicals and their quantivalence are given below. Examples of formulæ of salts containing univalent, bivalent, and trivalent radicals are appended.

Quantivalence of Common Radicals.

Univalent Radicals, or Monads.		Bivalent Radicals, or Dyads.		Trivalent Radicals, or Triads.	
Acidulous.	Basylous.	Acidulous.	Basylous.	Acidulous.	Basylous.
H	H	O	Ca	PO_4	As
Cl	K	SO_4	Mg	BO_3	Sb
I	Na	CO_3	Zn	$C_6H_5O_7$	Bi
HO	NH_4	C_2O_4	Cu	AsO_3	Fe^{iii}(ic)
NO_3	Ag	$C_4H_4O_6$	Hg(ic)	AsO_4	or
$C_2H_3O_2$	Hg(ous)	S	Fe(ous)	$C_4H_3O_5$	Fe^{vi}_2(ic)

Note.—The hydrogen (H) in the basylous parts of salts has entirely different functions to the hydrogen (H) in the acidulous part. The latter gives compounds commonly termed *hydrides* (*e. g.* CuH_2); in the former the element is the basylous radical of acids (*e. g.* HCl, H_2SO_4).

In compound radicals, *e. g.* $C_2H_3O_2$ or NH_4, the properties of hydrogen are no longer apparent: the chemical force resident with the atoms of such radicals seems to be mainly exerted in binding those atoms together, the excess only of the total amount of force giving the radical univalent, bivalent, or trivalent character. Thus in carbonate of potassium, K_2CO_3, the grouping CO_3 has two units of affinity in excess of those necessary for binding together the atoms (C=iv, O_3=vi); the four of the carbon uniting with four of the six of the oxygen leaves two free, and it is this excess which possibly gives the radical its bivalent character. On adding up the units of affinity, or the numbers expressing the quantivalence of each of the atoms of the radical $C_2H_3O_2$, or any of the univalent or trivalent radicals of which a Table has just been given, it will be found that an odd number is arrived at; such groupings may be expected to exhibit uneven quantivalence.

Examples of Formulæ containing Univalent, Bivalent, and Trivalent Radicals.

(R=any basylous Radical.) (*R*=any acidulous Radical.)

$\mathrm{R}'\mathit{R}'$. KI, NaCl, $NH_4C_2H_3O_2$, $AgNO_3$.
$\mathrm{R}''\mathit{R}'_2$. $CaCl_2$, $Zn2C_2H_3O_2$, $Pb2NO_3$ ($BaNO_3C_2H_3O_2$).
$\mathrm{R}'''\mathit{R}'_3$. $Bi3NO_3$, AsH_3, $SbCl_3$.
$\mathrm{R}'_2\mathit{R}''$. } { K_2CO_3, Na_2SO_4, $H_2C_4H_4O_6$.
$\mathrm{R}'\mathrm{R}'\mathit{R}''$. } { $KHCO_3$, $NaHSO_4$, $KHC_4H_4O_6$.
$\mathrm{R}'_3\mathit{R}'''$. } { Am_3PO_4, $K_3C_6H_5O_7$, H_3AsO_3.
$\mathrm{R}'_2\mathrm{R}'\mathit{R}'''$. } { Na_2HPO_4, Na_2HAsO_4.
$\mathrm{R}''\mathit{R}''$. $CaCO_3$, MgO, $CuSO_4$, HgO, $FeSO_4$.
$\mathrm{R}''_3\mathit{R}'''_2$. Ca_32PO_4, $Ca_32C_6H_5O_7$.
$\mathrm{R}''\mathrm{R}'\mathit{R}'''$. $MgAmPO_4$, $CuHAsO_3$.

$\mathrm{R}'''\mathit{R}''\mathit{R}$. $BiONO_3$.	$\mathrm{R}'''\mathit{R}'''$. $BiC_6H_5O_7$.
$\mathrm{R}'''_2\mathit{R}''_2\mathit{R}''$. $Bi_2O_2CO_3$.	$\mathrm{R}'''_2\mathit{R}'_6$. Fe_2Cl_6, Fe_26NO_3, $Fe_26C_2H_3O_2$.
$\mathrm{R}'''_2\mathit{R}''_3$. As_2O_3, Sb_2O_3.	$\mathrm{R}'''_2\mathit{R}''_3$. Fe_2O_3, Fe_23SO_4.

Quadrivalent Radicals or Tetrads, Quinquivalent Radicals or Pentads, and Sexivalent Radicals or Hexads, are known.

EXERCISE.

173. Write an exposition of the doctrine of Quantivalence within the limits of a sheet of note paper.

DIRECTIONS FOR APPLYING THE FOREGOING ANALYTICAL REACTIONS TO THE ANALYSIS OF AN AQUEOUS SOLUTION OF A SALT OF **ONE** OF THE METALS, BARIUM, CALCIUM, MAGNESIUM.

Add yellow chromate of potassium to a portion of the solution to be examined; a precipitate indicates barium.

If no barium is present, add chloride and carbonate of ammonium, and boil; a precipitate indicates calcium.

If barium and calcium are proved to be absent, add chloride of ammonium, ammonia, and then either phosphate of sodium or arseniate of ammonium; a white granular precipitate indicates magnesium.

Ammonia is here added to yield the necessary elements to ammonio-magnesian phosphate or ammonio-magnesian arseniate, both of which are highly characteristic precipitates; and chloride of ammonium is added to prevent a mere partial precipitate of the magnesium by the ammonia.

DIRECTIONS FOR APPLYING THE FOREGOING ANALYTICAL REACTIONS TO THE ANALYSIS OF AN AQUEOUS SOLUTION OF **ONE, TWO, OR ALL THREE** OF THE METALS, BARIUM, CALCIUM, MAGNESIUM.

Add chromate of potassium to the solution; barium, if present, is precipitated. Filter, if necessary, and add to the *filtrate* (that is, the liquid which has run through the filter) chloride, hydrate, and carbonate of ammonium, and boil; calcium, if present, is precipitated. Filter, if requisite, and add phosphate of sodium; magnesium, if present, is precipitated.

Note.—Red chromate of potassium must not be used in these operations, or a portion of the barium will remain in the liquid and be thrown down with, or in the place of, the carbonate of calcium (*vide* p. 76). The yellow chromate must not contain carbonate of potassium, or calcium will be precipitated with, or in the place of, barium. The absence of carbonate is proved by the non-occurrence of effervescence on the addition of hydrochloric acid to a little of the solution of the chromate, previously made hot in a test-tube. If the yellow chromate has been prepared by adding excess of ammonia to solution of red chromate of potassium, its addition to the liquid to be analyzed must be preceded by that of solution of chloride of ammonium; the precipitation of a portion of the magnesium (by the free ammonia in the yellow chromate) is thus prevented, for chloride-of-ammonium solution is a good solvent of hydrate (and carbonate) of magnesium.

TABLE OF SHORT DIRECTIONS FOR APPLYING THE FOREGOING ANALYTICAL REACTIONS TO THE ANALYSIS OF AN AQUEOUS SOLUTION OF SALTS CONTAINING **ANY OR ALL** OF THE METALLIC ELEMENTS HITHERTO CONSIDERED.

To the solution add AmCl, AmHO, Am_2CO_3; boil and filter.

<table>
<tr><td colspan="2">Precipitate
Ba Ca.
Wash, dissolve in $HC_2H_3O_2$,
add K_2CrO_4, and filter.</td><td colspan="2">Filtrate
Mg Am Na K.
Add Am_2HPO_4, shake, filter.</td></tr>
<tr><td>Precipitate
Ba.</td><td>Filtrate
Ca.
Test by
$Am_2C_2O_4$.</td><td>Precipitate
Mg.</td><td>Filtrate
Am Na K.
Evap. to dryness, ignite, dissolve residue in water.
Test for K by Pt Cl_4.
Test for Na by flame.
Test orig. sol. for Am.</td></tr>
</table>

Note 1.—The analysis of solutions containing the foregoing metals is commenced by the addition of chloride of ammonium (AmCl) and ammonia (AmHO), simply as a precautionary measure, the former compound preventing partial precipitation of magnesium, the latter neutralizing acids. The carbonate of ammonium (Am_2CO_3) is the important group-reagent—the precipitant of barium and calcium.

Note 2.—In the above, and in subsequent charts of analytical processes, the leading precipitants will be found to be ammonium salts. These being volatile, can be got rid of towards the end of the operations, and thus the detection of potassium and sodium be in no way prevented—an advantage which could not be had if such salts as chromate of potassium or phosphate of sodium were the group-precipitants employed.

Note 3.—Acetic, and not hydrochloric or nitric, acid is used in dissolving the barium and calcium carbonates, because chromate of barium, on the precipitation of which the detection of barium depends, is soluble in the stronger acids, and therefore could not be thrown down in their presence.

Note on Classification.—The compounds of barium, calcium, and magnesium, like those of the alkali metals, have many analogies; the carbonates, phosphates, and arseniates of each are insoluble, which sufficiently distinguishes them from the members of the class first studied. They possess, moreover, well-marked differences, so that their separation from each other is easy. The solubility of their hydrates in water mark their connection with the alkali metals; the slightness of that solubility, diminishing as we advance further and further from the alkalies, baryta being most and magnesia least soluble in water, points to their connection with the next class of metals, the hydrates of which are insoluble in water. These considerations must not, however, be over-valued. Though the solubility of their hydrates places barium nearest and magnesium furthest from the alkali metals, the solubility of their sulphates gives them the opposite order, magnesium-sulphate being most soluble, calcium-sulphate next, strontium-sulphate third (strontium is a rarer element, which will be mentioned subsequently), and barium-sulphate insoluble in water. These elements are sometimes spoken of as the metals of the alkaline earths.

Note.—In connection with the bivalence of the metals Barium, Calcium, and Magnesium, it is interesting to note that just as bivalent acidulous radicals give salts containing two atoms of univalent basylous radicals (K_2SO_4, $NaHSO_4$, H_2CO_3, $KNaC_4H_4O_6$), so bivalent basylous radicals yield salts containing two atoms of univalent acidulous radicals, as seen in acetonitrate of barium, $BaC_2H_3O_2NO_3$, a salt which is a definite compound, and not a mere mixture of acetate with nitrate of barium. A very large number of such salts is known.

Distillation.

The water with which, in analysis, solution of a salt or dilution of a liquid is effected should be pure. Well or river-water (*aqua*, U. S. P.) is unfit for the purpose, because containing alkaline and earthy salts (about 20 to 60 grains per gallon), derived from the soil through which the water percolates, and rain-water is not unfrequently contaminated with the dust and debris which fall on the roofs whence it is usually collected. Such water is purified by *distillation*, an operation in which the water is by ebullition converted into steam, and the steam condensed again to water in a separate vessel, the fixed earthy and other salts remaining in the vessel in which the water is boiled. On the large scale, ebullition is effected in metal boilers having a hood or head in which is a lateral opening through which passes the steam; on the small scale, either a common glass flask is employed, into the neck of which, by a cork, is inserted a glass tube bent to an acute angle, or a *retort* is used, a sort of long-necked Florence flask, dexterously bent near the body by the glass-worker to an appropriate angle (hence the name *retort*, from *retorqueo*, to bend back). *Condensation* is effected by surrounding the lateral steam-tube with cold water. In large stills the steam-tube, or *condensing-worm*, is usually a metal (tin) pipe, twisted into a spiral form for the sake of compactness, and so fixed in a tub that a few inches of one end of the pipe may pass through and closely fit a hole bored near the bottom of the tub. Cold water is kept in contact with the exterior of the pipe, provision being made for a continuous supply to the bottom, while the water heated by the condensing steams runs off from the top of the column. The condenser for a flask or retort may be a simple glass tube of any size, placed within a second much wider tube (a common long, narrow lamp-glass answers very well for experimental operations), the tube being connected at the extremities of the wider by bored corks; a stream of water passes into one end of the inclosed space (the end furthest from the retort), through a small glass tube inserted in the cork, and out at the other through a similar tube. The common (Liebig's) form of laboratory condenser is a glass tube three-fourths of an inch wide and a yard long, surrounded by a shorter tin or zinc tube two inches in diameter, and having at each extremity a neck, through which the glass tube passes. The ends of the necks of the tin tube, and small portions of the glass tube near them, are connected by means of a strip of sheet caoutchouc carefully bound round. An aperture near the lower part of the tin tube provides for the admission of a current of cold water, and a similar aperture near the top allows the escape of heated water. The inner tube may thus constantly be surrounded by cold water, and heated vapors passing through it be perfectly cooled and condensed.

In distilling several gallons of water for analytical or medicinal purposes (*Aqua Destillata*, B. P. and U. S. P.), the first two or three pints should be rejected, because likely to contain ammoniacal and other volatile impurities.

Rectification is the process of redistilling a distilled liquid. *Rectified spirit* is spirit of wine thus treated.

Dry or *destructive distillation* is distillation in which the condensed products are directly formed by the decomposing influence of the heat applied to the dry or non-volatile substances in the retort or still.

EXERCISE.

174. Write from memory two or three paragraphs descriptive of *distillation*.

ZINC, ALUMINIUM, IRON.

These three elements are classed together for analytical convenience rather than for more general analogies.

ZINC.

Symbol Zn. Atomic weight 65.

Source.—Zinc is tolerably abundant in nature as sulphide (ZnS) or *blende*, and carbonate ($ZnCO_3$) or *calamine* (from *calamus*, a reed, in allusion to the appearance of the mineral). The ores are roasted to expel sulphur, carbonic acid gas, and some impurities, and the resulting oxide distilled with charcoal, when the metal vaporizes and readily condenses.

Uses.—Its use as a metal is familiar; alloyed with nickel it yields german silver; with twice its weight of copper forms common brass, and as a coating on iron (the so-called *galvanized* iron) greatly retards the formation of rust. Most of the salts of zinc are prepared, directly or indirectly, from the metal (*Zincum*, B. P. and U. S. P.).

Quantivalence.—The atom of zinc is bivalent, Zn''.

REACTIONS HAVING (*a*) SYNTHETICAL AND (*b*) ANALYTICAL INTEREST.

(*a*) *Synthetical Reactions.*

Sulphate of Zinc.

First Synthetical Reaction.—Heat zinc (4 pts.) with water (20 pts.) and sulphuric acid (3 fl. pts.) in a test-tube (or larger vessel) until gas ceases to be evolved; solution of sulphate of zinc ($ZnSO_4$) results. Filter and concentrate the solution in an evaporating dish; on cooling, colorless, transparent, prismatic crystals of Sulphate of Zinc ($ZnSO_4, 7H_2O$) are deposited (*Zinci Sulphas*, B. P. and U. S. P.).

Note.—This reaction affords hydrogen and sulphate of zinc; it also gives electricity. Of several methods of evolving hydrogen, it is the most convenient; of the two or three means of preparing sulphate of zinc it is that most commonly employed; and of the many reactions which may be utilized in the development of dynamic electricity it is at present the cheapest and most manageable. The apparatus in which the reaction is effected differs according to the requirements of the operator; if the sulphate of zinc alone is wanted, an open dish is all that is necessary, the action being, perhaps, accelerated by heat; if hydrogen, a closed vessel and delivery-tube; if electricity, square vessels called cells and certain complementary materials, forming altogether what is termed a battery. In each operation for one product the other two are commonly wasted. It would not be difficult for the operator, as a matter of amusement, to construct an apparatus in which all three products should be collected.

Purification.—Impure sulphate of zinc may be purified in the same manner as impure chloride (see next reaction).

Chloride of Zinc.

Second Synthetical Reaction.—Dissolve zinc in hydrochloric acid mixed with half its bulk of water; the resulting solution contains chloride of zinc. Evaporate the liquid till no more steam escapes; Chloride of Zinc ($ZnCl_2$) in a state of fusion remains, and, on cooling, is obtained as a white opaque solid (*Zinci Chloridum*, B. P. and U. S. P.). It is soluble in water, alcohol, or ether.

$$\underset{\text{Zinc.}}{Zn} + \underset{\text{Hydrochloric acid.}}{2HCl} = \underset{\text{Chloride of zinc.}}{ZnCl_2} + \underset{\text{Hydrogen.}}{H_2}$$

This reaction is analogous to that previously described. The Burnett deodorizing or disinfecting liquid is solution of chloride of zinc.

Purification of Chloride or Sulphate of Zinc.—Zinc sometimes contains traces of iron or lead; and these, like zinc, are dissolved by most acids, with formation of soluble salts: they may be recognized in the liquids by applying the tests described hereafter to a little of the solution in a test-tube (p. 99). Should either be present in the above solution, a little chlorine water is added to the liquid till the odor of chlorine is permanent, and then the whole well shaken with some carbonate of zinc. In this way iron is precipitated as ferric hydrate, and lead as peroxide:—

$$\underset{\text{Ferrous chloride.}}{{}^{*}2FeCl_2} + \underset{\text{Chlorine.}}{Cl_2} = \underset{\text{Ferric chloride.}}{{}^{*}Fe_2Cl_6}$$

$$\underset{\text{Ferric chloride.}}{Fe_2Cl_6} + \underset{\text{Carbonate of zinc.}}{3ZnCO_3} + \underset{\text{Water.}}{3H_2O} = \underset{\text{Ferric hydrate.}}{Fe_2 6HO} + \underset{\text{Chloride of zinc.}}{3ZnCl_2} + \underset{\text{Carbonic acid gas.}}{3CO_2}$$

$$\underset{\text{Chloride of lead.}}{PbCl_2} + \underset{\text{Chlorine.}}{Cl_2} + \underset{\text{Carbonate of zinc.}}{2ZnCO_3} = \underset{\text{Peroxide of lead.}}{PbO_2} + \underset{\text{Chloride of zinc.}}{2ZnCl_2} + \underset{\text{Carbonic acid gas.}}{2CO_2}$$

In the British Pharmacopœia the presence of impurities in the zinc is assumed, and the process of purification just described incorporated with the process of preparation of *Zinci Chloridum*, *Liquor Zinci Chloridi*, and *Zinci Sulphas*. In the purification of the sulphate of zinc, the action of chlorine on any ferrous sulphate will result in the formation of ferric sulphate as well as ferric chloride:—

$$6FeSO_4 + Cl_6 = 2(Fe_2 3SO_4) + Fe_2Cl_6$$

carbonate of zinc will then give chloride as well as sulphate of zinc, and thus the whole quantity of sulphate of zinc be slightly contaminated by chloride. On evaporating and crystallizing, however, the chloride of zinc will be retained in the mother liquor.

For *Liquor Zinci Chloridi*, B. P., 1 pound of zinc is placed in a mixture of 44 fluidounces of hydrochloric acid and 20 of water, the mixture ultimately warmed until no more gas escapes, filtered into a bottle, chlorine water added until the liquid after shaking smells fairly of chlorine, about half an ounce or somewhat more of carbonate of zinc shaken up with the solution until a brown precipitate (of ferric hydrate, or peroxide of lead, or both) appears, the whole filtered and the filtrate evaporated to 40 fluidounces. If there is reason to believe that neither iron nor lead is present in the zinc, the treatment with chlorine, water, and carbonate of zinc may be omitted.

Carbonate of Zinc.

Third Synthetical Reaction.—To solution of any given quantity of sulphate of zinc in twice its weight of water (in a test-tube, evaporating basin, or other large or small

* It will be noticed that the iron is represented, in these equations, as exerting both bivalent and trivalent activity; this will be alluded to when iron comes under consideration.

vessel), add about an equal quantity of carbonate of sodium, also dissolved in twice its weight of water, and boil; the resulting white precipitate is so-called Carbonate of Zinc (*Zinci Carbonas*, B. P., *Zinci Carbonas Precipitata*, U. S. P.), a mixture of carbonate ($ZnCO_3$) and hydrate ($Zn2HO$), in the proportion of one molecule of the former and two of the latter, together with a molecule of water (H_2O). It may be washed, drained, and dried in the usual manner. It is used in the arts under the name of *zinc-white*, and frequently in medicine in the form of ointment (*Ceratum Zinci Carbonatis*, U. S. P.).

$$\underset{\text{Sulphate of zinc.}}{3ZnSO_4} + \underset{\text{Water.}}{2H_2O} + \underset{\text{Carbonate of sodium.}}{3Na_2CO_3} = \underset{\text{Official carbonate of zinc.}}{ZnCO_3,2ZnH_2O_2} + \underset{\text{Carbonic acid gas.}}{2CO_2} + \underset{\text{Sulphate of sodium.}}{3Na_2SO_4}$$

Acetate of Zinc.

Fourth Synthetical Reaction.—Collect in a filter the precipitate obtained in the last reaction, wash with distilled water, and dissolve a portion in strong acetic acid; the resulting solution contains acetate of zinc ($Zn2C_2H_3O_2$), and, on evaporating, and setting aside for a day, yields lamellar pearly crystals ($Zn2C_2H_3O_2,2H_2O$). This is the process for *Zinci Acetas*, B. P.

$$\underset{\text{Official carbonate of zinc.}}{ZnCO_3,2ZnH_2O_2} + \underset{\text{Acetic acid.}}{6HC_2H_3O_2} = \underset{\text{Acetate of zinc.}}{3(Zn2C_2H_3O_2)} + \underset{\text{Water.}}{5H_2O} + \underset{\text{Carbonic acid gas.}}{CO_2}$$

The U. S. P. process consists in precipitating by metallic zinc the lead in a solution of acetate of lead, evaporating and crystallizing.

Oxide of Zinc.

Fifth Synthetical Reaction.—Dry the remainder of the precipitated carbonate (by placing the open filter on a plate over a dish of water kept boiling), and then heat it in a small crucible till it ceases to effervesce on the addition of water and acid to trial samples taken out of the crucible from time to time; the product is Oxide of Zinc (*Zinci Oxidum*, B. P. and U. S. P.), much used in the form of ointment (*Unguentum Zinci*, B. P. and *Unguentum Zinci Oxidi*, U. S. P.).

$ZnCO_3, 2ZnH_2O_2$	=	$3ZnO$	+	$2H_2O$	+	CO_2
Official carbonate of zinc.		Oxide of zinc.		Water.		Carbonic acid gas.

Note.—This oxide is of a very pale yellow or buff tint, not nearly so white as oxide prepared by the combustion of zinc in air. The latter variety occurs in commerce under the name of Hubbuck's oxide of zinc. Its preparation can only be practically accomplished on the large scale, but the chief features of the action may be observed by heating a piece of zinc in a small porcelain crucible till it burns; flocks escape from the crucible, float about in the air, and slowly fall. These are the old *Flores Zinci, Lana Philosophica,* or *Nihilum Album.*

Valerianate of. Zinc.

Sixth Synthetical Reaction.—Valerianate of Zinc ($Zn2C_5H_9O_2$) *Zinci Valerianas,* B. P. and U. S. P.) is prepared by mixing strong solutions of sulphate of zinc and valerianate of sodium, cooling, separating the white pearly crystalline matter, evaporating at 200° to a low bulk, cooling, again separating the lamellar crystals, washing the whole product with a small quantity of cold distilled water, draining and drying by exposure to air at ordinary temperatures. Valerianate of zinc is soluble in ether, alcohol, or hot water.

$ZnSO_4$	+	$2NaC_5H_9O_2$	=	Na_2SO_4	+	$Zn2C_5H_9O_2$
Sulphate of zinc.		Valerianate of sodium.		Sulphate of sodium.		Valerianate of zinc.

The compounds of zinc described in the above six reactions are the only ones mentioned in the British Pharmacopœia; the processes are also those of that work. *Sulphide and Hydrate of Zinc* are mentioned in the following analytical paragraphs:—

(*b*) *Reactions having Analytical Interest* (*Tests*).

First Analytical Reaction.—To solution of a zinc salt (sulphate for example) in a test-tube, add solution of sulphydrate of ammonium (NH_4HS); white sulphide of zinc (ZnS) is precipitated, insoluble in acetic, but soluble in the stronger acids.

Note.—This is the only white sulphide that will be met with. Its formation, on the addition of the sulphydrate of ammonium, is therefore highly characteristic of zinc. If the zinc salt contains iron or lead as impurities the precipitate will have a dark appearance, the sulphides of those metals being black. Hydrate of aluminium, which is also white and precipitated by sulphydrate of ammonium, is the only substance sulphide of zinc is likely to be mistaken for, and *vice versâ;* but, as will be seen immediately, there are good means of distinguishing these from each other.

Second Analytical Reaction. To solution of a zinc salt add solution of ammonia; white hydrate of zinc (Zn2HO) is precipitated. Add excess of ammonia; the precipitate is redissolved.

This reaction at once distinguishes a zinc salt from an aluminium salt, hydrate of aluminium being insoluble in ammonia.

Other Analytical Reactions.—The fixed alkali hydrates afford a similar reaction to that just mentioned, the hydrate of zinc redissolving if the alkali is free from carbonate.—— Carbonate of ammonium yields a white precipitate of carbonate and hydrate, soluble in excess.——The fixed alkaline carbonates give a similar precipitate, which is not redissolved if the mixed solution and precipitate be well boiled.

Antidotes.—There are no efficient chemical means of counteracting the poisonous effects of zinc. Large doses, fortunately, act as powerful emetics. If vomiting has not occurred, or apparently to an insufficient extent, solution of carbonate of sodium (common washing salt) immediately followed by white of egg and demulcents may be administered.

QUESTIONS AND EXERCISES.

175. Give the sources and uses of metallic zinc.
176. Explain by a diagram what occurs when zinc is dissolved in dilute sulphuric acid.
177. How may solutions of Chloride or Sulphate of Zinc be purified from salts of iron? Give equations descriptive of the reactions.
178. State the formula of Carbonate of Zinc, and illustrate by a diagram the reaction which takes place in its production.
179. Give an equation showing the formation of Acetate of Zinc.
180. In what respect does Oxide of Zinc, resulting from the ignition of the carbonate, differ from that produced during the combustion of the metal?
181. How is Valerianate of Zinc prepared?
182. What are the properties of Valerianate of Zinc?
183. Name the more important tests for zinc.
184. How would you distinguish, chemically, between solutions of Sulphate of Zinc and Alum?
185. Describe the treatment in cases of poisoning by salts of zinc.

ALUMINIUM.

Symbol Al. Atomic weight 27.5.

Note.—In the formulæ of aluminium salts, it will be observed that to one atom of metal there are three atoms of other univalent radicals; hence, apparently, the atom of aluminium is trivalent, Al‴. But possibly it is quadrivalent; for one molecule of aluminium compounds includes two atoms of the metal, three-fourths only of whose power may be supposed to be exerted in retaining the other constituents of the molecule, the remaining fourth enabling the aluminium atoms themselves to keep together. This is graphically shown in the following formula of chloride of aluminium (Al_2Cl_6) from Frankland's "Lecture Notes for Chemical Students," which represents each

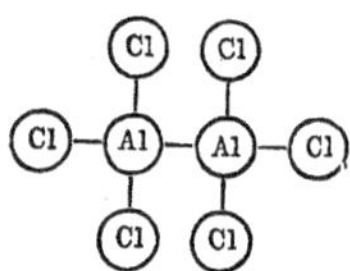

aluminium atom as a body having four arms or bonds, three of which are engaged in grasping the arms of univalent chlorine atoms, while the fourth grasps the corresponding arm of its brother aluminium atom. Such graphic formulæ, as they are called, are useful in facilitating the acquirement of hypotheses regarding the constitution of chemical substances, especially if the error be avoided of supposing that they are pictures either of the position or absolute power of atoms in a molecule, or indeed, the true representation of a molecule at all; for on this point man knows nothing.

Source.—Aluminium is very abundant in nature, chiefly as silicate, in clays, slate, marl, granite, basalt, and a large number of minerals. The sapphire and ruby are almost pure oxide of aluminium. The metal is obtained from the double chloride of aluminium and sodium, by the action of metallic sodium, the source of the chloride being the mineral *bauxite*.

Aluminium-bronze is an alloy of ten parts of aluminium with ninety of copper.

Alum (*Alumen*, B. P.), a double sulphate of aluminium and ammonium (Al_23SO_4, Am_2SO_4, $24H_2O$), (*Aluminæ et Ammoniæ Sulphas*, U. S. P.), is obtained from aluminous schist (from σχιστὸς, *schistos*, divided), a sort of pyritous slate or shale, by exposure to air; oxidation and chemical change produce sulphate of aluminium, sulphate of iron, and silica, from the silicate of aluminium and bisulphide of iron (iron pyrites) originally present in the shale. The sulphate of aluminium and sulphate of iron are dissolved out of the mass by water, and sulphate or chloride of ammonium added; on concentrating the liquids alum crystallizes out, while the more soluble iron salt remains in the mother-liquor.

Alums.—There are several *alums*, iron or chromium replacing aluminium, and potassium or sodium taking the place of ammonium, all crystallizing in one eight-sided form, the octahedron—a sort of double pyramid. These are, apparently, alike in chemical constitution, and their general formula (M=either metal) is $M'''_2 3SO_4$, M'_2SO_4, $24H_2O$. The alum of the manufacturer commonly occurs in colorless, transparent, octahedral crystals, massed in lumps, which are roughly broken up for trade purposes, but still exhibit the faces of octahedra.

Sulphate of Aluminium ($Al_2 3SO_4$, $9H_2O$), or *Alum Cake*, prepared from natural silicates in the manner just described, is a common article of trade, serving most of the manufacturing purposes for which alum was formerly employed. In the United States Pharmacopœia (*Aluminæ Sulphas*) it is directed to be made by dissolving hydrate of aluminium in diluted sulphuric acid with subsequent removal of water by evaporation.

$$Al_2 6HO + 3H_2SO_4 = Al_2 3SO_4 + 6H_2O.$$

The hydrate of aluminium is to be prepared by the addition of solution of alum to solution of carbonate of sodium, the precipitated hydrate being collected on a filter and well washed.

$$Al_2 3SO_4,\ Am_2SO_4 + 3Na_2CO_3 + 3H_2O = Al_2 6HO + Am_2SO_4 + 3Na_2SO_4 + 3CO_2.$$

Preparation of Alum.—Prepare alum by heating a small quantity of powdered pipeclay (silicate of aluminium) with about twice its weight of sulphuric acid for some time, dissolving out the resulting sulphate of aluminium and sulphuric acid by water, and adding only ammonia to the clear-filtered solution until, after well stirring, it is faintly acid to test-paper; on evaporating, crystals of alum are obtained.

The *Ammonio-ferric Alum* of American pharmacy (*Ferri et Ammoniæ Sulphas*, U. S. P.) is made by adding sulphate of ammonium to a hot solution of persulphate of iron, and setting the liquid aside to crystallize. It forms pale violet octohedral crystals. expressed by the formula $Fe_2 3SO_4, (NH_4)_2SO_4, 24H_2O$. *Alumen* (U. S. P.) is potassium alum, the sulphate of aluminium and potassium ($Al_2 3SO_4$, K_2SO_4, $24H_2O$).

Dried alum (*Alumen Exsiccatum*, B. P. and U. S. P.) is alum from which the water of crystallization has been expelled by heat, the temperature not exceeding 400°. By calculation from the molecular weight of alum, it will be found that the salt contains between 47 and 48 per cent. of water. At temperatures above 400° alum is decomposed, sulphate of ammonium and sulphuric anhydride escaping, and pure *alumina* (Al_2O_3) remaining. Dried alum rapidly reabsorbs water from the atmosphere. It is almost useless as a medicinal preparation.

Reactions having Analytical Interest.

First Analytical Reaction.—To a solution of an aluminium salt (alum, for example, which contains sulphate of aluminium) add sulphydrate of ammonium (NH_4HS); a gelatinous white precipitate of hydrate of aluminium falls:—

$$Al_2 3SO_4 + 6AmHS + 6H_2O = Al_2 6HO + 3Am_2SO_4 + 6H_2S.$$

Second Analytical Reaction.—To solution of alum add ammonia, NH_4HO; hydrate of aluminium falls: add excess of ammonia; the precipitate is insoluble.

Principle of Dyeing by help of Mordants.—The precipitated hydrate of aluminium, or alumina, has great affinity for vegetable coloring-matters, and also for the fibre of cloth. Once more perform the above experiment, but before adding the ammonia introduce some decoction of logwood, solution of cochineal, or other similar colored liquid, into the test-tube. Add now the ammonia, and set the tube aside for the alumina to fall; the latter takes down with it all the coloring principle. In dye-works the fabrics are passed through liquids holding the alumina but weakly in solution, and then through the coloring solutions; from the first bath the fibres abstract alumina, and from the second the alumina abstracts coloring matter. Some other metallic hydrates, notably those of tin and iron, resemble alumina in this property; they are all termed *mordants* (from *mordens*, biting); the substances they form with coloring-matters have the name of *lakes*.

Third Analytical Reaction.—To the alum add solution of potash; again hydrate of aluminium falls. Add excess of potash, and agitate; the precipitate dissolves.

Alumina may be precipitated from this solution by neutralizing the potash with hydrochloric acid, and adding ammonia until, after shaking, the mixture has an ammoniacal smell, or by adding solution of chloride of ammonium to the potash liquid. But the former way is the better; for it is difficult to know when a sufficiency of the chloride of ammonium has been poured in, whereas reaction with blue and red litmus-paper at once enables the operator to know when excess of hydrochloric acid or ammonia has been added.

Alkaline carbonates, phosphates, arseniates, and salts of other acidulous radicals also decompose solutions of aluminium salts and produce insoluble compounds of that metal, with the several acidulous radicals (except the carbonic), but the resulting precipitates are of no special interest.

QUESTIONS AND EXERCISES.

186. What is there remarkable about the quantivalence of aluminium?

187. Practically what is the quantivalence of the atom of aluminium?

188. Enumerate the chief natural compounds of aluminium.
189. Write down a formula which will represent either of the Alums.
190. Which *alum* is official, and commonly employed in the arts?
191. State the source, and explain the formation, of alum.
192. What is the crystalline form of alum? Work a sum showing how much Dried Alum is theoretically producible from 100 pounds of alum? Ans. 52 lbs. 6 ozs.
193. Show by figures how ordinary ammonium alum is capable of yielding 11.356 per cent. of alumina.
194. Why are aluminium compounds used in dyeing?
195. How are salts of aluminium analytically distinguished from those of zinc?

IRON.

Symbol Fe. Atomic weight 56.

Sources.—Compounds of iron are very abundant in nature. *Magnetic Iron Ore*, or *Loadstone* (*Lodestone* or *Leadstone*, from the Saxon *lædan*, to lead, in allusion to its use, or rather of magnets made from it, in navigation) is the chief ore from which Swedish iron is made; it is a mixture of ferrous and ferric oxide (FeO,Fe_2O_3). Much of the Russian iron is made from *Specular Iron Ore* (from *speculum*, a mirror, in allusion to the lustrous nature of the crystals of this mineral). This and *Red Hæmatite* (from αἷμα, *aima*, blood, so named from the color of its streak), an ore raised in Lancashire, are composed of ferric oxide only (Fe_2O_3). *Brown Hæmatite*, an oxyhydrate, is the source of much of the French iron. *Spathic Iron Ore* (from *spatha*, a slice, in allusion to the lamellar structure of the ore) is a ferrous carbonate ($FeCO_3$). An impure ferrous carbonate forms the *Clay Ironstone*, whence most of the English iron is derived. The chief Scotch ore is also an impure carbonate, containing much bituminous matter; it is known as *Black Band*. *Iron Pyrites* (from πῦρ, *pur*, fire, in allusion to the production of sparks when sharply struck) (FeS_2) is a yellow lustrous mineral, of use only for its sulphur. Ferrous carbonate ($FeCO_3$), chloride ($FeCl_2,4H_2O$), and sulphate ($FeSO_4,7H_2O$) sometimes occur in springs, the water of which is hence termed *chalybeate* (*chalybs*, steel).

Process.—Iron is obtained from its ores by processes of roasting, and reduction of the resulting impure oxide with coal or charcoal in the presence of chalk, the latter uniting with the sand, clay, &c., to form a fusible slag. The *cast iron* thus produced is converted into *wrought iron* (*Ferrum*, U. S. P.) by burning out the 4 or 5 per cent. of carbon, silicon, and other impurities present, by oxidation in a furnace, an operation termed *puddling*. *Steel* is wrought iron impregnated with from one to two per cent. of carbon by strongly heating in charcoal. The official variety of the metal (*Ferrum*, B. P.), the condition in which it is most easily employed for conversion into its compounds, is "wrought iron in the form of wire or nails free from oxide." In the form of a fine powder (see 17 Reac.) metallic iron is employed as a medicine.

Quantivalence.—Iron combines with other elements and radicals in two proportions; those salts in which the atom of iron appears to possess inferior affinities (in which the other radicals are in the less amount) are termed *ferrous*, the higher being *ferric* salts. In the former the iron exerts bivalent (Fe''), in the latter trivalent activity (Fe''' or Fe_2^{VI}).

The atom of iron is also sometimes considered to be sexivalent, on account of the analogy of its compounds with those of chromium, which is sexivalent, if the formula of its fluoride (CrF_6) be correct, and because the composition of *ferrate of potassium* (K_2FeO_4), a deep-purple salt obtained on passing chlorine through a concentrated solution of potash in which fresh ferric hydrate is suspended, is best explained on the assumption of the sexivalence of its iron.

Why the quantivalence of the atom of iron should vary is not at present known.

The Nomenclature of Iron Salts.—For educational and descriptive purposes the two classes of iron compounds are very conveniently spoken of as *ferrous* and *ferric*, the syllable "*ferr*" common to all indicating their allied ferruginous character, the syllable *ous* and *ic* indicating the lower and higher class respectively—functions fulfilled by these two syllables in other similar cases (sulphurous and sulphuric, mercurous and mercuric). Officially the iron salts are known by other names, thus, *Sulphate of Iron* (*Ferri Sulphas*), and *Phosphate of Iron* (*Ferri Phosphas*), names which are chemically inexplicit, for there are two sulphates, and two phosphates, and the terms do not define which salt is intended. Consistency and uniformity would demand that the names Ferrous Sulphate, Ferrous Phosphate, or similar terms should be employed. Practically, however, the old names cause no confusion, inasmuch as only one sulphate, phosphate, &c., are used in medicine; moreover, the higher salts usually have the prefix *per* attached (as persulphate, perchloride). These names are already well known, can be easily rendered in Latin, and then admit of simple abbreviations and adaptations such as are employed in prescriptions, advantages not possessed by the more rational terms. While therefore the comprehension of the chemistry of iron is rendered simple and intelligible by the use of the terms ferrous and ferric, the employment of older and less definite names may very well be continued in pharmacy as being practically more convenient.

Reactions having (*a*) Synthetical and (*b*) Analytical Interest.

(*a*) *Synthetical Reactions.*

FERROUS SALTS.

Green Sulphate of Iron. Ferrous Sulphate.

First Synthetical Reaction.—Place iron (small tacks) in sulphuric acid diluted with eight times its bulk of water (in a test-tube, basin, or other vessel of any required size), accelerating the action by heat until effervescence ceases.

$$Fe_2 + 2H_2SO_4 = 2FeSO_4 + 2H_2$$
Iron. Sulphuric acid. Ferrous sulphate. Hydrogen.

The solution contains what is generally known as Sulphate of Iron, that is Ferrous Sulphate, the lower of the two sulphates, and will yield crystals of that substance ($FeSO_4,7H_2O$) (*Ferri Sulphas*, B. P. and U. S. P.) on cooling or on further evaporation ; or if the hot concentrated solution be poured into alcohol, the mixture being well stirred, the sulphate is at once thrown down in minute crystals (*Ferri Sulphas Granulata*, B. P.). At a temperature of 400° F. ferrous sulphate loses six-sevenths of its water, and becomes the *Ferri Sulphas Exsiccata*, B. P. and U. S. P.

Other Sources of Ferrous Sulphate.—In the laboratory, ferrous sulphate is often obtained as a by-product in making sulphuretted hydrogen,

$$FeS + H_2SO_4 = H_2S + FeSO_4.$$

In manufactories it occurs as a by-product in the decomposition of aluminous shale, as already noticed (p. 103).

Ten grains of granulated sulphate of iron dissolved in one ounce of water constitutes "Solution of Sulphate of Iron," B. P. "The solution should be recently prepared."

Notes.—Ferrous sulphate is sometimes termed *green vitriol.* Vitriol (from *vitrum*, glass) was originally the name of any transparent crystalline substance, but afterwards restricted to the sulphates of zinc, iron, and copper, which were, and still are, occasionally known as white, green, and blue vitriol. *Copperas* (probably originally *Copper-rust*, a term applied to verdigris and other green incrustations of copper) is another name for this sulphate of iron, sometimes distinguished as *green copperas*, sulphate of copper being blue copperas. Solid sulphate of iron is a constituent of *Pilula Aloes et Ferri*, B. P.

Ferrous sulphate, when exposed to the air, gradually turns brown through absorption of oxygen, ferric oxysulphate (Fe_2O2SO_4) being formed. The latter is not completely dissolved by water owing to the formation of a still lower insoluble oxysalt ($Fe_4O_5SO_4$) and soluble ferric sulphate (Fe_23SO_4).

Iron heated with undiluted sulphuric acid gives sulphurous acid gas and ferrous sulphate:—

$$Fe_2 + 4H_2SO_4 = SO_2 + FeSO_4 + 2H_2O$$

Carbonate of Iron. Ferrous Carbonate.

Second Synthetical Reaction.—To solution of ferrous sulphate, boiling, in a test-tube, add a solution of carbonate of ammonium in recently boiled water; a white precipitate of ferrous carbonate ($FeCO_3$) is thrown down, rapidly becoming light green, bluish green, and, after a long time, red, through absorption of oxygen, evolution of carbonic acid gas, and formation of ferric oxyhydrate.

$$\underset{\text{Ferrous sulphate.}}{FeSO_4} + \underset{\text{Carbonate of ammonium.}}{Am_2CO_3} = \underset{\text{Ferrous carbonate.}}{FeCO_3} + \underset{\text{Sulphate of ammonium.}}{Am_2SO_4}$$

Saccharated Carbonate of Iron.—The above precipitate, rapidly washed with hot well-boiled distilled water, and the moist powder mixed with sugar and quickly dried—in short, all possible precautions taken to avoid exposure to air—forms the saccharated carbonate of iron (*Ferri Carbonas Saccharata*, B. P.).

The official proportions are two ounces of the sulphate and one ounce and a quarter of the carbonate, each dissolved in half a gallon of hot water; the solutions are mixed and set aside in a deep well-covered pan, the supernatant liquid poured off when the precipitate has subsided, the pan again filled up with boiling water, the liquid once more poured away, the precipitate transferred to a calico filter, drained, gently pressed, and while still somewhat moist rubbed in a mortar with one ounce of sugar, and finally dried over a water-bath.

Carbonate of Iron, mixed with a fourth its weight of Confection of Roses (Honey and Sugar, U. S. P.), forms the *Pilula Ferri Carbonatis*, B. P. and U. S. P.

Notes.—The *Subcarbonate of Iron* (*Ferri Subcarbonas*, U. S. P.) is precipitated on mixing solutions of sulphate of iron and carbonate of sodium. On washing and drying it is converted into reddish-brown oxyhydrate of iron, water being absorbed and carbonic acid gas being eliminated. This oxyhydrate of iron is best made by precipitating solution of persulphate of iron by solution of soda, and washing and drying the product.

Saccharated ferrous carbonate is said to be more easily dissolved in the stomach than any other iron preparation. It is so unstable and prone to oxidation, that it must be washed in water containing no dissolved air and mixed with the sugar (which protects it from oxidation) as quickly as possible. In making the official compound mixture of iron (*Mistura Ferri Composita*, B. P. and U. S. P.), "Griffith's mixture," the various ingredients, including the carbonate of potassium, should be placed in a bottle of the required size, space being left for the crystals or solution of ferrous sulphate, which should be added last, the bottle immediately filled up with rose-water, and securely corked; oxidation is thus prevented to the greatest possible extent. *Pilulæ Ferri Compositæ*, U. S. P., is made from myrrh, carbonate of sodium, sulphate of iron and syrup: carbonate of iron is gradually formed.

$$\underset{\text{Ferrous sulphate.}}{FeSO_4} + \underset{\text{Carbonate of potassium.}}{K_2CO_3} = \underset{\text{Ferrous carbonate.}}{FeCO_3} + \underset{\text{Sulphate of potassium.}}{K_2SO_4}$$

Arseniate of Iron. Ferrous Arseniate.

Third Synthetical Reaction, by which the lower arseniate of iron, ferrous arseniate (*Ferri Arsenias*, B. P.) (Fe_3

$2AsO_4$), partially oxidized, is formed. This will be noticed again under Arsenicum.

Phosphate of Iron. Ferrous Phosphate.

Fourth Synthetical Reaction.—To solution of ferrous sulphate in a test-tube add a little solution of acetate of sodium, then solution of phosphate of sodium; the lower phosphate of iron, ferrous phosphate (Fe_32PO_4), is precipitated (*Ferri Phosphas*, B. P. and U. S. P.).

$$\underset{\text{Ferrous sulphate.}}{3FeSO_4} + \underset{\text{Phosphate of sodium.}}{2Na_2HPO_4} + \underset{\text{Acetate of sodium.}}{2NaC_2H_3O_2}$$

$$= \underset{\text{Ferrous phosphate.}}{Fe_32PO_4} + \underset{\text{Sulphate of sodium.}}{3Na_2SO_4} + \underset{\text{Acetic acid.}}{2HC_2H_3O_2}$$

Officially, solutions of 3 ounces of sulphate of iron in a quart of water, and $2\frac{1}{2}$ ounces of phosphate and 1 of acetate of sodium in another quart of water, are well mixed, filtered, the precipitate well washed, and, to prevent oxidation as much as possible, dried at a temperature not exceeding 120° F. These proportions will be found to accord with the molecular weights of the crystalline salts, multiplied as indicated in the foregoing equation. $3(FeSO_4, 7H_2O)=834$; $2(Na_2HPO_4, 12H_2O)=716$; $2(NaC_2H_3O_2, 3H_2O)=272$.

The use of the acetate of sodium (not mentioned in the U. S. P. formula) is to insure the occurrence of acetic acid in the solution, where otherwise would be free sulphuric acid. Sulphuric acid is a solvent of ferrous phosphate; acetic acid is not. It is impossible to prevent the separation of sulphuric acid, if only ferrous sulphate and phosphate of sodium be employed. Ferrous phosphate is white, but soon oxidizes and becomes slate-blue.

The above reaction also occurs in making *Syrupus Ferri Phosphatis*, B. P.

Sulphide of Iron. Ferrous Sulphide.

Fifth Synthetical Reaction.—The formation of ferrous sulphide (FeS). In a gas- or spirit-flame strongly heat sulphur with about twice its weight of iron filings in a test-tube (or in an earthen crucible in a furnace); ferrous sulphide is formed. When cold, add water, then a few drops of sulphuric acid; sulphuretted hydrogen gas (H_2S), known by its odor, is evolved.

$$FeS + H_2SO_4 = FeSO_4 + H_2S.$$

Sticks of sulphur pressed against a white-hot bar of cast iron give the purest form of ferrous sulphide. The liquid sulphide thus formed is allowed to drop into a vessel of water (Sulphide of Iron, B. P.; Ferri Sulphuretum, U. S. P.).

Green Iodide of Iron. Ferrous Iodide.

Sixth Synthetical Reaction.—Place a piece of iodine, about the size of a pea, in a test-tube with a small quantity of water, and add a few iron filings, small nails, or iron wire. On gently warming, or merely shaking if longer time be allowed, the iodine disappears, and, on filtering, a clear light green solution of iodide of iron (FeI_2) is obtained.

The official Ferri Iodidum is formed by gently warming a mixture of 3 parts of iodine, 1½ of fine iron wire, and 12 of distilled water in an iron vessel. When combination is nearly complete (as shown by indications of a sea-green tint), boil for a short time until the whiteness of the froth proves that the iodine has entirely disappeared. The solution is then filtered and evaporated in a clean bright iron saucepan, ladle, or dish until a drop taken out on the end of an iron wire stirrer solidifies on cooling. The liquid is poured out on a clean smooth slab, broken up and preserved in a glass-stoppered bottle. Solid iodide of iron has a crystalline fracture, is "green with a tinge of brown; inodorous, deliquescent, and almost entirely soluble in water, forming a slightly green solution which gradually deposits a colored sediment and acquires a red color."

The solid iodide contains about 18 per cent. of water of crystallization, and a little oxide of iron.

Ferrous bromide ($FeBr_2$), occasionally used in medicine, could be made, as might be expected, in the same way as the iodide.

FERRIC SALTS.

Anhydrous Perchloride of Iron. Ferric Chloride.

Seventh Synthetical Reaction.—Pass chlorine (generated as usual, from black oxide of manganese and hydrochloric acid in a flask) through sulphuric acid contained in a small bottle, and thence by the ordinary narrow glass tubing to the bottom of a test-tube containing twenty or thirty small iron tacks (or a florence flask containing 2 or 3 ounces of iron tacks), the latter kept hot by a gas-flame; the higher chloride of iron, ferric chloride, or the perchloride* of iron (Fe_2Cl_6) is formed and condenses in the upper part of the tube or flask as a mass of small dark iridescent crystals.

* The prefixes *per* and *hyper* used here and elsewhere are from ὑπέρ, *uper* or *hyper*, over or above, and simply mean "the highest" of several. Thus perchloride, the highest *chloride*.

When a tolerably thick crust of the salt is formed, break off the part of the glass containing it, being careful that the remaining corroded tacks are excluded, and place it in ten or twenty times its weight of water; the resulting solution, poured off from any pieces of glass, is a pure neutral solution of hydrous ferric chloride, and will be serviceable in performing analytical reactions.

Precaution.—The above experiment must be conducted in the open air, or in a cupboard having a draught outwards.

Anhydrous Ferrous Chloride.—In breaking up the tube, small scales of a light buff color will be observed adhering to the nails; they are crystals of ferrous chloride ($FeCl_2$).

Note.—Solution of ferric chloride evolves some hydrochloric acid on boiling, while a darker-colored solution of ferric oxychloride remains.

Green Chloride of Iron. Hydrous ferrous Chloride. Solution of Hydrous Ferric Chloride.

Eighth Synthetical Reaction.—Dissolve iron tacks, in a test-tube, in hydrochloric acid; hydrogen escapes, and the solution on cooling, or on evaporation and cooling, deposits *crystallized ferrous chloride* ($FeCl_2,4H_2O$).

Through a portion of the solution of ferrous chloride pass chlorine gas; the ferrous chloride becomes *ferric chloride.*

The excess of chlorine dissolved by the liquid in this experiment may be removed by ebullition; but the ferric chloride is slightly decomposed at the same time, for the reason just stated. The free chlorine may also be carried off by passing a current of air through the liquid for some time.

Hydrous Ferric Chloride (another process).

Ninth Synthetical Reaction.—To another portion of the solution of ferrous chloride, in a test-tube, add a little more hydrochloric acid; heat the liquid, and continue to drop in nitric acid until the black color it first produces disappears; the resulting reddish-brown liquid is also solution of ferric chloride.

$$\underset{\text{Ferrous chloride.}}{6FeCl_2} + \underset{\text{Nitric acid.}}{2HNO_3} + \underset{\text{Hydrochloric acid.}}{6HCl} = \underset{\text{Ferric chloride.}}{3Fe_2Cl_6} + \underset{\text{Nitric oxide.}}{2NO} + \underset{\text{Water.}}{4H_2O}.$$

The black color is due to solution of nitric oxide gas (NO) in a portion of the ferrous salt; it is decomposed by heat.

This is the process for producing the *Liquor Ferri Perchloridi*

Fortior, B. P., 2 ounces of iron, 12 fluidounces of hydrochloric acid, 9 fluidrachms of nitric acid, and 8 ounces of water being employed, and the product boiled down to 10 fluidounces. Practically it is impossible so to apportion the acids that a solution shall result containing neither excess of acid nor of metal, nor contain ferric nitrate. For most medicinal purposes, however, solution of perchloride of iron containing hydrochloric acid is said to be unobjectionable.

Diluted with 3 volumes of water this strong solution gives the *Liquor Ferri Perchloridi*, B. P.—or with 3 volumes of rectified spirit the *Tinctura Ferri Perchloridi*, B. P. The *Tinctura Ferri Chloridi*, U. S. P., is a similar solution.

Note.—The spirit in the Tincture is unnecessary, useless, and deleterious; for it acts neither as a special solvent nor as a preservative, the offices usually performed by alcohol (*Tincturæ et Succi*, B. P. and U. S. P.); but, unless the liquid contain excess of acid, decomposes the ferric chloride and causes the formation of an insoluble oxychloride of iron. Even if the tincture be acid, it slowly loses color, ferrous chloride and chlorinated ethereal bodies being formed. A *Liquor*, of similar strength, is doubtless destined to displace the tincture altogether.

Solution of ferric chloride evaporated yields a mass of yellow crystals (*Ferri Chloridum*, U. S. P.) containing $Fe_2Cl_6\ 12H_2O$, or, rarely, red crystals having the formula $Fe_2Cl_6\ 5H_2O$. An old method of making solution of ferric chloride is to dissolve ferric oxide or hydrate in hydrochloric acid; but from the varying character of trade specimens of the ingredients, the liquid is more likely to contain excess or deficiency of iron than the proper proportion.

Persulphate of Iron. Ferric Sulphate.

Tenth Synthetical Reaction.—Dissolve about three-quarters of an ounce of ferrous sulphate and a sixth of its weight of sulphuric acid in an ounce and a half of water in an evaporating dish, heat the mixture and drop in nitric acid until the black color it first produces disappears; the resulting liquid, when made of a certain prescribed strength (*vide* 13*th Reac.*), is the solution of ferric sulphate, the higher sulphate or Persulphate of Iron (*Liquor Ferri Persulphatis*) of the British Pharmacopœia, a heavy dark-red liquid, sp. gr. 1.441. The *Liquor Ferri Tersulphatis*, U. S. P., is the same preparation but slightly stronger (sp. gr. 1.320). *Liquor Ferri Subsulphatis*, U. S. P. (Monsel's solution), is a similar fluid, made with less acids, probably containing, therefore, ferric oxysulphate and ferric oxynitrate (sp. gr. 1.552).

$$\underset{\text{Ferrous sulphate.}}{6FeSO_4} + \underset{\text{Sulphuric acid.}}{3H_2SO_4} + \underset{\text{Nitric acid.}}{2HNO_3} = \underset{\text{Ferric sulphate.}}{3(Fe_23SO_4)} + \underset{\text{Nitric oxide.}}{2NO} + \underset{\text{Water.}}{4H_2O}.$$

The black color, as in the previous reaction, is due to a compound of ferrous salt with nitric oxide ($2FeSO_4 + NO$).

Note.—In all the reactions in which iron passes from ferrous to ferric condition the element assumes different properties, the chief being an alteration from bivalent to trivalent activity.

Acetate of Iron. Ferric Acetate.

Eleventh Synthetical Reaction.—To a strong solution of ferric sulphate (from which free nitric acid has been removed by evaporating to dryness and redissolving in water) add an *alcoholic* solution of acetate of potassium ($KC_2H_3O_2$), and well shake the mixture; a crystalline precipitate of sulphate of potassium (K_2SO_4) falls, and ferric acetate ($Fe_26C_2H_3O_2$) remains in solution, forming, when filtered, and of definite strength, the *Tinctura Ferri Acetatis*, B.P. The preparation is unstable.

Fe_23SO_4	+	$6KC_2H_3O_2$	=	$3K_2SO_4$	+	$Fe_26C_2H_3O_2$
Ferric sulphate.		Acetate of potassium.		Sulphate of potassium.		Ferric acetate.

The official proportions are 2½ fluidounces of "Solution of Persulphate of Iron" (*vide* 10th Reac.) with 8 fluidounces of rectified spirit, mixed with a solution of 2 ounces of acetate of potassium in 10 fluidounces of spirit, the whole well shaken frequently during an hour, filtered, and the precipitated sulphate of potassium washed by pouring on spirit until the filtrate measures 1 pint. A solution four times this strength, made from ferric hydrate and glacial acetic acid, is stable: it is diluted with spirit as wanted (J. Deane and T. Jeaffreson).

Perhydrate of Iron. Ferric hydrate.

Twelfth Synthetical Reaction.—Pour a portion of the solution of ferric sulphate into excess of solution of soda (ammonia, U. S. P.); moist ferric hydrate is precipitated (*Ferri Peroxidum Humidum*, B. P., *Ferri Oxidum Hydratum*, U. S. P.).

Fe_23SO_4	+	$6NaHO$	=	Fe_26HO	+	$3Na_2SO_4$
Ferric sulphate.		Soda.		Ferric hydrate.		Sulphate of sodium.

Either of the other alkalies (potash or ammonia) will produce a similar reaction; but soda is cheapest and most convenient.

Ferric hydrate is an antidote to arsenic if administered directly after the poison has been taken.

It converts the soluble arsenic (As_2O_3) into insoluble ferrous arseniate:—

$$2(Fe_26HO) + As_2O_3 = Fe_32AsO_4 + 5H_2O + Fe2HO.$$

Dried ferric hydrate (then become an oxyhdrate—Fe_4O_44HO) (*Ferri Peroxidum Hydratum*, B. P.) has no action on arsenic. Even the moist recently prepared hydrate (Fe_26HO) ceases to react with arsenic as soon as it has become converted into an oxyhydrate (Fe_4O_36HO), a change which occurs though the hydrate be kept under water. According to T. and H. Smith this decomposition occurs gradually, but in an increasing ratio; so that after four months the power of the moist mass is reduced to one-half, and after five months to one-fourth. Now mere loss of water is not usually followed by any alteration of the essential chemical properties of a compound. It would seem, therefore, that ferric hydrate (two molecules) (Fe_412HO) probably suffers, on standing, actual decomposition into oxyhydrate (Fe_4O_36HO) and water ($3H_2O$), and does not merely lose water already existing in it as water. Ferric hydrate is also far more readily soluble in hydrochloric acid, tartaric acid, citric acid, and acid tartrate of potassium, than ferric oxyhydrate. Any formula exhibiting ferric hydrate (Fe_26HO) as a combination of ferric oxide and water ($Fe_2O_3,3H_2O$) is, apparently, for these and other reasons, incorrect.

Peroxyhydrate of Iron. Ferric Peroxyhydrate.

Collect the precipitate on a filter, wash, and dry on a plate over hot water; ferric oxyhydrate (*Ferri Peroxidum Hydratum*, B. P.) (Fe_2O_22HO) remains. When rubbed to powder it is fit for use in medicine.

$$Fe_26HO = Fe_2O_22HO + 2H_2O.$$

This oxyhydrate further decomposes when heated to low redness, ferric oxide (Fe_2O_3) remaining.

$$Fe_2O_22HO = Fe_2O_3 + H_2O.$$

Peroxyde of Iron. Ferric oxyde.

The six univalent atoms of the HO, the characteristic elements of all hydrates, are thus, by two successive steps, split up into water and oxygen. But between the hydrate and oxide there obviously may be another oxyhydrate, in which 4HO is displaced by O''_2, and such a compound is well known; it is a variety of brown iron ore. The other oxyhydrate, Fe_2O_22HO, is also native (needle iron ore), as well as being the *Ferri Peroxidum Hydratum*, B. P.

"Ferri Peroxidum Humidum"	$Fe'''_2 \quad 6HO$
A variety of brown iron ore	$Fe'''_2 \; O'' 4HO$
"Ferri Peroxidum Hydratum" (needle ore)	$Fe'''_2 \; O''_2 2HO$
Ferric oxide	$Fe'''_2 \; O''_3$

The moist ferric hydrate, when kept for some months, even under water, loses the elements of water (W. Procter, Jr.), and is converted into an oxyhydrate, having the formula $Fe_4H_6O_9$ (limonite or brown hæmatite), which is either a compound of the above oxyhydrates (Fe_2O4HO) + (Fe_2O_22HO), or is a definite intermediate oxyhydrate (Fe_4O_36HO).

By ebullition with water for seven or eight hours, ferric hydrate is decomposed into water, and an oxyhydrate having the formula $Fe_4H_2O_7$ (Saint-Giles), which is either a mixture of the official oxyhydrate (Fe_2O_22HO) with ferric oxide (Fe_2O_3), or a definite intermediate body (Fe_4O_52HO). The relation of these bodies to each other will be apparent from the following Table, in which, for convenience, the formulæ of ferric hydrate and oxide are doubled.

Ferric hydrate (B. P.) (as stalactite) . . .	Fe_4 12HO
Kilbride mineral (?)	Fe_4 O10HO
Brown iron ore (Huttenrode and Raschau) .	Fe_4 $O_2$8HO
Old ferric hydrate (limonite)	Fe_4 $O_3$6HO
Ferric oxyhydrate (B. P.) (gothite) . . .	Fe_4 $O_4$4HO
Boiled ferric hydrate (turgite)	Fe_4 $O_5$2HO
Ferric oxide (red hæmatite)	Fe_4 O_6

The official ferric oxyhydrate (Fe_2O_22HO), termed in the British Pharmacopœia *Hydrated Peroxide of Iron*, under the assumption that it is a compound of ferric oxide and water (Fe_2O_3,H_2O), was formerly made by mixing solutions of ferrous sulphate and carbonate of sodium and exposing the resulting ferrous carbonate to the air until it was nearly all converted into ferric oxyhydrate; hence its old name, still sometimes seen on old bottles, of *Ferri Carbonas* and *Ferri Subcarbonas*.

Ferric Oxide (another process).

Thirteenth Synthetical Reaction.—Roast a crystal or two of ferrous sulphate in a small crucible until fumes cease to be evolved; the residue is a variety of ferric oxide (Fe_2O_3) or peroxide of iron, known in trade as *red oxide of iron*, *colcothar*, *crocus*, *rouge* (mineral), or *Venetian red.* It has sometimes been used in pharmacy in mistake for the official oxyhydrates (*vide* 12th Synthet. Reac.), from which it differs not only in composition but in the important respect of being almost insoluble in acids.

The Scale Compounds of Iron.

Fourteenth Synthetical Reaction.—Repeat the previous (12th) reaction, introducing a little solution of citric or tartaric acid, or acid tartrate of potassium, before adding the alkali (soda, potash or ammonia), and notice that now no precipitation of ferric hydrate occurs. This is due to the formation of double compounds, termed Ammonio-Citrate, Potassio-Citrate, Ammonio-Tartrate, Potassio-Tartrate, and similar Sodium compounds of Iron, which remain in solution along with the secondary product—sulphate of the alkali metal. Such ferric compounds, made with certain prescribed proportions of recently prepared ferric hydrate (from which all alkaline sulphate has been washed), and the respective acids (tartaric or citric) or acid salts (acid tartrate of potassium), and the solutions evaporated to a syrupy consistence and spread on flat plates till dry, form the scaly preparations known as *Ferri et Ammoniæ Citras*, B. P. and U. S. P., Ferri Citras, U. S. P. (also *Liquor Ferri Citratis*, U. S. P.), *Ferri et Ammoniæ Tartras*, U. S. P., and *Ferri Potassio-tartras*, or rather, *Ferrum Tartaratum*, B. P., *Ferri et Potassæ Tartras*, U. S. P. A mixture of ferric citrate with citrate of quinine yields, by similar treatment, the well-known scales of *Ferri et Quinæ Citras*, B. P. and U. S. P. Specimens of these substances may be prepared by attending to the following details.

In the pharmacopœial processes for the three scaly compounds, the ferric hydrate is in each case fresh made from solution of ferric sulphate by precipitation with solution of ammonia:—

Fe_23SO_4	+	$6AmHO$	=	Fe_26HO	+	$3Am_2SO_4$
Ferric sulphate.		Hydrate of ammonium.		Ferric hydrate.		Sulphate of ammonium.

the solution of ferric sulphate being made of a definite strength from a known weight of ferrous sulphate. The reason for adopting this course is that ferric hydrate is unstable and cannot be weighed, because it cannot be dried without decomposing and becoming insoluble, as explained under the 12th reaction. This definite solution of ferric sulphate (*Liquor Ferri Persulphatis*, B. P., *Liquor Ferri Tersulphatis*, U. S. P.) is made by adding six fluidrachms of sulphuric acid to half a pint of water, warming, dissolving eight ounces of crystals of sulphate of iron in the liquid, pouring in nitric acid (six fluidrachms or rather more) slightly diluted until the mixture turns from a black to a reddish color, and ruddy nitrous vapors cease to be produced; the whole should measure eleven fluidounces, being diluted or further evaporated, as the case may be, to this bulk.

$$6FeSO_4 + 3H_2SO_4 + 2HNO_3 = 3(Fe_23SO_4) + 2NO + 4H_2O.$$

Ferri et Ammoniæ Citras, B. P. and U. S. P.—Ferric hydrate is dissolved in solution of citric acid, ammonia added, and the whole evaporated to dryness.

To prepare the ferric hydrate, dilute eight fluidounces of the above solution of ferric sulphate with about a quart of water; pour this into two or three pints of water containing excess of solution of ammonia (about 5 fluidounces of "Strong Solution of Ammonia," or 15 ounces of "Solution of Ammonia"). Thoroughly stir the mixture (if it does not then smell of ammonia, more of the latter should be added), allow the precipitate to subside, pour away the supernatant liquid, add more water, and repeat the washing until a little of the liquid tested for by-product (sulphate of ammonium) by solution of chloride or nitrate of barium ceases to give a white precipitate (sulphate of barium). Collect the ferric hydrate on a filter, drain, and place, while still moist, in a mortar with four ounces of citric acid. Set aside the mixture for a few hours, occasionally stirring to promote contact of the constituents, transfer to an evaporating basin, and heat over a water-bath, with frequent stirring, until the whole, or nearly the whole, of the hydrate has dissolved. To the solution, when cool, add nearly two fluidounces of strongest (or five and a half of weak) solution of ammonia, filter, evaporate over a water-bath to the consistence of syrup, spread on panes of glass, and dry (at a temperature not exceeding 100° F.). The product scales off the glass in deep red transparent laminæ.

Ferri et Quiniæ Citras, B. P. and U. S. P.—Ferric hydrate and pure quinia are dissolved in solution of citric acid, ammonia added, and the whole evaporated to dryness.

The ferric hydrate is obtained from four and a half fluidounces of the solution of ferric sulphate, with all the precautions described in the previous paragraph, a proportionate quantity of ammonia being employed.

While the ferric hydrate is being washed, prepare the quinia by dissolving one ounce of the ordinary sulphate of quinia in eight ounces of distilled water, acidified with sufficient sulphuric acid to dissolve the sulphate (about 12 fluidrachms of the official "diluted sulphuric acid"), and to the clear liquid add solution of ammonia, well mixing the product by stirring, until the whole of the quinia is precipitated (that is, until the mixture, after thorough agitation, smells of ammonia). Collect the precipitate on a filter, let it drain, and wash away adhering solution of sulphate of ammonium by passing through it about a pint and a half of distilled water. (It will be observed that the principle involved in the preparation of quinia from its sulphate is identical with that which obtains in the precipitation of alumina, ferric hydrate, or hydrate of zinc, &c. A soluble sulphate—or, indeed, any common soluble salt—has its acidulous constituent removed by the superior affinity of the basylous radical in ammonia, or other alkali, an insoluble precipitate and a new soluble sulphate being formed. The latter is washed away, leaving the former pure. In such manipulations, when economy has to be practised, soda is the alkali generally employed. Ammonia, however, has the advantage of showing the moment when its work of removing an acidulous radical is completed; for the salts which it forms with such acidulous radicals as SO_4, Cl, NO_3, and $C_2H_3O_2$ are inodorous, while it itself has a powerful odor; so long, therefore, as the salt to be decomposed is not wholly attacked, the addition of ammonia does not give an ammoniacal odor to the mixture, the ammonia, as such, being, in fact destroyed; but when the work is accomplished, the quantity of ammonia last added remains as ammonia, and communicates its natural smell to the liquid.)

The ferric hydrate and quinia being now washed and drained, dissolve the former, and afterwards the latter, in a solution of three ounces of citric acid in five of distilled water, the acid liquid being warmed over a water-bath, and portions of the precipitates stirred in as fast as solution is effected. "Let the solution cool, then add in small quantities at a time twelve fluidrachms of solution of ammonia diluted with two fluidounces of distilled water, stirring the solution briskly, and allowing the quinia which separates with each addition of ammonia to dissolve before the next addition is made. Filter the solution, evaporate to the consistence of a thin syrup, and then dry in thin layers on flat porcelain or glass plates at a temperature of 100°. Remove the dry salt in flakes, and keep it in a stoppered bottle." Long-continued exposure to sunlight causes opacity in the scales, and renders them difficultly soluble (Wood.)

Ferrum Tartaratum, B. P.; *Ferri et Potassæ Tartras*, U. S. P. —Ferric hydrate is dissolved in solution of acid tartrate of potassium, and the whole evaporated to dryness.

The ferric hydrate obtainable from five and a half fluidounces of the official solution of ferric sulphate by the action of ammonia, in the manner detailed in the previous paragraphs, is mixed (in a mortar), while still moist but well drained, with two ounces of acid tartrate of potassium. The whole is set aside for twenty-four hours, with occasionally rubbing to promote contact and reaction of the molecules (otherwise somewhat sluggish in attacking each other), and then heated in a dish over a water-bath to a temperature not exceeding 140° F.; a pint of distilled water is then added, and the mixture kept warm until nothing more will dissolve. Filter, evaporate at a temperature not exceeding 140° (greater heat causes decomposition), and when the mixture has the consistence of syrup, spread on panes of glass and dry (in any warm, light place shown by a thermometer to be not hotter than 140°). Remove the dry salt in flakes, and keep it in well-closed bottles.

Ferri et Ammoniæ Tartras, U. S. P., is made by saturating solution of acid tartrate of ammonium with ferric hydrate, evaporating, and scaling. The acid tartrate is prepared by exactly neutralizing half of any quantity of tartaric acid by carbonate of ammonium, and then adding the other half.

The foregoing are the only official scaly preparations of iron. Many others of similar character might be formed. None crystallize or give other indications of definite chemical composition. Their properties are only constant so long as made with unvarying proportions of constituents. Their want of chemical compactness, the loose state in which the iron is combined, precludes their recognition as well-defined chemical compounds, yet possibly enables them to be more readily assimilated as medicines than some of the more definite ferrous and ferric salts.

Wine of Iron, or "Steel" wine (*Vinum Ferri*, B. P.), made by digesting iron wire in sherry wine, probably contains tartrate of potassium and iron and other iron salts, formed by action of the metal on the acid tartrate of potassium and tartaric, citric, malic, and acetic acids present in the wine. *Vinum Ferri Citratis*, B. P., is a solution of ammonio citrate of iron in orange wine.

Black Hydrate of Iron. Ferro-ferric Hydrate.

Fifteenth Synthetical Reaction.—To two-thirds of a small quantity of a solution of ferrous sulphate add a little sulphuric acid; warm, and gradually add nitric acid, as described in the tenth reaction, care being taken not to allow one drop more nitric acid than necessary to fall into the test-tube. Add the other third of ferrous sulphate, shake, and pour the liquid into excess of an alkali; black hydrate of iron, or ferroso-ferric hydrate ($Fe_38HO = Fe2HO, Fe_26HO$), is produced.

$$\underset{\text{Ferric sulphate.}}{Fe_23SO_4} + \underset{\text{Ferrous sulphate.}}{FeSO_4} + \underset{\text{Soda.}}{8NaHO} = \underset{\text{Blk. hydrate of iron.}}{Fe_38HO} + \underset{\text{Sulphate of sodium.}}{4Na_2SO_4}$$

It is so readily attracted by a magnet, even when moist, as to collect round the latter when immersed in the supernatant liquid. Hence the B. P. name, *Ferri Oxidum Magneticum.*

In this process the nitric acid oxidizes the hydrogen of the sulphuric acid, the sulphuric radical uniting with the ferrous sulphate, whose iron is at the same time altered from the ferrous to the ferric condition, ferric sulphate being formed. If too much nitric acid be employed, the second portion of ferrous sulphate will also be converted into ferric salt, and the solution, on the addition of alkali, yield only red ferric hydrate. This result may be avoided by evaporating the solution of ferric sulphate nearly to dryness, thus boiling off excess of nitric acid, or by pouring first the ferric and then the ferrous liquid into the alkali and thoroughly stirring the mixture; the nitric acid is then neutralized and rendered incapable of oxidizing the ferrous sulphate subsequently added.

Black hydrate of iron is decomposed by heat, yielding, in a closed vessel, oxyhydrates and, finally, black oxide of iron or ferroso-ferric oxide. Heated in the air it absorbs oxygen and gives ferric oxide. The black *forge-scales*, which collect near the blacksmith's anvil, have the composition of ferroso-ferric oxide; the black magma formed on exposing a mixture of iron and water to the air is ferroso-ferric hydrate; but these varieties are apt to contain particles of metal and, hence, give hydrogen gas when dissolved in acids—a character which distinguishes them from the official preparation.

If a dried specimen of the black hydrate of iron be required, the mixture should be well boiled and then set aside for an hour or two to favor aggregation of the particles, the mixture filtered, and the precipitate washed until the washings contain no trace of sulphate (indicated by a white precipitate with chloride of barium). Black hydrate of iron absorbs oxygen even at the temperature of the water-bath; it should consequently be dried at 120°, a degree at which only slight oxidation occurs.

Pernitrate of Iron. Ferric Nitrate.

Sixteenth Synthetical Reaction.—Place a few iron tacks in dilute nitric acid and set aside; solution of ferric nitrate, or pernitrate of iron, is formed (Fe_26NO_3).

$$\underset{\text{Iron.}}{Fe_2} + \underset{\text{Nitric acid.}}{8HNO_3} = \underset{\text{Ferric nitrate.}}{Fe_26NO_3} + \underset{\text{Water.}}{4H_2O} + \underset{\text{Nitric oxide.}}{2NO}$$

This solution, made with care, and of a prescribed strength, forms the *Liquor Ferri Pernitratis*, B. B. (sp. gr. 1.107) and U. S. P. (sp. gr. 1.065).

Four and a half fluidounces of nitric acid are diluted with sixteen ounces of distilled water, and one ounce of iron wire, free from rust, dissolved in the mixture, the latter being kept cool to avoid violence of action. The liquid is finally filtered and diluted to thirty fluidounces.

Reduced Iron.

Seventeenth Synthetical Reaction.—Pass hydrogen gas (dried by passing over pieces of chloride of calcium contained in a tube, or through sulphuric acid in a wash-bottle) into a small quantity of ferric oxyhydrate or oxide ("subcarbonate," U. S. P.) contained in a tube arranged horizontally (a test-tube, the bottom of which has been accidentally broken, answers very well), the oxide being kept hot by a gas-flame; oxygen is removed from the oxide by the hydrogen, steam escapes at the open end of the tube, and after a short time, when moisture ceases to be evolved, metallic iron, in a minute state of division, remains.

$$\underset{\text{Ferric oxide.}}{Fe_2O_3} + \underset{\text{Hydrogen.}}{3H_2} = \underset{\text{Iron.}}{Fe_2} + \underset{\text{Water.}}{3H_2O}$$

While still hot throw the iron out into the air; it takes fire and falls to the ground as oxide.

If the ferric oxide is reduced in a gun-barrel heated by a strong furnace, the particles of iron aggregate to some extent, and, when cold, are only slowly oxidized in dry air. This latter form of reduced iron is *Fer réduit*, or *Quevenne's Iron, the Ferri pulvis*, or *Ferrum Redactum*, B. P. and U. S. P.—"a fine grayish-black powder, strongly attracted by the magnet, and exhibiting metallic streaks when rubbed with firm pressure in a mortar." It is often administered in the form of lozenges (*Trochisci Ferri Redacti*, B. P.) gum and sugar protecting the iron from oxidation as well as forming a vehicle for its administration.

Note.—The spontaneous ignition of the iron in the above experiment is an illustration of the influence of minute division on chemical affinity. The action is the same as occurs whenever iron rusts, and the heat evolved and amount of oxide formed is not greater from a given quantity of iron; but the surface exposed to the action of the oxygen of the air is, in the case of this variety of reduced iron, so enormous compared with the weight of the iron, that heat cannot be conducted away sufficiently fast to prevent elevation of temperature to a point at which the whole becomes incandescent. In the slow rusting of iron, escape of heat occurs, but is not observed, because spread over a length of time; in the spontaneous ignition of reduced iron the whole is evolved at one moment.

Ferric Pyrophosphate.

Eighteenth Synthetical Reaction.—To solution of pyrophosphate of sodium add solution of persulphate of iron; a yellowish-white precipitate of ferric pyrophosphate ($Fe_4 3P_2O_7, 9H_2O$) separates. This precipitate, dissolved in solution of citrate of ammonium, and evaporated, yields apple-green scales (*Ferri pyrophosphas*, U. S. P., containing forty-eight per cent. of anhydrous pyrophosphate).

(*b*) *Reactions having Analytical Interest* (Tests).

(The iron occurring as a ferrous salt.)

First Analytical Reaction.—Pass sulphuretted hydrogen (H_2S) through a solution of a ferrous salt (*e.g.*, ferrous sulphate) slightly acidulated by hydrochloric acid; no precipitate occurs.

This is a valuable negative fact, as will be evident presently.

Second Analytical Reaction.—Add sulphydrate of ammonium (NH_4HS) to solution of a ferrous salt; a black precipitate of ferrous sulphide (FeS) falls.

$$FeSO_4 + 2AmHS = FeS + Am_2SO_4 + H_2S.$$

Third Analytical Reaction.—Add solution of ferrocyanide of potassium (yellow prussiate of potash) $K_4Fe''Cy_6$, or K_4Fcy'''', to solution of a ferrous salt; a precipitate ($K_2Fe''Fcy$) falls, at first white, but rapidly becoming blue, owing to absorption of oxygen.

Fourth Analytical Reaction.—To solution of a ferrous salt add ferridcyanide of potassium (red prussiate of potash), $K_6Fe'''_2Cy_{12}$, or K_6Fdcy; a precipitate (Fe''_3Fdcy)

resembling Prussian blue (Turnbull's blue) is thrown down.

Other Analytical Reactions.—The precipitates produced from ferrous solutions on the addition of alkaline carbonates, phosphates, and arseniates, as already described in the synthetical reactions of ferrous salts, are characteristic, and hence have a certain amount of analytical interest, but are inferior in this respect to the four reactions above mentioned.

Note.—The alkalies (solution of potash, soda, or ammonia) are incomplete precipitants of ferrous salts, and are therefore almost useless as tests. To solution of a ferrous salt add ammonia (NH_4HO); on filtering and testing with sulphydrate of ammonium, iron will still be found in the solution. To another portion of the ferrous solution add a few drops of nitric acid and boil; this converts the ferrous into ferric salt, and now alkalies will wholly remove the iron, as already twice seen during the performance of the synthetical experiments.

In actual analysis, the separation of iron as ferric hydrate is an operation of frequent performance. This is always accomplished by the addition of alkali, and, if the iron occurs as a ferrous salt, by previous ebullition with a little nitric acid. Ferrocyanide and ferridcyanide of potassium are the tests used in distinguishing ferrous from ferric salts.

(The iron occurring as a ferric salt.)

Sixth Analytical Reaction.—Through a ferric solution (ferric chloride, *e. g.*) pass sulphuretted hydrogen; a white precipitate of the sulphur of the sulphuretted hydrogen falls, and the ferric is reduced to a ferrous salt, the latter remaining in solution. This reaction is of frequent occurrence in practical analysis.

$$2Fe_2Cl_6 + 2H_2S = 4FeCl_2 + 4HCl + S_2.$$

Seventh Analytical Reaction.—Add sulphydrate of ammonium to a ferric solution; the latter is reduced to the ferrous state, and black ferrous sulphide (FeS) is precipitated as in the second analytical reaction, sulphur being set free.

Eighth Analytical Reaction.—To a ferric solution add ferrocyanide of potassium (K_4FeCy_6, or K_4Fcy''''); a precipitate of prussian blue, the common pigment, occurs ($Fe'''_4 3Fe''Cy_6$, or $Fe'''_4Fcy''''_3$). (*Ferri Ferrocyanidum*, U. S. P.)

Ninth Analytical Reaction.—To a ferric solution add solution of ferridcyanide of potassium; no precipitate occurs, but the liquid is darkened to a greenish or olive hue, according to the strength.

Tenth Analytical Reaction.—This is the production of a red precipitate of ferric hydrate, on the addition of alkalies to ferric salts, and is identical with the twelfth synthetical reaction.

Note.—This reaction illustrates the conventional character of the terms synthesis and analysis. It is of equal importance to the manufacturer and the analyst, and is synthetical or analytical according to the intention with which it is performed.

Other ferric reactions have occasional analytical interest. In neutral ferric solutions the tannic acid in *tincture of galls* occasions a bluish-black inky precipitate, the basis of ordinary writing ink.——(The *Mistura Ferri Aromatica* of the British Pharmacopœia, made by digesting metallic iron in an infusion of various vegetable substances, contains tannate, or rather tannates of iron: it is commonly known in Ireland by the name of Heberden's Ink, after the physician by whom it was first used. It contains about 1 grain of iron in 1 pint.)——*Sulphocyanate of Potassium* (KCyS) causes the formation of ferric sulphocyanate, which is of a deep blood-red color.——There is no ferric carbonate; alkaline carbonates cause the precipitation of ferric hydrate, while carbonic acid gas escapes.

Note.—Cyanogen (NC, or Cy′), ferro-cyanogen (FeC_6N_6, or $FeCy_6$, or simply Fcy''''), and ferridcyanogen (Fe_2Cy_{12}, or $Fdcy^{VI}$), are radicals which play the part of non-metallic elements, just as ammonium in its chemical relations resembles the metallic elements. They will be again referred to.

Memorandum.—The reader must on no account omit to write out equations or diagrams expressive of each of the reactions of iron, analytical as well as synthetical. It is presumed that this has already been done immediately after each reaction has been performed.

DIRECTIONS FOR APPLYING THE FOREGOING ANALYTICAL REACTIONS TO THE ANALYSIS OF AN AQUEOUS SOLUTION OF SALTS CONTAINING **ONE** OF THE METALS, ZINC, ALUMINIUM, IRON.

Add solution of ammonia gradually:—

A dirty-green precipitate indicates iron in the state of a ferrous salt.

A red precipitate indicates iron in the state of a ferric salt.

A white precipitate, insoluble in excess, indicates the presence of an aluminium salt.

A white precipitate, soluble in excess, shows zinc.

These results may be confirmed by the application of some of the other tests to fresh portions of the solution.

TABLE OF SHORT DIRECTIONS FOR APPLYING THE FOREGOING ANALYTICAL REACTIONS TO THE ANALYSIS OF AN AQUEOUS SOLUTION OF SALTS OF **ONE, TWO, OR ALL THREE** OF THE METALS, ZINC, ALUMINIUM, IRON.

Boil about half a test-tubeful of the solution with a few drops of nitric acid. This insures the conversion of ferrous into ferric salts, and enables the next reagent (ammonia) *completely* to precipitate the iron. Add excess of ammonia, and shake the mixture. Filter.

<table>
<tr><td colspan="2">Precipitate
Al Fe.*
Dissolve in HCl, add excess of KHO, stir, filter.</td><td rowspan="2">Filtrate
Zn.
Test by AmHS.
(white ppt.).</td></tr>
<tr><td>Ppt.
Fe
(red ppt.).</td><td>Filtrate
Al.
Neutralize by HCl, and add excess of AmHO†
(white ppt.).</td></tr>
</table>

* The aluminium precipitate (Al_26HO) is white, the iron (Fe_26HO) red. If the precipitate is red, iron must be and aluminium may be present; if white, iron is absent, and further operation on the precipitate unnecessary.

† Alumina, when in small quantity, is sometimes prevented from being precipitated by ammonia through the presence of organic matter derived from the filter paper by action of the potash. In cases of doubt, therefore, before adding ammonia boil the liquid with a little nitric acid, which destroys any organic matter.

Note I.—If iron is present, portions of the original solution must be tested by ferridcyanide of potassium for ferrous, and by ferrocyanide for ferric salts; dark-blue precipitates with both indicate both salts.

Note II.—If no ferrous salt is present, ebullition with nitric acid is unnecessary. It is, perhaps, therefore advisable always to determine this point by previously testing a little of the original solution with ferridcyanide; if no blue precipitate occurs, the nitric acid treatment may be omitted.

CHART FOR ALL METALS HITHERTO CONSIDERED.

The following Table (*vide* Table, p. 126) is perhaps the best, but not the only adaptation of the ordinary reactions to systematic analysis. It is little else than the addition of the analytical scheme for the third group to that of the first two groups. As before, analysis is commenced by the addition of chloride of ammonium (NH_4Cl) to prevent partial precipitation of magnesium, and ammonia (NH_4HO) to neutralize any acid. The latter would attack the chief group-precipitant, sulphydrate of ammonium (NH_4HS), preventing its useful action, and causing a precipitation of the sulphur it commonly contains.

Note.—When a test gives no reaction, absence of the body sought for may be fairly inferred. If group-tests (that is, tests which precipitate a group of substances) give no reaction, the analyst is saved the trouble of looking for either member of that group.

TABLE OF SHORT DIRECTIONS FOR THE ANALYSIS OF AN AQUEOUS SOLUTION OF SALTS OF **ANY OR ALL** OF THE METALLIC ELEMENTS HITHERTO CONSIDERED.

Add AmCl; AmHO; AmHS; stir, filter.

<table>
<tr><td colspan="3">Precipitate
Fe Al Zn.
Wash, dissolve in HCl,* boil (to remove H_2S), filter (to remove S), add KHO, stir, filter.</td><td colspan="4">Filtrate
Ba Ca Mg Am Na K.
Add Am_2CO_3, boil, filter.</td></tr>
<tr><td rowspan="2">Ppt.
Fe
(test orig. sol. by K_4Fcy and K_6Fdcy).</td><td colspan="2">Filtrate
Al Zn.
Neutralize with HCl, add AmHO, stir, filter.</td><td colspan="2">Ppt.
Ba Ca
Dissolve in $HC_2H_3O_2$, add K_2CrO_4, filter.</td><td colspan="2">Filtrate
Mg Am Na K
Add Am_2HPO_4, stir, filter.</td></tr>
<tr><td>Ppt.
Al
(white).</td><td>Filtrate
Zn
add AmHS.
(white ppt.).</td><td>Ppt.
Ba
(yellow).</td><td>Filtrate
Ca
add $Am_2C_2O_4$
(white ppt.).</td><td>Ppt.
Mg
(white).</td><td>Filtrate
Am Na K.
Evap., ignite, dissolve.
Na by flame; K by $PtCl_4$;
orig. sol. for Am.</td></tr>
</table>

* Add, also, a few drops of HNO_3 if Fe be present—*i. e.*, if the ppt. be black. (*Vide* notes on pp. 122 and 125.)

QUESTIONS AND EXERCISES.

196. Name the chief ores of iron.
197. How is the metal obtained from the ores?
198. What is the chemical difference between cast iron, wrought iron, and steel?
199. What is the nature of chalybeate waters?
200. Illustrate by formulæ the difference between ferrous and ferric salts.
201. Under what different circumstances may the atom of iron be considered to exert bivalent, trivalent, and sexivalent activity?
202. Write a paragraph on the nomenclature of iron salts.
203. Give a diagram of the official process for the preparation of ferrous sulphate.
204. In what respects do Sulphate of Iron, Granulated Sulphate of Iron, and Dried Sulphate of Iron differ?
205. How is ferrous sulphate obtained on the large scale?
206. Mention the chemical names of white, green, and blue vitriol.
207. Why does ferrous sulphate become brown by prolonged exposure to air?
208. Give a diagram showing the formation of Ferrous Carbonate.
209. Describe the action of atmospheric oxygen on ferrous carbonate: can the effect be prevented?
210. In what order would you mix the ingredients of *Mistura Ferri Composita*, and why?
211. Write out an equation illustrative of the formation of the Phosphate of Iron.
212. Why is acetate of sodium used in the preparation of ferrous phosphate?
213. Which four compounds of iron may be formed by the direct union of their elements?
214. Give the official method for the preparation of Solution of Ferric Chloride.
215. Of what use is the spirit in Tincture of Perchloride of Iron?
216. How may Ferrous be converted into Ferric Sulphate?
217. What is the formula of Ferric Acetate? and how is it prepared for use in pharmacy?
218. Express, by formulæ, the difference between *Ferri Peroxidum Humidum*, B. P., and *Ferri Peroxidum Hydratum*, B. P.
219. What are the general characters and mode of production of the medicinal scale preparations of iron?
220. In what state is the iron in *Vinum Ferri*, B. P.?
221. What other form of Wine of Iron is official in Great Britain?
222. Give equations illustrating the chief steps in the artificial production of the so-called Magnetic Oxide of Iron.
223. How is precipitated magnetic oxide of iron distinguished from the varieties made directly from the metal?
224. Why is magnetic oxide of iron officially directed to be dried at a temperature not exceeding 120° Fahr.?
225. Give a diagram showing the formation of Ferric Nitrate.

226. Work out a sum showing how much anhydrous ferric oxide will yield, theoretically, one hundred-weight of iron. Ans. 160 lbs.

227. What are the properties of anhydrous ferric oxide?

228. Give the characteristic tests for iron, distinguishing between ferrous and ferric reactions, and illustrating each by an equation or a diagram:—

a. Sulphydrate of ammonium.
b. Ferrocyanide of potassium.
c. Ferridcyanide of potassium.
d. Caustic alkalies.
e. Sulphocyanate of potassium.

229. Describe the action of ammonia on salts of iron, aluminium, and zinc respectively.

230. What precautions must be used in testing for calcium in the presence of iron?

231. How is magnesium detected in the presence of zinc?

232. How is aluminium detected in presence of magnesium?

233. Draw up a scheme for the analysis of an aqueous liquid containing salts of iron, barium, and potassium.

234. How may zinc, magnesium, and ammonium be consecutively removed from aqueous solution?

ARSENICUM, ANTIMONY.

These two elements resemble metals in appearance and in the character of some of their compounds; but they are still more closely allied to the non-metals, especially to phosphorus and nitrogen. They are quinquivalent (As^{v}, Sb^{v}), as seen in arsenic anhydride (As_2O_5) and pentachloride of antimony ($SbCl_5$), but usually exert trivalent activity only (As^{III}, Sb^{III}), as seen in the hydrogen and other compounds (AsH_3, $AsCl_3$, $AsBr_3$, AsI_3). A few preparations of these elements are used in medicine; but all are more or less powerful poisons, and hence have considerable toxicological interest. The iodide (*Arsenici Iodidum*, U. S. P.) is made by cautiously fusing together atomic proportions of arsenicum and iodine. It is an orange-red crystalline solid soluble in water. The *Liquor Arsenici et Hydrargyri Iodidi*, U. S. P., is made by dissolving iodide of arsenicum and red iodide of mercury in water, in the proportion of 1 grain of each of the solids to 104 grains of water.

ARSENICUM.

Symbol As. Atomic weight 75.

Sources.—Arsenical ores are frequently met with in nature, the commonest being the arsenio-sulphide of iron (FeSAs). This mineral is roasted in a current of air, the oxygen of which, combining with the arsenicum, forms common white arsenic (As_2O_3) (*Acidum Arseni-*

osum, B. P. and U. S. P.), which is condensed in chambers or long flues. It commonly "occurs as a heavy white powder, or in sublimed masses, which usually present a stratified appearance, caused by the existence of separate layers, differing from each other in degrees of opacity." *Realgar* (red algar) is the red native sulphide (As_2S_2), and orpiment (*auripigmentum*, the golden pigment) the yellow native sulphide (As_2S_3) of arsenicum.

Reactions having (*a*) Synthetical and (*b*) Analytical Interest.

(*a*) *Reactions having Synthetical Interest.*

Alkaline Solution of Arsenic.

First Synthetical Reaction.—Boil a grain or two of powdered arsenic (As_2O_3) in water containing an equal weight of carbonate of potassium, and, if necessary, filter. The solution, colored with compound tincture of lavender, and containing 4 grains of arsenic per ounce, forms the *Liquor Arsenicalis*, B. P., or *Liquor Potassæ Arsenitis*, U. S. P. (*Fowler's Solution.*)

Note.—This official solution does not generally contain arsenite of potassium; for the arsenic does not decompose the carbonate of potassium, or only after long boiling. From concentrated solutions carbonic acid gas is more quickly eliminated.

Arsenious Acids and other Arsenites.

When arsenic (As_2O_3) is dissolved in excess of solutions of potash or soda, arsenites are formed having the formulæ KH_2AsO_3 and NaH_2AsO_3. Boiled with excess of arsenic, one molecule of these salts combines with one of arsenic. The usual character of such compounds is that of oily alkaline liquids. Arsenic or arsenious anhydride (the so-called arsenious acid), when dissolved in water, yields true arsenious acid (H_3AsO_3), the arsenite of hydrogen.

$$\underset{\text{Arsenious anhydride.}}{As_2O_3} + \underset{\text{Water.}}{3H_2O} = \underset{\text{Arsenious acid.}}{2H_3AsO_3}$$

Acid Solution of Arsenic.

Second Synthetical Reaction.—Boil arsenic with dilute hydrochloric acid. Such a solution made with prescribed proportions of acid and water, and containing 4 grains of arsenic (As_2O_3) per ounce, forms the *Liquor Arsenici Hydrochloricus*, B. P. (*De Valangin's Solution* contained a grain and a half per ounce.)

Note.—No decomposition occurs in this experiment. The liquid is simply a solution of arsenic in dilute hydrochloric acid. These two solutions may be preserved for analytical operations.

Mem.—The practical student should boil arsenic in water only, and thus have an acid, alkaline, and aqueous solution for analytical comparison.

Arsenicum.

Third Synthetical Reaction.—Place a grain or less of arsenic at the bottom of a narrow test-tube, cover it with about half an inch or an inch of small fragments of dry charcoal, and hold the tube, nearly horizontally, in a flame, the mouth being loosely covered by the thumb. At first let the bottom of the tube project slightly beyond the flame, so that the charcoal may become nearly red-hot; then heat the bottom of the tube. The arsenic will sublime, become deoxidized by the charcoal, carbonic oxide being formed, and arsenicum deposited in the cool part of the tube as a dark mirror-like metallic incrustation.

There is a characteristic odor, resembling garlic, emitted during this operation, probably due to a partially oxidized trace of arsenicum which escapes from the tube; for arsenic alone does not give this odor, neither, it is said, does arsenicum; moreover, arsenicum being a freely oxidizable element, its vaporous particles could scarcely exist in the air in an unoxidized state.

Metallic arsenicum (*Arsenicum,* U. S. P.) may be obtained in large quantities by the above process if the operation be conducted in vessels of commensurate size. But performed with great care, in narrow tubes, using not charcoal alone, but *black flux* (a mixture of charcoal and carbonate of potassium obtained by heating acid tartrate of potassium in a test-tube or other closed vessel till no more fumes are evolved), the reaction has considerable analytical interest, the garlic odor and the formation of the mirror-like ring being highly characteristic of arsenicum. Compounds of mercury and antimony, however, give sublimates which may be mistaken for arsenicum.

Arsenic Acid and other Arseniates.

Fourth Synthetical Reaction.—Boil a grain or two of arsenic with a few drops of nitric acid until red fumes cease to be evolved; evaporate the solution in a small dish to dryness, to remove excess of nitric acid; dissolve the residue in water: the product is Arsen′ic acid (H_3AsO_4).

Arsenic acid, when strongly heated, loses the elements of water, and arsenic anhydride remains (As_2O_5).

Arsenic anhydride readily absorbs water and becomes arsenic acid (H_3AsO_4). Arsenic acid is readily reduced to arsenious by the action of reducing agents such as sulphurous acid, $H_3AsO_4 + H_2SO_3 = H_3AsO_3 + H_2SO_4$.

Salts analogous to arsenic acid, the arseniate of hydrogen, are termed *arseniates*, and have the general formula R'_3AsO_4. The ammonium arseniate (Am_2HAsO_4) may be made by neutralizing arsenic acid with ammonia.——Arsenic acid is used as an oxidizing agent in the manufacture of the well-known dye, magenta.

Arsenite and arseniate of sodium are used in the cleansing operations of the calico-printer.

Pyroarseniate and Arseniate of Sodium.

Fifth Synthetical Reaction.—Fuse a minute fragment of common white arsenic (As_2O_3) with nitrate of sodium ($NaNO_3$) and dried carbonate of sodium (Na_2CO_3) in a porcelain crucible, and dissolve the mass in water; solution of arseniate of sodium (Na_2HAsO_4) results.

$$\underset{\text{Arsenic.}}{As_2O_3} + \underset{\text{Nitrate of sodium.}}{2NaNO_3} + \underset{\text{Carbonate of sodium.}}{Na_2CO_3} = \underset{\text{Pyroarseniate of sodium.}}{Na_4As_2O_7} + \underset{\text{Nitrous anhydride.}}{N_2O_3} + \underset{\text{Carbonic acid gas.}}{CO_2}$$

The official proportions (B. P.) are 10 of arsenic to 8½ of nitrate of sodium and 5½ of dried carbonate, each powdered, the whole well mixed, fused in a crucible at a red heat till effervescence ceases, and the liquid poured out on a slab. The product is pyroarseniate of sodium ($Na_4As_2O_7$). Dissolved in water, crystallized, and dried, the salt has the formula $Na_2HAsO_4, 7H_2O$ (*Sodæ Arsenias*, B. P.).

$$Na_4As_2O_7 + 15H_2O = 2(Na_2HAsO_4, 7H_2O).$$

Heated to 300° F. the crystals lose all water. A solution of 4 grains of the anhydrous salt (Na_2HAsO_4) in 1 ounce of water forms the *Liquor Sodæ Arseniatis*, B. P. The anhydrous salt is used in this preparation because the crystallized is of somewhat uncertain composition. The fresh crystals are represented by the formula $Na_2HAsO_4, 12H_2O$ (=53.7 per cent. of water); these soon effloresce and yield a stable salt having the formula $Na_2HAsO_4, 7H_2O$ (= 40.4 per cent. of water). To avoid the possible employment of a mixture of these bodies, the invariable anhydrous salt is officially used, constancy in the strength of a powerful preparation being thereby secured.

Arseniate of Iron. Ferrous Arseniate.

Sixth Synthetical Reaction.—To solution of arseniate of sodium add a little acetate of sodium and then solution of ferrous sulphate, a precipitate of ferrous arseniate occurs (Fe_32AsO_4) (*Ferri Arsenias*, B. P.). On the large scale 4 parts of dried arseniate and 3 of acetate dissolved in 40 of water, mixed with 9 of sulphate in 60 of water, may be employed. The precipitate should be collected on a calico filter, washed, squeezed, and dried at a low temperature (100° F.) over a wash-bath to avoid excessive oxidation.

$$\underset{\text{Arseniate of sodium.}}{2Na_2HAsO_4} + \underset{\text{Acetate of sodium.}}{2NaC_2H_3O_2} + \underset{\text{Ferrous sulphate.}}{3FeSO_4} = \underset{\text{Ferrous arseniate.}}{Fe_32AsO_4} + \underset{\text{Sulphate of sodium.}}{3Na_2SO_4} + \underset{\text{Acetic acid.}}{2HC_2H_3O_2}.$$

The use of the acetate of sodium is to insure the occurrence of acetic acid in solution, where otherwise would be free sulphuric acid. Sulphuric acid is a solvent of ferrous arseniate; acetic acid is not. It is impossible to prevent the separation of sulphuric acid, if only ferrous sulphate and arseniate of sodium be employed. At the instant of precipitation ferrous arseniate is white, but rapidly becomes of a green or greenish-blue color owing to absorption of oxygen and formation of a ferroso-ferric arseniate. It is a tasteless amorphous powder, soluble in acids.

The *Hydride* and *Sulphides* of *Arsenicum*, and the *Arsenites* and *Arseniates of Copper* and of *Silver* are mentioned in the following analytical paragraphs:—

(*b*) *Reactions having Analytical Interest* (Tests).

First Analytical Reaction.—Cut or break off portions of the tube containing the sublimate of arsenicum obtained in the third synthetical reaction, put them into a test-tube and heat the bottom of the latter, holding it nearly horizontally, and covering the mouth loosely with the finger or thumb; the arsenicum (As_2) will absorb oxygen from the air in the tube, and the resulting arsenious anhydride (As_2O_3) be deposited on the cool part of the tube in characteristic octahedral (ὀκτὼ, *okto*, eight; ἕδρα, *hedra*, side) crystals, more or less perfect.

Microscopic Test.—Prove that the crystals are identical in form with those of common white arsenic, by heating a grain or less of the latter in another test-tube, examining the two sublimates by a good lens or compound microscope.

Notes.—The production of arsenicum and its subsequent oxidation are test-reactions perhaps not quite so delicate as some that follow, requiring more material for their satisfactory performance; yet the form of the crystals is characteristic, no other volatile body being likely to be mistaken for them; and in toxicological cases it is desirable to obtain the arsenicum in a similar state to that in which probably it originally exerted its effects; the processes alluded to are therefore of considerable importance. Moreover, arsenicum, ready for sublimation to crystalline arsenic, is easily obtained from solution by the following reaction:—

Second Analytical Reaction.—Place a thin piece of copper, about a quarter inch wide and half inch long, in a solution of arsenic, acidified by hydrochloric acid, and boil (nitric acid must not be present, or the copper itself will be dissolved); arsenicum is deposited on the plate in a metallic condition, an equivalent portion of copper going into solution. Pour off the supernatant liquid from the copper, wash the latter once or twice with water, dry the piece of metal by holding in the fingers and passing through a flame, and finally place it at the bottom of a clean dry narrow test-tube; sublime as described in the last reaction, again noticing the form of the resulting crystals.

This is commonly known as Reinsch's test for arsenicum. The tube may be reserved for subsequent comparison with an antimonial sublimate (p. 144).

Note.—Copper itself frequently contains arsenicum, a fact that may not, perhaps, much trouble an operator so long as he is performing experiments in practical chemistry merely for educational purposes; but when he engages in the analysis of bodies of unknown composition, he must assure himself that neither his apparatus nor materials already contain the element of which he is in search.

The detection of arsenicum in metallic copper is best accomplished by distilling a mixture of a few grains of the sample with five or six times its weight of ferric hydrate or chloride (free from arsenicum) and excess of hydrochloric acid. The arsenicum is thus volatilized in the form of chloride of arsenicum, and may be condensed in water and detected by sulphuretted hydrogen (5th Analytical Reaction) or Reinsch's test. The ferric chloride solution is, if necessary, freed from any trace of arsenicum by evaporating once or twice to dryness with excess of hydrochloric acid (Odling).

Third Analytical Reaction—Marsh's test.—Generate hydrogen in the usual way from water by zinc and sulphuric acid, a bottle of about four or six ounces capacity being used, and a funnel-tube and short delivery-tube passing through the cork in the usual manner (described on page 69). Dry the escaping hydrogen (except in rough experiments, when it is unnecessary) by adapting to the delivery-tube, by a pierced cork, a short piece of wider tubing containing fragments of chloride of calcium. To the opposite end of the drying-tube fit a piece of narrow tubing ten or twelve inches long, made of hard German glass, and having its aperture narrowed by drawing out in the flame of the blowpipe. When the hydrogen has been escaping at such a rate and for a sufficient number of minutes as to warrant the operator in concluding that all the air originally existing in the bottle has been expelled, set light to the jet, and then pour eight or ten drops of the aqueous solution of arsenic, or three or four drops of the acid or alkaline solution of arsenic, previously prepared, into the funnel-tube, washing the liquid into the generating-bottle with a little water. The arsenic is at once reduced to the state of arsenicum, and the latter combines with some of the hydrogen to form hydride of arsenicum or arseniuretted hydrogen gas (AsH_3). Immediately hold a piece of earthenware or porcelain (the lid of a porcelain crucible, if at hand) in the hydrogen jet at the extremity of the delivery-tube; a brown spot of condensed arsenicum is deposited. Collect several of these spots, and retain them for future comparison with antimonial spots (p. 144).

The separation of arsenicum in the flame is due to the decomposition of the arseniuretted hydrogen by the heat of combustion. The cool porcelain at once condenses the arsenicum, and thus prevents its oxidation to white arsenic, which would otherwise take place at the outer edge of the flame.

Hold a small beaker or wide test-tube over the flame for a few minutes; a white film of arsenic (As_2O_3) will be slowly deposited, and may be further examined in contrast with a similar antimonial film (p. 144).

During these experiments the effect produced by the arsenical vapors on the color of the hydrogen-flame will have been noticed; they give it a dull livid bluish tint. This is characteristic.

Apply the flame of a gas-lamp to the middle of the hard delivery-tube; the arseniuretted hydrogen, as before, is decomposed by the heat, but the liberated arsenicum (As_2) immediately condenses in the cool part of the tube beyond the flame, forming a dark metallic mirror. The tube may be removed and kept for comparison with an antimonial deposit.

Note I.—Zinc, like copper, frequently itself contains arsenicum. When a specimen free from arsenicum is met with, it should be reserved for analytical experiments, or a quantity of guaranteed purity should be purchased of the chemical-apparatus maker. Sulphuric acid is more easily obtained free from arsenic.

Note II.—In delicate and important applications of Marsh's test, magnesium may be substituted for zinc with safety, as arsenicum has not yet been, nor is it likely to be, found in magnesium. Magnesium in rods is convenient for this purpose, and may be obtained from most dealers in chemicals.

Note III.—Arseniuretted hydrogen is decomposed by strong sulphuric acid; hence chloride of calcium is used in drying the gas.

Fourth Analytical Reaction—Fleitmann's test.—Generate hydrogen by heating to near the boiling-point a strong solution of caustic soda or potash and some pieces of zinc. Drop into the test-tube a little arsenical solution, and spread over the mouth of the tube a cap of filter-paper moistened with one drop of solution of nitrate of silver. Again heat the tube, taking care that the liquid itself shall not spirt up on to the cap; the arsenic is reduced to arsenicum, the latter uniting with the hydrogen as in Marsh's test; and the arseniuretted hydrogen passing up through the cap reacts on the nitrate of silver, causing the production of a purplish-black spot.

$$AsH_3 + 3H_2O + 6AgNO_3 = H_3AsO_3 + 6HNO_3 + 3Ag_2$$

Note.—This reaction is particularly valuable, enabling the analyst to quickly distinguish arsenicum in the presence of its sister element antimony, which, although it combines with the hydrogen evolved from dilute acid and zinc, does not combine with the hydrogen evolved from solution of alkali and zinc, and therefore does not give the effect just described.

Distinction between Arsenious and Arsenic combinations.—The above tests are those of arsenicum, whether existing in the arsenious or arsenic condition, though from the latter the element is not generally eliminated so quickly as from the former. Of the following reactions, that with nitrate of silver at once distinguishes arsenious acid and other arsenites from arsenic acid and other arseniates.

Mem.—The exact nature of all these analytical reactions will be more fully evident if traced out by diagrams or equations.

Fifth Analytical Reaction.—Through an acidified solution of arsenic pass sulphuretted hydrogen; a yellow precipitate of sulphide of arsenicum or arsenious sulphide (As_2S_3) quickly falls. Add an alkaline hydrate or sulphydrate to the precipitate, it readily dissolves. The precipitate consequently would not be obtained on passing sulphuretted hydrogen through an alkaline solution of arsenic.

Note I.—The only other metal which gives a yellow sulphide in an acid solution by action of sulphuretted hydrogen is cadmium; but this sulphide is insoluble in alkaline liquids.

Note II.—A trace of sulphide of arsenicum is sometimes met with in sulphur (distilled from arsenical pyrites). It may be detected by digesting the sulphur in solution of ammonia, filtering, and evaporating to dryness; a yellow residue of sulphide of arsenicum is obtained if that substance be present.

Sixth Analytical Reaction.—Through an acidified solution of arsenic acid, or any other arseniate, pass sulphuretted hydrogen; a yellow precipitate of arsenic sulphide (As_2S_5) slowly falls. This also is soluble in alkaline hydrates and sulphydrates.

Chemical Analogy of Sulphur and Oxygen.—The solubility of arsenious and arsenic sulphide in alkaline solutions is good evidence of the close chemical analogy between them and the corresponding oxygen compounds of arsenicum. The potassium arsenite and sulpharsenite, arseniate and sulph-arseniate, have the composition represented by the following formulæ:—

$$K_3AsO_3 \qquad K_3AsO_4$$
$$K_3AsS_3 \qquad K_3AsS_4;$$

and the corresponding ammonium and sodium salts have a similar composition:—

$$6AmHS + As_2S_3 = 2Am_3AsS_3 + 3H_2S$$
$$6AmHS + As_2S_5 = 2Am_3AsS_4 + 3H_2S.$$

Seventh Analytical Reaction.—To an aqueous solution of arsenic add two or three drops of solution of sulphate of copper, and then cautiously add diluted solution of ammonia, drop by drop, until a green precipitate is obtained. The production of this precipitate is characteristic of arsenicum. To a portion of the mixture add an acid; the precipitate dissolves. To another portion add alkali; the precipitate dissolves. These two experiments show the advantage of testing a suspected arsenical solution by litmus-paper before applying this reaction; if acid, cautiously adding alkali, if alkaline, adding acid, till neutrality is obtained. (Or a special copper reagent may be used; see a note to the Tenth Reaction, p. 137.)

The precipitate is arsenite of copper ($Cu''HAsO_3$) or *Scheele's Green.* More or less pure, or mixed with acetate or, occasionally, carbonate of copper, it is very largely used as a pigment under many names, such as Brunswick Green and Schweinfurth Green, by painters, paper-stainers, and others.

Eighth Analytical Reaction.—Apply the test just described to a solution of arsenic acid or other arseniate; a somewhat similar precipitate of arseniate of copper is obtained.

Ninth Analytical Reaction.—Repeat the seventh reaction, substituting nitrate of silver for sulphate of copper: in this case *yellow* arsenite of silver (Ag_3AsO_3) falls, also soluble in acids and alkalies.

Tenth Analytical Reaction.—Apply the test to a solution of arsenic acid or other arseniate; a *chocolate*-colored precipitate of arseniate of silver (Ag_3AsO_4) falls.

Copper and Silver Reagents for Arsenicum.—The last four reactions may be performed with increased delicacy and certainty of result, if the copper and silver reagents be previously prepared in the following manner: To solution of pure sulphate of copper (about 1 part in 20 of water) add ammonia until the blue precipitate at first formed is nearly all redissolved; filter and preserve the liquid as an arsenicum reagent, labelling it *solution of ammonio-sulphate of copper* (B. P.). Treat solution of nitrate of silver (about 1 part in 40) in the same way, and label it *solution of ammonio-nitrate of silver* (B. P.). The composition of these two salts will be referred to subsequently.

Arsenious and Arsenic Compounds.—While many reagents may be used for the detection of arsenicum, only nitrate of silver, as already stated, will readily indicate in which state of oxidation the arsenicum exists; for the two sulphides and the two copper precipitates, though differing in composition, resemble each other in appearance, whereas the two silver precipitates differ in color as well as in composition.

Soluble arseniates also give insoluble arseniates with barium, calcium, zinc, and some other metallic solutions.

Antidote.—In cases of poisoning by arsenic or arsenical preparations, the most effective antidote is recently precipitated moist ferric hydrate (*Ferri Peroxidum Humidum*, B. P.). It is perhaps best administered in the form of a mixture of solution of perchloride of iron (*Liquor* or *Tinctura*), with carbonate of sodium—two to three ounces of the former to about one ounce of the crystals of the latter. Instead of the carbonate of sodium about a quarter of an ounce of calcined magnesia may be used. These quantities will render at least 10 grains of arsenic insoluble. Emetics should also be given, and the stomach-pump applied as quickly as possible.

The above statements regarding the antidote for arsenic may be verified by mixing the various substances together, filtering, and proving the absence of arsenicum in the filtrate by applying some of the foregoing tests.

Mode of action of the Antidote.—The action of the carbonate of sodium or the magnesia is to precipitate ferric hydrate ($Fe_2 6HO$)—chloride of sodium (NaCl) or magnesium ($MgCl_2$) being formed, which are harmless, if not beneficial, under the circumstances. The reaction between the ferric hydrate and the arsenic results in the formation of insoluble ferrous arseniate.

$$\underset{\text{Ferric hydrate.}}{2(Fe_2 6HO)} + \underset{\text{Arsenic.}}{As_2O_3} = \underset{\text{Ferrous arseniate.}}{Fe_3 2AsO_4} + \underset{\text{Water.}}{5H_2O} + \underset{\text{Ferrous hydrate.}}{Fe2HO}$$

As already stated dried ferric hydrate (then become an oxyhydrate, $Fe_4O_4 4HO$) (*Ferri Peroxidum Hydratum*, B. P.) has no action on arsenic. Even the moist recently prepared hydrate ($Fe_2 6HO$) ceases to react with arsenic as soon as it has become converted into an oxyhydrate ($Fe_4O_3 6HO$), a change which occurs though the hydrate be kept under water. According to T. and H. Smith this decomposition occurs gradually, but in an increasing ratio; so that after four months the power of the moist mass is reduced to one-half, and after five months to one-fourth.

QUESTIONS AND EXERCISES.

235. In what form does arsenicum occur in nature?

236. Describe the characters of white arsenic.

237. Name the official preparations of arsenicum.

238. What proportion of arsenic (As_2O_3) is contained in *Liquor Arsenicalis*, B. P., and *Liquor Arsenici Hydrochloricus*, B. P.?

239. By what method may arsenic be reduced to arsenicum?

240. Give the formulæ of arsenious and arsenic acids.

241. Explain, by diagrams, the reactions which occur in converting arsenic into Arseniate of Sodium by the process of the British Pharmacopœia.

242. Why is anhydrous instead of crystallized arseniate of sodium employed in the preparation of *Liquor Sodæ Arseniatis*, B. P.?

243. In the preparation of Arseniate of Iron from ferrous sulphate and arseniate of sodium, why is acetate of sodium included?

244. Describe the manipulations necessary in distinguishing arsenic by its crystalline form.

245. How is Reinsch's test for arsenicum applied, and under what circumstances may its indications be fallacious?

246. Give the details of Marsh's test for arsenicum, and the precautions to be observed in its performance. Explain the reactions by diagrams.

247. What peculiar value has Fleitmann's test for arsenicum?

248. Describe the conditions under which sulphuretted hydrogen becomes a trustworthy test for arsenicum.

249. How may a trace of sulphide of arsenicum be detected in sulphur?

250. How are salts of copper and silver applied as reagents for the detection of arsenicum?

251. How are arsenites distinguished from arseniates?

252. Mention the best antidote in cases of poisoning by arsenic, explain the process by which it may be most quickly prepared, and describe its action.

253. What light does the action of arsenic on ferric hydrate throw on the constitution of the latter substance?

ANTIMONY.

Symbol Sb (stibium). Atomic weight 122.

Source and Uses.—Antimony occurs in nature chiefly as sulphide, Sb_2S_3. The *crude* or *black antimony* of pharmacy is this native sulphide freed from earthy impurities by fusion: it has a striated, crystalline, lustrous fracture; subsequently powdered it forms the grayish-black crystalline *Antimonium nigrum*, B. P., *Antimonii sulphuretum*, U. S. P. The metal is easily obtained from the sulphide by roasting, and then reducing with charcoal and carbonate of sodium. Metallic antimony is an important constituent of *Type-metal*, *Britannia metal* (tea and coffee pots, spoons, etc.), and the best varieties of *Pewter*. The old *pocula emetica*, or everlasting emetic cups, were made of antimony; wine kept in them for a day or two acquired a variable amount of emetic quality. The metal is not used in making the antimonial preparations of the Pharmacopœia, the sulphide alone being, directly or indirectly, employed for this purpose.

Antimony has very close chemical analogies with arsenicum. Its atom, in the official salts, exerts trivalent activity (*e.g.*, $SbCl_3$), but sometimes it is quinquivalent (*e.g.*, $SbCl_5$).

Reactions having (*a*) Synthetical and (*b*) Analytical Interest.

(*a*) *Reactions having Synthetical Interest.*

Chloride of Antimony. Antimonious Chloride.

First Synthetical Reaction.—Boil half an ounce or less of sulphide of antimony with four or five times its weight of hydrochloric acid in a dish in a fume-chamber or the open air; sulphuretted hydrogen is evolved and solution of chloride of antimony, $SbCl_3$, obtained.

$$\underset{\text{Sulphide of antimony.}}{Sb_2S_3} + \underset{\text{Hydrochloric acid.}}{6HCl} = \underset{\text{Chloride of antimony.}}{2SbCl_3} + \underset{\text{Sulphuretted hydrogen.}}{3H_2S}$$

This solution, cleared by subsidence, is what is commonly known as *Butter of antimony* (*Liquor Antimonii Chloridi*, B. P.). If pure sulphide has been used in its preparation the liquid is nearly colorless; but much of that met with in veterinary pharmacy is simply a by-product in the generation of sulphuretted hydrogen from native sulphide of antimony and hydrochloric acid, and is more or less brown from the presence of chloride of iron. It not unfrequently darkens in color on keeping; this is due to absorption of oxygen from the air and conversion of light-colored ferrous into dark-brown ferric chloride or oxychloride.

True butter of antimony ($SbCl_3$) is obtained on evaporating the above solution to a low bulk, and distilling the residue. The butter condenses as a white crystalline semi-transparent mass in the neck of the retort; at the close of the operation it may be easily melted and run down in a bottle, which should be subsequently well stoppered.

Pentachloride of antimony ($SbCl_5$), or antimonic chloride, is a fuming liquid, obtained on passing chlorine over the lower chloride.

Oxychloride of Antimony. Antimonious Oxychloride.

Second Synthetical Reaction.—Pour the solution of chloride of antimony produced in the last reaction into several ounces of water; a white precipitate of oxychloride of antimony ($2SbCl_3, 5Sb_2O_3$) falls, some chloride of antimony remaining in the supernatant acid liquid.

This is the old *pulvis Algarothi*, *pulvis angelicus*, or *mercurius vitæ*. On standing under water it gradually becomes crystalline.

$$\underset{\text{Chloride of antimony.}}{12SbCl_3} + \underset{\text{Water.}}{15H_2O} = \underset{\text{Oxychloride of antimony.}}{2SbCl_3,5Sb_2O_3} + \underset{\text{Hydrochloric acid.}}{30HCl}$$

Oxide of Antimony. Antimonious Oxide.

Well wash the precipitate with water, by decantation (*vide* p. 81), and add solution of carbonate of sodium; the terchloride remaining with the oxide is thus decomposed, and oxide of antimony (Sb_2O_3) alone remains. This is *Antimonii Oxidum*, B. P. and U. S. P. It is of a light buff or grayish-white color, insoluble in water, soluble in hydrochloric acid, fusible at a low red heat. The moist oxide of antimony may be well washed and employed for the next reaction, or dried over a water-bath. At temperatures above 212° oxygen is absorbed, and other oxides of antimony formed. The presence of the latter is detected on boiling the powder in solution of acid tartrate of potassium, in which oxide of antimony (Sb_2O_3) is soluble, but *antimonic anhydride* (Sb_2O_5) and the so-called *antimonious anhydride* (Sb_2O_4) insoluble.

$$\underset{\text{Oxychloride of antimony.}}{2SbCl_3,5Sb_2O_3} + \underset{\text{Carbonate of sodium.}}{3Na_2CO_3} = \underset{\text{Oxide of antimony.}}{6Sb_2O_3} + \underset{\text{Chloride of sodium.}}{6NaCl} + \underset{\text{Carbonic acid gas.}}{3CO_2}$$

A higher oxide of antimony (Sb_2O_5), termed antimonic oxide or anhydride, corresponding with arsenic anhydride, is obtained on decomposing the pentachloride by water, or on boiling metallic antimony with nitric acid. The variety obtained from the chloride differs in saturating-power from that obtained from the metal, and is termed metantimonic acid (μετὰ, *meta*, beyond).

Tartar Emetic.

Third Synthetical Reaction.—Mix the moist oxide of antimony obtained in the previous reaction with about an equal quantity of cream of tartar (6 of the latter to 5 of the dry oxide) and sufficient water to form a paste; set aside for a day to facilitate complete combination; boil the product with water, and filter; the resulting liquid contains the double tartrate of antimony and potassium ($KSbC_4H_4O_7$), potassio-tartrate of antimony, tartrated antimony or tartar emetic (emetic, from ἐμέω, *emeo*, I vomit; tartar from Τάρταρος, *tartaros*, see Index).

$$\underset{\text{Acid tartrate of potassium.}}{2KHC_4H_4O_6} + \underset{\text{Oxide of antimony.}}{Sb_2O_3} = \underset{\text{Tartar emetic.}}{2KSbC_4H_4O_7} + \underset{\text{Water.}}{H_2O}$$

On evaporation the salt is obtained in colorless transparent triangular-faced crystals of the above composition, with a molecule of water of crystallization, forming the *Antimonium Tartaratum*, B. P. ($KSbOC_4H_4O_6,H_2O$) the *Antimonii et Potassæ Tartras*, U. S. P.

The formula for tartar emetic is apparently inconsistent with the general formula for tartrates ($R'R'C_4H_4O_6$); this will be subsequently fully explained in connection with Tartaric Acid. The salt appears to be an oxytartrate ($KSbOC_4H_4O_6$).

Tartar emetic is soluble in water, and slightly so in proof spirit. Dissolved in sherry wine it forms the official *Vinum Antimoniale*, B. P., and *Vinum Antimonii*, U. S. P. It may be externally applied as an ointment, *Unguentum Antimonii Tartarati*, B. P. (*Unguentum Antimonii*, U. S. P.).

Sulphurated Antimony. Oxysulphide of Antimony.

Fourth Synthetical Reaction.—Boil a few grains of sulphide of antimony with solution of soda (potash, U. S. P.) in a test-tube (or larger quantities in larger vessels, 10 ounces of sulphide to 4½ pints of the official solution of soda for 2 hours, frequently stirring, and occasionally replacing water lost by evaporation), and filter; into the filtrate, before cool, stir diluted sulphuric acid until the liquid is slightly acid to test-paper; a brownish-red precipitate of oxysulphide of antimony, the *Antimonium Sulphuratum*, B. P. and U. S. P., falls; filter, wash, and dry over a water-bath. It is a mixture of sulphide of antimony (Sb_2S_3) with a small and variable amount of oxide (Sb_2O_3). The oxide results from the double decomposition of sulphide of antimony and soda (*Antimonii Oxysulphuratum*).

The United States Pharmacopœia in another preparation orders carbonate of sodium instead of the caustic alkali, and directs that only that precipitate be retained which separates from the alkaline liquid on cooling.

If a small quantity of sulphur be boiled with the sulphide of antimony in solution of soda, the precipitate on the addition of sulphuric acid will be bright orange-red, on account of the presence of a higher sulphide having a yellow color (Sb_2S_5).

There are some of the many varieties of *mineral kermes*, so called from their similarity in color to the *insect kermes*. Kermes is the name, now obsolete, of the *Coccus Ilicis*, a sort of cochineal-insect, full of reddish juice, and used for dyeing from the earliest times.

Explanation of process.—The sulphides of antimony, like those of arsenicum, unite with sulphides of metals to form soluble salts. In the hot solutions of these salts sulphide and oxide of antimony are soluble, and are reprecipitated in an indefinite state of combination, partially, on cooling, or wholly on the addition of acid. The acid also decomposes the sulphur-salt itself with precipitation of orange sulphide of antimony. The acid is added to the liquid before much oxysulphide has deposited (that is, before the solution is cool), in order to insure uniformity of product.

$$\underset{\text{Sulphide of antimony.}}{2Sb_2S_3} + \underset{\text{Soda.}}{6NaHO} = \underset{\text{Sulph-antimonite of sodium.}}{2Na_3SbS_3} + \underset{\text{Oxide of antimony.}}{Sb_2O_3} + \underset{\text{Water.}}{3H_2O}$$

$$\underset{\text{Sulph-antimonite of sodium.}}{2Na_3SbS_3} + \underset{\text{Sulphuric acid.}}{3H_2SO_4} = \underset{\text{Sulphate of sodium.}}{3Na_2SO_4} + \underset{\text{Sulphide of antimony.}}{Sb_2S_3} + \underset{\text{Sulphuretted hydrogen.}}{3H_2S}$$

The oxide and sulphide mentioned in these equations, together with excess of sulphide of antimony dissolved by the alkaline liquid and reprecipitated by the acid, form the *Sulphurated Antimony* of the Pharmacopœias, "an orange-red powder, readily dissolved by caustic soda, also by hydrochloric acid with the evolution of sulphuretted hydrogen and the separation of a little sulphur." Its antimony is detected by dissolving the precipitate in hydrochloric acid, or in solution of acid tartrate of potassium, and passing sulphuretted hydrogen through the liquid, as described in the first analytical reaction.

These four synthetical reactions illustrate the official processes for the respective substances. The solution of chloride of antimony is only used in the preparation of oxide; the oxide, besides its use in the preparation of tartar emetic, is mixed with twice its weight of phosphate of calcium (purified bone-earth) to form *Pulvis Antimonialis*, B. P.

The *sulphides* and *hydride* of antimony are incidentally mentioned in the following analytical paragraphs.

(*b*) *Reactions having Analytical Interest* (Tests).

First Analytical Reaction.—Through an acidified antimonial solution pass sulphuretted hydrogen; an orange precipitate of amorphous sulphide of antimony falls. It has the same composition as the crystalline black sulphide (Sb_2S_3), into which, indeed, it is quickly converted by heat. Like sulphide of arsenicum, it is soluble in alkaline solutions.

A higher sulphide of antimony (Sb_2S_5) corresponding to the higher sulphide of arsenicum, exists. It is formed on passing sulphuretted hydrogen through an acidified solution of the higher chloride ($SbCl_5$), or on boiling black sulphide of antimony and sulphur with an alkali, and decomposing the resulting filtered liquid by an acid.

Note.—The arsenious and antimonious compounds only are employed in medicine. The arseniates and antimoniates are sometimes useful in analysis, and the antimonic chloride in chemical research. The higher compounds of both elements are noticed here chiefly to draw attention to the close analogy existing between arsenicum and antimony, an analogy carried out in the numerous other compounds of these elements.

Second Analytical Reaction.—Dilute two or three drops of the solution of chloride of antimony with water; a precipitate of oxychloride occurs, the formation of which has been explained under the similar synthetical reaction. The occurrence of this precipitate distinguishes antimony from arsenicum, but is a reaction that cannot be fully relied upon in analysis, because requiring the presence of too much material and the observance of too many conditions. Add a sufficient quantity of hydrochloric acid to dissolve the precipitate, and boil a piece of copper in the solution as directed in the corresponding test for arsenicum (*vide* page 133); antimony is deposited on the copper. Wash, dry, and heat the copper in a test-tube as before; the antimony, like the arsenicum, is volatilized off the copper and condenses on the side of the tube as white oxide, but the sublimate, from its low degree of volatility, condenses close to the copper, and, moreover, is destitute of crystalline character, is amorphous (α, *a*, without; μορφή, *morphē*, shape).

Shake out the copper and boil water in the tube for several minutes. Do the same with the arsenical sublimate similarly obtained. The deposit of arsenic slowly dissolves, and may be recognized in the solution by ammonio-nitrate of silver; the antimonial sublimate is insoluble.

Third Analytical Reaction.—Perform the experiments described under Marsh's test for arsenicum (pp. 133–4), carefully observing all the details there mentioned, but using a few drops of solution of chloride of antimony or tartar emetic instead of the arsenical solution. Antimoniuretted hydrogen, or hydride of antimony (SbH_3), is formed and decomposed in the same way as arseniuretted hydrogen.

To one of the arsenicum spots on the porcelain lid (p. 134) add a drop of solution of "chloride of lime" (bleaching-powder); it quickly dissolves. Do the same with an antimony spot; it is unaffected.

Heat more quickly causes the volatilization of an arsenicum than an antimony spot; sulphydrate of ammonium more readily dissolves the antimony than the arsenicum.

Boil water for several minutes in the beaker or wide test-tube containing the arsenious sublimate (page 144); it slowly dissolves and may be recognized in the solution by the yellow precipitate given on the addition of solution of ammonio-nitrate of silver. The antimonial sublimate, similarly treated, gives no corresponding reaction.

Pass a slow current of sulphuretted hydrogen through the delivery-tube removed from the hydrogen-apparatus (page 134), and, when the air may be considered to have been expelled from the tube, gently heat that portion containing the deposit of arsenicum; the latter will be converted into a *yellow* sublimate of sulphide of arsenicum. Remove the tube from the sulphuretted-hydrogen apparatus, and repeat the experiment with a similar antimony deposit; it is converted into *orange* sulphide of antimony, which, moreover, owing to inferior volatility, condenses nearer to the flame than sulphide of arsenicum.

Pass dry hydrochloric acid gas through the two delivery-tubes. This is accomplished by adapting first one tube and then the other by a cork to a test-tube containing a few lumps of common salt, on which a little sulphuric acid is poured during the momentary removal of the cork. The sulphide of antimony dissolves and disappears; the sulphide of arsenicum is unaffected.

Thorough perception of the chemistry of arsenicum and antimony will be obtained on constructing equations or diagrams descriptive of each of the foregoing reactions.

Antidote.—The introduction of poisonous doses of antimonials into the stomach is fortunately quickly followed by vomiting. If vomiting has not occurred, or apparently to an insufficient extent, any form of tannic acid may be administered (infusion of tea, nutgalls, cinchona, oak-bark, or other astringent solutions or tinctures), an insoluble tannate of antimony being formed, and absorption of the poison consequently somewhat retarded. The stomach-pump must be as quickly as possible applied.

Recently precipitated moist ferric hydrate is also, according to T. and H. Smith, a perfect absorbent of antimony from its solutions, the chemical actions being probably, they say, similar to that which takes place between ferric hydrate and arsenious anhydride. It may be given in the form of a mixture of perchloride of iron with either carbonate of sodium or magnesia.

These statements may be verified by mixing together the various substances, filtering, and testing the filtrate for antimony in the usual manner.

DIRECTIONS FOR APPLYING THE FOREGOING REACTIONS TO THE ANALYSIS OF AN AQUEOUS SOLUTION OF SALTS OF ONE OF THE ELEMENTS ARSENICUM AND ANTIMONY.

Acidify the liquid with hydrochloric acid, and pass through it sulphuretted hydrogen:—

A *yellow* precipitate indicates arsenicum.

An *orange* precipitate indicates antimony.

The result may be confirmed by the application of other tests.

DIRECTIONS FOR APPLYING THE FOREGOING REACTIONS TO THE ANALYSIS OF AN AQUEOUS SOLUTION OF SALTS OF BOTH ARSENICUM AND ANTIMONY.

Acidify a small portion of the liquid with hydrochloric acid, and pass through it sulphuretted hydrogen.

Note I. If the precipitate by sulphuretted hydrogen is unmistakably orange, antimony may be put down as present, and arsenicum only further sought by the application of Fleitmann's test to the solution of the sulphides in aqua regia* freed from sulphur by boiling, or, better, to the original solution.

Note II. Sulphide of antimony is far less readily soluble than sulphide of arsenicum in solution of carbonate of ammonium. But this fact possesses limited analytical value; for the color of the sulphides is already sufficient to distinguish the one from the other when they are unmixed; and when mixed, much sulphide of antimony will prevent a little sulphide of arsenicum from being dissolved by the alkaline carbonate, while much sulphide of arsenicum will carry a little sulphide of antimony into the solution. When the proportions are, apparently, from the color of the precipitate, less wide, solution of carbonate of ammonium will be found useful in roughly separating the one sulphide from the other. On filtering and neutralizing the alkaline solution by an acid, the yellow sulphide of arsenicum is reprecipitated. The orange sulphide of antimony will remain on the filter.

Note III. Solution of bisulphate of potassium is said by Wöhler to be a good reagent for separating the sulphides of arsenicum and antimony, the former being soluble, the latter insoluble in the liquid.

Note IV. If the precipitate by sulphuretted hydrogen is unmistakably yellow, arsenicum may be put down as present, and any antimony detected by one of the following processes. These two processes are rather long, and require much care in their performance, but are indispensable, because at present we have no simple test for a small quantity of antimony in much arsenicum corresponding with Fleitmann's test for a small quantity of arsenicum in much antimony.

First process.—Generate hydrogen and pass it through a small wash-bottle containing solution of acetate of lead, to free the gas from any trace of sulphuretted hydrogen it may possess, and then through a dilute solution of nitrate of silver contained in a test-tube. When the apparatus is in good working order, pour into the generating-bottle the solution to be examined, adding it gradually to prevent violent action. After the gas has been passing for five or ten minutes, examine the contents of the nitrate-of-silver tube; arsenicum, if present, will be found in the solution in the state of arsenious acid,

$$AsH_3 + 3H_2O + 6AgNO_3 = H_3AsO_3 + 6HNO_3 + 3Ag_2;$$

* *Aqua regia* is a mixture of two parts hydrochloric and one part nitric acid. It was so called, from its property of dissolving gold, the "king" of metals.

while antimony, if present, will be found in the black precipitate that has fallen, according to the following equation:—

$$SbH_3 + 3AgNO_3 = SbAg_3 + 3HNO_3.$$

The arsenious radical may be detected in the clear, filtered, supernatant liquid, which still contains much nitrate of silver, by cautiously neutralizing with a very dilute solution of ammonia, or by adding a few drops of solution of ammonio-nitrate of silver, yellow arsenite of silver being produced. The antimony may be detected by washing the black precipitate, boiling it in an open dish with solution of tartaric acid, filtering, acidulating with hydrochloric acid, and passing sulphuretted hydrogen through the solution—the orange sulphide of antimony being precipitated (Hofmann).

Second process.—Obtain the metallic deposit in the middle of the delivery-tube as already described under Marsh's test. Act on the deposit by sulphuretted hydrogen gas, and then by hydrochloric acid gas, as detailed in the third analytical reaction of antimony (p. 144). If both arsenicum and antimony are present, the deposit, after the action of sulphuretted hydrogen, will be found to be of two colors, the yellow sulphide of arsenicum being usually further removed from the heated portion of the tube than the orange sulphide of antimony. Moreover, subsequent action of hydrochloric acid gas causes disappearance of the antimonial deposit, which is converted into chloride of antimony and carried off in the stream of gas.

The chief objection to this process is the liability of the operator mistaking sulphur, deposited from the sulphuretted hydrogen gas by heat, for sulphide of arsenicum. But the presence or absence of arsenicum is easily confirmed by applying Fleitmann's test to the original solution, while the process is most useful for the detection of a small quantity of salt of antimony when mixed with much arsenical compounds.

The laboratory student may now proceed to the analysis of aqueous solutions of salts of any of the metallic elements hitherto considered. The method followed may be that for the separation of the previous three groups, sulphuretted hydrogen being first passed through the solution to throw out arsenicum and antimony. The whole scheme of analysis is given on the next page. Three or four solutions should be examined before proceeding to the last group of metals.

Learners who have no opportunity of working at practical analysis will gain much knowledge by endeavoring not to remember, but to understand these methods of separating elements from each other in a solution containing several compounds.

TABLE OF SHORT DIRECTIONS FOR THE ANALYSIS OF AN AQUEOUS SOLUTION OF SALTS OF **ANY OR ALL** OR THE METALLIC ELEMENTS HITHERTO CONSIDERED.

Acidify with HCl, and pass H_2S through the solution; filter.

<table>
<tr><td rowspan="4">Precipitate
As Sb.
Wash, separate by carb. ammon.; or dissolve in a few drops HCl and HNO_3, and examine as described pages 146 and 147.</td><td colspan="7">Filtrate
Fe Al Zn Ba Ca Mg K Na Am.
Add AmCl; AmHO; AmHS; stir; filter.</td></tr>
<tr><td colspan="3">Precipitate*
Fe Al Zn.
Wash, dissolve in HCl, boil with HNO_3 (p. 124), add KHO, stir, filter.</td><td colspan="4">Filtrate
Ba Ca Mg K Na Am.
Add Am_2CO_3, boil, filter.</td></tr>
<tr><td rowspan="2">Precipitate
Fe.
Examine orig. solution for ferrous or ferric state.</td><td colspan="2">Filtrate
Al Zn.
Neut. by HCl, add AmHO, stir, filter.</td><td colspan="2">Precipitate
Ba Ca.
Dissolve in $HC_2H_3O_2$, add K_2CrO_4, filter.</td><td colspan="2">Filtrate
Mg K Na Am.
Add Am_2HPO_4, shake, filter.</td></tr>
<tr><td>Ppt.
Al</td><td>Sol.
Zn</td><td>Precipitate.
Ba.</td><td>Filtrate
Ca</td><td>Precipitate
Mg</td><td>Filtrate
Am Na K
(page 73).</td></tr>
</table>

* Much time may sometimes be saved by carefully remembering the color of the various hydrates and sulphides precipitated. Thus, if the AmHS precipitate is white, iron cannot be present, and AmHO, for Al and Zn may be at once added to the hydrochloric solution of the precipitate. The group-tests in this table are H_2S, AmHS, and Am_2CO_3.

QUESTIONS AND EXERCISES.

254. What is the composition and source of the *Black Antimony* of pharmacy?
255. In what alloys is metallic antimony a characteristic ingredient?
256. What is the quantivalence of antimony as far as indicated by the formulæ of the official preparations?
257. By a diagram show how "Butter of Antimony" is prepared.
258. Write out equations or diagrams expressive of the reactions which occur in converting chloride of antimony into oxide.
259. What is the formula of Tartar Emetic?
260. Explain the official process for the preparation of Oxysulphide of Antimony (*Antimonium Sulphuratum*, B. P.) by aid of diagrams.
261. Give a comparative statement of the tests for arsenicum and antimony.
262. How is antimony detected in the presence of arsenicum?
263. How may arsenicum and iron be distinguished analytically?
264. Describe a method by which antimony, magnesium, and iron may be separated from each other.
265. Draw out an analytical chart for the examination of an aqueous liquid containing salts of arsenicum, zinc, calcium, and ammonium.

COPPER, MERCURY, LEAD, SILVER.

These metals, like arsenicum and antimony, are precipitated from acidified solutions by sulphuretted hydrogen, in the form of sulphides; but the sulphides, unlike those of arsenicum and antimony, are insoluble in alkalies. The atom of copper is usually bivalent, Cu''; mercury bivalent in the mercuric salts, Hg'', and univalent in the mercurous salts, Hg'; lead sometimes quadrivalent, Pb'''', but generally exerting only bivalent activity, Pb''; and silver univalent, Ag'.

COPPER.

Symbol Cu. Atomic weight 63.5.

Source.—The commonest ore of this metal is *copper pyrites*, a double sulphide of copper and iron, raised in Cornwall; Australia and Russia supply *malachite*, a mixed carbonate and hydrate; much ore is also imported from South America. It is smelted in enormous quantities at Swansea, South Wales, a locality peculiarly fitted for the operation on account of its proximity to the coal-fields, and its position as a sea-coast town—these advantages at all times insuring cheap fuel and freightage to the different metallurgical establishments.

Alchemy.—The alchemists termed this metal *Venus*, perhaps on account of the beauty of its lustre, and gave it the symbol ♀, a compound hieroglyphic indicating that they thought it a mixture of gold ⊙ and a certain hypothetical substance called acrimony ✠, the corrosive nature of which was symbolized by the points of a Maltese cross. To this day the blue show-bottle in the shop-window of the pharmacist is occasionally ornamented by such a symbol, indicative, possibly, of the fact that the blue liquid in the vessel is a preparation of copper.

Coinage.—The material of British copper coinage is now a bronze mixture composed in 100 parts by weight of 95 copper, 4 tin, and 1 zinc, the same as in the copper coinage of France. The penny is coined at the rate of 48 pence in one pound avoirdupois, of 7000 grains, or 453.6 grammes; the halfpenny at 80 in the pound avoirdupois, and the farthing at 160. British copper pence are a legal tender in payments to the amount of 1*s.*; half-pence and farthings to the amount of 6*d.*

Metallic Copper (*Cuprum*, B. P.) in the form of fine wire, about No. 25, is used in preparing *Spiritus Ætheris Nitrosi*, B. P. *Copper Foil*, B. P., is "pure metallic copper, thin and bright."

Quantivalence.—Copper forms two classes of salts; in one the atom is bivalent (Cu''), in the other exerts univalent activity (Cu_2''). The former are of primary importance, the latter being for the most part unstable and wanting in technical interest. Their compounds are distinguished as cupric and cuprous; but those of the higher class only have general interest, and will be almost exclusively alluded to in the following paragraphs. Cuprous iodide (Cu_2I_2) will subsequently be referred to as a convenient form in which to remove iodine from solution, and the formation of cuprous oxide (Cu_2O), under given circumstances, as an indicator of the presence of sugar in a liquid.

Reactions having (*a*) Synthetical and (*b*) Analytical Interest.

(*a*) *Synthetical Reactions.*

The formation of the following salts includes the only synthetical copper-reactions having any medical or pharmaceutical interest: 1, cupric oxide, the black oxide of copper, by heating a piece of copper to low redness on a piece of earthenware in an open fire; 2, cupric sulphate, the common sulphate of copper, by boiling black oxide of copper and about an equal weight of sulphuric acid in water, filtering, and setting aside the solution so that crystals may form on cooling; and, 3, the preparation of solution of ammonio-sulphate of copper (see p. 153; also p. 137).

$$\underset{\text{Copper.}}{Cu_2} + \underset{\text{Oxygen.}}{O_2} = \underset{\text{Cupric oxide.}}{2CuO.}$$

$$\underset{\text{Cupric oxide.}}{CuO} + \underset{\text{Sulphuric acid.}}{H_2SO_4} = \underset{\text{Cupric sulphate.}}{CuSO_4} + \underset{\text{Water.}}{H_2O}$$

Sulphate of Copper (*Cupri Sulphas*, B. P. and U. S. P.) ($CuSO_4$, $5H_2O$), *blue vitriol*, *bluestone*, or *cupric sulphate*, is the only copper salt of much importance in Pharmacy. It is a by-product in silver-refining ($2Ag_2SO_4 + Cu_2 = 2CuSO_4 + 2Ag_2$). It is also formed by roasting copper pyrites. In the latter operation the sulphide of iron and sulphide of copper are oxidized to sulphates; but the low red heat employed decomposes the sulphate of iron, while the sulphate of copper is unaffected; it is purified by crystallization from a hot aqueous solution, though frequently much sulphate of iron remains in the crystals. Sulphate of copper results on dissolving in diluted sulphuric acid the black oxide (CuO) obtained in annealing copper plates; it may also be prepared by boiling copper with three times its weight of sulphuric acid ($2H_2SO_4 + Cu = CuSO_4 + SO_2 + 2H_2O$), diluting, filtering, evaporating, and crystallizing.

Anhydrous Sulphate of Copper ($CuSO_4$), is a yellowish-white powder prepared by depriving the ordinary blue crystals of sulphate of copper of their water of crystallization by exposing to a temperature of about 400° F. It is used in testing alcohol and similar liquids for water, becoming blue if the latter be present.

Verdigris (from *verde-gris*, Sp.), green-gray, is a Subacetate (*Cupri Subacetas*, U. S. P.) or Oxyacetate of Copper (B. P.) ($Cu_2O2C_2H_3O_2$), obtained by exposing alternate layers of copper and fermenting refuse grape-husks to the action of air. Digested with twice its weight of acetic acid and a little water, the mixture being evaporated to dryness and the residue dissolved in water, it forms the official Solution of Acetate of Copper ($Cu2C_2H_3O_2$).

The modes of forming *cupric sulphide, hydrate, oxide, ferrocyanide*, and *arsenite*, as well as the precipitation of *metallic copper*, are incidentally alluded to in the following analytical paragraphs.

(b) *Reactions having Analytical Interest* (*Tests*).

First Analytical Reaction.—Pass sulphuretted hydrogen through an acidified solution of a copper salt (sulphate, for example); black cupric sulphide (CuS) falls.

Second Analytical Reaction.—Add sulphydrate of ammonium to an aqueous copper solution; cupric sulphide is again precipitated, insoluble in excess.

Note.—Cupric sulphide is not altogether insoluble in sulphydrate of ammonium if free ammonia or much ammoniacal salt be present; it is quite insoluble in the fixed alkaline sulphides.

Third Analytical Reaction.—Immerse a piece of iron or steel, such as the point of a penknife or a piece of wire, in a few drops of a copper solution; the copper is deposited, of characteristic color, an equivalent quantity of iron passing into solution.

By this reaction copper may be recovered on the large scale from waste solutions, old hoop or other scrap iron being thrown into the liquors.

Fourth Analytical Reaction.—Add ammonia to a cupric solution; cupric hydrate (Cu2HO) of a light-blue color is precipitated. Add excess of ammonia; the precipitate is redissolved, forming a blue solution of ammonio-salt of copper, so deep in color as to render ammonia an exceedingly delicate test for this metal.

An ammonio-sulphate of copper may be obtained in large crystals by adding strongest solution of ammonia to powdered sulphate of copper until the salt is dissolved, placing the liquid in a test-glass or cylinder, cautiously pouring in twice its volume of strong alcohol or methylated spirit, taking care that the liquids do not become mixed, tying over the vessel with bladder, and setting aside for some weeks in a cool place. (Wittstein.) The constitution of ammonio-sulphate and other ammonio-salts of copper and corresponding salts of silver will be alluded to in connection with "white precipitate," the official "ammoniated mercury."

Cuprum Ammoniatum, U. S. P., is an ammonio-sulphate of copper prepared by rubbing together sulphate of copper and carbonate of ammonium until effervescence ceases, and drying the product.

Fifth Analytical Reaction.—Add solution of potash or soda to a cupric solution; cupric hydrate (Cu2HO) is precipitated, insoluble in excess. Boil the mixture in the test-tube; the hydrate is decomposed, losing the elements of water, and becoming the black anhydrous oxide (CuO).

Sixth Analytical Reaction.—Add solution of ferrocyanide of potassium (K_4Fcy) to an aqueous cupric solution; a reddish-brown precipitate of cupric ferrocyanide (Cu_2Fcy) falls. This also is a delicate test for copper.

Seventh Analytical Reaction.—To a cupric solution add solution of arsenic, and cautiously neutralize with alkali; green cupric arsenite ($CuHAsO_3$) falls.

Note.—This precipitate has been already mentioned under arsenicum. An arsenicum salt is thus a test for copper, as a copper salt is for arsenicum—a remark that may obviously be extended to most analytical reactions; for the *body acted upon characteristically by a reagent is as good a test for the reagent as the reagent is for it;* indeed it becomes a reagent when the other body is the object of search.

Antidotes.—In cases of poisoning by compounds of copper, iron filings should be administered, the action of which has just been explained (see third analytical reaction). Ferrocyanide of potassium may also be given (see sixth analytical reaction). Albumen forms, with copper, a compound insoluble in water; hence raw eggs should be swallowed, vomiting being induced or the stomach-pump applied as speedily as possible.

QUESTIONS AND EXERCISES.

266. What are the relations of copper, mercury, lead, and silver to each other and to arsenicum and antimony?

267. Name the sources of copper.

268. What proportion of copper is contained in English and French "copper" coins?

269. Give diagrams showing how Sulphate of Copper is prepared on the small and large scales.

270. Work out a sum showing how much Crystallized Sulphate of Copper may be obtained from 100 parts of sulphide?—*Ans.* 261¼.

271. How may Oxide of Copper be prepared?

272. Mention the formula of Verdigris.

273. Name a good clinical test for copper.

274. What is the analytical position of copper?

275. Mention the chief tests for copper.

276. How may copper be separated from arsenicum?

277. Why is finely divided iron an effective antidote in cases of poisoning by copper?

MERCURY.

Symbol Hg. Atomic weight 200.

Molecular weight 200 (*not* double the atomic weight).

Source.—Mercury occurs in nature as sulphide (HgS), forming the ore *cinnabar* (an Indian name expressive of something red). and is obtained from Spain, California, Eastern Hungary, China, Japan, and Peru.

Preparation.—The metal is separated by roasting off the sulphur and then distilling, or distilling with lime, which combines with and retains the sulphur.

Properties.—Mercury (*Hydrargyrum*, B. P. and U. S. P.) is a silver-white lustrous metal, liquid at common temperature. It boils at 662° F., and at —40° F. solidifies to a malleable mass of octohedral crystals. When quite free from other metals it does not tarnish, and its globules roll freely over a sheet of white paper without leaving any streak or losing their special form.

Medicinal Compounds.—The compounds of mercury used in medicine are all obtained from the metal. The metal itself, rubbed with chalk or with confection of roses and powdered liquorice-root, or with lard and suet, until globules are not visible *to the unaided eye*, is often used in medicine. The preparations are: the *Hydrargyrum cum Creta*, B. P. and U. S. P., or "Gray Powder;" *Pilula Hydrargyri*, B. P. and U. S. P., or "Blue Pill;" and *Unguentum Hydrargyri*, B. P. and U. S. P., or "Blue Ointment." There are also a Compound Ointment, a Plaster of Mercury, a Plaster of Ammoniacum and Mercury, a Liniment, and a Suppository. Their therapeutic effects are probably due to the black and red oxide which occur in them through the action of the oxygen of the air on the finely-divided metal. The proportion of oxide or oxides varies according to the age of the specimen.

Mercurous and Mercuric Compounds.—Mercury combines with other elements and radicals in two proportions: those compounds in which the other, acidulous, radicals are in the lesser amount are termed *mercurous*, the higher being *mercuric*. Thus, calomel ($HgCl$)* is mercurous chloride, while corrosive sublimate ($HgCl_2$) is mercuric chloride. In every pair of mercury compounds the mercuric contains *twice* as much complementary radical, in proportion to the mercury, as the mercurous.

Note on Nomenclature.—The remarks made concerning the two classes of iron salts, ferrous and ferric (p. 106), apply in the main to the two series of mercury salts. The latter are systematically distinguished in most modern works by the terms *mercurous* and *mercuric*. In the British and United States Pharmacopœias, however, which includes only a few in comparison with the whole number of mercury salts, older and more strongly contrasted names are employed, thus:—

Systematic names.	Official names.
Mercurous iodide	Green iodide of mercury.
Mercuric iodide	Red iodide of mercury.
Mercurous nitrate	Not mentioned in B. P.
Mercuric nitrate	Nitrate of mercury.
Mercurous sulphate . . .	Not mentioned in B. P.
Mercuric sulphate	Sulphate of mercury.
Mercurous chloride . . .	Subchloride of mercury.
Mercuric chloride	Perchloride of mercury.
Mercurous oxide	Black oxide of mercury.
Mercuric oxide	Red oxide of mercury.

Specific Gravity.—Mercury is 13.6 times as heavy as water.

Amalgams.—The compound formed in fusing metals together is

* The specific gravity of the vapor of calomel, and the fact that the salt is *not* decomposed at the temperature at which its specific gravity is taken, show that the formula of calomel is $HgCl$, and not Hg_2Cl_2.

usually termed an *alloy* (*ad* and *ligo*, to bind); but if mercury is a constituent, an *amalgam* (μάλαγμα, *malagma*, from μαλάσσω, *malasō*, to soften, the presence of mercury lowering the melting point of such a mixture).

Reaction having (*a*) Synthetical and (*b*) Analytical Interest.

(*a*) Synthetical Reactions.

The Two Iodides.

First Synthetical Reaction.—Rub together a small quantity of mercury and iodine, controlling the rapidity of combination by adding a few drops of spirit of wine, which, by evaporation, carries off heat, and thus keeps down temperature. The product of either mercuric iodide, mercurous iodide, or a mixture of the two, as well as mercury or iodine if excess of either has been employed. If the two elements have been previously weighed in single atomic proportions, 200 of mercury to 127 of iodine (about 8 to 5, or 1 ounce of mercury to 278 grains of iodine), the mercurous or green iodide results HgI (*Hydrargyri Iodidum Viride*, B. P. and U. S. P.); if in the proportion of one atom of mercury to two atoms of iodine (200 to twice 127, or about 4 to 5), the mercuric or red iodide, HgI_2, results, an iodide that is also official, but made in another way (*vide* p. 163).

Mercurous iodide is decomposed slowly by light, and quickly by heat, into mercuric iodide and mercury. Mercuric iodide occurring as an impurity in mercurous iodide may be detected by digesting in ether (in which mercurous iodide is insoluble), filtering and evaporating to dryness; mercuric iodide remains. Mercuric iodide is stable, and may be sublimed in scarlet crystals without decomposition. (For details of the method by which a specimen of the crystals may be obtained, and the precautions to be observed, *vide* "corrosive sublimate,' p. 158.)

Relation of Mercuric Iodide to Light.—In condensing, mercuric iodide is at first yellow, afterwards acquiring its characteristic scarlet color. This may be shown by smearing or rubbing a sheet of white paper with the red iodide, and then holding the sheet before a fire or over a flame for a few seconds. As soon as the paper becomes hot the red instantly changes to yellow, and the salt does not quickly regain its red color, even when cold, if the paper is carefully handled. But if a mark be made across the sheet by anything at hand, or the salt be pressed or rubbed in any way, the portions touched immediately return to the scarlet condition. According to Warington, this change is consequent upon rhomboidal crystals being converted into octahedra with a square base, and will serve as an excellent illustration of the influence of physical structure in causing color. The yellow modification so acts on the rays of white light shining on its particles as to absorb the violet and reflect the complementary hue, the yellow, which, entering the eye of the observer, strikes his retina, and thus conveys to the brain the impression of yellowness; and the red modification, though actually the same chemical substance, is sufficiently different in the structure of its particles to absorb the green constituent of white light and reflect the complementary ray, the red.

Illustration of the Chemical law of Multiple Proportions (p. 36).—Applying the atomic theory to the above iodides, it will at once be apparent why mercury and iodine should combine in the proportion of 200 of mercury with either 127 or 254 of iodine, and not with any intermediate quantity. For it is part of that theory that masses are composed of atoms, and that atoms are indivisible; and that the weight of the atom of mercury is to that of iodine as 200 is to 127. Mercury and iodine can only combine, therefore, in atomic proportions, atom to atom (which is the same as 200 to 127), or one atom to two atoms (which is the same as 200 to 254). To attempt to combine them in any intermediate proportion would be useless, a mere mixture of the two iodides would result. A higher proportion of mercury than 200 to 127 of iodine gives but a mixture of mercurous iodide and mercury; a higher proportion of iodine than 254 to 200 of mercury gives but a mixture of mercuric iodide and iodine. Or, for example, 200 grains of mercury mixed with, say, 200 of iodine would yield 139 grains of mercurous iodide, and 261 grains of mercuric iodide; for the 200 grains of mercury uniting with 127 grains of the iodine gives, for the moment, 327 grains of mercurous iodide and 73 grains of iodine still free. The 73 grains of iodine will immediately unite with 188 grains of the mercurous iodide (for if 127 of I require 327 of HgI to form HgI_2, 73 will require 188), and form 261 grains of mercuric iodide, diminishing the 327 grains of mercurous iodide to 139 grains.

The two Nitrates.

Second Synthetical Reaction.—Mix a little nitric acid in a test-tube with four or five times its bulk of water, add a small globule of mercury, and set the tube aside for a few hours, in a cool place; solution of mercurous nitrate ($HgNO_3$) will be formed, and nitric oxide (NO) evolved. The solution may be retained for subsequent analytical operations.

$$Hg_3 + 4HNO_3 = 3HgNO_3 + 2H_2O + NO.$$

Third Synthetical Reaction.—Place mercury in strong nitric acid, and warm the mixture; mercuric nitrate is formed, and will be deposited in crystals as the solution cools. Retain the product for a subsequent experiment.

The mercuric nitrates vary somewhat in composition, according to the proportion, strength, and temperature of the acid used in their formation. A mercuric nitrate may be obtained having the formula $Hg2NO_3$.

Hg_3	+	$8HNO_3$	=	$3(Hg2NO_3)$	+	$2NO$	+	$4H_2O$
Mercury.		Nitric acid.		Mercuric nitrate.		Nitric oxide.		Water.

Mercuric oxynitrates.—From the normal mercuric nitrate several oxynitrates may be obtained. Thus on merely evaporating a solution of mercuric nitrate, and cooling, crystals having the formula $Hg_6O_36NO_3$ are deposited. The latter, by washing with cold water, yield a *yellow* pulverulent oxynitrate, $Hg_6O_44NO_3$: mixed with lard, this has sometimes been used as an ointment. Boiled in water, the yellow gives a *brick-red* oxynitrate, $Hg_6O_52NO_3$.

The Pharmacopœial preparations of mercuric nitrate are *Liquor Hydrargyri Nitratis Acidus*, B. P. (sp. gr. 2.246; U. S. P., sp. gr. 2.165) and *Unguentum Hydrargyri Nitratis*, B. P. and U. S. P. The former (B. P.) is made by placing four ounces of mercury in five fluidounces of nitric acid diluted with an ounce and a half of water, and, when the metal is dissolved, boiling gently for fifteen minutes.

The Two Sulphates.

Fourth Synthetical Reaction.—Boil two or three grains of mercury with a few drops of strong sulphuric acid in a test-tube; sulphurous acid gas (SO_2) is evolved, and mercuric sulphate (*Hydrargyri Sulphas*, B. P.) ($HgSO_4$) results—a white heavy crystalline powder.

Hg	+	$2H_2SO_4$	=	$HgSO_4$	+	SO_2	+	$2H_2O$
Mercury.		Sulphuric acid.		Mercuric sulphate.		Sulphurous acid gas.		Water.

Between two and three ounces of mercuric sulphate may be prepared from a fluidrachm of mercury and a fluidounce of sulphuric acid boiled together in a small dish. These are the official proportions. The operation is completed and any excess of acid removed by evaporating the mixture of metal and acid to dryness, either in the open air or in a fume-chamber, sulphuric vapors being excessively irritating to the mucous membrane of the nose and throat; dry crystalline mercuric sulphate remains. If residual particles of mercury are observed, the mass should be damped with sulphuric acid and again heated.

By-products.—In chemical manufactories, secondary products, such as the sulphurous gas of the above reaction, are termed *by-products*, and, if of value, are utilized. In the present case the gas has no immediate interest, and is therefore allowed to escape. When very pure sulphurous acid gas is required for experiments on the small scale, this would be the best method of making it, a delivery-tube being adapted by a cork to the mouth of a flask containing the acid and metal. The sulphate of mercury would then become the by-product.

Mercuric oxysulphate.—Water decomposes mercuric sulphate into a soluble acid salt and an insoluble yellow oxysulphate ($Hg_3O_2SO_4$). The latter is called *Turpeth mineral*, from its resemblance in color to the powdered root of *Ipomea turpethum*, an Indian substitute for jalap. The yellow sulphate of mercury (*Hydrargyri Sulphas Flava*, U. S. P.) was formerly official in the pharmacopœia of Great Britain, but is now seldom used.

Fifth Synthetical Reaction.—Rub a portion of the dry mercuric sulphate of the previous reaction with as much mercury as it already contains; the product, when the two have thoroughly blended, is mercurous sulphate (Hg_2SO_4): it may be retained for a subsequent experiment.

Molecular Weight.—The exact proportion of mercury to sulphate is merely a matter of calculation; for the combining proportion of a compound (if it possess any combining-power) is the sum of the combining proportions of its constituents. *In other words, the combining weight of a molecule is simply the sum of the weights of its constituent atoms*, or, more generally, *the molecular weight of a compound is the sum of the atomic weights of its elements.* In accordance with this rule (sometimes called the fourth law of chemical combination, though only a deduction from the first—p. 36), 296 of mercuric sulphate and 200 of mercury (about 3 to 2) are the exact proportions necessary to the formation of mercurous sulphate.

The Two Chlorides.

Sixth Synthetical Reaction. — Mix thoroughly a few grains of dry mercuric sulphate with about four-fifths its weight of chloride of sodium, and heat the mixture slowly in a test-tube in a fume-chamber or in the open air to leeward of the operator; mercuric chloride ($HgCl_2$), or *corrosive sublimate* (*Hydrargyri Perchloridum*, B. P., *Hydrargyri Chloridum Corrosivum*, U. S. P.), sublimes and condenses in the upper part of the tube in heavy colorless crystals or a crystalline mass. Somewhat larger quantities (in the proportion of 20 of sulphate to 16 of salt, and, *vide infra*, 1 of black oxide of manganese) may be sublimed in a pair of two-ounce or three-ounce round-bottom gallipots, the one inverted over the other, and the joint luted by moist fireclay (the powdered clay kneaded with water to the consistence of dough). The luting having been allowed to dry (somewhat slowly, to avoid cracks), the pots are placed upright on a sand-tray (plate-shape answers very well), sand piled round the lower and a portion of the upper pot, and the whole heated over a good-sized gas-flame for an hour or more. Red Iodide of Mercury and Calomel may be sublimed in the same way. The former requires less, the latter more, heat than corrosive sublimate.

$HgSO_4$	+	$2NaCl$	=	$HgCl_2$	+	Na_2SO_4
Mercuric sulphate.		Chloride of sodium.		Mercuric chloride.		Sulphate of sodium.

Note.—If the mercuric sulphate contain any mercurous sulphate, some calomel may be formed. This result will be avoided if 2 or 3 per cent. of black oxide of manganese be previously mixed with the ingredients, the action of which is to eliminate chlorine from the excess of chloride of sodium used in the process, the chlorine converting any calomel into corrosive sublimate.

Precaution.—The operation is directed to be conducted with care in a fume-chamber or in the open air, because the vapor of corrosive sublimate ,which might possibly escape, is very acrid and highly poisonous. Its vulgar name is indicative of its properties.

Ten grains of perchloride of mercury and the same quantity of chloride of ammonium in one pint of water, form the *Liquor Hydrargyri Perchloridi*, B. P.

Seventh Synthetical Reaction.—Mix a few grains of the mercurous sulphate of the fifth reaction with about a third of its weight of chloride of sodium, and sublime in a test-tube; crystalline mercurous chloride (HgCl) or calomel (*Hydrargyri Subchloridum*, B. P., *Hydrargyri Chloridum Mite*, U. S. P.) results. Larger quantities may be prepared in the manner directed for corrosive sublimate, a somewhat higher temperature being employed; similar precautions must also be observed. The proportions are 10 of mercuric sulphate to 7 of mercury and 5 of dry chloride of sodium. "Moisten the sulphate of mercury with some of the water, and rub it and the mercury together until globules are no longer visible; add the chloride of sodium, and thoroughly mix the whole by continued trituration. When dry sublime by a suitable apparatus into a chamber of such size that the calomel, instead of adhering to its sides as a crystalline crust, shall fall as a fine (dull-white, powder on its floor. Wash this powder with boiling distilled water until the washings cease to be darkened by a drop of sulphydrate of ammonium. Finally, dry at a heat not exceeding 212°, and preserve in a jar or bottle impervious to light."

$$\underset{\text{Mercurous sulphate.}}{Hg_2SO_4} + \underset{\text{Chloride of sodium.}}{2NaCl} = \underset{\text{Mercurous chloride.}}{2HgCl} + \underset{\text{Sulphate of sodium.}}{Na_2SO_4}$$

The term calomel (καλὸς, *kalos*, good, and μέλας, *melas*, black) is said to relate to the use of the salt as a *good* remedy for *black* bile, but probably was simply indicative of the esteem in which black sulphide of mercury was held, the compound to which the name calomel was first applied.

Test for corrosive sublimate in calomel.—If the mercurous sulphate contains mercuric sulphate, some mercuric chloride will also be formed. Corrosive sublimate is soluble in water, calomel insoluble; the presence of the former may therefore be proved by boiling a few grains of the calomel in distilled water, filtering and testing by sulphuretted hydrogen or sulphydrate of ammonium as described hereafter. If corrosive sublimate is present, the whole bulk of the calomel must be washed with hot distilled water till the filtrate ceases to give any indications of mercury. Corrosive sublimate is more soluble in alcohol, and still more in ether, calomel insoluble. Ether in which calomel has been digested should, therefore, after filtration, yield no residue on evaporation. Calomel is converted by hydrocyanic acid into mercuric salt, with separation of metallic mercury.

Note.—The above process is that of the Pharmacopœias; but calomel may also be made by other methods. Calomel mixed with lard forms the *Unguentum Hydrargyri Subchloridi*, B. P., and with sulphurated antimony, guaiacum resin and castor oil, the *Pilula Hydrargyri Subchloridi Composita*, B. P., *Pilula Antimonii Composita*, U. S. P., or "Plummer's Pills."

The two Oxides.

Eighth Synthetical Reaction.—Evaporate the mercuric nitrate of the third reaction to dryness in a small dish, in a fume-chamber, or in the open air if more than a few grains have been prepared, and heat the residue till no more fumes are evolved; mercuric oxide (HgO), "Red Precipitate," the Red Oxide of Mercury (*Hydrargyri Oxidum Rubrum*, B. P. and U. S. P.) remains.

$$\underset{\text{Mercuric nitrate.}}{2(Hg2NO_3)} = \underset{\text{Mercuric oxide.}}{2HgO} + \underset{\text{Nitric peroxide.}}{4NO_2} + \underset{\text{Oxygen.}}{O_2}$$

The nitric constituents of the salt may be partially economized by previously thoroughly mixing with the dry mercuric nitrate as much mercury as is used in its preparation, or as much as it already contains (ascertained by calculation from the atomic weights and the weight of nitrate under operation, as in making mercurous sulphate p. 158), and well heating the mixture. In this case the free mercury is also converted into mercuric oxide. This is the official process, the Pharmacopœial quantities being four ounces of mercury dissolved in four and a half fluidounces of nitric acid diluted with two ounces of water, the solution evaporated to dryness, the residue thoroughly mixed with four ounces of mercury, and the whole heated until acid vapors cease to be evolved. (Mercuric oxide is tested for nitrate by heating a little of the sample in a test-tube, when orange nitrous vapors are produced and are visible in the upper part of the tube, if nitrate is present.)

$Hg2NO_3$	+	Hg	=	$2HgO$	+	$2NO_2$
Mercuric nitrate.		Mercury.		Mercuric oxide.		Nitric peroxide.

Mercuric oxide is an orange-red powder, more or less crystalline according to the extent to which it may have been stirred during preparation from the nitrate, much rubbing giving the crystals a pulverulent character. Mixed with yellow wax and oil of almonds it yields the *Unguentum Hydrargyri Oxidi Rubri*, B. P. (1 part in 8). A similar ointment is official in U. S. P.

Ninth Synthetical Reaction.—To solution of corrosive sublimate in a test-tube or larger vessel add solution of potash or soda, or lime-water; yellow oxide of mercury, or mercuric oxide (HgO), is precipitated.

$HgCl_2$	+	$Ca2HO$	=	HgO	+	$CaCl_2$	+	H_2O
Mercuric chloride.		Hydrate of calcium.		Mercuric oxide.		Chloride of calcium.		Water.

Eighteen grains of corrosive sublimate to ten ounces of lime-water form the *Lotio Hydrargyri Flava*, B. P. The precipitate only differs physically from the red mercuric oxide; the yellow is in a more minute state of division than the red.

Tenth Synthetical Reaction.—To calomel add solution of potash or soda, or lime-water; black oxide of mercury, or mercurous oxide (Hg_2O) is produced, and may be filtered off, washed, and dried. (This reaction and the formation of a white curdy precipitate, on the addition of solution of nitrate of silver to the filtrate from the mercurous oxide, acidified by nitric acid, form sufficient evidence of a powder being or containing calomel. The curdy precipitate is chloride of silver.)

Thirty grains of calomel to ten ounces of lime-water form the *Lotio Hydrargyri Nigra*, B. P.

$2HgCl$	+	$Ca2HO$	=	Hg_2O	+	$CaCl_2$	+	H_2O
Mercurous chloride.		Hydrate of calcium.		Mercurous oxide.		Chloride of calcium.		Water.

(*b*) *Analytical Reactions* (*Tests*).

MERCUROUS OR MERCURIC SALTS.

First Analytical Reaction.—The Copper Test. Deposition of mercury upon, and sublimation from copper.—Place a small piece of bright copper, about half an inch long and a quarter of an inch broad, in a solution of any salt of mercury, mercurous or mercuric, and heat in a test-tube; the copper becomes coated with mercury in a fine state of division. (The absence of any notable quantity of nitric acid must be insured, or the copper itself will be dissolved. See below.) Pour away the supernatant liquid from the copper, wash the latter once or twice by pouring water into, and then out of, the tube, remove the metal, take off excess of water by gentle pressure in a piece of filter-paper, dry the copper by passing it quickly through a flame, holding it by the fingers; finally, place the copper in a dry narrow test-tube, and heat to redness in a flame, the tube being held nearly horizontal; the mercury sublimes and condenses as a white sublimate of minute globules on the cool part of the tube outside the flame. The globules aggregate on gently pressing with a glass rod, and are especially visible where flattened between the rod and the side of the test-tube.

Notes on the test.—This is a valuable test, for several reasons: It is very delicate when performed with care. It brings before the observer the element itself—one which from its metallic lustre and fluidity cannot be mistaken for any other. It separates the element both from mercurous and mercuric salts. Mercury can in this way be readily eliminated in the presence of most other substances, organic or inorganic.

In performing the test the presence of any quantity of nitric acid may be avoided by adding an alkali until a slight permanent precipitate appears, and then reacidifying with a few drops of acetic or hydrochloric acid, or, if they fail to redissolve the precipitate, with a very few drops of nitric acid.

MERCURIC SALTS.

Second Analytical Reaction.—To a few drops of a solution of a mercuric salt (corrosive sublimate, for example) add solution of iodide of potassium, drop by drop; a precipitate of mercuric iodide (HgI_2) forms, and at first quickly redissolves, but is permanent when sufficient iodide of potassium has been added. Continue the addition of iodide of potassium; the precipitate is once more redissolved.

Notes.—When first precipitated, mercuric iodide is yellowish-red, but soon changes to a beautiful scarlet. Its solubility either in solution of the mercuric salt or in solution of iodide of potassium renders the detection of a small quantity of a mercuric salt by iodide of potassium, or a small quantity of an iodide by a mercuric solution, difficult, and hence lessens the value of the reaction as a test. But the reaction has synthetical interest, the method by precipitation being that adopted by the Pharmacopœias (*Hydrargyri Iodidum Rubrum*, B. P. and U. S. P.). Mercuric iodide thus made has the same composition as that prepared by direct combination of its elements. Equivalent proportions of the two salts must be used in making the preparation ($HgCl_2$=271; 2KI=332). About 4 parts of corrosive sublimate are dissolved in 50 or 60 of water (warmth quickens solution), and 5 of iodide of potassium in 15 or 20 of water, the solutions mixed and the precipitate collected on a filter, drained, washed twice with distilled water and dried on a plate over a water-bath. (For additional properties of mercuric iodide, see page 155.) The mercury in mercuric or mercurous iodide is set free and sublimes in globules on heating either powder with dried carbonate of sodium in a test-tube; the iodine may be detected by digesting with solution of soda, filtering, and to the solution of iodide of sodium thus formed adding starch paste and acidulating with nitric acid, when blue iodide of starch, results.

$$\underset{\text{Mercuric chloride.}}{HgCl_2} + \underset{\text{Iodide of potassium.}}{2KI} = \underset{\text{Mercuric iodide.}}{HgI_2} + \underset{\text{Chloride of potassium.}}{2KCl}$$

Red iodide of mercury mixed with white wax, lard, and oil forms the *Unguentum Hydrargyri Iodidi Rubri*, B. P. *Donovan's Solution* contained mercuric and arsenious iodides.

Third Analytical Reaction.—Add a solution of mercuric salt to solution of ammonia, taking care that the mixture, after well stirring, still smells of ammonia; a white precipitate falls.

Ammoniated Mercury.

Performed in a test-tube, this reaction is a very delicate test of the presence of a mercuric salt; performed in larger vessels, the mercuric salt being corrosive sublimate (3 ounces dissolved in 3 pints of distilled water, the solution poured into 4 fluidounces of Solution of Ammonia, and the precipitate washed and dried over a water-bath), it is the usual process for the preparation of "white precipitate," the old "ammonio-chloride," or "amido-chloride of mercury," now known as Ammoniated Mercury (*Hydrargyrum Ammoniatum*, B. P., and U. S. P.).

Constitution of Ammoniated Mercury.—This precipitate is considered to be the chloride of mercuric-ammonium ($NH_2Hg''Cl$)—that is, chloride of ammonium (NH_4Cl) in which two atoms of univalent hydrogen are replaced by one bivalent atom of mercury.

$$\underset{\text{Mercuric chloride.}}{HgCl_2} + \underset{\text{Ammonia.}}{2NH_4HO} = \underset{\text{"White precipitate."}}{NH_2Hg''Cl} + \underset{\text{Chloride of ammonium.}}{NH_4Cl} + \underset{\text{Water.}}{2H_2O}$$

Varieties of Ammoniated Mercury.—If the order of mixing be reversed and ammonia be added to solution of mercuric chloride, a double chloride of mercuric ammonium and mercury results ($NH_2HgCl, HgCl_2$): it contains 76.55 per cent. of mercury. Previously to the year 1826, "white precipitate" was officially made by adding a fixed alkali to a solution of equal parts of corrosive sublimate and sal-ammoniac; this gave a double chloride of mercuric ammonium and ammonium (NH_2HgCl, NH_4Cl), containing 65.57 per cent. of mercury. This compound is now known as "*fusible* white precipitate," because at a temperature somewhat below redness it fuses and then volatilizes. The "white precipitate" which has been official since 1826 contains 79.52 per cent. of mercury. The true compound may be distinguished as "*infusible* white precipitate," from the fact that when heated it volatilizes without fusing. An ointment of this body is official (*Unguentum Hydrargyri Ammoniati*, B. P. and U. S. P.). Prolonged washing with water converts "white precipitate" into a yellowish compound (NH_2HgCl, HgO); hence the official preparation is seldom thoroughly freed from the chloride of ammonium which is formed during its manufacture, and which, if present in larger proportion than seven or eight per cent., gives the character of partial or complete fusibility to the compound.

Note.—Chloride of mercuric ammonium is only one member of a large class of similar compounds, derivable from the various salts of ammonium by displacement of atoms of hydrogen by other atoms. The composition of ammonio-nitrate of silver and ammonio-sulphate of copper, made without excess of ammonia (p. 137), is consistent with this view.

$$\underset{\text{Chloride of ammonium.}}{N\left\{\begin{matrix}H\\H\\H\\H\end{matrix}\right\}Cl} \quad \underset{\text{Chloride of mercuric ammonium.}}{N\left\{\begin{matrix}Hg''\\H\\H\end{matrix}\right\}Cl} \quad \underset{\text{Nitrate of argent-ammon-ammonium.}}{N\left\{\begin{matrix}Ag\\Am\\H\\H\end{matrix}\right\}NO_3} \quad \underset{\text{Sulphate of cupr-ammon-ammonium.}}{N_2\left\{\begin{matrix}Cu''\\Am_2\\H_2\\H_2\end{matrix}\right\}SO_4}$$

The composition of the crystals of ammonio-sulphate of copper (p. 152) is consistent with the second of the following formulæ, the first being that of sulphate of ammonium:—

$$N_2\left\{\begin{matrix}H_2\\H_2\\H_2\\H_2\end{matrix}\right\}SO_4 \qquad N_2\left\{\begin{matrix}Cu''\\Am_2\\Am_2\\H_2\end{matrix}\right\}SO_4$$

Fourth Analytical Reaction.—Pass sulphuretted hydrogen through a mercuric solution; a black precipitate of mercuric sulphide (HgS) falls.

Note.—Sulphuretted hydrogen also precipitates mercurous sulphide (Hg_2S) from mercurous solutions; and in appearance the precipitates are alike; hence this reagent does not distinguish between mercurous and mercuric salts. But in the course of systematic analysis, mercuric salts are thrown down from solution as sulphide after mercurous salts have been otherwise removed. The sulphides are insoluble in sulphydrate of ammonium.

Note.—An insufficient amount of the gas gives a white or colored precipitate of oxysulphide.

Ethiops Mineral, the *Hydrargyri Sulphuretum cum Sulphure*, is a mixture of sulphide of mercury and sulphur, obtained on triturating the elements in a mortar till globules are no longer visible. Its name is probably in allusion to its similarity in color to the skin of the Æthiop. It was formerly official.

Vermilion is mercuric sulphide prepared by heating together sulphur and mercury, and subliming the mixture (*Hydraryri Sulphuretum Rubrum*, U. S. P.).

MERCUROUS SALTS.

Fifth Analytical Reaction.—To a solution of a mercurous salt (the mercurous nitrate obtained in the second synthetical reaction, for example) add hydrochloric acid, or any soluble chloride; a white precipitate of calomel (HgCl) occurs.

This reaction was formerly official in the Dublin Pharmacopœia as a process for the preparation of calomel.

Sixth Analytical Reaction.—To solution of a mercurous salt add iodide of potassium; green mercurous iodide (HgI) is precipitated.

Seventh Analytical Reaction.—To a mercurous salt, dissolved or undissolved (calomel), add ammonia; black salt (chloride) of mercurous ammonium (NH_2Hg_2Cl) is formed.

Other tests for Mercury.

The elimination of mercury in the actual state of metal by the copper test, coupled with the production or non-production of a white precipitate on the addition of hydrochloric acid to the original solution, is usually sufficient evidence of the presence of mercury and its existence as a mercurous or mercuric salt. But other tests may sometimes be applied with advantage. Thus, metallic mercury is deposited on placing a drop of the solution on a plate of gold (sovereign or half-sovereign), and touching the drop and the edge of the plate simultaneously with a key; an electric current passes, under these circumstances, from the gold to the key, and thence through the liquid to the gold, decomposing the salt, the mercury of which forms a white metallic spot on the gold, while the other elements go to the iron. This is called *the galvanic test*, and is useful for clinical purposes.——Solution of stannous chloride ($SnCl_2$), from the readiness with which the salt forms stannic chloride ($SnCl_4$), gives a white precipitate of mercurous chloride in mercuric solutions, and quickly still further reduces this mercurous chloride or other mercuric salts to a grayish mass of finely divided mercury; this is the old *magpie test*, probably so called from the white and gray appearance of the precipitate. The reaction may even be obtained from such insoluble mercury compounds as "white precipitate." ——Confirmatory tests for mercuric and mercurous salts will be found in the action of solution of potash, solution of soda, lime-water, solution of ammonia, and solution of iodide of potassium. (*Vide* pages 162 to 164.)——Normal alkaline carbonates produce yellowish mercurous carbonate, and brownish-red mercuric carbonate, both of them unstable. ——Alkaline bicarbonates give mercurous carbonate and white (soon becoming red) mercuric oxysalt.——Yellow chromate of potassium (K_2CrO_4) gives, with mercurous salts, a red precipitate of mercurous chromate (Hg_2CrO_4). ——Mercury and all its compounds are volatilized by heat: the experiment is most conveniently performed in a test-tube.

Antidote.—Albumen gives a white precipitate with solution of mercuric salts; hence the importance of administering white of egg while waiting for a stomach pump in case of poisoning by corrosive sublimate.

QUESTIONS AND EXERCISES.

278. Name the chief ore of mercury, and describe a process for the extraction of the metal.

279. In what state does mercury exist in "Gray Powder?"

280. What other preparations of metallic mercury itself are employed in medicine?

281. State the relation of the mercurous to the mercuric compounds.

282. Distinguish between an *alloy* and an *amalgam.*

283. State the formulæ of the two Iodides of Mercury.

284. Under what circumstances does mercuric iodide assume two different colors?

285. Illustrate the chemical law of Multiple Proportions as explained by the atomic theory, employing for that purpose the stated composition of the two iodides of mercury.

286. Write down the formulæ of Mercurous and Mercuric Nitrates and Sulphates.

287. How is Mercuric Sulphate prepared?

288. What is the formula of "Turpeth Mineral?"

289. Describe the processes necessary for the conversion of mercury into Calomel and Corrosive Sublimate, using diagrams.

290. Why is black oxide of manganese sometimes mixed with the other ingredients in the preparation of corrosive sublimate?

291. Give the chemical and physical points of difference between calomel and corrosive sublimate.

292. How may a small quantity of calomel in corrosive sublimate be detected?

293. Work out a sum showing how much mercury will be required in the manufacture of one ton of Calomel. *Ans.* 17 cwt. nearly.

294. Mention official preparations of the chlorides of mercury.

295. Give the formulæ and mode of formation of the Red, Yellow, and Black Oxides of Mercury, employing diagrams.

296. Explain the action of the chief general test for mercury.

297. How are mercurous and mercuric salts analytically distinguished?

298. Give a probable view of the constitution of *Hydrargyrum Ammoniatum*, and an equation showing how it is made.

299. What is the best temporary antidote in cases of poisoning by mercury?

LEAD.

Symbol Pb. Atomic weight 207.

Source.—The ores of lead are numerous; but the one from which the metal is chiefly obtained is the sulphide of lead (PbS), or *galena* (from γαλήνη, *galene*, tranquillity, perhaps from its supposed effect in allaying pain).

Preparation.—The ore is first roasted in a current of air; much sulphur is thus burnt off as sulphurous acid gas, while some of the metal is converted into oxide and a portion of the sulphide oxidized to sulphate. Oxidation being stopped when the mass presents certain appearances, the temperature is raised, and the oxide and sulphate, reacting on undecomposed sulphide, yield the metal and much sulphurous acid gas:—

$$2PbO + PbS = Pb_3 + SO_2$$
$$PbSO_4 + PbS = Pb_2 + 2SO_2.$$

Uses.—The uses of lead are well known. Alloyed with arsenicum it forms common *shot*, with antimony gives *type-metal*, with tin *solder*, and in smaller quantities enters into the composition of *Britannia metal*, *pewter*, and other alloys.

The salts of lead used in pharmacy and all other preparations of lead are obtained, directly or indirectly, from the metal itself. Heated in a current of air, lead combines with oxygen and forms oxide of lead (PbO) (*Plumbi Oxidum*, B. P. and U. S. P.), a yellow powder (*massicot*), or, if fused and solidified, a brighter reddish-yellow heavy mass of bright scales, termed *litharge* (from λίθος *lithos*, a stone, and ἄργυρος, *arguros*, silver). It is from this oxide that the chief lead compounds are obtained. Oxide of lead, by further roasting in a current of air, yields *red lead* (or *minium*), Pb_3O_4, or $PbO_2 2PbO$. Both oxides are much used by painters, paper-stainers, and glass-manufacturers. *White lead* is a mixture of carbonate ($PbCO_3$) and hydrate of lead (Pb2HO) (commonly 2 molecules of the former to 1 of the latter), usually ground up with about 7 per cent. of linseed oil; it is made by exposing lead, cast in spirals or little gratings, to the action of air, acetic fumes, and carbonic acid, the latter generated from decaying vegetable matter, such as spent tan; oxyacetate of lead slowly but continuously forms, and is as continuously decomposed by the carbonic acid with production of hydrate and carbonate, or *dry white lead*. The grating-like masses, when ground, form the heavy white pulverulent official *Plumbi Carbonas*, B. P. and U. S. P. The latter is the active constituent of *Unguentum Plumbi Carbonatis*, B. P. and U. S. P., the old *Unguentum Cerussæ*.

Lead compounds are poisonous, producing saturnine colic, or even paralysis. These effects are termed *saturnine* from an old name of lead, *Saturn*. The alchemists called lead Saturn, first, because they thought it the oldest of the seven then known metals, and it might therefore be compared to Saturn, who was supposed to be the father of the gods, and, secondly, because its power of dissolving other metals recalled a peculiarity of Saturn, who was said to be in the habit of devouring his own children.

Quantivalence.—The atom of lead is sometimes quadrivalent (Pb''''); but in most of the compounds used in medicine it exerts bivalent activity only (Pb'').

Reactions having (*a*) Synthetical and (*b*) Analytical Interest.

(*a*) *Synthetical Reactions.*

Acetate of Lead.

First Synthetical Reaction.—Place a few grains of oxide of lead in a test-tube, add about an equal weight of water and two and a half times its weight of acetic acid, and boil; the oxide dissolves and forms a solution of acetate of lead ($Pb2C_2H_3O_2$). When cold, or on evaporation (the solution being kept faintly acid), crystals of acetate of lead ($Pb2C_2H_3O_2, 3H_2O$) are deposited. Larger quantities are obtained by the same method.

$$\underset{\text{Oxide of lead.}}{PbO} + \underset{\text{Acetic acid.}}{2HC_2H_3O_2} = \underset{\text{Acetate of lead.}}{Pb2C_2H_3O_2} + \underset{\text{Water.}}{H_2O}$$

This is the official processs for *Plumbi Acetas*, B. P. and U. S. P. The salt is vulgarly termed *Sugar of Lead*, from its sweet taste. Besides its direct use in pharmacy, it forms three-fourths of the

Pilula Plumbi cum Opio, B. P., is the chief constituent of *Unguentum Plumbi Acetatis*, B. P., and an ingredient in *Suppositoria Plumbi Composita*, B. P.

Subacetate or Oxyacetate of Lead.

Second Synthetical Reaction.—Boil acetate of lead with about four times its weight of water and rather more than two-thirds its weight of oxide of lead; the resulting filtered liquid is solution of oxyacetate of lead, *Liquor Plumbi Subacetatis*, B. P. and U. S. P.

The official (B. P.) *Liquor* is made by boiling 5 ounces of acetate and 3½ of oxide in 1 pint of distilled water for half an hour (constantly stirring), filtering, and making up for any loss by evaporation by diluting the filtrate to 1 pint.

A similar solution was used by M. Goulard, who called it *Extractum Saturni*, and drew attention to it in 1770. It is now frequently termed *Goulard's Extract.* A more dilute solution, 1 of *Liquor* and 1 of spirit in 80 of distilled water, is also official in the Pharmacopœias, under the name of *Liquor Plumbi Subacetatis Dilutus.* The latter is commonly known as *Goulard Water.* The stronger solution is the chief ingredient in *Unguentum Plumbi Subacetatis Compositum*, B. P., a slight modification of the old *Goulard's Cerate.* Similar preparations are official in the United States Pharmacopœia.

Oxyacetates of lead.—The official subacetate of lead is not a definite chemical salt. It is probably a mixture of two subacetates of lead, which are well-known crystalline compounds, and which the author is disposed to regard as having a constitution similar to that he has already indicated for some other salts (see Iron, Antimony, and Bismuth).

	Acetate of Lead (3 molecules)	$Pb_3\ 6C_2H_3O_2$
B. P.	Pyro-oxyacetate of lead	$Pb_3O4C_2H_3O_2$
B. P.	Goulard's oxyacetate of lead	$Pb_3O_22C_2H_3O_2$
	Oxide of lead (3 molecules)	Pb_3O_3

$$\underset{\text{Oxide of lead.}}{PbO} + \underset{\text{Acetate of lead.}}{Pb2C_2H_3O_2} = \underset{\text{Official "subacetate."}}{Pb_2O2C_2H_3O_2}$$

$$\text{or } \underset{\text{Oxide of lead.}}{3PbO} + \underset{\text{Acetate of lead.}}{3(Pb2C_2H_3O_2)} = \underset{\text{Pyro-oxyacetate.}}{Pb_3O4C_2H_3O_2} + \underset{\text{Goulard's oxyacetate.}}{Pb_3O_22C_2H_3O_2}$$

The official "subacetate."

Third Synthetical Reaction.—Digest a few grains of red lead in nitric acid and water; nitrate of lead ($Pb2NO_3$) is formed, and remains in solution, while a puce colored peroxide of lead (PbO_2) is precipitated.

Nitrate of Lead. Red Lead. Peroxide of Lead.

Nitrate of lead (*Plumbi Nitras*, B. P. and U. S. P.) is more directly made by dissolving litharge (PbO) in nitric acid; but the above reaction serves to bring before the reader two other oxides of lead, namely, red lead (Pb_3O_4) and peroxide of lead (PbO_2). In the latter oxide the quadrivalent character of lead is obvious. Nitrate of lead is used officially in preparing iodide of lead; for this purpose the above mixture is filtered, the precipitate of peroxide of lead purified from adhering nitrate by passing hot water through the filter, the filtrate and washings evaporated to dryness to remove excess of nitric acid, the residual nitrate of lead redissolved by ebullition with a small quantity of hot water, and the solution set aside to crystallize, or a portion at once used for the following experiment. Nitrate of lead forms white crystals derived from octahedra.

Iodide of Lead.

Fourth Synthetical Reaction.—To a neutral solution of nitrate of lead add solution of iodide of potassium; a precipitate of iodide of lead (PbI_2) falls (*Plumbi Iodidum*, B. P. and U. S. P.). Equal weights of the salts may be used in making large quantities.

$$\underset{\text{Nitrate of lead.}}{Pb2NO_3} + \underset{\text{Iodide of potassium.}}{2KI} = \underset{\text{Iodide of lead.}}{PbI_2} + \underset{\text{Nitrate of potassium.}}{2KNO_3}$$

Iodide of lead is the chief ingredient in *Emplastrum Plumbi Iodidi*, B. P., and *Unguentum Plumbi Iodidi*, B. P.

Crystals of Iodide of Lead.—Heat the iodide of lead with the supernatant liquid, and, if necessary, filter; the salt is dissolved, and again separates in golden crystalline scales as the solution cools.

Oleate of Lead (Lead Plaster).

Fifth Synthetical Reaction.—Boil together in a small dish some very finely-powdered oxide of lead, with about twice its weight of olive oil, and ten or twenty times as much water, well stirring the mixture, and from time to time replacing water that has evaporated; the product is a white mass of oleate of lead ($Pb2C_{18}H_{33}O_2$) (*Emplastrum Plumbi*, B. P. and U. S. P.), glycerine remaining in solution in the water. Larger quantities are prepared in the same manner.

$$\underset{\text{Oxide of lead.}}{3PbO} + \underset{\text{Water.}}{3H_2O} + \underset{\text{Oleate of glyceryl (olive-oil or oleine).}}{2(C_3H_5 3C_{18}H_{33}O_2)} = \underset{\text{Oleate of lead (lead plaster).}}{3(Pb2C_{18}H_{33}O_2)} + \underset{\text{Hydrate of glyceryl (glycerine).}}{2(C_3H_5 3HO)}$$

The action between the oxide of lead and olive oil is slow, requiring several hours for its completion; but a sufficient amount of plaster to illustrate the operation is formed in a much shorter time.

The glycerine may be obtained by treating the aqueous product of the above reaction with sulphuretted hydrogen to remove a trace of lead, then digesting with animal charcoal, filtering and evaporating. But on the large scale glycerine is now usually produced as a by-product in the manufacture of candles; for its elements are found in all vegetable and animal fats. (*Vide* Index.)

Modes of forming *chloride, sulphide, chromate, sulphate, hydrate,* and other salts of lead are incidentally described in the following analytical paragraphs.

(*b*) *Reactions having Analytical Interest* (*Tests*).

First Analytical Reaction.—To a solution of lead salt (acetate, for example) add hydrochloric acid; a white precipitate of chloride of lead ($PbCl_2$) is obtained. Boil the precipitate with much water; it dissolves, but, on the solution cooling, is redeposited in small acicular crystals. Filter the cold solution, and pass sulphuretted hydrogen through it; a black precipitate (sulphide of lead, PbS) shows that the chloride of lead is soluble to a slight extent in cold water.

Note.—A white precipitate on the addition of hydrochloric acid, soluble in hot water, and blackened by sulphuretted hydrogen, sufficiently distinguishes lead salts from those of other metals, but the non-production of such a precipitate does not prove the absence of a small quantity of lead, chloride of lead being slightly soluble in cold water. Hydrochloric acid will be found to be a useful but not a delicate test for lead.

Second Analytical Reaction.—Through a dilute solution of a lead salt pass sulphuretted hydrogen; a black precipitate of sulphide of lead (PbS) occurs.

Lead in Water.—The foregoing is a very delicate test. Should a trace of lead be present in water used for drinking-purposes, sulphuretted hydrogen will detect it. On passing the gas through a pint of such water, a brownish tint, more or less deep, is produced. If the tint is scarcely perceptible, set the liquid aside for a day; the gas will become decomposed and a thin layer of sulphur be found at the bottom of the vessel, white if no lead be present, but more or less brown if it contain sulphide of lead.

Third Analytical Reaction.—To solution of a lead salt add sulphydrate of ammonium; a black precipitate of sulphide of lead falls, insoluble in excess.

Fourth Analytical Reaction.—To solution of a lead salt add solution of chromate of potassium (K_2CrO_4); a yellow precipitate of chromate of lead ($PbCrO_4$) is formed, insoluble in weak acids.

Chromes.—This reaction has technical as well as analytical interest. The precipitate is the common pigment termed *chrome yellow*, or *lemon chrome*. Boiled with lime and water, a portion of the chromic elements are removed, and an oxychromate, of a bright red or orange color (*orange chrome*), is produced.

Fifth Analytical Reaction.—To solution of a lead salt add dilute sulphuric acid, or solution of a sulphate; a white precipitate of sulphate of lead ($PbSO_4$) falls.

Sulphate of lead is slightly soluble in strong acids, and in solutions of alkaline salts; it is insoluble in acetic acid.

In dilute solutions this sulphuric reaction does not take place immediately; the precipitate, however, falls after a time; its appearance may be hastened by evaporating the solution nearly to dryness and then rediluting.

The white precipitate always noticed in the vessels in which diluted sulphuric acid is kept, is sulphate of lead, derived from the leaden chambers in which the acid is made; solubility in strong acid and insolubility in weak, explains its appearance.

Antidotes.—From the insolubility of sulphate of lead in water, the best *antidote* in a case of poisoning by the acetate or other soluble salt of lead, is a soluble sulphate, such as Epsom salt, sulphate of sodium or alum, vomiting being also induced, or the stomach-pump applied as quickly as possible.

Other tests for lead will be found in the reaction with *iodide of potassium* (*vide* p. 170); with *alkaline carbonates*, a white precipitate ($2PbCO_3 + Pb2HO$) insoluble in excess; with *alkalies*, a white precipitate ($Pb2HO$) more or less soluble in excess; with alkaline *phosphates*, *arseniates*, *ferrocyanides* and *cyanides*, precipitates mostly insoluble, but of no special analytical interest. Insoluble salts of lead are decomposed by solutions of potash (KHO) or soda ($NaHO$).

The metal is precipitated in a beautifully crystalline state by metallic zinc and some other metals; the *lead tree* is thus formed.——The *blowpipe-flame* decomposes solid lead compounds placed in a small cavity in a piece of charcoal, a soft malleable bead of metal being produced, and a yellowish ring of oxide deposited on the charcoal.

QUESTIONS AND EXERCISES.

300. Write down equations descriptive of the smelting of galena.
301. Mention some of the alloys of lead.
302. How is litharge produced?
303. Give the formulæ of white lead and red lead.
304. Describe the manufacture of white lead.
305. What is the quantivalence of lead?
306. Draw a diagram expressive of the formation of Acetate of Lead.
307. Describe the preparation and composition of *Liquor Plumbi Subacetatis*.
308. What is the action of nitric acid on red lead, litharge, and metallic lead?
309. How is the official Iodide of Lead prepared?
310. Describe the reaction between oxide of lead, water, and olive oil, at the temperature of boiling water, and give chemical formulæ explanatory of the constitution of the products.
311. Mention the chief tests for lead.
312. How would you search for lead in potable water?
313. What is the composition of chrome yellow?
314. State a method whereby lead, barium, and silver may be separated.
315. Name the best antidote in case of poisoning by salts of lead.

SILVER.

Symbol Ag. Atomic weight 108.

Source.—This element occurs in nature in the free state and as ore, the common variety being sulphide of silver (Ag_2S) in combination with much sulphide of lead, forming *argentiferous galena.*

Preparation.—The lead from galena (p. 167) is melted and slowly cooled; crystals of lead separate and are raked out from the still fluid mass, and thus an alloy very rich in silver is finally obtained: this is roasted in a current of air, whereby the lead is oxidized and removed as litharge, pure silver remaining. Other ores undergo various preparatory treatments according to their nature, and are then shaken with mercury, which amalgamates with and dissolves the particles of silver, the mercury being subsequently removed from the amalgam by distillation. Soils and minerals containing metallic silver are also treated in this way. An important improvement in the amalgamation process, by which the mercury more readily unites with the silver, consists in the addition of a small proportion of sodium to the mercury—a recent discovery, simultaneously made in England by Crookes, and in New York by Wurtz.

REACTIONS HAVING (*a*) SYNTHETICAL AND (*b*) ANALYTICAL INTEREST.

(*a*) *Synthetical Reactions.*

Impure Nitrate of Silver.

First Synthetical Reaction.—Dissolve a silver coin in nitric acid; nitric oxide gas (NO) and nitrous anhydride (N_2O_3) are evolved, and a solution of nitrates of silver and copper obtained.

Silver Coinage.—Pure silver is too soft for use as coin, it is therefore hardened by alloying with copper. The silver money of England contains 7.5, of France 10, and of Prussia 25 per cent. of copper. One pound troy of standard silver is coined into 66 shillings, of which the metal is worth from 60*s.* to 62*s.* according to the market price of silver. The standard fineness of silver is 0.925, three alloy in 40. The fineness of the French standard silver is 0.900 in the five-franc piece; but an inferior alloy of 0.835 is used for the lower denominations. The single-franc piece, composed of the latter alloy, is still made to weigh five grammes, the weight originally chosen for the franc as the unit of the monetary scale when the fineness of the coin was 0.900. It has now become a token, like the British shilling, of which the nominal value exceeds the metallic value. British silver coins are a legal tender in payments to the amount of 40*s.* only.

Chloride of Silver.

Second Synthetical Reaction.—To the product of the above reaction add water and hydrochloric acid or a soluble chloride; white chloride of silver (AgCl) is precipitated, copper still remaining in solution. Collect the precipitate on a filter, and wash with water; it is pure chloride of silver.

Note.—The nitrates of silver and copper may also be separated by evaporating the solution of the metals in nitric acid to dryness, and gently heating the residue, when the nitrate of copper is decomposed, but the nitrate of silver unaffected. The latter may be dissolved from the residual oxide of copper by water.

Pure Silver.

Third Synthetical Reaction.—Dissolve the chloride of silver of the previous reaction in slight excess of solution of ammonia, and immerse a piece of sheet copper in the liquid; metallic silver is precipitated, and after a time wholly removed from solution. Collect the precipitate on a filter and wash with water; it is pure metallic silver, and is readily fusible into a single button.

Note.—Chloride of silver may also be reduced by fusion, in a crucible, with about half its weight of carbonate of sodium. Chloride of silver may be obtained in crystals by evaporation of its solution in ammonia.

Pure Nitrate of Silver.

Fourth Synthetical Reaction.—Dissolve the pure silver of the previous reaction in nitric acid (3 of silver require about 2 or $2\frac{1}{2}$ of strong acid diluted with 5 of water), and remove excess of acid by evaporating the solution to dryness, slightly heating the residue; the product is pure nitrate of silver. Dissolve by heating with a small quantity of water; on the solution cooling, or on evaporation, colorless tabular crystals of nitrate of silver are obtained.

$$\underset{\text{Silver.}}{3Ag_2} + \underset{\text{Nitric acid.}}{8HNO_3} = \underset{\text{Nitric oxide.}}{2NO} + \underset{\text{Nitrate of silver.}}{6AgNO_3} + \underset{\text{Water.}}{4H_2O}$$

Notes.—The solution of pure or refined silver (*Argentum Purificatum*, B. P., *Argentum*, U. S. P.) in nitric acid, evaporation, and crystallization constitute the official process for the preparation of the nitrate (*Argenti Nitras*, B. P. and U. S. P.) The salt fused, and poured into proper moulds, yields the white cylindrical sticks or rods (*Argenti Nitras Fusa*, U. S. P.) commonly termed *caustic* (from καίω, *kaio*, I burn), or *lunar caustic*. (The alchemists called silver *Diana* or *Luna*, from its supposed mysterious connection with the moon.) The specimen of nitrate of silver obtained in the above reaction, dissolved in water, will be found useful as an analytical reagent. Nitrate of silver is soluble in rectified spirit; but after a time reaction and decomposition occur.

Marking Ink.—Silver salts are decomposed when in contact with organic matter, especially in the presence of light or heat, a black insoluble compound being formed. Hence the use of the nitrate in the manufacture of indelible ink for marking linen.

Oxide of Silver.

Fifth Synthetical Reaction.—To a few drops of solution of nitrate of silver add solution of potash or soda or lime-water; an olive-brown precipitate of oxide of silver (Ag_2O) occurs. The washed and dry oxide, like most silver compounds, is decomposed by heat with production of metal.

The *Argenti Oxidum*, B. P. and U. S. P., is thus made, lime-water (solution of potash U. S. P.) being the precipitant employed. Three and a half pints of lime-water will decompose half an ounce of nitrate of silver.

$$\underset{\text{Nitrate of silver.}}{2AgNO_3} + \underset{\text{Hydrate of calcium.}}{Ca2HO} = \underset{\text{Oxide of silver.}}{Ag_2O} + \underset{\text{Nitrate of calcium.}}{Ca2NO_3} + \underset{\text{Water.}}{H_2O}$$

Methods of forming several other salts of silver are incidentally mentioned in the following analytical paragraphs.

(*a*) *Reactions having Analytical Interest.* (*Tests.*)

First Analytical Reaction.—To a solution of a silver salt add hydrochloric acid or other soluble chloride; a white curdy precipitate of chloride of silver falls. Add nitric acid, and boil; the precipitate does not dissolve. Pour off the acid and add solution of ammonia; the precipitate dissolves. Neutralize the ammoniacal solution by an acid; the chloride of silver is re-precipitated.

This is the most characteristic test for silver. The precipitated chloride is also soluble in solutions of hyposulphite of sodium or cyanide of potassium—facts of considerable importance in photograhic operations.

Other analytical reagents than the above are occasionally useful.——Sulphuretted hydrogen, or sulphydrate of ammonium, gives a black precipitate, sulphide of silver (Ag_2S), insoluble in alkalies.——Solutions of potash or soda give a brown precipitate, oxide of silver (Ag_2O), converted into a fulminating compound by prolonged contact with ammonia.——Phosphate of sodium gives a pale yellow precipitate, phosphate of silver (Ag_3PO_4), soluble in nitric acid and in ammonia.——Arseniate of ammonium gives a chocolate-colored precipitate, arseniate of silver (Ag_3AsO_4), already noticed in connection with arsenic acid.——Iodide or bromide of potassium gives a yellowish-white precipitate, iodide or bromide of silver (AgI or $AgBr$), insoluble in acids and only slightly soluble in ammonia.——Cyanide of potassium gives a white precipitate, cyanide of silver ($AgCy$), soluble in excess, sparingly soluble in ammonia, insoluble in dilute nitric acid, soluble in boiling concentrated nitric acid. *Argenti cyanidum*, U. S. P. is made by distilling a mixture of ferrocyanide of potassium and diluted sulphuric acid and passing the resulting hydrocyanic acid into solution of nitrate of silver: $HCy + AgNO_3 = AgCy + HNO_3$, the precipitate is well washed and dried.) ——Yellow chromate of potassium (K_2CrO_4) gives a red precipitate, chromate of silver (Ag_2CrO_4).——Red chromate of potassium also gives a red precipitate, acid chromate of silver (Ag_2CrO_4,CrO_3).——Many organic acids afford insoluble salts of silver.——Several metals displace silver from solution, mercury forming in this way a crystalline compound known as the silver tree, or *Arbor Dianæ.* ——In the blowpipe flame, silver salts, placed on charcoal with a little carbonate of sodium, yield bright globules of metal, accompanied by no incrustation as in the corresponding reaction with lead salts; the experiment may be performed with the nitrate, which first melts and then, like all nitrates, deflagrates, yielding a white metallic coating of silver which slowly aggregates to a button.

Antidotes.—Solution of common salt, sal-ammoniac, or any other inert chloride should obviously be administered where large doses of nitrate of silver have been swallowed. A quantity of sea-water or brine would convert the silver into insoluble chloride, and at the same time produce vomiting.

QUESTIONS AND EXERCISES.

316. By what process is silver obtained from argentiferous galena?
317. What weight of English silver coin will yield one pound of pure nitrate of silver?
318. How may the metal be recovered from an impure mixture of silver salts?
319. Give a diagram showing the formation of nitrate of silver from the metal.
320. Describe the reaction of lime-water and nitrate of silver.
321. Mention the chief test for silver, and the precautions to be observed in order that it may be distinguished from lead and mercury.
322. Name the antidote for silver.

DIRECTIONS FOR APPLYING SOME OF THE FOREGOING REACTIONS TO THE ANALYSIS OF AN AQUEOUS SOLUTION OF SALTS OF ONE OF THE METALS COPPER, MERCURY (EITHER AS MERCUROUS OR MERCURIC SALT), LEAD, SILVER.

Add hydrochloric acid:—

Silver is indicated by a white curdy precipitate, soluble in ammonia.

Mercurous salts also by a white precipitate, turned black by ammonia.

Lead by a white precipitate, insoluble in ammonia. Confirm by boiling another portion of the hydrochloric precipitate in water; it dissolves.

If hydrochloric acid gives no precipitate, silver and mercurous salts are absent. Lead can only be present in very small quantity. Mercuric salts may be present. Copper may be present. Divide the liquid into three portions, and apply a direct test for each metal.

Lead is best detected by the sulphuric test; the tube being set aside for a time if the precipitate does not appear at once.

Mercury is best detected by the copper test. If present, it occurs as mercuric salt.

Copper betrays itself by the blue color of the liquid under examination. Confirm by the ammonia test.

If the above reactions are not thoroughly conclusive, confirmatory evidence should be obtained by the application of some of the other reagents for copper, mercury, lead or silver.

TABLE OF SHORT DIRECTIONS FOR APPLYING SOME OF THE FOREGOING REACTIONS TO THE ANALYSIS OF AN AQUEOUS SOLUTION OF SALTS OF **ANY OR ALL** OF THE METALS COPPER, MERCURY (EITHER MERCUROUS OR MERCURIC SALT, OR BOTH), LEAD, SILVER.

Add hydrochloric acid, filter, and wash the precipitate with a small quantity of cold water.

<table>
<tr><td colspan="3">Ppt.
Pb Hg Ag.
Wash with boiling water.</td><td rowspan="3">Filtrate
Cu Hg Pb.
Divide into three portions.
Test for
Cu by AmHO; blue sol.
Hg (mercuric) by Cu; globules.
Pb by H_2SO_4; white ppt.</td></tr>
<tr><td colspan="2">Ppt.
Hg Ag.
Add AmHO.</td><td rowspan="2">Filtrate
Pb.
Add H_2SO_4, white ppt.*</td></tr>
<tr><td>Precipitate
Hg.
(mercurous)
black.</td><td>Filtrate
Ag.
Add HNO_3, white ppt.</td></tr>
</table>

* Liquids containing only a small quantity of lead do not readily yield sulphate of lead on the addition of sulphuric acid. Before lead can be said to be absent, therefore, the liquid should be evaporated to dryness with one drop of sulphuric acid, and the residue digested in water; any sulphate of lead then remains as a heavy white insoluble powder.

SHORT DIRECTIONS FOR THE ANALYSIS OF AN AQUEOUS SOLUTION OF ORDINARY SALTS OF **ONE** OF THE ELEMENTS HITHERTO CONSIDERED.

Add hydrochloric acid.

<table>
<tr>
<td rowspan="3">Ppt.
Hg(ous) Pb Ag.
Add AmHO.
Hg, black ppt.
Pb, ppt. still white.
Ag, ppt. dissolved.
If HCl gave no precipitate, neither Hg, Pb, nor Ag is present.
Hg obtained here must have existed in the solution as a mercurous salt.
Sb is also precipitated by HCl, but is dissolved on adding more HCl; the Hg, Pb, and Ag precipitates are not soluble in excess of HCl.</td>
<td colspan="3">If HCl gave no precipitate the metal is still in the liquid; pass H_2S through it.</td>
</tr>
<tr>
<td rowspan="2">Ppt.
Cu Hg(ic) Pb As Sb.
As, yellow ppt.
Sb, orange ppt.
Cu } Hg } black ppt. Pb }
Test original solution for
Cu by AmHO; blue sol.
Hg by Cu; globules.
Pb by H_2SO_4; white ppt.
If H_2S gave no precipitate, neither Cu, Hg, Pb, As, nor Sb is present.</td>
<td colspan="2">If H_2S gave no precipitate the metal is still in the liquid; add AmCl, AmHO, and AmHS.</td>
</tr>
<tr>
<td>Ppt.
Fe Al Zn
Fe, black ppt.
Test original solution for ferric salt by K_4Fcy (dark blue ppt.); ferrous salt by K_6Fdcy (dark blue ppt.).
Al } Zn } white ppt.
Test original solution by AmHO.
Al, white ppt. insoluble in excess.
Zn, white ppt. soluble in excess.</td>
<td>If AmHS, &c. gave no precipitate, the liquid may still contain either Ba, Ca, Mg, K, Na, or Am; add successively $KCrO_4$ for Ba, $Am_2C_2O_4$ for Ca, Na_2HPO_4 for Mg.
If neither Ba, Ca, nor Mg is found, examine the original solution for Am by KHO, Na by the flame test, and K $PtCl_4$.</td>
</tr>
</table>

TABLE OF SHORT DIRECTIONS FOR APPLYING SOME OF THE FOREGOING ANALYTICAL REACTIONS TO THE ANALYSIS OF AN AQUEOUS SOLUTION OF ORDINARY SALTS OF **ANY OR ALL** OF THE ELEMENTS HITHERTO CONSIDERED.

Add hydrochloric acid, and filter.

<table>
<tr><td colspan="3">Precipitate
Hg(ous) Pb Ag.
Wash, boil with water, filter.</td><td colspan="10">Filtrate
Cu Hg(ic) Pb As Sb Fe Al Zn Ba Ca Mg K Na Am.
Pass H_2S through the liquid ; filter.</td></tr>
<tr><td colspan="2">Precipitate
Hg Ag.
Add AmHO.</td><td rowspan="4">Filtrate
Pb.
Add
H_2SO_4;
white
precipi-
tate.</td><td colspan="3">Precipitate
Cu Hg Pb As Sb.
Wash, digest in AmHS ; filter.</td><td colspan="7">Filtrate.
Fe Al Zn Ba Ca Mg K Na Am.
Add AmHO, AmHS, and filter.</td></tr>
<tr><td rowspan="3">Precipitate
Hg.
Black pre-
cipitate.</td><td rowspan="3">Filtrate
Ag.
Add
HNO_3;
white
precipi-
tate.</td><td rowspan="3">Precipitate
Cu Hg Pb.
Wash, dissolve in a few drops of HNO_3 and HCl ; evap. nearly to dry-ness ; redissolve in H_2O, divide into three, and test for
Cu by AmHO ; blue solution.
Hg by Cu ; globules.
Pb by H_2SO_4 ; white precip.</td><td colspan="2">Filtrate
As Sb.
Add $HC_2H_3O_2$, and boil ; digest the pre-cipitate in Am_2CO_3 ; filter.</td><td colspan="3">Precipitate
Fe Al Zn.
Wash, dissolve in HCl, boil (with a few drops of HNO_3 if necessary, p. 124) ; add KHO, stir, filter.</td><td colspan="4">Filtrate
Ba Ca Mg K Na Am.
Add Am_2CO_3 ; boil, filter.</td></tr>
<tr><td>Precip.
Sb.
Orange.</td><td>Filtrate
As.
Add
$HC_2H_3O_2$.
Yellow
preciptate</td><td rowspan="2">Precipitate
Fe.
? Ferric or ferrous.
Test origi-nal solu-tion by yellow and red prussiate.</td><td colspan="2">Filtrate
Al Zn.
Neutralize by HCl ; add AmHO, stir, filter.</td><td colspan="2">Precipitate
Ba Ca.
Wash, dissolve in $HC_2H_3O_2$; add K_2CrO_4, filter.</td><td colspan="2">Filtrate.
Mg K Na Am.
Add Am_2HAsO_4 ; stir, filter.</td></tr>
<tr><td colspan="2">Confirm by testing original solution by the H tests.</td><td>Precipitate
Al.
White pre-
cipitate.</td><td>Filtrate
Zn.
Add
AmHS ;
white pre-
cipitate,</td><td>Precip.
Ba.
Yellow.</td><td>Filtrate
Ca.
Add
$Am_2C_2O_4$;
white
precipi-
tate.</td><td>Precip.
Mg.
White.</td><td>Filtrate
K Na Am.
Evap. ignite, dis. in H_2O, & test for K by $PtCl_4$, yel. precip. Na by flame; yel. Am in orig. sol. by NaHO.</td></tr>
</table>

The group-tests of this Table are HCl, H_2S, NH_4HS, and $(NH_4)_2CO_3$.

OUTLINE OF THE PRECEDING TABLES.

H Cl	H_2S		AmHS	Am_2CO_3	$Am_2H\,AsO_4$	
Hg (as mercurous salt)	Cu	Insoluble in AmHS.	Zn	Ba	Mg	K
Pb	Hg (as mercuric salt)		Al	Ca		Na
Ag	Pb		Fe			Am
	As	Soluble in AmHS.				
	Sb					

The practical student should examine solutions containing the above metals until he is able to analyze with facility and accuracy. In this way he will best perceive the peculiarities of each element and their general relations to each other. As the rarer metals are not included here, the tables are not complete analytical schemes; further remarks concerning them, therefore, are for the present deferred.

QUESTIONS AND EXERCISES.

323. Give processes for the qualitative analysis of liquids containing the following substances:—

a. Antimony and Mercurous salt.
b. Lead and Calcium.
c. Silver and Mercurous salt.
d. Lead and Mercuric salt.
e. Copper and Arsenicum.
f. Arsenicum and Antimony.
g. Aluminium and Zinc.
h. Iron and Copper.
i. Magnesium, Calcium, and Potassium.
j Silver, Antimony, Zinc, Barium, and Ammonium.

324. Enumerate the so-called group-tests.

325. Give a general sketch of the method of analyzing a solution suspected to contain two or more salts of common metals.

326. Classify the common metals according to their analytical relations.

METALS OF MINOR PHARMACEUTICAL IMPORTANCE.

Thus far has been considered, somewhat in detail, the chemistry of the common metals, salts of which are frequently used in medicine or in testing medicinal substances. These are:—

Potassium,	Barium,	Zinc,	Arsenicum,	Mercury,
Sodium,	Calcium,	Aluminium,	Antimony,	Lead,
Ammonium (?)	Magnesium,	Iron,	Copper,	Silver.

There still remain eleven metals, eight of which are mentioned in the British Pharmacopœia, namely:—

Lithium,	Chromium,	Gold,	Cadmium,
Manganese,	Tin,	Platinum,	Bismuth.

Compounds of the remaining three are sufficiently common to occasionally come under notice:—

Strontium, Cobalt, Nickel.

These eleven metals of minor pharmaceutical interest may be shortly studied, a few only of the reactions of each (just those mentioned in the following pages) being performed. When all have been thus treated, their respective positions in the analytical groups will be indicated and a tabular scheme by which an analysis of a solution containing any metal may be effected. Thus, step by step, we may learn how to analyze almost any substance that may occur, and know to what extent the presence of a rarer will interfere with the ordinary tests for a common element: additional illustrations of the working of chemical laws will be acquired, and the store of chemical and pharmaceutical facts increased. The opportunity thus afforded for improvement in habits of neatness in manipulation, precision, and classification is another and no mean reason why such experiments should be prosecuted, the direct value of which may not be considerable.

LITHIUM.

Symbol L. Atomic weight 7.

Lithium is widely distributed in nature, but usually in minute proportions compared with other elements. A trace of it may be found in most soils and waters, a Cornish spring containing even considerable quantities as chloride.

One salt used in medicine is the *Citrate* ($L_3C_6H_5O_7$) (*Lithiæ Citras*, B. P.), occurring in white deliquescent crystals or powder, prepared by dissolving 50 grains of the *Carbonate* (L_2CO_3) and 90 of citric acid in 1 ounce of water, evaporating to a low bulk and setting aside in a dry place to crystallize, or at once evaporating to dryness and powdering the residue.

$$3L_2CO_3 + 2H_3C_6H_5O_7 = 2L_3C_6H_5O_7 + 3H_2O + 3CO_2$$

Carbonate of lithium. Citric acid. Citrate of lithium. Water. Carbonic acid gas.

The carbonate (*Lithiæ Carbonas*, B. P. and U. S. P.) is a white granular powder obtained from the minerals which contain lithium; namely, lepidolite (from λεπὶς, *lepis*, a scale, and λίθος, *lithos*, a stone; it has a scaly appearance), triphane (from τρεῖς, *treis*, three, and φαίνω *phainō*, I shine), or spodumene (from σποδόω, *spodŏō*, to reduce to ashes, in allusion to its exfoliation in the blowpipe-flame), and petalite (from πέταλον, *petalon*, a leaf; its character is leafy and laminated). Each contains silicate of aluminium, with fluoride of potassium and lithium in the case of lepidolite, and silicate of sodium and lithium in the others. *Liquor Lithiæ Effervescens*, B. P., is a solution of 10 grains of carbonate of lithium in 1 pint of water charged with 7 times its volume of carbonic acid gas and kept in ordinary aërated water-bottles. "Half a pint, evaporated to dryness, yields 5 grains of a white solid residue, answering to the tests for carbonate of lithium. . . . . Ten grains of the latter salt neutralized with sulphuric acid, and afterwards heated to redness, leave 14.86 grains of dry sulphate of lithium, which, when redissolved in distilled water, yields no precipitate with oxalate of ammonium or solution of lime," indicating absence of salts of calcium and aluminium. Citrate of lithium should yield by incineration 52.8 per cent. of white carbonate of lithium.

*Urate of lithium** is more soluble than urate of sodium; hence lithium preparations are administered to gouty patients in the hope that urate of sodium, with which such systems are loaded, may be converted into urate of lithium and removed.

In chemical position lithium stands between the alkaline and the alkaline-earth metals, its hydrate, carbonate, and phosphate being slightly soluble in water. Its atom is univalent, L′.

Analytical Reaction.—Moisten the end of a platinum wire with solution of a minute particle of solid lithium salt, and introduce it into the flame of a Bunsen burner or other slightly colored flame (spirit-lamp or blowpipe-flame); a magnificent crimson tinge is imparted.

The light emitted by ignited lithium vapor is of a purer scarlet than that given by strontium, the next element. When the flames are examined by spectral analysis (physically analyzed by a prism), the red rays are, in the case of strontium, found to be associated with blue and yellow, neither of which is present in the lithium light.

* Urates will be considered subsequently in connection with uric acid.

STRONTIUM.

Symbol Sr. Atomic weight 87.5.

Source.—Strontium is not widely distributed in nature; but the carbonate ($SrCO_3$), known as *strontianite*, and the sulphate ($SrSO_4$), known as *celestine* (from *cœlum*, the sky, in allusion to its occasional bluish color), are by no means rare minerals.

Salts of strontium are not employed in medicine. They are chiefly used by firework manufacturers in preparing red fire. The color they impart to flame is a beautiful crimson—ignited strontium vapor emitting red rays, as already explained. Nitrate of strontium ($Sr2NO_3$) is best for pyrotechnic compositions, its oxygen enabling it to burn freely when mixed with charcoal, sulphur, &c. It, or any salts, may be obtained by dissolving the carbonate in the appropriate acid, or by igniting the cheaper sulphate with coal, whereby sulphide (SrS) is produced, and dissolving this in acid.

The position of strontium among the chemical elements is between barium and calcium; its sulphate is very sparingly soluble in water. Its atom, like those of barium and calcium, is bivalent (Sr'').

Analytical Reactions (Tests).

First Analytical Reaction.—To solution of a strontium salt ($Sr2NO_3$ or $SrCl_2$) add carbonate of ammonium; a white precipitate of carbonate of strontium ($SrCO_3$) falls.

Second Analytical Reaction.—To a solution of a strontium salt add sulphuric acid previously so diluted that it will not precipitate calcium salts or an equally dilute solution of any other sulphate; a white precipitate of sulphate of strontium ($SrSO_4$) falls. The formation of this precipitate is promoted by stirring and by setting the liquid aside for some time.

Barium is precipitated immediately under similar circumstances.

Third Analytical Reaction.—To a dilute solution of a strontium salt add yellow chromate of potassium; no precipitate falls.

Barium may be separated from strontium by chromate of potassium, that reagent at once precipitating barium from aqueous or acetic solutions.

Fourth Analytical Reaction.—Insert a fragment of a strontium salt in the blowpipe-flame, or other equally colorless flame, or hold the end of a platinum wire dipped into a strontium solution in the flame; a crimson color is imparted.

Other Analytical Reactions.—Alkaline phosphates, arseniates, and oxalates give white insoluble precipitates with strontium as with barium and calcium.——Strontium, like calcium, but unlike barium, is not precipitated by hydrofluosilicic acid.

CERIUM. Ce. At. wt. 22.—This element occurs in the mineral cerite (a silicate of iron, calcium, and the three rare metals, cerium, lanthanium, and didymium); also occasionally as impure fluoride, carbonate, and phosphate. The oxalate of cerium, a white granular powder, is the only official salt; it may be obtained from cerite by boiling the powdered mineral in strong hydrochloric acid for several hours, evaporating, diluting, and filtering to separate silica; adding ammonia to precipitate hydrates of all the metals except calcium; filtering off, washing, redissolving in hydrochloric acid, and adding oxalic acid to precipitate oxalate of cerium. The preparation will still contain oxalates of lanthanium and didymium; it is therefore strongly calcined, the resulting oxides of lanthanium and didymium dissolved out by boiling with a concentrated solution of chloride of ammonium, the residual oxide of cerium dissolved in hydrochloric acid, and oxalate of ammonium added to precipitate pure oxalate of cerium ($Ce''C_2O_4$, $3H_2O$).

Oxalate of cerium (*Cerii Oxalas*, B. P.) is decomposed at a dull red heat, a salmon-colored mixture of oxides remaining; usually a little didymium is present, giving the ignited residue a reddish-brown color; it is then soluble in boiling hydrochloric acid (without effervescence; indicating, indirectly, absence of earthy and other carbonates or oxalates), and the solution gives, with excess of a saturated solution of sulphate of potassium, a crystalline precipitate of double sulphate of cerium and potassium. Alumina mixed with oxalate of cerium may be detected by boiling with solution of potash, filtering, and adding excess of solution of chloride of ammonium, when a white flocculent precipitate of hydrate of aluminium will be obtained. The oxalic radical is recognized by neutralizing the potash solution by acetic acid and adding chloride of calcium; white oxalate of calcium is then precipitated; this precipitate though insoluble in acetic, should be wholly dissolved by hydrochloric acid.

MANGANESE.

Symbol Mn. Atomic weight 55.

Source.—Manganese is a constituent of many minerals, and as black oxide (MnO_2) *Manganesii Oxidum Nigrum*, B. P. and U. S. P.), or *pyrolusite* (from πῦρ, *pur*, fire, and λύσις, *lusis*, a loosing or resolving, in allusion to the readiness with which it is split up by heat into a lower oxide and oxygen), occurs frequently in abundance in the southwest of England, Aberdeenshire, and most of the countries of Europe.

The chemical position of manganese is close to iron and three other metals still to be considered—cobalt, nickel, and chromium. Its atom apparently has sexivalent affinities, as seen in manganate of potassium (K_2MnO_4); but commonly it is quadrivalent (Mn^{iv}) or bivalent (Mn'').

Uses.—Metallic manganese is only used in alloy with iron in the manufacture of some varieties of steel. The black oxide is an important agent in the production of chlorine, the preparation of green and red disinfecting manganates, purple glass, and black glazes for earthenware.

Reactions having either Synthetical or Analytical Interest, or both.

First Reaction.—Boil a few grains of black oxide of manganese with some drops of hydrochloric acid until chlorine ceases to be evolved; add water, and filter; the filtrate is a solution of manganous chloride ($MnCl_2$).

$$MnO_2 + 4HCl = MnCl_2 + 2H_2O + Cl_2.$$

This is the reaction commonly applied in the preparation of chlorine gas. It is also a ready method of preparing a manganous salt for analytical experiments. Coupled with the application of reagents to the filtrate, the reaction is that by which a black powder or mineral would be recognized as black oxide of manganese.

Second Reaction.—Heat a particle of a manganese compound with a grain or two of carbonate and hydrate of potassium and a fragment of nitrate or chlorate of potassium on platinum foil in the blowpipe-flame; a green mass containing *manganate of potassium* (K_2MnO_4) results. Boil the foil in a little water; the green manganate dissolves and soon changes to solution of the purple *permanganate of potassium* ($K_2Mn_2O_8$).

This is a delicate analytical test for manganese.

The reaction is similar to that by which permanganate of potassium (*Potassæ Permanganas*, B. P. and U. S. P.) is directed to be prepared for use in volumetric analysis. *Liquor Potassæ Permanganatis*, B. P., is a solution of 80 grains of permanganate of potassium in 1 pint of distilled water. Equations showing the exact action which occurs in making the salt according to the process of the British Pharmacopœia have already been given in connection with the compounds of potassium (*vide* p. 53). The proportions of ingredients and details of the operation are as follows:—

Reduce 3½ parts of chlorate of potassium to fine powder, and mix it with 4 of black oxide of manganese; put the mixture into a porcelain basin, and add to it 5 parts of solid caustic potash, previously dissolved in 4 parts of water. Evaporate to dryness, stirring diligently to prevent spirting. Pulverize the mass, put it into a covered Hessian or Cornish crucible, and expose it to a dull red heat for an hour, or till it has assumed the condition of a semifused mass. Allow to cool, pulverize, and boil with about 30 parts of water. Let the insoluble matter subside, decant the fluid, boil again with about 10 parts of water, again decant, neutralize the united liquors accurately with diluted sulphuric acid (or, better, carbonic acid gas), and evaporate till a pellicle forms. Set aside to cool and crystallize. Drain the crystalline mass, boil it in 6 parts of water, and strain through a funnel the throat of which is lightly obstructed by a little asbestos. Let the fluid cool and crystallize, drain the dark purple slender prismatic crystals, and dry them by placing under a bell jar over a vessel containing sulphuric acid.

Instead of converting the manganate into permanganate by ebullition, by which one-third of the manganese is lost, Städeler recommends chlorine to be passed through the cold solution until the green color is entirely changed to purple.

Solutions of the manganates of potassium are in common use as disinfectants under the name of Condy's fluid. They act by oxidizing organic matter, the manganic or permanganic radical being reduced to black manganic oxide, or even a lower oxide.

The changes in color which the green mass of the above process undergoes when dropped into warm water procured for it the old name of *mineral chameleon*.

Third Reaction.—Make a borax bead by heating a fragment of the salt on the looped end of a platinum wire in the blowpipe-flame until a clear transparent globule is obtained. Place on the bead a minute portion of a manganese compound, or touch it with a drop of solution. Again fuse the borax; a bead of a violet or amethystine tint is produced.

This is a good analytical reaction. It has also synthetical interest, illustrating the use of black oxide of manganese in producing common purple-tinted glass.

Expose the bead to the reducing part of the flame, the part nearer to the blowpipe, where there are highly heated hydro-carbon gases greedy of oxygen ; the color disappears.

This is owing to the reduction of the manganic compound to a manganous condition, in which it no longer possesses peculiar coloring-power. This action also illustrates the use of black oxide of manganese in glass-manufacture. Glass when first made is usually of a green tint, owing to the presence of ferrous impurities; the addition of manganic oxide to the materials converts the ferrous into ferric compounds, which have comparatively little colorific power, it itself being thereby reduced to manganous oxide, which also gives but little color. If excess of manganic oxide be added, a purple tint is produced.

Fourth Reaction.—Through a solution of a manganous salt acidified by hydrochloric acid pass sulphuretted hydrogen; no decomposition occurs. Add ammonia; the sulphydrate of ammonium thus formed causes the precipitation of a yellowish pink or flesh-tinted precipitate of manganous sulphide (MnS) in a hydrous state.

This reaction is characteristic, sulphide of manganese being the only flesh-colored sulphide known. The salt used may be the manganous cloride obtained in the first reaction; but such crude solutions usually give a black precipitate with sulphydrate of ammonium, owing to the presence of iron. The latter element may be removed, however, on boiling the manganous solution with a little carbonate of sodium, which throws the ferric salt out of solution before the manganous. *Pure* manganous chloride may be similarly obtained on boiling the impure solution with manganous carbonate; the latter decomposes the ferric chloride with production of ferric hydrate and more manganous chloride, and evolution of carbonic acid gas.

To the recently precipitated manganous sulphide add acetic acid; it is dissolved.

This solubility enables manganese to be separated from nickel, cobalt, and zinc, whose sulphides are insoluble in weak acetic acid. To express the fact in another way—manganese is not precipitated by sulphuretted hydrogen from a solution containing free acetic acid only.

Fifth Reaction.—To solution of manganous salt add ammonia drop by drop; a white precipitate of manganous hydrate (Mn2HO) falls. Add excess of ammonia; the precipitate is dissolved.

The fixed alkalies give a similar precipitate *insoluble* in excess. The precipitate rapidly absorbs oxygen, becomes brown, and gradually passes into a higher oxide.

Sixth Reaction.—Heat a little black oxide of manganese in a test-tube with sulphuric acid; oxygen is evolved and sulphate of manganese formed (*Manganesii Sulphas*, U.S.P.), add water, boil, filter, evaporate and set aside to crystallize. Larger quantities are made in a similar manner.

Sulphate of manganese ($MnSO_4,5H_2O$) occurs in colorless, or pale rose-colored, transparent crystals, which, when deposited from a solution at a temperature between 68° and 86°, have the form of right rhombic prisms, and contain four molecules of water. This salt is very soluble in water. The solution is not colored by tincture of nutgall a black (a black shows iron), but affords with caustic alkalies a white precipitate (Mn2HO), which, by exposure to the air, soon absorbs oxygen, and becomes brown. Sulphydrate of ammonium throws down a flesh-colored precipitate (MnS), and ferrocyanide of potassium, a white one (MnFcy).

Many other reactions occur between manganese salts and various reagents, but are of no particular synthetical or analytical interest. A good method proposed by Crom, for detecting minute quantities of manganese consists in adding diluted nitric acid and the puce-colored oxide or peroxide of lead to the solution, and then boiling; a red tint, due to permanganic acid, is imparted to the liquid.

COBALT.

Symbol Co. Atomic weight 58.8.

Source.—Cobalt occurs sparingly in nature as the arsenide ($CoAs_2$), or *tin-white cobalt*, and occasionally as a double arsenide and sulphide ($CoAs_2, CoS_2$), or *cobalt-glance* (from *glanz*, brightness, in allusion to its lustre).

Uses.—Its chief use is in the manufactory of blue glass, the color of which is due to a compound of cobalt. Cobalt is also the coloring constituent of *smalt* (from *smelt*, a corruption of *melt*), a finely-ground sort of glass used as a blue pigment by paper-stainers and others, and employed also by laundresses to neutralize the yellowish appearance of washed linen.

The salts of cobalt may be obtained from the oxide (CoO), and the oxide from *zaffre*, a mixture of sand and roasted ore.

Quantivalence.—Cobalt often exhibits quadrivalent affinities, but still more often exerts only bivalent powers (Co''). It has analytical relations with zinc, nickel, and manganese, and may be regarded as a member of the iron group.

Analytical Reactions (Tests).

First Analytical Reaction.—Pass sulphuretted hydrogen through a solution of a salt of cobalt—the chloride ($CoCl_2$) or nitrate ($Co2NO_3$) for example; no decomposition occurs. Add ammonia; the sulphydrate of ammonium thus formed causes the precipitation of black sulphide of cobalt (CoS).

The moist precipitate slowly absorbs oxygen from the air, becoming converted into sulphate of cobalt ($CoSO_4$).

Second Analytical Reaction.—Add ammonia gradually to a cobalt solution; a blue precipitate of impure hydrate of cobalt (Co2HO) falls. Add excess of ammonia; the precipitate is dissolved.

A similar precipitate is given by the fixed alkalies, *insoluble* in excess.

Third Analytical Reaction.—Make a borax bead by heating a fragment of the salt on the looped end of a platinum wire in a blowpipe-flame until a clear transparent globule is obtained. Place on the head a minute portion of cobalt compound, or touch it with a drop of solution. Again, fuse the borax; a blue bead results.

This is a delicate test for cobalt. From what has previously been said, it will be seen that this experiment has also considerable synthetical interest.

Fourth Analytical Reaction.—To a solution of a salt of cobalt add two or three drops of hydrochloric acid, then excess of solution of cyanide of potassium, and boil for ten minutes; oxygen is absorbed, and cobalticyanide of potassium (K_3CoCy_6) formed. Add hydrochloric acid, and boil the mixture (in a fume-cupboard, to avoid inhalation of any hydrocyanic acid); the excess of cyanide of potassium is thus decomposed, but the cobalticyanide is unaffected. Now add excess of solution of potash; the cobalticyanide of potassium is decomposed, the hydrate of cobalt formed remaining dissolved in the alkaline liquid.

Nickel under similar circumstances is precipitated, the reaction thus affording means of separating these closely allied metals from each other.

Other reactions between a cobalt solution and different reagents may be performed, and various precipitates obtained; but these have no special analytical interest.

Invisible Ink.—The salts of cobalt containing water of crystallization are light red, the anhydrous more or less blue. Prove this by writing some words on paper with a solution of chloride of cobalt sufficiently dilute for the characters to be invisible when dry; hold the sheet before a fire or over a flame; the letters at once become visible, distinct, and of a blue color. Breathe on the words, or set the sheet aside for a while; the characters are once more invisible, owing to absorption of moisture. Hence solution of chloride of cobalt forms one of the so-called *sympathetic inks*.

NICKEL.

Symbol Ni. Atomic weight 58.8.

Nickel is, chemically, closely allied to cobalt, the ores of the two metals being commonly associated in nature. Indeed it is from *speiss*, an arsenio-sulphide of nickel obtained in the manufacture of smalt, a pigment of cobalt already mentioned, that most of the nickel met with in commerce is obtained. It is much used in the preparation of the white alloy known as German or nickel silver.

Quantivalence.—Nickel exerts bivalent activity (Ni″) in its ordinary compounds. Its salts and their solutions are usually green. They are chiefly made, directly or indirectly, from the metal itself.

Analytical Reactions (Tests).

First Analytical Reaction.—Pass sulphuretted hydrogen through a solution of a salt of nickel—chloride ($NiCl_2$), nitrate ($Ni2NO_3$), or sulphate ($NiSO_4$); no decomposition occurs. Add ammonia; the sulphydrate of ammonium thus formed causes the precipitation of black sulphide of nickel (NiS).

Note.—When sulphide of nickel is precipitated by the direct addition of the common yellow solution of sulphydrate of ammonium, which always contains sulphur, there is much difficulty in filtering the mixture, owing to the slight solubility of the sulphide of nickel in the reagent and the formation of some sulphate of nickel ($NiSO_4$), oxygen being absorbed from the air by the sulphide. This may be avoided by warming the mixture and using freshly-made sulphydrate of ammonium, in which the sulphide of nickel is insoluble; or, where practicable, the salt of nickel may be precipitated from an ammoniacal solution by sulphuretted hydrogen.

Second Analytical Reaction.—Add ammonia drop by drop to a nickel solution; a pale-green precipitate of hydrate of nickel (Ni2HO) falls. Add excess of ammonia; the precipitate dissolves.

A similar precipitate is given by the fixed alkalies, *insoluble* in excess.

Third Analytical Reaction.—Nickel salts color a borax bead, when hot, a reddish-yellow tint; the reaction is not very serviceable analytically.

Fourth Analytical Reaction.—To a solution of a salt of nickel add solution of cyanide of potassium; cyanide of nickel ($NiCy_2$) is precipitated. Add excess of solution of cyanide of potassium; the precipitate is dissolved with formation of double cyanide of nickel and potassium ($NiCy_2,2KCy$). Next add hydrochloric acid, and boil the mixture (in a fume-cupboard), adding a little hydrochloric acid from time to time until all smell of hydrocyanic acid has disappeared. Lastly, add excess of solution of potash; hydrate of nickel is precipitated.

This reaction serves for the separation of nickel from cobalt. On adding excess of hydrochloric acid to a solution containing the two metals, together with cyanide of potassium, a precipitate of cyanide of nickel and cobalticyanide of nickel occurs. By ebullition with excess of hydrochloric acid the cyanide of nickel is decomposed, chloride of nickel going into solution. On then adding excess of potash hydrate of nickel is precipitated. The cobalticyanide of nickel is not decomposed by the acid; but it is by the alkali, its cobalt going into solution and its nickel remaining insoluble as hydrate.

After filtering off the nickel, cobalt is detected in the filtrate by evaporating to dryness and testing the residue with borax in the blowpipe-flame.

Other reactions between a nickel solution and various reagents give, in many cases, insoluble precipitates which, from their green color, are occasionally useful in distinguishing nickel from allied elements.

CHROMIUM.

Symbol Cr. Atomic weight 52.5.

Source.—The chief ore of chromium is chrome ironstone, a mixture of the oxides of the metals (FeO, Cr_2O_3), occurring chiefly in the United States and Sweden.

Preparation of Red Chromate of Potassium.—On fusing the powdered ore with carbonate of potassium and nitre, yellow chromate of potassium (K_2CrO_4) is obtained; the mass, treated with acid, yields red or bichromate (K_2CrO_4, CrO_3) (*Potassæ Bichromas*, B. P. and U. S. P.); from this salt other chromates are prepared, and by reduction, as presently explained, the salts of chromium itself. The yellow and orange chromates of lead are largely used as pigments.

Note on Constitution.—Red chromate of potassium is a somewhat abnormal salt, containing, probably, neutral chromate associated with chromic anhydride; it seems to be analogous in constitution to borax and some other compounds. The value of chromates as chemical reagents is alluded to in connection with chromate of barium (p. 76). Heated strongly in a crucible, red chromate of potassium splits up into yellow chromate, glistening oxide of chromium, and oxygen.

Quantivalence.—Chromium stands in close chemical relation to iron, aluminium, and manganese. Its atom is sexivalent if the formula of the fluoride (CrF_6) be correct. Like iron and aluminium, it is trivalent, as seen in chromic chloride (Cr_2Cl_6), but sometimes exerts only bivalent activity, as in chromous chloride ($CrCl_2$).

Passage of chromium from the acidulous to the basylous side of salts.—Through an acidified solution of red chromate of potassium pass sulphuretted hydrogen; sulphur is deposited, and a green salt of chromium remains in solution—chloride (Cr_2Cl_6) if hydrochloric acid be used, and sulphate (Cr_23SO_4) if sulphuric be the acid employed. Boil the liquid to expel excess of sulphuretted hydrogen, filter, and reserve the solution for subsequent experiments.

Alcohol, sugar, or almost any substance which is tolerably liable to oxidation will answer as well as sulphuretted hydrogen.

Sulphate of chromium ($Cr_2 3SO_4$), like sulphate of aluminium ($Al_2 3SO_4$), unites with alkaline sulphates to form *alums*, which resemble common alum both in crystalline form and, as far as we know, in internal structure: they are of a purple color.

Reactions.

Chromium as *chromic acid*, or other *chromate*.—This is the state in which chromium will usually be met with, the most common salt being the red chromate or bichromate of potassium. Mix four volumes of a cold, saturated aqueous solution of red chromate of potassium with five of oil of vitriol; on cooling, *chromic anhydride* (CrO_3), *acidum chromium*, U. S. P., separates in crimson needles. After well draining, the crystals may be freed from adhering sulphuric acid by washing once or twice with nitric acid: the latter may be removed by passing dried and slightly warmed air through a tube containing the crystals. In contact with moisture chromic anhydride takes up water and forms solution of true chromic acid (H_2CrO_4). Chromic anhydride is a powerfully corrosive oxidizing agent. It melts between 356° and 374°.

The oxygen in chromic acid and other chromates, and in manganates, permanganates, black oxide of manganese and puce colored oxide of lead is in a physically different state to that in peroxide of hydrogen, peroxide of barium, and similar compounds. On bringing chromic acid or the above acidified solution of red chromate of potassium into contact with solution of peroxide of hydrogen a strong effervescence of oxygen ensues. According to Schönbein and Brodie the oxygen of chromic acid is in the negative or ozonic state, while that of peroxide of hydrogen is in the positive or antozonic condition. Both are equally active, but neutralize each other forming neutral or ordinary oxygen.

In the analytical examination of solutions containing chromates, the chromium will always come out in the state of green chromic hydrate along with ferric hydrate and alumina, the prior treatment by sulphuretted hydrogen reducing the molecule to the lower state, thus:—

$$K_2CrO_4, CrO_3 + 8HCl + 3H_2S = Cr_2Cl_6 + 2KCl + 7H_2O + S_3.$$

Chromium having been found in a solution, its condition as chromate may be ascertained by applying to the original solution salts of barium, mercury, lead, and silver. (See the various paragraphs relating to those metals.)

$Ba2NO_3$	gives	yellow	$BaCrO_4$	with chromates.
Hg_22NO_3	"	red	Hg_2CrO_4	"
$AgNO_3$	"	red	Ag_2CrO_4	"
"	"	"	Ag_2CrO_4, CrO_3	with bichromates.
$Pb2C_2H_3O_2$	"	yellow	$PbCrO_4$	with both.

Nitrate of barium does not completely precipitate bichromates, bichromate of barium being soluble in water; the chromate of barium is insoluble in water or acetic acid, but soluble in hydrochloric or nitric acid. Mercurous nitrate does not wholly precipitate bichromates: mercuric nitrate or chloride only partially precipitates chromates, and does not precipitate bichromates. The mercurous chromate is insoluble, or nearly so, in diluted nitric acid. Acetate of lead precipitates chromates and bichromates, acetic acid being set free in the latter case. The silver chromates are soluble in acids and alkalies.

A delicate reaction for dry chromates will be found in the formation of *chlorochromic acid* (CrO_2Cl_2). A small portion of the chromate is placed in a test-tube with a fragment of dry chloride of sodium and a drop or two of oil of vitriol, and the mixture heated; red irritating fumes of chlorochromic acid are evolved, and condense in dark red drops on the side of the tube.

Large quantities of pure distilled chlorochromic acid are obtained by the same reaction, the operation being conducted in a retort, with thoroughly dry materials. It may be regarded as chromic anhydride in which an atom of oxygen is displaced by an equivalent quantity (two atoms) of chlorine. It is not used in medicine, but is of interest to the chemical student as being an illustration of a large class of similar bodies—*chloro-acidulous compounds.*

Analytical Reactions of Chromium Salts (Tests).

First Analytical Reaction.—To solution of a salt of chromium (chloride, sulphate, or chrome alum) add sulphydrate of ammonium; a bulky green precipitate of chromic hydrate (Cr_26HO), containing a large quantity of water (7 molecules, $7H_2O$), is precipitated.

$$Cr_2Cl_6 + 6AmHS + 6H_2O = Cr_26HO + 6AmCl + 6H_2S.$$

Second Analytical Reaction.—To solution of a chromium salt add ammonia; chromic hydrate is precipitated, insoluble in excess.

Third Analytical Reaction.—To solution of a chromium salt add solution of potash or soda drop by drop; chromic hydrate is precipitated. Add excess of the fixed alkali; the precipitate is dissolved. Well boil the solution; the chromic hydrate is reprecipitated.

Iron, Chromium, and Aluminium Salts, chemically so alike, may be separated by this reaction. Ferric hydrate is insoluble in solutions of the fixed alkalies, cold or hot; chromium hydrate soluble in cold but not in hot; hydrate of aluminium in both. To a solution containing all three metals, therefore, add potash or soda, stir, and filter; the iron is thrown out: boil the filtrate, and filter: the chromium is thrown out: neutralize the filtrate by acid, and then add ammonia; the aluminium is thrown out. The three hydrates are insoluble in ammonia, and may therefore be easily separated from the hydrates of the somewhat analogous metals zinc, cobalt, nickel, and manganese.

Fourth Analytical Reaction.—Add a salt of chromium (either of the above precipitates of chromic oxide or the dry residue of the evaporation of a few drops of a solution of a chromium salt) to a few grains of nitre and carbonate of sodium on platinum foil, and fuse the mixture in the blowpipe-flame; a yellow mass of chromate of potassium and sodium ($KNaCrO_4$) is formed. Dissolve the mass in water, add acetic acid to decompose excess of carbonate, and apply the reagents for chromates.

This is a delicate and useful reaction if carefully performed.

TIN.

Symbol Sn. Atomic weight 118.

Source.—The chief ore of tin is stannic oxide (SnO_2), occurring in veins under the name of *tinstone*, or in alluvial deposits as *stream-tin*. The principal mines are those of Cornwall.

Preparation.—The metal is obtained by reducing the roasted and washed ore by charcoal or anthracite* coal at a high temperature, and is purified by slowly heating, when the pure tin, fusing first, is run off, a somewhat less fusible alloy of tin with small quantities of arsenic, copper, iron, or lead remaining. The latter is known as *block tin;* the former heated till brittle and then hammered or let fall from a height splits into prismatic fragments resembling starch

* *Anthracite* (from ἄνθραξ, *anthrax*, a burning coal) or *stone coal* differs from the ordinary *bituminous* or *caking coal*, in containing less volatile matter, and, therefore, in burning without flame. It gives a higher temperature, and from its non-caking properties is, in furnace operations, more manageable than bituminous coal.

or basalt, and is named *dropped* or *grain tin*. Good tin emits a crackling noise in bending, termed the cry of tin, caused by the friction of its crystalline particles on each other.

Uses.—Tin is an important constituent of such alloys as pewter, Britannia metal, solder, speculum-metal, bell-metal, gun-metal, and bronze. It is very ductile, and may be rolled into plates or leaves, known as *tin foil*, varying from $\frac{1}{250}$ to $\frac{1}{1000}$ of an inch in thickness. Common tin foil, however, usually contains a large proportion of lead. The reflecting surface of most *looking-glasses* is an amalgam of tin and mercury, produced by carefully sliding a plate of glass over a sheet of tin foil on which mercury has been rubbed, and then excess of mercury poured. *Pins* are made of brass wire on which tin is deposited. *Tin plate*, of which common utensils are made, is iron alloyed with tin by dipping the cleansed sheet into melted tin. *Tin tacks* are in reality tinned iron tacks, a tin nail would be too soft to drive into wood. Tin may be granulated by melting and triturating briskly in a hot mortar, by shaking melted tin in a box on the inner sides of which chalk has been rubbed, or, in thin little bells or corrugated fragments (Granulated Tin, B. P.), by melting in a ladle and, as soon as fluid, pouring from the height of a few feet into water.

The chemical position of tin among the metals is close to that of arsenicum and antimony. Its atom is quadrivalent and bivalent. The two classes of salts are termed stannic and stannous respectively. They are all made directly or indirectly from the metal itself.

REACTIONS HAVING (*a*) SYNTHETICAL AND (*b*) ANALYTICAL INTEREST.

(*a*) *Synthetical Reactions.*

Chloride of Tin. Stannous Chloride.

First Synthetical Reaction.—Warm a fragment of tin with hydrochloric acid; hydrogen escapes and solution of stannous chloride ($SnCl_2$) is formed. It may be retained for future experiments.

One ounce of tin dissolved in three fluidounces of hydrochloric acid and one of water, and the resulting solution diluted to five fluidounces, constitutes the "Solution of Chloride of Tin," B. P.

Solid stannous chloride.—By evaporation of the above solution stannous chloride is obtainable in crystals ($SnCl_2,2H_2O$). It is a powerful reducing agent, even a dilute solution precipitating gold, silver, and mercury from their solutions, converting ferric and cupric into ferrous and cuprous salts, and partially deoxidizing arsenic, manganic, and chromic acids. It absorbs oxygen from the air, and is decomposed when added to a large quantity of water unless some acid be present. It is used as a mordant in dyeing and calico-printing.

Perchloride of Tin. Stannic Chloride.

Second Synthetical Reaction.—Through a portion of the solution of the stannous chloride of the previous reaction pass chlorine gas; solution of stannic chloride ($SnCl_4$) is formed. Or add hydrochloric acid to the stannous solution, boil, and slowly drop in nitric acid until no more fumes are evolved; again stannic chloride results. Reserve the solutions for subsequent experiments.

Stannic Oxide, or Anhydride, and Stannates.

Third Synthetical Reaction.—Boil a fragment of tin with nitric acid, evaporate to dryness, and strongly calcine the residue; white stannic anhydride (SnO_2) is produced. Heat the stannic anhydride with excess of potash or soda; stannate of the alkali metal (K_2SnO_3 or Na_2SnO_3) results. Dissolve the stannate in water, and add hydrochloric acid; white, gelatinous *stannic acid* (H_2SnO_3) is precipitated. Stannic acid is also obtained on adding an alkali to solution of stannic chloride; it is soluble in excess of acid or alkali.

The product of the action of nitric acid on tin is also an acid, but, from its insolubility in hydrochloric and other acids, is different from ordinary stannic acid. It is termed *metastannic acid* (from *μετὰ*, *meta*, beyond), and probably has a composition expressed by the formula $H_{10}Sn_5O_{15}$. It is also produced on gently heating stannic acid:—

$$\underset{\text{Stannic acid.}}{5H_2SnO_3} = \underset{\text{Metastannic acid.}}{H_{10}Sn_5O_{15}}$$

Metastannates may be formed; their general formula is $M_2H_8Sn_5O_{15}$. Both acids yield buff-colored stannic oxide or anhydride (SnO_2) when strongly heated; it is employed in polishing plate under the name of *putty powder*. *Stannate of sodium* ($Na_2SnO_3,4H_2O$) is used as a mordant by dyers and calico-printers under the name of *tin prepare-liquor*.

(*b*) *Reactions having Analytical Interest* (*Tests*).

STANNOUS SALTS.

First Analytical Reaction.—Through a solution of a stannous salt (stannous chloride, for example) pass sulphuretted hydrogen; brown stannous sulphide (SnS) is precipitated. Pour off the supernatant liquid, add ammonia to the moist precipitate (to neutralize acid), and lastly, yellow sulphydrate of ammonium; the precipitate is dissolved.

Aqueous solution of sulphydrate of ammonium becomes yellow when a day or two old, and then contains excess of sulphur, that element having become displaced by oxygen absorbed from the air; hence, in the above reaction, the stannous sulphide (SnS), in dissolving, becomes stannic sulphide (SnS_2); for the latter is precipitated on decomposing the alkaline liquid by an acid.

Second Analytical Reaction.—To solution of a stannous salt add solution of potash or soda; white stannous hydrate falls (Sn2HO). Add excess of the alkali; the precipitate dissolves. Boil the solution; some of the tin is reprecipitated as black stannous oxide (SnO).

Ammonia gives a similar precipitate, insoluble in excess. The alkaline carbonates do the same, carbonic acid gas escaping.

STANNIC SALTS.

Third Analytical Reaction.—Through solution of a stannic salt (stannic chloride, for example) pass sulphuretted hydrogen; yellow stannic sulphide (SnS_2) is precipitated. Pour off the supernatant liquid, and to the moist precipitate add ammonia (to neutralize acid), and then sulphydrate of ammonium; the precipitate dissolves.

Note.—In precipitating stannic sulphide the presence of too much hydrochloric acid must be avoided; the formation of the precipitate is also facilitated if the solution be warmed. Stannic sulphide, like the sulphide of arsenicum and antimony, dissolves in solutions of any alkaline sulphide, with formation of definite crystallizable salts.

Anhydrous stannic sulphide, prepared by sublimation, has a yellow or orange lustrous appearance, and is used by decorators as *bronzing-powder*. It is sometimes termed *mosaic gold*.

Fourth Analytical Reaction.—To solution of a stannic salt add potash or soda; white stannic acid falls (H_2SnO_3), Add excess of the alkali; the precipitate dissolves. Boil the precipitate; no reprecipitation occurs—a fact enabling stannic to be distinguished from stannous salts.

Ammonia gives a similar precipitate, soluble, but not readily, in excess. The fixed-alkaline carbonates do the same, carbonic acid gas escaping; after a time the stannic salt is again deposited, probably as stannate of the alkali metal. Carbonate of ammonium and acid carbonates of alkali metals give a precipitate of stannic acid insoluble in excess.

Antidotes.—In cases of poisoning by tin salts (dyers' tin liquor *e. g.*), solution of carbonate of ammonium should be given. White of egg is also said to form an insoluble precipitate with compounds of tin. Vomiting should be speedily induced, and the stomach pump quickly supplied.

GOLD.

Symbol Au. Atomic weight 196.7.

Source.—Gold occurs in the free state in nature, occasionally in nodules or *nuggets*, but commonly in a finer state of division termed *gold dust.*

Preparation.—Gold is separated from the sand, crushed quartz, or other earthy matter with which it may be associated, by agitation with water, when the gold from its relatively greater specific gravity, falls to the bottom of the vessels first, the lighter mineral matter being allowed to run off with the water. From this rich sand the gold is dissolved out by mercury, the latter filtered, and the amalgam distilled, when the mercury volatilizes and gold remains. The amalgamation may be much facilitated by the use of a small proportion of sodium, as described under silver.

Pure gold is too soft for general use as a circulating medium. *Gold coin* is an alloy of copper and gold, that of Great Britain containing 1 of the former to 11 of the latter, or $8\frac{1}{3}$ per cent. of copper, that of France, Germany, and the United States about 10 per cent. *Jewellers' gold* varies in quality, every 24 parts containing 18, 15, 12, or 9 parts of gold, the alloys being technically termed 18, 15, 12, or 9 *carat fine.* Articles made of the better qualities are usually stamped by authority. Trinkets of inferior intrinsic worth are commonly thinly coated with pure gold by electro-deposition or otherwise. *Gold leaf* is nearly pure gold passed between rollers till it is about $\frac{1}{800}$ of an inch in thickness and then hammered between sheets of animal membrane, termed gold-beater's skin and calf-skin vellum, till it is $\frac{1}{100000}$ or $\frac{1}{200000}$ of an inch in thickness. It may even be hammered till 280,000 leaves would be required to form a pile an inch thick.

Gold coinage.—The weight of gold is expressed in Great Britain in ounces troy and decimal parts of an ounce, and the metal is always taken to be of standard fineness (11 gold and 1 alloy) unless otherwise described. The degree of fineness of gold, as ascertained by assay, is expressed decimally, fine pure gold ("gold free from metallic impurities," B. P.), being taken as unity, or 1.000. Thus gold of British standard is said to be 0.9166 fine, of French standard 0.900 fine. The legal weight of the sovereign is 0.2568 ounce of standard gold, or 123.274 grains. The weight came from one pound of standard gold (5760 grains) being coined into $44\frac{1}{2}$ guineas. Sovereigns are legal tender to any amount, provided that the weight of each does not fall below 122.5 grains, or in the case of a half sovereign 61.125 grains; these are the "least current" weights of the coins.

Note.—In chemical analysis gold comes out among the sulphides of the metals precipitated by sulphuretted hydrogen; and of those sulphides, it, like the sulphides of tin, antimony, and arsenicum, is soluble in sulphydrate of ammonium.

Quantivalence.—Gold is trivalent (Au‴), but in some compounds univalent (Au′).

Reactions.

Synthetical Reaction.—Place a fragment of gold (*e. g.*, gold leaf) in ten or twenty drops of aqua regia (a mixture of one part of nitric and two or three of hydrochloric acid), and set the test-tube aside in a warm place; solution of perchloride of gold or auric chloride ($AuCl_3$) results. When the metal is dissolved, evaporate nearly to dryness to remove most of the excess of fluid, dilute with water, and retain the solution for subsequent experiments. Sixty grains of gold treated thus, and the resulting chloride dissolved in five ounces of distilled water, constitutes "Solution of Chloride of Gold," B. P.

$$Au_2 + 2HNO_3 + 6HCl = 2AuCl_3 + 2NO + 4H_2O$$

This reaction has analytical interest also; for in examining a substance suspected to be or contain metallic gold, solution would have to be effected in the above way before reagents could be applied. Gold is insoluble in hydrochloric, nitric, and the weaker acids.

Analytical Reactions (Tests).

First Analytical Reaction.—Through a few drops of solution of an auric salt (the chloride, $AuCl_3$, is the only convenient one) pass sulphuretted hydrogen; brown auric sulphide (Au_2S_3) is precipitated. Filter, wash, and add sulphydrate of ammonium; the precipitate dissolves.

Second Analytical Reaction.—To solution of a salt of gold add ferrous chloride or sulphate, and set the tube aside; metallic gold is precipitated, a ferric salt remaining in solution.

This is a convenient way of preparing pure gold, or *fine gold* as it is termed, or of working up the gold residues of laboratory operations. The precipitate, after boiling with hydrochloric acid, washing, and drying, may be obtained in a button by mixing with an equal weight of borax or acid sulphate of potassium and fusing in a good furnace.

Third Analytical Reaction.—Add a few drops of dilute solutions of stannous and stannic chloride to a considerable quantity of distilled water; pour the liquid, a small quantity at a time, into a dilute solution of auric chloride

($AuCl_3$), well stirring; the mixture assumes a purple tint, and flocks of a precipitate, known as the *Purple of Cassius*, (from the name of the discoverer, M. Cassius), are produced.

The same compound is formed on immersing a piece of tin foil in solution of auric chloride; it is said to be a mixture of auric, aurous, stannic, and stannous oxides. It is the coloring agent in the finer varieties of ruby glass.

PLATINUM.

Symbol Pt. Atomic weight 198.

Source.—Platinum, like gold, usually occurs in nature in the free state, the chief sources of supply being Mexico, Brazil, and Siberia. It is separated from the alluvial soil by washing.

Uses.—The chief use of platinum is in the construction of foil, wire, crucibles, spatulas, capsules, evaporating-dishes, and stills, for the use of the chemical analyst or manufacturer. It is tolerably hard, fusible with very great difficulty, not dissolved by hydrochloric, nitric, or sulphuric acid, and only slightly affected by alkaline substances. It is attacked by aqua regia with production of perchloride of platinum or platinic chloride ($PtCl_4$). It forms fusible alloys with lead and other metals, and with phosphorus a phosphide, which easily melts. Neither of these substances, therefore, nor mixtures which may yield a metal, should be heated in platinum vessels.

The chemical position of platinum among the elements is close to that of gold. Its atom is quadrivalent in some compounds, in others apparently bivalent (Pt''). The higher salts are termed *platinic*, the lower *platinous*.

REACTIONS.

Perchloride of Platinum. Platinic Chloride.

Synthetical Reaction.—Place a fragment of platinum in a little aqua regia and set the vessel aside in a warm place, adding more acid from time to time if necessary; solution of perchloride of platinum ($PtCl_4$) results. Evaporate the solution to remove excess of acid, and complete the desiccation over a water-bath. Dissolve the residue in water and retain the solution for subsequent experiments, and as a reagent for the precipitation of salts of potassium and ammonium.

A quarter of an ounce of platinum treated in the above manner, and the resulting chloride dissolved in five ounces of water, constitutes "Solution of Perchloride of Platinum," B. P.

This reaction has analytical interest also; for in examining a substance suspected to be or to contain metallic platinum, solution would have to be thus effected before reagents could be applied.

Analytical Reactions (Tests).

First Analytical Reaction.—Through a few drops of a solution of a platinic salt ($PtCl_4$ is the only convenient one) to which an equal quantity of solution of chloride of sodium has been added, pass sulphuretted hydrogen; dark brown platinic sulphide (PtS_2) is precipitated. Filter, wash, and add sulphydrate of ammonium; the precipitate dissolves.

If chloride of sodium be not present in the above reaction, the precipitated sulphide will contain platinous chloride, and detonate when heated.

Second Analytical Reaction.—Add excess of solution of carbonate of sodium and some sugar to solution of perchloride of platinum and boil; a precipitate of metallic platinum falls.

Platinum Black (B. P.) is the name of this precipitate. It possesses in a high degree a quality common to many substances, but largely possessed by platinum, namely, that by absorbing or occluding gases. In its ordinary state, after well washing and drying, it absorbs from the air and retains many times its bulk of oxygen. A drop of ether or alcohol placed on it is rapidly oxydized, the platinum becoming hot. This action may be prettily shown by pouring a few drops of ether into a beaker (one having portions of the top and sides broken off answers best), loosely covering the vessel with a card, and suspending within the beaker a platinum wire, one end being attached to the card by passing through its centre, the other terminating in a short coil or helix near the surface of the ether; on now warming the helix in a flame and then rapidly introducing it into the beaker, it will become red-hot and continue to glow so long as there is ether in the vessel. In this experiment real combustion goes on between the ether vapor and the concentrated oxygen of the air, the products of the oxidation revealing themselves by their odor.

Third Analytical Reaction.—To solution of perchloride of platinum add solution of chloride of ammonium; a yellow granular precipitate of double chloride of platinum and ammonium ($PtCl_4, 2AmCl$) falls. When slowly formed in dilute solutions, the precipitate is obtained in minute orange prisms.

Chloride of potassium (KCl) gives a similar precipitate ($PtCl_4$ $2KCl$). Platinic chloride having been stated to be a test for potassium and ammonium salts, the reader is prepared to find that potassium and ammonium salts are tests for platinic salts. The double sodium compound ($PtCl_4 2NaCl$) is soluble in water.

Collect the precipitate, dry, and heat in a small crucible; it is decomposed, and metal, in the finely divided state of *spongy platinum*, remains.

$$3(PtCl_4 2NH_4Cl) = Pt_3 + 2NH_4Cl + 16HCl + 2N_2$$

Heat decomposes the potassium salt into $Pt + 2KCl + Cl_4$, the chlorine escaping and the chloride of potassium remaining with the platinum.

In working up the platinum residues of laboratory operations, the mixture should be dried, burnt, boiled successively with hydrochloric acid, water, nitric acid, water, then dissolved in aqua regia, excess of acid removed by evaporation, chloride of ammonium added, the precipitate washed with water, dried, ignited, and the resulting spongy platinum retained or converted into perchloride for use as a reagent for alkali-metals. It is by this process that the native platinum is treated to free it from the rare metals palladium, rhodium, osmium, ruthenium, and iridium. The spongy platinum is converted into the massive condition by a refinement on the blacksmith's process of *welding* (German *wellen*, to join), or by fusing in a flame of pure oxygen and hydrogen gases—the oxyhydrogen blowpipe.

Occlusion by spongy platinum.—Spongy platinum has great power of occlusion. A small piece held in a jet of hydrogen causes ignition of the gas, owing to the close approximation of particles of oxygen (from the air) and hydrogen. Dobereiner's lamp is constructed on this principle—the apparatus being essentially a vessel in which hydrogen is generated by the action of diluted sulphuric acid on zinc, and a cage for holding the spongy platinum.

CADMIUM.

Symbol Cd. Atomic weight 112.

In most of its chemical relations cadmium (*Cadmium*, U. S. P.) resembles zinc. In nature it occurs chiefly as an occasional constituent of the ores of that metal. In distilling zinc containing cadmium, the latter, being the more volatile, passes over first. In analytical operations cadmium, unlike zinc, comes down among the metals precipitated by sulphuretted hydrogen; that is, its sulphide is insoluble in dilute hydrochloric acid, while sulphide of zinc is soluble. It is a white malleable metal nearly as volatile as mercury. Sp. gr. 8.7.

Beyond the occasional employment of the sulphide as a pigment (*jaune brillant*), and the iodide in photography and medicine, cadmium and its salts are but little used. The atom of cadmium is bivalent (Cd'').

Reactions.

Iodide of Cadmium.

First Synthetical Reaction.—Digest metallic cadmium in water in which a fragment of iodine is placed, until the color of the iodine disappears; solution of iodide of cadmium (*Cadmii Iodidum*, B. P.) (CdI_2) remains. Pearly micaceous crystals may be obtained on evaporating the solution.

This is the process alluded to in the British Pharmacopœia. The compound is used in medicine in the form of ointment, *Unguentum Cadmii Iodidi*, B. P. The salt is also employed, with other iodides, in iodizing collodion for photographic purposes. It melts when heated, and is soluble in water or spirit, the solution reddening litmus paper.

Sulphate of Cadmium.

Second Synthetical Reaction.—Dissolve cadmium in nitric acid; pour the resulting solution of nitrate of cadmium ($Cd2NO_3$) into a solution of carbonate of sodium; dissolve the precipitate of carbonate of cadmium ($CdCO_3$) in dilute sulphuric acid, separate and crystallize. Sulphate of cadmium ($CdSO_4$) is a white crystalline salt soluble in water, (U. S. P.)

First Analytical Reaction.—Through solution of a cadmium salt (CdI_2 or $CdCl_2$) pass sulphuretted hydrogen; a yellow precipitate of sulphide of cadmium (CdS) falls, resembling in appearance arsenious, arsenic, and stannic sulphides. Add sulphydrate of ammonium; the precipitate, unlike the sulphides just mentioned, does not dissolve.

Sulphides of cadmium and copper may be separated by solution of cyanide of potassium, in which sulphide of copper is soluble and sulphide of cadmium insoluble.

Second Analytical Reaction.—To a cadmium solution add solution of potash; white hydrate of cadmium (Cd2HO) is precipitated, insoluble in excess of the potash.

Hydrate of zinc (Zn2HO), precipitated under similar circumstances, is soluble in solution of potash; the filtrate from the hydrate of cadmium may therefore be tested for any zinc occurring as an impurity by applying the appropriate reagent—sulphydrate of ammonium.

Before the blowpipe-flame, on charcoal, cadmium salts give a brown deposit of oxide of cadmium (CdO).

BISMUTH.

Symbol Bi. Atomic weight 208.

Source.—Bismuth occurs in the metallic state in nature. It is freed from adherent quartz, &c., by simply heating, when the metal melts, runs off, and is collected in appropriate vessels. It is also met with in combination with other elements. Bismuth is grayish-white, with a distinct pinkish tinge.

Uses.—Beyond the employment of some of its compounds in medicine, bismuth is but little used. Melted bismuth expands considerably on solidifying, and hence is valuable in taking sharp impressions of dies. It is a constituent of some kinds of type-metal and of pewter-solder.

The position of bismuth among the metals is close to that of arsenicum and antimony. Its atom is rarely quinquivalent (Bi^{v}); but in most compounds trivalent (Bi''').

Reactions having (*a*) Synthetical and (*b*) Analytical Interest.

(*a*) *Reactions having Synthetical Interest.*

Nitrate of Bismuth.

First Synthetical Reaction.—To a few drops of nitric acid and an equal quantity of water in a test-tube, add a little powdered bismuth, heating the mixture if necessary; nitric oxide (NO) escapes and solution of *nitrate of bismuth* ($Bi3NO_3$) results.

$$\underset{\text{Bismuth.}}{Bi_2} + \underset{\text{Nitric acid.}}{8HNO_3} = \underset{\text{Nitrate of bismuth.}}{2(Bi3NO_3)} + \underset{\text{Nitric oxide.}}{2NO} + \underset{\text{Water.}}{4H_2O}$$

The solution evaporated gives crystals ($Bi3NO_3, 5H_2O$), any arsenicum which the bismuth might contain remaining in the mother-liquor. Native bismuth (*Bismuthum*, B. P. and U. S. P.) commonly contains arsenicum, most of which is removed by roasting or by fusing two or three times with a tenth of its weight of nitre (*Bismuthum Purificatum*, B. P.), or, finally, by converting the metal into oxynitrate, as described in the next reaction, and reducing this with charcoal at a high temperature.

To make *nitrate* of bismuth and other salts on a larger scale, 2 ounces of the metal, in small fragments, are gradually added to a mixture of 4 fluidounces of nitric acid and 3 of water, and when effervescence (due to escape of nitric oxide) has ceased, the mixture heated for ten minutes, poured off from any insoluble matter, evaporated to 2 fluidounces to remove excess of acid, and then either set aside for *crystals* to form, poured into half a gallon of water to form the *oxynitrate* of bismuth, or into a solution of 6 ounces of carbonate of ammonium in a quart of water to form the *oxycarbonate* as described in the following reactions. The precipitates should be washed with cold water and dried at a temperature not exceeding 150° F. Exposed in the moist state to 212° for any length of time, they undergo slight decomposition.

Subnitrate or Oxynitrate of Bismuth.

Second Synthetical Reaction.—Pour some of the above solution into a considerable quantity of water; decomposition occurs and oxynitrate of bismuth ($BiONO_3$) in a hydrous state ($BiONO_3, H_2O$) (*Bismuthi Subnitras*, B. P.) is precipitated:—

$$\underset{\text{Nitrate of bismuth.}}{Bi3NO_3} + \underset{\text{Water.}}{H_2O} = \underset{\text{Oxynitrate of bismuth.}}{BiONO_3} + \underset{\text{Nitric acid.}}{2HNO_3}$$

Filter, and test the filtrate for bismuth by adding excess of carbonate of sodium; a precipitate shows that some bismuth remains in solution. The following equation, therefore, probably more nearly represents the decomposition:—

$$\underset{\text{Nitrate of bismuth.}}{5(Bi3NO_3)} + \underset{\text{Water.}}{8H_2O} = \underset{\text{Oxynitrate of bismuth.}}{4(BiONO_3, H_2O)} + \underset{\text{Nitrate of bismuth in acid.}}{Bi3NO_3, 8HNO_3}$$

Decomposition of nitrate of bismuth by water is the process of the British Pharmacopœia for the preparation of oxynitrate or "subnitrate" of bismuth for use in medicine. For this purpose the original metal must contain no arsenicum. In manufacturing the compound, therefore, before pouring the solution of nitrate into water, the liquid should be tested for arsenicum by one of the hydrogen tests; if that element be present, the solution must be evaporated and only the deposited crystals be used in the preparation of the oxynitrate. For on pouring an arsenical solution of nitrate of bismuth into water, the arsenicum is not wholly removed in the supernatant liquid, unless the oxynitrate be redissolved and reprecipitated several times, according to the amount of arsenicum present.

In the United States Pharmacopœia the solution of nitrate (made from washed carbonate) is directed to be poured into dilute solution of ammonia. Such a product will probably contain more oxhydrate than oxynitrate.

Subnitrate of Bismuth is sometimes administered in the form of a lozenge (*Trochisci Bismuthi*, B. P.). It is used as a cosmetic under the name of *Pearl-white* (*Blanc de Perle*).

Oxysalts of Bismuth.—It will be noticed that the formula for subnitrate of bismuth ($BiNO_4$) does not accord with that of other nitrates, the characteristic elements of which are NO_3. Analogy would seem to indicate, however, that the fourth atom of oxygen has different functions to the three in the NO_3; for on pouring solution of chloride of bismuth ($BiCl_3$) into water, oxychloride is produced

($BiOCl$) (a white powder used as a cosmetic, also in enamels, and in some varieties of sealing-wax). The bromide ($BiBr_3$) and iodide (BiI_3) similarly yield oxybromide ($BiOBr$) and oxyiodide ($BiOI$). The subnitrate ($BiNO_4$) is, therefore, probably an analogous compound, an oxynitrate ($BiONO_3$). The sulphate (Bi_23SO_4) also decomposes when placed in water, giving what may be termed an oxysulphate ($Bi_2O_2SO_4$).

Subcarbonate or Oxycarbonate of Bismuth.

Third Synthetical Reaction.—To solution of nitrate of bismuth add carbonate of ammonium; a white precipitate of hydrous oxycarbonate ($2Bi_2O_2CO_3$, H_2O) (*Bismuthi Carbonas*, B. P.) falls.

$2(Bi3NO_3)$	+ $3Am_2CO_3$	= $6AmNO_3$	+ $Bi_2O_2CO_3$	+ $2CO_2$
Nitrate of bismuth.	Carbonate of ammonium.	Nitrate of ammonium.	Oxycarbonate of bismuth.	Carbonic acid gas.

According to the United States Pharmacopœia the oxycarbonate (*Bismuthi Subcarbonas*) is made by precipitating with carbonate of sodium a solution of the nitrate prepared from washed hydrate of bismuth.

This compound may be regarded as similar in constitution to the oxysalts just described. In Bi_2CO_5 one scarcely recognizes the characteristic elements of carbonates; but considering the preparation to be an oxycarbonate ($Bi_2O_2CO_3$) its relations to carbonates and oxides are evident. These subsalts may all be viewed as normal bismuth salts in which an atom of oxygen replaces an equivalent proportion of other acidulous atoms or radicals:—

Chloride	$Bi3Cl$	Oxychloride .	$BiOCl$
Bromide	$Bi3Br$	Oxybromide .	$BiOBr$
Iodide	$Bi3I$	Oxyiodide . .	$BiOI$
Nitrate	$Bi3NO_3$	Oxynitrate .	$BiONO_3$
Sulphate	Bi_23SO_4	Oxysulphate .	$Bi_2O_2SO_4$
Carbonate (unknown)	Bi_23CO_3	Oxycarbonate	$Bi_2O_2CO_3$

They may be viewed, in short, as salts in process of conversion to oxide; continue the substitution a little further, and each yields oxide of bismuth (Bi_2O_3). They have also been considered to be salts of a hypothetical univalent radical bismuthyl (BiO).

Citrate of Bismuth.

Fourth Synthetical Reaction.—To solution of nitrate of bismuth add citric acid and then solution of ammonia until the precipitate at first formed is redissolved, and the liquid after shaking has a slight ammoniacal odor. The product contains citrate of bismuth dissolved in solution of citrate and nitrate of ammonium. Made with definite quantities of ingredients and an amount of bismuth salt equivalent to the three grains of oxide (Bi_2O_3) in a fluidrachm, the solution forms the *Liquor Bismuthi et Ammoniæ Citratis*, B. P.

(*b*) *Reactions having Analytical Interest* (*Tests*).

First Analytical Reaction.—Through solution of a bismuth salt pass sulphuretted hydrogen; a black precipitate of sulphide of bismuth (Bi_2S_3) falls. Add ammonia (to neutralize acid) and then sulphydrate of ammonium; the precipitate, unlike As_2S_3 and Sb_2S_3, is insoluble.

Second Analytical Reaction.—Concentrate almost any acid solution of a bismuth salt and pour into water; a white salt is precipitated.

This reaction is characteristic of bismuth salts; it has already been amply explained. The precipitate is distinguished from one formed by antimony under similar circumstances, by being insoluble in solution of tartaric acid.

The reader is again advised to trace out the exact nature of each of the foregoing reactions, chiefly by aid of equations or diagrams.

QUESTIONS AND EXERCISES.

327. Enumerate the 15 commoner metals.
328. Mention the 11 rarer metals.
329. Name the sources and official compounds of lithium.
330. Give an equation explanatory of the formation of Citrate of Lithium.
331. What is the strength of *Liquor Lithiæ Effervescens?*
332. On what chemical hypothesis are lithium compounds administered to gouty patients?
333. Describe the relation of lithium to other metals.
334. What is the chief test for lithium?
335. Write a paragraph on strontium, its natural compounds, chemical relations, technical applications, and tests.
336. What are the formulæ and properties of oxalate of cerium?
337. Name the commonest ore of manganese, and give an equation descriptive of its reaction with hydrochloric acid.
338. Explain the formation of permanganate of potassium, employing diagrams or equations.
339. In what manner do the manganates of potassium act as disinfectants?
340. What are the chief tests for manganese?

341. What are the chief uses of the compounds of cobalt?

342. How are salts of cobalt analytically distinguished from those of nickel?

343. Mention an application of nickel in the arts.

344. What is the general color of nickel salts?

345. State the method of preparation of red chromate of potassium.

346. Give the formulæ of red and yellow chromates of potassium.

347. How is red chromate of potassium obtained?

348. Describe the action of sulphuretted hydrogen on acidified solutions of chromates.

349. What is the formula of chrome alum?

350. Mention the chief tests for the chromic radical, and for chromium.

351. How would you detect iron, chromium, and aluminium in a solution?

352. Define the terms tinstone, stream-tin, block-tin, grain-tin, tin-plate.

353. Describe the position occupied by tin in relation to other metals.

354. What is the difference between stannic acid and meta-stannic acid?

355. State the applications of tin in the arts.

356. Mention the chief tests for stannous and stannic salts.

357. Name the best antidote in cases of poisoning by tin solutions.

358. How is gold dust separated from the earthy matter with which it is naturally associated?

359. How much pure gold is contained in English coin, and in jewellers' gold?

360. State the average thickness of gold leaf.

361. What is the weight of a sovereign?

362. Explain the term "fineness" as applied to gold.

363. What effect is produced on gold by hydrochloric, nitric, and nitrohydrochloric acids respectively?

364. By what reagents is metallic gold precipitated from solutions of its salts?

365. How is Purple of Cassius prepared?

366. Whence is platinum obtained?

367. Why are platinum utensils peculiarly adapted for use in chemical laboratories?

368. How is perchloride of platinum prepared?

369. Name the chief tests for platinum.

370. What is "platinum black?"

371. Describe an experiment demonstrative of the large amount of attraction for gases possessed by metallic platinum.

372. How is "spongy platinum" produced?

373. By what process may the metal be recovered from platinum residues?

374. What is *occlusion* in chemistry?

375. In what condition does cadmium occur in nature?

376. By what process may Iodide of Cadmium be prepared? and in what form is it used in medicine?

377. Mention the chief test for cadmium.

378. Distinguish sulphide of cadmium from other sulphides of similar color.

379. How is cadmium separated from zinc?

380. How does bismuth occur in nature?

381. What is the quantivalence of bismuth?

382. Write down equations descriptive of the action of nitric acid on bismuth, and water on nitrate of bismuth.

383. How may pure salts be prepared from bismuth containing arsenicum?

384. Give a diagram of the process for the so-called Carbonate of Bismuth.

385. Write formulæ showing the accordance of the official Subnitrate and Carbonate with the other salts of Bismuth, and with ordinary Nitrates and Carbonates.

386. How is *Liquor Bismuthi et Ammoniæ Citratis* prepared?

387. What are the tests for Bismuth?

Practical Analysis.

Bismuth is the last of the metals whose synthetical or analytical relations are of general interest. The position of the rarer among the common metals, and the influence which either has on the other during the manipulations of analysis, will now be considered. These objects will be best accomplished, and a more intimate acquaintance with all the metals be obtained, by analyzing, or studying the methods of analyzing, solutions containing one or more metallic salts.

Of the following Tables, the first includes directions for the analysis of an aqueous or only slightly acid solution containing but one salt of any of the metals hitherto considered. Here the color of the precipitate or precipitates afforded by a metal under given circumstances must be relied on to a considerable extent in attempting the detection of the various elements.

The second Table is intended as a chart for the analysis of solutions containing salts of more than one of the common and rarer metals. It is simply a compilation from the foregoing reactions—an extension of the scheme for the analysis of salts of the ordinary metals. Hence it often may be altered or varied in arrangement to suit the requirements of the analyst.

The third is a mere outline of the preceding Tables. It gives the position of the metals in relation to each other, and will much aid the memory in recollecting that relation.

TABLE OF SHORT DIRECTIONS FOR THE ANALYSIS OF AN AQUEOUS OR ONLY SLIGHTLY ACID SOLUTION OF ORDINARY SALTS OF ONE OF THE ELEMENTS HITHERTO CONSIDERED—THE COMMON AND RARER METALS.

Add hydrochloric acid.

<table>
<tr><td rowspan="6">Precipitate
Hg(ous) Pb Ag.
Collect, wash, and add AmHO.
Hg ppt., blackened.
Pb ppt., still white.
Ag ppt., dissolved.
Sb and Bi may also be precipitated by HCl, but are dissolved on adding more HCl.</td><td colspan="6">If HCl gave no precipitate the metal is still in the liquid; pass H_2S through the solution.</td></tr>
<tr><td rowspan="5">Precipitate.
Cd Cu Hg(ic) Pb Bi As Sb Sn Au Pt.
Collect, wash, add AmHS.
Insoluble.
Cd, yellow
Cu, Hg(ic), Pb, Bi } black.
Soluble.
As(ous & ic), Sn(ic) } yellow.
Sb, orange
Sn(ous), Au, Pt } black.
Apply special tests for each to the original solution. For these, see the previous pages.</td><td colspan="5">If H_2S gave no precipitate add AmCl, AmHO, and AmHS.</td></tr>
<tr><td rowspan="4">Precipitate
Zn Mn Co Ni Al Fe Cr.
Zn, Al } white.
Cr, green.
Mn, skin-tint.
Ni, Co, Fe } black.
Test specially for each in original solution. See previous pages.</td><td colspan="4">If AmHS gave no precipitate add Am_2CO_3</td></tr>
<tr><td colspan="2">Precipitate
Ba Sr Ca.
Collect, wash, dissolve in $HC_2H_3O_2$, add K_2CrO_4.</td><td colspan="2">If Am_2CO_3 gave no precipitate add Am_2HAsO_4.</td></tr>
<tr><td rowspan="2">Ppt.
Ba.</td><td>Sol.
Sr Ca.
Add dil. H_2SO_4.</td><td rowspan="2">Ppt.
Mg.</td><td rowspan="2">If no precipitate, test original solution in flame on loop of Pt. wire.
L, crimson.
Na, yellow.
K, violet.
If neither, test orig. sol. for Am.</td></tr>
<tr><td>Ppt. Sol.
Sr.—Ca.</td></tr>
</table>

OUTLINE OF THE PRECEDING TABLES.

HCl	H_2S		AmHS		Am_2CO_3	Am_2HAsO_4	
Hg (as mercurous salt)	Cd	Insoluble in AmHS.	Zn	Hydrates soluble in AmHO.	Ba	Mg	K
	Cu						
Pb (some)	Hg (as mercuric salt)		Mn		Sr		Na
			Co		Ca		Am
Ag	Pb (a little)						
	Bi		Ni				
	As (as arsenious or arsenic salt)	Soluble in AmHS.	Al	Hydrates insol. in AmHO.			L
			Fe				
	Sb						
	Sn (as stannous or stannic salt)		Cr				
	Au						
	Pt						

The laboratory student should practise the examination of aqueous solutions of salts of the above metals until able to analyze with facility and accuracy.

Memoranda relating to the preceding Analytical Tables.

General Memoranda.

These charts are constructed for the analysis of salts more or less soluble in water.——The student has still to learn how substances insoluble in water are to be brought into a state of solution; but, once dissolved, their analysis is effected by the same scheme as that just given. The second Table may therefore be regarded as fairly representing the method by which metallic constituents of chemical substances are separated from each other and recognized.——The methods of isolation of the complementary constituent of the salt (the reactions of non-metals and acidulous radicals) will form the next object of practical study.

The group-tests adopted in the Tables are, obviously, hydrochloric acid, sulphuretted hydrogen, sulphydrate of ammonium, carbonate of ammonium, and arseniate of ammonium. If a group-test produces no precipitate, it is self-evident that there can be no member of the group present. At first, therefore, add only a small quantity of a group-test, and if it produces no effect add no more; for it is not advisable to overload a solution with useless reagents; substances expected to come down as precipitates are not unfrequently held in the liquid by excess of acid, alkali, or strong aqueous solution of some group reagent, thoughtlessly added. Indeed, experienced manipulators not unfrequently make preliminary trials with group-reagents on a few drops only of the liquid under examination; if a precipitate is produced, it is added to the bulk of the original liquid and the addition of the group-reagent continued; if a precipitate is not produced, the few drops are thrown away and the unnecessary addition of a group-reagent thus avoided altogether, an advantage fully making up for the extra trouble of making a preliminary trial.—— While shunning excess, however, care must be taken to avoid deficiency; a substance only partially removed from solution through the addition of an insufficient amount of a reagent will appear where not expected, be consequently mistaken for something else, and cause much trouble; this will not occur if the appearance, odor, or reaction of the liquid on test-paper be duly observed. It is also a good plan, when a group-reagent has produced a precipitate and the latter has been filtered out, to add a little more of the reagent to the clear filtrate; if more precipitate is produced, an insufficient amount of the group-test was introduced in the first instance; but the error is corrected by simply refiltering; if no precipitate occurs, the mind is satisfied and the way cleared for further operations.

Group-precipitates, or any precipitates still requiring examination, should, as a rule, be well washed before further testing; this is to remove the aqueous solution of other substances adhering to the precipitate (the mother-liquor as it is termed), so that subsequent reactions may take place fairly between the reagent used and the precipitate only.——A precipitate is sometimes in so fine a state of division as to retard filtration by clogging the pores of the paper, or even to pass through the filter altogether; in these cases the mixture may be warmed or boiled, which usually causes aggregation of the particles of a precipitate, and hence facilitates the passage of liquids.

Division of Work.—It is immaterial whether a solution be first divided into group-precipitates or each precipitate be examined as soon as produced; if the former method be adopted, confusion will be avoided by labelling or marking the funnels or papers holding the precipitate "the HCl ppt.," "the H_2S ppt.," and so on.

The colors and general appearance of the various sulphides and hydrates precipitated should be borne in mind, as the absence of other bodies, as well as the presence of those thrown down, is often at once thus indicated. For example, if a precipitate by sulphydrate of ammonium is white, neither cobalt, nickel, nor iron can be present, and only small quantities of manganese and chromium.

Application of confirmatory tests must be frequent.

Results of analyses should be recorded neatly in a memorandum-book.

The various reactions which occur in an analysis have already come before the reader in going through the tests for the individual metals or in other analytical operations, it is unnecessary, therefore, again to draw out equations or diagrams. But the reactions should be thought over, and, if not perfectly clear to the mind, be written out again and again till thoroughly understood.

Special Memoranda.

The hydrochloric-acid precipitate may at first include some antimony and bismuth as oxychlorides, readily dissolved, however, by excess of acid.——If either of these elements be present the washings of the precipitate will probably be milky; in that case add a few drops of hydrochloric acid, which will clear the liquid and make way for the application of the test for lead.

The sulphuretted-hydrogen precipitate may be white, in which case it is nothing but sulphur; for, as already indicated, ferric salts are reduced to ferrous, and chromates to the lower salts of chromium by sulphuretted hydrogen, sulphur being deposited:—

$$2Fe_2Cl_6 + 2H_2S = 4FeCl_2 + 4HCl + S_2;$$
$$4H_2CrO_4 + 6H_2S + 12HCl = 2Cr_2Cl_6 + 16H_2O + 3S_2.$$

The proportion of the sulphuretted-hydrogen precipitate dissolved by sulphydrate of ammonium may include a trace of copper, sulphide of copper being not altogether insoluble in sulphydrate of ammonium.——On adding hydrochloric acid to the sulphydrate-of-ammonium solution, a white precipitate of sulphur only may be precipitated, the sulphydrate of ammonium nearly always containing free sulphur.——Carbonate of ammonium does not readily dissolve small quantities of sulphide of arsenicum out of much sulphide of antimony; and, on the other hand, carbonate of ammonium takes into solution a small quantity of sulphide of antimony if much sulphide of arsenicum is present. The original solution should therefore always be examined by the hydrogen tests for arsenicum and antimony if any doubt exists concerning the presence or absence of either. Tin remains in the hydrogen-bottle in the metallic state, deposited as a black powder on the zinc used in the experiment. The contents of the bottle are turned out into a dish, ebullition continued until evolution of hydrogen ceases, and the zinc is taken up by the excess of sulphuric acid employed; any tin is then filtered out, washed, dissolved in a few drops of hydrochloric acid, and the liquid tested for tin by the usual reagents.

The portion of the sulphuretted-hydrogen precipitate not dissolved by the sulphydrate of ammonium may leave a yellow semi-fused globule of sulphur on boiling with nitric acid. This globule may be black, not only from presence of mercuric sulphide, but also from inclosed particles of other sulphides protected by the sulphur from the action of the acid. It may also contain sulphate of lead, produced by the action of nitric acid on sulphide of lead. In cases of doubt the mass must be removed from the liquid, boiled with nitric acid till dissolved, the solution evaporated to remove excess of acid, and the residue examined; but usually it may be disregarded. ——In testing for lead by sulphuric acid the liquid should be diluted and set aside for some time.

Mercury may also be isolated by digesting the sulphuretted-hydrogen precipitate in sulphydrate of sodium instead of sulphydrate of ammonium. The sulphides of arsenicum, antimony, tin, and mercury are thus dissolved out. The mixture is then filtered, excess of hydrochloric acid added to it, and the precipitated sulphides collected on a filter, washed, and digested in sulphydrate of ammonium; sulphide of mercury remains insoluble, while the sulphides of arsenicum, antimony, and tin are dissolved. By this method copper also appears in its right place only, sulphide of copper being quite insoluble in sulphydrate of sodium. The other metals are then separated in the usual way.

The sulphydrate-of-ammonium precipitate may, if the original solution was acid, contain Phosphates, Oxalates, Silicates, and Borates of Barium, Calcium, and Magnesium. These will subsequently come out with the iron, and, being white, give the iron precipitate a light-colored appearance; their examination must be conducted separately, by a method described subsequently in connection with the treatment of substances insoluble in water.——Precipitates containing aluminium, iron, and chromium often carry down some manganese, which afterwards comes out with the iron. This manganese may be detected by washing the ferric hydrate to remove all trace of chlorides, boiling with nitric acid, adding puce-colored oxide of lead, and setting the vessel aside; permanganic acid is formed, recognized in the clear liquid by its purple tint.——Sulphide of nickel is not easily removed by filtration (vide p. 191) until most of the excess of sulphydrate of ammonium has been dissipated by prolonged ebullition.

The carbonate-of-ammonium precipitate may not contain the whole of the barium, strontium, and calcium in the mixture, unless free ammonia be present; for the carbonates of those metals are soluble in water charged with carbonic acid. If, therefore, the liquid is not distinctly ammoniacal, solution of ammonia should be added. ——Neither carbonate nor hydrate of ammonium wholly precipitates magnesian salts; and as a partial precipitation is undesirable, a solvent, in the form of an alkaline salt (chloride of ammonium), if not already in the liquid, should be added.

Lithium.—The search for lithium may usually be omitted. Should a precipitate, supposed to be due to lithium, be obtained, it must be tested in a flame (= scarlet tint), as a little magnesium not unfrequently shows itself under similar circumstances.

Spectral Analysis.—If present only in minute proportions, the lithium may also remain with the alkalies; it can then only be detected by physical analysis (by a prism) of the light emitted from a tinged flame—by, in short, an instrument termed a spectroscope. Such a method of examination is called spectral analysis, a subject of much interest and of no great difficulty, but scarcely within the range of Pharmaceutical Chemistry; it will be briefly described in connection with the methods of analyzing solid substances.

QUESTIONS AND EXERCISES.

388. Describe a general method of analysis by which the metal of a single salt in a solution could be quickly detected.

389. Give illustrations of black, white, light pink, yellow, and orange sulphides.

390. Mention the group-tests generally employed in analysis.

391. Under what circumstances may a hydrochloric precipitate contain antimony or bismuth?

392. If a sulphuretted-hydrogen precipitate is white, what substances are indicated?

393. Give processes for the qualitative analysis of liquids containing the following substances:—

a. Arsenicum and Cadmium.
b. Bismuth and Antimony.
c. Ferrous and Ferric salts.
d. Aluminium, Iron, and Chromium.
e. Arsenicum, Antimony, and Tin.
f. Lead and Strontium.
g. Iron and Phosphate of Calcium.
h. Mercury, Manganese, and Magnesium.
i. Zinc, Manganese, Nickel, and Cobalt.
j. Barium, Strontium, and Calcium.

THE ACIDULOUS RADICALS.

Introduction.—The twenty-six radicals which have up to this point mainly occupied attention are (admitting ammonium, NH_4) metals; and they have been almost exclusively studied not in the free state, but in the condition in which they exist in salts. Moreover these metals have been treated as if they formed the more important constituent, the stronger half, the foundation or base, of salts. Attention has been continuously directed to the metallic or *basylous* side of salts. There is, indeed, still one more basylous radical worthy of a passing notice, though it usually is supposed to play only a subordinate part in reactions—Hydrogen. Unlike the salts of most metals, those of hydrogen are never, in medicine or the arts generally, professedly used for the sake of their hydrogen, but always for the other half of the salt, the *acidulous* side. And it is not for their basylous radical that these hydrogen salts are now commended to notice,* but in order to study, under the most favorable circumstances, those acidulous groupings which have continually presented themselves in operations on salts, but which were for the time of secondary importance. They may now be treated as the primary object of attention; and there is no better way of doing so than in operating on their compounds with hydrogen, the relatively inferior medicinal importance of which element, as compared with potassium, iron, and other basylous radicals, will serve to give the desired prominence to the *acidulous radicals* in question.

Common Acids.—These salts of hydrogen are the ordinary, sharp, sour bodies termed *acids* (from the Latin root *acies*, an edge). The following Table includes the formulæ and names of the most important; others will be noticed subsequently. A few of those mentioned are unstable or somewhat rare; in such cases a common metallic salt containing the acidulous radical may be used for reactions.

* It must not be forgotten that the commonest salt of any radical whatsoever is a salt of hydrogen, the oxide of hydrogen (H_2O), or hydrate of hydrogen (HHO), *water*. In the reactions already performed, the value of this compound has been constantly recognized, both for its hydrogen and for its oxygen, but most of all as the vehicle or medium by which nearly all other atoms are enabled to come into that contact with each other without which their existence would be almost useless; for some atoms are like some animals, out of water they are as inactive as fishes. It is true that both fishes and salts have usually to be removed from water to be utilized by man; but before they can be assimilated, either as food or as medicine, they must again seek the agency of water—become dissolved.

HCl	hydrochloric acid.
HBr	hydrobromic acid.
HI	hydriodic acid.
HCN (HCy)	hydrocyanic acid.
HNO_3	nitric acid.
$HClO_3$	chloric acid.
$HC_2H_3O_2$	acetic acid.*
H_2S	hydrosulphuric acid †.
H_2SO_3	sulphurous acid.
H_2SO_4	sulphuric acid.
H_2CO_3?	carbonic acid.
$H_2C_2O_4$	oxalic acid.
$H_2C_4H_4O_6$	tartaric acid.
$H_3C_6H_5O_7$	citric acid.
H_3PO_4	phosphoric acid.
H_3BO_3	boracic acid.

A prominent point of difference will at once be noticed between the basylous radicals met with up to the present time and the acidulous groupings included in the above tabular list. The former are nearly all elements, ammonium only being a compound; the latter are mostly compounds, chlorine, bromine, iodine, and sulphur being the only elements. This difference will not, however, be so apparent when the chemistry of alcohols, ethers, and such bodies has been mastered, for they are all salts of *compound* basylous radicals.

Rarer Acids.—The above acids contain the only acidulous groupings that commonly present themselves in analysis, or in pharmaceutical operations. There are, however, several other acids (such as hypochlorous, nitrous, hypophosphorous, valerianic, benzoic, gallic, tannic, uric, hyposulphurous, hydroferrocyanic, hydroferridcyanic, and lactic) with which it is desirable to be more or less familiar; reactions concerning these will therefore be described. Arsenious, arsenic, stannic, manganic, and chromic acids have already been treated of in connection with the metals they contain; in practical analysis they always become sufficiently altered to come out among the metals.

Quantivalence.—A glance at the foregoing Table is sufficient to show the quantivalence of the acidulous radicals. The first seven

* The hydrogen on the acidulous side must not be confounded with the basylous hydrogen in all these hydrogen salts or acids; the two perform entirely different functions. Hydrogen in the acidulous portion is like the hydrogen in the basylous radical ammonium, it has combined with other atoms, to form a group which plays more or less the part of an elementary radical, and to which a single symbol is not unfrequently applied (Am; Cy, $\overline{A}$, $\overline{O}$, $\overline{T}$, $\overline{C}$, &c.). Cobalt, chromium, iron, platinum, &c. resemble hydrogen in this respect in often uniting with other atoms to form definite acidulous radicals, in which the usual basylous character of the metals has for the time disappeared. In *hydrides* (p. 92) hydrogen itself is an acidulous radical.

† Synonyms: sulphydric acid and sulphuretted hydrogen.

are clearly univalent; then follow six bivalent, leaving three trivalent.

These all combine with equivalent amounts of basylous radicals to form various salts; hence they may be termed monobasylous, dibasylous, and tribasylous radicals. The acids themselves were formerly spoken of as monobasic, dibasic, and tribasic respectively, or monobasic and polybasic, in reference to the amount of *base* (hydrates or oxides) they could decompose; but the terms are no longer definite, and hence but little used in mineral chemistry.

Analysis.—The practical study of the acidulous side of salts will occupy far less time than the basylous. Salts will then be briefly examined as a whole.

One word of caution. It is only for convenience in the division of chemistry for systematic study that salts may be considered to contain basylous and acidulous radicals, or separate sides, so to speak; for we possess no absolute knowledge of the internal arrangement of the atoms (admitting that there are such things) in the molecule of a salt. We only know that certain groups of atoms may be transferred from compound to compound in mass (that is, without apparent decomposition); hence the assumption that these groups are radicals. A salt is probably, however, a whole, having no such sides as those mentioned.

QUESTIONS AND EXERCISES.

394. Mention the basylous radical of acids.

395. Give illustrations of univalent, bivalent, and trivalent acidulous radicals, and monobasylous, dibasylous, and tribasylous salts.

396. What is the difference between an elementary and a compound acidulous radical?

397. Name the grounds on which salts may be assumed to contain basylous and acidulous radicals.

HYDROCHLORIC ACID AND OTHER CHLORIDES.

Formula of hydrochloric acid HCl. Molecular weight* 36.5.

The acidulous radical of hydrochloric acid and of other chlorides is the element chlorine (Cl). It occurs in nature chiefly as chloride of sodium (NaCl), either solid, under the name of *rock-salt*, mines of which are not unfrequently met with, or in solution in the water of all seas. Common table-salt is more or less pure chloride of sodium in minute crystals. Chlorine, like hydrogen, is univalent (Cl′); its atomic weight is 35.5. Its molecule is symbolized thus, Cl_2, chloride of chlorine.

* The weight of a molecule is the sum of the weights of its atoms.

Reactions.

Hydrochloric Acid.

First Synthetical Reaction.—To a few fragments of chloride of sodium in a test-tube or small flask add about an equal weight of sulphuric acid; colorless and invisible gaseous hydrochloric acid is evolved, a sulphate of sodium remaining. Adapt to the mouth of the vessel, by a perforated cork, a piece of glass tubing bent to a right angle, heat the mixture, and convey the gas into a small bottle containing a little water; solution of hydrochloric acid results.

$$\underset{\text{Chloride of sodium.}}{NaCl} + \underset{\text{Sulphuric acid.}}{H_2SO_4} = \underset{\text{Hydrochloric acid.}}{HCl} + \underset{\text{Acid sulphate of sodium.}}{NaHSO_4}$$

Hydrochloric Acid.—The product of this operation is the nearly colorless and very sour liquor commonly termed hydrochloric acid. When of certain given strengths (estimated by volumetric analysis) it forms *Acidum Hydrochloricum*, B. P. and U. S. P., and *Acidum Hydrochloricum Dilutum*, B. P. (and U. S. P., specific gr. 1.038). The former has a specific gravity of 1.16 (1.1578), and contains 31.8 per cent. of real acid, the latter specific gravity 1.052, with 10.58 per cent. of real acid, and is made by diluting 8 fluid parts of the strong acid with water until the mixture measures 26½ fluid parts. The above process is that of the Pharmacopœias—larger vessels being employed, and the gas being freed from any trace of sulphuric acid by washing. Other chlorides yield hydrochloric acid when heated with sulphuric acid; but chloride of sodium is always used because cheap and common. The acid is a by-product in the manufacture of carbonate of sodium from common salt, a process in which the chloride of sodium is first converted into sulphate, hydrochloric acid being liberated.

The official (B. P.) *process* is as follows:—

"Take of chloride of sodium, dried, 48 ounces, sulphuric acid 44 fluidounces, water 36 fluidounces, distilled water 50 fluidounces; pour the sulphuric acid slowly into thirty-two ounces of the water, and, when the mixture has cooled, add it to the chloride of sodium previously introduced into a flask having the capacity of at least one gallon. Connect the flask by corks and a bent glass tube with a three-necked wash-bottle, furnished with a safety tube, and containing the remaining four ounces of the water; then, applying heat to the flask, conduct the disengaged gas through the wash-bottle into a second bottle containing the distilled water, by means of a bent tube dipping about half an inch below the surface, and let the process be continued until the product measures sixty-six ounces, or the liquid has acquired a specific gravity of 1.16. The bottle containing the distilled water must be kept cool during the whole operation."

Invisible gaseous hydrochloric acid forms visible grayish-white fumes on coming into contact with air. This is due to combination with the moisture of the air. The intense greediness of hydrochloric gas and water for each other is strikingly demonstrated on opening a test-tube full of the gas under water; the latter rushes into and instantly fills the tube. If the water is tinged with blue litmus, the acid character of the gas is prettily shown at the same time. The test-tube, which should be perfectly dry, may be filled from the delivery-tube direct; for the gas is somewhat heavier than, and therefore readily displaces, air. The mouth may be closed by the thumb of the operator.

Note.—The process, as described in the British Pharmacopœia, includes the use of as much sulphuric acid as is theoretically necessary for the production of acid sulphate of sodium ($NaHSO_4$) which remains in the generating vessel. A hot solution of this residue carefully neutralized by carbonate of sodium, filtered and set aside, yields normal sulphate (*Sodæ Sulphas*, B. P. and U. S. P.), in the form of transparent oblique efflorescent prisms ($Na_2SO_4, 10H_2O$).

$$2NaHSO_4 + Na_2CO_3 = 2Na_2SO_4 + H_2O + CO_2$$

$2NaHSO_4$	Na_2CO_3	$2Na_2SO_4$	H_2O	CO_2
Acid sulphate of sodium.	Carbonate of sodium.	Sulphate of sodium.	Water.	Carbonic acid gas.

Chlorine.

Second Synthetical Reaction.—To some drops of hydrochloric acid (that is, the common aqueous solution of the gas) add a few grains of black oxide of manganese, and warm the mixture; *chlorine*, the acidulous radical of all chlorides, is evolved, and may be recognized by its peculiar odor, or irritating effect on the nose and air-passages.

$$4HCl + MnO_2 = Cl_2 + 2H_2O + MnCl_2$$

Chlorine-water.—This is the process of the Pharmacopœias for the production of chlorine-water (*Liquor Chlori*, B. P., *Aqua Chlorinii*, U. S. P.), the gas being first washed and then passed into water. Six fluidounces of hydrochloric acid diluted with two ounces of water, and the gas passed through a wash-bottle containing about two ounces of water, yield enough chlorine to produce about a pint and a half of chlorine water. On the small scale, less than half the acid is utilized through incomplete decomposition and incomplete absorption of the chlorine gas. Chlorine slowly decomposes water with production of hydrochloric acid; it is best preserved in a green-glass well-stoppered bottle in a cool and dark place.

Note.—To obtain the chlorine from other chlorides, sulphuric acid, as well as black oxide of manganese, must be added. Hydrochloric acid is first formed. The action described in the above equation then goes on, except that half instead of the whole of the oxygen of the black oxide is available for the removal of the hydrogen from the chlorine of the hydrochloric acid, the other half being taken up by the hydrogen of the sulphuric acid. Thus, supposing common salt to be the chloride used, the following equations may represent the supposed steps of the process:—

$$2NaCl + H_2SO_4 = Na_2SO_4 + 2HCl,$$
$$MnO_2 + H_2SO_4 = MnSO_4 + H_2O + O;$$
$$\text{then the } 2HCl + O = H_2O + Cl_2;$$

or the whole may be included in one equation:

$$2NaCl + MnO_2 + 2H_2SO_4 = Na_2SO_4 + MnSO_4 + 2H_2O + Cl_2.$$

This reaction may have occasional analytical interest, a very small quantity of combined chlorine being recognized by its means. But the following reaction is nearly always applicable for the detection of this element, and leaves nothing to be desired in point of delicacy.

Analytical Reaction (Test).

To a drop of hydrochloric acid, or to a dilute solution of any other chloride, add solution of nitrate of silver; a white curdy precipitate falls. Pour off most of the supernatant liquid, add nitric acid, and boil; the precipitate does not dissolve. Pour off the acid, and add ammonia; the precipitate quickly dissolves. Neutralize the solution by an acid, chloride of silver is once more precipitated.

The formation of this white precipitate, its appearance, insolubility in boiling nitric acid, solubility in ammonia, and reprecipitation by an acid, form abundant evidence of the presence of chlorine. Its occurrence as a chloride of a metal is determined by testing for the metal with the appropriate reagents; its occurrence as hydrochloric acid is considered to be indicated by the odor, if strong, and the sour taste, if weak, of the liquid, and the action of the liquid on the litmus paper, which, like other acids, it reddens. If hydrochloric acid be present in excessive quantity it will, in addition to the above reactions, give rise to strong effervescence on the addition of a carbonate, a chloride being formed. The chlorine in insoluble chlorides, such as calomel, "white precipitate," &c., may be detected by boiling with caustic potash, filtering, acidulating the filtrate by nitric acid, and then adding the nitrate of silver.

Antidotes.—In cases of poisoning by strong hydrochloric acid, solution of carbonate of sodium (common washing-soda) or a mixture of magnesia and water may be administered as an antidote.

QUESTIONS AND EXERCISES.

398. A specimen of official Hydrochloric Acid contains 31.8 per cent. by weight of gas, and its specific gravity is 1.16; work out a sum showing what volume of it will be required, theoretically, to mix with black oxide of manganese for the production of one gallon of chlo-

rine-water, one fluidounce of which contains 2.66 grains of chlorine. Ans. 5½ fluidounces, nearly,

399. Why does hydrochloric acid gas give visible fumes on coming into contact with air?

400. How much chloride of sodium will be required to furnish one pound of chlorine?

401. Give the analytical reactions of chlorides.

402. What antidotes may be administered in cases of poisoning by hydrochloric acid?

HYDROBROMIC ACID AND OTHER BROMIDES.

Formula of Hydrobromic Acid HBr. Molecular weight 81.

Bromine. Source, Preparation, and Properties.—The acidulous radical of hydrobromic acid and other bromides is the element bromine, Br (*Bromum*, B. P., *Brominium*, U. S. P.). It occurs in nature chiefly as bromide of magnesium in sea-water and certain saline springs. It may be liberated from its compounds by the process for chlorine from chlorides—that is, by heating with black oxide of manganese and sulphuric acid. It is a dark-red volatile liquid, emitting an odor more irritating, if possible, than chlorine—of specific gravity 2.966, boiling-point 117°.

Quantivalence.—The atom of bromine, like that of chlorine, is univalent (Br'); its atomic weight is 80. Free bromine has the molecular formula Br_2, bromide of bromine.

Hydrobromic Acid.—The bromide of hydrogen, hydrobromic acid, is made by decomposing bromide of phosphorus by water—$PBr_5 + 4H_2O = 5HBr + H_3PO_4$.

Bromide of Potassium (KBr) is occasionally employed in pharmacy, and is the salt, therefore, which may be used in studying the reactions of this acidulous radical. The official method of making the salt has been alluded to under the salts of potassium (page 52).

Other bromides are seldom used; they may be prepared in the same way as, and closely resemble, the corresponding chlorides or iodides.

Bromide of Ammonium (AmBr) (*Ammonii Bromidum*, B. P.) may be made by saturating hydrobromic acid with ammonia: $HBr + NH_4HO = NH_4Br + H_2O$. It forms colorless crystals which become slightly yellow on exposure to air, is readily soluble in water, less so in spirit, and, when heated, sublimes.

Solution of Bromine, B. P., 10 minims in 5 ounces, is an aqueous solution, bromine being slightly soluble in water.

Hypobromites, Bromates, Perbromates, analogous to hypochlorites, chlorates, and perchlorates, are producible.

Analytical Reactions (Tests).

First Analytical Reaction.—To a few drops of solution of a bromide (KBr, or NH_4Br) add solution of nitrate of silver; a yellowish-white precipitate of bromide of silver ($AgBr$) falls. Treat the precipitate successively with nitric acid and ammonia, as described for the chloride of silver; it is only sparingly dissolved by the ammonia.

Second Analytical Reaction.—To solution of a bromide add a drop or two of chlorine-water, or a bubble or two of chlorine gas; then add a few drops of chloroform or ether, shake the mixture, and set the test-tube aside; the chlorine, from the greater strength of its affinities, liberates the bromine, which is dissolved by the chloroform or ether, the solution falling to the bottom of the tube in the case of the heavy chloroform, or rising to the top in the case of the light ether. Either solution has a distinct yellow, or reddish-yellow or red color, according to the amount of bromine present.

Notes.—This reaction serves for the isolation of bromine when mixed with many other substances. Excess of chlorine must be avoided, as colorless chloride of bromine is then formed. Iodides give a somewhat similar result; the absence of iodine must therefore be insured by a process given in the next section. The above solution in chloroform or ether may be removed from the tube by drawing up into a *pipette* (small pipe, a narrow glass tube, usually having a bulb or expanded portion in the centre) the bromine fixed by the addition of a drop of solution of potash or soda, the chloroform or ether evaporated off, and the residue tested as described in the next reaction.

The above operation is frequently employed for synthetical purposes.

Third Analytical Reaction.—Liberate bromine from a bromide by the cautious addition of chlorine or chlorine-water, then add a few drops of cold decoction of starch; a yellow combination of bromine and starch, commonly termed "bromide of starch," is formed.

Decoction of starch is made by rubbing down two or three grains of starch with some drops of cold water, then adding much more water and boiling the mixture.

The above reaction may be varied by liberating the bromine by a little black oxide of manganese and a drop of sulphuric acid, the upper part of the inside of the test-tube being smeared over with some thick decoction of starch or thin starch-paste.

HYDRIODIC ACID AND OTHER IODIDES.

Formula of Hydriodic Acid HI. Molecular weight 128.

Source.—The acidulous radical of hydriodic acid and other iodides is the element iodine (I). It occurs in nature chiefly as iodide of sodium and of magnesium in sea-water. Seaweeds, sponges, and other marine organisms, which derive much of their nourishment from sea-water, store up iodides in their tissues, and it is from the ashes of these that supplies of iodine (*Iodum*, B. P., *Iodinium*, U. S. P.) are obtained.

Process.—Iodine is liberated from iodides as bromine from bromides, or chlorine from chlorides—namely, by the action of black oxide of manganese and sulphuric acid.

Properties.—Iodine is a crystalline purplish-black substance; its vapor, readily seen on heating a fragment in a test-tube, is dark violet. Its vapors are irritating to the lungs; but a trace may be inhaled with safety (*Vapor Iodi*, B. P.). It melts at 239°, boils at about 392°, and is entirely volatilized, the first portions containing any cyanide of iodine that may be present. The latter body occurs in slender colorless prisms, emitting a pungent odor.

Quantivalence. The atom of iodine, like those of bromine and chlorine, is univalent* (I′); its atomic weight is 127, its molecular formula I_2.

The Iodide of Hydrogen, or Hydriodic Acid, is a heavy, colorless gas. Its solution in water (*Acidum Hydriodicum Dilutum*, U. S. P.) is made by passing sulphuretted hydrogen through water in which iodine is suspended, $2H_2S + 2I_2 = S_2 + 4HI$. *Iodide of potassium* (KI) is largely used in medicine, and hence is the most convenient iodide on which to experiment in studying the reactions of this acidulous radical. Solid iodine itself might be taken for the purpose; but its use and action in that state have already been alluded to in describing the iodides of potassium, cadmium, and mercury; its analytical reactions in the combined condition are those which may now occupy attention.

Solution of Iodine.—Iodine is slightly soluble in water (iodine-water), and readily soluble in an aqueous solution of iodide of potassium. Twenty grains of iodine and 30 of iodide of potassium, dissolved in 1 ounce of distilled water, form *Liquor Iodi*, B. P.; *Liquor Iodinii Compositus*, U. S. P., is of the same character and about the same strength; 32 grains of iodine and 32 of iodide of potassium, rubbed with 1 fluidrachm of proof spirit, and 2 ounces of lard gradually mixed in, form *Unguentum Iodi*, B. P. *Unguentum Iodinii Compositum*, U. S. P., and *Unguentum Iodinii*, U. S. P., are similar preparations. It is more soluble in spirit (*Tinctura*

* There is a compound of iodine having the formula ICl_3. Iodine would therefore seem to be a trivalent element (I‴); and bromine and fluorine, from their close chemical analogy with iodine, would necessarily be regarded as trivalent also. From this aspect the position of chlorine would be anomalous.

Iodinii, U. S. P.), or in a spirituous solution of iodide of potassium (*Tinctura Iodi*, B. P., *Tinctura Iodinii Composita*, U. S. P.). It combines with sulphur, forming an unstable grayish-black solid iodide ($S_2 I_2$), having a radiated crystalline structure (*Sulphuris Iodum*, B. P. and U. S. P., and *Unguentum Sulphuris Iodidi*). "If 100 grains be thoroughly boiled with water the iodine will pass off in vapor, and about 20 grains of sulphur remain."—*Brit. Pharm.*

Analytical Reactions (Tests).

First Analytical Reaction.—To a few drops of an aqueous solution of an iodide (*e. g.* KI) add solution of nitrate of silver; a yellowish-white precipitate of iodide of silver (AgI) falls. Pour away the supernatant liquid and treat the precipitate with nitric acid, it is not dissolved; add ammonia, it is only sparingly dissolved.

This reaction is useful in separating iodine from most other acidulous radicals, but does not distinguish iodine from bromine.

Ammonia, it will be remembered, dissolves chloride of silver readily; hence the presence of chloride of potassium in bromide or iodide may be detected by dissolving in water, adding excess of nitrate of silver, collecting the precipitate, washing, digesting in ammonia, filtering and adding excess of nitric acid to the filtrate; a white curdy precipitate indicates a chloride (of potassium).

Second Analytical Reaction.—Liberate iodine from an iodide by the cautious addition of chlorine, then add cold decoction of starch; a deep-blue combination of iodine and starch, commonly termed "iodide of starch," is formed.

Starch is highly sensitive to the action of iodine; this reaction is consequently very delicate and characteristic. Excess of chlorine must be avoided, or colorless chloride of iodine will be produced. Nitrous acid, or a nitrite acidulated with sulphuric acid, may be used instead of chlorine. The reaction is not observed in hot liquids.

In testing bromine for iodine the bromine must be nearly all removed by solution of sulphurous acid before the decoction of starch is added.

Ozone (O_3).—Papers soaked in mucilage of starch containing iodide of potassium, form a test for free chlorine and nitrous acid, and are also employed by meteorologists to detect an allotropic and energetic form of oxygen termed by Schönbein *ozone* (from ὄζω, *ozō*, to smell). This substance liberates iodine from iodide of potassium (with formation of iodide of starch), and is supposed to occur normally in the atmosphere, the salubrity or insalubrity of which is said to be dependent to some extent on the presence or absence of ozone. The possible occurrence of nitrous or chlorinoid gases in the air, however, renders the test untrustworthy. Houzeau proposes to test for ozone by exposing litmus paper of a neutral tint soaked in a dilute solution of iodide of potassium; the potash set free by action of the ozone turns the paper blue. The same paper without iodide would indicate the extent to which the effect might be due to ammonia vapor. Ozone, or rather ozonized air, is produced artificially in large quantities on passing air through a box (Beane's Ozone-generator) highly charged with electricity. Small quantities may be obtained by exposing in a loosely closed bottle a stick of phosphorus partially covered by water. It is a powerful bleaching, disinfecting, and general oxidizing agent; insoluble in water, soluble in oils of turpentine, cinnamon, and some other liquids. From experiments that have been made by Soret on the specific gravity of ozone, its molecular formula would seem to be O_3, that of ordinary oxygen being O_2. Its smell is peculiar.

Third Analytical Reaction.—To a neutral aqueous solution of an iodide add a solution containing one part of sulphate of copper to two parts of green sulphate of iron; a dirty-white precipitate of cuprous iodide (Cu_2I_2) falls.

$$2KI + 2CuSO_4 + 2FeSO_4 = Cu_2I_2 + K_2SO_4 + Fe_23SO_4$$

Separation of Chlorides, Bromides, and Iodides.—Chlorides and bromides are not affected in this way; the reaction is useful, therefore, in removing iodine from a solution in which chlorides and bromides have to be sought. The total removal of iodine by this process is insured by supplementing the addition of the cupric and ferrous sulphate by a few drops of ammonia, any acid which might be keeping cuprous iodide in solution being thereby neutralized, ferric or ferrous hydrate, precipitated at the same time, not affecting the reaction. Chloride of the rare metal palladium performs a similar useful office in removing iodine, but not bromine or chlorine, from solutions. Chlorides may be separated from bromides by taking advantage of the ready solubility of chloride of silver, and almost complete insolubility of bromide of silver in ammonia.

Fourth Analytical Reaction.—Iodides have been shown to be useful in testing for mercuric salts (see the Mercury reactions, p. 155); a mercuric salt (corrosive sublimate, for example) may therefore be used in testing for iodides, a scarlet precipitate of mercuric iodide (HgI_2) being produced.

This reaction may be employed where large quantities of an iodide are present; but its usefulness in analysis is much impaired by the fact that the precipitate is soluble in excess of the dissolved iodide, or in excess of the mercuric reagent. Its color and insolubility in water distinguish it from mercuric chloride, bromide, and cyanide, which are white soluble salts.

Fifth Analytical Reaction.—Iodides have also (see the Lead reactions, p. 172) been shown to be useful in testing for lead salts; similarly a lead salt (acetate, for example) may be used in testing for iodides, a yellow precipitate of iodide of lead (PbI_2), soluble in hot water and crystallizing in yellow scales on cooling, being produced.

Chloride, bromide, and cyanide of lead are white; hence the above reaction may occasionally be useful in distinguishing iodine from the allied radicals. But iodide of lead is slightly soluble in cold water; hence small quantities of iodine cannot be detected by this reaction. (For *Iodates* see p. 244.)

QUESTIONS AND EXERCISES.

403. State the method by which Bromine is obtained from its natural compounds.
404. Mention the properties of bromine.
405. How may the Bromides of Potassium and Ammonium be made?
406. By what reagents may bromides be distinguished from chlorides?
407. Whence is iodine obtained?
408. By what process is iodine isolated?
409. State the properties of iodine.
410. What is the nature of Iodide of Sulphur?
411. Give the analytical reactions of iodides.
412. Which three substances may be detected by a mixture of iodide of potassium and mucilage of starch?
413. Describe a method by which iodides may be removed from a solution containing chlorides and bromides.

HYDROCYANIC ACID AND OTHER CYANIDES.

Formula of Hydrocyanic Acid HNC or HCy.
Molecular weight 27.

History of Cyanogen.—The acidulous radical of hydrocyanic acid and other cyanides is a compound body, cyanogen (Cy). It is so named from κύανος, *kuanos*, blue, and γεννάω, *gennaō*, I generate, in allusion to its prominent chemical character of forming, with iron, the different varieties of Prussian blue. It was from Prussian blue that Scheele, in 1782, first obtained what we now, from our knowledge of its composition, term hydrocyanic acid, but which he called Prussic acid. Cyanogen was isolated by Gay-Lussac in 1814, and was the first compound radical distinctly proved to exist.

Sources.—Cyanogen does not occur in nature, and is only formed from its elements under certain circumstances. It is found in small quantities among the gases of iron-furnaces, and is produced to a slight extent in distilling coals for gas. In the form of ferrocyanide of potassium it is obtained abundantly by heating animal refuse containing nitrogen, such as the scrapings of horns, hoofs, and hides (5 parts) with carbonate of potassium (2 parts) and waste iron (filings, &c.) in a covered iron pot. The residual mass is boiled with water, the mixture filtered, and the filtrate evaporated and set aside for crystals to form. The cyanogen, produced from the carbon and nitrogen of the animal matter, unites with the potassium and then with iron to form what is known as the yellow prussiate of potash (*Potassæ Prussias Flava*, B. P.), or ferrocyanide of potassium ($K'_4Fe''Cy'_6$), (*Potassii Ferrocyanidum*, U. S. P.), a compound occurring in four-sided tabular yellow crystals. It contains the elements of cyanogen, yet it is not a cyanide, for it is not poisonous, and is otherwise different from cyanides; it will be further noticed subsequently. From this salt all cyanides are directly or indirectly prepared.

Cyanide of potassium (KCy), (*Potassii Cyanidum*, U. S. P.), which is the most common, is procured by fusing ferrocyanide of potassium in a crucible; carbonic acid gas (CO_2) is evolved, iron (Fe) is set free, and cyanate of potassium (KCyO), a body that will be subsequently noticed, is formed at the same time :—

$$2K_4FeCy_6 + 2K_2CO_3 = 10KCy + 2KCyO + Fe_2 + 2CO_2.$$

Double cyanides exist, such as the cyanide of sodium and silver (NaCy,AgCy), formed in the process (subsequently described) of quantitatively determining the amount of hydrocyanic acid in a liquid by a standard solution of nitrate of silver: these compounds have, more or less, the properties of their constituents. But other cyanogen compounds, not double cyanides, occur in which the cyanogen is so intimately united with a metal as to form a distinct radical: such are ferrocyanides and ferridcyanides—salts which will be noticed in due course.

Cyanogen, like chlorine, bromine, and iodine, is univalent (Cy'). It may be isolated by simply heating mercuric cyanide ($HgCy_2$) or cyanide of silver (AgCy). It is a colorless gas, burning, when ignited, with a beautiful peach-blossom-colored flame.

Mercuric cyanide is produced in crystals on dissolving 1 part of ferrocyanide of potassium in 15 parts of boiling water, adding 2 parts of mercuric sulphate, keeping the whole hot for ten or fifteen minutes, and then filtering and setting aside to cool. In addition to mercuric cyanide ($HgCy_2$), mercury (Hg), ferric sulphate (Fe_23SO_4) and sulphate of potassium (K_2SO_4), are formed. Any excess of ferrocyanide also gives Prussian blue by reaction with ferric sulphate. It (*Hydrargyri Cyanidum*, U. S. P.) may also be made by dissolving red oxide of mercury in diluted hydrocyanic acid. A small flame of cyanogen may be obtained on heating a few crystals of mercuric cyanide in a short piece of glass tubing closed at one end, and applying a light to the other end as soon as evolution of gas commences.

Reactions.

Diluted Hydrocyanic Acid.

Synthetical Reaction.—Dissolve 2 or 3 grains of ferrocyanide of potassium in 5 or 6 times its weight of water in a test-tube, add a few drops of sulphuric acid and boil the mixture, conveying the evolved gas by a bent glass tube (adapted to the test-tube by a cork) into another test-tube containing a little water; the product is a dilute solution of hydrocyanic acid. Made by this process in large quantities of a certain definite strength (2 per cent.), this solution is the *Acidum Hydrocyanicum Dilutum*, B. P., and U. S. P. "A colorless liquid of a peculiar odor. Specific gravity 0.997."

$$2K_4FeCy_6 + 6H_2SO_4 = Fe''K_2FeCy_6 + 6KHSO_4 + 6HCy.$$

The details of the official process are as follows: Dissolve $2\frac{1}{4}$ ounces of ferrocyanide of potassium in 10 ounces of water, add 1 fluidounce of sulphuric acid previously diluted with four ounces of the water and cooled. Put the solution into a flask or other suitable apparatus of glass or earthenware, to which are attached a condenser and a receiver arranged for distillation; and having put 8 ounces of distilled water into the receiver, and provided efficient means for keeping the condenser and receiver cold, apply heat to the flask, until, by slow distillation, the liquid in the receiver is increased to 17 fluidounces. Add to this 3 ounces of distilled water, or as much as may be sufficient to bring the acid to the required strength, so that 100 grains (or 110 minims) of it, precipitated with a solution of nitrate of silver (*vide* paragraphs on quantitative analysis), shall yield 10 grains of dry cyanide of silver.

The residue of this reaction is acid sulphate of potassium ($KHSO_4$), which remains in solution, and ferrocyanide of potassium and iron ($Fe''K_2FeCy_6$), an insoluble powder sometimes termed Everitt's yellow salt, from the name of the chemist who first made out the nature of the reaction. The latter compound becomes bluish-green during the reaction, owing to absorption of oxygen. *Diluted hydrocyanic acid* may also be prepared by reaction of cyanide of silver and diluted hydrochloric acid.

Pure anhydrous hydrocyanic acid is a colorless, highly volatile, intensely poisonous liquid, solidifying when cooled to a low temperature. It may be made by passing sulphuretted hydrogen over mercuric cyanide.

Note.—A few drops of diluted hydrocyanic acid so placed that its vapor may be inhaled, forms the *Vapor Acidi Hydrocyanici*, B. P., or Inhalation of Hydrocyanic Acid.

Hydrocyanic acid also occurs in cherry-laurel water and bitter-almond water (*vide* Index).

The methods of determining the strength of solutions of hydrocyanic acid will be described in connection with volumetric and gravimetric quantitative analysis.

Analytical Reactions (Tests).

First Analytical Reaction.—To a few drops of the hydrocyanic acid solution produced in the above reaction, or to any solution of a cyanide, add solution of nitrate of silver; a white precipitate of cyanide of silver (AgCy) falls. When the precipitate has subsided, pour away the supernatant liquid, and place half of the residue in another test-tube: to one portion add nitric acid, and notice that the precipitate does not dissolve; to the other add ammonia, and observe that the precipitate is insoluble or only sparingly soluble. (Chloride of silver, which is also white, is readily soluble in ammonia.)

Solubility of precipitate in strong solutions of salts. Cyanide of silver and many other precipitates insoluble in acids or alkalies are often soluble in the strong saline liquids formed by the addition of acids to alkalies. Hence the precaution of adding the latter reagents to separate portions of a precipitate, or of not adding the one until the other has been poured away.

Cyanogen in an insoluble cyanide, such as cyanide of silver itself, is readily recognized on heating the substance in a short piece of glass tubing closed at one end like a test-tube and drawn out at the other end, so as to have but a small opening; on applying a flame, the escaping cyanogen ignites and burns with a characteristic peach-blossom-tint.

Antidote.

Second Analytical Reaction.—To a dilute solution of hydrocyanic acid, or a soluble cyanide, add a few drops of solution of a ferrous salt and a drop or two of solution of a ferric salt (ferrous sulphate and ferric chloride are usually at hand); to the mixture add potash or soda, and then hydrochloric acid; a precipitate of Prussian blue remains. The decompositions may be traced in the following equations:—

$$\begin{array}{llllll} HCy & + & KHO & = & KCy & + H_2O \\ 2KCy & + & FeSO_4 & = & FeCy_2 & + K_2SO_4 \\ 4KCy & + & FeCy_2 & = & K_4FeCy_6 & \text{or } K_4Fcy \\ 3K_4Fcy & + & 2Fe_2Cl_6 & = & 12KCl & + Fe_4Fcy_3. \end{array}$$

The test depends on the conversion of the cyanogen into ferrocyanogen by the iron of a ferrous salt, and the combination of the ferrocyanogen, so produced, with the iron of a ferric salt.

Hence a mixture of green sulphate of iron, solution of perchloride of iron, and either magnesia or carbonate of sodium, is the recognized *antidote* in cases of poisoning by hydrocyanic acid or cyanide of potassium.

In such an alkaline mixture the poisonous cyanide, by reaction with ferrous hydrate, is at once converted into innocuous ferrocyanide of potassium or sodium: should the mixture become acid, the ferric salt present reacts with the soluble ferrocyanide forming insoluble Prussian blue, which is also inert. From the rapidity of the action of these poisons, however, there is seldom time to prepare an antidote. Emetics, the stomach-pump, the application of a stream of cold water to the spine, and the above antidote form the usual treatment.

Third Analytical Reaction.—To solution of hydrocyanic acid add ammonia, and common yellow sulphydrate of ammonium, and evaporate the liquid nearly or quite to dryness in a small dish, occasionally adding ammonia till the excess of sulphydrate of ammonium is decomposed; acidify the liquid with hydrochloric acid, and then add a drop of solution of a ferric salt; a blood-red solution of sulphocyanate of iron will be formed.

This is a very delicate reaction. Some free sulphur in the yellow sulphydrate of ammonium unites with the alkaline cyanide and forms sulphocyanate ($2AmCy+S_2=2AmCyS$); the ammonia combines with excess of free sulphur and forms, among other salts, sulphydrate of ammonium, the whole of which is removed by the ebullition. If the liquid has not been evaporated far enough, sulphydrate of ammonium may still be present, and give black sulphide of iron on the addition of the ferric salt.

Hydrocyanic acid in the blood.—According to Buchner the blood of animals poisoned by hydrocyanic acid, instead of coagulating as usual, remains liquid and of a clear cherry-red color for several days. In one case he obtained the reactions of the acid on diluting and distilling the blood fifteen days after death, and applying the usual reagents to the distillate. Aqueous solution of peroxide of hydrogen (p. 76) changes such blood to a deep brown color.

QUESTIONS AND EXERCISES.

414. Write a paragraph on the history of cyanogen.
415. Mention the source of the cyanogen of all cyanides.
416. How is Ferrocyanide of Potassium prepared?
417. What is the formula of ferrocyanide of potassium?
418. Is ferrocyanide of potassium poisonous?
419. Write an equation expressive of the reaction which ensues when ferrocyanide and carbonate of potassium are brought together at a high temperature.

420. What are the properties of cyanogen? How may it be obtained in a pure condition?

421. How is mercuric cyanide prepared?

422. How much real hydrocyanic acid is contained in the official liquid?

423. Give details of the preparation of hydrocyanic acid, and an equation of the reaction.

424. State the proportion of water that must be added to an aqueous solution containing 15 per cent. of hydrocyanic acid to reduce the strength to 2 per cent.—*Ans.* 6½ to 1.

425. What are the characters of pure hydrocyanic acid? How may it be obtained?

426. Enumerate the tests for cyanogen, giving equations.

427. Explain the action of the best antidote in cases of poisoning by hydrocyanic acid or cyanide of potassium.

NITRIC ACID AND OTHER NITRATES.

Formula of Nitric Acid HNO_3. Molecular weight 63.

Introduction.—The group of elements represented by the formula NO_3 is that characteristic of nitric acid and all other nitrates; hence it is expedient to regard these elements as forming an acidulous radical, which may be termed *the nitric radical.* Like the hypothetical basylous radical ammonium (NH_4), this supposed acidulous radical (NO_3) has not been isolated. Possibly it is liberated when chlorine is brought into contact with nitrate of silver; but if so, its decomposition into white crystalline nitric anhydride (N_2O_5) and oxygen (O) is too rapid to admit of its identification.

Sources.—The nitrogen and oxygen of the air combine and ultimately form nitric acid whenever a current of electricity (as in the occurrence of lightning) passes. Nitrates are commonly met with in waters, soils, and the juices of plants. Nitric acid and other nitrates are obtained from nitrates of potassium and sodium, and these from the surface soil of tropical countries. *Nitrate of potassium* or *prismatic nitre* (from the form of its crystals) is chiefly produced in and about the villages of India. The natives simply scrape the surface of waste grounds, mud heaps, banks, and other spots where a slight incrustation indicates the presence of appreciable quantities of nitre, mix the scrapings with wood-ashes (carbonate of potassium, to decompose the nitrate of calcium always present), digest the mixture in water, and evaporate the liquor. The impure product is purified by careful recrystallizations, and is sent into commerce in the form of white crystalline masses or fragments of striated six-sided prisms. Besides its use in medicine (*Potassæ Nitras*, B. P. and U. S. P.), it is employed in very large quantities in the manufacture of gunpowder. *Nitrate of Sodium* (*Sodæ Nitras*, B. P.) occurs in more distinct incrustations on the surface of the ground in Peru, Bolivia, and Chili, more especially in the district of Atacama; it is distinguished as Chili saltpetre or (from the form of its crystals—

obtuse rhomboids) cubic nitre, and is chiefly used as a manure and as a source of nitric acid, its tendency to absorb moisture unfitting it for use in gunpowder. In many parts of Europe nitrate of potassium is made artificially by exposing heaps of animal manure, refuse, ashes, and soil to the action of the air and the heat of the sun: in the course of a year or two the nitrogen of the animal matter becomes oxidized to nitrates, and the latter are removed by washing.

Note.—The word *nitric* is from *nitre*, the English equivalent of the Greek νίτρον (nitron), a name applied to certain natural deposits of *natron* (carbonate of sodium), for which nitrate of potassium seems at first to have been mistaken. *Saltpetre* is simply *sal petræ*, salt of the rock, in allusion to the natural origin of nitrate of potassium. *Sal prunella* (from *sal*, a salt, and *pruna*, a live coal) is nitrate of potassium melted over a fire and cast into cakes or bullets.

The nitric radical is univalent (NO_3').

Constitution of Salts.

It is here necessary again to caution the reader against regarding salts as invariably possessing a known constitution, or supposing that they always possess two or more sides, or contain definite radicals. The erroneous conception which, of all others, is most likely to be imperceptibly formed is that of considering salts binary bodies. For, first, the names of salts are necessarily binary. A student hears the names "sulphate of iron," "sulphate of copper," and simultaneously receives the impression that each salt has two sides, copper or iron occupying one and something indicated by the words "sulphate of" the other. Such words "vitriol," green or blue, or "nitre," would perhaps implant unitary ideas in the mind; but it is simply impossible to give such names to all salts as will convey the impression that each salt is a whole, and therefore unitary. The name "sulphate of potash" produces binary impressions; and the less incorrect name, "sulphate of potassium," is in this respect no better. Secondly, it is impracticable to study salts as a whole. Teachers are unanimous in the opinion that students should first master the reactions characteristic of the metals in salts, and then the residues which, with those metals, make up the salts, or *vice versâ*. It is not only impracticable, but impossible, to study salts as a whole; binary ideas concerning them are therefore almost inevitably imbibed. We come to regard a salt as a body which splits up in one direction only, look upon nitre, for instance, and all other nitrates, as containing NO_3 and a metal, K; whereas KNO_3 may be split up into KNO_2 and O; or into K_2O, N_2, and O_5; or may contain K_2O and N_2O_5. These are the chief disadvantages attending the employment of the binary hypothesis in studying chemical compounds: if they be borne in mind, the hypothesis may be freely used without much danger of permanent mental bias. Thus in nitre let the group of elements (NO_3) which, with potassium, makes up the whole salt be called the nitric radical, the name of the latter being directly derived from its hydrogen salt. Similarly allow the acidulous residues of other salts of metals to be termed respectively the chloric, acetic, sulphurous, sulphuric, carbonic, oxalic, tartaric, phosphoric, citric, boracic radicals. In short, these compound radicals should be regarded as groupings common to many salts, and which may usually be transferred without any apparent breaking or splitting; at the same time we must be prepared to find that occasionally a salt divides in other directions. In this way perhaps erroneous impressions will gain least hold on the mind, and a way be left open for the easy entrance of new truths, should the real constitution of salts be discovered.

Formerly salts (such as sulphate of magnesium) were regarded as containing (*a*) an oxide of a metal (MgO) and an anhydride (SO_3), the latter being incorrectly called an acid (sulphuric acid), or (*b*) as containing two simple radicals (*e. g.* KI, NaCl, KCy, HgS)—the former being called *oxyacid salts*, or *oxysalts*, and the latter *haloid salts* (from ἅλς, *als*, seasalt, and εἶδος, *eidos*, likeness). Such distinction is no longer maintained, the two classes being merged. This is an important educational gain on the side of simplicity; for, whereas under the old system much time was necessarily expended before salts of a metal and salts of the oxide of that metal could be distinguished (*e. g.* KI and MgO,SO_3), now, all salts being regarded as salts of the metals themselves (*e. g.* KI and $MgSO_4$), no such distinction is necessary.

REACTIONS.

Nitric Acid.

Synthetical Reaction.—To a fragment of nitrate of potassium or nitrate of sodium in a test-tube add a drop or two of sulphuric acid, and warm; nitric acid (HNO_3) is evolved in vapor. The fumes may be condensed by a bent tube fitted to the test-tube, not by a cork as for hydrochloric acid, because the nitric vapors would strongly act on it, but by plaster of Paris, a paste of which sets hard on being set aside for a short time, and is unaffected by the acid.

On a somewhat larger scale nitric acid may be prepared by heating, in a stoppered or plain retort, a mixture of equal weights of nitrate of potassium and sulphuric acid; the acid distils over, and acid sulphate of potassium remains behind:—

$$\underset{\text{Nitrate of potassium.}}{KNO_3} + \underset{\text{Sulphuric acid.}}{H_2SO_4} = \underset{\text{Nitric acid.}}{HNO_3} + \underset{\text{Acid sulphate of potassium.}}{KHSO_4}$$

Half the quantity of sulphuric acid may be taken; but in that case neutral sulphate of potassium (K_2SO_4) is produced, which, from its hard, slightly soluble character, is removed with difficulty from the retort. On the manufacturing scale the less proportion is used; but instead of retorts iron cylinders are employed, from which the residual salt is removed by chisels. Moreover the cheaper sodium salt is the nitrate from which manufacturers usually prepare nitric acid, seven parts of nitrate of sodium and four of sulphuric being employed.

Note.—The acid sulphate of potassium is readily converted into neutral sulphate (*Potassæ Sulphas*, B. P. and U. S. P.) by dissolving in water, adding carbonate of potassium until effervescence ceases to occur, filtering, and setting aside to crystallize.

Pure nitric acid (HNO_3) is a colorless liquid, somewhat difficult of preparation; its specific gravity is 1.52. The strongest acid met with in commerce has a sp. gr. of 1.5, and contains 93 per cent. of real nitric acid (HNO_3); it fumes disagreeably, is unstable, and, except as an escharotic, is seldom used. The British and United States Pharmacopœias contain two acids: *Acidum Nitricum*, prepared as above, of sp. gr. 1.42 (also in U. S. P.), and containing 70 per cent. of real acid (HNO_3); and another, *Acidum Nitricum Dilutum*, sp. gr. 1.101 (U. S. P. 1.068), containing nearly 17½ (17.44) per cent. Either of the stronger liquids, although containing water, is usually simply termed "nitric acid." The official nitric acid, of sp. 1.42, is a definite hydrous acid ($2HNO_3, 3H_2O$); it distils at 250° F. without change. If a weaker acid be heated it loses water, if a stronger acid be heated it loses nitric acid, until the density of 1.42 is reached. *Aqua fortis* is an old name for nitric acid (*Aqua fortis simplex*, sp. gr. 1.22 to 1.25; *Aqua fortis duplex*, 1.36). The strength of a specimen of nitric acid is determined by volumetric analysis. *Nitric anhydride* (N_2O_5) sometimes, but erroneously called *anhydrous nitric acid*, is a solid crystalline substance formed on passing dry chlorine over dry nitrate of silver.

Aqua Regia.—Three fluidounces of nitric acid (B. P.), four of hydrochloric acid (B. P.), (3 to 5 by weight forms the *Acidum Nitromuriaticum*, U. S. P.), and twenty-five of water, give the *Acidum Nitrohydrochloricum Dilutum* of the British Pharmacopœia. The acids must be mixed twenty-four hours before dilution to insure mutual decomposition and full development of the chief active product, chlorine:—

$$\underset{\text{Nitric acid.}}{2HNO_3} + \underset{\text{Hydrochloric acid.}}{6HCl} = \underset{\text{Chloronitric gas.}}{N_2O_2Cl_4} + \underset{\text{Water.}}{4H_2O} + \underset{\text{Chlorine.}}{Cl_2}$$

In the later stages of the reaction, the decomposition expressed in the following equation also probably occurs:—

$$\underset{\text{Nitric acid.}}{HNO_3} + \underset{\text{Hydrochloric acid.}}{3HCl} = \underset{\text{Chloronitrous gas.}}{NOCl} + \underset{\text{Water.}}{2H_2O} + \underset{\text{Chlorine.}}{Cl_2}$$

The same reaction occurs if the acids are mixed after dilution, but is not complete for a week or a fortnight (Tilden). The undiluted mixture of acids is known as *aqua regia*, so called from its property of dissolving gold, the "king" of metals.

Analytical Reactions (Tests).

First Analytical Reaction.—To a solution of any nitrate (*e.g.* KNO_3) add sulphuric acid, and then copper turnings, and warm; colorless nitric oxide gas (NO) is evolved, which at once unites with the oxygen in the tube, giving *red fumes* of nitric peroxide or peroxide of nitrogen (NO_2).

$$2KNO_3 + 5H_2SO_4 + Cu_3 = 2NO + 3CuSO_4 + 4H_2O + 2KHSO_4;$$
$$2NO + O_2 = 2NO_2.$$

Performed on a larger scale, in a vessel to which a delivery-tube is attached, this reaction becomes of synthetical interest, being the process for the preparation of nitric oxide gas for the purposes of chemical experiment.

Small amounts of a nitrate may be overlooked by this test, the color of the red fumes not being very intense.

Undiluted nitric acid poured on to copper turnings gives dense red vapors of *nitrous acid* (HNO_2), *nitrous anhydrate* (N_2O_3), and *nitric peroxide* (NO_2).

Second Analytical Reaction.—To a cold solution of the nitrate, even if very dilute, add three or four crystals of sulphate of iron, shake gently for a minute in order that some of the sulphate may become dissolved, and then pour eight or ten drops of strong sulphuric acid down the side of the test-tube, so that it may form a layer at the bottom of the vessel; a reddish purple or black coloration will appear between the acid and the supernatant liquid.

This is a very delicate test for the presence of nitrates. The black color is due to a solution or, perhaps, combination of nitric oxide with a portion of the ferrous salt. The nitric oxide is liberated from the nitrate by the reducing action of the hydrogen of the sulphuric acid, the sulphuric radical of which is absorbed by the ferrous sulphate, the latter salt becoming ferric sulphate.

$$2HNO_3 + 3H_2SO_4 + 6FeSO_4 = 4H_2O + 3(Fe_23SO_4) + 2NO.$$

The process of oxidation is one frequently employed in experimental chemistry; and nitrates, from their richness in oxygen, but more especially because always at hand, are the oxidizers usually selected for the purpose. In the operation they generally split up in one way, namely into oxide of their basylous radical, nitric oxide gas, and available oxygen. Thus hydrogen nitrate (nitric acid) yields oxide of hydrogen (water) and the other bodies mentioned, as shown in the following equation:—

$$4NHO_3 = 2H_2O + 4NO + 3O_2.$$

When nitrates, other than nitric acid, are used for the purpose of oxidation, a stronger acid, generally sulphuric, is commonly added in order that nitric acid may be formed; the hydrogen nitrate splitting up more readily than other nitrates.

Nitrate of ammonium (readily formed on neutralizing nitric acid with carbonate of ammonium), when heated, yields *nitrous oxide*, or laughing-gas (N_2O).

$$NH_4NO_3 = N_2O + 2H_2O.$$

Nitrous oxide is thus prepared for use as an anæsthetic. When required for inhalation, it should be washed from any possible trace of acid or nitric oxide, by being passed through solution of potash, and through solution of ferrous sulphate.

Nitrous oxide is slightly soluble in warm water, more so in cold. By pressure it may be liquefied, and by simultaneous cooling solidified. It supports combustion almost as well as oxygen.

The five oxides of nitrogen have now been mentioned, namely:—

Nitrous oxide	N_2O		N_2O
Nitric oxide*	NO		N_2O_2
Nitrous anhydride . . .	N_2O_3	or	N_2O_3
Nitric peroxide*	NO_2		N_2O_4
Nitric anhydride	N_2O_5		N_2O_5

The two anhydrides by absorbing water yield respectively nitrous acid (HNO_2) and nitric acid (HNO_3). This series of compounds forms a good illustration of the doctrine of multiple proportions (p. 36).

Third Analytical Reaction.—Direct the blowpipe-flame on to charcoal until a spot is red-hot; now place on the spot a fragment of a nitrate; deflagration ensues.

This reaction does not distinguish nitrates from chlorates. It is insufficient for the recognition of very small quantities of either class of salts, especially when they are mixed with other substances.

Gunpowder is an intimate mechanical mixture of 75 parts of nitre, 15 to 12½ parts of charcoal, and 10 to 12½ parts of sulphur. In burning it may be said to give sulphide of potassium (the white smoke, K_2S), nitrogen (N), carbonic oxide (CO), and carbonic acid (CO_2) gases, though the decomposition is seldom complete. The sudden production of a large quantity of heated gas from a small quantity of a cold solid is sufficient to account for all the effects of gunpowder.

Fourth Analytical Reaction.—To nitric acid or other nitrate add solution of "sulphate of indigo;" the color is discharged.

"*Solution of Sulphate of Indigo*," B. P. (Sulphindylic or Sulphindigotic Acid), is made by digesting 5 grains of dry finely powdered indigo in a small quantity of strong sulphuric acid in a test-tube for an hour, the mixture being kept hot by a water-bath; the blue liquid is then poured into 10 ounces of sulphuric acid, the whole

* The specific gravities of these gases indicate that NO and NO_2 are the correct formulæ, and not N_2O_2 and N_2O_4.

well shaken, set aside, and the clear liquid decanted. Free chlorine also destroys the color of this reagent.

Indigo B. P. (C_8H_5NO) is a blue coloring-matter deposited when infusion of various species of *Indigofera* is exposed to air and slight warmth. Under these circumstances, *indican*, a yellow transparent amorphous substance, soluble in water, breaks up into indigo, which is insoluble and falls as a sediment, and a sort of sugar termed *indiglucin*. The indigo is collected, drained, pressed, and dried. By action of deoxidizing agents indigo is converted into soluble colorless *indigogen, reduced indigo*, or *white indigo:* 1 part of powdered indigo, 2 of green sulphate of iron, 3 of slaked lime, and 200 of water, shaken together and set aside in a well-closed bottle, gives this colorless indigo. A piece of yarn, calico, or similar fabric, dipped into such a solution, and exposed to air, becomes dyed blue, deposition of insoluble indigo-blue occurring within the cells and vessels of the fibre. This operation is readily performed on the small scale, and forms a good illustration of the characteristic feature of the art of dyeing, namely, the introduction of soluble coloring-matter into a fabric by permeation of the walls of its cellular and vascular tissue, and the imprisonment of that coloring-matter by conversion into a solid and insoluble form (*vide* also p. 104).

Distinction between nitric acid and other nitrates.—Presence of the nitric radical in a solution having been proved by the above reactions, its occurrence as the nitrate of a metal is demonstrated by the neutral, or nearly neutral, deportment of the liquid with test-paper and the detection of the metal—its occurrence as nitric acid by the sourness of the liquid to the taste and the effervescence produced on the addition of a carbonate.

Antidote.—In cases of poisoning by strong nitric acid, solution of carbonate of sodium (common washing-soda) or a mixture of magnesia and water may be administered as antidotes.

QUESTIONS AND EXERCISES.

428. Trace the origin of nitrates.

429. In what does cubic nitre differ, chemically, from prismatic nitre?

430. Describe a process by which nitrate of potassium may be obtained artificially.

431. State the difference between nitrate of potassium, nitre, saltpetre, and sal prunella.

432. What group of elements is characteristic of all nitrates? and what claim has this group to the title of radical?

433. Mention the usual theory regarding the manner in which atoms are arranged in reference to each other in such salts as nitrate of potassium.

434. How is Nitric Acid prepared?

435. Give the properties of nitric acid.

436. What reactions occur when strong nitric and hydrochloric acids are mixed?

437. How is nitric oxide prepared?

438. Enumerate and explain the tests for nitrates.

439. Into what substances does nitric acid usually split when employed as an oxidizing agent?

440. How is nitrous oxide prepared?

441. Enumerate the five oxides of nitrogen.

442. What is the nature of gunpowder?

443. Write a few sentences on the chemistry of indigo, one of the tests for nitric acid.

444. How is nitric acid distinguished from other nitrates?

445. What quantity of cubic nitre will be required to produce ten carboys of official nitric acid, each containing 114 pounds?—*Ans.* $1076\frac{4}{5}$ pounds.

CHLORIC ACID AND OTHER CHLORATES.

Formula of Chloric Acid $HClO_3$. Molecular weight 84.5.

Hypochlorous Acid (HClO), and other Hypochlorites.

Place a few grains of red oxide of mercury in a test-tube, half-fill the tube with chlorine-water and well shake the mixture; the resulting liquid is a solution of hypochlorous acid, mercuric oxychloride remaining undissolved:—

$$2HgO + 2Cl_2 + H_2O = 2HClO + Hg_2OCl_2.$$

By the double decomposition of hypochlorous acid and oxides or hydrates, other pure hydrochlorites are formed:—

$$HClO + NaHO = NaClO + H_2O.$$

The direct action of chlorine on metallic hydrates is supposed to give a mixture of chloride and hypochlorite, as described in connection with the synthetical reactions of Sodium (p. 61, *Liquor Sodæ Chloratæ*, B. P.) and Calcium (p. 84, *Calx chlorata*, B. P.).

$$Cl_2 + 2NaHO = NaCl,NaClO + H_2O;$$
$$2Cl_2 + 2CaH_2O_2 = CaCl_2,Ca2ClO + 2H_2O.$$

But the presence of chlorides cannot be directly demonstrated in these bodies; so that their constitution is not definitely determined. The action of acids on them results in the evolution of chlorine; hence the great value of the calcium compound (chlorinated lime, or chloride of lime) in bleaching operations:—

$$CaCl_2,Ca2ClO + 2H_2SO_4 = 2Cl_2 + 2CaSO_4 + 2H_2O.$$

The solubility of hypochlorites in water, their peculiar odor, greatly intensified on the addition of acid, and their bleaching-powers (see the above calcium reaction) are the characters on which to rely in searching for hypochlorites.

Chlorates.

The group of elementary atoms represented by the formula ClO_3 is that characteristic of chloric acid and all other chlorates; hence it is expedient to regard it as being an acidulous radical, which may be termed the chloric radical. Like the nitric radical, it has not been isolated. Chloric anhydride also (Cl_2O_5), unlike nitric anhydride, has not yet been obtained in the free condition.

Chlorates are artificial salts. They are formed by simply boiling aqueous solutions of the common bleaching salts (chlorinated lime, chlorinated soda, chlorinated potash). Heat thus converts

$3(NaCl, NaClO)$ Chlorinated soda.	into	$NaClO_3$ Chlorate of sodium.	and	$5NaCl$ Chloride of sodium.
$3(KCl, KClO)$ Chlorinated potash.	into	$KClO_3$ Chlorate of potassium.	and	$5KCl$ Chloride of potassium.
$3(CaCl_2, Ca2ClO)$ Chlorinated lime.	into	$Ca2ClO_3$ Chlorate of calcium.	and	$5CaCl_2$ Chloride of calcium.

One chlorate may also be made from another by double decomposition. In making chlorates economically the chlorinated salt is specially prepared for, and in the same vessel as, the chlorate.

Chlorate of Potassium.

Thus Chlorate of Potassium (*Potassæ Chloras*, B. P. and U. S. P.) is commercially made by saturating with chlorine gas a moistened mixture of three parts of chloride of potassium and 10 of slaked lime, and well boiling the product. Chlorinated lime is first formed; this, on boiling with water, splits up into chloride of calcium and chlorate of calcium, and the latter reacting on the chloride of potassium yields chloride of calcium and chlorate of potassium.

$$6(Ca2HO) + 6Cl_2 = 3(CaCl_2,Ca2ClO) + 6H_2O;$$
$$3(CaCl_2,Ca2ClO) = Ca2ClO_3 + 5CaCl_2;$$
$$Ca2ClO_3 + 2KCl = CaCl_2 + 2KClO_3.$$

The operation may be conducted on a small scale by rubbing together in a mortar the above proportions of ingredients in ounces or half-ounces, adding enough water to make the whole assume the character of damp lumps, placing the porous mass in a funnel (loosely plugged with stones or pieces of glass) and passing chlorine gas (p. 15) up through the neck of the funnel. When the whole mass has become of a slight pink tint (due to a trace of permanganate) it should be turned into a dish, well boiled with water, filtered, the filtrate evaporated if necessary, and set aside; the chlorate of potassium crystallizes out in colorless rhomboidal plates, chloride of calcium remaining in the mother-liquor.

In the official process, carbonate of potassium instead of chloride is used; but otherwise it is similar to the method just described. Chlorinated potash and chlorinated lime are first formed—

$$K_2CO_3 + Ca2HO + Cl_2 = KCl, KClO + CaCO_3 + H_2O,$$
$$6(Ca2HO) + 6Cl_2 = 3(CaCl_2, Ca2ClO) + 6H_2O;$$

these, on boiling with water split up into chlorates and chlorides—

$$3(KCl, KClO) = KClO_3 + 5KCl$$
$$3(CaCl_2, Ca2ClO) = Ca2ClO_3 + 5CaCl_2,$$

the whole of the chloride of potassium and chlorate of calcium finally yielding chlorate of potassium and chloride of calcium,

$$2KCl + Ca2ClO_3 = CaCl_2 + 2KClO_3.$$

Neglecting intermediate decompositions, the reactions may be represented by the following equation:—

$$\underset{\text{Chlorine.}}{6Cl_2} + \underset{\text{Carbonate of potassium.}}{K_2CO_3} + \underset{\text{Hydrate of calcium.}}{6CaH_2O_2} = \underset{\text{Chlorate of potassium.}}{2KClO_3} + \underset{\text{Carbonate of calcium.}}{CaCO_3} + \underset{\text{Chloride of calcium.}}{5CaCl_2} + \underset{\text{Water.}}{6H_2O}.$$

Chlorate of potassium is soluble in water to the extent of 6 or 7 parts in 100 at common temperatures. It is usually administered medicinally in aqueous solution, sometimes also in lozenges (*Trochisci Potassæ Chloratis*, B. P.). Chlorate of potassium must, on no account, be rubbed with sulphur in a mortar, friction of such a mixture resulting in violent explosion.

Chlorate of potassium, when heated, yields chloride of potassium and oxygen, and is the salt commonly employed in the preparation of the gas for experimental purposes. But if the action be arrested when one-third of the oxygen has escaped, the residual salt is found to contain perchlorate of potassium ($KClO_4$):—

$$2KClO_3 = KClO_4 + KCl + O_2.$$

Chloric acid ($HClO_3$) may be isolated, but is unstable, quickly decomposing into chlorine, oxygen, and perchloric acid; some other chlorate (*e. g.* $KClO_3$) must therefore be used in studying the reactions of the chloric radical. *Perchloric acid* ($HClO_4$) may be obtained by distilling perchlorate of potassium with sulphuric acid; it is quite stable, and is occasionally administered in medicine.

Table of the Chlorine Acids.

Hydrochloric acid	HCl.
Hypochlorous acid	$HClO$.
Chlorous acid	$HClO_2$.
Chloric acid	$HClO_3$.
Perchloric acid	$HClO_4$.

The chloric radical is univalent (ClO_3). The acidulous radicals of the other chlorine acids are also univalent.

Analytical Reactions (Tests).

First Analytical Reaction.—To solution of a chlorate (*e.g.* chlorate of potassium) add solution of nitrate of silver; no precipitate falls, showing that the chlorine must be performing different functions to those it possesses in chlorides. Evaporate the solution to dryness, and place the residue in a small dry test-tube, or at once drop a fragment of a chlorate into a test-tube, and heat strongly; oxygen is evolved, and may be recognized by its power of reinflaming an incandescent match inserted in the tube. Boil the residue with water, and again add solution of nitrate of silver; a white precipitate falls, having all the characters of chloride of silver, as described under hydrochloric acid.

This is a trustworthy test, and, omitting the recognition of the oxygen, may be applied in the detection of small quantities of chlorates.

Second Analytical Reaction.—To a fragment of a chlorate add two or three drops of strong sulphuric acid; an explosive gas (Cl_2O_4) is evolved, having a peculiar odor somewhat like chlorine, but deeper in color than that element.

$$3KClO_3 + H_2SO_4 = Cl_2O_4 + KClO_4 + K_2SO_4 + H_2O.$$

Warm the upper part of the test-tube to 150° or 200° F., or introduce a hot wire; a sharp explosion ensues, due to decomposition of the gas, peroxide of chlorine, into its elements.

Third Analytical Reaction.—Heat a small fragment of a chlorate with hydrochloric acid; a yellowish-green explosive gas termed *euchlorine*, is evolved. Its color is deeper than that of chlorine, hence the name (from εὖ, *eu*, well, and χλωρός, *chlōros*, green). In odor it resembles chlorine, and is probably a mixture of that element with one of the oxides of chlorine.

Fourth Analytical Reaction.—Direct the blowpipe-flame on to charcoal until a spot is red-hot, and then place on the spot a fragment of a chlorate; deflagration ensues as with nitrates.

Bromates.

Bromates are salts closely resembling chlorates and iodates. The formula of Bromic acid is $HBrO_3$.

Iodates.

Iodic Acid (HIO_3).—Iodine is boiled with several times its weight of strong nitric acid, in a fume-cupboard, until all action ceases. The liquid is evaporated to dryness to remove excess of nitric acid, the residue dissolved in a small quantity of boiling water and the solution set aside to crystallize.

Iodate of Potassium (KIO_3).—Powder together equal weights of iodine and chlorate of potassium; to the mixture add twice its weight of water and about one-eighth of its weight of nitric acid; warm the whole until iodine disappears, and evaporate quite to dryness over a water-bath. The residue dissolved in water forms "Solution of Iodate of Potash," B. P. (The reaction is complicated. *Vide* Naquet's Modern Chemistry, Eng. edit. p. 107.)

Ferric Iodate, or rather *Oxyiodate* (Fe_2O4IO_3, $8H_2O$), is precipitated on adding solution of ferric chloride to solution of iodate of potassium.

QUESTIONS AND EXERCISES.

446. How may hypochlorous acid be formed?

447. What are the relations of hypochlorous acid to common bleaching powder?

448. By what reaction is chlorine eliminated from hypochlorites?

449. State the general reaction by which chlorates are formed.

450. Give details of the preparation of chlorate of potassium.

451. Mention the properties of chlorate of potassium.

452. What decompositions occur when chlorate of potassium is heated?

453. Find the molecular weight of chlorate of potassium.

454. What weight of oxygen is yielded when 1 oz. of chlorate of potassium is completely decomposed, and how much chloride of potassium remains?

455. One hundred cubic inches of oxygen, at 60° F. and barometer

at 30 inches, weighing 34.203 grains, and 1 gallon containing 277¼ cubic inches, what weight of chlorate of potassium will be required to yield 10 gallons of the gas?—*Ans.* 5½ ozs.

456. How many cubic inches of oxygen are producible from 1 oz. of chlorate of potassium?

457. Calculate the weight of chlorate of potassium theoretically obtainable from 100 parts of chloride.

458. How is perchloric acid prepared?

459. Enumerate the chlorine acids.

460. How may the presence of chlorides in chlorates be demonstrated?

461. Mention the tests for chlorates.

462. Give the formula of peroxide of chlorine.

463. What is euchlorine?

464. How may iodic acid be made?

465. Describe the preparation of iodate of potassium.

ACETIC ACID AND OTHER ACETATES.

Formula of Acetic Acid $HC_2H_3O_2$, or $H\overline{A}$. Molecular weight 60.

Source.—Acetic acid is said to occur naturally in certain plant-juices and animal fluids in minute proportions, but otherwise is an artificial product. Much is furnished by the destructive distillation of wood, hence the term *pyroligneous acid* for the crude product, a hybrid word from πῦρ, *pūr*, fire, and *lignum*, wood. In Germany and France large quantities are made by the spontaneous oxidation of the alcohol in inferior wines, hence the *white-* and *red-wine vinegar* (*vinegar*, from the French *vin*, wine, and *aigre*, sour). In England also the domestic form of acetic acid (brown vinegar) has a similar origin: infusion of malt and unmalted grain is fermented; and the resulting oxidation of its sugar, instead of being arrested when the product is an alcoholic liquid, a sort of beer, is allowed to go on to the next stage, acetic acid; it usually contains from 3 to 6 per cent. of real acetic acid ($HC_2H_3O_2$).

Vinegars.—The official vinegar (*Acetum*, B. P. and U. S. P.) contains nearly 5½ (5.4) per cent. The so-called Vinegar of Cantharides (*Acetum Cantharidis*, B. P.) is a solution of the active principle of cantharides in very strong acetic acid, not in vinegar. The Vinegar of Squill (*Acetum Scillæ*, B. P. and U. S. P.) is also a solution of the active principle of squill in dilute acetic acid, not in true vinegar. The same may be said of *Acetum Colchici*, U. S. P., *Acetum Lobeliæ*, U. S. P., *Acetum Opii*, U. S. P., and *Acetum Sanguinariæ*, U. S. P. (Vinegar of Bloodroot). Distilled vinegar (*Acetum Destillatum*, U. S. P.) is a form of Dilute Acetic Acid not now official in Great Britain. The *Acetum Opii* or *Black Drop* of America is made from nutmeg, saffron, and sugar, as well as Opium and Diluted Acetic Acid. In the British Pharmacopœia, vinegar, except its use for its own sake, is only employed in the preparation of *Emplastrum Cerati Saponis.*

The Acetic Radical.—The group of elements represented by the formula $C_2H_3O_2$ is that characteristic of acetic acid and other acetates, and may, for convenience of study, be assumed to be an acidulous univalent radical. It has not been isolated, unless indeed a compound of similar composition, resulting from the action of peroxide of barium on acetic anhydride, is the radical in question.

$C_2H_3O_2$, the characteristic grouping in acetates, is frequently considered to contain, rather than to be, a radical—C_2H_3O, termed *acetyl.* Acetates may be made to yield a body having the composition C_2H_3OCl, which is regarded as chloride of acetyl; from this may be obtained acetic anhydride ($C_4H_6O_3$), which by absorbing water becomes acetic acid.

$$\left.\begin{matrix}C_2H_3O\\Cl\end{matrix}\right\} \qquad \left.\begin{matrix}C_2H_3O\\C_2H_3O\end{matrix}\right\}O \qquad \left.\begin{matrix}C_2H_3O\\H\end{matrix}\right\}O \qquad \left.\begin{matrix}C_2H_3O\\M\end{matrix}\right\}O$$

Chloride of acetyl. Acetic anhydride. Acetic acid. Metallic acetates.

The relation of acetic acid to alcohol will be evident from the following equation representing empirically the formation of the acid:—

$$\underset{\text{Alcohol.}}{C_2H_6O} + O_2 = \underset{\text{Acetic acid.}}{C_2H_4O_2} + H_2O$$

Acetic Acid.

Synthetical Reaction.—To a few grains of acetate of sodium in a test-tube add a little water and some sulphuric acid, and heat the mixture; acetic acid is evolved, and may be condensed by a bent tube adapted to the test-tube by a cork in the usual way.

Acetic Acid.—This is the process by which acetate of sodium or calcium (the neutralized products of the distillation of wood) is made to yield acetic acid on the large scale. As with nitric and hydrochloric acids, the loose term "acetic acid" is that usually applied to aqueous solutions of acetic acid. The *Acidum Aceticum*, B. P., contains nearly 33 per cent. of real acid—that is, of $HC_2H_3O_2$; for it contains only 28 per cent. of acetic anhydride ($C_4H_6O_3$). Its specific gravity is 1.044, the specific gravity of *Acidum Aceticum*, U.S. P., being 1.047. *Acidum Aceticum Dilutum*, B. P. and U. S. P., contains 4½ per cent. of $HC_2H_3O_2$. Glacial acetic acid ($HC_2H_3O_2$) contains no water. It solidifies to a crystalline mass at temperatures below 63° F., hence the appellation *glacial* (from *glacies*, ice). Good commercial glacial acetic acid (*Acidum Aceticum Glaciale*, B. P.) does not contain more than 1 per cent. of water, corresponding to 84.15 per cent. of acetic anhydride; it solidifies at 34°, and again liquefies at 48°: its specific gravity is 1.065. Although water is lighter than this acetic acid, yet the addition of water at first renders the acid heavier; evidently therefore condensation, or contraction in bulk, occurs on mixing the liquids: after 10 per cent. has been added, the addition of more water produces the usual effect of dilution of a heavy liquid by a lighter, namely, reduction of relative weight. This matter will be better understood after the subject of specific gravity has been studied.

The following equation is expressive of the above reaction:—

$$\underset{\text{Acetate of sodium.}}{NaC_2H_3O_2} + \underset{\text{Sulphuric acid.}}{H_2SO_4} = \underset{\text{Acetic acid.}}{HC_2H_3O_2} + \underset{\text{Acid sulphate of sodium.}}{NaHSO_4}$$

or, assuming the existence of acetyl (C_2H_3O) in acetic acid, and a corresponding radical sulphuryl (SO_2) in sulphuric acid,

$$\left.\begin{matrix}C_2H_3O\\ Na\end{matrix}\right\}O + \left.\begin{matrix}SO_2\\ H_2\end{matrix}\right\}O_2 = \left.\begin{matrix}C_2H_3O\\ H\end{matrix}\right\}O + \left.\begin{matrix}SO_2\\ NaH\end{matrix}\right\}O_2;$$

or, thirdly, on the assumption that salts contain the oxide of a basylous radical united with the anhydride of an acid (the old view under which such names as acetate of soda were formed),

$$Na_2O,C_4H_6O_3 + 2H_2O,SO_3 = Na_2O,H_2O,2SO_3 + H_2O,C_4H_6O_3.$$

Note on Constitution of Salts.

Which of these three equations, or, more broadly, which of the three views of the constitution of salts illustrated by the equations, is correct, it is impossible to say. Whether it is $C_2H_3O_2$, C_2H_3O, or $C_4H_6O_3$, which migrates from one acetic compound to another, whether it is SO_4, SO_2, or SO_3, which migrates from one sulphuric compound to another, and so on with other acidulous groupings, cannot at present be determined. There are strong objections to each view; and possibly neither is right. Either the given radicals cannot be isolated, or application of the forces of heat, light, and electricity do not confirm views arrived at by the results of operations with the chemical force; or a salt comes to be regarded as having so large a number of constituent parts that the view, however true, breaks down in practice from the sheer inability of the mind to grasp the complicated analogies involved. Yet for the purposes of description, study, and conversation some system must be adopted. Let the first, then, be generally taken, over-reliance on it being checked by the use of general instead of special names for the hypothetical radicals, and other systems be employed in certain cases. (See also p. 243.)

Impurity.—Acetic acid often contains sulphurous acid. The method by which this impurity is detected will be described hereafter in connection with sulphurous acid.

Analytical Reactions (Tests).

First Analytical Reaction.—To an acetate add sulphuric acid and heat the mixture; acetic acid, recognized by its odor, is evolved.

Note 1.—Iodine, sulphurous acid, and other substances of powerful odor mask that of acetic acid; they must be removed, therefore, usually by precipitation or oxidation, before applying this test.

Note 2.—It will be noticed that this reaction is identical with the previous one; it has synthetical or analytical interest, according to the object and method of its performance.

Second Analytical Reaction.—Repeat the above action, a few drops of spirit of wine being added to the mixture before applying heat; acetic ether (acetate of ethyl, $C_2H_5C_2H_3O_2$), also of characteristic odor, is evolved.

The basylous radical ethyl (C_2H_5) will be referred to subsequently.

Third Analytical Reaction.—Heat a fragment of a dry acetate in a test-tube, and again notice the odor of the gaseous products of the decomposition; among them is *acetone* (C_3H_6O), the smell of which is characteristic. Carbonate of the metal remains in the test-tube.

Fourth Analytical Reaction.—To a solution of an acetate, made neutral by the addition of acid or alkali, as the case may be, add a few drops of neutral solution of perchloride of iron; a deep-red liquid results, owing to the formation of ferric acetate ($Fe_26C_2H_3O_2$).

Note.—It will be noticed that the formation of characteristic precipitates, the usual method of removing radicals from solution for recognition, is not carried out in the qualitative analysis of acetates. This is because all acetates are soluble. Acetate of silver ($AgC_2H_3O_2$) and mercurous acetate ($HgC_2H_3O_2$) are only sparingly soluble in cold water, but the fact can seldom be utilized in analysis. Hence peculiarities of color and odor, the next best characters on which to rely, are adopted as means by which acetates may be detected. Acetates, like other organic compounds, char when heated to a high temperature.

QUESTIONS AND EXERCISES.

466. What is the formula of acetic acid?
467. State the relation of acetic acid to other acetates.
468. What is the molecular weight of acetic acid?
469. Name the sources of acetic acid.
470. What is pyroligneous acid?
471. From what compound is the acetic acid of foreign and English vinegar immediately derived?
472. How much real acid is contained in official vinegar?
473. What is the nature of the "Vinegars" of Pharmacy?
474. How may acetic acid be obtained from acetate of sodium?
475. How much real acid is contained in the official acetic acid?

476. Mention the strength of commercial glacial acetic acid.

477. Give three or more views of the constitution of acetates, illustrating each by formulæ.

478. Enumerate the tests for acetates.

HYDROSULPHURIC ACID AND OTHER SULPHIDES.

Formula of Hydrosulphuric Acid H_2S. Molecular weight 34.

Source and Varieties.—The acidulous radical of *hydrosulphuric acid, sulphydric acid,* or *sulphuretted hydrogen* and other sulphides, is the element sulphur (S). It occurs in nature in combination with metals, as already stated in describing the ores of some of the metals, and also in the free state. Most of the sulphur used in medicine is imported from Sicily, where it occurs chiefly associated with blue clay. It is purified by fusion, sublimation, or distillation. Melted and poured into moulds, it constitutes a crystalline mass termed *roll sulphur.* If distilled and the vapor carried into large chambers, so that it may be rapidly condensed, the crystals are so minute as to give the sulphur a pulverulent character; this is *sublimed sulphur* (*Sulphur Sublimatum,* B. P. and U. S. P.) or *flowers of sulphur:* the same washed constitutes *Sulphur Lotum,* U. S. P. The third common form, *milk of sulphur,* will be noticed subsequently. Sulphur also occurs in nature in combination as a constituent of animal and vegetable tissues, as sulphurous acid gas (SO_2) in volcanic vapors, and as sulphuretted hydrogen in some waters, as those of Harrogate.

Quantivalence.—Sulphur is sexivalent, as seen in sulphuric anhydride (SO_3), a substance which will be noticed under sulphuric acid. It also occasionally exhibits quadrivalent (SO_2) and still oftener bivalent affinities (H_2S).

Acid Salts.—Sulphur (S'') being the first acidulous radical of bivalent activity met with in these sections on acids, it is desirable here to draw attention to a new class of salts to which such a radical will generally give rise. These are acid salts, which are intermediate between normal salts and acids. Univalent radicals with an atom of hydrogen give an acid, and with an atom of other basylous radicals an ordinary or normal salt. But bivalent radicals, from the fact that they give with two atoms of hydrogen an acid, and with two atoms of univalent metals a normal salt, may obviously give intermediate bodies containing one atom of hydrogen and one atom of metal; these are appropriately termed acid salts: they are neither normal acids nor normal salts, but *acid salts.* (Examples:—$KHCO_3$, $NaHSO_4$, $KHC_4H_4O_6$, Na_2HPO_4, $CuHAsO_3$, CaH_42PO_4.) Whether or not these salts give an acid reaction with blue litmus paper depends on the strength of the respective radicals. Usually they do redden the test-paper, but sometimes not; thus the acid sulphide or sulphydrate of potassium (KHS), of sodium (NaHS), or ammonium (AmHS) has alkaline properties.*

* Some chemists regard these sulphydrates as compounds of basylous radicals with HS, a univalent grouping termed hydrosulphyl

Synthetical Reactions.

Sulphuretted Hydrogen.

First Synthetical Reaction. The preparation of sulphuretted hydrogen.—This operation was described on page 69, and probably has already been studied by the reader.

Precipitated Sulphur.

Second Synthetical Reaction.—Prepare the variety of the radical of sulphides known as *Precipitated Sulphur* (*Sulphur Præcipitatum*, B. P. and U. S. P.) by boiling a few grains of flowers of sulphur (5 parts) with slaked lime (3 parts) (10 parts U. S. P.) and some water (20 parts) in a test-tube (larger quantities in an evaporating-basin), filtering, and (reserving a small portion of the filtrate) adding dilute hydrochloric acid until the well-stirred liquid has a faint acid reaction on test-paper; sulphur is precipitated, and may be collected on a filter, washed, and dried (at about 120°). Excess of acid must be avoided, or hydrosulphyl, the liquid persulphide of hydrogen (H_2S_2) will be formed, causing the particles of sulphur to aggregate to a gummy mass.

This is the process of the Pharmacopœias. Polysulphide of calcium and hyposulphite of calcium are formed:—

$3CaH_2O_2$	+	$6S_2$	=	$2CaS_5$	+	CaS_2O_3	+	$3H_2O$
Hydrate of calcium.		Sulphur.		Polysulphide of calcium.		Hyposulphite of calcium.		Water.

On adding the acid, both salts are decomposed and sulphur separates:—

$2CaS_5$	+	CaS_2O_3	+	$6HCl$	=	$3CaCl_2$	+	$3H_2O$	+	$6S_2$
Polysulphide of calcium.		Hyposulphite of calcium.		Hydrochloric acid.		Chloride of calcium.		Water.		Sulphur.

Polysulphide of calcium alone would yield sulphuretted hydrogen as well as sulphur on the addition of acid. Hyposulphite of calcium alone would yield sulphurous acid gas as well as sulphur. If these gases are formed in the above operation, they at once react and give sulphur and water, very little, if any, sulphuretted hydrogen escaping.

$$4H_2S + 2SO_2 = 3S_2 + 4H_2O.$$

(persulphide of hydrogen, H_2S_2), just as hydrates are similarly viewed as compounds of the univalent radical hydroxyl (HO) (peroxide of hydrogen, H_2O_2),—H_2S becoming HHS or HHs (hydrosulphylide of hydrogen), and H_2O becoming HHO or HHo (hydroxylide of hydrogen).

Impure Precipitated Sulphur.—To a sulphur solution prepared as before (or to the reserved portion) add sulphuric acid; the precipitate is in this case largely contaminated with sulphate of calcium:—

$2CaS_5$	+	CaS_2O_3	+	$3H_2SO_4$	=	$3CaSO_4$	+	$3H_2O$	+	$6S_2$
Polysulphide of calcium.		Hyposulphite of calcium.		Sulphuric acid.		Sulphate of calcium.		Water.		Sulphur.

Place a little of each of these specimens of precipitated sulphur with a drop of the supernatant liquid on a strip of glass, cover each spot with a piece of thin glass, and examine the precipitates under a microscope; the pure sulphur will be found to consist of minute grains or globules, the impure to contain comparatively large crystals (sulphate of calcium).

Note.—By far the larger proportion of precipitated sulphur met with in commerce is still (1871) adulterated with sulphate of calcium, most specimens containing two-thirds of their weight of that substance. Moreover, this adulteration has been so persistently practised that many persons have become sufficiently accustomed to the satiny appearance of the impure article to regard the pure article with suspicion, sometimes refusing to purchase it.

To ascertain the amount of sulphate of calcium in an impure specimen of precipitated sulphur, place a weighed quantity in a tared crucible and heat till no more vapors are evolved. The weight of the residual anhydrous sulphate of calcium ($CaSO_4 = 136$), with one-fourth thereof added, is the amount of crystalline sulphate of calcium ($CaSO_4, 2H_2O = 172$) present in the original quantity of impure sulphur.

Pharmacists should refuse all parcels of sulphur which yield a white ash when a little is burnt off on the end of a table-knife or spatula. (No more damage is done to the steel than a rub on a knife-board will remove.)

Analytical Reactions (Tests).

To a sulphide add a few drops of hydrochloric acid; sulphuretted hydrogen will probably be evolved, well known by its smell. If the sulphide is not acted upon by the acid, or if free sulphur be under examination, mix a minute portion with a fragment of solid caustic potash or soda, and fuse on a silver coin or spoon. When cold, place a drop of dilute hydrochloric acid on the spot, sulphuretted hydrogen is evolved, and a black stain, due to sulphide of silver (Ag_2S), left on the coin.

Other sulphur reactions may be adopted as tests, but the above are sufficient for all ordinary purposes. The most convenient reagent for detecting sulphur in solution of ammonia is ammonio-sulphate of copper, which gives a black precipitate of sulphide of copper if sulphur be present.

QUESTIONS AND EXERCISES.

479. In what form does sulphur occur in nature?
480. State the modes of preparation of the three chief commercial varieties of sulphur.
481. To what extent does the atom of sulphur vary in quantivalence?
482. State the relations of acid salts to acids and to normal salts.
483. Define sulphides and sulphydrates.
484. Describe the preparation of sulphuretted hydrogen.
485. What are the characters of pure precipitated sulphur?
486. Give equations explanatory of the reactions which occur in precipitating sulphur according to the official process.
487. Describe the microscopic test for impure precipitated sulphur.
488. Mention a ready physical method of detecting the adulteration of precipitated sulphur by sulphate of calcium.
489. Mention the tests for sulphides, and the character by which sulphuretted hydrogen is distinguished from other sulphides.
490. How are sulphides insoluble in acids tested for sulphur?
491. Give a method for the detection of a trace of sulphur in solution of ammonia.

SULPHUROUS ACID AND OTHER SULPHITES.

Formula of sulphurous acid H_2SO_3. Formula of sulphurous acid gas or sulphurous anhydride, commonly termed sulphurous acid, SO_2. Molecular weight of sulphurous acid 82.

When sulphur is burned in the air it combines with oxygen and forms sulphurous acid gas (SO_2), more correctly termed sulphurous anhydride, or commonly, but erroneously, sulphurous acid. It is a pungent, colorless gas, readily liquefied on being passed through a tube externally cooled by a *freezing-mixture* composed of two parts of well-powdered ice (or, better, snow) with one part of common salt. If sulphurous acid gas becomes moist or is passed into water, heat is evolved and true sulphurous acid (H_2SO_3) formed. The latter body may be obtained in crystals; but it is very unstable, and hence the properties of the sulphurous radical must be studied under the form of some other sulphite; sulphite of calcium ($CaSO_3$), or sulphite of sodium (Na_2SO_3), may be used for the purpose.

Quantivalence.—The radical of the sulphites is bivalent (SO_3''), and hence forms acid sulphites, such as acid sulphite of potassium ($KHSO_3$) and normal sulphites, such as sulphite of sodium (Na_2SO_3).

Note on Nomenclature.—The sulphites are so named from the

usual rule, that salts corresponding with acids whose names end in *ous* have a name ending in *ite*. They are generally made by passing sulphurous acid gas over moist oxides or carbonates—in the latter case carbonic acid gas escaping.

Synthetical Reaction.—To a few drops of sulphuric acid in a test-tube add a piece of charcoal and apply heat; sulphurous acid gas is evolved, and may be conveyed by a bent tube into a small quantity of cold water in another test-tube. Larger quantities may be made in a Florence flask. The product is the *Acidum Sulphurosum*, B. P. and U. S. P. It is said to contain, if saturated, nearly 12 (11.79) per cent. of sulphurous acid (H_2SO_3), or about 9 (9.2) per cent. of the gas (SO_2). The process is also that described in the Pharmacopœia, except that the gas is purified by passing through a small wash-bottle before final collection. Specific gravity 1.04 (1.035, U. S. P.).

If in this process the water were replaced by solutions of or solid metallic oxides or carbonates, sulphites of the various metals would be formed. The formula of sulphite of sodium (*Sodæ Sulphis*, U. S. P.) is $Na_2SO_3,7H_2O$; of the bisulphite or acid sulphite $NaHSO_3$. The former is used for removing traces of chlorine from paper pulp, and is termed *antichlor*.

$$\underset{\text{Sulphuric acid.}}{4H_2SO_4} + \underset{\text{Carbon (charcoal).}}{C_2} = \underset{\text{Carbonic acid gas.}}{2CO_2} + \underset{\text{Water.}}{4H_2O} + \underset{\text{Sulphurous acid gas.}}{4SO_2}$$

$$\underset{\text{Sulphurous acid gas.}}{SO_2} + \underset{\text{Water.}}{H_2O} = \underset{\text{Sulphurous acid.}}{H_2SO_3}$$

Analytical Reactions (Tests).

First Analytical Reaction.—To a sulphite add a drop or two of dilute hydrochloric acid; sulphurous acid gas escapes, known by its peculiar pungent smell.

This smell is the same as that evolved on burning lucifer matches that have been tipped with sulphur. It is due, probably, not to the gas (SO_2), but to sulphurous acid (H_2SO_3) formed by the union of sulphurous acid gas with either the moisture of the air or that on the surface of the mucous membrane of the nose. It is highly suffocating.

Second Analytical Reaction.—To a sulphite add a little water, a fragment or two of zinc, and then hydrochloric acid; sulphuretted hydrogen will be evolved, known by its putrid odor and action on a piece of paper placed like a cap on the mouth of the test-tube, and moistened with a drop of solution of acetate of lead, black sulphide of lead being formed. Sulphurous acid may be detected in acetic acid, or in hydrochloric acid, by this test.

$$H_2SO_3 + H_6 = H_2S + 3H_2O.$$

Other Analytical Reactions.

To solutions of neutral sulphites add nitrate or chloride of barium, chloride of calcium, or nitrate of silver; in each case white sulphites of the various metals are precipitated. The barium sulphite is soluble in weak hydrochloric acid; but if a drop or two of chlorine-water is first added, barium sulphate is formed, which is insoluble in acids. The other precipitates are also soluble in acids. The silver sulphite is decomposed on boiling, sulphuric acid being formed, and metallic silver set free.

To recognize the three radicals in an aqueous solution of sulphides, sulphites, and sulphates, add chloride of barium, filter, and wash the precipitate. In the filtrate sulphides are detected by the sulphuretted hydrogen involved on adding an acid. In the precipitate sulphites are detected by the odor of sulphurous acid produced on adding hydrochloric acid, and sulphates by their insolubility in the acid.

QUESTIONS AND EXERCISES.

492. What are the differences between sulphurous acid and sulphurous acid gas, sulphites and acid sulphites?

493. State the characters of sulphurous acid gas.

494. How is the official Sulphurous Acid prepared?

495. By what test may sulphurous acid be recognized in acetic acid?

496. Give a method by which sulphites may be detected in presence of sulphides and sulphates.

SULPHURIC ACID AND OTHER SULPHATES.

Formula of Sulphuric Acid H_2SO_4. Molecular weight 98.

Sulphates occur in nature; but the common and highly important hydrogen sulphate, sulphuric acid, is made artificially.

Preparation of Sulphuric Acid. General nature of the process.—Sulphur itself, or sometimes the sulphur in iron pyrites, is first converted into sulphurous acid gas by burning in air, and this gas, by moisture and oxygen, into sulphuric acid ($SO_2 + H_2O + O = H_2SO_4$).

Details of the process.—The oxygen necessary to oxidize the sulphurous acid gas cannot directly be obtained from air, but indirectly, the agency of nitric oxide (NO) being employed—this gas becoming nitric peroxide (NO_2) by action of the air, and the nitric peroxide again becoming nitric oxide by the action of the sulphurous acid gas, and so on. A small quantity of nitric oxide gas will in this way act as carrier of oxygen from the air to very large quantities of sulphurous acid. The nitric peroxide is in the first instance obtained from nitric acid, and this from nitrate of potassium or sodium by the action of a small quantity of the sulphuric acid of a previous operation.

Other processes.—Sulphuric acid may be obtained by other processes, as by distilling the sulphate of iron resulting from the natural oxidation of iron pyrites by air; but it is seldom so made at the present day.

Explanation of the Commercial Process.—The following equations represent various steps in the usual process:—

$2NaNO_3$	$+$	H_2SO_4	$=$	Na_2SO_4	$+$	$2HNO_3$
Nitrate of sodium.		Sulphuric acid.		Sulphate of sodium.		Nitric acid.

S_2	$+$	$2O_2$	$=$	$2SO_2$
Sulphur.		Oxygen (of the air).		Sulphurous acid gas.

SO_2	$+$	H_2O	$=$	H_2SO_3
Sulphurous acid gas.		Water.		Sulphurous acid.

$3H_2SO_3$	$+$	$2HNO_3$	$=$	$3H_2SO_4$	$+$	H_2O	$+$	$2NO$
Sulphurous acid.		Nitric acid.		Sulphuric acid.		Water.		Nitric oxide.

$2NO$	$+$	O_2	$=$	$2NO_2$
Nitric oxide.		Oxygen (of the air).		Nitric peroxide.

NO_2	$+$	H_2SO_3	$=$	H_2SO_4	$+$	NO
Nitric peroxide.		Sulphurous acid.		Sulphuric acid.		Nitric oxide.

On the large scale the sulphurous acid gas is produced by burning sulphur in furnaces; it is carried, together with the nitric vapors, by flues into leaden chambers, where jets of steam supply the necessary moisture; the steam also, condensing, prevents other reactions. The resulting dilute sulphuric acid is concentrated by evaporation in leaden vessels.

Experiment.—For purposes of practical study, a small quantity may be made by passing, *a*, sulphurous acid gas (p. 252), *b*, nitric oxide (p. 237), *c*, air (forced through by aid of bellows or a gas-holder), and, occasionally, *d*, steam (generated in a Florence flask) through glass tubes, nearly to the bottom of a two- or three-quart flask.

$$SO_2 + H_2O = H_2SO_3; \quad | \quad 2NO + O_2 = 2NO_2;$$
$$H_2SO_3 + NO_2 = H_2SO_4 + NO.$$

A slow current of sulphurous acid gas, air, and steam, and a small quantity of nitric oxide, will furnish, in the course of a few minutes, enough sulphuric acid for recognition by the first of the following analytical reactions.

Purification.—Sulphuric acid may contain arsenic, nitrous compounds, and salts. Arsenic may be detected by the hydrogen-test (p. 133), nitrous compounds by powdered sulphate of iron (which acquires a violet tint if they are present), and salts by the residue left on boiling a little to dryness in a crucible in a fume-chamber. If only nitrous compounds are present, the acid may be purified by heating with about half per cent. of sulphate of ammonium—water and nitrogen being produced (Pelouze). If arsenic occurs, heat with a little nitric acid, which converts arsenious (As_2O_3) into arsenic anhydride (As_2O_5), then add sulphate of ammonium, and distil in a retort containing pieces of quartz and heated by an annular-shaped burner (to prevent "bumping"). The arsenic anhydride remains in the retort. (Arsenious anhydride would be carried over with the sulphuric-acid vapors.) By distillation the acid is also purified from salts (such as $NaHSO_4$) which are not volatile.

Quantivalence.—The sulphuric radical being bivalent (SO_4''), acid as well as normal sulphates may exist. Acid sulphate of potassium ($KHSO_4$) is an illustration of the former, sulphate of sodium (Na_2SO_4) of the latter; *double sulphates* may also occur, such as that of potassium and magnesium ($K_2SO_4, MgSO_4, 6H_2O$). Sulphates generally contain water of crystallization.

Pure sulphuric acid (H_2SO_4) is of specific gravity 1.848. The best "oil of vitriol" of commerce, a colorless liquid of oily consistence, is of specific gravity 1.843, and contains 96.8 per cent. of real acid (H_2SO_4). This is the *Acidum Sulphuricum*, B. P. and U. S. P. The *Acidum Sulphuricum Dilutum*, B. P., sp. gr. 1.094 (U. S. P. 1.082) contains about 13½ (13.64) per cent. of acid (H_2SO_4); and the *Acidum Sulphuricum Aromaticum*, B. B. and U. S. P., a dilute acid in which are dissolved the soluble aromatic parts of cinnamon and ginger, also contains nearly 13½ (13.36) per cent. of acid (H_2SO_4). There are some definite compounds of sulphuric acid with water; the first (H_2SO_4, H_2O) may be obtained in crystals.

Sulphuric anhydride (SO_3) is a white silky crystalline solid, having no acid properties. It is made by distilling sulphuric acid with phosphoric anhydride ($3H_2SO_4 + P_2O_5 = 2H_3PO_4 + 3SO_3$). It appears to unite with sulphuric acid and some other normal sulphates to form compounds (R_2SO_4, SO_3) resembling in constitution red chromate of potassium or borax. The fuming sulphuric acid (H_2SO_4, SO_3), made at Nordhausen in Saxony, seems to be such a body.

Note.—Sulphuric acid is a most valuable compound to all chemists and manufacturers of chemical substances. It is the key by which hundreds of chemical salts are unlocked, and their contents utilized. To describe its uses would be to write a work on chemistry.

Analytical Reactions (Tests).

First Analytical Reaction.—To solution of a sulphate add solution of a barium salt; a white precipitate of sulphate of barium ($BaSO_4$) falls. Add nitric acid and boil the mixture, the precipitate does not dissolve.

This reaction is as highly characteristic of sulphates as it has been stated to be of barium salts (*vide* page 76). The only error likely to be made in its application is that of overlooking the fact that nitrate and chloride of barium are less soluble in strong acid than in water. On adding the barium salt to the acid liquid, therefore, a white precipitate may be obtained, which is simply the nitrate or chloride of barium. The appearance of such a precipitate differs considerably from that of the barium sulphate; hence a careful operator will not be misled. Should any doubt remain, water should be added, which will dissolve the nitrate or chloride, but not affect the sulphate.

Second Analytical Reaction.—Mix a fragment of an insoluble sulphate ($BaSO_4$ *e. g.*) with carbonate of potassium or of sodium; or, better, with both carbonates, and fuse the mixture in a small crucible. Digest the residue when cold, in water, and filter; the filtrate may be tested for the sulphuric radical.

This is a convenient method of qualitatively analyzing insoluble sulphates, such as those of barium and lead.

Third Analytical Reaction.—Mix a fragment of an insoluble sulphate with a little alkaline carbonate on a piece of charcoal, taking care that some of the charcoal-dust is included in the mixture. Heat the little heap in the blowpipe-flame until it fuses, and, when cold, add a drop of acid; sulphuretted hydrogen is evolved, recognized by its odor.

This is another process for the recognition of insoluble sulphates. Other preparations of sulphur, and sulphur itself, give a similar result. It is therefore rather a test for sulphur and its compounds than sulphates only; but the absence of other salts can generally, if necessary, be previously determined.

Note.—The presence of the sulphuric radical in a solution having been proved by the above reactions, its occurrence as the normal sulphate of a metal is demonstrated by the neutral, or nearly neutral, deportment of the liquid with test-paper, and the detection of the metal—its occurrence as sulphuric acid or an acid sulphate by the sourness of the liquid to the taste, and the effervescence produced on the addition of a carbonate.

Antidote.—In cases of poisoning by strong sulphuric acid, solution of carbonate of sodium (common washing-soda), magnesia and water, &c., may be administered as antidotes.

22*

QUESTIONS AND EXERCISES.

497. What is the formula of sulphuric acid, and what its molecular weight?

498. How is it related to other sulphates?

499. Write a short article on the manufacture of sulphuric acid, giving diagrams.

500. How may nitrous compounds be detected in, and eliminated from, sulphuric acid?

501. State the method by which the presence of arsenic is detected in sulphuric acid, and explain the process by which it may be removed.

502. Define sulphates, acid sulphates, and double sulphates.

503. What percentage of real acid is contained in commercial oil of vitriol?

504. State the strength of the official "diluted" and "aromatic" sulphuric acid.

505. By what process is sulphuric anhydride obtained from Nordhausen sulphuric acid?

506. Explain the reactions which occur in testing for sulphates.

507. Ascertain by calculation the weight of oil of vitriol (of 96.8 per cent.) necessary for the production of one ton of dry sulphate of ammonium.—*Ans.* 1718 pounds.

508. Name the antidotes in cases of poisoning by strong sulphuric acid.

CARBONIC ACID AND OTHER CARBONATES.

Formula of carbonic acid H_2CO_3. Molecular weight 62. Formula of carbonic acid gas, or carbonic anhydride, commonly termed carbonic acid, CO_2.

Sources.—Carbonates (compounds containing the grouping CO_3) are very common in nature, the calcium carbonate ($CaCO_3$) being widely distributed as chalk, limestone, or marble. The hydrogen carbonate, true carbonic acid, is not known, unless, indeed, carbonic acid gas assumes that condition on dissolving in water (*Aqua Acidi Carbonici*, U. S. P.). Such a solution (see page 60) changes the color of blue litmus-paper, and the gas does not; this may be because only the true acid (H_2CO_3) affects the litmus, or because the gas (CO_2) cannot come into real contact with the litmus without a medium. From the commonest natural carbonate, carbonate of calcium, are derived the carbonic constituents of the one most frequently used in medicine, carbonate of sodium.

Carbonate of sodium is prepared from the chief natural salt, the chloride. After the chloride has been converted into sulphate (salt-cake) by sulphuric acid,

$$2NaCl + H_2SO_4 = Na_2SO_4 + 2HCl,$$

the sulphate is roasted with limestone and small coal, by which carbonate of sodium and an oxysulphide of calcium are formed:—

$$5Na_2SO_4 + C_{20} + 7CaCO_3 = 5Na_2CO_3 + 5CaS.2CaO + 20CO + 2CO_2.$$

Carbonic oxide gas and some carbonic acid gas escape; the residual mass (black ash) is digested in water, in which the carbonate of sodium dissolves, the double oxide and sulphide of calcium remaining insoluble. The solution is evaporated to dryness, and yields crude carbonate of sodium. This is roasted with a small quantity of saw-dust, to convert any caustic soda into carbonate. The product is *soda-ash.* Dissolved in water and crystallized, it constitutes the ordinary "soda" used for washing purposes: recrystallized and sometimes ground, it forms the official carbonate of sodium (*Sodæ Carbonas,* B. P. and U. S. P.) ($Na_2CO_3, 10H_2O$). The reaction is rendered more intelligible by regarding it as occurring in three stages: 1st, the reduction of the sulphate of sodium to sulphide by the carbon of the coal,

$$Na_2SO_4 + C_4 = Na_2S + 4CO;$$

2d, the reaction of the sulphide of sodium and carbonate of calcium, giving soluble carbonate of sodium, thus—

$$Na_2S + CaCO_3 = Na_2CO_3 + CaS;$$

and, 3d, the combination of sulphide of calcium with lime from the chalk, giving insoluble oxysulphide of calcium—

$$5CaS + 2CaCO_3 = 5CaS, 2CaO + 2CO_2.$$

Carbonic acid gas (CO_2) is a product of the combustion of all carbonaceous matters. It is constantly exhaled by animals and inhaled by plants, its intermediate storehouse being the atmosphere, throughout which it is equally distributed by *diffusion* (*vide* p. 21) to the extent of about 4 parts in 10,000. A larger proportion than that just mentioned gives to confined air depressing effects, 4 or 5 per cent. rendering the atmosphere poisonous when taken into the blood from the lungs. Carbonic acid, however, may be taken into the stomach with beneficial sedative effects; hence, probably, much of the value of such effervescing liquids as soda-water, lemonade, and solutions of the various granulated preparations and effervescing powders (*vide* p. 62). The gas liquefies on being compressed, and the liquid solidifies on being cooled. Carbonic acid gas is twenty-two times as heavy as hydrogen.

REACTIONS.

Synthetical and Analytical Reactions.—1. To a fragment of marble in a test-tube add water and then hydrochloric acid; carbonic acid gas (CO_2) is evolved, and may be conveyed into water or solutions of salts by the usual delivery-tube.

This is the process of the British Pharmacopœia, and the one usually adopted for experimental purposes. Passed into carbonate of sodium, the gas gives *Sodæ Bicarbonas* (p. 47), and into carbonate of potassium, *Potassæ Bicarbonas* (p. 58). On the large scale the gas is prepared from chalk and sulphuric acid, frequent stirring promoting its escape.

2. Pass the gas into lime-water; a white precipitate of carbonate of calcium ($CaCO_3$) falls. Solution of subacetate of lead may be used instead of, and is perhaps even a more delicate test than, lime-water.

The evolution of a gas on adding an acid to a salt, warming the mixture if necessary, the gas being inodorous and giving a white precipitate with lime-water, is sufficient evidence of the presence of a carbonate. Carbonates in solution of ammonia, potash, or soda, may be detected by the direct addition of solution of lime.

3. Blow air from the lungs through a glass tube into lime-water; the presence of carbonic acid gas is at once indicated.

The passage of a considerable quantity of normal air through lime-water produces a similar effect. A bottle containing lime-water soon becomes coated with carbonate of calcium from absorption of carbonic acid gas.

4. Fill a dry test-tube with the gas, by passing the delivery-tube of the above apparatus to the bottom of the test-tube. Being rather more than once and a half as heavy as the air (1.529), it will displace the latter. Prove the presence of the gas by pouring it slowly, as if a visible liquid, into another test-tube containing lime-water; the characteristic cloudiness and precipitate are obtained on gently shaking the lime-water.

In testing for carbonates by bringing evolved gas into contact with lime-water, the preparation and adaptation of a delivery-tube may often be avoided by pouring the gas from the generating-tube into that containing the lime-water in the manner just indicated.

5. Pass carbonic acid gas through lime-water until the precipitate at first formed is dissolved. The resulting liquid is a solution of carbonate of calcium in carbonic acid water. Boil the solution; carbonic acid gas escapes, and the carbonate is again precipitated.

This experiment will serve to show how chalk is kept in solution in ordinary well-waters, giving the property of "hardness," and how the *fur* or stone-like deposit in tea-kettles and boilers is formed. It should be here stated that sulphate of calcium produces the same result, and that these, with the sulphate and carbonate of magnesium, constitute the hardening constituents of well-waters, a curd (oleate of calcium or magnesium) being formed whenever soap is used with such waters. An enormous amount of soap is wasted through the employment of hard water for washing-purposes.

QUESTIONS AND EXERCISES.

509. Name the chief natural carbonates.

510. What are the formulæ of carbonic acid and carbonic acid gas?

511. Adduce evidence of the existence of true carbonic acid.

512. Trace the steps by which the carbonic constituents of chalk are transferred to sodium by the process usually adopted in alkali-works—the manufacture of "soda."

513. Carbonic acid gas is constantly exhaled from the lungs of animals; why does it not accumulate in the atmosphere?

514. What is the effect of pressure on carbonic acid gas?

515. State the specific gravity of carbonic acid gas.

516. By what processes may carbonic acid gas be obtained for experimental and manufacturing-purposes?

517. Describe the action of carbonic acid gas on the carbonates of potassium or sodium.

518. How may carbonic acid be detected in expired air?

519. To what extent is carbonic acid gas heavier than air?

520. What quantity of chalk (90 per cent. pure) will be required to furnish the carbonate acid necessary to convert one ton of carbonate of potassium (containing 83 per cent. of K_2CO_3) into acid carbonate, supposing no gas to be wasted?—*Ans.* 1500 lbs.

521. Define "hardness" in water.

522. How may the presence of carbonates be demonstrated?

OXALIC ACID AND OTHER OXALATES.

Formula of Oxalic Acid $H_2C_2O_4, 2H_2O$. Molecular weight 126.

Sources.—Oxalates occur in nature in the juices of some plants, as wood-sorrel, rhubarb, the common dock, and certain lichens; but the hydrogen oxalate (oxalic acid) and other oxalates are all made artificially. Many organic substances yield oxalic acid when boiled with nitric acid, and an alkaline oxalate when roasted with a mixture of the hydrates of potassium and sodium.

Experimental process.—On the small scale, a mixture of nitric acid and loaf sugar yields the acid in the purest form, the two being boiled together for some time.

Manufacturing process.—On the large scale, sawdust is roasted with alkalies, resulting oxalate of sodium decomposed by lime with formation of oxalate of calcium, the latter digested with sulphuric acid, and the liberated oxalic acid (Oxalic Acid of Commerce, B. P.) purified by recrystallization (Oxalic Acid, Purified, B. P.).

Quantivalence.—The elements represented by the formula C_2O_4 are those characteristic of oxalates. They form a bivalent grouping; hence normal oxalates ($R'_2C_2O_4$), and acid oxalates ($R'HC_2O_4$) exist.

Salt of sorrel is a crystalline compound of oxalic acid with acid potassium oxalate ($KHC_2O_4, H_2C_2O_4$) the crystals containing two molecules of water of crystallization.

Analytical Reactions (Tests).

First Analytical Reaction.—To solution of an oxalate (oxalate of ammonium *e. g.*) add solution of chloride of calcium; a white precipitate falls. Add to the precipitate excess of acetic acid; it is insoluble. Add hydrochloric acid; the precipitate is dissolved.

The formation of a white precipitate on adding a calcium or barium salt, insoluble in acetic but soluble in hydrochloric or nitric acid, is usually sufficient proof of the presence of an oxalate. The action of the liquid on litmus paper, effervescence with carbonate of sodium, and absence of metals, would indicate that the oxalate is that of hydrogen, oxalic acid.

Antidote.—In cases of poisoning by oxalic acid or salt of sorrel, chalk and water may be administered as a chemical antidote (with the view of producing the insoluble oxalate of calcium), emetics and the stomach-pump being used as soon as possible.

Second Analytical Reaction.—Heat a fragment of a fixed metallic oxalate (an oxalate of potassium for example) in a test-tube; decomposition occurs, carbonic oxide (CO) (a gas that will be noticed subsequently) is liberated, and a carbonate of the metal remains. Add water and then an acid to the residue; effervescence occurs.

This is a ready test for insoluble oxalates, and is trustworthy if, on heating the substance, no charring occurs. Organic salts of metals decompose when heated, and leave a residue of carbonate, but except in the case of oxalate, the residue is always accompanied by much charcoal.

Other Analytical Reactions.—Nitrate of silver gives, with oxalates, white oxalate of silver ($Ag_2C_2O_4$).——Dry oxalates are decomposed when heated with strong sulphuric acid, carbonic oxide, and carbonic acid gases escaping. If much of the substance be operated on, the gas may be washed with an alkali, the carbonic acid be thus removed, and the carbonic oxide be ignited; it will be found to burn with a characteristic bluish flame.——Oxalates, when mixed with water, black oxide of manganese (free from carbonates), and sulphuric acid, yield carbonic acid gas, which may be tested by lime-water in the usual manner.——Insoluble oxalates, such as those of calcium and magnesium, may be decomposed by ebullition with solution of carbonate of sodium; after filtration the oxalic radical will be found in the clear liquid as soluble oxalate of sodium.

Test of Purity.—"Purified oxalic acid . . . . is entirely dissipated by a heat below 350° F." (B. P.)

QUESTIONS AND EXERCISES.

523. Explain the constitution of oxalates.
524. State how oxalates are obtained.
525. What is the quantivalence of the oxalic radical?
526. Give the formula of "salt of sorrel."
527. Mention the chief test for oxalic acid and other soluble oxalates.
528. Name the antidote for oxalic acid, and describe its action.
529. By what reactions are insoluble oxalates recognized?

TARTARIC ACID AND OTHER TARTRATES.

Formula of Tartaric Acid $H_2C_4H_4O_6$, or $H_2\overline{T}$.

Molecular weight 150.

Sources.—Tartrates exist in the juice of many fruits; but it is from that of the grape that our supplies are usually obtained. Grape-juice contains much acid tartrate of potassium, which is gradually deposited when the juice is fermented, as in making wine; for acid tartrate of potassium, not very soluble in aqueous liquids, is still less so in spirituous, and hence crystallizes out as the sugar of the grape-juice is gradually converted into alcohol. It is found with tartrate of calcium lining the vessels in which wine is kept; and it is from this crude tartar* (argal or argol), as well as from what tartar may be remaining in the marc left after the juice has been pressed from the grapes, that tartaric acid and other tartrates are prepared.

Cream of tartar, purified by crystallization (*Potassæ Tartras Acida*, B. P., *Potassæ Bitartras*, U. S. P.), occurs as a "gritty white powder, or fragments of cakes crystallized on one surface;" of a pleasant acid taste, soluble in 180 parts of cold and 6 of boiling water, insoluble in spirit.

Quantivalence.—The elements represented by the formula $C_4H_4O_6$ are those characteristic of tartrates. They form a bivalent grouping; hence normal tartrates ($R'_2\overline{T}$) and acid tartrates ($R'H\overline{T}$) exist. Tartrate of potassium, the *Potassæ Tartras* of the U. S. Pharmacopœia ($K_2C_4H_4O_6$) and Rochelle Salt, or tartrate of potassium and sodium ($KNaC_4H_4O_6$, $4H_2O$), the official *Potassæ et Sodæ Tartras* (*Soda Tartarata*, B. P.), are illustrations of normal tarates, while Cream of Tartar is an example of acid tartrates. The

* "It is called *tartar*," says Paracelsus, "because it produces oil, water, tincture and salt, which burn the patient as tartarus does." *Tartarus* is Latin (Τάρταρος, Tartaros, Greek) for *hell*. The products of its destructive distillation are certainly somewhat irritating in taste and smell; and the "salt" (carbonate of potassium) that is left is diuretic, and, in larger quantities, powerfully corrosive.

A boiling solution of tartar yields a floating crust of minute crystals on cooling, hence the term *cream* of tartar.

only official tartrate not apparently included in these general formulæ is tartar-emetic (*Antimonium Tartaratum*, B. P., *Antimonii et Potassæ Tartras*, U. S. P.), which is sometimes regarded as the double tartrate of potassium and a hypothetical radical, antimonyl (SbO), thus, $KSbOC_4H_4O_6$. Possibly, however, it is but an oxytartrate of antimony ($Sb_2O_2\overline{T}$) with normal tartrate of potassium ($K_2\overline{T}$); for there are several oxycompounds of antimony analogous to the oxycompounds of bismuth that have been described (p. 207), normal salts partially decomposed by water into oxides, and many of these oxycompounds readily unite with normal salts of other basylous radicals. Tartar emetic would thus be oxytartrate of antimony with tartrate of potassium ($Sb_2O_2\overline{T}$, $K_2\overline{T}$, or $Sb_2O_2C_4H_4O_6$, $K_2C_4H_4O_6$).

Tartaric Acid.

Tartaric Acid (*Acidum Tartaricum*, B. P. and U. S. P.) is obtained, according to the British Pharmacopœia, by boiling cream of tartar (*Potassæ Tartras Acida*, B. P., *Potassæ Bitartras*, U. S. P.) with water, adding chalk till effervescence ceases, and then chloride of calcium so long as a precipitate falls; the two portions of tartrate of calcium thus consecutively formed are thoroughly washed, treated with sulphuric acid, the mixture boiled for a short time, resulting sulphate of calcium mostly separated by filtration, the filtrate concentrated by evaporation, any sulphate of calcium that may have deposited removed as before, and concentration continued until the solution is strong enough to crystallize. Tartrate of calcium from 9 ounces of cream of tartar requires 5 ounces by weight of sulphuric acid for complete decomposition.

$2KH\overline{T}$	+	$CaCO_3$	=	$Ca\overline{T}$	+	$K_2\overline{T}$	+	H_2O	+	CO_2
Acid tartrate of potassium.		Carbonate of calcium.		Tartrate of calcium.		Tartrate of potassium.		Water.		Carbonic acid gas.

$K_2\overline{T}$	+	$CaCl_2$	=	$Ca\overline{T}$	+	$2KCl$
Tartrate of potassium.		Chloride of calcium.		Tartrate of calcium.		Chloride of potassium.

$2Ca\overline{T}$	+	$2H_2SO_4$	=	$2CaSO_4$	+	$2H_2\overline{T}$
Tartrate of calcium.		Sulphuric acid.		Sulphate of calcium.		Tartaric acid.

Tartaric acid occurs in colorless crystals, or the same powdered. It is strongly acid and readily soluble in water or spirit. One part in 8 of water and 2 of spirit of wine forms "Solution of Tartaric Acid," B. P. Its aqueous solution is not stable.

Reactions.

Tartrate of Potassium.

Synthetical Reactions.—To a small quantity of a strong solution of carbonate of potassium add acid tartrate of potassium so long as effervescence occurs; the resulting liquid is solution of normal tartrate of potassium (*Potassæ

Tartras, B. P. and U. S. P.) ($K_2\overline{T}$), crystals of which may be obtained on evaporation.

Note.—This is a common method of converting an acid salt of a bivalent acidulous radical into a normal salt. The carbonate added need not be a carbonate of the same, but may be of a different metal; compounds like Rochelle salt ($KNa\overline{T}$) are then obtained. Thus:—

Tartrate of Potassium and Sodium.

To a strong hot solution of carbonate of sodium add acid tartrate of potassium until effervescence ceases; the resulting liquid is solution of tartrate of potassium and sodium: on cooling, it yields crystals. This is the official process (*Soda Tartarata*, B. P., *Potassæ et Sodæ Tartras*, U. S. P.) ($KNa\overline{T},4H_2O$).

Equivalent Weights *of Tartaric Acid, Carbonate of Potassium, Bicarbonate of Potassium, Carbonate of Sodium, Bicarbonate of Sodium, and Carbonates of Ammonium and Magnesium: repeated for* 20 *parts of each* (and, incidentally, for other proportions).

Tart. Acid........	$H_2C_4H_4O_6$................ = 150	**20**	**18¼**	**15**	**10½**	**17¾**	**25½**	**31½**
Carb. Potas......	K_2CO_3 (of 83 per cent.)... = 166	**22**	**20**	16½	11½	19⅓	28	34⅓
Bicarb. Pot.......	2($KHCO_3$)................ = 200	**26¾**	24¼	**20**	14	23¾	34	42
Carb. Soda (cryst.)	$Na_2CO_3,10H_2O$........... = 286	**38**	34¾	28½	**20**	34	48½	60
Bicarb. Sod......	2($NaHCO_3$)............... = 168	**22½**	20¼	16¾	11¾	**20**	28½	35¼
Carb. Ammon....	($N_4H_{16}C_3O_8$)÷2........... = 118	**15¾**	14¼	11¾	8¼	14	**20**	24¾
Carb. Magnes....	$(MgCO_3)_3Mg2HO, 4H_2$÷04 = 95.5	**12¾**	11½	9¾	6¾	11¼	16	**20**

Thus 20 parts (grains, or other weights) of tartaric acid neutralize 22 of carbonate of potassium, 26¾ of bicarbonate of potassium, 38 of carbonate of sodium, 22½ of bicarbonate of sodium, 15¾ of carbonate of ammonium, or 12¾ of carbonate of magnesium. Other quantities of tartaric acid (18¼, 15, 10½, 17¾, 25½, 31½) saturate the amounts of salts mentioned in the other columns and *vice versâ*. A similar Table for Citric Acid will be found at page 269, and for both acids in the Appendix. These Tables afford good illustrations of the laws of chemical combination (page 36). The reader should verify a few of the numbers by calculation from the atomic weights of the elements concerned in the reactions, remembering that the salts formed are considered to be neutral in constitution. In medical practice effervescing saline draughts are often designedly prescribed to contain an amount of acid or alkali considerably in excess of the proportions required for perfect neutrality.

A common form of *Seidlitz Powder* consists of 3 parts of Rochelle salt (120 grains) with 1 (40 grains) of acid carbonate of sodium (the mixture usually wrapped in blue paper), and 1 (40 grains) of tartaric acid (wrapped in white paper). When administered, the latter is dissolved in a tumbler rather more than half full of water, the former added, and the mixture drank during effervescence. It will be seen that the salts swallowed are tartrate of potassium and sodium ($KNa\overline{T},4H_2O$), tartrate of sodium ($Na_2\overline{T},2H_2O$), and acid tartrate of sodium ($Na_2H\overline{T},H_2O$). The last-mentioned salt results because $11\frac{1}{4}$ per cent. ($4\frac{1}{2}$ grains) of the tartaric acid is in excess of the quantity necessary for the formation of neutral tartrate of sodium. This amount of acid salt gives agreeable acidity to the draught. The United States formula (*Pulveres Effervescentes Aperientes*, U.S. P.) includes rather less tartaric acid, so that only neutral salts are formed.

Analytical Reactions (Tests).

First Analytical Reaction.—To solution of any normal tartrate, or tartaric acid made neutral by solution of soda, add solution of chloride of calcium; a white precipitate, tartrate of calcium, falls. Collect the precipitate on a filter, wash, place a small quantity in a test-tube, and add solution of potash; on stirring the mixture the precipitate dissolves. Heat the solution; the tartrate of calcium is again precipitated.

The solubility of tartrate of calcium in cold potash solution enables the analyst to distinguish between tartrates and citrates, otherwise a difficult matter. Citrate of calcium is not soluble in the alkali. The absence of much ammoniacal salt must be insured in both cases, the precipitates being soluble in such liquids.

Second Analytical Reaction.—Acidulate a solution of a tartrate with acetic acid, add acetate of potassium, and well stir the mixture; a crystalline precipitate of acid tartrate of potassium slowly separates. The precipitate being insoluble in alcohol, the addition of a little spirit of wine renders the test more delicate.

This reaction is not applicable in testing for very small quantities of tartrates, the acid tartrate of potassium being not altogether insoluble.

Third Analytical Reaction.—To a neutral solution of a tartrate add solution of nitrate of silver; a white precipitate of tartrate of silver, $Ag_2C_4H_4O_6$, falls. Boil the mixture; it turns black, owing to the reduction of the salt to metallic silver.

Other Reactions.—Tartrates heated with strong sulphuric acid char immediately.——Tartaric acid and the soluble tartrates prevent the precipitation of ferric and other hydrates by alkalies, soluble double tartrates being formed (which on evaporation yield liquids that do not crystallize, but, spread on sheets of glass, dry up to thin transparent plates or scales). The ferri et potassæ tartras, U. S. P. (*Ferrum Tartaratum*, B. P.), is a preparation of this kind. ——Tartrates decompose when heated, carbonates being formed and carbon set free, the gaseous products having a peculiar, more or less characteristic smell, resembling that of burnt sugar.

QUESTIONS AND EXERCISES.

530. State the origin of tartaric acid and other tartrates, and explain the deposition of argol, crude acid tartrate of potassium, during the manufacture of wine.

531. What are the chemical formula and characters of "cream of tartar?"

532. Mention the formula and quantivalence of the tartaric radical.

533. Write formulæ of normal, acid, and double tartrates, tartar-emetic being treated as an oxytartrate of antimony with tartrate of potassium.

534. Give equations or diagrams illustrative of the production of tartaric acid from cream of tartar.

535. By what general process may normal or double tartrates be obtained from acid tartrate of potassium?

536. Work out sums proving the correctness of some of the figures given on p. 265 as showing the saturating-power of tartaric acid for various quantities of different carbonates, and give diagrams or equations of the reactions.

537. State the names and quantities of the salts resulting from the admixture of 120 grains of tartrate of potassium and sodium, 40 grains of acid carbonate of sodium, and 40 grains of tartaric acid (Seidlitz powder).

538. Enumerate the tests for tartrates, and explain the effects of heat on tartrates of the metals.

CITRIC ACID AND OTHER CITRATES.

Formula of Citric Acid $H_3C_6H_5O_7, H_2O$ or $H_3\bar{C}iAq$.
Molecular weight 210.

Source.—Citric acid (*Acidum Citricum*, B. P. and U. S. P.) exists in the juice of many of our common garden fruits; thus the pulp of the fruit of *Tamarindus indica* (*Tamarindus*, B. P. and U. S. P.) contains nearly 10 per cent. (in addition to 1.5 of tartaric acid, .5

of malic acid, and 3 per cent. of acid tartrate of potassium). But it is from the lemon or lime that the acid of commerce is usually obtained.

Process.—The British Pharmacopœia directs that the hot lemon-juice (4 pints) be saturated by powdered chalk (4½ ounces), the resulting citrate of calcium collected on a filter, washed with hot water till the liquor passes from it colorless, then mixed with cold water (1 pint), decomposed by sulphuric acid (2½ fluidounces in 1½ pint of water), the mixture boiled for half an hour, filtered, the solution evaporated to a density of 1.21, set aside for 24 hours, then poured off from any deposit of crystalline sulphate of calcium, further concentrated and set aside to crystallize.

$$\underset{\text{Citric acid (impure).}}{2H_3C_6H_5O_7} + \underset{\text{Carbonate of calcium.}}{3CaCO_3} = \underset{\text{Citrate of calcium.}}{Ca_32C_6H_5O_7} + \underset{\text{Water.}}{3H_2O} + \underset{\text{Carbonic acid gas.}}{3CO_2}$$

$$\underset{\text{Citrate of calcium.}}{Ca_32C_6H_5O_7} + \underset{\text{Sulphuric acid.}}{3H_2SO_4} = \underset{\text{Citric acid (pure).}}{2H_3C_6H_5O_7} + \underset{\text{Sulphate of calcium.}}{3CaSO_4}$$

Quantivalence.—The elements represented by the formula $C_6H_5O_7$ are those characteristic of citrates. They form a trivalent grouping; hence three classes of salts may exist—one, two, or three atoms of the basylous hydrogen in the acid, $H_3C_6H_5O_7$, being displaced by equivalent proportions of other basylous radicals.

Citric acid itself is the only citric compound of much direct importance to the pharmacist. It usually occurs in colorless crystals soluble in half their weight of boiling and three-fourths of cold water, less soluble in spirit, and insoluble in ether. A solution of about 34 grains in 1 ounce of water forms a sort of artificial lemon-juice. Citrates heated with strong sulphuric acid to about 212° F. evolve carbonic oxide gas, and at higher temperatures acetone and carbonic acid gas.

"*Effervescing Citrate of Magnesia,*" so-called, is generally a mixture of bicarbonate of sodium, citric acid, tartaric acid, sugar, either carbonate or sulphate of magnesium (sometimes neither) and occasionally essence of lemon. True citrate of magnesium is easily made by heating together calcined magnesia and citric acid; it is frequently prescribed in France in doses of two ounces. *Liquor Magnesiæ Citratis*, U. S. P., is a bottled mixture of magnesia, citric acid, and syrup, with bicarbonate of potassium, and sufficient water to nearly fill the bottle which is closed by a cork secured with twine.

The official Lemon Juice (*Succus Limonum*, B. P., *Limonis Succus*, U. S. P.) is to be freshly expressed from the ripe fruit, and contain an average of 32.5 grains of citric acid in 1 fluidounce. The acidity may be ascertained by adding solution of potash or soda (the strength of which has been previously determined with pure crystals of citric acid) till red litmus paper is fairly turned blue. Before applying this test to commercial specimens, the absence of notable quantities of sulphuric, hydrochloric, acetic, tartaric, or other acid must be insured by application of appropriate reagents.

Mistura Potassæ Citratis, U. S. P., is lemon juice completely neutralized by bicarbonate of potassium. It is a slightly impure but flavored solution of citrate of potassium.

Equivalent Weights *of Citric Acid, Carbonate of Potassium, Bicarbonate of Potassium, Carbonate of Sodium, Bicarbonate of Sodium, and Carbonates of Ammonium and Magnesium; repeated for* 20 *parts of each* (and, incidentally, for other proportions).

Citric Acid.......	$H_3C_6H_5O_7, H_2O$ .... = 210	**20**	**17**	**14**	**9¾**	**16¾**	**23¾**	**29¼**
Carb. Potas.	(K_2CO_3; of 83 p.ct.)÷2×3 = 249	**23½**	**20**	16⅙	11½	19¾	28	34¼
Bicarb. Pot.......	3($KHCO_3$) .... = 300	**28½**	24¼	**20**	14	24	34	41¾
Carb. Sod. (cryst.)	(Na_2CO_3, $10H_2O$)÷2×3... = 429	**40¾**	34¾	28½	**20**	34¼	48½	60
Bicarb. Sod.	3($NaHCO_3$).............. = 252	**24**	20½	16¾	11¾	**20**	28½	35
Carb. Ammon. ...	($N_4H_{16}C_3O_8$)÷4×3 .... = 177	**16¾**	14¼	11¾	8¼	14	**20**	24¾
Carb. Magnes. ...	($(MgCO_3)_3Mg2HO$, $4H_2O$) ÷8×3 = 143¼	**13½**	11¾	9½	6¾	11½	16¼	**20**

Thus 20 parts (grains, or other weights) of citric acid neutralize 23¾ of carbonate of potassium, 28½ of bicarbonate of potassium, 40¾ of carbonate of sodium, 24 of bicarbonate of sodium, 16¾ of carbonate of ammonium, or 13½ of carb. of magnesium. Other quantities of acid (17, 14, 9¾, 16¾, 23¾, 29¼) saturate the amounts of salts mentioned in the other columns, and *vice versâ*.

This Table, the similar one for tartaric acid (p. 265), and that for both acids (*vide* Appendix) afford good illustrations of some of the laws of chemical combination (p. 36). The reader should verify a few of the numbers by calculation from the atomic weights of the elements concerned in the reactions, remembering that the salts formed are considered to be neutral in constitution. In medical practice, effervescing saline draughts are often designedly prescribed to contain an amount of acid or alkali considerably in excess of the proportions required for perfect neutrality.

Analytical Reactions (Tests).

First Analytical Reaction.—To a dilute solution of any neutral citrate, or citric acid carefully neutralized by alkali, add solution of chloride of calcium and boil; a white precipitate, citrate of calcium ($Ca_3\overline{Ci}_2$), falls. Treat the precipitate as for tartrate of calcium (p. 266); it is *not* dissolved by the potash.

A mixture of citrates and tartrates can be separated by this reaction. They are precipitated as calcium salts, and the washed precipitate mixed with solution of potash, diluted and filtered; the filtrate contains the tartrate, which is shown to be present by reprecipitation on boiling. The precipitate still on the filter is washed, dissolved in solution of chloride of ammonium, and the solution boiled; the citrate of calcium is reprecipitated. The presence of much sugar interferes with this reaction. A dilute solution of a citrate is not precipitated by chloride of calcium until the liquid is heated: precipitation from a strong solution, also, is not thoroughly complete without ebullition of the mixture.

Second Analytical Reaction.—To a neutral solution of a citrate add solution of nitrate of silver; a white precipitate of citrate of silver ($Ag_3\overline{Ci}$) falls. Boil the mixture; the precipitate does not turn black as tartrate of silver does.

Other Analytical Reactions.—Citric acid forms no precipitate corresponding with the acid tartrate of potassium. ——Lime-water, in excess, gives no precipitate with citric acid or citrates, unless the solution is boiled, citrate of calcium being slightly soluble in cold but not in hot water; it usually precipitates tartrates in the cold.——Citrates, when heated with strong sulphuric acid, do not char immediately.——Citric acid and citrates prevent the precipitation of oxide of iron by alkalies, soluble double compounds being formed. The *Ferri et Ammoniæ Citras*, B. P. and U. S. P., is a preparation of this kind.——Metallic citrates decompose when heated, carbonates being formed and carbon set free: the odor of the gaseous products is not so characteristic as that of tartrates.

QUESTIONS AND EXERCISES.

539. What is the source of citric acid?

540. Describe the method by which citric acid is prepared, giving diagrams.

541. Illustrate by formulæ the various classes of tartrates and citrates.

542. State the average proportion of citric acid in lemon-juice.

543. Work out the sums proving the correctness of some of the figures given on page 269 as showing the saturating-power of citric acid for various carbonates.

544. What are the tests for citrates?

545. How are the tartrates separated from citrates?

PHOSPHORIC ACID AND OTHER PHOSPHATES.

Formula of Phosphoric Acid H_3PO_4. Molecular weight 98.

Source.—The source of the ordinary normal phosphates and of phosphorus itself (*Phosphorus*, B. P. and U. S. P.) is the normal phosphate of calcium (Ca_32PO_4). It is the chief constituent of the bones of animals, being derived from the plants on which they feed, plants again obtaining it from the soil.

Process.—Phosphorus is obtained from bones by the following processes: The bones are burnt to remove all traces of animal matter. The resulting *bone-earth* is treated with sulphuric acid, by which an acid phosphate (CaH_42PO_4), often called *superphosphate of lime*, is produced:—

$$Ca_32PO_4 + 2H_2SO_4 = CaH_42PO_4 + 2CaSO_4.$$

The acid phosphate is mixed with charcoal and strongly heated in a retort, when it splits up into normal phosphate of calcium and phosphoric acid—

$$3CaH_42PO_4 = Ca_32PO_4 + 4H_3PO_4,$$

the phosphoric acid being reduced by the charcoal to phosphorus and hydrogen, and carbonic oxide gas liberated:—

$$H_3PO_4 + C_4 = P + H_3 + 4CO.$$

Phosphorus is "a semitransparent, colorless, wax-like solid, which emits white vapors when exposed to the air. Specific gravity 1.77. It is soft and flexible at common temperatures, melts at 110°, ignites in the air at a temperature a little above its melting-point, burning with a luminous flame and producing dense white fumes. Insoluble in water, but soluble in ether and in boiling oil of turpentine," also in bisulphide of carbon.

Quantivalence.—The atom of phosphorus is quinquivalent, as seen in the pentachloride (PCl_5) and oxychloride (PCl_3O), but it often exhibits trivalent activity as seen in the trichloride and trihydride.

Phosphoric Acid.

The chief use of phosphorus in pharmacy is in the formation of Diluted Phosphoric Acid. Phosphorus is boiled with nitric acid and water until dissolved. The solution, evaporated to a low bulk to remove nitrous compounds, and rediluted so as to contain nearly 14 (13.8) per cent. of acid (H_3PO_4), equivalent to 10 per cent. of phosphoric anhydride (P_2O_5), constitutes the *Acidum Phosphoricum Dilutum*, B. P. and U. S. P., a colorless sour liquid of specific gravity 1.08 (1.056 U. S. P.). If the necessary appliances are at hand, four or five ounces of this acid may be prepared as follows: A quarter of a pint is made by boiling together, in a retort attached to a Liebig's condenser, 103 grains of phosphorus, 1½ fluidounce of the official nitric acid, and 2 ounces of water. When about 1 oz. of water has distilled over it should be returned to the retort, and the operation repeated until the phosphorus has disappeared.

$$\underset{\text{Phosphorus.}}{P_6} + \underset{\text{Nitric acid.}}{10HNO_3} + \underset{\text{Water.}}{4H_2O} = \underset{\text{Phosphoric acid}}{6H_3PO_4} + \underset{\text{Nitric oxide.}}{10NO}$$

The liquid remaining in the retort is then transferred to a dish (preferably of platinum), evaporated down to about half an ounce, and, lastly, diluted with distilled water to 5 fluidounces.

The use of the water in this process is to moderate the reaction. Strong hot nitric acid oxidizes phosphorus with almost explosive rapidity, hence must not only be diluted in the first instance, but be rediluted, from time to time, to prevent its becoming too strong by loss of water. Deficiency of nitric acid must also be avoided, or some phosphorous acid (H_2PHO_2) will be formed. A flask, in the neck of which a funnel is inserted, and a second funnel inverted, so that its mouth rests within the mouth of the first, is an efficient and convenient arrangement of apparatus for this process, especially if the operation be conducted slowly.

Solution of phosphoric acid evaporated leaves a residue which melts at a low red heat, yielding *pyrophosphoric acid*, and, finally, *metaphosphoric acid* (*Glacial Phosphoric Acid*).

Quantivalence.—The elements represented by the formula PO_4 are those characteristic of phosphates. The grouping is trivalent; hence there may exist trimetallic or normal phosphate (M'_3PO_4), dimetallic acid phosphates (M'_2HPO_4), monometallic acid phosphates ($M'H_2PO_4$), and, lastly, trihydric phosphate (H_3PO_4), or common phosphoric acid. These are the ordinary phosphates met with in nature or used in pharmacy; the rarer pyrophosphates, metaphosphates, phosphites, and hypophosphites will be mentioned subsequently.

Analytical Reactions (Tests).

First Analytical Reaction.—To an aqueous solution of a phosphate (*e.g.* Na_2HPO_4) add solution of sulphate of magnesium with which chloride of ammonium and ammonia have been mixed; a white crystalline precipitate of ammonio-magnesium phosphate falls ($MgAmPO_4$).

Chloride of ammonium is added to prevent the precipitation of hydrate of magnesium. Arseniates, from their close analogy to phosphates, give a similar precipitate with the magnesium reagent.

Second Analytical Reaction.—To an aqueous solution of a phosphate add solution of nitrate of silver; light-yellow phosphate of silver (Ag_3PO_4) is precipitated. To a portion of the precipitate add ammonia; it dissolves. To another portion add nitric acid; it dissolves.

By this reaction phosphates may be distinguished from their close allies the arseniates, arseniate of silver being of a chocolate color.

Third Analytical Reaction.—To a solution (in a few drops of acid) of a phosphate insoluble in water (*e.g.* Ca_32PO_4) add an alkaline acetate (that is, a mixture of soda or ammonia with excess of acetic acid), and then a drop or two of solution of perchloride of iron; yellowish-white ferric phosphate (Fe_2PO_4) is precipitated.

Too much of the ferric chloride must not be added, or ferric acetate will be produced, in which ferric phosphate is to some extent soluble.

To remove the whole of the phosphoric radical from the solution, add ferric chloride so long as a precipitate is produced, and then boil the mixture; ferric phosphate and ferric oxyacetate are precipitated.

To obtain confirmatory evidence of the presence of phosphate in this precipitate, and to separate the phosphoric radical as a pure unmixed phosphate, collect the precipitate on a filter, wash, drop some solution of ammonia on it, then sulphydrate of ammonium, and finally wash with water; black ferrous sulphide remains on the filter, while phosphate of ammonium occurs in the filtrate. To the filtrate add a mixture of solutions of sulphate of magnesium and chloride of ammonium, and well stir; ammonio-magnesian phosphate is precipitated.

The above reaction is useful in the analysis of bone-earth, other earthy phosphates, phosphate of iron, and all phosphates insoluble in water. Only arseniates give similar appearance; but the acid solution of these may be decomposed by sulphuretted hydrogen (H_2S), especially after agitation with sulphurous acid and subsequent ebullition.

Other Analytical Reactions.—Solutions of barium and calcium salts give, with aqueous solutions of phosphates, white precipitates of the respective phosphates $BaHPO_4$, or Ba_32PO_4, and $CaHPO_4$, or Ca_32PO_4, all of which are soluble in acetic and the stronger acids.

Vanadium, V. 51.3, is a very rare element, and is here mentioned only because of its exceedingly interesting relationship to nitrogen, phosphorus, and arsenicum. Discovered but not isolated by Sefstrom, and its compounds investigated by Berzelius, it has only recently been obtained in the free state and fully studied by Roscoe.

N_2O_5, N_2O_4, N_2O_3, N_2O_2, N_2O. V_2O_5, V_2O_4, V_2O_3, V_2O_2, V_2O

Oxides of Nitrogen.		Oxides of Vanadium.	
Orthophosphates	$R_3'PO_4$	Orthovanadates	$R_3'VO_4$
Pyrophosphates	$R_4'P_2O_7$	Pyrovanadates	$R_4'V_2O_7$
Metaphosphates	$R'PO_3$	Metavanadates	$R'VO_3$

Isomorphous Minerals.

Apatite	$3(Ca_32PO_4),CaFl_2$
Pyromorphite	$3(Pb_32PO_4),PbCl_2$
Mimetesite	$3(Pb_32AsO_4),PbCl_2$
Vanadinite	$3(Pb_32VO_4),PbCl_2$

QUESTIONS AND EXERCISES.

546. State the source of phosphorus.

547. Give equations or diagrams explanatory of the isolation of phosphorus from its natural compounds.

548. What is the composition of farmers' "superphosphate," and how prepared?

549. Enumerate the properties of phosphorus.

550. Mention some solvents of phosphorus.

551. How is the official Diluted Phosphoric Acid made?

552. Describe the precautions necessary to be observed in making this acid.

553. What is the strength of the official acid?

554. Write formulæ illustrative of all classes of orthophosphates.

555. Mention the chief tests for soluble and insoluble phosphates.

556. By what reactions may phosphates be distinguished from arseniates?

BORACIC ACID AND OTHER BORATES.

Formula of Boracic Acid H_3BO_3. Molecular weight 62.

The composition of artificial boracic acid is expressed by the formula H_3BO_3; but at a temperature of 212° F. this body loses the elements of water and yields metaboracic acid, HBO_2. The latter acid exists in the jets of steam (*fumerolles* or *suffioni*) that issue from the earth in some districts of Tuscany, and collects in the water of the *lagoni* (lagoons or little lakes) formed at the orifice of the steam-channel. Neutralized by carbonate of sodium the acid liquid gives common borax ($2NaBO_2, B_2O_3, 10H_2O$), a salt containing, probably, metaborate of sodium, boracic anhydride, and water of crystallization: it appears to be analogous in constitution to the red chromate of potassium and other similar abnormal salts. It occurs "in transparent colorless crystals, sometimes slightly effloresced, with a weak alkaline reaction; insoluble in rectified spirit, soluble in water." Borax is also found native, particularly in Thibet. Fused borax readily dissolves metallic oxides, as will have been already noticed in testing for cobalt and manganese. Hence, besides its use in medicine (*Sodæ Borax*, U. S. P.; *Borax; Mel Boracis*, B. P., or *Mel Sodæ Boratis*, U. S. P., and *Glycerinum Boracis*, B. P.), it is employed as a flux in refining and other metallurgic and ceramic operations.

Quantivalence.—The boracic radical is trivalent (BO_3'''), the metaboracic, univalent (BO_2'); they have not been isolated. The element boron, like carbon, occurs in the amorphous, graphitoidal, and crystalline conditions. It is a trivalent element (B'''), yielding definite salts, such as the chloride (BCl_3) and fluoride (BF_3). Its atomic weight is 11.

Reactions.

First Synthetical Reaction.—To a hot solution of a crystal of borax add a few drops of sulphuric acid and set aside; on cooling, crystalline scales of boracic acid (H_3BO_3) are deposited. They may be purified by collecting on a filter, slightly washing, drying, digesting in hot alcohol, filtering, and setting aside; pure boracic acid (B. P.) is deposited. The acid may also be recrystallized from water. Fifty grains dissolved in one ounce of rectified spirit constitutes "Solution of Boracic Acid," B. P.

When heated, these crystals lose water and yield, first, metaboracic acid (HBO_2), and subsequently, when fused, boracic anhydride (B_2O_3).

Second Synthetical Reaction.—Mix together 1 part of boracic acid, 4 of acid tartrate of potassium, and 10 or 20 of water; evaporate to a syrupy consistence, spread on plates, and set aside for dry scales to form. The resulting substance is far more readily dissolved by water than its constituents, and is known as *boro-tartrate of potassium*, *soluble tartar*, or *soluble cream of tartar*. The Prussian *tartarus boraxatus* differs from the foregoing French variety in containing 1 part of *borax* to 3 of acid tartrate of potassium.

Analytical Reactions (Tests).

First Analytical Reaction.—Dip a piece of turmeric paper (paper soaked in tincture of turmeric tubers and dried) into a solution of boracic acid; it is colored brown-red, as by alkalies.

The usual way of applying this test is as follows: Add to the borate a few drops of hydrochloric acid, immerse half of a slip of turmeric paper in the liquid, then remove the hydrochloric acid by drying the paper over a flame. Concentrated hydrochloric acid and ferric chloride produce a somewhat similar effect.

Second Analytical Reaction.—To a fragment of a borate (borax, for example) in a small dish or watch-glass add a drop of sulphuric acid and then a little alcohol, warm the mixture and set light to the spirit; the resulting flame will be tinged of a greenish color at its edges by the volatilized boracic acid.

The liquid should be well stirred while burning. Salts of copper and some metallic chlorides produce a somewhat similar color.

Other Analytical Reactions.—In solutions of normal borates (Na_3BO_3 *e. g.*) barium salts give a white precipitate of barium borate (Ba_32BO_3) soluble in acids and alkaline salts. Nitrate of silver gives borate of silver (Ag_3BO_3) soluble in nitric acid and in ammonia. Chloride of calcium, if the solution is not too dilute, gives white borate of calcium.

The foregoing acids and other salts contain the only acidulous radicals that are commonly met with in analysis or in ordinary pharmaceutical operations. There are, however, many others which occasionally present themselves. The chief of these will now be shortly noticed; they are arranged in alphabetical order to facilitate reference.

SALTS OF RARER ACIDULOUS RADICALS.

BENZOIC ACID ($HC_7H_5O_2$) AND OTHER BENZOATES.—Slowly heat a fragment of benzoin (*Benzoinum*, B. P. and U. S. P.) in a test-tube; benzoic acid (*Acidum Benzoicum*, B. P. and U. S. P.) rises in vapor and condenses in small, white, feathery plates and needles, on the cool sides of the tube. Or boil the benzoin with one-fourth its weight of lime, filter, concentrate, decompose the solution of benzoate of calcium by hydrochloric acid, collect the precipitated benzoic acid, press between paper, dry, and sublime in a tube or other vessel.

$$\underset{\text{Benzoic acid (impure).}}{2HC_7H_5O_2} + \underset{\text{Hydrate of calcium.}}{Ca2HO} = \underset{\text{Benzoate of calcium.}}{Ca2C_7H_5O_2} + \underset{\text{Water.}}{2H_2O}$$

$$\underset{\text{Benzoate of calcium.}}{Ca2C_7H_5O_2} + \underset{\text{Hydrochloric acid.}}{2HCl} = \underset{\text{Chloride of calcium.}}{CaCl_2} + \underset{\text{Benzoic acid (pure).}}{2HC_7H_5O_2}$$

There is always associated with the product a minute quantity of a volatile oil of agreeable odor, suggesting that of hay.

Benzoate of Ammonium.—To a little benzoic acid add a few drops of solution of ammonia; it readily dissolves, forming benzoate of ammonium (*Ammoniæ Benzoas*, B. P. ($NH_4C_7H_5O_2$).

$$\underset{\text{Benzoic acid.}}{HC_7H_5O_2} + \underset{\text{Ammonia.}}{NH_4HO} = \underset{\text{Benzoate of ammonium.}}{NH_4C_7H_5O_2} + \underset{\text{Water.}}{H_2O}$$

On evaporation, acid crystals or, ammonia being added, neutral crystals of benzoate of ammonium are deposited.

Properties.—Benzoic acid is also soluble in other alkaline liquids, forming benzoates. It is slightly soluble in cold water, more so in hot, and readily soluble in rectified spirit. It melts at 248° F., and boils at 462°, evaporating with only a slight residue.

Tests.—The following are the *tests* for benzoic acid: To a portion of the above solution of benzoate of ammonium add a drop or two of sulphuric or hydrochloric acid; a white crystalline precipitate of benzoic acid separates. To another portion, carefully made neutral, add a drop or two of neutral solution of perchloride of iron; reddish ferric benzoate is precipitated. Benzoic acid is distinguished from an allied body, cinnamic acid (occurring in Balsams of Peru, Tolu, and Storax), by not yielding hydride of benzoyl (C_7H_5OH) (oil of bitter almonds) when distilled with chromic acid—that is, with a mixture of red chromate of potassium and sulphuric acid.

Benzoic acid is said to be largely produced at a cheap rate from naphthalin, one of the by-products in the distillation of coal for gas (*Chemical News*, xvi. p. 296.)

Carminic Acid ($C_{14}H_{14}O_8$).—This is the coloring principle of cochineal (*Coccus*, B. P. and U. S. P.). The *carmine* of trade, when unadulterated (*vide* Pharmaceutical Journal, 1859–60, p. 546), is carminic acid united with about five per cent. of alumina, or, occasionally, of oxide of tin or albumen. It should be wholly soluble in solution of ammonia. Carmine, with French chalk, or starch, constitutes *face-rouge* or *animal rouge*.

Cetraric Acid ($H_2C_{34}H_{30}C_{16}$) is the bitter principle of Iceland moss (*Cetraria*, B. P. and U. S. P.). In the lichen it is associated with much starch.

Chrysophanic Acid ($C_{10}H_8O_3$?). This acid is the chief coloring-matter of various species of rhubarb root (*Rhei Radix*, B. P., *Rheum*, U. S. P.) and parmelia. It may be obtained in crystals of a golden-yellow color, hence the name (from χρυσὸς, *chrusos*, gold, and φαίνω, *phainō*, I shine). Its synonyms are *Rhaponticin*, *Rheic acid*, *Rhein*, *Rheumin*, *Rhubarbaric acid*, *Rhubarbarin*, *Rumicin*. Chrysophanic acid, black, red-brown, and red resins (*Aporetine*, *Phæore-*

tine, and *Erythroretine*), a bitter principle, and tannic acid are considered to be the conjoint source of the therapeutic properties of rhubarb.

CYANIC ACID (HCyO) AND OTHER CYANATES.—The valuable reducing-power of cyanide of potassium (KCy) (or ferrocyanide, K_4Fcy) on metallic compounds is due to the avidity with which it forms cyanate (KCyO).

Process.—Fuse a few grains of cyanide of potassium in a small porcelain crucible, and add powdered oxide of lead; a globule of metallic lead is at once set free, excess of the oxide converting the whole of the cyanide of potassium into cyanate of potassium.

Urea.—Cyanate of potassium (KCNO), or, better, cyanate of lead (Pb2CNO), treated with sulphate of ammonium, yields cyanate of ammonium (NH_4CNO); and solution of cyanate of ammonium, when simply heated, changes to artificial *urea* (CH_4N_2O), the most important constituent of urine, and the chief form in which the nitrogen of food is eliminated from the animal system. The process will be more fully described subsequently in connection with urea.

FORMIC ACID ($HCHO_2$).—The red ant (*Formica rufa*) and several other insects, when irritated, eject a strongly acid, acrid liquid, having a composition expressed by the above formula, and which has appropriately received the name of formic acid; it is also contained in the leaves of the stinging-nettle.

Process.—It may be artificially prepared by heating equal weights of oxalic acid and glycerine to a temperature of from 212° to 220° for fifteen hours. The glycerine has, apparently, no chemical action, but, for some unknown reason, induces decomposition of the oxalic acid at a lower temperature than would otherwise be necessary; at a higher temperature the formic acid itself is decomposed. On distilling the mixture with water the formic acid slowly passes over. The dilute acid may be concentrated by neutralizing with carbonate of lead, filtering, evaporating to a small bulk, collecting the deposited crystalline formate of lead, drying, decomposing in a current of sulphuretted hydrogen, and separating the resulting syrupy acid, or distilling the formate of lead with strong sulphuric acid.

$$\underset{\text{Oxalic acid.}}{H_2C_2O_4} = \underset{\text{Formic acid.}}{HCHO_2} + \underset{\text{Carbonic acid gas.}}{CO_2}$$

Formic acid may be instructively though not economically prepared by the oxidation of methylic alcohol (wood-spirit), just as acetic acid and valerianic acid are obtained from ethylic alcohol and amylic alcohol respectively.

$$\underset{\text{Wood spirit.}}{CH_3HO} + \underset{\text{Oxygen.}}{O_2} = \underset{\text{Formic acid.}}{HCHO_2} + \underset{\text{Water.}}{H_2O}$$

Tests.—Formic acid does not char when heated alone or with sulphuric acid, but splits up into carbonic oxide gas and water. It is recognized by this property and by its reducing-action on salts of gold, platinum, mercury, and silver. It is solid below 32°.

GALLIC ACID.—See *Tannic Acid.*

HEMIDESMIC ACID.—The supposed active principle of hemidesmus root (*Hemidesmi Radix*, B. P.).

HIPPURIC ACID ($HC_9H_8NO_3$) is a constituent of human urine (much increased on taking benzoic acid), but is best prepared from the urine of the horse (hence the name, from ἵππος, *hippos*, a horse), or, better, from that of the cow. To such urine add a little milk of lime, boil for a few minutes, remove precipitated phosphates by filtration, drop in hydrochloric acid until the liquid, after well stirring, is exactly neutral to test-paper, concentrate to about one-eighth the original bulk, and add excess of strong hydrochloric acid; impure hippuric acid is deposited. From a solution of the impure acid in hot water chlorine gas removes the color, and the liquid deposits crystals of pure hippuric acid on cooling. Its constitution is that of *benzoic glycocine*, $C_2H_2(C_7H_5O)(NH_2)O_2$.

Tests.—To a solution of hippurate add neutral solution of ferric chloride; a brown precipitate (ferric hippurate) results. Salts of silver and mercury give white precipitates. Heat hippuric acid in a test-tube; it chars, benzoic acid sublimes, and vapors of characteristic odor are evolved; they contain, amongst other bodies, hydrocyanic acid and a substance smelling somewhat like Tonka bean.——The crystalline form of hippuric acid is characteristic; it will be described in connection with the subject of urine.

QUESTIONS AND EXERCISES.

557. Give the preparation, composition, properties, and tests of benzoic acid, employing equations or diagrams.
558. What is the nature of carmine?
559. Name the bitter principle of Iceland moss.
560. Mention the coloring principle of rhubarb.
561. To what is rhubarb considered to owe its medicinal activity?
562. How is cyanate of potassium prepared, how converted into an ammonium salt, and what the relations of the latter to urea?
563. Give the formulæ of cyanic acid, cyanate of ammonium, and urea.
564. What is the chemical formula of formic acid?
565. Describe the artificial production of formic acid.
566. Describe the relation of formic acid to wood-spirit.
567. State the sources, characters, and tests of hippuric acid.

HYDROFERROCYANIC ACID ($H_4Fe''Cy_6$, or H_4Fcy'''') AND OTHER FERROCYANIDES.—The ferrocyanide of most interest is that of potassium (*Potassii Ferrocyanidum*, U. S. P.), the yellow prussiate of potash (*Potassæ Prussias Flava*, B. P.) ($K_4FeC_6N_6$, $3H_2O$), the formation of which was alluded to in connection with hydrocyanic acid (see page 229). It cannot be regarded as simply a double salt of cyanide of potassium with cyanide of iron ($FeCy_2$, $4KCy$), its chemical properties being entirely different from either of those substances; moreover, unlike cyanide of potassium, it is not poisonous. Most of its reactions point to the conclusion that its iron and cyanogen are intimately united to form a definite quadrivalent radical appropriately termed *ferrocyanogen* ($FeCy_6$, or Fcy). One part of ferrocyanide of potassium in 20 of water forms the official "Solution of Yellow Prussiate of Potash," B. P.

Tests.—Many of the ferrocyanides are insoluble, and are therefore precipitated when solution of ferrocyanide of potassium is added to the various salts. Those of iron and copper being of characteristic color, are adopted as tests of the presence of the metals or of the ferrocyanogen, as the case may be.

$$3K_4Fcy + 2(Fe_23SO_4) = Fe_4Fcy_3 + 6K_2SO_4.$$

To solution of ferrocyanide of potassium add a ferric salt; ferrocyanide of iron (Fe_4Fcy_3) (Prussian Blue) (*Ferri Ferrocyanidum*, U. S. P.) is precipitated.

To another portion add solution of a copper salt; reddish-brown ferrocyanide of copper (Cu_2Fcy) is precipitated.

Note.—The ferrocyanogen in ferrocyanide of potassium is broken up when the salt is heated with sulphuric acid, *carbonic oxide* being involved if the acid is strong, and *hydrocyanic acid* if weak:—

$$K_4FeC_6N_6 + 6H_2O + 6H_2SO_4 = 2K_2SO_4 + FeSO_4 + 3(NH_4)_2SO_4 + 6CO.$$

$$2K_4FeCy_6 + 6H_2SO_4 + xH_2O = FeK_2FeCy_6 + 6KHSO_4 + 6HCy + xH_2O.$$

Hydrocyanic Acid has already been described. (*Vide* p. 230.)

Carbonic oxide (CO).—Heat two or three fragments of ferrocyanide of potassium with eight or ten times their weight of sulphuric acid, and, as soon as the gas begins to be evolved, remove the test-tube from the flame; for the action, when once set up, proceeds somewhat tumultuously. Ignite the carbonic oxide at the mouth of the tube; it burns with a pale blue flame, the product of combustion being carbonic acid gas (CO_2).

Carbonic oxide is a direct poison. It is generated whenever coke, charcoal, or coal burns with an insufficient supply of air. Hence the danger of open fires in the more or less closed apartments of ordinary dwellings.

Carbonic oxide may also be obtained from oxalic acid. (*Vide* p. 262).

HYDROFERRIDCYANIC ACID ($H_6Fe'''_2Cy_{12}$, or $H^I_6Fdcy^{VI}$) AND OTHER FERRIDCYANIDES.—Pass chlorine gas through solution of ferrocyanide of potassium until the liquid ceases to give a blue precipitate, when a minute portion is taken out on the end of a glass rod and brought into contact with a drop of a dilute solution of a ferric salt; it now contains ferridcyanide of potassium ($K_6Fe'''_2Cy_{12}$, or $K^I_6Fdcy^{VI}$), *red prussiate of potash* (B. P.), as it is termed from the color of its crystals:—

$$2K'_4Fe''Cy'_6 + Cl'_2 = 2K'Cl' + K'_6Fe_2'''Cy'_{12}.$$

Note.—The removal of two atoms of potassium from the ferrocyanide is the only change of composition that occurs; but the ferrocyanogen is altered in quality, its iron passing from the ferrous to the ferric condition, from bivalent to trivalent activity, a condition in which it no longer precipitates ferric salts, but, on the other hand, gives a dark-blue precipitate with ferrous salts. The radical is distinguished as ferridcyanogen.

Test.—To a portion of the solution add solution of ferrous sulphate; a precipitate falls. This precipitate is ferridcyanide of iron (Turnbull's blue), $Fe''_3Fe'''_2Cy'_{12}$, or $Fe^{II}_3Fdcy^{VI}$.

$$K_6Fdcy + 3FeSO_4 = Fe_3Fdcy + 3K_2SO_4.$$

It will be noticed that this change in the condition of the iron keeps up the balance of the atomic values of the various parts of the radicals or of the salts; the quantivalential equilibrium is maintained.

A solution of 1 of ferridcyanide of potassium in 20 of water constitutes the "Solution of Red Prussiate of Potash," B. P.

HYDROFLUORIC ACID (HF) AND OTHER FLUORIDES.—Molecular weight of HF, 20. The chief use of hydrofluoric acid is in the etching on glass. The operation, performed on the small scale, also constitutes the best test for fluorine, the elementary radical of all fluorides.

Process and Test.—Warm any odd piece of window-glass, having an inch or two of surface, until a piece of beeswax rubbed on one side yields a thin oily film. When cool make a cross, letter, or other mark on the glass by pressing a pointed piece of wood, a penknife, or file, through the wax. Place two or three grains of powdered fluor spar, the commonest natural fluoride, in a small porcelain crucible, add a drop or two of sulphuric acid, cover the crucible with the prepared glass, waxed side downwards, and gently warm the bottom of the crucible in a fume-chamber or in the open air, in such a way as not to melt the wax. After a few minutes remove the glass, wash the waxed side by pouring water over it, scrape off most of the wax, then warm the glass, and wipe off the remainder; the marks made through the wax will be found to be permanently etched on the glass; the acid has eaten into or *etched* (from the German *ätzen*, to corrode) the glass.

In the above operation the fluoride of calcium and sulphuric acid yield hydrofluoric acid, thus:—

$$CaF_2 + H_2SO_4 = CaSO_4 + 2HF.$$

The hydrofluoric acid gas and the silica of the glass then yield gaseous fluoride of silicon (SiF_4), which escapes, and water, thus:—

$$4HF + SiO_2 = 2H_2O + SiF_4.$$

The silica being removed from the glass, leaves furrows or etched portions.

Note.—In the experiment just described, the liberated hydrofluoric acid also attacks the siliceous glazing of the porcelain crucible; so that in important cases, where search is made for very small quantities of fluorine, vessels of platinum or lead must be employed.

Uses.—The aqueous solution of hydrofluoric acid used by etchers, and commonly termed simply hydrofluoric acid, or fluoric acid, is prepared in leaden stills and receivers, and kept in leaden or gutta-percha bottles. Except these materials, as well as platinum and fluor spar, hydrofluoric acid rapidly attacks any substance of which bottles and basins are usually made. It quickly cauterizes the skin, producing a painful slow-healing sore.

Quantivalence.—The atom of fluorine, like that of chlorine, bromine, or iodine, is univalent (F'). The great analogy existing between these radicals extends to their compounds.

Fluorine is said to be a colorless gas; but, from the avidity with which it combines with all elements (except oxygen), it is so difficult of isolation as hitherto to preclude satisfactory study of its physical properties.

HYPOPHOSPHOROUS ACID (H_3PO_2, or HPH_2O_2) AND OTHER HYPOPHOSPHITES.—Boil together, in a fume-chamber, a grain or two of phosphorus, a few grains of slaked lime, and about a quarter of an ounce of water until phosphoretted hydrogen, a spontaneously inflammable, badly smelling gas, ceases to be evolved. The mixture, filtered, yields solution of hypophosphite of calcium ($Ca2PH_2O_2$).

$$P_8 + 6H_2O + 3CaH_2O_2 = 3(Ca2PH_2O_2) + 2PH_3.$$

The solution, when concentrated by evaporation, has been known to explode, probably from formation of phosphoretted hydrogen. This may be prevented, it is said, by evaporating at a low temperature, especially towards the close of the operation; or by adding alcohol, which decomposes any traces of liquid phosphoretted hydrogen (PH_2) or solid phosphoretted hydrogen (P_2H) which possibly may be present, and to which it is conceivable explosion may be due.

Phosphoretted hydrogen (PH_3).—The above reaction is also that by which phosphoretted hydrogen, the third hydride of phosphorus,, may be prepared. If the gas is to be collected, the phosphorus and water may first be boiled in a flask until spontaneously a jet of phosphorus vapor escapes, with steam, from the end of the attached delivery-tube. Strong solution of caustic potash or soda is next very gradually poured into the flask through a funnel tube previously fitted into the cork, the liquid being kept boiling. Phosphoretted hydrogen is then evolved, and if the delivery-tube dip under water may be collected, or allowed to slowly pass up through the water bubble by bubble so as to form the peculiar rings of smoke (phosphoric anhydride) characteristic of the experiment.

Hypophosphite of calcium may be obtained in crystals; but the solution is usually at once evaporated to dryness, a white pulverulent salt being obtained. Other hypophosphites may be obtained in the same way from other hydrates, or by double decomposition of the calcium salt and carbonates. Hypophosphorous acid, the hydrogen hypophosphite, may be prepared by decomposing the calcium salt by oxalic acid; hypophosphite of quinine by dissolving the alkaloid in hypophosphorous acid, or by decomposing sulphate of quinine by hypophosphite of barium. The hypophosphites are often used in medicine in the form of syrups. The term hypophosphite is in allusion to the smaller amount (ὑπὸ, *hupo*, under or deficiency) of oxygen in these compounds (R'_3PO_2) than in the phosphites (R_3PO_3), a class of salts having again less oxygen in their molecules than exists in those of the phosphates (R_3PO_4). The prefix *hypo* has similar significance in such words as hyposulphite and hypochlorite.

Tests.—To a portion of the above solution of hypophosphite of calcium add solution of chloride of barium, chloride of calcium, or acetate of lead; in neither case is a precipitate obtained, whereas soluble phosphates and phosphites yield white precipitates of phosphate or phosphite of barium, calcium, or lead. To other portions add solutions of nitrate of silver and mercuric chloride; the respective metals are precipitated as by phosphites. To another small portion add zinc and dilute sulphuric acid; hydrogen and phosphoretted hydrogen are evolved as from phosphites. To another portion add sufficient oxalic acid to remove the calcium; filter; to the solution of hypophosphorous acid add solution of sulphate of copper and slowly warm the mixture; solid brown hydride of copper is precipitated; increase the heat to the boiling-point; hydrogen is evolved and metallic copper set free. Heat a small quantity of a solid hypophosphite on the end of a spatula in a flame; it splits up into pyrophosphate, phosphoretted hydrogen, and water, burning with a phosphorescent light.

$$2(Ca2PH_2O_2) = Ca_2P_2O_7 + 2PH_3 + H_2O.$$

HYPOSULPHUROUS ACID ($H_2S_2O_3$) AND OTHER HYPOSULPHITES.—The only hyposulphite of much interest in pharmacy is the sodium salt (Hyposulphite of Soda, B. P.) ($Na_2S_2O_3, 5H_2O$).

Process.—Heat together gently, or set aside in a warm place, a mixture of solution of sulphite of sodium (Na_2SO_3), and a little powdered sulphur; combination slowly takes place, and hyposulphite of sodium is formed. The solution, filtered from excess of sulphur, readily yields crystals. [The solution of sulphite of sodium may be made by saturating a solution of soda with sulphurous acid gas.]

Use of hyposulphite of sodium in quantitative analysis. —In the British Pharmacopœia hyposulphite of sodium is given as a reagent for the quantitative estimation of free iodine in volumetric analysis. To a few drops of iodine-water add cold mucilage of starch; a deep-blue color (starch iodide) is produced. To the product add solution of hyposulphite of sodium until the blue color just disappears. This absorption of iodine is sufficiently definite and delicate to admit of application for quantitative purposes. It depends on the combination of the iodine with half of the sodium in two molecules of the hyposulphite, the hyposulphurous radicals of the two molecules apparently coalescing to form a new radical, the tetrathionic (from τέτρας, *tetras*, four, and θεῖον, *theion*, sulphur),—tetrathionate ($Na_2S_4O_6$) and iodide of sodium being formed.

Sulphur oxyacids.—It will be as well here to give the formulæ of three other oxyacids of sulphur, forming with the four already mentioned a series that is as useful as the series of compounds of nitrogen and oxygen in illustrating the soundness of Dalton's atomic theory (p. 36).

Sulphurous Acid	H_2SO_3
Sulphuric Acid	H_2SO_4
Hyposulphurous Acid	$H_2S_2O_3$
Dithionic Acid	$H_2S_2O_6$
Trithionic Acid	$H_2S_3O_6$
Tetrathionic Acid	$H_2S_4O_6$
Pentathionic Acid	$H_2S_5O_6$

Use of "Hypo" in Photography.—The sodium hyposulphite is largely used in photography to dissolve chloride, bromide, or iodide of silver off plates which have been exposed in the camera. Prepare a little chloride of silver by adding a chloride (chloride of sodium) to a few drops of solution of nitrate of silver. Collect the precipitated chloride on a filter, wash, and add a few drops of solution of hyposulphite of sodium; the silver salt is dissolved, solution of double hyposulphite of sodium and silver being formed. The solution of this double hyposulphite has a remarkably sweet taste, sweeter than syrup. The double hyposulphite of sodium and gold is employed for giving a pleasant tint to photographic prints.

Test.—To solution of a hyposulphite add a few drops of dilute sulphuric or other acid; hyposulphurous acid is set free, but at once begins to decompose into sulphurous acid, recognized by its odor, and free sulphur ($2H_2S_2O_3 = 2H_2SO_3 + S_2$). This reaction constitutes the best test for hyposulphites. Another good test of a soluble simple hyposulphite is its power of dissolving chloride of silver with production of a sweet solution.

QUESTIONS AND EXERCISES.

568. Give the formula of ferrocyanide of potassium.

569. What is the supposed constitution of ferrocyanide of potassium?

570. Enumerate the tests for ferrocyanogen.

571. What are the respective reactions of ferrocyanide of potassium with strong and weak sulphuric acid?

572. Mention and explain a common source of carbonic oxide in households?

573. Write equations or diagrams illustrative of the changes effected on ferrocyanide of potassium during its conversion into ferridcyanide.

574. By what reactions may the presence of a ferridcyanide in a solution be demonstrated?

575. State the difference between Prussian blue and Turnbull's blue.

576. Describe the source, mode of preparation, chief use of, and test for hydrofluoric acid.

577. Illustrate by a diagram the preparation and composition of hyposulphite of sodium.

578. Mention the uses and characteristic reactions of hyposulphite of sodium.

579. Give the names and formulæ of seven acids, each containing hydrogen, sulphur, and oxygen.

Lactic Acid ($H_2C_3H_4O_3$) and other Lactates.—When milk turns sour its sugar has become converted into an acid appropriately termed lactic (*lac, lactis*). Other saccharine and amylaceous substances also by fermentation yield lactic acid. Neither the hydrogen lactate (lactic acid) nor other lactates are much used in England, but the former is official in America (*Acidum Lacticum*, U. S. P.).

Process.—Lactate of calcium and lactic acid may be prepared as follows: Mix together eight parts of sugar, one of common cheese, three of chalk, and fifty of water, and set aside in a warm place (about 80° F.) for two or three weeks; a mass of small crystals of lactate of calcium results. Remove these, recrystallize from hot water, decompose by sulphuric acid, avoiding excess, digest in alcohol, filter off the sulphate of calcium, evaporate the clear solution to a syrup; this residue is lactic acid; sp. gr. 1.212.

Lactate of Iron (*Ferri Lactas*, U. S. P.) is made by digesting iron filings in warm diluted lactic acid (1 acid to 16 water) till effervescence of hydrogen ceases, filtering and setting aside to cool and crystallize. The crystals are collected, washed with alcohol, and dried. This ferrous lactate occurs in greenish-white crystalline crusts or grains, of a mild, sweetish, ferruginous taste, soluble in forty-eight parts of cold, and twelve of boiling water, but insoluble in alcohol. Exposed to heat it froths up, gives out thick, white, acid fumes, and becomes black; sesquioxide of iron being left. If it be boiled for fifteen minutes with nitric acid of the specific gravity 1.20, a white, granular deposit of mucic acid will occur on the cooling of the liquid.

Test.—No single reaction of lactic acid is sufficiently distinctive to form a test. The crystalline form of the lactate of calcium, as seen by the microscope, is characteristic. The production of this salt, and the isolation of the syrupy acid itself, are the only means, short of quantitative analysis, on which reliance can be placed.

A variety of lactic acid has been obtained from the juice of fish; it is termed *sarcolactic* acid (from σάρξ, gen. σαρκός, flesh).

MALIC ACID ($H_3C_4H_3O_5$) AND OTHER MALATES (from *malum*, an apple).—The juice of unripe apples, gooseberries, currants, rhubarb stalks, &c., contains malic acid and malate of potassium. When isolated it occurs in deliquescent prismatic crystals.

Tests.—Malate of calcium ($CaHC_4H_3O_5$) is soluble in water; hence the aqueous solution of malic acid or other malate is not precipitated by lime-water or chloride of calcium; but on adding spirit of wine a white precipitate falls, owing to the insolubility of the calcium malate in alcohol. Malates are precipitated by lead-salts; on warming the malate of lead with acetic acid it dissolves, separating out in acicular crystals on cooling. If the mixture be heated without acid the malate of lead agglutinates and fuses.

Hot strong sulphuric acid chars malic acid far less readily than it does nearly all other organic acids.

Malic acid is one of the chief products of the action of nitrous acid on asparagin ($C_4H_8N_2O_3,H_2O$), a crystalline body extracted from asparagus and marshmallow (*Althea*, U. S. P.).

MECONIC ACID ($H_3C_7HO_7$).—Opium contains meconic acid (from μήκων *mēkōn*, a poppy) partially combined with morphia. To concentrated infusion of opium, nearly neutralized by ammonia, add solution of chloride of calcium, meconate of calcium is precipitated. Wash the precipitate, place it in a small quantity of hot water, and add a little hydrochloric acid; the clear liquid (filtered, if necessary) deposits scales of meconic acid on cooling.

Test.—To solution of meconic acid or other meconate, or to infusion of opium, add a *neutral* solution of ferric chloride; a red solution of meconate of iron is produced. To a portion of the mixture add solution of corrosive sublimate; the color is not destroyed: to another portion add hydrochloric acid; the color is discharged. (These reagents act on sulphocyanate of iron, which is of similar tint, in exactly the opposite manner.)

The normal meconates of potassium, sodium, and ammonium are soluble in water, the acid meconates very slightly soluble, the meconates of barium, calcium, lead, copper, and silver insoluble in water but soluble in acetic acid.

METAPHOSPHORIC ACID (HPO_3) AND OTHER METAPHOSPHATES.—Prepare phosphoric anhydride (P_2O_5) by burning a small piece of phosphorus in a porcelain crucible placed on a plate and covered by an inverted test-glass, tumbler, half-pint measure-glass, or some such vessel. After waiting a few minutes for the phosphoric anhydride to fall, pour a little water on the plate and filter the liquid; the product is solution of metaphosphoric acid (from μετὰ, *meta*, a preposition denoting change).

$$P_2O_5 + H_2O = 2HPO_3.$$

Tests.—To solution of metaphosphoric acid add ammonio-nitrate of silver, or to a neutral metaphosphate add solution of nitrate of silver; a white precipitate ($AgPO_3$)

is obtained. This reaction sufficiently distinguishes metaphosphates from the ordinary phosphates or orthophosphates (from ὀρθὸς, *orthos*, straight), as the common phosphates may, for distinction, be termed (which give, it will be remembered, a *yellow* precipitate with nitrate of silver). Another variety of phosphates shortly to be considered, the pyrophosphates, also give a white precipitate with nitrate of silver. To the solution of metaphosphoric acid obtained as above or by the action of acetic acid on a metaphosphate, add an aqueous solution of white of egg; coagulation of the albumen ensues. Neither orthophosphoric nor pyrophosphoric acid coagulates albumen. Boil the aqueous solution of metaphosphoric acid for some time; on testing the solution the acid will be found to have been converted into orthophosphoric acid:—

$$HPO_3 + H_2O = H_3PO_4.$$

The ordinary medicinal phosphoric acid is made from phosphorus and nitric acid, the liquid being evaporated to a syrupy consistence to remove the last traces of nitric acid. It may contain pyrophosphoric and metaphosphoric acids, if the heat employed be high enough to remove the elements of water:—

$$H_3PO_4 - H_2O = HPO_3.$$

On redilution the metaphosphoric acid only slowly reabsorbs water. If, therefore, on testing, metaphosphoric be found to be present, the solution should be boiled until conversion to orthophosphoric acid has occurred.

NITROUS ACID (HNO_2) AND OTHER NITRITES.—Strongly heat a fragment of nitrate of potassium or of sodium on a piece of platinum foil; oxygen is evolved and nitrate of potassium remains.

Test.—Dissolve the residue in water, add a few drops of dilute sulphuric acid, then a little weak solution of iodide of potassium, and, lastly, some mucilage of starch; the deep-blue compound of iodine and starch is at once produced. Repeat this experiment, using nitrate instead of nitrite; no blue color is produced.

$$2HI + 2HNO_2 = 2H_2O + 2NO + I_2.$$

Test for Nitrites in Water.—This liberation of iodine by nitrites and not by nitrates is a reaction of considerable value in searching for nitrites in ordinary drinking-waters, the occurrence of such salts being held to indicate the presence of nitrogenous organic matter in a state of oxidation or decay. The sulphuric acid used in the operation must be pure, and the iodide of potassium free from iodate.

Commercial Nitrous Acid.—The liquid commonly termed in pharmacy nitrous acid is simply nitric acid impure from the presence of nitrous acid.

The only nitrite used in medicine is a nitrite of an organic basylous radical, ethyl; nitrite of ethyl ($C_2H_5NO_2$), or nitrous ether, is the chief constituent of "*sweet spirit of nitre*" (*Spiritus Ætheris Nitrosi*, B. P. and U. S. P.: *vide* Index).

Phosphorous Acid (H_3PO_3, or H_2PHO_3).—It is necessary to notice this compound in order that the reader may have brought before him the three acids of phosphorus, namely, phosphoric acid (H_3PO_4), phosphorous acid (H_2PHO_3), and hypophosphorous acid (HPH_2O_2): it will be noticed that in composition they differ from each other simply in the proportion of oxygen, the molecules containing four, three, and two atoms respectively. In constitution they differ by the hypothetical phosphoric radical or grouping being trivalent, the phosphorous bivalent, and the hypophosphorous univalent. These three acids and corresponding salts must not be confounded with pyrophosphoric and metaphosphoric acids and salts; the former are acids of phosphorus; the latter, varieties of phosphoric acid: the former, in composition, differ from each other in the proportion of oxygen they contain; the latter, by the elements of water:—

Acids of Phosphorus.	*Varieties of phosphoric acid.*
H_3PO_4 phosphoric acid.	H_3PO_4 (ortho)phosphoric acid.
H_2PHO_3 phosphorous acid.	$H_4P_2O_7$ pyrophosphoric acid.
HPH_2O_2 hypophosphorous acid.	HPO_3 metaphosphoric acid.

When hypophosphorous acid is exposed to the air, oxygen is absorbed and phosphorous acid results; by prolonged exposure more oxygen is absorbed and phosphoric acid is obtained. When phosphoric acid, or rather, for distinction, orthophosphoric acid is heated, every two molecules yield the elements of a molecule of water, and pyrophosphoric acid results; by prolonged exposure to heat more water is evolved, and metaphosphoric acid is obtained. These differences will be further evident if the formulæ be written empirically, nearly all being doubled, thus:—

$H_6P_2O_4$ hypophosphorous acid.
$H_6P_2O_6$ phosphorous acid.
$H_6P_2O_8$ { phosphoric acid, or orthophosphoric acid.
$H_4P_2O_7$ pyrophosphoric acid.
$H_2P_2O_6$ metaphosphoric acid.

Or thus:—

phosphoric acid
$H_6P_2O_8$.

phosphorous acid	pyrophosphoric acid
$H_6P_2O_6$.	$H_4P_2O_7$.
hypophosphorous acid	metaphosphoric acid
$H_6P_2O_4$.	$H_2P_2O_6$.

From the central compound, phosphoric acid, the acids of phosphorus differ by regularly diminishing proportions of the element oxygen (see previous page), the varieties of phosphoric acid by regularly diminishing proportions of the elements of water.

Prepare phosphorous acid by exposing a moist stick of phosphorus to the air; a thin stream of heavy white vapor falls, which is the acid in question. The best method of collection is to place the stick in an old test-tube having a hole in the bottom, to support this tube by a funnel or otherwise, the neck of the funnel being supported in a bottle, test-glass, or tube, at the bottom of which is a little water. Having collected some phosphorous acid in this way, apply the various tests already alluded to under *Hypophosphorous Acid*, first carefully neutralizing the phosphorous acid by an alkali. The means by which the varieties of phosphoric acid are distinguished have been given under *Metaphosphoric Acid.*

Other soluble phosphites are prepared by neutralizing phosphorous acid with alkalies, and the insoluble phosphites by double decomposition.

PYROGALLIC ACID.—See *Tannic Acid.*

PYROPHOSPHORIC ACID ($H_4P_2O_7$) AND OTHER PYROPHOSPHATES.—Heat ordinary phosphate of sodium (Na_2HPO_4, $12H_2O$) in a crucible; water of crystallization is first evolved, and dry phosphate (Na_2HPO_4) remains. Continue the heat to redness; two molecules of the salt yield one molecule of water, and a salt having new properties is obtained:—

$$2Na_2HPO_4 - H_2O = Na_4P_2O_7.$$

It is termed pyrophosphate of sodium, in allusion to its origin (πῦρ, *pūr*, fire). Other pyrophosphates are produced in a similar way, or by double decomposition and precipitation, or by neutralizing pyrophosphoric acid by an oxide, hydrate, or carbonate. Possibly the pyrophosphates are only compounds of orthophosphates with metaphosphates:—

$$Na_4P_2O_7 = Na_3PO_4, NaPO_3.$$

Tests.—To solution of a pyrophosphate add solution of nitrate of silver; white pyrophosphate of silver ($Ag_4P_2O_7$) falls as a dense white powder, differing much in appearance from the white gelatinous metaphosphate of silver or the yellow orthophosphate. To pyrophosphoric acid, or to a pyrophosphate mixed with acetic acid, add an aqueous solution of albumen (white of egg); no precipitate occurs. Metaphosphoric acid, it will be remembered, gives a white precipitate with albumen.

QUESTIONS AND EXERCISES.

580. What are the sources of lactic acid?
581. How is lactic acid usually prepared?
582. Name some of the plants in which malic acid is found.
583. Whence is meconic acid derived?
584. By what process may meconic acid be isolated?
585. Which is the best test for the meconic radical?
586. Distinguish meconates from sulphocyanates.
587. Give the mode of manufacture of hypophosphites.
588. How is the phosphoretted hydrogen prepared?
589. By what ready method may metaphosphoric acid be obtained for experimental purposes?
590. Name the tests for metaphosphates.
591. How may meta- or pyro-phosphoric acid be converted into orthophosphoric acid?
592. Describe the preparation of phosphorous acid.
593. State the relations which the acids of phosphorus bear to each other.
594. How are pyrophosphates prepared?
595. Offer two views of the constitution of pyrophosphates.
596. Define, by formulæ, metaphosphates, pyrophosphates, orthophosphates, phosphites, and hypophosphites.
597. Mention the tests by which meta-, pyro-, and orthophosphates are analytically distinguished.
598. Name the reactions by which hypophosphites and phosphites are detected.

Silicic Acid (H_4SiO_4) and other Silicates.—Silicates of various kinds are among the commonest of minerals. The ordinary *sandstones* are chiefly silicates; *meerschaum* is an acid silicate of magnesium; the various *clays* are aluminium silicates; *sand, flint, quartz, agate, chalcedony,* and *opal,* are silicic anhydride or *silica* (SiO_2). Artificial silicates are familiar under the forms of *glass* and *earthenware.* Common English window-glass is usually silicate of calcium, sodium, and aluminium; French glass, silicate of calcium and sodium; Bohemian, chiefly silicate of potassium and calcium; English flint- or crystal-glass for ornamental, table, and optical purposes, is mainly silicate of potassium and lead. Earthenware is mostly silicate of aluminium (clay), with more or less of silicate of calcium, sodium, and potassium, and, in the commoner forms, iron. The various kinds of *porcelain* (China, Sèvres, Meissen, Berlin, English), *Wedgwood-ware,* and *stoneware* are varieties of earthenware. *Crucibles, bricks,* and *tiles* are clay-silicates. *Mortar* is essentially silicate of calcium. *Portland, Roman,* and other hydraulic *cements* are silicates of calcium with more or less silicate of aluminium.

Mix together a few grains of powdered flint or sand with about five or six times its weight of carbonate of sodium and an equal quantity of carbonate of potassium, and fuse a little of the mixture on platinum-foil in the blowpipe-flame; the product is a kind of *soluble glass*. Boil the foil in water for a few minutes; filter; to a portion add excess of hydrochloric acid, evaporate the solution to dryness, and again boil the residue in water and acid; oxide of silicon or *silica* (SiO_2) remains as a light, flaky, insoluble powder.

The *soluble glass* or *glass liquor* of trade commonly contains 10 or 12 per cent. of soda ($NaHO$) to 20 or 25 per cent. of silica (SiO_2).

The foregoing operation constitutes the *test* for silicates. By fusion with alkali the silicate is decomposed, and a soluble alkaline silicate formed. On addition of acid, silicic acid (H_4SiO_4) is set free, but remains in solution if sufficient water is present. The heat subsequently applied eliminates water and reduces the silicic acid to silica (SiO_2), which is insoluble in water or acid. By the addition of hydrochloric acid to soluble glass, and removal of the resulting alkaline chloride and excess of hydrochloric acid by dialysis (a process to be subsequently described), a pure aqueous solution of silicic acid may be obtained; it readily changes into a gelatinous mass of silicic acid. Possibly some of the natural crystallized varieties of silica may have been obtained from the silica contained in such an aqueous solution, nearly all waters yielding a small quantity of silica when treated as above described.

Siliciuretted hydrogen, or hydride of silicon (SiH_4), is a spontaneously inflammable gas formed on treating silicide of magnesium with hydrochloric acid. It is the analogue of light carburetted hydrogen (CH_4). A liquid chloride of silicon ($SiCl_4$) and a gaseous fluoride (SiF_4) also exist.

SUCCINIC ACID ($H_2C_4H_4O_4$).—Amber (*Succinum*) is a peculiar resin usually occurring in association with coal and lignite. From the fact that fragments of coniferous fruit are frequently found in amber, and impressions of bark on its surface, it is considered to have been an exudation from a species of Pinus now probably extinct. Heated in a retort, amber yields, first, a sour aqueous liquid containing acetic acid and another characteristic body appropriately termed *succinic acid;* second, a volatile liquid known as *oil of amber* (*Oleum Succini Rectificatum*, U. S. P.) resembling the oil yielded by most resinous substances under similar circumstances; and, third, a pitchy residue allied to asphalt. The succinic acid is a normal constituent of the amber, the acetic acid is produced during distillation. Succinic acid has also been found in wormwood, in several pine-resins, and in certain animal fluids, such as those of hydatid cysts and hydrocele. It may be obtained artificially from butyric, stearic, or margaric acid by oxidation. Tartaric, malic, and succinic acids are also convertible the one into the other.

The *succinates* are normal ($R'_2C_4H_4O_4$) and acid ($R'HC_4H_4O_4$); a double succinate of potassium and hydrogen ($KHC_4H_4O_4,H_2C_4H_4O_4,H_2O$), analogous to the superacid oxalate, salt of sorrel, also exists.

Soluble succinates give a bulky brown precipitate with neutral ferric chloride, only less voluminous than ferric benzoate; a white precipitate with acetate of lead, soluble in excess of either reagent; with nitrate of silver a white precipitate after a time; with chloride of barium no precipitate at first, but a white one of succinate of barium on the addition of ammonia and alcohol. Succinates are distinguished from benzoates by the last-named reaction, and by not yielding a precipitate on the addition of acids (*vide* p. 277).

Sulphocyanic Acid (HCyS) and other Sulphocyanates.—Boil together sulphur and solution of *pure* cyanide of potassium; solution of sulphocyanate of potassium (KCyS) is formed.

Tests.—Filter, and to a small portion of the solution add a ferric salt (Fe_2Cl_6); a deep-blood-red solution of ferric sulphocyanate is formed. To a portion of the red liquid add hydrochloric acid; the color is not discharged (meconate of iron, a salt of similar tint, is decomposed by hydrochloric acid). In the acid liquid place a fragment or two of zinc, sulphuretted hydrogen is evolved, and the red color disappears. To another portion of the ferric sulphocyanate add solution of corrosive sublimate; the color is at once discharged. (Ferric meconate is unaffected by corrosive sublimate.) The ferric is the best test of the presence of a sulphocyanate; indirectly, it is a good test of the presence of hydrocyanic acid or cyanogen.

To solution of a sulphocyanate add solution of mercuric nitrate; mercuric sulphocyanate is precipitated as a white powder.

Pharaoh's Serpents.—Mercuric sulphocyanate, thoroughly washed and made up into little cones, forms the toy called Pharaoh's serpent. It readily burns when ignited, the chief product being a light solid matter (mellon, C_9N_{13}, and the melam, $C_3H_6N_6$), which issues from the cone in a snake-like coil of extraordinary length. The other products are mercuric sulphide (of which part remains in the snake and part is volatilized), nitrogen, sulphurous and carbonic acid gases, and vapor of metallic mercury. (For details concerning the economical manufacture of sulphocyanates see *Pharmaceutical Journal*, second series, vol. vii. p. 581, and p. 152.)

The sulphocyanic radical (CyS) is often termed sulphocyanogen (Scy), and its compounds regarded as *sulphocyanides*.

Tannic Acid or Tannin ($C_{27}H_{22}O_{17}$).—This is a common astringent constituent of plants, but is contained in largest quantity in galls (excrescences on the oak formed by the puncture and deposited ova of an insect). English galls contain from 14 to 28 per cent. of tannic acid; Aleppo galls (*Galla*, B. P. and U. S. P.) from 25 to 65 per cent. (*Acidum Tannicum*, B. P. and U. S. P.)

Process.—"Expose powdered galls (about an ounce is sufficient for the purpose of study) to a damp atmosphere for two or three days, and afterwards add sufficient ether to form a soft paste. Let this stand in a well-closed vessel for twenty-four hours, then, having quickly enveloped it in a linen cloth, submit it to strong pressure so as to separate the liquid portion, which contains the bulk of the tannin in solution. Reduce the pressed cake to powder, mix it with sufficient ether, to which one-sixteenth of its bulk of water has been added, to form again a soft paste, and press this as before. Mix the expressed liquids, and expose the mixture to spontaneous evaporation until, by the aid subsequently of a little heat, it has acquired the consistence of a soft extract; then place it on earthen plates or dishes, and dry it in a hot-air chamber at a temperature not exceeding 212°."

The resulting tannic acid occurs in "pale yellow vesicular masses or thin glistening scales, with a strongly astringent taste, and an acid reaction, readily soluble in water and rectified spirit, very sparingly soluble in ether."

Medicinal Uses.—Tannic acid is very soluble in water, and in this form is usually administered in medicine. Its official preparations are *Glycerinum Acidi Tannici*, *Suppositoria Acidi Tannici*, and *Trochisci Acidi Tannici*.

Tests.—To an aqueous solution of tannic acid add aqueous solution of gelatine, a yellowish-white flocculent compound of the two substances is precipitated. This is a good test of the presence of tannic acid.

Tanning.—The above reaction also serves to explain the chemical principle involved in *tanning*—the operation of converting skin into leather. In that process the skin is soaked in infusion of oak-bark (*Quercus Cortex*), the tannic acid of which uniting with the gelatinous tissues of the skin yields a compound very well represented by the above precipitate. Other infusions and extracts besides that of oak-bark are largely used by tanners; but they appear to act too quickly, and give a harsh, hard, less durable leather. The tannic acid of these preparations is probably slightly different from that of oak-bark.

To an aqueous solution of tannic acid add a neutral solution of a ferric salt; dark bluish-black tannate of iron is slowly precipitated. This is an excellent test for the presence of tannic acid in vegetable infusions. The precipitate is the basis of nearly all black writing-ink. Ferrous salts give at first only a slight reaction with tannic acid; but the liquid gradually darkens. Characters written with this liquid become quite black in a few hours, and are very permanent.

To an aqueous solution of tannic acid add solution of tartar-emetic; tannate of antimony is precipitated. This reaction and that with gelatine are useful in the quantitative estimation of the amount of tannic acid in various substances.

Tannic acid is a glucoside; that is, like several other substances, it yields glucose (grape-sugar) when boiled with dilute sulphuric or hydrochloric acid, the other product being gallic acid:—

$$C_{27}H_{22}O_{17} + 4H_2O = C_6H_{12}O_6 + 3H_3C_7H_3O_5.$$

Catechu (*Catechu*, U. S. P., *Catechu pallidum*, B. P.), *Gambir*, or *Terra Japonica*, *Kino* (*Kino*, B. P. and U. S. P.), *Elm Bark* (*Ulmi Cortex*, B. P.), and Slippery Elm Bark (*Ulmus fulva*, U. S. P.), and some other vegetable products contain a variety of tannic acid (*mimo-tannic acid*), which gives a greenish precipitate with neutral solutions of ferric salts.

Bael fruit (*Belæ fructus*, B. P.), from the *Ægle Marmelos*, is said to owe its astringency to a variety of tannic acid. In India a jelly and preserve have long been made from the Marmelos—whence the word *marmalade* for similar preserves. The astringency of Pomegranate-root Bark (*Granati Radicis Cortex*, B. P. and U. S. P.), and *Fruit* (*Granati Fructus Cortex*, U. S. P.), is due to tannic acid (its anthelmintic properties probably to a resinoid matter); and the same may be said of logwood (*Hæmatoxyli Lignum*, B. P. and U. S. P., the *color* of which is due to oxidized *hæmatoxylin*). *Rhatany*-root (*Krameriæ Radix*, B. P. and U. S. P.) contains about 40 per cent. of tannic acid, its active astringent principle; rhubarb-root about 9 per cent. *Bearberry*-leaves (*Uvæ Ursi Folia*, B. P. and U. S. P.) owe most of their therapeutic power to about 35 per cent. of tannic acid. (The cause of their influence on the kidneys is not yet traced.)

Gallic acid ($H_3C_7H_3O_5,H_2O$) (*Acidum Gallicum*, B. P. and U. S. P.) occurs in small quantity in oak-galls and other vegetable substances, but is always prepared from tannic acid. Powdered galls are moistened with water and set aside in a warm place for five or six weeks, occasionally being remoistened; fermentation occurs, and impure gallic acid is formed. The product is treated with about three times its weight of water, boiled to dissolve the gallic acid, filtered, the solution set aside to cool, deposited gallic acid collected, drained, pressed between folds of paper to remove all mother-liquor, and, if necessary, purified by recrystallization from water, or by solution in hot water and treatment with animal charcoal, which absorbs coloring-matter. On filtering and cooling, most of the acid separates in the form of fawn-colored slender acicular crystals. Gallic acid is soluble in about 100 times its weight of cold or 3 of boiling water, freely in spirit, sparingly in ether.

The nature of the action by which gallic acid is thus produced is probably similar to that of the action of dilute acids on tannic acid. During the process oxygen is absorbed and carbonic acid gas evolved, the sugar being thus broken up or perhaps prevented from being formed.

Test.—To an aqueous solution of gallic acid add a neutral solution of ferric salt; a bluish-black precipitate of gallate of iron falls, similar in appearance to tannate of iron. Ferrous salts also are blackened by gallic acid. To more of the solution add an aqueous solution of gelatine; no precipitate occurs. By the latter test gallic is distinguished from tannic acid.

Pyrogallic Acid ($C_6H_6O_3$).—This substance sublimes in light feathery crystals when gallic acid is heated. To an aqueous solution add a neutral solution of a ferric salt; a red color is produced. To another portion add a ferrous salt; a deep-blue color results.

Test for the three acids.—To three separate small quantities of milk of lime in test-tubes add, respectively tannic, gallic, and pyrogallic acids; the first slowly turns brown, the second more rapidly, while the pyrogallic mixture at once assumes a beautiful purplish-red color changing to brown. These reactions are highly characteristic. They are accompanied by absorption of oxygen from the air.

Use of Pyrogallic Acid in Gas-analysis.—A mixture of pyrogallic acid and solution of potash absorbs oxygen with such rapidity and completeness that a strong solution of each, passed up successively by a pipette into a graduated tube containing air or other gas, forms an excellent means of estimating free oxygen. The value of this method may be roughly proved by pouring a small quantity of each solution into a phial, immediately and firmly closing its mouth with a cork, thoroughly shaking the mixture and then removing the cork under water; the water rushes in and occupies about one-fifth of the previous volume of air, indicating that the atmosphere contains one-fifth of its bulk of oxygen. The small amount of carbonic acid gas present in the air is also absorbed by the alkaline liquid; in delicate experiments this should be removed by the alkali before the addition of pyrogallic acid.

URIC ACID ($H_2C_5H_2N_4O_3$) AND OTHER URATES.—Acidulate a few ounces of human urine with hydrochloric acid, and set aside for twenty-four hours; a few minute crystals of uric acid will be found adhering to the sides and bottom of the vessel and floating on the surface of the liquid.

Microscopical Test.—Remove some of the floating particles by a slip of glass, and examine by a powerful lens or microscope; the chief portion will be found to be in yellowish semitransparent crystals, more or less square, two of the sides of which are even, and two very jagged; but other forms are common (*vide* Frontispiece).

Chemical Test.—Collect more of the deposit, place in a watch-glass or small white evaporating-dish, remove adherent moisture by a piece of blotting- or filter-paper, add a drop or two of strong nitric acid, and evaporate to dryness; the residue will be red. When the dish is cold, add a drop of solution of ammonia; a purplish-crimson color results. The color is deepened on the addition of a drop of solution of potash.

Notes.—Uric acid and urates of sodium, potassium, calcium, and ammonium are common constituents of animal excretions. Human urine contains about one part of urate (usually urate of sodium) in 1000. When more than this is present the urate is often deposited as a sediment in the excreted urine, either at once, or after standing a short time. Uric acid or other urate is also occasionally deposited before leaving the bladder, and, slowly accumulating there, forms a common variety of urinary calculus.——Some urates are not definitely crystalline; but when treated with dilute nitric acid or a drop of solution of potash and then a drop or two of acetic acid, jagged microscope crystals of uric acid are usually formed.—All urates yield the crimson color when treated as above described.—This color is due to a definite substance, *murexid* ($C_8H_8N_6O_6$) (from the *murex*, a shell-fish of similar tint); and the test is known as *the murexid test*. The formation of murexid is due to the action of ammonia on *alloxan* ($C_4H_2N_2O_4,4H_2O$) and other white crystalline products of the oxidation of uric acid by nitric acid. Murexid is a good dye; it may be prepared from *guano* (the excrement of sea-fowl), which contains a large quantity of urate of ammonium. The excrement of the serpent is almost pure ammonium urate.

Uric acid and the urates will be again alluded to in connection with the subject of morbid urine.

Valerianic Acid or Valeric Acid ($HC_5H_9O_2$) and other Valerianates.—In a test-tube place a few drops of amylic alcohol (fousel oil) with a little dilute sulphuric acid and a grain or two of red chromate of potassium, cork the tube, set aside for a few hours, and then heat the mixture; valerianic acid, of characteristic valerian-like odor, is evolved.

Valerianic acid occurs naturally in valerian-root, but is usually prepared artificially, by the foregoing process, from amylic alcohol, to which it bears the same relation as acetic acid does to common alcohol :—

$$C_2H_5HO + O_2 = HC_2H_3O_2 + H_2O$$
$$C_5H_{11}HO + O_2 = HC_5H_9O_2 + H_2O.$$

Valerianate of Sodium ($NaC_5H_9O_2$) (*Sodæ Valerianas*, B. P. and U. S. P.) is prepared from the valerianic acid obtained on distilling the mixture of amylic alcohol (4 fl. ozs.), sulphuric acid ($6\frac{1}{2}$ fl. ozs. with 10 of water), and red chromate of potassium (9 ozs. in 70 of water). The mixture should stand for a few hours before heat is applied.

$$\underset{\text{Red chromate of potassium.}}{2(K_2CrO_4,CrO_3)} + \underset{\text{Sulphuric acid.}}{8H_2SO_4} = \underset{\text{Sulphate of chromium.}}{2(Cr_23SO_4)} + \underset{\text{Sulphate of potassium.}}{2K_2SO_4} + \underset{\text{Water.}}{8H_2O} + \underset{\text{Oxygen.}}{3O_2}$$

$$\underset{\text{Amylic alcohol.}}{C_5H_{11}HO} + \underset{\text{Oxygen.}}{O_2} = \underset{\text{Valerianic acid.}}{HC_5H_9O_2} + \underset{\text{Water.}}{H_2O}$$

$$\underset{\text{Amylic alcohol.}}{2C_5H_{11}HO} + \underset{\text{Oxygen.}}{O_2} = \underset{\text{Valerianate of amyl.}}{C_5H_{11}C_5H_9O_2} + \underset{\text{Water.}}{2H_2O}$$

The distillate (70 or 80 ozs.) is saturated with soda, which not only yields valerianate of sodium with the free valerianic acid, but decomposes the valerianate of amyl produced at the same time, more valerianate of sodium being formed and some amylic alcohol set free, according to the following equations :—

$$\underset{\text{Valerianic acid.}}{HC_5H_9O_2} + \underset{\text{Soda.}}{NaHO} = \underset{\text{Valerianate of sodium.}}{NaC_5H_9O_2} + \underset{\text{Water.}}{H_2O}$$

$$\underset{\text{Valerianate of amyl.}}{C_5H_{11}C_5H_9O_2} + \underset{\text{Soda.}}{NaHO} = \underset{\text{Valerianate of sodium.}}{NaC_5H_9O_2} + \underset{\text{Amylic alcohol.}}{C_5H_{11}HO}$$

From the solution of valerianate of sodium (which should be made neutral to test-paper by careful addition of soda solution) the solid white salt is obtained by evaporation to dryness and cautious fusion of the residue. The mass obtained on cooling should be broken up and kept in a well-closed bottle. It is entirely soluble in spirit.

Other Valerianates, as valerianate of zinc (*Zinci Valerianas*, B. P.) and ferric valerianate, may be made by double decomposition of valerianate of sodium with the sulphate or other salt of the metal the valerianate of which is desired, the new valerianate precipitating or crystallizing out.

Tests.—Heated with diluted sulphuric acid, valerianates of the metals give valerianic acid, which has a highly characteristic smell. Valerianate of sodium thus treated, and the resulting oily acid liquid purified by agitation with sulphuric acid and distillation furnishes the *Acidum Valerianicum* of the United States Pharmacopœia. Sp. gr. 933. Dry ammonia gas passed into valerianic acid gives white lamellar crystals of valerianate of ammonium (*Ammoniæ Valerianas*, U. S. P.).

The amylic alcohol ($C_5H_{11}HO$) from which valerianates are prepared may contain the next lower homologue, *butylic alcohol* (C_4H_9HO). This, during oxidation, will be converted into *butyric acid* ($HC_4H_7O_2$), the next lower homologue of valerianic acid ($HC_5H_9O_2$), and hence the various valerianates be contaminated by some *butyrates*. These are detected by distillation with diluted sulphuric acid and addition of solution of acetate of copper to the distillate, which at once becomes turbid if butyric acid be present. In this reaction valerianic and butyric acids are produced by double decomposition of the valerianate and butyrate by the sulphuric acid, and distil over on the application of heat. On the addition of acetate of copper ($Cu2C_2H_3O_2$) butyrate of copper ($Cu2C_4H_7O_2, H_2O$) is formed, and, being almost insoluble in water, is at once precipitated, or remains suspended, giving a bluish-white opalescent liquid. Valerianate of copper ($Cu2C_5H_9O_2$) is also formed after some time, but is far more soluble than the butyrate, and only slowly collects in the form of greenish oily drops, which gradually pass into greenish-blue hydrous crystalline valerianate of copper (Larocque and Huralt).

QUESTIONS AND EXERCISES.

599. What is the constitution of nitrites?
600. Mention a test for nitrites in potable waters.
601. Which nitrite is official?
602. Give the names of some natural and artificial silicates.
603. What is "soluble glass?"
604. Distinguish between silica and silicic acid.
605. How are silicates detected?
606. What is the quantivalence of silicon?
607. Mention the sources, formulæ, and analytical reactions of succinates.
608. State the mode of manufacture and tests of sulphocyanates.
609. What proportion of tannic acid is contained in galls?
610. Describe the official process for the preparation of Tannic Acid.
611. Explain the chemistry of "tanning."
612. Enumerate the tests for tannic acid.
613. What is the assumed constitution of tannic acid?
614. Mention other official substances whose astringency is due to tannic acid.
615. How is gallic acid prepared?
616. By what reaction is gallic distinguished from tannic acid?
617. Mention the characteristic properties of pyrogallic acid.
618. Explain the murexid test for uric acid.

619. Describe the artificial preparation of valerianic acid and other valerianates, giving diagrams or equations.
620. What is the formula of valerianic acid?
621. How are butyrates detected in presence of valerianates?

DETECTION OF THE ACIDULOUS RADICALS OF SALTS SOLUBLE IN WATER.

Analytical operations may now be resumed, the detection of acidulous radicals being practised for two or three days, and then full analyses made, both for basylous and acidulous radicals. To this end a few compounds of stated metals (potassium, sodium, or ammonium) should be placed in the hands of the practical student for examination according to the following paragraphs and Tables. Mixtures in which both basylous and acidulous radicals may be sought should then be analyzed.

In examining salts soluble in water, and concerning which no general information is obtainable, search must first be made for any basylous radicals by the appropriate methods (*vide* pages 178 or 210). Certain metals having been thus detected, a little reflection on the character of their salts will at once indicate what acidulous radicals may be, and what cannot be, present. Thus, for instance, if the substance under examination is freely soluble in water, and lead is found, only the nitric and acetic radicals need be sought, none other of the lead salts than nitrate or acetate being freely soluble in water. Moreover, the salt is more likely to be acetate than nitrate of lead, for two reasons: the former is more soluble than the latter, and is by far the commoner salt of the two. Medical and pharmaceutical students have probably, in dispensing, already learned much concerning the solubility of salts, and whether a salt is rarely employed or in common use. And although but little dependence can be placed on the chances of a salt being present or absent according to its rarity, still the point may have its proper weight. If, in a mixture of salts, ammonium, potassium, and magnesium have been found associated with the sulphuric, nitric, and hydrochloric radicals, and we are asked how we suppose these bodies may exist in the mixture, it is far more in accordance with common sense to suggest that sal-ammoniac, nitre, and Epsom salt were originally mixed together than to suppose any other possible combination. Such appeals to experience regarding the solubility or rarity of salts cannot be made by any one not previously acquainted, or insufficiently acquainted, with the characters of salts; in such cases the relation of a salt to water and acids can be ascertained by referring to the following Table (p. 302) of the solubility or insolubility of about five hundred of the common or rarer salts met with in chemical operations.

The opposite course to the above (namely, to ascertain what acidulous radicals are present in a mixture, and then to appeal to experience to tell what basylous radicals may be and what cannot be present) is impracticable; for acidulous radicals cannot be separated out, one after the other, from one and the same quantity of substance by a similar treatment to that already given for basylous radicals. Indeed such a sifting of acidulous radicals could scarcely be accomplished at all, or only by a vast deal of labor. The basylous radicals must, therefore, be first detected.

Even when the basylous radicals have been found, the acidulous radicals which may be present must be sought for singly, the only additional aid which can be brought in being the action of sulphuric acid, a barium salt, a calcium salt, nitrate of silver, and ferric chloride on *separate* small portions of the solution under examination, as detailed in the second of the following Tables.

Commence the analysis of an aqueous solution of a salt or salts, the basylous radicals in which are known, by writing out a list of the acidulous radicals which may be, or, if more convenient, of those which cannot be present. To this end consult the following Table (p. 302) of the solubility of salts in water. Look for the name of the metal of the salt in the vertical column; the letters S and I indicate which salts are soluble and which insoluble in water, an asterisk attached to the S meaning that the salt is slightly soluble. The acidulous part of the name is given in the top line of the Table. All the names are in alphabetical order, for facility of reference.

Some of the salts marked as insoluble in water are soluble in aqueous solutions of soluble salts, a few forming soluble double salts. To characterize salts as soluble, slightly soluble, or insoluble, only roughly indicates their relation to water: on the one hand, very few salts are absolutely insoluble in water; on the other, there is a limit to the solubility of every salt.

If only one, two, or perhaps three given acidulous radicals can be in the liquid, test directly for it or them according to the reactions given in the previous pages. If several may be present, pour small portions of the solutions, rendered neutral if necessary by ammonia, into five test-tubes, and add respectively sulphuric acid, nitrate or chloride of barium, chloride of calcium, nitrate of silver, and ferric chloride; then consult the Table on page 303, *in order to correctly interpret the effects these reagents may have produced.*

TABLE OF THE SOLUBILITY OR INSOLUBILITY OF SALTS IN WATER.

	Acetate.	Arseniate.	Arsenite.	Carbonate.	Chloride.	Citrate.	Chromate.	Cyanide	Hydrate.	Iodide.	Nitrate.	Oxalate.	Oxide.	Phosphate.	Sulphate.	Sulphide.	Sulphite.	Tartrate.
Aluminium	S	I	I	I	S	S*	I	?	I	?	S	I	I	I	S	I	I	S
Ammonium	S	S	S	S	S	S	S	S	S	S	S	S	?	S	S	S	S	S
Antimony	S	I	I	?	S	?	I	?	I	I	?	S*	I	I	I	I	I	I
Barium	S	I	I	I	S	S*	I	S	S	S	S	I	S	I	I	S	I	I
Bismuth	S	I	?	I	S	S*	I	?	I	I	S	I	I	I	S	I	I	I
Cadmium	S	?	?	I	S	S*	?	?	I	S	S	I	I	I	S	I	S	S*
Calcium	S	I	I	I	S	S*	S	S	S*	S	S	I	S*	I	S*	S*	S*	S*
Chromium	S	I	?	I	S	S	I	I	I	S	S	S	I	I	S	I	S	S
Cobalt	S	I	I	I	S	S	?	I	I	S	S	I	I	I	S	I	S*	S
Copper	S	I	I	I	S	S	S	I	I	I	S	I	I	I	S	I	I	S*
Ferric	S	I	I	?	S	S	S	?	I	S	S	S*	I	I	S	I	?	S
Ferrous	S	I	I	I	S	S	?	I	I	S	S	S*	I	I	S	I	S*	S*
Gold	?	I	?	?	S	?	?	I	I	I	?	?	I	?	?	I	?	?
Lead	S	I	I	I	S*	S*	I	I	S*	S*	S	I	I	I	I	I	I	I
Magnesium	S	I	I	I	S	S	S	?	I	S	S	I	I	I	S	?	S	S
Manganese	S	I	?	I	S	I	S	I	I	S	S	I	I	I	S	I	S*	S*
Mercuric	S	I	I	I	S	?	S*	S	I	I	S	I	I	I	S	I	?	I
Mercurous	S*	I	I	I	I	I	I	?	?	I	S	I	I	I	S*	I	?	I
Nickel	S	I	I	I	S	S	I	I	I	S	S	I	I	I	S	I	S*	S*
Platinum	?	I	?	?	S	?	?	?	I	S*	S	?	I	?	S	I	S	?
Potassium	S	S	S	S	S	S	S	S	S	S	S	S	S	S	S	S	S	S
Silver	S*	I	I	I	I	I	I	I	?	I	S	I	I	I	S*	I	I	I
Sodium	S	S	S	S	S	S	S	S	S	S	S	S	S	S	S	S	S	S
Stannic	S	?	I	?	S	?	I	?	I	S	S	S	I	I	S	I	?	?
Stannous	S	I	I	?	S	?	I	?	I	S	S	I	I	I	S	I	I	S
Strontium	S	I	I	I	S	I	I	S	S	S	S	I	S	I	I	S	I	S*
Zinc	S	I	?	I	S	S*	S	I	?	S	S	I	I	I	S	I	S*	S*

TABLE TO AID IN THE DETECTION OF CHLORIDES, BROMIDES, IODIDES, CYANIDES, NITRATES, CHLORATES, BORATES, ACETATES, SULPHIDES, SULPHITES, SULPHATES, CARBONATES, OXALATES, TARTRATES, PHOSPHATES, AND CITRATES, IN A **NEUTRAL** AQUEOUS SOLUTION.

(For remarks concerning this Table see next page.)

Sulphuric acid decomposes	**Chloride of Barium precipitates**	**Chloride of Calcium precipitates**	**Nitrate of Silver precipitates**	**Ferric Chloride precipitates**	**Not precipitated**
Sulphides. Sulphites. Carbonates, with effervescence—hydrosulphuric, sulphurous, and carbonic acid gases, known by smell, being evolved. Cyanides, with production of the odor of hydrocyanic acid. Acetates, with production of the odor of acetic acid when the solution is warmed.	Borates. Sulphites. Sulphates. Carbonates. Oxalates. Tartrates. Phosphates. Citrates. Of these white barium precipitates, the sulphate is the only one insoluble in hydrochloric acid; the tartrate and citrate char when heated on platinum foil; the sulphite and carbonate are decomposed with effervescence by acids.	Borates. Oxalates. Sulphites. Tartrates. Sulphates. Phosphates. Carbonates. Citrates. Of these white calcium precipitates, the sulphate only is soluble in much water; the borate, tartrate, and citrate are soluble in solution of chloride of ammonium; all are soluble in acetic acid except oxalate and some sulphate; all are soluble in hydrochloric acid, much sulphate excepted; the dry tartrate and citrate char when heated; the sulphite and carbonate effervesce with acids.	Chlorides, white. Bromides, white. Iodides, yellow. Cyanides, white. Borates, white. Sulphides, black. Sulphites, white. Carbonates, white. Oxalates, white. Tartrates, white. Phosphates, yellow. Citrates, white. Of these silver precipitates, the chloride, bromide, iodide, cyanide, and sulphide are insoluble in dilute nitric acid; the rest soluble.	Borates, yellowish. Sulphides, black. Carbonates, reddish. Oxalates, yellow. Phosphates, yel.-white. Gives red color with acetates, if neutral.	Nitrates. Chlorates. Apply special tests.

Note.—The student should practise the examination of aqueous solutions of salts until able to detect acidulous radicals with facility and precision. For this purpose he may finish the analyses of salts or solutions already examined for common and rarer metals, or have aqueous solutions of salts, or the salts themselves, specially prepared for present use, the metals of the salts being stated. He will then be in a position to effectively study the analysis of salts which may or may not be soluble in water, examining them for both basylous and acidulous radicals.

REMARKS ON THE PRECEDING TABLE.

The first point of value to be noticed in connection with this Table is one of a negative character; namely, if either of the re-agents gives no reaction it is self-evident that the salts which it decomposes with production of a precipitate must be absent. Then, again, if the action of one of the reagents indicates the absence of certain acidulous radicals, those radicals cannot be precipitated by the other reagents; thus, if the action of sulphuric acid points to the absence of sulphides, sulphites, carbonates, cyanides, and acetates, these salts may be struck out of the other lists, and the examination of subsequent precipitates be so far simplified. Or, if the barium precipitate is soluble in hydrochloric acid and the calcium precipitate in acetic acid, neither sulphates nor oxalates can be present. Observing these and other points of difference, which will be seen on careful and thoughtful reflection, and remembering the facts suggested by a knowledge of what basylous radicals are present, one acidulous radical after the other may be struck off as absent or present, leaving only one or two as the objects of special experiment. Among the chief difficulties to be encountered will be the separation from each other of chlorides, bromides, iodides, and cyanides, or of tartrates from citrates, and confirmatory tests of the presence of certain compounds. These may all be surmounted on referring back to the reactions of the various radicals, as described under their hydrogen salts, the acids.

The rarer acidulous radicals will very seldom be met with. *Benzoates*, *hippurates* (which give benzoic acid), *hypochlorites*, *hyposulphites*, *nitrites*, and *valerianates* show themselves under the sulphuric treatment. *Ferrocyanides*, *ferridcyanides*, *meconates*, *succinates*, *sulphocyanates*, *tannates*, and *gallates* appear among the salts whose presence is indicated by ferric chloride; *formiates*, *hypophosphites*, *malates*, and others by nitrate of silver. *Urates* char when heated, giving an odor resembling that of burnt feathers.

In actual practice the analyst nearly always has some clue to the nature of rarer substances placed in his hands.

If chromium and arsenicum have been detected among the basylous radicals, those elements may be present in the form of *chromates*, *arseniates*, and *arsenites*, yielding with chloride of barium yellow chromate of barium and white arseniate and arsenite of barium, and with nitrate of silver red chromate, brown arseniate, and yellow arsenite of silver.

QUESTIONS AND EXERCISES.

622. In analyzing an aqueous solution of salts, for which radicals would you first search, the basylous or the acidulous? and why?

623. In an aqueous solution there have been found magnesium (Mg) and potassium (K), with the sulphuric radical (SO_4) and iodine (I); state the nature of the salts which were originally dis-

solved in the water, and mention the principles which guide you to the conclusions.

624. Give a sketch of the method by which to analyze a neutral or only faintly acid aqueous liquid for the acidulous radicals of salts. In what stage of the process would the following salts be detected?

a. Carbonates and Sulphates.
b. Oxalates.
c. Tartrates and Nitrates.
d. Acetates and Sulphites.
e. Bromides and Cyanides.
f. Borates.
g. Iodides and Phosphates.
h. Chlorates, Oxalates, and Acetates.
i. Chlorides and Iodides.
j. Sulphites.
k. Sulphides, Carbonates, and Nitrates.
l. Citrates and Sulphates.

625. Nitrate of silver gives no precipitate in an aqueous solution; what salts may be present?

626. Chloride of barium gives no precipitates in a neutral solution, but nitrate of silver a white; what acidulous radicals are indicated?

627. Ferric chloride produces a deep red color in a solution, chloride of calcium yielding no precipitate; what salts may be present, and how might they be distinguished from each other?

628. Ferric chloride gives a black precipitate in a solution in which sulphuric acid develops no odor; to what is the effect due?

ANALYSIS OF SALTS,

SINGLE OR MIXED, SOLUBLE OR INSOLUBLE.

Thus far all material substances, especially those of pharmaceutical interest, have been regarded as being definite compounds, and as having certain well-defined parts, termed, for convenience, basylous and acidulous respectively: moreover attention has been designedly restricted to those definite compounds which are soluble in water. But there are many substances having no definite or known composition; and of those having definite composition there are many having no definite or ascertained parts. Again, of those having definite composition, and whose constitution admits of the entertainment of theory, there are many insoluble in water.

Chemical substances of whose composition or constitution little or nothing is at present known, are chiefly of animal and vegetable origin, and figure in tables of analysis under the convenient collective title of "extractive matter;" they are not of immediate importance, and may be omitted.

Of substances which are definite in composition, but whose parts or radicals, if they have any, are unknown or imperfectly known, there are only a few (such as the alkaloids, amylaceous and saccharine matters, the glucosides, alcoholic bodies, albumenoid, fatty, resinoid, and colorific substances) which have any considerable amount of pharmaceutical interest; these will be noticed subsequently.

Definite compounds most frequently present themselves; and of these by far the larger proportion (namely, the salts soluble in water) have already been fully studied. There remain, however, many salts which are insoluble in water, but which must be brought into a state of solution before they can be effectively studied from an analytical, pharmaceutical, or a physiological point of view. The next subject of laboratory work is therefore the analysis of substances which may or may not be soluble in water. This will involve no other analytical schemes than those which have been given, will in only one or two cases increase the difficulty of the analysis of a precipitate produced by a group-reagent, but will give roundness, completeness, and a practical bearing to the reader's analytical knowledge. Such a procedure will at the same time bring into notice the methods by which substances insoluble in water are manipulated for pharmaceutical purposes, or made available for use as food by plants, or as food and medicine by man and animals generally.

Preliminary Examination of Solid (chiefly mineral) Salts.

Before attempting to dissolve a salt for analysis, its appearance and other physical properties should be noted, and the influence of heat and strong sulphuric acid be ascertained. If the operator knows how to interpret what is thus observed, and to what extent to place confidence in the observations, he may more certainly obtain a high degree of precision in analysis, and will always gain some valuable negative information. But if he has only slight experience of the appearance and general properties of bodies, or has the habit of turning what should be inferences from tentative processes into foregone conclusions, he should omit the preliminary examination altogether, or only follow it out under the guidance of a judicious tutor; for it is impracticable here to do more than hint at the results which may be obtained by such an examination, or to so adapt descriptions as to prevent a student from allowing unnecessary weight to preconceived ideas.

Whatever be the course pursued, short memoranda describing results should invariably be entered in the note-book.

1. Examine the physical characters of the salt in various ways, but never, or only rarely, by the palate, on account of the danger to be apprehended.

If the salt is white, colored substances cannot be present; if colored, the tint may indicate the nature of the substance or of one of its constituents, supposing that the learner is already acquainted with the colors of salts. Closer observation, aided perhaps by a lens, may reveal the occurrence, in a pulverulent mixture, of small crystals or pieces of a single substance; these should be picked out by a needle and examined separately. The body may present an undoubted metallic appearance, in which case only the metals existing under ordinary atmospheric conditions need be sought. Peculiarity in smell reveals the presence of ammonia, hydrocyanic acid, hydrosulphuric acid, &c. Between the fingers a substance is, perhaps, hard, soft, or gritty; consequent inferences follow. Or the matter may be heavy, like the salts of barium or lead; or light, like the carbonates and hydrates of magnesium.

2. Place a grain or two of the salt in a small dry test-tube or in a piece of ordinary tubing, closed at one end, and heat it, at first gently, then more strongly, and finally, if necessary, by the blowpipe.

Gases or vapors of characteristic appearance or odor may be evolved; such as iodine, nitrous fumes, sulphurous, hydrocyanic, or ammoniacal gases. Much steam given by a dry substance indicates either hydrates or salts containing water of crystallization. (A small quantity of interstitial moisture often causes heated crystalline substance to *decrepitate*—from *decrepo*, to crackle—that is, break up with slight explosive violence, owing to the expansive force of the steam suddenly generated.) A sublimate may be obtained, due to salts of mercury or arsenicum, to oxalic or benzoic acid, or to sulphur free or as a sulphide—a salt wholly volatile containing such substances only. The compound may blacken, pointing to the presence of organic matter—which, in common definite salts, will probably be in the form of acetates, tartrates, and citrates, or as common salts of the alkaloids morphia, quinia, strychnia, or as starch, sugar, salicin, or in other definite or indefinite forms common in pharmacy and for which tests will be given in subsequent pages. If no charring occurs, the important fact that no organic matter is present is established. The residue may change color from presence or development of oxide of zinc, oxide of iron, &c., or melt from the presence of a fusible salt and absence of any large proportion of infusible salt, or be unaltered, showing the absence of any large amount of such substances.

3. Place a grain or two of the salt in a test-tube, add a drop or two of strong sulphuric acid, cautiously smelling any gas that may be evolved; afterward slowly heat the mixture, noticing the effect, and stopping the experiment when any sulphuric fumes begin to escape.

Iodine, bromine, and nitrous or chlorinoid fumes will reveal themselves by their color, indicating the presence of iodides, bromides, iodates, bromates, nitrates, and chlorates. The evolution of a colorless gas fuming on coming into contact with air, and having an irritating odor, points to chlorides, fluorides, or nitrates. Gaseous products having a greenish color and odor of chlorine indicate chlorates, hypochlorites, or chlorides mixed with other substances. Slight sharp explosions betoken chlorates. Evolution of colorless gas may proceed from cyanides, acetates, sulphides, sulphites, carbonates, or oxalates. Charring will be due to citrates, tartrates, or other organic matter. If none of these effects are produced, most of the bodies are absent or only present in minute quantity. The substances apparently unaffected by the treatment are metallic oxides, borates, sulphates, and phosphates.

4. Exposure of the substance to the blowpipe-flame, on platinum wire with or without a bead of borax or of microcosmic salt (phosphate of sodium, ammonium, and hydrogen, $NaAmHPO_4$)—on platinum foil in a porcelain crucible, or on a crucible lid with or without carbonate of sodium—on charcoal, alone or in conjunction with carbonate of sodium, cyanide of potassium, or nitrate of cobalt, will sometimes yield important information, especially to one who has devoted much attention to reactions producible by the blowpipe-flame. The interior portions of the flame consist of hydrocarbon gases heated to a temperature at which they combine with oxygen with great avidity, abstracting that element from metallic oxides or other oxidized substance which may be brought within their influence; the exterior portions, on the other hand, contain excess of heated oxygen; the former is the *reducing*, the latter the *oxidizing* part of the flame. The medical or pharmaceutical student, however, will seldom have time to work out this subject to an extent sufficient to make it a trustworthy guide in analysis. (See Plattner and Muspratt "On the Use of the Blowpipe," and a chapter in Galloway's "Manual of Qualitative Analysis.")

Methods of dissolving and analyzing single or mixed solid substances.

Having submitted the substance to preliminary examination, proceed to dissolve and analyze by the following methods. These operations consist in treating a substance well powdered, consecutively with cold or hot water, hydrochloric acid, nitric acid, nitro-hydrochloric acid, or fusion with alkaline carbonates and solution of the product in water and acid. Resulting liquids are analyzed in the manner already described, or by slightly modified processes as detailed in the following paragraphs.

Solution in Water.—Boil a grain or two of the salt presented for analysis in about a third of a test-tubeful of water. If it dissolves prepare a solution of about 20 or 30 grains in half an ounce or more of water, and *proceed with the analysis in the usual way*, testing first for the basylous radical or radicals by the proper group-reagents (HCl, H_2S, AmHS, Am_2CO_3, Am_2HPO_4), pp. 181 or 212, and then for the acidulous radical or radicals, directly or by aid of the prescribed reagents (H_2SO_4, $BaCl_2$, $CaCl_2$, $AgNO_3$, Fe_2Cl_6), p. 303.

If the salt is not *wholly* dissolved by the water, ascertain whether or not any has entered into solution, by filtering, if necessary, and evaporating a drop or two of the clear liquid to dryness on platinum foil; the presence or absence of a residue gives the information sought. If anything is dissolved, prepare a sufficient quantity of solution for analysis and proceed as usual, reserving the insoluble portion of the mixture, after thoroughly exhausting with water, for subsequent treatment by acids.

Solution in Hydrochloric Acid.—If the salt is insoluble in water, digest about a grain of it (or of the insoluble portion of a mixed salt) in a few drops of hydrochloric acid, adding water, and boiling if necessary. If the salt wholly dissolves, prepare a sufficient quantity of the liquid, noticing whether or not any effervescence (due to the presence of sulphides, sulphites, carbonates, or cyanides) occurs, and proceed with the analysis as before, except that the first step, the addition of hydrochloric acid, may be omitted.

The analysis of this solution will in most respects be simpler than that of an aqueous solution, inasmuch as the majority of salts (all those soluble in water) will be absent. This acid solution will, in short, only contain: chlorides produced by the action of the hydrochloric acid on sulphides, sulphites, carbonates, cyanides, oxides, and hydrates; and certain borates, oxalates, phosphates, tartrates, and citrates (possibly silicates and fluorides), which are insoluble in water but soluble in acids without apparent decomposition. The first four—sulphides, sulphites, carbonates, and cyanides—will have revealed themselves by the occurrence of effervescence during solution; and the presence of oxides and hydrates may often be inferred by the absence of compatible acidulous radicals. The borates, oxalates, phosphates, tartrates, and citrates alluded to will be reprecipitated in the general analysis as soon as the acid of the solution is neutralized; that is, will come down in their original state when ammonia and sulphydrate of ammonium are added in the usual course. Of these precipitates, only the oxalate of calcium and the phosphates of calcium and magnesium need occupy attention now; for oxalate and phosphate of barium seldom or never occur, and the borates, tartrates, and citrates met with in medicine or in general analysis are all soluble in water. These phosphates and oxalates, then, will be precipitated in the course of analysis along with iron, their presence not interfering with the detection of any other metal. If, from the unusual light color of the ferric precipitate, phosphates and oxalates are suspected, the precipitate is treated according to the following Table (reference to which should be inserted in the Table for metals, under Fe, pp. 181 and 212).

PRECIPITATE OF PHOSPHATES, OXALATES, AND FERRIC HYDRATE.

Dissolve in HCl, add citric acid, then NH_4HO, and filter.

<table>
<tr><td rowspan="3">Filtrate
Fe.
Add HCl and
K_4Fcy
Blue ppt.</td><td colspan="2">Precipitate.
$Ca_3 2PO_4$, CaC_2O_4, $Mg_3 2PO_4$.
Boil in acetic acid and filter.</td></tr>
<tr><td rowspan="2">Insoluble
CaC_2O_4.
White.</td><td>Filtrate
$Ca_3 2PO_4$, $Mg_3 2PO_4$
Add $Am_2C_2O_4$, stir, filter.</td></tr>
<tr><td>Precipitate
white, indicating
$Ca_3 2PO_4$.</td></tr>
</table>

<table>
<tr><td>Filtrate,
Add AmHO.
White ppt.
$MgNH_4PO_4$.</td></tr>
</table>

In analyzing phosphates and oxalates advantage is also frequently taken of the facts that the phosphoric radical is wholly removed from solution of phosphates in acid by the addition of an alkaline acetate, ferric chloride, and subsequent ebullition, as described under "Phosphoric Acid" (p. 298), and that dry oxalates are converted into carbonates by heat, as mentioned under "Oxalic Acid" (p. 287).

Certain arseniates and arsenites, insoluble in water but soluble in hydrochloric acid, may accompany the above phosphates and oxalates if from any cause hydrosulphuric acid gas has not been previously passed through the solution, or passed for an insufficient length of time.

If the substance insoluble in water does not *wholly* dissolve in hydrochloric acid, ascertain if any has entered into solution, by filtering, if necessary, and evaporating a drop of the clear liquid to dryness on platinum foil; the presence or absence of a residue gives the information sought. If anything is dissolved, prepare a sufficient quantity of solution for analysis, and proceed as usual, reserving the insoluble portion of the mixture, after thoroughly exhausting with hydrochloric acid and well washing with water, for the following treatment by nitric acid.

Solution in Nitric Acid.—If the salt is insoluble in water and hydrochloric acid, boil it (or that part of it which is insoluble in those menstrua) in a few drops of nitric acid. If it wholly dissolves, remove excess of acid by evaporation, dilute with water, and proceed with the analysis.

This nitric solution can contain only very few substances; for nearly all salts soluble in nitric acid are also soluble in hydrochloric acid, and therefore will have been previously removed. Some of the metals, however (Ag, Cu, Hg, Pb, Bi), as well as amalgams and alloys, unaffected or scarcely affected by hydrochloric acid, are readily attacked and dissolved by nitric acid. Many of the sulphides, also insoluble in hydrochloric acid, are dissolved by nitric acid, usually with separation of sulphur. Calomel is converted, by long boiling with nitric acid, into mercuric chloride and nitrate. The nitrates here produced are soluble in water.

This nitric solution, as well as the hydrochloric and aqueous solutions, should be examined separately. Apparently time would be saved by mixing the three solutions together and making one analysis. But the object of the analyst is to separate every radical from every other; and when this has been partially accomplished by solvents, it would be unwise to again mix and separate a second time. Moreover, solvents often do what the chemical reagents cannot—namely, separate *salts* from each other. This is important, inasmuch as the end to be obtained in analysis is not only an enumeration of the radicals present, but a statement of the actual condition in which they are present; the analyst must, if possible, state of what salts a given mixture was originally formed—how the basylous and acidulous radicals were originally distributed. In attempting this, much must be left to theoretical considerations; but a process by which the salts themselves are separated is of trustworthy practical assistance; hence the chief advantage of analyzing separately the solutions resulting from the action of water and acids on a solid substance.

Solution in Nitro-Hydrochloric Acid.—If the salt or any part of a mixture of salts is insoluble in water, hydrochloric acid, and nitric acid, digest it in nitro-hydrochloric acid, boiling if necessary; evaporate to remove excess of acid, dilute, and proceed as before.

Sulphide of mercury and substances only slowly attacked by hydrochloric or nitric acid, as, for example, calomel and ignited ferric oxide, are sufficiently altered by the free chlorine of aqua regia to become soluble.

If the substance is insoluble in water and acids, it is one or more of the following substances: Sand and certain silicates, such as pipeclay and other clays; fluor spar; cryolite ($3NaF,AlF_3$); sulphates of barium, strontium, and possibly calcium; tinstone; glass; felspar (double silicate of aluminium and other metals); chloride of silver; sulphate of lead. It may also be or contain carbon or carbonaceous matter, in which case it is black and combustible, burning entirely or partially away when heated in the air—or be or contain sulphur, in which case sulphurous gas is evolved, detected by its odor, when the substance is exposed to heat. For the other substances proceed according to the following (Bloxam's) method:—

Four or five grains of the substance are intimately mixed with twice the quantity of dried carbonate of sodium, and this mixture well rubbed in a mortar with five times its weight of *deflagrating flux* (1 of finely powdered charcoal to 6 of nitre). The resulting powder is placed in a thin porcelain dish, or crucible, or clean iron tray, and a lighted match applied to the centre of the heap. Deflagration ensues, and decomposition of the various substances occurs, the acidulous radicals going to the alkali-metals to form salts soluble in water, the basylous radicals being simultaneously converted into carbonates or oxides. The mass is boiled in water for a few minutes, the mixture filtered, and the residue well washed. The filtrate may then be examined for acidulous radicals and aluminium, and the residue dissolved in dilute hydrochloric acid and analyzed by the ordinary method.

The only substance which resists this treatment is chrome-iron-ore. To detect alkali in felspar, glass, or cryolite, Bloxam recommends deflagration of the powdered mineral with one part of sulphur and six of nitrate of barium. The mass is boiled in water, the mixture filtered, hydrate and carbonate of ammonium added to remove barium, the mixture again filtered, and the filtrate evaporated and examined for alkalies by the usual process.

QUALITATIVE ANALYSIS OF SUBSTANCES HAVING UNKNOWN PROPERTIES.

Substances are presented to the analyst in one of the three forms in which all matter exists—namely, solid, liquid, or gaseous.

The method of analysis in the case of solid bodies has just been described (pp. 306–312).

In the case of liquids, the solvents as well as the dissolved matters claim attention. A few drops are evaporated to dryness on platinum foil to ascertain if solid matter of any kind is present; the liquid is tested by red and blue litmus paper to ascertain if free alkalies, free acids, or neither are present; a few drops are heated in a test-tube and the odor of any vapor noticed, a piece of glass tubing bent to a right angle being, if necessary, adapted to the test-tube by a cork, and some of the distilled liquid collected and examined; finally, the usual group-reagents for the several basylous and acidulous radicals are consecutively applied.

Proceeding in this way, the student, who has already had some experience in pharmacy, will not be likely to overlook such solvents as water, acids, alcohol, ether, fixed oils, and essential oils, or to miss the substances which these menstrua may hold in solution. He must not, however, suppose that he will always be able to qualitatively analyze, say, a bottle of medicine; for the various infusions, decoctions, tinctures, wines, syrups, liniments, confections, extracts, pill-masses, and powders contain vegetable matters, most of which at present are quite beyond the reach of the analyst. Neither the highest skill in analysis nor the largest amount of experience concerning the odor, appearance, taste, and uses of drugs is sufficient for the detection of all these vegetable matters. Skill and experience combined, however, will do much, and in most cases even so difficult a task as the one just mentioned be accomplished with reasonable success. Qualitative analysis alone will not enable the experimenter to produce a mixture of substances similar to that analyzed; to this end recourse must be had to quantitative analysis, a subject reserved for subsequent consideration.

Gas-analysis, or *Eudiometry* (from εὐδία, *eudia*, calm air, and μέτρον, *metron*, a measure, in allusion to the *eudiometer*, an instrument used in measuring the proportion and, as the early chemists thought, the salubrity of the gases of the air), is a branch of experimental investigation, chiefly of a quantitative character, concerning which information must be sought in other treatises. The analysis of atmospheric air from various localities, coal-gas, and gases obtained in chemical researches, involves operations which are scarcely within the sphere of Chemistry applied to Medicine. Beyond the recognition, therefore, of oxygen, hydrogen, nitrogen, carbonic, sulphurous, and hydrosulphuric acid gases, the experimental consideration of the chemistry of gaseous bodies may be omitted. Their study, however, should not be neglected, as existing conceptions of the constitution of chemical substances are largely dependent on the observed relations of the volumes of gaseous compounds to their elements. The best work on this subject is a small book by Hofmann, 'Introduction to Modern Chemistry.'

Spectral Analysis.—It may be as well to state here that the preliminary and final examinations of minute quantities of solid matter may, in certain cases, profitably include their exposure to a temperature at which they emit light, the flame being physically analyzed

27

by a spectroscope. A spectroscope consists essentially of a prism to decompose a ray of light into its constituent colors, with tubes and lenses to collect and transmit the ray or rays to the eye of an observer. The material to be examined is placed on the end of a platinum wire, which is then brought within the edge of a spirit-lamp or other smokeless flame; volatilization, attended usually in the case of a compound by decomposition, at once occurs, and the whole flame is tinged with a characteristic hue. A flat ribbon of rays is next cut off by bringing near to the flame a brass tube, the cap of which is pierced by a narrow slit. At the other end of the tube, at focal distance for parallel rays, is a lens, through which the ribbon of light passes to a prism; the prism decomposes the ribbon, spreading out its constituent colors like a partially opened fan, and the spectrum thus produced is then examined by help of a telescope attached by a movable joint to the stand which carries the prism and object-tube. Sodium compounds, under these circumstances, give yellow light only, indicated by a double band of light in a position corresponding to the yellow part of an ordinary solar spectrum. The potassium spectrum is mainly composed of a red and violet band; lithium a crimson, and at very high temperatures a blue band. Most of the other elements give equally characteristic spectra.

QUESTIONS AND EXERCISES.

629. Describe the preliminary treatment to which a salt may be subjected prior to systematic analysis.

630. Mention substances which might be recognized by smell.

631. Which classes of salts are heavy, and which light?

632. Name some bodies detectable by their color.

633. What inference may be drawn from the appearance of steam when dry substances are heated?

634. Why do certain crystals decrepitate?

635. If a powder sublimes on being heated, to what classes of compounds may it belong?

636. When heat causes charring, what conclusion is drawn?

637. No change occurring by heat, which substances cannot be present?

638. Give examples of salts which are identified by their reaction with strong sulphuric acid; by their comportment in the blowpipe-flame, with or without borax or microcosmic salt.

639. What are the solvents usually employed in endeavoring to obtain a substance in a state of solution, and what is the order of their application?

640. Name a few salts which may be present in an aqueous solution.

641. Mention some common compounds insoluble in water, but soluble in hydrochloric acid?

642. What substances are attacked only by nitric acid or nitro-hydrochloric acid?

643. Sketch out a method for the complete analysis of a liquid suspected to be an aqueous solution of neutral salts.

644. How can earthy phosphates and oxalates with ferric oxide be separated from each other?

645. By what process may substances insoluble in water or acids be analyzed?

646. How are different solvents recognized?

647. By what methods would you attempt the analysis of a bottle of medicine?

648. Give a short sketch of spectral analysis.

CHEMISTRY OF CERTAIN SUBSTANCES OF VEGETABLE AND ANIMAL ORIGIN.

Except alcohol and a few acids, the compounds which have hitherto engaged notice have been of mineral origin. But the two other kingdoms of nature, the animal and vegetable, furnish a large number of medicinal substances. These, indeed, when discovered, were producible only by highly organized living structures, and were hence termed *organic* compounds.*

A few of these compounds, of common occurrence in pharmacy and possessing prominent characteristics, may now occupy attention; reactions of the alkaloids and some other principles may be performed, and the methods of examining morbid urine be experimentally studied. There will then remain certain galenical, as distinguished from chemical, substances, solid and liquid, which can only be fairly regarded from a pharmacist's point of view, and a still larger number, doubtless, not yet brought within the grasp of the chemist, and of which, therefore, we must at present be content to remain in ignorance. An opportunity, however, will be afforded of noticing the effect of a mixture of definite and indefinite organic matter, such as a vomit or the contents of a stomach, in masking or preventing the reaction by which mineral and vegetable poisons are detected.

ALKALOIDS.

Constitution of Alkaloids or Organic Bases.

The alkaloids, or alkali-like (εἶδος, *eidos*, likeness) bodies have many analogies with ammonia. Their constitution is not yet known;

* *Organic*, from ὄργανον, *organon*, an organ. A large number of organic compounds can now be obtained artificially—without the aid of a living organism; hence the distinction formerly drawn between organic and inorganic compounds, organic and inorganic chemistry, is fast breaking down.

but they are probably derivative of a single molecule of ammonia (NH_3), or of double, triple, or quadruple molecules (N_2H_6, N_3H_9, N_4H_{12}). A large number of artificial alkaloids or organic bases having such a constitution have already been formed. Those are termed *amines*, and are primary, secondary, and tertiary according as one, two, or three atoms of hydrogen in ammonia (the tri-hydrogen amine) have been displaced by radicals, as seen in the following general formulæ (R=any univalent radical. *Vide* Index, "Alcohol radicals")—

$$\left.\begin{matrix}R\\H\\H\end{matrix}\right\}N \qquad \left.\begin{matrix}R\\R\\H\end{matrix}\right\}N \qquad \left.\begin{matrix}R\\R\\R\end{matrix}\right\}N;$$

or the following examples—

$$\left.\begin{matrix}C_2H_5\\H\\H\end{matrix}\right\}N \qquad \left.\begin{matrix}C_2H_5\\C_2H_5\\H\end{matrix}\right\}N \qquad \left.\begin{matrix}C_2H_5\\C_2H_5\\C_2H_5\end{matrix}\right\}N.$$

Ethylamine or ethylia. Diethylamine or diethylia. Triethylamine or triethylia.

The three classes have also been termed amidogen-, imidogen-, and nitrile-bases. *Propylamine* or *tritylia* (C_3H_7HHN) is a volatile oil, one of the products resulting from the destructive distillation of bones and other animal matters.

The displacing radicals may be similar or different; and while the radical displacing one atom of hydrogen is keeping its place, any of the many known radicals may occupy the position of one or both of the other atoms of hydrogen. Thus, for example, we have methyl-ethyl-amyl-amine ($CH_3C_2H_5C_5H_{11}N$, or MeEtAyN), a colorless, oily body, of agreeable aromatic odor.

The organic bases derived from one molecule of ammonia are termed monamines; from two molecules, diamines; from three, triamines; and from four, tetramines:—

$$\left.\begin{matrix}R\\R\\R\end{matrix}\right\}N \qquad \left.\begin{matrix}R_2\\R_2\\R_2\end{matrix}\right\}N_2 \qquad \left.\begin{matrix}R_3\\R_3\\R_3\end{matrix}\right\}N_3 \qquad \left.\begin{matrix}R_4\\R_4\\R_4\end{matrix}\right\}N_4$$

In these amines, any bivalent, trivalent, or quadrivalent radical may occupy the place of two, three, or four univalent radicals.

Attempts to form artificially the natural organic bases have hitherto failed; but the primary, secondary, or tertiary character of some of them has been indicated by the introduction or elimination of methyl, ethyl, and other radicals for hydrogen.

Note on Nomenclature.—The first syllables of the names of the natural alkaloids recall the name of the plant whence they were obtained, or some characteristic property. It is to be regretted that the last syllable is not either *ine* or *ia*, instead of sometimes one and sometimes the other: general usage seems to be in favor of the latter, a plan that distinguishes the alkaloids from some other substances the names of which end in *ine*, as chlorine, bromine, iodine, fluorine, glycerine, gelatine, &c. The names of the salts of the alkaloids are given on the assumption that the acid unites with the alkaloid without decomposition. Thus hydrochlorate of morphia is regarded as morphia with hydrochloric acid just as we might assume sal-ammoniac to be ammonia (NH_3) with hydrochloric acid (HCl), and name it hydrochlorate of ammonia (NH_3HCl) instead of chloride of ammonium (NH_4Cl).

Antidotes.—In cases of poisoning by alkaloids, emetics and the stomach-pump must be relied on rather than chemical agents. Astringent liquids may be administered, as tannic acid precipitates many of the alkaloids from their aqueous solution, absorption of the poison being thus possibly retarded.

MORPHIA, OR MORPHINE.

Formula $C_{17}H_{19}NO_3, H_2O$. Molecular weight 303.

Occurrence.—Morphia occurs in opium (the inspissated juice of the fruit, *Papaveris capsulæ*, of the White Poppy, *Papaver somniferum*) as meconate of morphia.

Morphia, U. S. P., is made by adding to infusion of opium an equal bulk of alcohol, then slight excess of ammonia, and setting aside for crystalline morphia to separate. It is purified by recrystallization.

Process for Hydrochlorate.—The hydrochlorate, $C_{17}H_{19}NO_3, HCl, 3H_2O$ (*Morphiæ Hydrochloras,* B. P.), occurs in slender white acicular crystals; it is prepared by simply decomposing an aqueous infusion of opium with chloride of calcium, meconate of calcium and hydrochlorate of morphia being produced. (If the infusion, which is always acid, be first nearly neutralized by the cautious addition of small quantities of a very dilute solution of ammonia, the chloride of calcium then at once causes a precipitate of meconate of calcium, which can be filtered off, leaving a colored solution of hydrochlorate of morphia. On the large scale—*vide* B. P.—the details are somewhat different.) The salt is partially purified by crystallization from the evaporated liquid, then by treatment of the solution of the impure hydrochlorate by animal charcoal, and lastly by precipitation of the morphia from the still colored liquid by ammonia and resolution of the morphia in hot dilute hydrochloric acid; hydrochlorate of morphia separates out on cooling. The process of U. S. P. consists in neutralizing morphia by hydrochloric acid. (*Morphiæ Murias,* U. S. P.):

Morphiæ Sulphas, U. S. P., by neutralizing morphia with sulphuric acid.

Process for Acetate.—Acetate of morphia ($C_{17}H_{19}NO_3C_2H_4O_2$) (*Morphiæ Acetas,* B. P. and U. S. P.) is a white pulverulent salt prepared by dissolving pure morphia in acetic acid, the morphia being prepared (B. P.) from a solution of the hydrochlorate by precipitation with ammonia. Eight parts of hydrochlorate yield about seven of acetate.

Both the hydrochlorate and acetate of morphia are soluble in water, but the solution is not stable unless acidulated and containing alcohol; hence the official solutions, 4 grains in one ounce—1 in 110

(*Liquor Morphiæ Hydrochloratis*, B. P., and *Liquor Morphiæ Acetatis*, B. P.), consists of three parts water and one part rectified spirit, a few minims per ounce of hydrochloric or acetic acid being added. *Liquor Morphiæ Sulphatis*, U. S. P., is a solution in water, 1 in 456. The other official preparations are *Suppositoria Morphiæ, Trochisci Morphiæ*, and *Trochisci Morphiæ et Ipecacuanhæ.*

Analytical Reactions.

First Analytical Reaction.—To a minute fragment of a salt of morphia add one drop of water, and warm the mixture until the salt dissolves, then stir the liquid with a glass rod moistened by a strong *neutral* solution of perchloride of iron; a dirty blue color is produced. This effect is not observed in dilute solutions.

Second Analytical Reaction.—To a drop or two of a strong solution of a morphia salt in a test-tube add a minute fragment of iodic acid (HIO_3, page 244); iodine is set free. Into the upper part of the tube insert a glass rod covered with mucilage of starch, and warm the solution; dark-blue starch iodide is produced.

This reaction is only confirmatory of others, as albuminous matters also reduce iodic acid.

Third Analytical Reaction.—To a few drops of an aqueous infusion of opium add a drop of *neutral* solution of perchloride of iron; a red solution of meconate of iron is produced. Add solution of corrosive sublimate; the color is not destroyed (as it is in the case of sulphocyanide of iron, a salt of similar tint).

In cases of poisoning by a preparation of opium, this test is almost as conclusive as a direct reaction of morphia (the poison itself), meconic acid being obtainable from opium only.

Other Reactions.—Add carbonate of sodium to a solution of a salt of morphia; a white precipitate of morphia falls, slowly and of a crystalline character if the solution is dilute. Collect this precipitate and moisten it with neutral solution of perchloride of iron; the bluish tint above referred to is produced.——Add an alkali to a solution of hydrochlorate or acetate of the alkaloid; morphia is precipitated, soluble in excess of the fixed alkali, far less readily so in ammonia.——Moisten a particle of a morphia salt with nitric acid; an orange-red coloration is produced.——Heat morphia on platinum foil; it burns entirely away.

Apomorphia ($C_{17}H_{17}NO_2$).

Apomorphia (ἀπὸ, *apo*, from, and *morphia*) is an alkaloid recently obtained from morphia by Matthiessen and Wright. It possesses remarkable physiological effects; $\frac{1}{10}$ of a grain (in aqueous solution) injected under the skin, or $\frac{1}{4}$ of a grain taken into the stomach, is said to produce vomiting in from four to ten minutes.

Process.—Hydrochlorate of morphia is hermetically sealed in a thick tube with considerable excess of hydrochloric acid, and heated to nearly 300° F. for two or three hours. The product is purified by diluting the contents of the tube with water, precipitating with bicarbonate of sodium, and treating the precipitate with ether or chloroform.——On shaking up the ethereal or chloroform solution with a very small quantity of strong hydrochloric acid, the sides of the vessel become covered with crystals of the hydrochlorate of the new base. These may be drained from the mother-liquor, washed with a little cold water, in which the salt is sparingly soluble, recrystallized from hot water, and dried on bibulous paper or over sulphuric acid. The formula ($C_{17}H_{17}NO_2,HCl$) indicates that the new alkaloid is derived from morphia by abstraction of the elements of water.

Codeia, another alkaloid of opium also, according to the same chemists, yields apomorphia by similar treatment, a reaction that would seem to indicate that codeia is methyl-morphia:—

$$\underset{\text{Codeia.}}{C_{17}H_{17}CH_3HNO_3} + HCl = \underset{\text{Chl. of methyl.}}{CH_3Cl} + H_2O + \underset{\text{Apomorphia.}}{C_{17}H_{17}NO_2}$$

QUESTIONS AND EXERCISES.

649. Write some general formulæ of artificial alkaloids.

650. Name the substances represented by the following formulæ:—

$$\left.\begin{matrix}C_3H_7\\H\\H\end{matrix}\right\}N,\quad \left.\begin{matrix}C_3H_7\\C_3H_7\\H\end{matrix}\right\}N,\quad \left.\begin{matrix}CH_3\\C_2H_5\\C_5H_{11}\end{matrix}\right\}N.$$

$$\left.\begin{matrix}CH_3\\H\\H\end{matrix}\right\}N,\quad \left.\begin{matrix}CH_3\\CH_3\\H\end{matrix}\right\}N,\quad \left.\begin{matrix}CH_3\\CH_3\\CH_3\end{matrix}\right\}N.$$

651. What is the assumed constitution of the salts of the alkaloids?

652. Describe the treatment in cases of poisoning by alkaloids.

653. Give the process for the preparation of Hydrochlorate of Morphia. In what form does morphia occur in opium?

654. How is Acetate of Morphia prepared?

655. What plan is adopted for preventing the decomposition of solutions of morphia?

656. Mention the analytical reactions of morphia.

657. In addition to the reaction of morphia, what test may be employed in searching for opium in a liquid or semifluid material?

658. How is apomorphia prepared, and what are its properties?

659. Describe the relation of morphia to codeia.

QUINIA, OR QUININE.

Formula $C_{20}H_{24}N_2O_2,3H_2O$. Molecular weight 378.

Source.—Quinia and other similar alkaloids exist in cinchona-bark as kinates. In the yellow bark (*Cinchonæ Flavæ Cortex*, B. P. and U. S. P.) quinia is almost exclusively present; in the pale bark (*Cinchonæ Pallidæ Cortex*, B. P. and U. S. P.) cinchonia is equally characteristic; while in the red bark (*Cinchonæ Rubræ Cortex*, B. P. and U. S. P.) these alkaloids occur in more nearly equal proportions.

Process for Sulphate.—Sulphate of quinia (*Quiniæ Sulphas*, B. P.) is prepared according to the British Pharmacopœia by treating the yellow bark with dilute hydrochloric acid, precipitating the resulting solution of hydrochlorate of quinia by soda, and redissolving the precipitated quinia in the proper proportion of hot dilute sulphuric acid. The sulphate crystallizes out on cooling in silky acicular crystals containing two atoms of quinia ($2C_{20}H_{24}N_2O_2$), one of sulphuric acid (H_2SO_4), and seven of water of crystallization ($7H_2O$).

In the process of the United States Pharmacopœia lime is used instead of soda and the precipitated quinia is dissolved in boiling alcohol, the latter recovered by distillation, the residue quinia neutralized by diluted sulphuric acid, the solution treated with animal charcoal, filtered while hot, set aside to crystallize, and recrystallized if necessary.

Sulphate of quinia, or, more correctly, disulphate, is only slightly soluble in water; on the addition of dilute sulphuric acid a neutral sulphate is formed which is freely soluble. The latter salt may be obtained in large rectangular prisms, having a composition expressed by the formula $C_{20}H_{24}N_2O_2$, H_2SO_4, $7H_2O$. The ordinary disulphate of quinia is more soluble in alcohol or alcoholic liquids than in water; hence the *Tinctura Quiniæ*, B. P., which is a solution (saturated at 55° or 60° F.) of the salt in tincture of orange-peel (eight grains in the ounce). Quinia wine (*Vinum Quiniæ*, B. P.) is a solution of neutral sulphate and citrate of quinia in orange wine, made by dissolving the disulphate (one grain in the ounce) in orange-wine by the help of citric acid. The only official preparation of the pure disulphate is *Pilula Quiniæ*, containing three parts salt to one of confection of hips (gum arabic and honey, U. S. P.). The remaining Pharmacopœial preparation of quinia is the mixed citrates of iron, ammonium, and quinia (*Ferri et Quiniæ Citras*, B. P. and U. S. P.), the well-known scaly compound. It is made by dissolving ferric hydrate, prepared from ferric sulphate, and quinia, prepared from the sulphate, in solution of citric acid, ammonia also being added: the liquid, evaporated to a syrupy consistence and dried in thin layers on glass plates, yields the usual greenish-yellow scales (*vide* p. 115).

Quiniæ Valeriana, U. S. P., is made by dissolving precipitated quinia in warm aqueous solution of valerianic acid and setting aside to crystallize.

Reactions.

First Analytical Reaction.—To a solution of quinia or its salts in faintly acid water add fresh chlorine-water and then solution of ammonia; a green coloration is produced.

Second Analytical Reaction.—Repeat the foregoing reaction, but precede the addition of ammonia by solution of ferrocyanide of potassium; an evanescent red coloration is produced (Livonius and Vogel).

Third Analytical Reaction.—Quinia may be impure from the presence of the other alkaloids (chiefly quinidia and cinchonia) of cinchona-bark; the following tests will determine the point. The first is Stoddart's modification of Liebig's process.

Into a glass tube or bottle put ten grains of the suspected salt, dissolve in 10 minims of dilute sulphuric acid and 60 minims of distilled water; to this add 150 minims of *pure* ether, 3 minims of spirit of wine, and 40 minims of a solution of soda (1 part of solid hydrate to 12 of water). Agitate well and set aside for twelve hours, when, if the slightest trace of quinidia or cinchonia be present, they will be seen at the line of separation between the ether and solution of sulphate of sodium.

If only a small percentage of quinidia be present, it will appear as an oily substratum, appearing under a lens as dust, from the minuteness of its particles. Cinchonia will appear more decidedly crystalline. With a little practice the eye will easily distinguish which of the alkaloids is deposited.

Fourth Analytical Reaction.—This is Stoddart's chemico-microscopic test. Into an ounce of distilled water drop 10 drops of dilute sulphuric acid (British Pharmacopœia strength). To this add 14 grains (or as much as will saturate the acid) of the suspected salt. Filter through paper, and to a little of the filtered solution add a few drops of solution of sulphocyanide of potassium (180 grains in 1½ ounce of water). An immediate precipitate of the several alkaloids takes place, each of which is distinct and characteristic. If quinia, quinidia, and cinchonia be present they will all be seen on the slide, becoming more and more distinct during the first hour. A good plan is to place on a glass slip a drop of the solution to be tested, and to put another of the sulphocyanide by its side—the drops not being larger than good-sized pin-heads. Over both place a piece of thin glass, which will cause the drops to touch.

Examine the line of junction under a half-inch object-glass, when the crystals are readily seen and recognized. By this method $\frac{1}{10000}$ of a grain of quinidia or cinchonia may be easily detected. The particles arrange themselves into the respective groups—the long slender needles of the quinia salt, the round crystalline masses of the quinidia, and the large well-formed prisms of the cinchonia salts. This reaction is sufficiently constant to enable an observer who has accustomed himself to the general appearance to at once distinguish the respective salts from each other.

The sulphocyanide-of-potassium solution should be of the strength indicated. If not at hand it may quickly be made, sufficiently pure for this reaction, by the following process: Cyanide of potassium (fused), sublimed sulphur, of each 120 grains; distilled water an ounce and a half. Boil in a glass flask for fifteen minutes, filter, and make up the quantity to 1½ ounce with sufficient distilled water.

A small quantity of quinia in much cinchonia or quinidia cannot be recognized by the above reaction. Therefore, before concluding that no quinia is present in a specimen of those alkaloids, the sample should be treated with ether, filtered, the solution evaporated to dryness, and the residue, if any, examined for quinia.

Other Characters.—Concentrated sulphuric acid dissolves quinia with production of only a faint yellow color; salicin, with which quinia may possibly be adulterated, slowly gives, under the same circumstances, a deep red.

Concentrated nitric acid dissolves quinia, yielding a colorless solution; on heating, the solution becomes yellowish.

Quinia and its salts, heated on platinum foil, burn entirely away.

Salicin in quinia may be detected by several other tests (*vide* p. 345).

CINCHONIA OR CINCHONINE ($C_{20}H_{24}N_2O$) and quinia are distinguished from morphia by non-solubility of the alkaloid precipitated by a fixed alkali in excess of the alkaline solution. They are distinguished from each other by the solubility of the precipitated quinia and insolubility of cinchonia when ether is added to the alkaline mixture. Cinchonia, moreover, does not give the green coloration with chlorine-water and ammonia. Strychnia is also precipitated by fixed alkalies and insoluble in excess, but this alkaloid has such strongly marked reaction of its own as to preclude confusion.

Sulphate of Cinchonia (*Cinchoniæ Sulphas*, U. S. P.) occurs in the mother-liquors of sulphate of quinia, and is directly prepared from several kinds of bark. It forms white, shining crystals, having the form of short, oblique prisms, with dihedral summits. When heated, it fuses to a resinoid mass of a rich red color. It dissolves in fifty-four parts of cold water, in much less boiling water, in seven parts of alcohol, and very sparingly in ether. Its aqueous solution gives with terchloride of gold a yellow precipitate, and with chloride of calcium a white one. Ammonia, added to its solution in chlorine water, causes a white precipitate. If the salt be rubbed with water of ammonia, and then treated with ether, the cinchonia, separated by the former, will not be dissolved by the latter.

Quinidia or *Quinidine* is an isomer of quinia, and *Cinchonidia* or *Cinchonidine* an isomer of cinchonia. *Cinchovatia* or *Cinchovatine* occurs in a particular variety of cinchona-bark. *Quinicia* or *Quinicine* and *Cinchonicia* or *Cinchonicine* are the products of the action of heat on quinia and cinchonia.

STRYCHNIA, OR STRYCHNINE.

Formula $C_{21}H_{22}N_2O_2$. Molecular weight 334

Source.—This alkaloid exists in Nux Vomica (*Strychnos Nux Vomica*, B. P. and U. S. P.) and in St. Ignatius's bean (*Strychnos Ignatia*) (*Ignatia*, U. S. P.) chiefly in combination with lactic acid.

Process.—According to the British official process for its preparation (*Strychnia*, B. P.) the nuts, disintegrated by subjection to steam and, after drying, grinding in a coffee-mill, are exhausted with spirit, the latter removed by distillation, the extract dissolved in water, coloring and acid matters precipitated by acetate of lead, the filtered liquid evaporated to a small bulk, the strychnia precipitated by ammonia, the precipitate washed, dried, and exhausted with spirit, the spirit recovered by distillation, and the residual liquid set aside to crystallize. Crystals of strychnia having formed, the mother-liquor (which contains the brucia of the seeds) is poured away, and the crystals of strychnia washed with spirit (to remove any brucia) and recrystallized.

In the U. S. P. process the rasped Nux Vomica is exhausted by very dilute hydrochloric acid, milk of lime added to the evaporated decoction to decompose the hydrochlorate of strychnia, the precipitated and dried mixture of strychnia and lime treated with diluted alcohol to remove brucia, and then with strong hot alcohol to dissolve out strychnia: the alcohol having been recovered by distillation, the residual impure strychnia is dissolved in very dilute sulphuric acid, the solution decolorized by animal charcoal, evaporated, and set aside to crystallize, the crystals of sulphate of strychnia (*Strychniæ Sulphas*, U. S. P.) redissolved in water, ammonia added to precipitate pure strychnia, and the latter dried.

Properties.—Strychnia occurs "in right square octahedrons or prisms, colorless and inodorous; sparingly soluble in water, but communicating to it its intensely bitter taste; soluble in boiling rectified spirit, and in chloroform, but not in absolute alcohol or in ether."

Reactions.

First Analytical Reaction.—Place a minute particle of strychnia on a white plate, and near to it a small fragment of red chromate of potassium; to each add one drop of concentrated sulphuric acid: after waiting a minute or so for the chromate to fairly tinge the acid, draw the latter, by a glass rod, over the strychnia spot; a beautiful purple color is produced, quickly fading into a yellowish-red. The following oxidizing agents may be used in the place of the chromate: puce-colored oxide of lead, fragments of black oxide of manganese, ferridcyanide of potassium, or permanganate of potassium.

This reaction is highly characteristic; a minute fragment dissolved in much dilute alcohol, or, better, chloroform, and one drop of the liquid evaporated to dryness on a porcelain crucible-lid or other white surface, yields a residue which immediately gives the purple color on being oxidized in the manner directed.

Other Reactions.—Strong sulphuric acid does not act on strychnia, even at the temperature of boiling water, a fact of which advantage is taken in separating strychnia from other organic matter for purposes of toxicological analysis.——Sulphocyanide of potassium produces, even in dilute solutions of strychnia, a white precipitate, which, under the microscope, is seen to consist of tufts of acicular crystals.——Strong nitric acid does not color strychnia in the cold, and on heating only turns it yellow.

The Physiological Test.—A small frog placed in an ounce of water to which $\frac{1}{100}$ of a grain of a salt (acetate) of strychnia is added, is, in two or three hours, seized with tetanic spasms on the slightest touch, and dies shortly afterwards.

Strychnia has an intensely bitter taste. Cold water dissolves only $\frac{1}{2000}$ part; yet this solution, even when largely diluted, is distinctly bitter. Alcohol is a somewhat better solvent. The salts of the alkaloid are more soluble. The official solution (*Liquor Strychniæ*, B. P.) contains four grains of strychnia to the ounce, the solvent being three parts water, one part spirit, and a few minims (6 per ounce) of hydrochloric acid (rather more than sufficient to form hydrochlorate of strychnia).

Brucia, or Brucine ($C_{23}H_{26}N_2O_4,4H_2O$), is an alkaloid accompanying strychnia in Nux Vomica. It is readily distinguished by the intense red color produced when nitric acid is added to it. *Igasuria* is another alkaloid of Nux Vomica. This alkaloid is said to occur in no less than nine varieties, each slightly differing from the other in chemical composition. They resemble strychnia in physical properties.

Distinction of Brucia from Morphia.—The red coloration produced by the action of nitric acid on brucia is distinguished from that yielded by morphia by the action of reducing agents (such as stannous chloride, hyposulphite of sodium, sulphydrate of sodium), which decolorize the morphia-red, but change that of the brucia to violet and green (Cotton).

QUESTIONS AND EXERCISES.

660. What alkaloids are more or less characteristic of the different varieties of cinchona-bark? In what form do they occur?
661. By what method is Disulphate of Quinia obtained?
662. Give the characters of disulphate of quinia.
663. Describe the tests for quinia.
664. How is the adulteration of disulphate of quinia by salicin detected?
665. Show how the sulphates of quinidia or cinchonia may be proved to be present in commercial quinia.
666. How are cinchonia and quinia distinguished from morphia?
667. Whence is Strychnia obtained?
668. Describe the official process for the isolation of strychnia.
669. Give the characters of strychnia.
670. Enumerate the tests for strychnia, and describe their mode of application.
671. By what reagent is brucia distinguished from strychnia?
672. Distinguish between brucia and morphia.

ALKALOIDS OF LESS FREQUENT OCCURRENCE.

Aconitia, Aconitina, or Aconitine ($C_{30}H_{47}NO_7$) is an alkaloid obtained from aconite (*Aconitum Napellus*)-leaves (*Aconiti Folia* B. P. and U. S. P.) and root (*Aconiti Radix*, B. P. and U. S. P.). The alkaloid itself is only slightly soluble in water; it occurs in the plant in combination with a vegetable acid, forming a soluble salt.

Process.—The official process for its preparation (*Aconitia*, B. P. and U. S. P.) consists in dissolving out the natural salt of the alkaloid from the root by rectified spirit, recovering the latter by distillation, mixing the residue with water, filtering, precipitating the aconitia by ammonia, drying the precipitate and digesting it in ether (in which some of the accompanying impurities are insoluble), recovering the ether by distillation, dissolving the dry residue in the retort in water acidulated by sulphuric acid, again precipitating the alkaloid by ammonia, and finally washing and drying.

Properties.—Aconitia usually occurs as a white powder, soluble in 150 parts of cold water, 50 of hot, and much more soluble in alcohol and in ether. The chemical reactions of aconitia are not sufficiently well marked to admit of application as qualitative tests. It is one of the most violent poisons known. "When rubbed on the skin it causes a tingling sensation, followed by prolonged numbness."

Unguentum Aconitiæ, B. P., contains eight grains of the alkaloid to one ounce of prepared lard.

ATROPIA, or ATROPINE ($C_{17}H_{23}NO_3$), exists in the Belladonna, or Deadly Nightshade (*Atropa Belladonna: Belladonnæ Folia et Radix*, B. P. and U. S. P.), as soluble acid malate of atropia.

Process.—It is obtained in the pure state by exhausting the root with spirit, precipitating the acid and some coloring-matter by lime, filtering, adding sulphuric acid to form sulphate of atropia (which is somewhat less liable to decomposition during subsequent operations than the alkaloid itself), recovering most of the spirit by distillation, adding water to the residue, and evaporating till the remaining spirit is removed; solution of carbonate of potassium is then poured in till the liquid is nearly but not quite neutral, by which resinous matter is precipitated; the latter is filtered away, excess of carbonate of potassium then added, and the liberated atropia dissolved out by shaking the liquid with chloroform. The latter solution, having subsided, is removed, the chloroform recovered by distillation, the residual atropia dissolved in warm spirit, coloring matter separated by digesting the liquid with animal charcoal, the solution filtered, evaporated, and set aside to deposit crystals.

Solubility.—Atropia is sparingly soluble in water, the liquid giving an alkaline reaction—more soluble in alcohol and ether.

Tests.—Atropia-solutions give with perchloride of gold a yellow precipitate. One drop of a dilute aqueous solution (two grains to the ounce) powerfully dilates the pupil of the eye. It is applied on a piece of thin tissue paper or small disk placed between the eyelid and the eye.

Preparations.—The alkaloid itself (*Atropia*), its sulphate (*Atropiæ Sulphas*, a colorless powder soluble in water, made by neutralizing atropia with sulphuric acid), their solutions (*Liquor Atropiæ*, four grains per ounce, and *Liquor Atropiæ Sulphatis*, four grains per ounce), and an ointment (*Unguentum Atropiæ*, eight grains per ounce) are the preparations official in the British Pharmacopœia. The alkaloid and its sulphate are official in the United States Pharmacopœia.

Daturia or *Daturine*, an alkaloid in *Datura Stramonium* or Thorn-apple (*Stramonii Folia et Semina*, B. P. and U. S. P.), appears to be identical with atropia.

BEBERIA, or BEBERINE ($C_{19}H_{21}NO_3$), is an alkaloid existing in the bark of Bebeeru (*Nectandra Rodiæi*).

Process.—According to the British Pharmacopœia, it, or rather its sulphate, $C_{38}H_{42}N_2O_6$, H_2SO_4 (*Beberiæ Sulphas*, B. P.), may be prepared by exhausting the bark (*Nectandræ Cortex*, B. P. and U. S. P.) with water acidulated by sulphuric acid, concentrating, removing most of the acid by lime, filtering, precipitating the alkaloid by ammonia, filtering, drying, dissolving in spirit (in which some accompanying matters are insoluble), recovering most of the spirit by distillation, neutralizing by dilute sulphuric acid, evaporating to dryness, dissolving the residual sulphate in water, evaporating to the consistence of a syrup, and spreading on glass plates, drying the product at 140°. Thus obtained, it occurs in thin dark-brown translucent scales, yellow when powdered, strongly bitter, soluble in water and in alcohol.

Tests.—Alkalies give a pale yellow precipitate of beberia when added to an aqueous solution of a salt of the alkaloid; the precipitate is soluble in ether, With red chromate of potassium and sulphuric acid beberia gives a black resin, and with nitric acid a yellow resin.

Nectandria ($C_{20}H_{23}NO_4$).—Drs. Maclagan and Gamgee have recently discovered this second alkaloid in Bebeeru bark. It differs from beberia in fusing when placed in boiling water, in being much less soluble in ether, in giving with strong sulphuric acid and black oxide of manganese a beautiful green and then violet coloration, and in having a distinct molecular weight. They are of opinion that two other alkaloids exist in Bebeeru bark.

Berberia, or Berberine ($C_{20}H_{17}NO_4$), is an alkaloid existing in several plants of the natural order *Berberideæ*, in Calumba-root (*Calumbæ Radix*, B. P. and U.S. P.), *Goldthread* (*Coptis trifolia*, U. S. P.) according to Mayer, and in many yellow woods. The color of the tissues of these vegetables is apparently due to berberia; for the alkaloid itself is remarkable for its beautiful yellow color.

Tests.—When a dilute solution of iodine in iodide of potassium is added to solution of any salt of berberia in hot spirit, excess of iodine being carefully avoided, brilliant green spangles are deposited. The reaction is sufficiently delicate to form, according to Perrins, an excellent test of the presence of berberia. This iodo-compound polarizes light, and has other analogies with a similar quinine-salt termed herapathite.

Berberia is not an official alkaloid; but the plants in which it occurs are used as medicinal agents in all parts of the world.

Process.—Berberia is readily extracted by boiling the raw material with water, evaporating the strained liquid to a soft extract, digesting the residue in alcohol, recovering the alcohol by distillation, boiling the residue with diluted sulphuric acid, filtering and setting aside; the sulphate of berberia separates out, and may be purified by recrystallization from hot water. The alkaloid itself is obtained by shaking hydrate of lead with a hot aqueous solution of the sulphate of berberia (Proctor).

Podophyllum-root (*Podophylli Radix*, B. P., *Podophyllum*, U. S. P.), contains berberia. In preparing the resin of podophyllum or May-apple (*Podophylli Resina*, B. P. and U. S. P.) an alcoholic extract of the root is poured into water acidulated by hydrochloric acid, whereby the whole of the hydrochlorate of berberia, which is almost insoluble in dilute mineral acids, is precipitated with the resin (Maisch). No acid is ordered in U. S. P.

Capsicia, or Capsicine, is an alkaloid occurring in Cayenne pepper or Capsicum-fruit (*Capsici Fructus*, B. P. and U. S. P.), associated with resin and volatile oil. It is crystalline, and forms crystallizable salts with acids.

Cissampelia, Cissampeline, Pelosia, or Pelosine ($C_{18}H_{21}NO_3$), is an alkaloid occurring in the root (*Pareiræ Radix*, B. P. and U. S. P.) of *Cissampelos Pareira*. It is the tonic and diuretic principle of the drug.

CONIA, CONYLIA, CONINE, CONICINE, or CICUTINE.—Formula $C_8H_{15}N$, or $(C_8H_{14})''HN$. This alkaloid is a volatile liquid, occurring in hemlock (*Conium maculatum*). It is not official.

Process.—It may be obtained by distilling hemlock-fruit (*Conii Fructus*, B. P.) with water rendered slightly alkaline by caustic soda or potash, or by similarly treating the fresh juice of the leaves. The alkaloid is a yellow oily liquid, floating on the water that distils over; by redistillation it is obtained colorless and transparent.

The salts of conia have no odor, but when moistened with solution of an alkali yield the alkaloid, the strong smell of which, at once recalling hemlock, is characteristic. Extract of hemlock leaves (*Conii Folia*, B. P. and U. S. P.), to which solution of potash and boiling water have been added, forms the official Inhalation of Conia (*Vapor Coniæ*, B. P.).

Tests.—Sulphuric acid turns conia purplish-red, changing to olive-green, nitric acid a blood-red; perchloride of gold produces a yellowish-white precipitate, perchloride of platinum no precipitate, in aqueous solutions.

Hemlock also contains *methyl-conia* $(C_8H_{14})''$ CH_3N (Kekulé and Van Planta).

EMETIA or EMETINE $(C_{30}H_{44}N_2O_8)$.—This alkaloid is the active emetic principle of *Cephælis ipecacuanha* (*Ipecacuanha*, B. P. and U. S. P.). It occurs in combination with ipecacuanhic acid. The nitrate is peculiarly slightly soluble in water (Lefort). In the *Pulvis Ipecacuanhæ*, B. P. and U. S. P., or "Dover's Powder" (Powdered Ipecacuanha, 1 part; Powdered Opium, 1 part; and Sulphate of Potassium, 8 parts), minute division of the active ingredients is promoted by prolonged trituration with sulphate of potassium, which is a very hard salt.

HYOSCYAMIA, or HYOSCYAMINE, a volatile alkaloid, is said to occur in the leaves (*Hyoscyami Folia*, B. P. and U. S. P., *Hyoscyami Semen*, U. S. P.), and other parts of Henbane.

LOBELIA, or LOBELINE.—A volatile alkaloid first isolated from the dried flowering herb *Lobelia inflata* (*Lobelia*, B. P. and U. S. P.) by Bastick.

NECTANDRIA, *vide* BEBERIA.

NICOTIA, NICOTINA, NICOTYLIA, or NICOTINE.—Formula $C_{10}H_{14}N_2$, or $(C_5H_7)'''_2N_2$. This is also a volatile liquid alkaloid, forming the active principle of tobacco (*Nicotiana tabacum*), malate and citrate of nicotina being the forms in which it occurs in the leaf (*Tabaci Folia*, B. B. and U. S. P.). Its odor is characteristic; like conia, it yields a precipitate with perchloride of gold; but, unlike that alkaloid, its aqueous solutions are precipitated yellowish-white by perchloride of platinum. It is not official.

PHYSOSTIGMIA, or PHYSOSTIGMINE.—An alkaloid contained in the Calabar Bean (*Physostigmatis Faba*), the seed of *Physostigma venenosum* (Jobst and Hesse). A trace of it powerfully contracts the pupil of the eye; a small quantity is highly poisonous. Fraser also isolated this principle, and termed it *Eseria*, from Eserĕ, the name of this ordeal-poison at Calabar.

PIPERIA, or PIPERINE ($C_{17}H_{19}NO_3$), is a feeble alkaloid occurring in *white*, *black* (*Piper Nigrum*, B. P. and U. S. P.), *long*, and *cubeb pepper* (*Cubeba*, B. P. and U. S. P.), associated with volatile oil and resin; to these three substances the odor, flavor, and acridity belong. Piperia is obtained on boiling white pepper with alcohol, and evaporating the liquid with solution of potash, which retains resin. Recrystallized from alcohol, piperia forms colorless prisms fusible at 212°. With acids it forms salts, and distilled with strong alkali yields *piperidia* or *piperidine*, an alkaloid of strong chemical properties.

Sanguinarina, or *Sanguinarine* ($C_{37}H_{64}N_4O_8$) is a colorless alkaloid obtained from the rhizome of *Sanguinaria Canadensis* (U. S. P.) or Blood-root. Its salts have a red, crimson, or scarlet color.

SOLANIA, or SOLANINE ($C_{43}H_{70}NO_{16}$).—An alkaloid said to exist in the Woody Nightshade or Bitter-sweet (*Solanum dulcamara*). The dried young branches of the plant are official (*Dulcamara*, B. B. and U. S. P.).

SPARTEIA, or SPARTEINE ($C_{15}H_{26}N$), is a poisonous volatile alkaloid occurring in Broom-tops (*Scoparii Cacumina*, B. P. and U. S. P.). Its discoverer, Stenhouse, considers that the diuretic principle of broom is *Scoparin*, a non-poisonous body.

THEIA, THEINE, or CAFFEINE ($C_8H_{10}N_4O_2+H_2O$.)—This alkaloid occurs in tea, coffee (*Caffea*, U. S. P.), Paraguay tea, guarana, and the kola-nut. Infusions and preparations of these vegetable products are used chiefly as beverages by three-fourths of the human race. It is remarkable that the instinct of man, even in his savage state, should have led him to select, as the bases of common beverages, just the four or five plants which out of many thousands are the only ones, so far as we know, containing theia.

Test.—Concentrated nitric acid, or a mixture of chlorate of potassium and hydrochloric acid, rapidly oxidizes theia, forming compounds which with ammonia yield a beautiful purple-red color, resembling the murexid obtained under similar circumstances from uric acid; the oxidation must not be carried too far. Theine boiled with caustic potash yields methylamine (CH_3HHN), the vapor of which has a peculiar, characteristic odor.

The chemical action of theia on the system is not yet made out. Liebig thinks it may aid in the production of a substance a normal amount of which is so necessary, an abnormal so unpleasant—namely, bile. Most chemists agree that it arrests the rapid consumption of tissue and consequent feeling of fatigue which is especially experienced after hard work with mind or body.

VERATRIA, or VERATRINE ($C_{32}H_{52}N_2O_8$).—This alkaloid occurs as gallate of veratria in various species of *Veratrum* (Hellebore) (as *Veratrum Album*, U. S. P., *Veratri Viridis Radix*, B. P. and U. S. P.), in *Cevadilla* (*Sabadilla*, B. P. and U. S. P.), and in the cormus or so-called root of *Colchicum autumnale* (*Colchici Cormus*; *Colchici Semina*, B. P. and U. S. P.). White Hellebore is also said to contain three other alkaloids, *sabadillia* or *sabadilline*, *colchicia* or *colchicine*, and *jervia* or *jervine*. A mere trace of veratria brought into contact with the mucous membrane of the nose causes violent fits of sneezing. Fuming sulphuric acid colors it yellow, red, and violet in succession.

The official process for the preparation of the alkaloid (*Veratria*, B. P.) consists in exhausting the disintegrated cevadilla seeds by alcohol, recovering most of the spirit by distillation, pouring the residue into water, by which much resin is precipitated, filtering, and precipitating the veratria from the aqueous solution by ammonia. It is purified by washing with water, solution in dilute hydrochloric acid, decolorization of the liquid by animal charcoal, reprecipitation by ammonia, washing and drying. The U. S. P. process is similar, but includes treatment of the first crude veratria by diluted sulphuric acid and precipitation of alkaloid by magnesia.

Unguentum Veratriæ, B. P., contains eight grains of the slightly impure alkaloid obtained as just described, rubbed down with half a drachm of olive oil and diffused through one ounce of prepared lard.

QUESTIONS AND EXERCISES.

673. How is Aconitia prepared?
674. Give the strengths of the official preparations of Atropia.
675. Describe the properties of atropia.
676. What is the active principle of stramonium?
677. Mention pharmacopœial substances containing beberia and berberia respectively.
678. Give the characters of beberia.
679. In what does nectandria differ from beberia?
680. Mention the characteristics of conia.
681. What is the active principle of Ipecacuanha?
682. Name the alkaloid of Tobacco.
683. Give the name and properties of the active principle of Calabar Bean.
684. What are the sources of piperia?
685. Whence is theia obtained?
686. Describe the preparations of Veratria.
687. State the properties of veratria.

BITTER (TONIC) SUBSTANCES.

The following official articles, commonly employed medicinally in such forms as Decoction, Extract, Infusion, Tincture, contain active principles which have not yet been thoroughly examined. Some of these principles have been isolated, and a few have been obtained in the crystalline condition; but their constitution has not been sufficiently well made out to admit of the classification of the bodies either among alkaloids, glucosides, acids, or other well-marked principles.

Absinthium (Absinthin).
Anthemidis flores.
Aurantii cortex.
Buchu folia.
Canellæ albæ cortex.
Cascarillæ cortex.
Chirata.
Chimaphila.
Cuspariæ cortex, or *Angustura*, U. S. P., contains Cusparin or Angusturin.
Gentianæ radix.
Lactuca (Lactucin).
Lupulus.
Maticæ folia.
Marrubium.
Quassiæ lignum (Quassin, $C_{10}H_{12}O_3$).
Serpentariæ radix.
Spigelia marilandica.
Taraxaci radix (Taraxacin).

AMYLACEOUS AND SACCHARINE SUBSTANCES.

STARCH.

Formula $C_6H_{10}O_5$.

Processes.—Rasp or grate, or, with a knife, scrape a portion of a clean raw potato, letting the pulp fall on to a piece of muslin placed over a small dish or test-glass, and then pour a slow stream of water over the pulp; minute particles or *granules* of starch pass through the muslin and sink to the bottom of the vessel, fibrous matter remaining on the sieve. This is potato-starch. Wheat-starch (*Amylum*, B. P. and U. S. P.) may be obtained by tying up some flour in a piece of calico and kneading the bag in a slow stream of water flowing from a tap, the washings running into a deep vessel, at the bottom of which the white starch collects: the sticky matter remaining in the bag is *gluten*. The *blue starch* of the shops is artificially colored with smalt or indigo, to neutralize the yellow tint of recently washed linen; it should not be used for medicinal purposes. Starch dried in mass splits up into curious columnar masses, resembling the basaltic pillars of Fingal's Cave in Staffa, or those of the Giant's Causeway in the North of Ireland. The cause of the phenomenon, which may also be seen in grain-tin, is not conclusively known.

Gluten is the body which gives tenacity to dough and bread. It seems to be a mixture of vegetable fibrin, vegetable casein, and an albuminous matter termed glutin. These substances and gluten itself are closely allied; each contains about 16 per cent. of nitrogen. *Wheaten Flour* (*Farina Tritici*, B. P.) contains about 72 per cent. of starch and 11 of gluten, as well as sugar, gum, fine bran, water, and ash. The compactness of barley, well seen in Husked or Pearl Barley (*Hordeum Decorticatum* B. P. and U. S. P.), is said to be due to the large amount of vegetable fibrin present. During germination the fibrin is destroyed, hence, probably, the cretaceous character of malt. *Oatmeal* (*Avenæ Farina*, U. S. P.) is very rich in albuminoid or flesh-forming constituents, containing nearly 16 per cent. *Sago*, U. S. P., is granulated starch from the Sago Palm. *Tapioca*, U. S. P., is granulated starch from the Bitter Cassava.

Mucilage of Starch.—Mix two or three grains of starch with first a little and then more water, and heat to the boiling-point, mucilage of starch (*Mucilago Amyli*, B. P.) results.

This mucilage or paste is not a true solution; by long boiling, however, a portion of the starch becomes dissolved. In the latter case the starch probably becomes somewhat altered.

Chemical Test.—To some of the mucilage add a little free iodine; a deep-blue color is produced.

This reaction is a very delicate test of the presence of either iodine or starch. The starch must be in the state of mucilage; hence in testing for starch the substance supposed to contain it must be first boiled in water. The solutions used in the reactions should also be cold, or nearly so, as the blue color disappears on heating, though it is partially restored on cooling. The iodine reagent may be iodine-water or tincture of iodine. In testing for iodine its occurrence in the free state must be insured by the addition of a drop, or even less, of chlorine-water. Excess of chlorine must be avoided, or chloride of iodine will be formed, which does not color starch.

The so-called *iodide of starch* scarcely merits the name of a chemical compound, the state of union of its constituents being feeble. Substances that attack free iodine remove that element from iodide of starch. The alkalies, hydrosulphuric acid, sulphurous acid, and other reducing agents destroy the blue color.

Microscopical test.—All kinds of starch yield the blue color with iodine, showing their chemical similarity. But physically the granules of starch from different sources differ much in size and appearance when examined by the microscope with or without the aid of polarized light. The granules of potato-starch are large, of rice-starch very small, arrowroot (*Maranta*, U. S. P.), and wheat-starch being intermediate. By polarized light the granules of potato-starch appear as if traversed by a black cross, the wheat-starch granules, as seen in common flour, yielding no such effect. (See the frontispiece plates of the original edition of Pereira's "Materia Medica.") The granules of *Tous les Mois* (*Canna*, U. S. P.) are very large.

DEXTRIN.—Mix a grain or two of starch with about half a test-tubeful of cold water and a drop or two of sulphuric acid, and boil the mixture for a few minutes; no mucilage is formed, and the liquid, if sufficiently boiled, yields no blue color with iodine; the starch has become converted into *dextrin*. The same effect is produced if the starch is maintained at a temperature of about 320° F. for a short time. Dextrin is now largely manufactured in this way, and a paste of it used by calico-printers as a vehicle for colors; it is termed *British gum.* The change may also be effected by *diastase*, a peculiar ferment existing in malt. Mix two equal quantities of starch with equal amounts of water, adding to one a little ground malt, then heat both slowly to the boiling-point; the mixture without malt thickens to a paste or pudding, that with malt remains thin, its starch having become converted into dextrin.

Diastase is probably the vegetable fibrin of gluten in a state of decomposition; it is so named from διάστασις (*diastasis*), *separation*, in allusion to the separation, or rather alteration, it effects among the constituent atoms of starch.

Malt (the word malt is said to be derived from the Welsh *mall*, soft) is simply barley which has been softened by steeping in water, allowed to germinate slightly, and further change then arrested by the application of heat in a kiln. During germination the gluten breaks up and yields a glutinous substance termed vegetable gelatine, diastase, and other matters. To the vegetable gelatine is due much of the "body" of well-malted and slightly-hopped beer; it is precipitated by tannic acid, hence the thinness of ale (pale or bitter) brewed with a large proportion of hop or other materials containing tannic acid. A portion of the diastase reacting on the starch of the barley converts it into dextrin, and, indeed, carries conversion to the further stage of grape-sugar, as will be explained immediately. The temperature to which the malt is heated is made to vary, so that the sugar of the malt may or may not be partially altered to a dark-brown coloring material; if great, the malt is said to be *high-dried*, and is used in porter-brewing; if low, the product is of lighter color, and is used for ale. The diastase remaining in malt is still capable of converting a large quantity of starch into dextrin and sugar; hence the makers or distillers of the various spirits operate on a mixture of malted and unmalted grain in preparing liquors for fermentation.

Gum is a frequent constituent of vegetable juices, existing in large quantity in several species of acacia. According to Frémy gum is a calcium salt, sometimes partially a potassium salt of the *gummic* or *arabic* radical. The formula of gummic acid is said to be $H_2C_{12}H_{18}O_{10}, H_2O$. Gum differs from dextrin in yielding oxalic acid but no mucic acid when oxidized by nitric acid. *Cerasin* or *cherry-tree gum* is an insoluble modification of acacia gum. *Bassorin* ($C_{12}H_{20}O_{10}$) is a form of gum which is insoluble in water, but absorbs a large quantity of that liquid and forms a gelatinoid mass. It occurs largely in Tragacanth, combined, like arabin, with calcium. *Pectin* or *vegetable jelly* ($C_{32}H_{40}O_{28}, 4H_2O$) is the body which gives to expressed vegetable juices the property of gelatinizing. It forms the chief portion of Irish or Carrageen moss (*Chondrus crispus*, U. S. P.).

Isomerism. Allotropy. Polymorphism.

The composition of dextrin is represented by the same formula as that of starch, namely $C_6H_{10}O_5$; for it has the same percentage composition as starch. There are many other bodies similar in centesimal composition, but dissimilar in properties; such substances are termed *isomeric* (from ἴσος, *isos*, equal, and μέρος, *meros*, part); and their condition is spoken of as one of *isomerism*. There is sometimes good reason for doubling or otherwise multiplying the formula of one of two isomeric bodies. Thus olefiant gas (ethylene), the chief illuminating constituent of coal-gas, is represented by the formula C_2H_4, while amylene, an anæsthetic liquid hydrocarbon, obtained from amylic alcohol, though having the same percentage composition as olefiant gas, is represented by the formula C_5H_{10}; for the latter, when gaseous, is about twice and a half as heavy as the former, and must contain, therefore, in equal volumes, twice and a half as many atoms; its formula is, consequently, for this and other reasons, constructed to represent those proportions. This variety of isomerism is termed *polymerism* (from πολὺς, *polūs*, many or much, and μέρος, part). Metastannic acid (*vide* p. 197) is a polymeric variety of stannic acid. An illustration of a second variety of isomerism is seen in the case of cyanate of ammonium and urea, bodies already alluded to in connection with cyanic acid. These and several other pairs of chemical substances have dissimilar properties, yet are similar not only in elementary composition and in the centesimal proportion of the elements, but also in the fact that each molecule possesses the same number of atoms. But the reactions of these bodies indicate the probable nature of their construction; and this is shown in their formula by the disposition of the symbols. Thus cyanate of ammonium is represented by the formula NH_4CNO, urea by CH_4N_2O. Such bodies are termed *metameric* (from μετὰ, *meta*, a preposition denoting change, and μέρος), and their condition spoken of as one of *metamerism*. The isomerism of starch and dextrin may be of a polymeric or of a metameric character; but we do not yet know which, and must therefore at present give them identical formulæ. Substances similar in composition and constitution, yet differing in properties, are termed *allotropic* (ἄλλος, *allos*, another, τρόπος, *tropos*, condition). Thus ordinary phosphorus, kept at a temperature of about 450° Fahr., in an atmosphere from which air is excluded, becomes red, opaque, insoluble in liquids in which ordinary phosphorus is soluble, oxidizes extremely slowly, and only ignites when heated to near 500° Fahr. (red or amorphous phosphorus). Another illustration of *allotropy* is seen in certain varieties of tartaric acid, which have different optical properties, but otherwise are identical; they are in neither of the above-mentioned states of isomerism, but are allotropic modifications of the same substance. Occasionally one and the same substance crystallizes in two distinct forms, its state is then described as one of *polymorphism* (πολὺς, *polūs*, many, μορφή, *morphē*, form). Sulphur is polymorphous. It crystallizes by slow cooling in (1) prismatic crystals of sp. gr. 1.98, while in nature it occurs in (2) octahedra of sp. gr. 2.07. Melted and poured into water, sulphur takes up the form of (3) caoutchouc of sp. gr. 1.96. These differences warrant the statement that sulphur occurs in three distinct allotropic conditions.

Cellulin or *cellulose*, the woody fibre of plants, familiar, in the nearly pure state, under the forms of "cotton-wool" (*Gossypium*, B. P. and U. S. P., "hairs of the seed of various species of Gossypium"), paper, linen, and pith is another substance isomeric, probably polymeric, with starch. Lignin is a closely allied body, lining the interior of woody cells and vessels. By the action of nitric acid of various strengths on cellulin, peroxide of nitrogen (NO_2) is substituted for one, two, or three atoms of hydrogen—mono-, di-, or trinitrocellulin being formed:—

$$\underset{\text{Cellulin.}}{C_6H_{10}O_5} + \underset{\text{Nitric acid.}}{HNO_3} = \underset{\text{Mononitrocellulin.}}{C_6\left\{\begin{matrix}H_9\\NO_2\end{matrix}\right\}O_5} + \underset{\text{Water.}}{H_2O}$$

$$\underset{\text{Cellulin.}}{C_6H_{10}O_5} + \underset{\text{Nitric acid.}}{2HNO_3} = \underset{\text{Dinitrocellulin.}}{C_6\left\{\begin{matrix}H_8\\2NO_2\end{matrix}\right\}O_5} + \underset{\text{Water.}}{2H_2O}$$

$$\underset{\text{Cellulin.}}{C_6H_{10}O_5} + \underset{\text{Nitric acid.}}{3HNO_3} = \underset{\text{Trinitrocellulin.}}{C_6\left\{\begin{matrix}H_7\\3NO_2\end{matrix}\right\}O_5} + \underset{\text{Water.}}{3H_2O}$$

Trinitrocellulin is highly explosive gun-cotton; dinitrocellulin is not sufficiently explosive for use instead of gunpowder; mononitrocellulin is scarcely at all explosive.

Dinitrocellulin (*Pyroxylin*, B. P.) may be prepared by the following process: Mix 5 fluidounces of sulphuric acid and 5 of nitric in an earthenware mortar, immerse 1 ounce of cotton-wool in the mixture, and stir it for three minutes with a glass rod, until it is thoroughly wetted by the acids. Transfer the cotton to a vessel containing water, stir it well with a glass rod, decant the liquid, pour more water upon the mass, agitate again, and repeat the affusion, agitation, and decantation until the washing ceases to give a precipitate with chloride of barium. Drain the product on filtering paper, and dry in a water-bath.

Mononitrocellulin and *trinitrocellulin* are insoluble in a mixture of alcohol and ether; *dinitrocellulin* or *pyroxylin* is soluble, the solution forming ordinary collodion (*Collodium*, B. P. and U. S. P.). The official proportions are 1 ounce of pyroxylin dissolved in a mixture of 36 fluidounces of ether and 12 of rectified spirit. After digesting for a few days, the liquid is decanted from any insoluble matter and preserved in a well-corked bottle. It is "a colorless highly inflammable liquid with ethereal odor, which dries rapidly upon exposure to the air, and leaves a thin transparent film, insoluble in water or rectified spirit." Flexible collodion (*Collodium Flexile*, B. P.) is a mixture of collodion (6 fluidounces), Canada Balsam (120 grains), and castor oil (1 fluidrachm).

QUESTIONS AND EXERCISES.

688. How is wheat-starch or potato-starch isolated?
689. Define gluten and glutin.
690. Enumerate the proximate principles of wheaten flour.
691. Is starch soluble in water?
692. Which is the best chemical test for starch?
693. Distinguish physically between the varieties of starch.
694. Into what compound is starch converted by heat?
695. What occurs when a mixture of starch and water is allowed to flow into hot diluted sulphuric acid?
696. If equal amounts of starch and water be heated, one containing a small quantity of ground malt, what effects ensue?
697. Write a short article on the chemistry of "malting."
698. Explain *isomerism*, as illustrated by starch and dextrin.
699. Give examples of polymeric bodies.
700. State the formula of a body metameric with urea.
701. Define *allotropy* and *polymorphism*, giving illustrations.
702. What form of cellulin is official?
703. Mention the properties of the products of the action of nitric acid of various strengths on cellulin.
704. How is pyroxylin prepared?

SUGAR.

Formula $C_{12}H_{22}O_{11}$.

Artificial formation of Grape-sugar from Cane-sugar.—Tests for Sugar.—Dissolve a grain or two of common cane-sugar in water. To a portion of this solution placed in a test-tube add more water, two or three drops of solution of sulphate of copper, a considerable quantity of solution of potash or soda (enough to turn the color of the liquid from a light to a dark blue), and heat the mixture to the boiling-point; no obvious change occurs. To another portion of the syrup add a drop of sulphuric acid, and boil for ten or twenty minutes, then add the copper solution and alkali, and heat as before; a yellowish-red precipitate of cuprous oxide (Cu_2O) falls. This test is exceedingly delicate.

The above reaction is due to the conversion of the *cane-sugar* ($C_{12}H_{22}O_{11}$) into a kind of *grape-sugar* ($C_{12}H_{24}O_{12}$, or $2C_6H_{12}O_6$) by the influence of the sulphuric acid, and to the reducing action of the grape sugar on the cupric solution. The formation of a precipitate immediately, without the action of acid, shows the presence of grape-sugar—its formation only after ebullition with acid indicating, in the absence of starch or dextrin, cane-sugar. In this process the sugar is oxidized and broken up into several substances; the exact nature of the reaction has not been ascertained.

Cane-sugar or *sucrose* (*Saccharum Purificatum* B. P. and U. S. P.) is a frequent constituent of vegetable juices. Thus it forms the chief portion of cassia-pulp (*Cassiæ Pulpa*, B. P.) and Fig (*Ficus*, B. P. and U. S. P.) but is most plentiful in the sugar-cane: much, however, is now obtained from the sugar-maple and beetroot. On the evaporation of the juice, common *brown* or *moist sugar* crystallizes out; this by resolution, filtration through animal charcoal, evaporation to a strong syrup, and crystallization in moulds, yields the compact crystalline conical loaves known in trade as *lump-sugar*. From a slightly less strong syrup, slowly cooled, the crystals termed *sugar-candy* are deposited, white or colored according to the color of the syrup. Grape sugar or *glucose* (from γλυκὺς, *glucūs*, sweet) is often seen in the crystallized state, in dried grapes or raisins and other fruits; it is also the variety of sugar met with in diabetic urine. Both varieties twist a ray of polarized light from left to right, to an extent dependent on the amount of sugar present—a fact easy of application in estimating the amount of sugar in syrups or in diabetic urine.

Both cane-sugar and grape-sugar yield alcohol and carbonic acid gas by fermentation, the cane-sugar probably always passing into grape-sugar before the production of alcohol commences.

$$\underset{\text{Grape-sugar.}}{C_6H_{12}O_6} = \underset{\text{Alcohol.}}{2C_2H_5HO} + \underset{\text{Carbonic acid gas.}}{2CO_2}.$$

In *bread-making*, some of the starch is converted into dextrin, and this into sugar by the ferment. The above action then goes on, the liberation of gas producing the *rising* or swelling of the mixture of flour, water, and yeast (dough)—the temperature to which the mass is subjected in the oven causing escape of alcohol, and further expansion of the bubbles of carbonic acid gas in every part of the now spongy loaf. The carbonic acid gas gradually evolved when flour is worked up for bread with a mixture of dry bicarbonate of sodium and tartaric acid (best preserved by previous admixture with a little dried flour)—*baking-powder*—exerts similar influence. The least objectionable method of introducing carbonic acid gas, however, is that of Dauglish, whose patent Aërated Bread is made from flour by mere admixture with carbonic-acid water under pressure. On removal from the cylinder, the resulting dough expands by the natural elasticity of the imprisoned carbonic acid, and the bake-oven completes the process. The crumb of bread is official (*Mica Panis*, B. P.).

Milk-sugar or *lactose* (*Saccharum Lactis*, B. P. and U. S. P.), the sweet principle of the milk of various animals, is not susceptible of alcoholic or vinous fermentation; but it resembles grape-sugar in reducing an alkaline solution of copper with precipitation of suboxide. It is readily obtained from milk by adding a few drops of acid, stirring, setting aside for the *curds* to separate, filtering, evaporating the *whey* to a small bulk, filtering again if necessary, and allowing to cool and crystallize. It usually occurs in trade "in cylindrical masses, two inches in diameter, with a cord or stick in the axis, or in fragments of cakes—grayish-white, crystalline on the surface and in its texture, translucent, hard, scentless, faintly sweet, gritty when chewed." It is soluble in 6 parts of cold and 3 of boiling water; slightly soluble in alcohol; insoluble in ether.

Action of Alkali on Sugar.—To a little solution of grape-sugar add solution of potash or soda, or solution of carbonate of potassium, and warm the mixture; the liquid is darkened in color from amber to brown, according to the amount of sugar present.

Tests.—The copper-reaction, the fermentation process, and the effect of alkalies form three good tests of the presence of grape-sugar, and, indirectly, of cane-sugar. A piece of merino or other woollen material, previously dipped in a solution of stannic chloride and dried, becomes of a brown or black color when dipped in a solution of glucose and heated to about 300° F. by holding before a fire.

Sugar from Starch.—Boil the starch with a little water and a drop of sulphuric acid as for dextrin, but continue the ebullition for several minutes: on testing a portion of the cooled liquid with iodine, and another portion with the heated alkaline solution of a copper salt as described on page 336, it will be found that the starch has nearly all become converted into grape-sugar, or *starch-sugar* as it is sometimes termed. When made on a large scale, a warm (131° F) mixture of starch and water of the consistence of cream is slowly poured into a boiling solution of one part of sulphuric acid in one hundred of water, the whole boiled for some time, the acid neutralized by chalk, the mixture filtered, the liquid evaporated to a thick syrup and set aside; in a few days it crystallizes to a granular mass resembling honey. In this operation a small quantity of dextrin remains with the glucose; but if the process be conducted under pressure, conversion, according to Manbré, is complete.

The sugar in fresh fruits is mainly cane-sugar; but by the action of the acid, or possibly of a ferment in the juice, it is gradually converted into *inverted sugar*, a variety differing from cane-sugar in being uncrystallizable, and in having an inverted or opposite influence on polarized light, twisting the ray from right to left (lævogyrate, having lævo-rotation—hence sometimes termed *levulose*). Ripe Hips (*Rosæ Caninæ Fructus*, B. P.) contain 30 per cent. of such sugar. Fruit-sugar, as gathered in the form of syrup by bees, is probably a mixture of these two varieties. It is gradually altered to a crystalline or granular mass of grape-sugar, as seen in dried fruits, such as Raisins (*Uvæ*, B. P., *Uva Passa*, U. S. P), and the Prune (*Prunum*, B. P. and U. S. P.), and in solidified honey (*Mel*, B. P. and U. S. P.). This, the common form of grape-sugar, is dextrogyrate, and hence is sometimes termed *dextrose*, to distinguish it from levulose. Honey often contains flocculent matters which cause it to ferment and yield mannite (Stoddart), alcohol, and acetic acid; hence for use in medicine it is directed (*Mel Depuratum*, B. P. and U. S. P.) to be clarified by melting and straining, while hot, through flannel previously moistened with warm water. A mixture of clarified honey 80 per cent., acetic acid 10 per cent., and water 10 per cent., is official under the name of *Oxymel* (from ὀξύς, *oxūs*, acid, and μέλι, *meli*, honey). A similar mixture of honey with acetic acid containing the soluble portions of squill-bulbs (*Scilla*, B. P. and U. S. P.) is known as Oxymel of Squill (*Oxymel Scillæ*, B. P.). Honey or cane-sugar are the bases of the official *Confections*.

Barley sugar is made by simply heating cane-sugar till it fuses, a change from the crystalline to the uncrystallizable condition occurring. *Treacle* (*Theriaca*, B. P.), *Molasses*, (*Syrupus Fuscus*, U. S. P.), or *Melasses* (from *Mel*, honey), chiefly results from the application of too much heat in evaporating the syrups of the sugar cane; it is a mixture of cane-sugar with uncrystallizable sugar and coloring-matter. Liquorice-root (*Glycyrrhizæ Radix*, B. P.), contains a considerable quantity of uncrystallizable sugar (*Glycyrrhizin*).

Caramel.—Carefully heat a grain or two of sugar in a test-tube until it blackens; the product is *caramel* or *burnt sugar* (the *Saccharum Ustum* of pharmacy). It is used as a coloring agent for gravies, confectioneries, spirits, and similar materials.

Mannite ($C_6H_{14}O_6$).—Boil manna with alcohol, filter, and set aside; mannite separates in colorless shining crystals or acicular masses, to the extent of from 60 to 80 per cent. of the manna.

Manna, B. P. and U. S. P., is "a concrete saccharine exudation from the stem of *Fraxinus Ornus* and *F. rotundifolia;* it is obtained by making incisions in the stem of the trees." It occurs in "stalactiform pieces from one to six inches in length, and one or two inches in width, uneven, porous, and friable, curved on one side, of a yellowish-white color, with a faintly nauseous odor, and a sweetish taste."

Mannite is an alcohol, the radical of which is sexivalent $(C_6H_8)^{vi}$ 6HO (Wanklyn). It is closely related to the sugars, glucose becoming mannite by action of nascent hydrogen:—

$$\underset{\text{Glucose.}}{C_6H_{12}O_6} + \underset{\text{Hydrogen.}}{H_2} = \underset{\text{Mannite.}}{C_6H_{14}O_6}$$

Indeed, glucose itself is probably an alcohol of another radical $(C_6H_6)^{vi}$6HO. Mannite does not undergo vinous fermentation in contact with yeast. In is soluble in 5 times its weight of cold water.

Mucic Acid ($H_2C_6H_8O_8$) and *Saccharic Acid* ($H_2C_6H_8O_8$) are two isomeric bodies formed by the action of dilute nitric acid on gum, sugar, and mannite.

QUESTIONS AND EXERCISES.

705. How are cane-sugar and grape-sugar analytically distinguished?
706. Describe the methods of extracting and purifying cane-sugar.
707. Mention the chief sources of cane-sugar.
708. Give chemical explanations of the different processes of bread-making.
709. How is milk-sugar obtained, and in what respects does it differ from other sugar?
710. By what process may starch be entirely converted into sugar?
711. What is the difference between fruit-sugar and honey?
712. What is Oxymel?
713. Describe the effect of heat on cane-sugar.
714. Describe the source and character of manna.
715. Give the latest view of the constitution of mannite.
716. Whence are mucic and saccharic acids obtained?

THE GLUCOSIDES.

Source.—The Glucosides are certain proximate vegetable principles which, by ebullition with dilute acid, or other method of decomposition, take up the elements of water and yield glucose, accompanied by a second substance, which differs in each case according to the body operated on. Twelve of the glucosides are of pharmaceutical interest, namely: Aloin, Amygdalin, Cathartic acid, Convolvulin, Digitalin, Elaterin, Guaiacin, Jalapin, Salicin, Santonin, Scammonin. Tannin, or tannic acid, is also a glucoside; it has been described among the acids.

Note on Nomenclature.—The first syllable of the names of glucosides and neutral principles generally are commonly given in allusion to origin; the last syllable is *in*, which sufficiently distinguishes them as a class.

Aloin ($C_{34}H_{36}O_{14},H_2O$).—This substance, first obtained by T. & H. Smith, occurs in minute crystals in that portion of aloes which is soluble in water. According to the experiments of Kosmann it seems to be a glucoside, the aqueous extract of aloes yielding, by ebullition with dilute acid, glucose and *Aloesetic acid*. The portion of aloes insoluble in water is also a glucoside; for Kosmann by similar treatment obtained from it glucose, *aloeresinic acid* and *aloeretinic acid*. The aloes of Pharmacy (*Aloe Barbadensis*, B. P. and U. S. P., *Aloe Socotrina*, B. P. and U. S. P., and *Aloe Capensis*, U. S. P.), is an evaporated juice, doubtless much altered by the temperature to which it is subjected.

AMYGDALIN ($C_{20}H_{27}NO_{11}, 3H_2O$).—This is a white crystalline substance, existing in the bitter (*Amygdala Amara*, B. P. and U. S. P.), but not in the sweet almond (*Amygdala Dulcis*, B. P. and U. S. P.). It is readily extracted by alcohol from the cake left when the fixed oil has been expressed from bitter almonds. From the concentrated alcoholic solution ether precipitates the amygdalin.

Make an emulsion of two or three sweet almonds by bruising and rubbing them with water, and notice that it has no odor of essential oil of bitter almonds; add a grain or two of amygdalin, an odor of essential oil of bitter almonds is at once developed. Bruise two or three bitter almonds and rub with water; the volatile oil is again developed (*Oleum Amygdalæ Amaræ*, U. S. P.).

Bitter Almond-water (*Aqua Amygdalæ Amaræ*, U. S. P.) is made by filtering a mixture of 16 minims of the oil with 60 grains of carbonate of magnesium and 2 wine-pints of distilled water.

The source of the hydride of benzoyl, or essential oil of bitter almonds, in these reactions is the amygdalin, which, under the influence of *synaptase* or *emulsin*, a ferment existing in both bitter and sweet almonds, splits up into the essential oil, hydrocyanic acid, and glucose:—

$$\underset{\text{Amygdalin.}}{C_{20}H_{27}NO_{11}} + \underset{\text{Water.}}{2H_2O} = \underset{\text{Hydride of benzoyl.}}{C_7H_5OH} + \underset{\text{Hydrocyanic acid.}}{HCN} + \underset{\text{Glucose.}}{2C_6H_{12}O_6}$$

As each molecule of amygdalin yields one of hydrocyanic acid, a simple calculation shows that 17 grains (mixed with emulsion of sweet almonds) will be required to form one grain of real hydrocyanic acid, a quantity equivalent to 50 minims of the dilute hydrocyanic acid of the British Pharmacopœia.

Test.—The reaction between synaptase and amygdalin is applicable as a test of the presence of one by the addition of the other, even when mixed with much organic matter.

Cherry-Laurel-water (*Aqua Laurocerasi*, B. P., by distillation with water from *Laurocerasi Folia*, B. P.), contains hydrocyanic acid derived from a reaction similar to, if not identical with, that just described. But the proportion of amygadalin or analogous body in cherry-laurel-leaves is most variable; hence the strength of the water is highly uncertain. The preparation is worse than useless.

Caution.—Essential oil of almonds is highly poisonous. The purified oil or hydride of benzoyl is almost innocuous. Artificial oil of bitter almonds or nitrobenzol ($C_6H_5(NO_2)$) when taken in quantity has been known to produce death.

CATHARTIC ACID.—"The glucoside acid that now is known to confer on the Senna of Alexandria (*Senna Alexandriana*, B. P.), Tinnevely (*Senna Indica*, B. P., *Senna*, U. S. P.), and probably on American Senna (*Cassia Marilandica*, U. S. P.), its purgative property, has been named by its discoverers (Dragendorf and Kubly) Cathartic acid. Its formula has been stated as $C_{180}H_{192}N_4SO_{82}$, which, if true, accounts for its extreme stability. It is insoluble in water, strong alcohol, and ether, but enters readily into watery solution when combined with alkaline and earthy bases. Its ammonium salts give brownish flocculent precipitates with salts of silver, tin, mercury, copper, and lead. Antimonial salts, tannin, yellow and red prussiates have no effect upon it. Alkalies, aided by heat, act destructively upon it. Boiled with a mineral acid it splits into a peculiar kind of glucose and an acid that has been named Cathartogenic; its formula is said to be $C_{132}H_{116}N_4SO_{44}$. Cathartic acid, in a combined state and of tolerable purity, is prepared by partially precipitating by strong spirit a watery infusion of senna, concentrated to a syrupy state by evaporation *in vacuo*. The filtrate is now treated with a much larger bulk of absolute alcohol, and the precipitate thus obtained is purified by repeated solution in water and precipitation by alcohol. To obtain the pure acid, advantage is taken of its colloidal properties; the crude cathartate is dissolved in moderately strong hydrochloric acid, and subjected to dialysis on a diaphragm of parchment paper. The minimum dose of this pure acid was found to be about 1½ grains, which caused several stools with decided griping.

"The carthartic combinations that I have made are, the cathartate of ammonium, prepared from cathartate of lead by my original process, and the mixed cathartates, prepared according to Dragendorf's method as modified by myself. Of the former nearly pure salt, I have found 3¾ grains to purge fairly as to amount, but slowly as to time, and with considerable griping. Of the latter, 7½ grains purged violently with much griping and sickness, which continued through the greater part of the day. It obviously would be improper to combine senna with any of its metallic precipitants, should such be desired, which is not likely. It is here satisfactory to observe that the cathartate of magnesium is soluble, and that the old-fashioned black draught agrees with new-fashioned science." (Groves.)

Buckthorn juice (*Rhamni Succus*, B. P.) owes its cathartic properties to a substance apparently identical with cathartic acid.

COLOCYNTHIN ($C_{56}H_{84}O_{23}$?).—This substance is the active bitter and purgative principle of colocynth-fruit (*Colocynthidis Pulpa*, B. P., *Colocynthis*, U.S. P.): it is soluble in water and alcohol, but not in ether. By ebullition with acids it furnishes glucose and a resinoid body.

CONVOLVULIN.—See JALAPIN.

DIGITALIN ($C_{27}H_{45}O_{15}$).—This is an active principle of the Foxglove (*Digitalis*, B. P.). Boil a grain of digitalin (*Digitalinum*, B. P.) with sulphuric acid for some time; flocks of *digitaliretin* ($C_{15}H_{25}O_5$) separate, and glucose may be detected in the liquid.

$$\underset{\text{Digitalin.}}{C_{27}H_{45}O_{15}} + \underset{\text{Water.}}{2H_2O} = \underset{\text{Digitaliretin.}}{C_{15}H_{25}O_5} + \underset{\text{Glucose.}}{2C_6H_{12}O_6}$$

Properties.—Digitalin occurs "in porous mammillated masses or small scales, white, inodorous, and intensely bitter, readily soluble in spirit, but almost insoluble in water and in pure ether, dissolves in acids, but does not form with them neutral compounds; its solution in hydrochloric acid is of a faint yellow color, but rapidly becomes green. It leaves no residue when burned with free access of air. It powerfully irritates the nostrils, and is an active poison."

Process.—The official process for the preparation of digitalin consists in dissolving the glucoside out of the digitalis leaf (*Digitalis Folia*, B. P. and U. S. P.) by alcohol, removing the alcohol by distillation, dissolving the residue in water by the help of a small quantity of acetic acid, removing much of the color from the solution by animal charcoal, neutralizing most of the acetic acid by ammonia, precipitating the digitalin by tannic acid (with which it forms an insoluble compound), washing the precipitate, rubbing and heating it with spirit and oxide of lead (which removes the acid in the form of insoluble tannate of lead), again decolorizing by animal charcoal, evaporating to dryness, washing out impurities still remaining by ether, and drying the residual digitalin. In this form digitalin is uncrystallizable.

Pure Digitalin.—On treating commercial digitalin with chloroform only an inert substance remains undissolved. The solution yields pure digitalin on evaporation; it may be crystallized from spirit in radiating needles. (Nativelle.) The therapeutic power of the pure substance has not been determined.

Elaterin ($C_{20}H_{28}O_5$).—Boil elaterium (*Elaterium*, B. P. and U. S. P.), the dried sediment from the juice of the squirting-cucumber fruit (*Ecbalii Fructus*, B. P.), in a small quantity of spirits of wine, and filter; fibrous and amylaceous matter remain insoluble, while elaterin and resin are dissolved. The filtrate, concentrated and poured into a warm solution of potash, yields, on cooling, crystals of elaterin, resin being retained by the alkali. It is purified by recrystallization from spirit. Boil elaterium in dilute sulphuric acid for an hour or two, filter, and test the clear liquid for glucose; a reddish precipitate of cuprous oxide falls. This reaction is readily obtained with elaterium, but not always with elaterin; hence probably the latter is not a true glucoside.

Elaterin is the active principle of the so-called elaterium. Elaterium occurs "in light friable slightly incurved cakes, about one line ($\frac{1}{12}$ inch) thick, greenish-gray, acrid and bitter; fracture finely granular." Good specimens of this drug should yield, according to the British Pharmacopœia, not less than 20 per cent. of elaterin by the above process. Elaterium is sometimes adulterated with chalk and other substances.

Guaiacin.—Resin of guaiacum (*Guaiaci Resina*, B. P. and U. S. P), an exudation from the wood (*Guaiaci Lig-*

num, B. P. and U. S. P.) of *Guaiacum officinale*, is probably a mixture of several substances, among which are *Guaiaretinic acid* ($C_{20}H_{26}O_4$) (Hlasiwetz) and *Guaiacin*, a glucoside. On boiling guaiacum-resin with dilute sulphuric acid for some time, glucose is found in the liquid, a green resinous substance (*guaiaretin*) remaining insoluble (Kosmann). Most oxidizing agents, and even atmospheric air, especially under the influence of certain organic substances, produce a blue, then green, and finally a brown color, when brought into contact with an alcoholic solution of guaiacum-resin.

These effects are said to be due to three stages of oxidation (Jonas). They may be observed on adding the solution to the inner surface of a paring of raw potato.

JALAPIN ($C_{31}H_{50}O_{16}$) AND CONVOLVULIN ($C_{34}H_{56}O_{16}$).—According to Keyser and Meyer, jalap-resin contains two distinct substances—convolvulin, chiefly obtained from Mexican male jalap, and jalapin, most largely contained in the true jalap; the former is soluble in ether, the latter insoluble. Boil jalap-resin with dilute sulphuric acid for some time and filter; a substance, which is probably a mixture of *jalapinol* ($C_{13}H_{24}O_3$) and *convolvulinol* ($C_{16}H_{30}O_3$), separates; and glucose may be detected in the clear liquid. (It is to be regretted that the authors transpose the above names, terming the old well-known jalapin convolvulin.)

$$\underset{\text{Jalapin.}}{C_{31}H_{50}O_{16}} + \underset{\text{Water.}}{5H_2O} = \underset{\text{Jalapinol.}}{C_{13}H_{24}O_3} + \underset{\text{Glucose.}}{3C_6H_{12}O_6}$$

Jalapic acid.—This is contained in the portion of jalap-resin soluble in ether. It may also be obtained from jalapin by ebullition with alkalies:—

$$\underset{\text{Jalapin.}}{2C_{31}H_{50}O_{16}} + 3H_2O = \underset{\text{Jalapic acid.}}{C_{62}H_{106}O_{35}}$$

Jalap-resin (*Jalapæ Resina*, B. P. and U. S. P.) is obtained by digesting and percolating jalap tubercles (*Jalapa*, B. P. and U. S. P.) with spirit of wine, adding a little water, distilling off the spirit, pouring away the aqueous portion which contains much saccharine matter, and washing and drying the residual resin. The tincture is sometimes decolorized by animal charcoal, and the evaporated product sold as jalapin.

Jalap-resin is insoluble in oil of turpentine; common resin, or rosin, soluble. If the presence of the latter is suspected, the specimen should be powdered, digested in turpentine, the mixture filtered, and the filtrate evaporated; no residue, or not more than yielded by the turpentine itself, should be obtained.

Salicin ($C_{13}H_{18}O_7$).—This substance is contained in and easily extracted from willow-bark.

Tests.—1. To a small portion of salicin placed on a white plate or dish add a drop of strong sulphuric acid; a deep-red color is produced.

2. Boil salicin with dilute sulphuric acid for some time; it is converted into *saligenin* ($C_7H_8O_2$) and glucose.

$$\underset{\text{Salicin.}}{C_{13}H_{18}O_7} + \underset{\text{Water.}}{H_2O} = \underset{\text{Saligenin.}}{C_7H_8O_2} + \underset{\text{Glucose.}}{C_6H_{12}O_6}$$

Examine a portion of the solution for grape-sugar by the copper test.

3. To another portion of the liquid, carefully neutralized, add a persalt of iron; a purplish-blue color is produced, due to the reaction of the saligenin and the ferric salt.

4. Heat a mixture of about 1 part of salicin, 1 of red chromate of potassium, $1\frac{1}{2}$ of sulphuric acid, and 20 of water in a test-tube; a fragrant characteristic odor is evolved, due to the formation of hydride of salicyl ($C_7H_5O_2H$), an essential oil identical with that existing in meadow-sweet (*Spiræa ulmaria*) and in heliotrope.

$$\underset{\text{Saligenin.}}{2C_7H_8O_2} + \underset{\text{Oxygen.}}{O_2} = \underset{\text{Hydride of salicyl.}}{2C_7H_5O_2H} + \underset{\text{Water.}}{2H_2O}$$

Santonin ($C_{15}H_{18}O_3$).—This substance is a weak acid, insoluble in ammonia, but forming a soluble calcium salt. From a solution of santonate of calcium the santonin is precipitated by acids. Boiled for some time with dilute sulphuric acid it yields 87 per cent. of an insoluble resinous substance (*santoniretin*) and glucose (Kosmann). Santonin (*Santoninum*, B. P. and U. S. P.) is official.

Process.—The process for its preparation consists in boiling *santonica*, B. P. and U. S. P. (the unexpanded flower-heads of an undetermined species of *Artemisia*) with milk of lime (whereby santonate of calcium is formed), straining, precipitating the santonin or santonic acid by hydrochloric acid (acetic acid, U. S. P.), washing with ammonia to remove resin, dissolving in spirit and digesting with animal charcoal to get rid of coloring-matter, setting the spirituous solution aside to deposit crystals of santonin, and purifying by recrystallization from spirit. (Mialhe).

Saponin ($C_{12}H_{20}O_7$?) is a peculiar glucoside occurring in Soapwort, the root of the common Pink, and many other plants: its solution in water, even though very dilute, froths like a solution of soap. Pereira considered *smilacin*, one of the principles of the supposed activity of Sarsaparilla (*Sarzæ Radix*, B. P., *Sarsaparilla*, U. S. P.), to be closely allied to, if not identical with, saponin.

Saponin is also met with in the root of *Polygala Senega* (*Senegæ Radix*, B. P., *Senega*, U. S. P.), though the active principle of senega is said to reside in *polygalic acid*, probably a glucoside derivative of saponin.

Scammonin ($C_{32}H_{52}O_{16}$).—Boil resin of scammony (*Scammoniæ Resina*, B. P. and U. S. P.) with dilute sulphuric acid for some time; glucose may then be detected in the liquid, a resinous acid termed *scammoniol* ($C_{14}H_{13}O_3$?) being produced at the same time.

Natural scammony (*Scammonium*, B. P. and U. S. P.) is an exudation from incisions in the living root (*Scammoniæ Radix*, B. P.) of *Convolvulus Scammonia*. It contains from 10 to 20 per cent. of gum. The British official resin of scammony contains no gum, and is made by digesting the root in spirit, adding water, distilling off the alcohol, and washing the residual resin with hot water till free from gum.

The U. S. P. process consists in exhausting scammony in alcohol, recovering the latter by distillation, treating the residue with water, and drying the separated resin.

QUESTIONS AND EXERCISES.

717. Define glucosides, and mention those of pharmaceutical interest.

718. What is Aloes, and what crystalline principle may be obtained from it?

719. Draw out an equation illustrative of the development of Oil of Bitter Almonds.

720. To what does Cherry-Laurel-water owe activity? Is the preparation trustworthy?

721. Mention the active principle of Senna.

722. By what process is the glucoside of the purple foxglove prepared?

723. State the circumstances under which Guaiacum-Resin and Jalap-Resin yield glucose.

724. Mention a test for guaiacum-resin.

725. How may the adulteration of jalap-resin by rosin be detected?

726. Enumerate the tests for Salicin.

727. How is Santonin officially prepared?

728. Name sources of saponin.

729. What is the difference between Scammony and Resin of Scammony?

ALCOHOL AND ALLIED BODIES.

ALCOHOL.

Formation of Alcohol.—Ferment two or three grains of sugar by dissolving in a test-tube full of water, adding a little yeast (*Cerevisiæ Fermentum*, B. P., *Fermentum*, U. S. P.), or piece of the so-called German or dried yeast, and setting the whole aside in a warm place at a temperature of 70° or 75°; carbonic acid gas is evolved, and, if the tube be inverted in a small dish containing water, may be collected in the upper part of the tube and subsequently tested: the solution contains alcohol. If the experiment be made on large quantities (four ounces of sugar, one of yeast, and a pint of water) the fermented liquid should be distilled, one half being collected, shaken with a little lime, soda, or potash, to neutralize any acetic acid, and decompose ethereal salts, and again distilled till one half has passed over; the product is dilute spirit of wine. It may be still further concentrated or rectified by repeating this process of *fractional distillation.*

Both cane-sugar and grape-sugar yield alcohol by fermentation, the cane-sugar probably always passing into grape-sugar before the production of alcohol commences.

$$\underset{\text{Grape-sugar.}}{C_6H_{12}O_6} = \underset{\text{Alcohol.}}{2C_2H_5HO} + \underset{\text{Carbonic acid gas.}}{2CO_2}\ .$$

Hence the spirit of the various kinds of wine, beer, and liqueurs, such as Orange Wine (*Vinum Aurantii*, B. P.) made "by the fermentation of a saccharine solution, to which the fresh peel of the bitter orange has been added;" Sherry Wine (*Vinum Xericum*, B. P. and U. S. P.), the fermented juice of the grape.

Port Wine (*Vinum Portense*, U. S. P.), Whiskey (*Spiritus Frumenti*, U. S. P.), containing from 48 to 56 per cent. of pure alcohol; *Spirit of Myrcia* or *Bay Rum* (*Spiritus Myrciæ*, U. S. P.), prepared by distilling rum with leaves of *Myrcia acris*, and others.

Varieties of alcohol.—The weak spirit concentrated by distillation till it contains 84 per cent. by weight of pure alcohol is an ordinary article of commerce; its specific gravity at 60° is 0.8382. This is common *Spirit of Wine*, the *Spiritus Rectificatus* of the British Pharmacopœia. *Alcohol*, U. S. P., has sp. gr. 0.835; *Alcohol Fortius*, U. S. P., sp. gr. 0.817. The official *Proof Spirit** (*Spiritus Tenuior*, B. P.) contains 49 per cent. by weight of alcohol, and is made by diluting 100 volumes of Rectified Spirit with water until the well-stirred product measures 156 volumes. Sixty volumes of water will be required for this purpose, the liquids occupying less

* *Proof spirit* is so termed from the fact that in olden times a proof of its strength was supposed to be afforded by moistening a small quantity of gunpowder and setting light to the spirit; if it fired the powder it was said to be "over proof;" if not, "under proof." The weakest spirit that would stand this test was what we should now describe as of sp. gr. 0.920.

bulk after than before admixture. In the language of the Excise authorities the rectified spirit of the Pharmacopœia would be described as "56 per cent. over proof" (56 per cent. O. P.); that is 100 volumes contains as much alcohol as is present in 156 volumes of proof spirit. Obviously, proof spirit may be made by diluting with water rectified spirit of any other strength than that mentioned above. Thus 100 fluidounces of a spirit of "seventy over proof" may be diluted to 170, or the same quantity of a spirit of "fifty over proof" may be diluted to 150, and so on. The specific gravity of proof spirit at 60° is 0.920. (*Alcohol Dilutum*, U. S. P., has sp. gr. 0.941.)

Composition of Alcohol.—Alcohol, by quantitative analysis, is found to contain the elements carbon, hydrogen, and oxygen in the following proportions:—

Centisimal composition of Alcohol.

Carbon	52.174
Hydrogen . . .	13.043
Oxygen	34.783
	100.000

From these numbers a formula is obtained in the usual way. Thus, on dividing these figures by the atomic weights of the respective elements (C=12, H=1, O=16), and reducing the products to the simplest whole numbers, alcohol will be found to contain two atoms of carbon to every six of hydrogen and to every one of oxygen, and its possible or *empirical formula* to be C_2H_6O.

Constitution of Alcohol,—There is good reason to believe that alcohol is the hydrate of a basylous radical *ethyl* (C_2H_5 or Et); hence we derive the *rational formula* C_2H_5HO or EtHO.

Salts of Ethyl.—Alcohol is, then, a body analogous in constitution to hydrate of potassium (KHO); and there are other compounds of ethyl analogous in constitution to ordinary inorganic salts, such as those of potassium. The oxide of ethyl (Et_2O) is common ether; the nitrate of ethyl ($EtNO_2$) is the body which, dissolved in spirit of wine, constitutes "sweet spirit of nitre;" the acid sulphate of ethyl ($EtHSO_4$), or sulphethylic or sulphovinic acid, is a liquid met with in the preparation of ether. The iodide (EtI), hydride (EtH), acetate ($Et\bar{A}$) and other salts are of considerable chemical interest, but not used in medicine.

Absolute or Real Alcohol.—(C_2H_5HO) may be prepared from spirit of wine by removing the water which the latter contains. This is accomplished, partially, by the agency of carbonate of potassium, and finally and entirely by recently burned quicklime. In operating on, say, one pint, 1½ ounces of dried carbonate of potassium is placed in a bottle that can be well closed, and frequently shaken during two days with the spirit. Meanwhile, about half a pound of good quicklime, if not already at hand, is made from 10 or 11 ounces of slaked lime by heating to redness in a covered crucible for half an hour. The spirit having been decanted from the denser aqueous solution of carbonate of potassium and placed in a quart flask, retort, or tin can, the lime, as soon as cold, is added, and the whole occasionally shaken during a day. The vessel is now placed in a saucepan or other bath containing water, quickly connected with a condenser (in the case of the flask or can by a bent tube and cork previously prepared; for absolute alcohol must not be exposed to air, or water in the form of moisture will be rapidly reabsorbed) and heat applied to the bath. Rejecting the first ounce or ounce and a half, as likely to contain traces of moisture absorbed from the air or apparatus, continue distillation until nothing more passes over, the water in the bath being kept just below the boiling-point (about 200° F.). These details are those of the British Pharmacopœia. Specific gravity 0.7938.

Tests.—There are no specific tests for alcohol when mixed with complex matters. It is, however, easily isolated and concentrated by fractional distillation, and is then recognizable by conjoint physical and chemical characters. Thus its odor and taste are characteristic; it is lighter than water, volatile, colorless, and, when tolerably strong, inflammable, burning with an almost non-luminous flame; it readily yields aldehyd (see below) and acetic ether (*vide* p. 248), each of which has a characteristic odor; lastly, in presence of hot acid, alcohol reduces red chromate of potassium to a green salt of chromium.

Tests of purity.—Oil or resin is precipitated on diluting spirit of wine with distilled water, giving an opalescent appearance to the mixture. The specific gravity should be 0.838. Fusel oil, aldehyd, and aldehydic acid are detected by nitrate of silver (*vide* Index, "Alcohol"). Water in absolute alcohol may be detected by adding to a small quantity a little highly dried sulphate of copper, which becomes blue ($CuSO_4,5H_2O$) if water is present, but retains its yellowish-white anhydrous character ($CuSO_4$) if water be absent.

ALDEHYD (C_2H_4O).—Place together, in a capacious test-tube, or a flask, spirit of wine, black oxide of manganese, sulphuric acid, and water, and gently warm the mixture; aldehyd (*al*cohol *dehyd*rogenatus), a highly volatile liquid, is immediately formed, and its vapor evolved, recognized by its peculiar, somewhat fragrant odor. Adapt a cork and rather long bent tube to the test-tube, and let some of the aldehyd slowly distil over into another test-tube, the condensing-tube being kept as cool as possible. Set the distillate aside for a day or two; the aldehyd will have nearly all disappeared, and acetic acid be found in the tube. Test the exposed liquid by litmus paper; it will be found to have an acid reaction: make it slightly alkaline by a drop or two of solution of carbonate of sodium, then boil to remove any alcohol and aldehyd present, add sulphuric acid, and notice the characteristic odor of the acetic acid evolved.

These experiments will enable the process of acetification described in connection with acetic acid to be more fully understood. Pure diluted alcohol is not oxidized by exposure to air; but in presence of fermentive matter, or vegetable matter undergoing decay or change, it is oxidized first to aldehyd and then to acetic acid.

In the above process the black oxide of manganese and sulphuric acid furnish nascent oxygen:—

$$\underset{\text{Black oxide of manganese.}}{2MnO_2} + \underset{\text{Sulphuric acid.}}{2H_2SO_4} = \underset{\text{Sulphate of manganese.}}{2MnSO_4} + \underset{\text{Oxygen.}}{O_2} + \underset{\text{Water.}}{2H_2O}$$

One molecule of the nascent oxygen then acts on two molecules of the alcohol, just as the oxygen of the air acts on the alcohol in fermented infusion of malt, beer, or wine, giving aldehyd:—

$$\underset{\text{Alcohol.}}{2C_2H_6O} + \underset{\text{Oxygen.}}{O_2} = \underset{\text{Aldehyd.}}{2C_2H_4O} + \underset{\text{Water.}}{2H_2O}$$

The aldehyd rapidly, even when pure (more rapidly when impure), absorbs oxygen and yields acetic acid:—

$$\underset{\text{Aldehyd.}}{2C_2H_4O} + \underset{\text{Oxygen.}}{O_2} = \underset{\text{Acetic acid.}}{2C_2H_4O_2}$$

Spirit of French Wine (*Spiritus Vini Gallici*, B. P. and U.S.P.) or *Brandy* is a colored and flavored variety of alcohol distilled from French wine. Its color is that of light sherry, and is derived from the cask in which it has been kept, but is commonly deepened by the addition of burnt sugar. Its taste is due to the volatile flavoring constituent of the wine, often increased by the addition of artificial essences. It should contain from 48 to 56 per cent. of alcohol.

QUESTIONS AND EXERCISES.

730. Write a few sentences on the formation, purification, and concentration of alcohol, and explain the difference between Rectified Spirit, Proof Spirit, and Absolute Alcohol.

731. What quantity of water must be added to one gallon of spirit of wine, 56 degrees over proof, to convert it into proof spirit?

732. To what volume must 5 pints of spirit of wine of 53 degrees be diluted before it becomes proof spirit?—*Ans.* 7 pints, 13 ounces.

733. State the specific gravity of proof spirit.

734. Show how the formula of alcohol is obtained from its centesimal composition:—

Carbon	52.174
Hydrogen	13.043
Oxygen	34.783
	100.000

735. Give the formulæ of some of the salts of ethyl.

736. By what processes may pure hydrate of ethyl be obtained?

737. Enumerate the characters of alcohol.

738. Mention a chemical test to distinguish rectified spirit from absolute alcohol.
739. From the formula of aldehyd calculate its composition in 100 parts.
740. What is the relation of aldehyd to alcohol and to acetic acid?
741. Whence is brandy obtained, and to what are due its color and flavor?

ETHER.

Formula $C_4H_{10}O$, or $(C_2H_5)_2O$, or Et_2O.

Experimental Process.—Into a capacious test-tube put a small quantity of spirit of wine and about half its bulk of sulphuric acid, mix, and gently warm; the vapor of ether, recognized by its odor, is evolved. Adapt a cork and long bent tube to the test-tube and slowly distil over the ether into another test-tube. Half the original quantity of alcohol now placed in the generating-tube will again give ether; and this operation may be repeated many times.

On the large scale, and according to the following official process (*Æther,* B. P. and U. S. P.), the addition of alcohol, instead of being intermitting, is continuous, a tube conveying alcohol from a reservoir into the generating-vessel. Mix 10 fluidounces of sulphuric acid with 12 fluidounces of rectified spirit in a glass flask capable of containing at least two pints, and, not allowing the mixture to cool, connect the flask by means of a bent glass tube with a Liebig's condenser, and distil with a heat sufficient to maintain the liquid in brisk ebullition. If a thermometer be used the temperature may be still more carefully regulated—between 284° and 290° F. As soon as the ethereal fluid begins to pass over, supply fresh spirit in a continuous stream, and in such quantity as to equal the volume of the fluid which distils over. For this purpose use a tube furnished with a stopcock to regulate the supply, connecting one end of the tube with a vessel containing the spirit supported above the level of the flask, and passing the other end through the cork of the flask into the liquid. When a total of 50 fluidounces of spirit has been added, and 42 fluidounces of ether have distilled over, the process may be stopped.

To *partially purify* the liquid, dissolve 10 ounces of chloride of calcium in 13 ounces of water, add half an ounce of lime, and agitate the mixture in a bottle with the impure ether. Leave the mixture at rest for ten minutes, pour off the light supernatant fluid, and distil it with a gentle heat until a glass bead of specific gravity 0.735 placed in the receiver begins to float. The ether and spirit retained by the chloride of calcium and by the residue of each rectification may be recovered by distillation and used in a subsequent operation,

Explanation of Process.—On the addition of sulphuric acid to alcohol in equal volumes, one molecule of each react and give a molecule of sulphethylic acid and one of water:—

$$\underset{\text{Alcohol.}}{EtHO} + \underset{\text{Sulphuric acid.}}{H_2S_4O} = \underset{\text{Sulphethylic acid.}}{EtHSO_4} + \underset{\text{Water.}}{H_2O}$$

More alcohol then gives ether and sulphuric acid by the reaction of one molecule of the alcohol on one of sulphethylic acid:—

$$\underset{\text{Alcohol.}}{EtHO} + \underset{\text{Sulphethylic acid.}}{EtHSO_4} = \underset{\text{Ether.}}{Et_2O} + \underset{\text{Sulphuric acid.}}{H_2SO_4}$$

The water of the first reaction and the ether of the second distil over, while the sulphuric acid, as fast as liberated, is attacked by alcohol and reconverted into sulphethylic acid,

$$\underset{\text{Alcohol.}}{EtHO} + \underset{\text{Sulphuric acid.}}{H_2SO_4} = \underset{\text{Sulphethylic acid.}}{EtHSO_4} = \underset{\text{Water.}}{H_2O}$$

so that the sulphuric acid originally employed finally remains in the retort in the form of sulphethylic acid. The effect, however, of a small quantity of sulphuric acid in thus converting a large quantity of alcohol into ether is limited, secondary reactions occurring to some extent after a time.

Properties.—Pure ether is gaseous at temperatures above 95° F.; hence the condensing-tubes employed in its distillation must be kept as cool as possible. At all ordinary temperatures it rapidly evaporates, absorbing much heat from the surface on which it is placed. A few drops evaporated consecutively from the back of the hand produce great cold; if blown in the form of spray, the cooling effect is so rapid and intense as to produce local anæsthesia. Its vapor is very heavy, more than twice and one-half that of air, and in a still atmosphere will flow a considerable distance along a table or floor before complete diffusion occurs; the vapor is also highly inflammable; hence the importance of keeping candle and other flames at a distance during manipulations with ether.

Purification.—To imitate the process of partial purification above described, add to the small quantity of ether obtained in the foregoing operation a strong solution of chloride of calcium and a little slaked lime; the latter absorbs any sulphurous acid that may have been produced by secondary decompositions, while the former absorbs water; on shaking the mixture and then setting aside for a minute or two, the ether will be found floating on the surface of the solution of chloride of calcium.

This ether, redistilled until the distillate has a sp. gr. not higher than 0.735 (0.750, U. S. P.) and boiling-point not higher than 105° F., is the ether of the British Pharmacopœia. It still contains about 8 per cent. of alcohol. The latter may be removed by well shaking the ether with half of its bulk of water, setting aside, separating the floating ether and again shaking it with water; alcohol is thus washed out. This washed ether containing water (for water and ether are to some extent soluble the one in the other; 50 measures agitated with an equal volume of water are reduced to 45 by an absorption of 10 per cent.) is next placed in a retort with solid chloride of calcium and a little caustic lime, and once more distilled; pure dry ether (*Æther Purus*, B. P., *Æther Fortior*, U. S. P.) results. Sp. gr. not exceeding 0.720 (0.728, U. S. P.).

Spiritus Ætheris, B. P., is a mixture of common ether (*Æther*, B. P.) with twice its bulk of rectified spirit.

NITROUS ETHER, OR NITRITE OF ETHYL.

Formula $EtNO_2$.

Process.—To a third of a test-tubeful of rectified spirit add about a tenth of its bulk of sulphuric acid, rather more of nitric acid, and some copper-wire or turnings, and warm the mixture as soon as ebullition commences, the vapor of nitrous ether is evolved, recognized by its odor. A long bent tube, kept cool, may be adapted by a perforated cork to the test-tube, and thus a few drops of impure nitrous ether be condensed and collected.

The above process conducted on a larger scale, with definite quantities of materials, temperature regulated by a thermometer, and a well-cooled condenser, is the official (Redwood's) process for the preparation of a concentrated solution of nitrous ether in spirit; diluted with nearly three times its bulk of rectified spirit it forms the "sweet spirit of nitre" (*Spiritus Ætheris Nitrosi*, B. P. and U. S. P.) of pharmacy.

"Take of

Nitric Acid	3 fluidounces,
Sulphuric Acid	2 fluidounces,
Copper, in fine wire (about No. 25)	2 ounces,
Rectified Spirit	a sufficiency.

"To one pint of the spirit add gradually the sulphuric acid, stirring them together; then add, in the same way, two and a half ounces of the nitric acid. Put the mixture into a retort or other suitable apparatus, into which the copper has been introduced, and to which a thermometer is fitted. Attach now an efficient condenser, and, applying a gentle heat, let the spirit distil at a temperature commencing at 170° and rising to 175°, but not exceeding 180°, until 12 fluidounces have passed over and been collected in a bottle kept cool, if necessary, with ice-cold water; then withdraw the heat, and, having allowed the contents of the retort to cool, introduce the remaining half ounce of nitric acid, and resume the distillation as before, until the distilled product has been increased to 15 fluidounces. Mix this with two pints of the rectified spirit, or as much as will make the product correspond to the tests of specific gravity and percentage of liquid separated by chloride of calcium (*vide infra*). Preserve it in well-closed vessels.

Disregarding secondary products, the following equation probably represents the decompositions that occur in the operation. The main point in the reaction is the reduction of the nitric to the nitrous radical by the indirect agency of the copper.

$$\underset{\text{Alcohol.}}{EtHO} + \underset{\text{Nitric acid.}}{HNO_3} + \underset{\text{Sulphuric acid.}}{H_2SO_4} + \underset{\text{Copper.}}{Cu} = \underset{\text{Nitrous ether.}}{EtNO_2} + \underset{\text{Water.}}{2H_2O} + \underset{\text{Sulphate of copper.}}{CuSO_4}$$

Properties.—Spirit of Nitrous Ether "is transparent and nearly colorless, with a very slight tinge of yellow, mobile, inflammable, of a peculiar penetrating apple-like odor, and sweetish cooling sharp taste. Specific gravity, 0.845. It effervesces feebly, or not at all, when shaken with a little bicarbonate of soda" (showing absence of appreciable quantities of free acid).

Test.—The nitrous radical may be detected by adding sulphate of iron and sulphuric acid to some of the spirit of nitrous ether, a brown or black compound being produced, already explained in connection with nitric acid (p. 237).

Test of strength.—To some of the official Spirit of Nitrous Ether add twice its bulk of a saturated solution of chloride of calcium and mix the liquids; on setting aside, nitrous ether will rise to the surface. If the spirit of nitrous ether be of official strength, not less than 2 per cent. of its volume will thus separate, indicating the presence of 10 per cent. of the ether, 8 per cent. still remaining dissolved. A graduated tube is obviously most convenient for this purpose.

Spiritus Ætheris Nitrosi, U. S. P., is made by the old process of distilling a mixture of alcohol and nitric acid, and redistilling from carbonate of potassium, which retains any traces of nitric acid. Sp. gr. 0.837. Strength in nitrous ether 4.3 to 5 per cent.

Iodide of Ethyl (EtI) may be prepared by mixing amorphous phosphorus with *absolute* alcohol and then adding iodine.

$$\underset{\text{Alcohol.}}{5EtHO} + \underset{\text{Iodide of phosphorus.}}{PI_5} = \underset{\text{Iodide of ethyl.}}{5EtI} + \underset{\text{Phosphoric acid.}}{H_3PO_4} + \underset{\text{Water.}}{H_2O}$$

The reaction at first proceeds rapidly, and is complete after the mixture has been set aside for a few hours. The iodide of ethyl may then be isolated by careful distillation, freed from any excess of iodine by washing with a very small quantity of solution of potash or soda, washed with water, dried over chloride of calcium, and again distilled. It should be kept in a dark place, as light favors decomposition and liberation of iodine.

ETHYL.—This gaseous radical, $(C_2H_5)_2$ or Et_2, is obtained on digesting together at about 250° F., in a strong sealed tube, dry freshly granulated zinc with iodide of ethyl (Frankland).

Zn	+	$2EtI$	=	ZnI_2	+	Et_2
Zinc.		Iodide of ethyl.		Iodide of zinc.		Ethyl.

On cautiously opening the tube the ethyl escapes, and may be ignited or collected over water. There remains with the iodide of zinc a body termed by Frankland *zinc-ethyl* $(ZnEt_2)$; it is a spontaneously inflammable liquid, but may easily be distilled and otherwise manipulated if a few simple precautions be observed. If water be allowed to flow down the tube, the solid compound of iodide of zinc and zinc-ethyl will be decomposed, a gas, *hydride of ethyl* (EtH), resulting, which also may be inflamed or collected over water:—

$$ZnEt_2 + 2H_2O = Zn2HO + 2EtH.$$

QUESTIONS AND EXERCISES.

742. Describe the official process for the preparation of Ether, giving equations.

743. Offer a physical explanation of the mode of producing local anæsthesia.

744. How is commercial ether purified?

745. Explain Redwood's process for the preparation of "sweet spirit of nitre."

746. Give the properties of spirit of nitrous ether.

747. By what method is the strength of "sweet spirit of nitre" estimated?

748. How is iodide of ethyl made?

749. Adduce evidence of the existence of ethyl.

OTHER ALCOHOL RADICALS AND THEIR SALTS.

What has been stated concerning the chemistry of ethyl and its compounds may be applied to other radicals known to exist, some of the compounds of each of which are of common occurrence. These basylous radicals are closely related to each other, to hydrogen, and to the metals. Starting from hydrogen, their formulæ may be built up by successive additions of CH_2, thus:—

Hydrogen	H
Methyl	CH_3, or Me
Ethyl	C_2H_5, or Et
Propyl (or Trityl)	C_3H_7, or Pr
Butyl (or Tetryl)	C_4H_9, or Bu
Amyl	C_5H_{11}, or Ay
Caproyl (or Hexyl)	C_6H_{13}, or Cp

The above list is an illustration of an *homologous* series (from ὁμὸς, *homos*, the same, and λόγος, *logos*, description) of compounds. It will be observed that the relation of the number of hydrogen atoms to carbon is twice as many with one added; hence the series is often termed the C_nH_{2n+1} series (n=any number). The oxides of these radicals are known as *ethers*, their hydrates *alcohols*, their compounds with the acetic and similar acidulous radicals *ethereal salts*. Every alcohol furnishes a body corresponding to the aldehyd of spirit of wine, the class being termed *aldehyds;* each also yields an acid corresponding with acetic acid. Any one of these classes constitutes an homologous series. Or, taking the hydride, oxide, hydrate, acid, of any single radical, we get a *heterologous* (ἕτερος, *heteros*, another) series of compounds. Hydride of methyl (MeH or CH_3H) is ordinary *marsh-gas*, *fire-damp*, or *light carburetted hydrogen;* it is a diluent or non-luminiferous constituent of ordinary coal-gas to the extent of 30 to 40 per cent.*; *formic acid*, the acid of the methyl series; *butyric acid*, the acid of the butyl series; *sulphocyanate of butyl*, the essential oil of horseradish; *valerianic acid*, the acid of the amyl series.

Homologous and Heterologous Series of the C_nH_{2n+1} *Radicals.*

Radicals.	Hydrides.	Oxides (or ethers).	Hydrates (or alcohols).	Aldehyds.	Acids.
$(CH_3)_2$	CH_3H	$(CH_3)_2O$	CH_3HO	CH_2O ?	CH_2O_2
$(C_2H_5)_2$	C_2H_5H	$(C_2H_5)_2O$	C_2H_5HO	C_2H_4O	$C_2H_4O_2$
$(C_3H_7)_2$	C_3H_7H	$(C_3H_7)_2O$	C_3H_7HO	C_3H_6O	$C_3H_6O_2$
$(C_4H_9)_2$	C_4H_9H	$(C_4H_9)_2O$	C_4H_9HO	C_4H_8O	$C_4H_8O_2$
$(C_5H_{11})_2$	$C_5H_{11}H$	$(C_5H_{11})_2O$	$C_5H_{11}HO$	$C_5H_{10}O$	$C_5H_{10}O_2$
&c.	&c.	&c.	&c.	&c.	&c.

* *Coal-gas.*—The other diluents, or vehicles for the illuminating constituents, of coal-gas are hydrogen (40 to 50 per cent.) and carbonic oxide (6 to 7 per cent.). The illuminating constituents are olefiant gas (p. 364) and its homologues, existing to the extent of from 5 to 7 per cent. The impurities are nitrogen, air, carbonic acid, bisulphide of carbon CS_2 (a volatile liquid easily made from its elements), and other badly smelling sulphur compounds. Upwards of fifty distinct chemical substances have been obtained from the solid, liquid, and gaseous products of the destructive distillation of coal.

QUESTIONS AND EXERCISES.

750. Mention several radicals homologous with ethyl, and give their formulæ.
751. Define ethers, hydrides, alcohols, ethereal salts, aldehyds.
752. What is the difference between homologous and heterologous series?
753. Give the systematic name of *fire-damp*.
754. Enumerate the chief constituents of coal-gas.
755. State the formulæ of formic, butyric, and valerianic acids.
756. Write the formulæ of butyl, its hydride, ether, alcohol, aldehyd, and acid.

MYTHYLIC ALCOHOL.

Methylic Alcohol (CH_3HO, or MeHO), Wood-Spirit, or Pyroxylic Spirit, is a product of the destructive distillation of wood. Spirit of wine containing 10 per cent. of wood-spirit constitutes ordinary *methylated spirit*, a spirit issued duty free, for the use of manufacturers, the methylic alcohol not interfering with technical applications. From its nauseous taste and odor, however, it cannot take the place of gin, brandy, or other spirit; hence, while industry is benefited, intemperance is discouraged and the revenue not injured.

Detection of Methylic Alcohol in presence of Ethylic Alcohol.—Three or four methods have been proposed for the detection of methylated spirit in various liquids; that open to least objection is by J. T. Miller. For the application of the test to tinctures and similar spirituous mixtures, some of the spirit is first separated by distilling off a drachm or so from about half an ounce of the liquid placed in a small flask or test-tube having a long bent tube attached. Into a similar apparatus put 30 grains of powdered red chromate of potassium, half an ounce of water, 25 minims of strong sulphuric acid, and 30 or 40 minims of the spirit to be tested. Set the mixture aside for a quarter of an hour and then distil half a fluidounce. Place the distillate in a small dish, add a very slight excess of carbonate of sodium, boil down to about a quarter of an ounce, add enough acetic acid to impart a distinct but feeble acid reaction, pour the liquid into a test-tube, add a grain of nitrate of silver dissolved in about 30 drops of water, and heat gently for a couple of minutes. If the liquid then merely darkens a little, but continues quite translucent, the spirit is free from methylic alcohol; but if a copious precipitate of dark-brown or black metallic silver separates, and the tube, after being rinsed out and filled with clean water, has a distinct film of silver, which appears brown by transmitted light (best seen by holding it against white paper), the spirit is methylated.

Explanation.—This test depends for its action on the reducing-powers of formic acid. In the above operation the ethylic alcohol becomes oxidized to acetic acid (the natural acid of the ethyl series), which does not reduce silver salts, a minute quantity only of formic acid being produced, while the methylic alcohol yields formic acid (the natural acid of the methyl series) in a comparatively large quantity. Aldehyd, which is also a reducing agent, is simultaneously produced, but removed in the subsequent ebullition with carbonate of sodium.

Methylated Sweet Spirit of Nitre.—The preparation of spirit of nitrous ether from methylated spirit is illegal, but, nevertheless, occasionally practised. For the detection of methylic alcohol in this liquid, Mr. Miller suggests the following modification of the above process.

Shake about an ounce of the sample with 20 or 30 grains of anhydrous carbonate of potassium, and, if needful, add fresh portions of the salt until it ceases to be dissolved, then pour off the supernatant spirit. This serves to neutralize acid and to remove water, in which some samples are remarkably rich. Introduce half a fluidounce of the spirit into a small flask; add 150 grains of anhydrous chloride of calcium in powder, and stir well together; then, having connected the flask with a condenser, place it in a bath of boiling water, and distil a fluidrachm and a half, or continue the distillation until scarcely anything more comes over. The operation is rather slow, but needs little attention, and should be done thoroughly. The distillate contains nearly the whole of the nitrous ether and other interfering substances. Now add to the contents of the flask a fluidrachm of water, and draw over the half drachm of spirit required for testing. Add to it the usual oxidizing solution composed of 30 grains of red chromate of potassium, 25 minims of strong sulphuric acid, and half an ounce of water; let the mixture stand a quarter of an hour, then distil half a fluidounce. Treat the distillate with a slight excess of carbonate of sodium, boil rapidly down to two fluidrachms, and drop in, cautiously, enough acetic acid to impart a faint acid reaction; pour the liquid into a test-tube about three-quarters of an inch in diameter; add two drops of *diluted* acetic acid, and one grain of nitrate of silver in half a drachm of pure water; apply heat, and boil gently for two minutes. If the spirit is free from methylic alcohol the solution darkens and often assumes transiently a purplish tinge, but continues quite translucent, and the test-tube, after being rinsed out and filled with water, appears clean or nearly so. But if the spirit contains only 1 per cent. of methylic alcohol the liquid turns first brown, then almost black and opaque, and a film of silver, which is brown by transmitted light, is deposited on the tube. When the sample is methylated to the extent of 3 or 4 per cent., the film is sufficiently thick to form a brilliant mirror. To insure accuracy, the experiments should be performed by daylight.

CHLOROFORM.

Formula $CHCl_3$.

Process.—Should the necessary appliances be at hand, a small quantity of this liquid may easily be prepared by the official process. One fluidounce and a half of spirit and 24 of water are placed in a retort or flask of at least a quart capacity; 8 oz. of chlorinated lime and 4 of slaked lime are added, the vessel connected with a condenser, and the mixture heated until distillation commences, the source of heat then being withdrawn. The condensed liquid should fall into a small flask containing water at the bottom of which about a drachm of chloroform will slowly collect.

Explanation of Process.—The hypochlorite of calcium ($Ca2ClO$) believed to be present in the chlorinated lime (see remarks in connection with hypochlorous acid) readily yields up oxygen and chlorine to organic substances, the calcium being liberated as hydrate, $4\,(Ca2ClO)+4H_2O=4(Ca2HO)+2O_2+4Cl_2$. The alcohol used in making chloroform is thus reduced first to aldehyd:—

$$\underset{\text{Alcohol.}}{2C_2H_6O} + \underset{\text{Oxygen.}}{O_2} = \underset{\text{Aldehyd.}}{2C_2H_4O} + \underset{\text{Water.}}{2H_2O}$$

The action of chlorine on aldehyd then probably gives chloral (*chlor-al*dehyd):—

$$\underset{\text{Aldehyd.}}{C_2H_4O} + \underset{\text{Chlorine.}}{3Cl_2} = \underset{\text{Chloral.}}{C_2HCl_3O} + \underset{\text{Hydrochl. acid.}}{3HCl}$$

The hydrochloric acid being at once neutralized by some of the liberated hydrate of calcium to form chloride of calcium and water, more freed hydrate of calcium and chloral give formate of calcium and chloroform.

$$\underset{\text{Chloral.}}{2C_2HCl_3O} + \underset{\text{Hydrate of calcium.}}{Ca2HO} = \underset{\text{Formate of calcium.}}{Ca2CHO_2} + \underset{\text{Chloroform.}}{2CHCl_3}$$

Or, neglecting the probable steps in the process, and regarding only the materials and the products, 4 molecules of alcohol and 8 of hypochlorite of calcium give 2 of chloroform, 3 of formate of calcium, 5 of chloride of calcium, and 8 of water, thus:—

$$\underset{\text{Alcohol.}}{4C_2H_6O} + \underset{\text{Hypochlorite of calcium.}}{8CaCl_2O_2} = \underset{\text{Chloroform.}}{2CHCl_3} + \underset{\text{Formate of calcium.}}{3(Ca2CHO_2)} + \underset{\text{Chloride of calcium.}}{5CaCl_2} + \underset{\text{Water.}}{1H_2O}$$

The hydrate of calcium placed in the generating-vessels is not essential, but is useful in preventing secondary decompositions, the hydrate of calcium obtainable from the reaction being insufficient for this purpose.

Constitution.—Chloroform is sometimes considered to be the chloride of a trivalent radical methenyl (CH), the first member of a series C_nH_{2n-1}. Glycerine is the hydrate of another member—*glyceryl* or *propenyl*, C_3H_5 (p. 364).

Chloroform may also be regarded as the chloride of dichlor-methyl; it may be formed from methylic compounds, thus:—

$$\underset{\text{Methylic alcohol.}}{2CH_4O} + \underset{\text{Chlorinated lime.}}{2(CaCl_2,CaCl_2O_2)} = \underset{\text{Chloroform.}}{2CHCl_3} + \underset{\text{Oxychloride of calcium.}}{CaCl_23CaO} + \underset{\text{Water.}}{3H_2O}$$

Chlorine converts it into tetrachloride of carbon, completing a series of *substitution products* of chloride of methyl.

$$\underset{\text{Chloride of methyl.}}{C\left\{\begin{matrix}H\\H\\H\end{matrix}\right\}Cl} \quad \underset{\text{Chloride of mono-chlor-methyl.}}{C\left\{\begin{matrix}H\\H\\Cl\end{matrix}\right\}Cl} \quad \underset{\text{Chloride of di-chlor-methyl.}}{C\left\{\begin{matrix}H\\Cl\\Cl\end{matrix}\right\}Cl} \quad \underset{\text{Chloride of tri-chlor-methyl, or Tetrachloride of carbon.}}{C\left\{\begin{matrix}Cl\\Cl\\Cl\end{matrix}\right\}Cl \text{ or } CCl_4}$$

The chloride of mono-chlor-methyl, under the name of dichloride of methylene, has been used as an anæsthetic.

Chloroform is purified by shaking it with water and then with sulphuric acid, which chars and removes hydrocarbons, but does not affect chloroform. It is freed from any trace of acid by agitation with lime, and from moisture by solid chloride of calcium.

Properties.—The sp. gr. of purified chloroform is 1.49 (1.49 to 1.494 U. S. P.). It readily and entirely volatilizes with characteristic odor at common temperatures. It has a sweetish taste, is limpid, colorless, soluble in alcohol and ether, and slightly in water, but burns with a sluggish green smoky flame.

Chloral.

Process.—Pass a rapid stream of dry chlorine into pure absolute alcohol so long as absorption occurs. During the first hour or two the alcohol must be kept cool, afterwards gradually warmed till ultimately the boiling point is reached. The preparation of a considerable quantity occupies several days. The crude product is mixed with three times its volume of oil of vitriol and distilled, again mixed with a similar quantity of oil of vitriol and again distilled, and finally rectified from quicklime.

Properties.—The formula of chloral is C_2HCl_3O. It is a colorless liquid of oily consistence. Sp. gr. 1.502. Boiling point 201.2. Its vapor has a penetrating smell and is somewhat irritating to the eyes. Mixed with water heat is disengaged and solid, white, crystallizable, *hydrous chloral* results. The latter fuses at 110.8 and boils at 293° F., subliming as a white crystalline powder. Both chloral and hydrous chloral are soluble in water, alcohol, ether, and oils. The aqueous solution should be neutral and give no reaction with nitrate of silver. Hydrous chloral is said somtimes to undergo a spontaneous change into an opaque white isomeric modification, insoluble in water, alcohol, or ether, but convertible by prolonged contact with water or by distillation into the ordinary condition. By action of weak alkalies chloral yields formiate of the alkali metal and chloroform:—

$$C_2HCl_3O + KHO = KCHO_2 + CHCl_3$$

Chloral, or rather strong aqueous solution of hydrous chloral (3 in 4) injected beneath the skin yields nascent chloroform by action of the alkali of the blood, and produces narcotic effects. (Liebreich. Personne.) Chloroform itself admits of similar hypodermic use (Richardson). If administered by the stomach thirty to eighty grains of solid hydrous chloral are required. The final product of the reaction of chloroform and blood are chloride and formiate of sodium. A spirituous solution of potash effects the same transformation.

$$CHCl_3 + 4NaHO = NaCHO_2 + 3NaCl + 2H_2O$$

AMYLIC ALCOHOL.

AMYLIC ALCOHOL (*Alcohol Amylicum,* B. P. and U. S. P.) ($C_5H_{11}HO$, or AyHO) is a constant accompaniment of ethylic or common alcohol (C_2H_5HO, or EtHO) when the latter is prepared from sugar which has been derived from starch; hence the name, from *amylum* starch. The sugar of potato-starch yields a considerable quantity; hence the alcohol is often called *potato-oil.* It is also termed *fousel-oil,* or *fusel-oil* (from φύω, *phuō,* to produce), in allusion to the circumstance that the supposed oil is not simply educed from a substance already containing it, as is usually the case with oils, but is actually produced during the operation. It was described as oil probably because it resembled oil in not readily mixing with water; but it is soluble to some extent in water, and is a true spirit, homologous with spirit of wine. See also VALERIANIC ACID.

Amylic alcohol is "a colorless liquid with a penetrating and oppressive odor, and a burning taste. When pure its specific gravity is 0.818; boiling-point 279°. Sparingly soluble in water, but soluble in all proportions in alcohol, ether, and essential oils. Exposed to the air in contact with platinum-black, it is slowly oxidized, yielding valerianic acid." Two allotropic varieties of amylic alcohol exist, one dextro-rotating a polarized ray.

ACETATE OF AMYL ($C_5H_{11}C_2H_3O_2$, or $Ay\bar{A}$). To a small quantity of amylic alcohol in a test-tube add some acetate of potassium and a little sulphuric acid, and warm the mixture; the vapor of acetate of amyl is evolved, recognized by its odor, which is that of the jargonelle pear. If a condensing-tube be attached, the essence may be distilled over, washed by agitation with water to free it from alcohol, and separated by a pipette.

$$\underset{\text{Acetate of potassium.}}{K\bar{A}} + \underset{\text{Amylic alcohol.}}{AyHO} + \underset{\text{Sulphuric acid.}}{H_2SO_4} = \underset{\text{Acetate of amyl.}}{Ay\bar{A}} + \underset{\text{Acid sulphate of potassium.}}{KHSO_4} + \underset{\text{Water.}}{H_2O}$$

Fruit-Essences.

Acetate of amyl, prepared with the proper equivalent proportions of constituents as indicated by the above equation, is largely manufactured for use as a flavoring agent by confectioners. Valerianate of amyl ($C_5H_{11}C_5H_9O_2$) is similarly used under the name of apple-oil. Butyrate of ethyl ($C_2H_5C_4H_7O_2$) closely resembles the odor and flavor of the pine-apple; œnanthylate of ethyl ($C_2H_5C_7H_{13}O_2$) recalls green-gage; pelargonate of ethyl ($C_2H_5C_9H_{17}O_2$) quince; suberate of ethyl ($Et_2C_8H_{12}O_4$) mulberry; sebacate of ethyl ($Et_2C_{10}H_{16}O_4$) melon. Hydride of salicyl ($C_7H_5O_2H$), or salicylous acid, is the essential oil of meadow-sweet (*Spiræa ulmaria*), and may be prepared artificially by the oxidation of salicin (*vide* p. 345). Salicylate of methyl ($CH_3C_7H_5O_3$), or gaultheric acid (*Oleum gaultheriæ*, U. S. P.), is the essential oil of winter-green (*Gaultheria procumbens*), and may also be prepared artificially from salicin. By mixing these ethereal salts with each other and with essential oils in various proportions, the odor and flavor of nearly every fruit may be fairly imitated.

QUESTIONS AND EXERCISES.

757. Name the source of methylic alcohol.

758. What is "methylated spirit"?

759. Describe the method by which methylated spirit is detected in a tincture.

760. In what relation does formic acid stand to methylic alcohol?

761. How would you proceed to ascertain whether or not a specimen of sweet spirit of nitre had been made from methylated spirit?

762. Give details of the production of chloroform from alcohol, tracing the various steps by equations.

763. Is chloroform an ethylic compound? What is its probable constitution?

764. How is chloroform purified?

765. State the character of pure chloroform.

766. Whence is amylic alcohol obtained?

767. Has valerianic acid any chemical relation to amylic alcohol?

768. Mention the systematic names of several artificial fruit-essences.

SALTS AND DERIVATIVES OF RADICALS OF OTHER SERIES THAN THE C_nH_{2n+1}.

What has been stated regarding radicals having the general formula C_nH_{2n+1} and their salts, may be applied to the radicals of other series. The series C_nH_{2n-7} includes *phenyl* (C_6H_5), the hydride of which (C_6H_5H, or PhH) is common *benzol* (B. P.), a colorless volatile liquid obtained from coal-tar. Benzol is a powerful solvent of grease, and under the name of *Benzine Collas* was introduced by M. Collas, in 1848, for cleansing stuffs. By the action of strong nitric acid, benzol yields *nitrobenzol* ($C_6H_5(NO_2)$), a liquid termed, from its odor, *artificial oil of bitter almonds*, or *essence of mirbane*. The odor of this essence, however, is not exactly that of essential oil of almonds, and its composition is very different; so that it is not truly an artificial volatile oil, the natural oil (C_7H_5OH) being a hydride of the negative radical benzoyl, a radical derived from the next higher homologue of phenyl by displacement of hydrogen by oxygen. The hydrate of phenyl (C_6H_5HO), or *phenic alcohol*, or *phenol*, is the *phenic acid* or *carbolic acid* of commerce (*Acidum Carbolicum*, B. P.), a colorless crystalline substance, obtained from coal-tar oil by fractional distillation and subsequent purification. At temperatures above 95° F. it is an oily liquid. It is only slightly soluble in water, but readily dissolved by alcohol, ether, and glycerine (*Glycerinum Acidi Carbolici*, B. P.). In odor, taste, and solubility (and in appearance when liquefied by heat or by the addition of 5 per cent. of water) it resembles creasote ($C_8H_{10}O_2$), a wood-tar product for which carbolic acid is often substituted. Certain coloring-matters may be obtained by the oxidation of carbolic acid; ammonia mixed with it, and then a small quantity of solution of a hypochlorite gives a blue liquid; a similar effect is produced on dipping a chip of deal into carbolic acid (or into creasote), then into hydrochloric acid, and afterwards exposing it to the air. By the following tests carbolic acid may be distinguished from creasote. The former boils only at 370°, while the latter readily dries up at 212°. Carbolic acid does not affect a ray of polarized light; creasote twists it to the right. Carbolic acid is either solid or may be solidified by cooling; creasote is not solidified by the cold produced by a mixture of hydrochloric acid and sulphate of sodium. Creasote from coal (impure or crude carbolic acid) gives a jelly when shaken with collodion; creasote from wood (*Creasotum*, B. P. and U. S. P.)

is unaffected by collodion (Rust). Coal-creasote is soluble in solution of potash, wood-creasote insoluble. The coal product is soluble in a large volume of water, and a neutral solution of ferric chloride strikes a blue color with the liquid: wood-creasote is less soluble (*Aqua Creasoti*, U. S. P. is said to contain 1 in 129) and not altered by ferric chloride. An alcoholic solution of the coal-oil is colored brown by ferric chloride, a similar solution of true creasote green. Carbolic acid is a powerful *antiseptic* (ἀντὶ, *anti*, against, and σήπω, *sepo*, to putrefy). In large doses it is poisonous, the best *antidote* being olive oil and castor oil, freely administered. Both carbolic acid and benzol are secondary products, obtained in the manufacture of coal-gas; hence, indeed the word *phenic* and thence *phenyl* (from φαίνω, *phainō*, I light, in allusion to the use of coal-gas). *Aniline*, or *phenylamine*, is a product of the action of nascent hydrogen on nitrobenzol.

$$\underset{\text{Nitrobenzol.}}{C_6H_5NO_2} + \underset{\text{Hydrogen.}}{3H_2} = N\left\{\begin{array}{l} C_6H_5 \\ H \\ H \end{array}\right. + 2H_2O,$$

the substance whence, by oxidation, &c., aniline-red (magenta), -orange, -yellow, -green, -blue, -violet (mauve), and -black are produced. Tri-nitro-carbolic acid ($C_6H_3(NO_2)_3O$) is the yellow dye known as *picric acid*; most of the picrates are explosive by percussion. In the series $C_nH_{2n-1}{}'$ we have the univalent radical *allyl* (C_3H_5), whose sulphide ($(C_3H_5)_2S$) is *essential oil of garlic* (*Allium*, U. S. P.) and sulphocyanate (C_3H_5CyS) the *essential oil of mustard*. *Mustard* (*Sinapis*, B. P. and U. S. P.) is a powdered mixture of black and white mustard-seeds. The black contains a ferment resembling the *emulsin* of almonds (p. 341) and *myronate* of potassium. The latter is the body which, under the influence of the former, yields the oil.

$$\underset{\text{Myronate of potassium.}}{K_2C_{20}H_{38}N_2S_4O_{19}} = \underset{\text{Acid sulphite of potassium.}}{2(KHSO_3)} + \underset{\text{Oil of Mustard.}}{2C_3H_5CNS} + \underset{\text{Glucose.}}{2C_6H_{12}O_6} + \underset{\text{Water.}}{H_2O}$$

Allyl compounds are also met with in several other liliaceous and cruciferous plants. In the C_nH_{2n} series occurs *ethylene* or *olefiant gas* (C_2H_4), the chief illuminating constituent of coal-gas (readily made on heating alcohol with twice its volume of strong sulphuric acid), a bivalent radical, the alcohol of which is *glycol* (C_2H_42HO). *Etherol*, or *Ethereal Oil* (*Oleum Ethereum*, U. S. P.), or *light oil of wine* ($C_{16}H_{32}$?) a hydrocarbon polymeric with olefiant gas, is one of the products of the action of excess of sulphuric acid on alcohol: its sp. gr. is 0.917. In the $C_nH_{2n-1}{}'''$ the trivalent hypothetical radical *glyceryl* (C_3H_5) is found, the hydrate of which (C_3H_53HO) is glycerine. The homologues of glycol are termed *glycols*, the homologues of glycerine *glycerines*.

Glycerine.

Glycerine, or *Glyceric Alcohol* (C_3H_53HO).—Glycerine is the hydrate of *glyceryl*, *glycyl*, or *propenyl*—the basylous radical of most oils and fats. These latter are mainly oleates, palmitates, and stearates of glyceryl; and when heated with metallic hydrates (even with water—hydrate of hydrogen, HHO—at a temp. of 500° or 600° F.) yield oleate, palmitate or stearate of the metal, and hydrate of glyceryl or glycerine. Hence glycerine is a by-product in the manufacture of soap, hard candles, and lead-plaster (*vide* pp. 170 and 371).

Properties.—Glycerine is viscid when pure, specific gravity 1.28 (not below 1.25, B. P.), has a sweet taste, is soluble in water or alcohol in all proportions. It has remarkable powers as a solvent, is a valuable *antiseptic* even when diluted with 10 parts of water, and useful as an emollient.

Test.—Heat one or two drops of glycerine in a test-tube, alone or with strong sulphuric acid, acid sulphate of potassium, or other salt powerfully absorbent of water; vapors of acrolein (from *acer*, sharp, and *oleum*, oil) are evolved, recognized by their powerfully irritating effects on the eyes and respiratory passages. If the glycerine be in solution in water, it must be evaporated as low as possible before applying this test. Besides glycerine itself (*Glycerinum*, B. P., *Glycerina*, U. S. P.), there are several official preparations of glycerine—solutions of carbolic, gallic, and tannic acids and borax in glycerine, and a sort of mucilage of starch in glycerine (*Glycerinum Acidi Carbolici*, *Glycerinum Acidi Gallici*, *Glycerinum Acidi Tannici*, *Glycerinum Boracis*, and *Glycerinum Amyli*).

QUESTIONS AND EXERCISES.

769. Give the names and formulæ of compounds of radicals having the general formulæ C_nH_{2n-7}', C_nH_{2n-1}', C_nH_{2n-1}''', and C_nH_{2n}'',—*e. g.*, benzol, essential oil of mustard, glycerine, and glycol.

770. State the difference in composition of natural and artificial oil of bitter almonds.

771. How is the so-called artificial oil of bitter almonds prepared?

772. What are the uses, composition, source, and properties of Carbolic Acid?

773. State the characters by which carbolic acid is distinguished from Creasote.

774. Draw out an equation explanatory of the production of aniline.

775. Mention the chief properties of Glycerine.

776. What is the specific gravity of glycerine?

777. By what test is glycerine recognized?

778. Enumerate some official preparations in which glycerine is employed as a solvent.

ALBUMENOID SUBSTANCES.

Albumen.—Agitate, thoroughly, white of egg (*Albumen Ovi*, B. P.) with water, and strain or pour off the liquid from the flocculent membranous insoluble matter. One white to 4 ozs. of water forms the "Solution of Albumen," B. P.

Test.—Heat a portion of this solution of albumen to the boiling-point; the albumen becomes insoluble, separating in clots or coagula of characteristic appearance.

Other Reactions.—Add to small quantities of aqueous solution of albumen solutions of corrosive sublimate, nitrate of silver, sulphate of copper, acetate of lead, alum, perchloride of tin; the various salts not only coagulate but form insoluble compounds with albumen. Hence the value of an egg as a temporary antidote in cases of poisoning by many metallic salts, its administration retarding the absorption of the poison until the stomach-pump or other measures can be applied. Sulphuric, nitric, and hydrochloric acids precipitate albumen; the coagulum is slowly redissolved by aid of heat, a brown, yellow, or purplish-red color being produced. Neither acetic, tartaric, nor organic acids, generally, except gallo-tannic, coagulate albumen. Alkalies prevent the precipitation of albumen.

Yolk or *Yelk of Egg* (*Ovi Vitellus*, B. P.) contains only 3 per cent. of albumen—the white 12½. The yolk also contains only 30 per cent. of yellow fat and 14 of casein. The whole egg (*Ovum*, U. S. P.) is also official.

Albumen is met with in large quantities in the serum of blood, in smaller quantity in chyle and lymph, and in the brain, kidneys, liver, muscles, and pancreas. It is not a normal constituent of saliva, gastric juice, bile, or mucus, but occurs in those secretions during inflammation. It is found in the urine and feces only under certain diseased states of the system.

The cause of the coagulation of albumen by heat has not yet been discovered.

Albumen has never been obtained sufficiently pure to admit of its composition being expressed by a trustworthy formula; Gerhardt regarded it as a sodium compound ($HNaC_{72}H_{110}N_{18}SO_{22},H_2O$).

Fibrin, Casein, Legumin.

Fibrin is the chief constituent of the muscular tissue of animals. It occurs in solution in the blood; and its spontaneous solidification or coagulation is the cause of the *clotting* of blood shortly after being drawn from the body—a phenomenon which cannot at present be explained satisfactorily. Fibrin may be obtained by whipping fresh blood with a bundle of twigs, separating the adherent fibres, and washing in water till colorless.

Average Composition of Blood (in 1000 parts).
(Compiled by Kirkes.)

	Water		784
	Albumen		70
	Fibrin		2.2
	Red Corpuscles: Globulin		123.5
	Hæmatin		7.5
Fatty matters.	Cholesterin	0.08	1.3
	Cerebrin	0.40	
	Serolin		
	Oleic and margaric acids		
	Volatile and odorous fatty acid		
	Fat containing Phosphorus		
Inorganic salts.	Chloride of sodium		3.6
	Chloride of potassium		.36
	Phosphate of sodium (Na_3PO_4)		.2
	Carbonate of sodium		.84
	Sulphate of sodium		.28
	Phosphates of calcium and magnesium		.25
	Oxide and phosphate of iron		.50
	Extractive matters, biliary-coloring-matter, gases, and accidental substances		5.47
			1000.

Percentage proportion of the *chief* constituents of Blood.

Water	78.4
Red corpuscles	13.1
Albumen of serum	7.0
Inorganic salts	.603
Extractive, fatty, and other matters	.677
Fibrin	.22
	100.

Casein occurs in Cow's Milk (*Lac*, B. P.) to the extent of 3 per cent., dissolved by a trace of alkaline salt. Its solution does not spontaneously coagulate like that of fibrin, nor by heat like albumen; but acids cause its precipitation from milk in the form of a curd (cheese) containing the fat (butter)-globules previously suspended in the milk, a clear yellow liquid (or whey) remaining. *Curds and whey* are also produced on adding to milk a piece, or an infusion, of *rennet*, the salted and dried inner membrane of the fourth stomach of the calf. The exact action of rennet is not known.

Average composition of 1000 *parts of Milk.*

	Specific gravity.	Water.	Solid constituents.	Casein and extractive	Sugar.	Butter.	Salts.
Woman	1.033	889	111	40	44	27	2
Cow	1.034	864	136	55	38	36	7

Specific gravity alone, as taken by the form of hydrometer termed a *lactometer*, or even by more delicate means, is of little value as an indication of the richness of milk, the butter and the other solids exerting an influence in opposite directions. Good cow's milk affords from 11 to 13 per cent. by volume of cream, and 3 to 3½ per cent. of butter. The water of milk seldom or never varies more than from 86½ to 87½ per cent., and the solid constituents from 13½ to 12½. Town milk is commonly 3 and sometimes 2 parts milk and 1 part water. Under the microscope milk is seen to consist of minute corpuscles floating in a transparent medium. These corpuscles consist of fatty matter (butter) contained in a filmy albumenoid envelope.

Legumin or *vegetable casein* is found in most leguminous seeds, such as sweet and bitter almonds. Peas contain about 25 per cent. of legumin.

Vegetable albumen is contained in many plant-juices, and is deposited in flocculi on heating such liquids. *Vegetable fibrin* is the name given by Liebig and Dumas to that portion of the gluten of wheat which is insoluble in alcohol and ether (*vide* p. 368).

Albumenoid substances are nearly identical in percentage composition. Albumen (and fibrin) contains 53.5 of carbon, 7 of hydrogen, 15.5 of nitrogen, 22 of oxygen, 1.6 of sulphur, and .4 of phosphorus. Casein contains no phosphorus. These three bodies are often termed the *plastic elements of nutrition*, under the assumption that animals directly assimilate them in forming muscles, nerves, and other tissues, —starch, sugar, and similar matter forming the *respiratory* materials of food, because more immediately concerned in keeping up the temperature of the body by the combustion going on between them, and their products, and the oxygen of the air in the blood.

Musk (*Moschus*, B. P. and U. S. P.), "the inspissated and dried secretion from the preputial follicles of *Moschus moschiferus*" (the Musk-Deer), is a mixture of albumenoid, fatty, and other animal matters with a volatile odorous substance of unknown composition.

GELATIGENOUS SUBSTANCES.

This group of nitrogenous bodies differs from true albumenoid in containing less carbon and sulphur and more nitrogen. They are contained in certain animal tissues, and on boiling with water yield a solution which has the remarkable property of solidifying to a jelly on cooling. The tendons, ligaments, bones, skin, and serous membranes afford *gelatine* proper; the cartilages give *chondrine,* which differs from gelatine in composition and in being precipitated by vegetable acids, alum, and the acetates of lead. The purest variety of gelatine is *isinglass*, B. P. (*Icthyocolla*, U. S. P.), "the swimming-bladder or sound of various species of *Acipenser*, Linn., prepared and cut in fine shreds." Small quantities are more easily disintegrated by a file than a knife. Fifty grains dissolved in 5 ounces of distilled water forms the official "Solution of Gelatine," B. P. *Glue* is an impure variety of gelatine, made from the trimmings of hides; *size* is glue of inferior tenacity, prepared from the parings of parchment and thin skins. "Among the varieties of gelatine derived from different tissues and from the same sources at different ages, much diversity exists as to the firmness and other characters of the solid formed on the cooling of the solutions. The differences between isinglass, size, and glue, in these respects, are familiarly known, and afford good examples of the varieties called weak and strong, or low and high, gelatines. The differences are sometimes ascribed to the quantities of water combined in each case with the pure or anhydrous gelatine, part of which water seems to be chemically combined with the gelatine; for no artificial addition of water to glue would give it the character of size, nor would any abstraction of water from isinglass or size convert it into the hard dry substance of glue. But such a change is effected in the gradual process of nutrition of the tissues; for, as a general rule, the tissues of an old animal yield a much firmer or stronger jelly than the corresponding parts of a young animal of the same species." (Kirke's Physiology.) Gelatine appears to unite chemically with a portion of the water in which it is soaked when used for culinary and manufacturing purposes, for a solution of glue in hot anhydrous glycerine does not yield an ordinary jelly on cooling.

PEPSINE.

Pepsine (from πέπτω, *peptō*, to digest) is a nitrogenous substance existing in the gastric juice, and as a viscid matter in the *peptic* glands and on the walls of the stomachs of animals. The mucous membrane of the stomach (of the hog, sheep, or calf, killed fasting) is scraped, and macerated in cold water for twelve hours; the pepsine in the strained liquid is then precipitated by acetate of lead, the deposit washed once or twice by decantation, sulphuretted hydrogen passed through the mixture of the deposit with a little water to remove the whole of the lead, and the filtered liquid evaporated to dryness at a temperature not exceeding 105° F. Pepsine is a powerful promoter of digestion; its solution is hence frequently termed *artificial gastric juice.* As met with in pharmacy its strength varies greatly. It is often prepared by simply mixing with starch the thick liquid obtained on macerating the scraped stomach with water, and evaporating to dryness. (Vide *Pharmaceutical Journal*, 1865-66, p. 112).

QUESTIONS AND EXERCISES.

779. In what form is albumen familiar?
780. Name the chief test for albumen
781. Why is the administration of albumen useful in cases of poisoning?
782. Mention the points of difference between yolk and white of egg.
783. From what sources other than egg may albumen be obtained?
784. In what respects does fibrin differ from albumen?
785. Enumerate the chief constituents of blood.
786. How may fibrin be obtained from blood?
787. State the difference between casein, fibrin, and albumen.
788. What are the relations of cream, butter, curds and whey, and cheese, to milk?
789. Describe the microscopic appearances of blood and of milk.
790. How much cream should be obtained from good milk?
791. What is the percentage of water in genuine milk?
792. Name sources of vegetable casein and vegetable albumen.
793. Give the percentage of nitrogen in albumenoid substances.
794. Describe the chemical nature of musk.
795. In what lie the peculiarities of gelatine?
796. To what extent do isinglass, glue, and size differ?
797. Whence is pepsine obtained?
798. How is pepsine prepared?

FATTY BODIES.

SOAPS, SOLID FATS, FIXED OILS, VOLATILE OILS, CAMPHORS.

General relations.—Oils and fats are, apparently, almost as simple in constitution as ordinary inorganic salts. Just as acetate of potassium ($KC_2H_3O_2$) is regarded as a compound of potassium (K) with the characteristic elements of all acetates ($C_2H_3O_2$), so soft soap is considered to be a compound of potassium (K) with the elements characteristic of all oleates ($C_{18}H_{33}O_2$), and hence is chemically termed oleate of potassium ($KC_{18}H_{33}O_2$). Olive oil, from which soap is commonly prepared, is mainly oleate of the trivalent radical *glyceryl* (C_3H_5), the formula of pure fluid oil being $C_3H_53C_{18}H_{33}O_2$, and its name *oleine*. The formation of a soap, therefore, on bringing together oil and a moist oxide or hydrate, is a simple case of double decomposition, as seen already in connection with lead plaster (p. 170), or in the following equation relating to the formation of common hard soap:—

$$\underset{\text{Hydrate of sodium (caustic soda).}}{3NaHO} + \underset{\text{Oleate of glyceryl (vegetable oil).}}{C_3H_53C_{18}H_{33}O_2} = \underset{\text{Oleate of sodium (hard soap).}}{3NaC_{18}H_{33}O_2} + \underset{\text{Hydrate of glyceryl (glycerine).}}{C_3H_53HO}$$

Berthelot has succeeded in preparing oil artificially from oleic acid and glycerine; and it is said to be identical with the pure of oleine of olive and of other fixed oils. Hard fats chiefly consist of *stearine*—that is, of tristearate of glyceryl ($C_3H_53C_{18}H_{35}O_2$). Mr. Wilson, of Price's Candle Company, obtains stearic and oleic acids and glycerine by simply passing steam, heated to 500° or 600° F., through melted fat. Both the glycerine and fat acids distil over in the current of steam, the glycerine dissolving in the condensed water, the fat-acids floating on the aqueous liquid.

Soaps.—Olive oil boiled with solution of potash yields potassium soap, or *soft soap* (*Sapo Mollis*, B. P.); with soda, sodium soap, or *hard soap* (*Sapo Durus*, B. P. and U. S. P.); mixed with ammonia, an ammonium soap (*Linimentum Ammoniæ*, B. P. and U. S. P.); and with lime-water, calcium soap (*Linimentum Calcis*, B. P. and—flax-seed oil—U. S. P.),—all oleates, chiefly of the respective basylous radicals. The alkali soaps are soluble in alcohol, the others insoluble. The official characters of Hard Soap are: "grayish-white, dry, inodorous; horny and pulverizable when kept in dry warm air; easily moulded when heated; soluble in rectified spirit; not imparting an oily stain to paper; incinerated it yields an ash which does not deliquesce." And of Soft Soap: "yellowish-green, inodorous, of a gelatinous consistence: soluble in rectified spirit; not imparting an oily stain to paper: incinerated it yields an ash which is very deliquescent."

Bile, the gall of the ox (*Bos taurus*, Linn.), freed from mucus by agitating with twice its bulk of rectified spirit (in which mucus is insoluble), filtering, and evaporating, yields the official Purified Ox-Bile (*Fel Bovinum Purificatum*, B. P.): the latter has a resinous appearance, but is chiefly composed of two crystalline substances having the constitution of a soap; the one is *glycocholate*, or simply *cholate, of sodium* ($NaC_{26}H_{42}NO_6$), the other is termed *taurocholate of sodium* ($NaC_{26}H_{44}NO_7S$). Both taurocholates and glycocholates are conjugated bodies readily yielding, the former *cholalic acid* ($H_2C_{14}H_{39}O_5$) and *taurine* ($C_2H_7NO_3S$), the latter cholalic acid and *glycocine* or *glycocoll* ($C_2H_5NO_2$), a body having interesting physiological relations, inasmuch as it is obtainable from gelatine (hence the name glycocoll, from γλυκὺς, *glucūs*, sweet, and κόλλα, *kolla*, glue) and hippuric acid.

Solid Fats.—1. *Lard* (*Adeps Præparatus*, B. P. and U. S. P.) is the purified internal fat of the abdomen of the hog—the perfectly fresh *omentum* or *flare*, washed, melted, strained, and dried. 2. *Benzoated Lard* (*Adeps Benzoatus*, B. P.) is prepared lard heated over a water-bath with benzoin (10 grains per ounce), which communicates an agreeable odor and prevents or retards rancidity. Purified lard is a mixture of oleine and stearine; *margarine*, the margarate of glyceryl, was formerly supposed to be a constituent of lard and other soft fats, but is now regarded as a mere mixture of *palmitine* (the chief fat of palm oil) and stearine. 3. *Yellow Wax* (*Cera Flava*,

B. P. and U. S. P.), the prepared honeycomb of the Hive-Bee, and the same bleached by exposure to sunlight. 4. *White Wax* (*Cera Alba*, B. P. and U. S. P.), according to Brodie, is chiefly a mixture of *Cerotic Acid* ($HC_{27}H_{53}O_2$), *Palmitate of Melissyl* ($C_{30}H_{61}C_{16}H_{31}O_2$), and about 5 per cent. of *Ceroleine*, the body to which the color, odor, and tenacity of wax are due. 5. *Spermaceti* (*Cetaceum*, B. P. and U. S. P.) is the *palmitate of cetyl* ($C_{16}H_{33}C_{16}H_{31}O_2$), or *cetine*; when saponified it yields not glycerine, the hydrate of glyceryl (C_3H_53HO), but *ethal*, the hydrate of cetyl ($C_{16}H_{33}HO$); it is the solid crystalline fat accompanying *sperm* oil in the head of the spermaceti-whale. 6. *Suet*, the internal fat of the abdomen of the sheep, purified by melting and straining, forms the official *Prepared Suet* (*Sevum Præparatum*, B. P. and U. S. P.); it is almost exclusively composed of stearin ($C_3H_53C_{18}H_{35}O_2$). 7. Expressed oil of *nutmeg* (*Oleum Myristicæ Expressum*, B. P.) is a mixture of a little volatile oil with much yellow and white fat, the latter a myristate of glyceryl ($C_3H_53C_{14}H_{27}O_2$). 8. Oil of *theobroma*, or *Cacao-butter* (*Oleum Theobromæ*, B. P. and U. S. P.), is a solid product of the ground seeds or *cocoa nibs* of the *Theobroma cacao*, which also furnish *cocoa* and *chocolate*. 9. *Cocoa-nut* oil, a soft fat largely contained in the edible portion of the nut of *Cocos nucifera*, or common cocoa-nut of the shops, a body containing glyceryl united with no less than six different univalent acidulous radicals, namely, the caproic ($C_6H_{11}O_2$), caprylic ($C_8H_{15}O_2$), rutic ($C_{16}H_{19}O_2$), lauric ($C_{12}H_{23}O_2$), myristic ($C_{14}H_{27}O_2$), and palmitic ($C_{16}H_{31}O_2$)—radicals which, like some from common resin, when united with sodium, form a soap differing from ordinary hard soap (oleate of sodium) by being tolerably soluble in a solution of chloride of sodium; hence the use of cocoa-nut oil and resin in making *marine soap*, a soap which, for the reason just indicated, readily yields a lather in sea-water.

Fixed Oils.—*Fixed* and *Volatile* oils are naturally distinguished by their behavior when heated; they also differ in chemical constitution, a fixed oil being, apparently, a combination of a basylous with an acidulous radical, while a volatile oil is commonly a neutral hydrocarbon.

Drying and Non-drying Oils.—Among fixed oils, most of which are oleate with a little palmitate and stearate of glyceryl, a few, such as, 1, *linseed* (*Oleum Lini*, B. P. and U. S. P., contained in *Lini Semina*, B. P., *Linum*, U. S. P., or Flaxseed, the ground residue of which, after removal of the oil, is *linseed meal*, *Lini Farina*, U. S. P.), and, 2, *cod-liver* (*Oleum Morrhuæ*, B. P. and U. S. P.), and, to some extent, castor and croton, are known as *drying oils*, from the readiness with which they absorb oxygen and become hardened to a resin. Among the *non-drying oils* are: 3, *almond* oil, indifferently yielded by the bitter (*Amygdala Amara*, B. P. and U. S. P.) or sweet seed (*Amygdala Dulcis*, B. P. and U. S. P.); 4, *croton* oil (*Oleum Crotonis*, B. P., *Oleum Tiglii*, U. S. P.), which seems to contain *crotonate of glyceryl* ($C_3H_53C_4H_5O_2$); 5, *olive* oil (*Oleum Olivæ*, B. P. and U. S. P.), already noticed; 6, *castor* oil (*Oleum Ricini*, B. P. and U. S. P.), a *ricinoleate of glyceryl* ($C_3H_53C_{18}H_{33}O_3$) or ricinoleine, a slightly oxidized oleine, soluble, unlike most fixed oils, in alcohol; 7, oil of *male fern* (*Filix Mas*, B. P. and U. S. P.), a vermifuge obtained by exhausting the rhizome with ether and removing the ether by evaporation—a dark-colored oil containing a little volatile oil and resin, and officially termed an extract (*Extractum Filicis Liquidum*, B. P.); 8, fixed oil of *mustard*, a bland, inodorous yellow or amber oil, yielding by saponification, and action of sulphuric acid, glycerine, oleic acid and *erucic acid*, $HC_{22}H_{41}O_2$ (Darby); 9, *Lycopodium Oil* from the sporules of Club-moss; 10, *Neat's-foot Oil* (*Oleum Bubulum*, U. S. P.).

Their physical qualities and the formulæ of their acidulous radicals show that the fatty bodies are closely related, and indicate that the natural processes by which they are formed are probably as closely related. The following Table, from Miller's "Elements of Chemistry," well shows the homology of the fat-acids, and gives their names, formulæ, melting-points, boiling-points, and natural and artificial sources.

:ids.	Formulæ. Molec. Vol. = 2.	Melting point.		Boiling-point.		Whence obtained.
		°F.	°C.	°F.	°C.	
c	$HC\ H\ O_2$	21	—6	221	105.3	Red ants; distillation of oxalic acid; and oxidation of amylaceous and other organic bodies.
!	$HC_2\ H_3\ O_2$	63	17	243	117	Distillation of wood; oxidation of alcohol, &c.
)nic ...	$HC_3\ H_5\ O_2$	...	...	284	140	Fermentation of glycerin, &c.
ic.......	$HC_4\ H_7\ O_2$	below 0	—20	314	157	Butter; fermentation of lactic acid, &c.
.anic...	$HC_5\ H_9\ O_2$	"	"	347	175	Valerian-root; oxidation of fousel oil.
ic.......	$HC_6\ H_{11}O_2$	...	...	392	200	Butter.
thylic.	$HC_7\ H_{12}$	"	"	298?	148?	Castor oil by distillation, &c.
lic......	$HC_8\ H_{15}O_2$	59	15	457	236	Butter; cocoa-nut oil.
;onic...	$HC_9\ H_{17}O_2$	...	...	500	260	Leaves of the geranium.
....	$HC_{10}H_{19}O_2$	86	30	...	...	Butter; oil of rue by oxidation.
;........	$HC_{12}H_{23}O_2$	110	43	...	...	Cocoa-nut oil; berries of the bay tree.
.ic......	$HC_{14}H_{27}O_2$	129	54	...	...	Nutmeg-butter; cocoa-nut oil, &c.
tic.....	$HC_{16}H_{31}O_2$	143.6	62	...	...	Palm oil; butter; beeswax, &c.
;........	$HC_{18}H_{35}O_2$	159	70.5	...	...	Most solid animal fats.
idic....	$HC_{20}H_{39}O_2$	167	75	...	...	Butter; oil of ground-nut.
ɔ	$HC_{27}H_{53}O_2$	174	79	...	...	Beeswax.
ic	$HC_{30}H_{59}O_2$	192	89	...	...	Beeswax.

(Bracketed against the second to ninth rows: By oxidation of oleic acid with nitric acid.)

QUESTIONS AND EXERCISES.

799. Give a sketch of the general chemistry of fixed oils, fats and soaps.
800. What is the difference between Hard and Soft Soap?
801. Which soaps are official?
802. Name the source of lard, and state how "Prepared Lard" is obtained.
803. State the composition of Beeswax.
804. In what does Spermaceti differ from other solid fats?
805. Mention the chief constituent of Suet.
806. Whence is Cacao-Butter obtained?
807. Why is *marine soap* so called, and from what fatty matter is it exclusively prepared?
808. What do you understand by *drying* and *non-drying* oils?
809. In what respect does Castor Oil differ from other oils?
810. How is oil of male fern (*Ex. Filicis Liquidum*) prepared?
811. Mention the sources and formulæ of the following fat-acids: formic, acetic, propionic, butyric, valerianic, caproic, œnanthylic, caprylic, pelargonic, and rutic.

VOLATILE OILS.—The *Volatile* or *Essential Oils* exist in various parts of plants probably as mere combinations of carbon and hydrogen; but such *hydrocarbons* are prone to change when in contact with oxygen or moisture; hence these liquids as they occur in pharmacy are usually mixtures of liquid hydrocarbons or *elæoptens* with oxidized hydrocarbons, which are commonly solid or camphor-like bodies termed *stearoptens*. On cooling a volatile oil, a stearopten (from στέαρ, *stear*, suet) often crystallizes out; or on distilling an oil, it remains in the retort, being less volatile than an elæopten (from ἔλαιον, *elaion*, oil, and ὄπτομαι, *optomai*, to see). Volatile oils should be preserved in well-closed bottles.

The process by which volatile oils are usually obtained from herbs, flowers, fruits, or seeds, may be imitated on the small scale by placing the material (bruised cloves or caraways for instance) in a tubulated retort, adapting the retort to a Liebig's condenser, and passing steam, generated in a Florence flask, through a glass tube to the bottom of the retort. The steam in its passage upward through the substance will carry the oil over the neck of the retort into the condenser, and thence, liquefied and cooled, into the receiving vessel, where the oil will be found floating on the water. It may be collected by running off the distillate through a glass funnel having a stopcock in the neck, or by letting the water from the condenser drop into an old test-tube which has a small hole in the bottom, or any similar tube placed in a larger vessel, the water and oil being subsequently run off separately from the tube as from a pipette. The water will in most cases be the ordinary official medicated water of the material operated on (*Aqua Aurantii Floris*, *Anethi*, *Carui*, *Cinnamomi*, *Fœniculi*, *Menthæ Piperitæ*, *Menthæ Viridis*, *Pimentæ*, *Rosæ*—from *Rosæ Centifoliæ Petala*, B. P. and U. S. P.—*Sambuci*). Volatile oils, like fixed oils, stain paper, but the stain of the former is not permanent like that of the latter. Oils of lemon and orange are sometimes obtained by mere pressure of the rind of the fruit.

A large number of volatile oils are employed in medicine, either in the pure state, in the form of saturated aqueous solution (medicated waters), solution in spirit of wine, 1 in 5 (*Essentia Anisi* and *Essentia Menthæ Piperitæ*, B. P.) and 1 in 50 (*Spiritus Cajuputi*, *Juniperi*, *Lavandulæ*, *Menthæ piperitæ*, *Myristicæ*, *Rosmarini*), or as leading constituents in various barks, roots, leaves, &c. The strength of *Spiritus Anisi*, U. S. P.; *Sp. Cinnamomi*, U. S. P.; *Sp. Menthæ Piperitæ*, U. S. P. and *Sp. Menth. Viridis*, U. S. P., is 1 of oil to 15 of spirit of wine. *Perfumes* ("scents" or "essences," including "Lavender-Water" and "Eau de Cologne") are for the most part solutions of essential oils in spirit of wine, or spirituous infusions of materials containing essential oils. The following oils are, directly or indirectly, official in the British Pharmacopœia. 1. Volatile oil of *Bitter Almond* (p. 341). 2. Oil of *Dill* (*Oleum Anethi*, B. P.), a pale yellow, pungent, acrid liquid distilled from dill-fruit. 3. Oil of *Aniseed* (*Oleum Anisi*, B. P.), a colorless or pale yellow liquid, of sweetish warm flavor, distilled in Europe from the Anise-fruit (*Pimpinella anisum*), and in China from the fruit of Star-Anis (*Illicium anisatum*); it is a mixture of a hydrocarbon isomeric with oil of turpentine and a stearopten ($C_{10}H_{12}O$), which crystallizes out at low temperatures. 4. Oil of *Chamomile* (*Oleum Anthemidis*, B. P.), a bluish or, when old, yellow oil, of characteristic odor and taste, distilled from chamomile-flowers (*Anthemidis flores*, B. P.): the official variety (*Anthemis nobilis*) yields an oil composed of a hydrocarbon ($C_{10}H_{16}$) and an oxidized portion ($C_{10}H_{16}O_2$ or C_5H_8O) which, heated with potash, gives *angelate of potassium* ($KC_5H_7O_2$), whence is obtained *angelic acid* ($HC_5H_7O_2$); while the flowers of another variety (*Matricaria Chamomilla*, U. S. P.) contain a stearopten ($C_{10}H_{16}O$) having the composition of laurel-camphor. 5. Oil of *Horseradish*-root (*Armoraciæ Radix*, B. P.) is, according to Hofmann, the sulphocyanate of butyl (C_4H_9CNS), p. 356: it is the chief active ingredient of *Spiritus Armoraciæ Compositus*, B. P. 6. Oil of Sweet-Orange Peel (*Aurantii Dulcis Cortex*, U. S. P.) and Oil of Bitter-Orange rind (*Aurantii Amari Cortex*, B. P. and U. S. P.), the flavoring constituent of the official syrup of the *peel* (*Syrupus Aurantii*, B. P.), and the oils of, 7, *lemon* (*Oleum Limonis*, B. P. and U. S. P.), from Lemon Peel (*Limonis Cortex*, U. S. P.); 8, *lime;* 9, *bergamot* (*Oleum Bergamii*, U. S. P.);

10, *citron* and a variety of citron termed *cedra*, resemble each other in composition, containing a hydrocarbon ($C_{10}H_{16}$) and a small quantity of oxidized hydrocarbons ($C_{10}H_{10}O_5$ and $C_{15}H_{10}O_5$). 11. Oil of *Neroli* or *Orange-Flower*, the aqueous solution of which is official in the forms of water (*Aqua Aurantii Floris*, B. P. and U. S. P.) and syrup (*Syrupus Aurantii Floris*, B. P. and U. S. P.), contains a fragrant hydrocarbon ($C_{10}H_{16}$), colorless when fresh, but becoming red on exposure to light, and an inodorous oxidized hydrocarbon. 12. Oil of *Buchu-leaves* (*Buchu Folia*, B. P. and U. S. P.) consists of a hydrocarbon holding in solution a crystalline stearopten. 13. Oil of *Cardamoms*, from the seeds of the capsules (*Cardamomum*, B. P. and U. S. P.), is chiefly a hydrocarbon ($C_{10}H_{16}$) isomeric with oil of turpentine. 14. Oil of *Cajuput* (*Oleum Cajuputi*, B. P. and U. S. P.) is a mobile bluish liquid the composition of which ($C_{10}H_{18}O$) seems to be that of the common hydrocarbon associated with the elements of water. 15. Oil of *Caraway*-fruit (*Carum*, U. S. P.) (*Oleum Carui*, B. P., *Oleum Cari*, U. S. P.) is a mixture of *carvene* ($C_{10}H_{16}$) and *carvol* ($C_{10}H_{14}O$). 16. Oil of *Cloves* (*Oleum Caryophylli*, B. P. and U. S. P.) and of *Pimento* (*Oleum Pimentæ*, B. P. and U. S. P.), both heavier than water, contain a liquid hydrocarbon ($C_{10}H_{16}$), *eugenic acid* ($C_{10}H_{12}O_2$), a solid body, *eugenin*, isomeric with eugenic acid, and a second crystalline substance, *caryophyllin* ($C_{10}H_{16}O$), isomeric with common camphor. 17. Oil of *Cascarilla*-bark (*Cascarillæ Cortex*, B. P. and U. S. P.) has not been fully examined. 18. Oil of *Cinnamon*-bark (*Cinnamomi Cortex*, B. P. and U. S. P.) and 19, of *Cassia*-bark is mostly hydride of cinnamyl (C_9H_7OH). Boiled with nitric acid it furnishes hydride of benzoyl (C_7H_5OH) and benzoic acid ($HC_7H_5O_2$), with chloride of lime yields benzoate of calcium ($Ca2C_7H_5O_2$), and with caustic potash gives cinnamate of potassium ($KC_9H_7O_2$). The specific gravity of oil of cinnamon (*Oleum Cinnamomi*, B. P. and U. S. P.) varies from 1.025 to 1.050. 20. Oil of *Copaiva* (*Oleum Copaibæ*, B. P. and U. S. P.) and, 21, of *Cubebs* (*Oleum Cubebæ*, B. P. and U. S. P.) are hydrocarbons having the formula $C_{25}H_{24}$. 22. Oil of *Coriander* (*Coriandri fructus*, B. P., *Coriandrum*, U. S. P., *Oleum Coriandri*, B. P.) seems to have the composition of hydrous oil of turpentine ($C_{10}H_{16}H_2O$). 23. Oil of *Juniper* (*Oleum Juniperi*, B. P. and U. S. P.), the active constituent of Juniper Tops and Berries (*Juniperus*, U. S. P.), is a hydrocarbon ($C_{10}H_{16}$) which by contact with water yields a white crystalline hydrous compound ($C_{10}H_{16}H_2O$). 24. Oil of *Fennel*-fruit (*Oleum Fœniculi*, U. S. P.) (*Fœniculi Fructus*, B. P. and U. S. P.) differs in odor, but contains the same proximate constituents as oil of anise. 25. Oil of *Lavender* (*Oleum Lavandulæ*, B. P. and U. S. P.) contains a hydrocarbon which by oxidation yields common camphor. 25*a*. Oil or Butter of *Orris* (*Iris Florentina*) is a soft camphor ($C_8H_{16}O_2$), lighter than water. 26. Oil of *Peppermint* (*Oleum Menthæ Piperitæ*, B. P. and U. S. P.) consists of a hydrocarbon, *menthene* ($C_{10}H_{18}$), differs from that of most volatile oils, and hydrous menthene ($C_{10}H_{18}H_2O$), a crystalline stearopten. 27. Oil of *Spearmint* (*Oleum Menthæ Viridis*, B. P. and U. S. P.) is expressed by the formula $C_{10}H_{20}O$. 28. Oil of *Nutmeg* (*Oleum Myristicæ*, B. P.

and U. S. P.) and of the arillus of the nutmeg or mace (*Macis*, U. S. P.) is composed of a hydrocarbon and the same more or less oxidized. 29. Oil or Otto or Attar of *Cabbage-Rose petals* (*Rosæ Centifoliæ Petals*, B. P. and U. S. P., *Oleum Rosæ*, U. S. P.) gives the fragrance to Rose-water (*Aqua Rosæ*, B. P.). It resembles most other volatile oils in being composed of a hydrocarbon and an oxidized portion, but differs from all in this respect, that the hydrocarbon is solid and is destitute of odor, while the oxygenated constituent is liquid and the source of the perfume. According to Flückiger the solid hydrocarbon (C_8H_{16}) yields succinic acid as the chief product of its oxidation by nitric acid, and in other respects affords evidence of belonging to the paraffin series of fats. 30. Oil of *Rosemary-tops* (*Oleum Rosmarini*, B. P. and U. S. P.) is a mixture of hydrocarbon, oxygenized oil, and stearopten in variable proportions. 31. Oil of *Rue* (*Oleum Rutæ*, B. P.) contains a small quantity of hydrocarbon ($C_{10}H_{16}$) with some rutic aldehyd ($C_{10}H_{20}O$), but according to Greville Williams is chiefly euodic aldehyd ($C_{11}H_{22}O$), some lauric aldehyd ($C_{12}H_{24}O$) also being present. 32. Oil of *Savin* (*Oleum Sabinæ*, B. P. and U. S. P.) is isomeric with oil of turpentine ($C_{10}H_{16}$). 33. Oil of *Elder-flowers* (*Sambuci Flores*, B. P. and U. S. P.) occurs in very small quantity; it has a butyraceous consistence. 34. Oil of *Sassafras-root* (*Oleum Sassafras*, U. S. P.) specific gravity 1.094 (*Sassafras Radix*, B. P. and U. S. P.) yields *safren* ($C_{10}H_{16}$) and large quantities of a stearopten, *sassafrol* ($C_{10}H_{10}O_2$). 35. Oil of *Mustard* (*Oleum Sinapis*, B. P.) is the sulphocyanate of allyl (p. 364). If adulterated with alcohol, its specific gravity is below 1.015. 36. Oil of *Turpentine* (*Oleum Terebinthinæ*, B. P. and U. S. P.). Turpentine itself is really an oleoresin of about the consistence of fresh honey. It flows naturally or by incision from the wood of most coniferous trees, larch (*Larix Europæa*) yielding *Venice Turpentine*, *Abies balsamea* furnishing *Canadian Turpentine*, Balsam of Fir or *Canada Balsam* (*Terebinthina Canadensis*, B. P. and U. S. P.), *Pistachia terebinthus*, the variety termed *Chian Turpentine*, and the *Pinus palustris*, *Pinus abies*, and *Pinus pinaster* affording American Turpentine, *Terebinthus*, U. S. P. *Pinus maritima* gives the French or Bordeaux Turpentine. By distillation turpentine is separated into *rosin* or *resin* (which remains in the still), and *essential oil of turpentine*, often termed simply *turpentine*, *spirit of turpentine*, or "*turps*" (which distils over). Mixed with alkali to saturate resinous acids, and redistilled, oil of turpentine furnishes *rectified oil of turpentine*. Under the influence of heat, chemical agents, or both, oil of turpentine ($C_{10}H_{16}$) yields many derivatives of considerable chemical interest. 37. Oil of *Valerian-root* (*Valerianæ Radix*, B. P. and U. S. P.) (*Oleum Valerianæ*, U. S. P.) is a mixture of a hydrocarbon ($C_{10}H_{16}$) and *valerol* ($C_6H_{10}O$). Valerol slowly oxidizes to valerianic acid, known by its smell. A similar change occurs at once if the oil of valerian be allowed to fall, drop by drop, on heated caustic potash: $C_6H_{10}O+3KHO+H_2O=K_2CO_3+KC_5H_9O_2+3H_2$. By the action of sulphuric acid on the valerianate of potassium thus produced, valerianic acid is obtained. 38. Oil of *Ginger* (*Zingiber*,

B. P. and U. S. P.) has the composition of hydrous oil of turpentine. 39. *Wormseed* (*Chenopodium*, U. S. P.) contains a volatile oil. 40. Oil of *Thyme* (*Oleum Thymi*, U. S. P.) is a mixture of *thymene* ($C_{10}H_{16}$) and *thymol* ($C_{10}H_{14}O$), a solid white crystalline body. Thymol is also contained in, 41, Oil of Horsemint (*Monarda*, U. S. P.).

Camphors.—In addition to the stearoptens or camphors already mentioned as being contained in or formed from volatile oils, there is one that is a common article of trade. It is obtained from the wood of *Camphora officinarum*, or Camphor-Laurel in Japan (termed, in Europe, Dutch camphor, because imported by the Dutch) and in China (known as Formosa camphor), by a rough process of distillation with water, and is resublimed in this country (*Camphora*, B. P. and U. S. P.). The formula of laurel-camphor is $C_{10}H_{16}O$. The essential oil (*Oleum Camphoræ*, U. S. P.), from which doubtless camphor is derived by oxidation, is easily obtained from the wood, and is occasionally met with in commerce under the name of *liquid camphor* or *camphor oil;* its formula is $C_{20}H_{32}O$; by exposure to air it becomes oxidized and deposits common camphor, $C_{20}H_{32}O+O=2C_{10}H_{16}O$. There is another kind of camphor in European markets less common than laurel-camphor, but highly esteemed by the Chinese; it is obtained from the *Dryobalanops aromatica*, and denominated Sumatra or Borneo camphor. It differs slightly from laurel-camphor in containing more hydrogen, its formula being $C_{10}H_{18}O$. It is accompanied in the tree by a volatile oil ($C_{10}H_{16}$) isomeric with oil of turpentine. This oil *borneène*, is also occasionally met with in trade under the name of *liquid camphor* or *camphor oil*, but differs from laurel-camphor oil in not depositing crystals on exposure to air.

Camphor is soluble to a slight extent in water (40 grains per gallon, Pooley). The official Camphor-water (*Aqua Camphoræ*, B. P. and U. S. P.) or *Camphor mixture*, is such a solution.

Cantharidin ($C_5H_6O_2$?), the active blistering principle of cantharides (*Cantharides*, B. P., *Cantharis*, U. S. P.) and other vesicating insects, has most of the properties of a camphor or stearopten. It slowly crystallizes, from an alcoholic tincture of the beetles, in fusible, volatile, micaceous plates. The following process for the extraction of cantharidin is by Fumouze: Powdered cantharides are macerated with chloroform for twenty-four hours; and this treatment is repeated twice with fresh quantities of solvent, the residue having been well squeezed each time. The collected solutions are then distilled, and the dark green residue treated with bisulphide of carbon, which dissolves fatty, resinous, and other matters, and precipitates the cantharidin. The precipitate is thrown on a filter, washed with bisulphide of carbon, and recrystallized from chloroform. The same process, omitting the final recrystallization, may be used for the quantitative estimation of cantharidin in cantharides. The average quantity found is from four to five parts in one thousand.

QUESTIONS AND EXERCISES.

812. How do volatile oils differ chemically from fixed oils?
813. What are the general chemical characters of volatile oils?
814. Describe the usual process by which volatile oils are obtained.
815. Mention the differences in composition between the volatile oils of *Anthemis nobilis* and *Matricaria chamomilla.*
816. Give the systematic name of oil of horseradish.
817. State the general composition of the oil of lemon, lime, bergamot, citron, and cedra.
818. Name the constituents of oil of cloves.
819. In what respect does oil (or otto) of roses differ from other volatile oils?
820. To what class of substances do the constituents of oil of rue belong?
821. How does natural turpentine differ from the turpentine of trade?
822. With what object is commercial turpentine rectified?
823. How is camphor oil related to camphor?
824. In what respects do Borneo or Sumatra camphor and camphor oil differ from the corresponding products of Japan and China?
825. What is the nature of cantharidin?

RESINOID SUBSTANCES.

RESINS, OLEO-RESINS, GUM-RESINS, BALSAMS.

Resins occur in plants generally in association with volatile oils. They closely resemble camphors or stearoptens, but are not volatile, and differ from oils and fats mainly in being solid and brittle. *Oleo-resins* are mixtures of a resin and a volatile oil. *Gum-resins* are mixtures of a resin or oleo-resins and gum. *Balsams* are commonly described as resins or oleo-resins which yield benzoic or cinnamic acid; but oleo-resins containing neither of these acids are often termed balsams, *e. g.* balsam of copaiva and Canada balsam.

Resins.—1. *Resin, rosin,* or *colophony* (*Resina,* B. P. and U. S. P.) is the type of this class. Its source is the oleo-resin or true turpentine of the conifers, a body which by distillation yields spirit of turpentine and a residuum of rosin. The chief constituents of resin are *pinic acid* ($HC_{20}H_{29}O_2$) and *sylvic acid*, identical in composition, but differing in properties (*vide* Isomerism), the former being soluble and the latter insoluble in alcohol of sp. gr. 0.883. Pinic acid heated yields *colophonic* or *colopholic acid.* Among the products of the destructive distillation of resin, Tichborne has recently found "*colophonic hydrate*" ($C_{10}H_{22}O_3$, H_2O), a white inodorous crystalline substance, and by depriving this of water obtained white crystalline *colophonine* ($C_{10}H_{22}O_3$). Resin is soluble in oil of turpentine. It is a constituent of eight of the fourteen Plasters (*Emplastra*) of the

British Pharmacopœia. 2. *Arnicin*, the chief acrid if not the only active principle of Arnica (*Arnicæ Radix*, B. P., *Arnicæ Flores*, U. S. P.), is a resin. 3. *Cannabin*, said to be the active principle of *Indian Hemp* (*Cannabis Indica*, B. P., *Extractum Cannabis*, U. S. P.), is usually described as a resin. 4. *Capsicum-fruit* contains resin (p. 327). 5. *Castorin*, a resinous matter, is the name given to the chief constituent of *Castor* (*Castoreum*, B. P. and U. S. P.), the dried preputial follicles and included secretion of the Beaver (*Castor Fiber*). 6. *Ergotin* is a very active resinoid constituent of *Ergot* (*Ergota*, B. P. and U. S. P.), or "the sclerotium (compact mycelium or spawn) of *Claviceps purpurea*, produced within the paleæ of the common rye, *Secale cereale*." 7. *Guaiacum-resin* is a mixture of several substances (p. 343). 8. *Jalap-resin* (p. 344). 9. *Kousso* (*Cusso*, B. P.) is said to owe its anthelmintic property to a neutral bitter acrid resin. 10. *Mastic* (*Mastiche*, B. P. and U. S. P.) is a resinous exudation obtained by incision from the stem of the Mastic or Lentisk tree. Nine-tenths of Mastic is *mastichic acid* ($C_{20}H_{31}O_2$), a resin soluble in alcohol; the remaining tenth, *masticin* ($C_{20}H_{31}O$), a tenacious elastic resin. 11. *Mezereon*, the dried bark (*Mezerei Cortex*, B. P. and U. S. P.) of *Daphne mezereum*, Mezereon, and *Daphne laureola*, Spurge Laurel, owes its acridity to a resin. 12. *Pepper* contains a resin (p. 329). 13. *Burgundy Pitch* (*Pix Burgundica*, B. P. and U. S. P.) is the melted and strained exudation from the stem of the Spruce Fir, *Abies Excelsa*. The term Burgundy is a misnomer, the resin never having been collected at or near Burgundy; Finland, and to a smaller extent Baden, and Austria being the countries whence it is derived. Its constituents closely resemble those of common Resin. It is often adulterated and imitated by a mixture of resin with palm-oil, water, &c., from which it may be readily distinguished by its duller yellow color, highly aromatic odor, greater solubility in alcohol, and almost complete solubility in twice its weight of glacial acetic acid (Hanbury). 14. *Podophyllum-resin* (p. 327). 15. *Pyrethrin* is the name of the acrid resinous active principle of *Pellitory-root* (*Pyrethri Radix*, B. P.). 16. The resins of Rhubarb have already been alluded to in connection with Chrysophanic acid (p. 277). 17. *Rottlerin* is the name given by Anderson to a crystalline resin from Kamala (*Kamala*, B. P.), the minute glands that cover the capsules of *Rottlera tinctoria*: to this, and, apparently, allied resins, Kamala owes its activity as an anthelmintic.

Oleo-resins.—1. *Copaiva* (*Copaiba*, B. P. and U. S. P.) is a mixture of about 40 per cent. of essential oil ($C_{15}H_{24}$), with two or more per cent. of brown soft resin, and 50 or more of a yellow dark resin termed *Copaivic acid* ($C_{20}H_{30}O_2$). Copaiva heated with a fourth of its weight of the official carbonate of magnesium yields a transparent fluid, owing to the formation of copaivate of magnesium and solution of this soap in the essential oil. With an equal weight of the carbonate enough soap is produced to take up the whole of the essential oil, and form a mass capable of being rolled into pills. A much smaller quantity of calcined magnesia, as might be expected, effects the same result; but more time, often several days, is required before complete reaction is effected. Quicklime has a similar effect. Perhaps carbonate reacts more quickly because of its fine state of division and admixture of hydrate—in which case hydrates of calcium and magnesium may be expected to act better than the calcined preparations, and in much smaller quantity than carbonate of magnesium. Copaiva is soluble in its own bulk of benzol, and, unlike, 2, Wood-oil, a similar oleo-resin from the *Dipterocarpus turbinatus*, does not become gelatinous when heated to 270° F. Copaiva, also, is not fluorescent. 3. *Elemi* (*Elemi*, B. P.) is an exudation from an unknown tree (probably *Canarium commune*). It consists of volatile oil with 80 or more per cent. of two resins, the one ($C_{20}H_{32}O_2$) soluble in cold alcohol, the other ($C_{20}H_{33}O$) almost insoluble. 4. *Wood-Tar* (*Pix Liquida*, B. P. and U. S. P.) is a mixture of several resinoid and oily bodies (amongst others Creasote, p. 363) obtained by destructive distillation from the wood of *Pinus sylvestris* and other pines. When heated it yields a terebinthinate oil and a residue of *pitch*. 5. *Turpentines*. These oleo-resins have been mentioned in connection with oil of turpentine, their volatile, and resin, their fixed constituent. 6. *Common Frankincense* (*Thus Americanum*, B. P.) is the concrete turpentine of *Pinus tæda*. 7. *Canada Balsam* (*Terebinthina Canadensis*, B. P.) is the turpentine or oleo-resin of the Balm of Gilead Fir (*Abies balsamea*). 8. *Sumbul-root* (*Sumbul Radix*, B. P.) seems to owe its stimulating property to two oleo-resins, one soluble in ether, the other in alcohol. 9. *Oleo-resin of Lupulin* (U. S. P.) is an ethereal extract of the yellow powder (*Lupulina*, U. S. P.) attached to the small nuts at the base of the scales which form the aggregate fruit of the Hop (*Humulus Lupulus*). It contains essential oil of hop and oxidized oil or resin. *Oleoresinæ Capsici*, *Cubebæ*, *Piperis* and *Zingiberis* are also official in the United States Pharmacopœia. 10. *Pix Canadensis*, U. S. P., is the concrete juice of *Abies Canadensis*.

Gum-resins.—1. *Ammoniacum* (*Ammoniacum*, B. P. and U. S. P.) is an exudation from the *Dorema Ammoniacum*. It contains nearly 20 per cent. of gum and about 70 of resin ($C_{40}H_{50}O_9$—Johnston). 2. *Assafœtida* (*Assafœtida*, B. P.) is a gum-resin obtained, by incision, from the living root of *Narthex assafœtida*. It contains from 50 to 70 per cent. of resin, 25 to 30 per cent. of gum (about two-thirds arabin, one-third bassorin, p. 85), and 3 to 5 per cent. of volatile oil. 3. *Gamboge* (*Gambogia*, B. P. and U. S. P.) is obtained from the *Garcinia morella*. When of best quality it contains from 20 to 25 per cent. of gum, and 80 to 75 per cent. of a resin termed *gambogic acid* ($C_{20}H_{23}O_4$). 4. *Galbanum* (*Galbanum*, B. P. and U. S. P.) contains from 20 to 25 per cent. of gum, and about 65 per cent. of resin ($C_{40}H_{54}O_7$), and 3 or 4 per cent. of volatile oil. 5. *Myrrh* (*Myrrha*, B. P. and U. S. P.), an exudation from the stem of *Balsamodendron myrrha*, contains about half its weight of soluble gum (probably arabin), 10 per cent. of insoluble gum (probably bassorin), 2½ of volatile oil, and about 25 per cent. of resin (myrrhic acid). 6. *Scammony* (p. 346).

Gum-resins need only be finely powdered and rubbed in a mortar with water to yield a medicinal *emulsion*, in which the fine particles of resin are held in suspension by the aqueous solution of gum.

BALSAMS.—1. *Benzoin* (*Benzoinum*, B. P. and U. S. P.) is obtained from incisions of the bark of *Styrax benzoin*. It contains 12 to 15 per cent. of benzoic acid (p. 276), about 50 per cent. of a resin (α) soluble in ether, 25 to 30 per cent. of a resin (β) soluble in alcohol only, and 3 to 4 per cent. of a resin (γ) soluble in solution of carbonate of sodium. The α resin is considered to be a compound of the β ($C_{40}H_{46}O_9$) and the γ ($C_{30}H_{40}O_5$). The balsams of Peru, Tolu, and Storax differ from benzoin in containing cinnamic (p. 377) in place of benzoic acid; hence they yield, by oxidation, hydride of benzoyl (oil of bitter almonds). 2. *Balsam of Peru* (*Balsamum Peruvianum*, B. P. and U. S. P.), from the *Myroxylon Pereiræ*, is a mixture of 70 per cent. of oily with about 23 of resinous matter, and 6 per cent. of cinnamic acid. The oil (cinnaméin), by action of potash, yields cinnamic acid ($HC_9H_7O_2$) and *cinnamic alcohol* (HC_9H_9O), otherwise known as *peruvine* or *styrone;* it also often holds in solution *metacinnaméin* or *styracin* ($C_{18}H_{16}O_2$), isomeric with hydride of cinnamyl (C_9H_7OH). The resin of balsam of Peru seems to result from the action of moisture on the oil. The constituents of *Vanilla*, U. S. P., somewhat resemble those of Balsam of Peru. 3. *Balsam of Tolu* (*Balsamum Tolutanum*, B. B. and U. S. P.) is an exudation from incisions in the bark of *Myroxylon toluifera;* it closely resembles balsam of Peru, but is more susceptible of resinification. Old hard balsam of tolu is a convenient source of cinnamic acid, which is extracted by the same process as that by which benzoic acid is obtained from benzoin, namely, ebullition with alkali, filtration, and precipitation by hydrochloric acid. 4. *Storax* is an oleo-resin obtained from the *Liquidambar orientale*. It contains a volatile oil termed *styrol* (C_8H_8), cinnamic acid, styracin, and a soft and a hard resin. Styrol differs from similar hydrocarbons in being converted into a polymeric solid termed *metastyrol* or *draconyl* on the mere application of a temperature of about 400° F. For medicinal use, storax (*Styrax Præpuratus*, B. P. and U. S. P.) is purified by solution in alcohol, filtration, and removal of the alcohol by distillation.

Caoutchouc or *India-rubber*, and *Gutta Percha*.

Caoutchouc is the hardened juice of *Hevea* (*Siphonia*) *Braziliensis*, *Castilloa elastica*, *Urceola elastica*, *Ficus elastica*, and other plants (Collins). Heated moderately with sulphur it takes up 2 or 3 per cent., and forms *vulcanized India-rubber;* at a higher temperature a hard horny product, termed *ebonite* or *vulcanite*, results. *Gutta Percha* (U. S. P.) is the concrete drop or juice of the *percha* (Malay) tree, the *Isonandra gutta*, and of other Sapotaceous plants. It is soluble in chloroform (*Liquor Gutta-percha*, U. S. P.), benzoyl, and essential oils.

These two elastic substances, in the pure state, are hydrocarbons (xC_5H_4), usually slightly oxidized.

QUESTIONS AND EXERCISES.

826. Distinguish between resins and camphors. Mention the points of difference of resins, oleo-resins, gum-resins, and balsams.
827. Name the constituents of common Resin.
828. Enumerate some official articles of which the active constituents are resins.
829. Give the chief distinguishing characters of Burgundy Pitch.
830. What is the average proportion of oil in Copaiva?
831. Explain the effect of magnesia or lime on copaiva.
832. State the nature of Wood-Tar.
833. Why do Ammoniacum, Assafœtida, Gamboge, Galbanum, and Myrrh give an emulsion by mere trituration with water?
834. In what respect does Benzoin differ from the Balsams of Peru, Tolu, and Storax?
835. What is the chemical nature of India-rubber and Gutta Percha?
836. How is India-rubber *vulcanized* and converted into *ebonite* or *vulcanite?*

COLORING-MATTERS.

The animal, vegetable, and mineral kingdoms abound in substances or pigments which powerfully decompose light, absorbing certain of its constituent colors, and reflecting some others. Thus, for example, most leaves contain a body termed chlorophyll, which has the property of absorbing red light and reflecting green; these reflected rays entering the eye of an observer, and striking on the retina (the expanded extremity of the optic nerve), always communicate the same impression to the brain; in popular language the leaf is said to be green. Art has added largely to the number of natural coloring-matters.

YELLOW.—1. *Chrome-yellow* occurs in more than a dozen shades (see *Lead, chromate of*). 2. *Fustic* or *yellow wood* is the wood of the *Rhus cotinus.* 3. *Gamboge* (see *Gamboge*). 4. *Ochre* is met with of many tints, under the names of *yellow ochre, gold yellow, gold earth* or *ochre, yellow sienna, chinese yellow.* It is chiefly a mixture of oxyhydrates of iron with alumina and lime. 5. *Orpiment* is a sulphide of arsenicum (As_2S_3). 6. *Persian berries* or *Avignon grains* contain a principle termed *chrysorhamnin* ($C_{23}H_{22}O_{11}$). They are the product of the *Rhamnus infectorius.* 7. *Purree* or *Indian yellow* is said by Stenhouse to owe its color to *purrate* or *euxanthate of magnesium* ($MgC_{42}H_{34}O_{22}$). 8. *Quercitron* is the bark of *Quercus tinctoria,* U. S. P. or Black Oak. It contains the yellow glucoside, *quercitrin* ($C_{18}H_{18}O_{10},H_2O$). 9. *Rhubarb* (see *Chrysophanic acid,* p. 277). 10. *Saffron* (*Crocus,* B. P. and U. S. P.), the dried stigma and part of the style of *Crocus sativus,* yields *saffranin* or *polychroite,* a yellow principle whose chemistry is but little known. 11. *Turmeric,* the rhizome of *Curcuma longa,* owes its yellow color to *curcumin*, a resinous matter. 12. *Weld* (*Reseda luteola*) contains a durable yellow matter termed *luteolin* ($C_{20}H_{14}O_3$). 13. *Picric* or *carbazotic acid* (p. 364) is a very powerful yellow dye.

RED.—1. *Alkanet*, the root of *Alkanna tinctoria*, Tausch, *Anchusa tinctoria*, Desf., yields *anchusin* ($C_{35}H_{40}O_8$), a resinoid matter soluble in oils and fats. 2. *Annatto* or *Arnotto*, a paste prepared from the seeds of *Bixa orellana*, contains *bixin*, an orange-red, and *orellin*, a yellow principle. 3. *Brazil-wood* (*Cæsalpinia brasiliensis*) furnishes *brezilin*, the basis of several lakes. *Sapan-wood* and *Cam-wood* probably contain the same substance. 4. *Cinnabar*, Chinese red, Vermilion, or Paris red, is mercuric sulphide. 5. *Chrome-red* is an oxychromate of lead. 6. *Cochineal* (p. 277). 7. *Madder*, the root of *Rubia tinctorum*, powdered and treated with sulphuric acid and acidulated water to effect the removal of earthy and other inert matters, furnishes a residual powder termed *garancin*. Garancin yields to pure water *alizarin* ($C_{14}H_{10}O_4$, $3H_2O$), the red, neutral, crystallizable coloring-matter of madder. Alizarin does not exist ready formed in the plant, but is derived, by fermentation, from rubian, a yellowish resinoid substance. 8. *Mulberry-juice* (*Mori Succus*, B. B.) contains a violet-red coloring-matter which has not been chemically examined. 9. *Red lead* (p. 170). 10. *Red oxide of iron*, of shades varying from light to brown red, is found native. The common names of it are Armenian bole, Berlin-red, colcothar, English red, red ochre, burnt ochre, red earth, terra di sienna, mineral purple, stone red, and Indian red. 11. *Red Sandal-wood* (*Pterocarpi Lignum*, B. P. and U. S. P.), the billets and chips of *Pterocarpus santalinus*, owes its color to *santalin* ($C_{16}H_{16}O_3$), a resinoid matter. 12. *Red-Poppy Petals* (*Rhœdos Petula*, B. P.), from the *papaver rhœas*, contains a red coloring principle which has not yet been isolated. 13. *Red-Rose Petals* (*Rosæ Gallicæ Petala*, B. P. and U. S. P.) also yield a red substance which has not been analyzed. 14. *Safflower* or *Bastard Saffron*, the florets of *Carthamus tinctorius*, contains an unimportant yellow dye, and *carthamin* ($C_{14}H_{16}O_7$), an uncrystallizable red dye, the pigment of the old *pink saucers*. Mixed with French chalk, carthamin is used as a cosmetic under the name of *vegetable rouge*—*carmine* being *animal rouge*, and *peroxide of iron mineral rouge*. 15. *Lac-dye* is a cheap form of cochineal, and is also yielded by a species of *Coccus*. 16. *Logwood* (*Hæmatoxyli Lignum*, B. P.) contains a yellow substance, *hæmatoxylin* ($C_{16}H_{14}O_6H_2O$ or $3H_2O$), which, under the influence of air and alkali, assumes an intense red color. 17. *Red enamel* colors, for glass-staining and ceremic operations, are produced either by cuprous silicate or purple of Cassius (p. 200).

BLUE.—1. *Cobalt oxide* precipitated in combination or admixture with alumina or phosphate of calcium forms *Thénard's blue*, *cobalt-blue*, *Hoffner's blue*, and *cobaltic ultramarine*. 2. *Smalt*, *Saxony blue*, or *King's blue*, are rough cobalt glass in fine powder (p. 189). 3. *Copper-blue*, *mountain-blue*, and *English* or *Hambro' blue* are carbonates or oxycarbonates of copper. 4. *Indigo* (p. 239). 5. *Litmus*, *lichen-blue*, *turnsole*, *orchil* or *archil*, and *cudbear* are products of the action of air and alkalies on certain colorless principles, as *orcin* ($C_7H_8O_2$), derived from different species of lichen—*Roccella, Variolaria*, and *Lecanora*. 6. *Prussian blue* (p. 280) and *Turnbull's blue* (p. 281), the ferro- and ferridcyanides of iron, are met with under the names of *Erlangen, Louisa, Saxon, Paris* or *Berlin blue*. 7. *Ultramarine* is made on a large scale by roasting a mixture of fine white clay, carbonate of sodium, sulphur, and charcoal. Its constitution is not well made out. Acids decompose it, sulphuretted hydrogen escaping.

GREEN.—1. *Cupro-arsenical* green pigments (p. 136). 2. *Chlorophyll, Leaf-green*, or *Chromule*. A method of extracting chlorophyll is given on p. 406. It is of a resinoid nature, soluble in alcohol and ether, but insoluble in water, and, according to Frémy, consists of a blue substance, *phyllocyanin* ($C_{34}H_{68}N_4O_{17}$?), and a yellow, *phylloxanthin*; the yellow tints in fading autumnal leaves, he says, are due to the latter principle, the former being the first to fade. 3. *Sap-green, buckthorn-, vegetable-*, or *bladder-green* is obtained by evaporating to dryness a mixture of lime and the juice (*Rhamni Succus*, B. P.) of the berries of the Buckthorn (*Rhamnus catharticus*). It is soluble in water, slightly in alcohol, and insoluble in ether and oils. 4. *Green ultramarine* is made by a process similar to that for blue ultramarine. 5. Mixtures of blue and yellow pigments and dyes are common sources of green colors. 6. Glass and earthenware are colored green by oxide of chromium and black oxide of copper.

BROWN.—1. *Umber, Sienna*, or *Chestnut-brown* is found native. By heat it is darkened in tint, and is then known as *burnt umber*. It is a mixture of oxide of iron, silica, and alumina. 2. *Sepia* is a dried fluid from the ink-bag of cuttlefishes (*Sepiadæ*); by its ejection into adjacent water the animal obtains opportunity of escape from enemies. 3. *Catechu* (p. 295) furnishes a brown coloring-matter.

BLACK.—1. *Blacklead* (p. 26), *bone-black* (p. 82), or *ivory-black* and *lampblack*, the latter a deposited soot from the incomplete combustion of resin and tar, are varieties of carbon. 2. *Burnt sugar* or *caramel* (p. 377). 3. *Indian ink* is usually a dried mixture of fine lampblack and size, or thin glue. 4. *Black ink* is essentially tannates and gallates of iron suspended in water containing a little gum in solution. 5. *Printer's ink* is well boiled linseed or other oil, mixed with good lampblack, vermilion, or other pigment. 6. *Black dyes* are of the same nature as ink.

WHITE PIGMENTS.—1. *Chalk* or *Whiting* (p. 82). 2. *French chalk, steatite*, or *soapstone*, a silicate of magnesium. 3. *Heavy white* (p. 75). 4. *Pearl-white* (p. 206). 5. *Plaster of Paris* (p. 78). 6. *Starch* (p. 348). 7. *White lead* (p. 168). 8. *Zinc-white* (p. 99). 9. Oxides of tin and zinc and phosphate of calcium are employed for giving a white opacity to glass.

ANILINE COLORS. *Coal-tar colors.*—Within the last ten years nearly every shade of color seen in the animal or vegetable kingdoms has been successfully imitated by certain dyes and pigments primarily derived from a mineral, coal. Coal distilled for gas furnishes tar or gas-tar. Coal-tar contains some aniline; but especially it contains a liquid convertible into aniline, namely benzol (C_6H_5H), first discovered by Faraday in compressed oil-gas. From aniline, by oxidation, Runge obtained the violet color-reaction, the body producing which Perkin afterwards studied and isolated, and manufactured under the name of *mauve*. *Aniline-red* (*fuchsine*, *magenta*, or *roseaniline*), *aniline-yellow*, *aniline-green*, *aniline-blue*, and, in short, aniline-dyes, lakes, and pigments of every hue of the rainbow, are now common articles of trade. Their application has revolutionized the arts of the dyer and color-printer.

QUESTIONS AND EXERCISES.

837. Explain the production of color.
838. Mention the chief yellow coloring-matters.
839. What is annatto?
840. Name the colorific constituent of madder.
841. State the source of Litmus.
842. Distinguish between Prussian blue and Turnbull's blue.
843. How is blue ultramarine obtained?
844. Describe the coloring principle of green leaves.
845. By what agents is glass colored green?
846. Whence is sepia obtained?
847. Describe the chemistry of black ink.
848. Write a few sentences on *aniline colors*.

CHEMICAL TOXICOLOGY.

In cases of criminal and accidental poisoning, the substances presented to the chemical analyst for examination are usually articles of food, medicines, vomited matters, or the liver, kidney, intestines, stomach and contents, removed in course of post-mortem examination. In these cases some special operations are necessary before the poison can be isolated in a state of sufficient purity for the application of the usual tests; for in most instances the large quantity of animal and vegetable, or, in one word, organic matter present prevents or masks the characteristic reactions on which the tests are founded. These operations will now be described;* they form the chemical part of the subject of Toxicology (τοξικὸν, *toxicon*, poison, and λόγος, *logos*, discourse). Substances occurring in the form of an apparently definite salt or unmixed with organic matter need no special treatment, they are analyzed by the ordinary methods already given, attention being restricted to poisonous compounds only.

* Materials for these experiments are readily obtained for educational purposes by dissolving the poison in infusions of tea, coffee, porter, or in water to which some mucilage of starch or linseed-meal, pieces of bread, potato, and fat, have been added.

EXAMINATION OF AN ORGANIC MIXTURE SUSPECTED TO CONTAIN: MERCURY, ARSENICUM, ANTIMONY, LEAD, OR COPPER; SULPHURIC ACID, NITRIC ACID, HYDROCHLORIC ACID, OXALIC ACID, OR HYDROCYANIC ACID; STRYCHNIA OR MORPHIA.

Preliminary Examination.

Odor, Appearance, Taste.—Smell the mixture, with the view of ascertaining the presence or absence of any notable quantity of free hydrocyanic acid. Look carefully for any small solid particles, such as arsenic, corrosive sublimate, or verdigris, and for any appearance which may be regarded as abnormal, any character unusual to the coffee, tea, beer, medicine, vomit, coats of stomach, kidney, liver, or other organ, tissue, or solid matter under examination. If liquid or semifluid, taste the mixture, or add to a small portion some solution of carbonate of sodium, with the view of ascertaining by excessive sourness or strong effervescence the presence of any large, poisonous quantity of sulphuric, nitric, or hydrochloric acid.

If this preliminary examination does not indicate the method to be pursued, proceed as follows, treating a portion (not more than one-fourth) of the mixture for the poisonous metals, another for the acids, and a third for alkaloids, reserving the remainder for any special experiments which may suggest themselves in the course of the analysis.

Examination for Mercury, Arsenicum, Antimony, Lead, Copper, Zinc.

If a liquid, acidulate with hydrochloric acid and boil for a short time. If solid or semisolid, cut up the matter into small pieces, add enough water to form a fluid mixture, stir in ten or twenty per cent. of ordinary liquid hydrochloric acid, and boil until, from partial aggregation and solution of the solid matter, filtration can be easily effected.

Heat a portion of the clear liquid with a thin piece of bright copper or copper gauze, about an inch long and a quarter of an inch broad, for about ten or twenty minutes; metallic *mercury*, *arsenicum*, or *antimony* will be deposited on the copper, darkening it considerably in color. Pour off the liquid from the copper, carefully rinse the latter with a little cold water, dry the piece of metal by holding it over or near a flame (using fingers, not tongs, or it may become sufficiently hot for loss of mercury or arsenicum to occur by volatilization), introduce it into a narrow test-tube or piece of glass tubing closed at one end, and heat the bottom of the tube in a flame, holding it horizontally that the upper part of the tube may be kept cool, and partially closing the mouth with the finger to prevent escape of vapor. Under these circumstances any *Mercury* will volatilize from the copper and condense on the cool part of the tube in a ring or patch of white sublimate, readily aggregating into visible globules on being pressed by the side of a thin glass rod inserted into the tube; *Arsenicum* will volatilize from the copper, and, absorbing oxygen from the air in the tube, condense on the cool part of the glass in a ring or patch of white sublimate of arsenic (gray or even darker if much arsenicum as well as arsenic be present), not running into globules when rubbed, but occurring in small crystals, the characteristic octahedral form of which is readily seen by aid of a good hand lens, or the lower part of a microscope; *Antimony* volatilizes from the copper, if strongly heated, and, absorbing oxygen, immediately condenses as a slight white deposit close to the metal.

Confirmatory Tests.—1. Nothing short of the production of globules should be accepted as evidence of the presence of mercury. It will usually have existed as corrosive sublimate.

2. To confirm indications of the presence of arsenicum, a portion of the acid liquid may be subjected to the hydrogen tests (pp. 133, 135); or the tube containing the white crystalline arsenic may be broken, and the part on which the sublimate occurs boiled for some time in water, and the hydrosulphuric-acid, ammonio-nitrate-of-silver, and ammonio-sulphate-of-copper tests (pp. 135, 137) applied to the aqueous solution.

3. For antimony, a portion of the acid liquid must always be introduced into the hydrogen-apparatus with the usual precautions. (*Vide* p. 144.)

For *Lead* and *Copper*, pass hydrosulphuric acid gas through the clear acid liquid for some time, warming the liquid if no precipitate is produced, or diluting and partially neutralizing the acid by ammonia if much acid has been added. Collect on a filter any black precipitate that may have formed; wash, dissolve in a few drops of aqua regia, dilute, and apply the tests, ammonia for copper, sulphuric acid for lead, and any other of the ordinary reagents (pp. 151, 171).

Copper may often be at once detected in a small quantity of acidulated liquid by immersing the point of a penknife or a piece of bright iron wire—a deposit of copper, in its characteristic color, quickly or slowly appearing, according to the amount present (p. 151).

Zinc.—To the acid liquid through which sulphuretted hydrogen has been passed, add excess of ammonia (or to the original acid fluid add excess of ammonia, and then sulphydrate of ammonium); a precipitate falls which may contain alumina, phosphates, and zinc; it is usually blackish from the presence of sulphide of iron. Collect the precipitate on a filter, wash, dissolve in a little hydrochloric acid, add a few drops of nitric acid, boil, pour in excess of ammonia, filter, and test the filtrate with sulphydrate of ammonium—a white precipitate indicates zinc.

Examination for Mineral Acids, Oxalic Acid, or Hydrocyanic Acid.

To detect *Hydrochloric*, *Nitric*, or *Sulphuric Acid* in any liquid containing organic matter, dilute with water and apply to small portions the usual tests for each acid, disregarding indications of small quantities. (*Vide* pp. 222, 237, 257.)

Excessive sourness, copious evolution of carbonic acid gas on the addition of carbonate of sodium, and abundant evidence of acid on applying the various tests to small portions of the fluid presented for analysis, collectively form sufficient evidence of the occurrence of a poisonous amount of either of the three common mineral acids. Small quantities of the hydrochloric, nitric, and sulphuric radicals occurring as metallic salts or acids, are common normal constituents of food, hence the direction to disregard insignificant indications. If the fluid under examination is a vomit or the contents of a stomach, and an antidote has been administered, free acid will not be found, but, instead, a large amount of corresponding salt.

For *Oxalic Acid*, filter or strain a portion of the liquid, if not already clear, and add solution of acetate of lead so long as a precipitate occurs; collect the precipitate, which is partly oxalate of lead, on a filter, wash, transfer it to a test-tube or test-glass, add a little water, and pass hydrosulphuric gas through the mixture for a short time; the lead is thus converted into the insoluble form of sulphide, while oxalic acid is set free in the solution. Filter, boil to get rid of hydrosulphuric gas, and apply the usual tests for oxalic acid (see p. 262) to the clear filtrate.

For *Hydrocyanic Acid*, the three chief tests may be applied at once to the liquid or semiliquid organic mixture, whether it has an odor of hydrocyanic acid or not. First: half fill a small porcelain crucible with the material, add eight or ten drops of strong sulphuric acid, stir gently with a glass rod, and invert over the mouth of the crucible a watch-glass moistened with a small drop of solution of nitrate of silver; a white film on the silver solution is probably cyanide of silver, formed by the action of the gaseous hydrocyanic acid on the nitrate of silver. Second: prepare a small quantity of the organic mixture as before, slightly moistening the centre of the watch-glass with solution of potash; here again the heat generated by the action of the strong acid is sufficient to volatilize some of the hydrocyanic acid, which, reacting on the potash, forms cyanide of potassium. On removing the watch-glass and stirring into it successively solution of a ferrous salt, a ferric salt, and hydrochloric acid, flocks of prussian blue are produced if hydrocyanic acid is present. Third: proceed as before, moistening the watch-glass with sulphydrate of ammonium; after exposure to the hydrocyanic gas for five or ten minutes, add a drop of solution of ammonia, evaporate to dryness at a low temperature, and add a drop of hydrochloric acid and of solution of perchloride of iron; a blood-red color, due to sulphocyanate of iron, is produced if cyanogen is present.

If the above reactions are not well marked, the organic mixture may be carefully and slowly distilled in a small retort, the neck of which passes into a bottle and dips beneath the surface of a little water at the bottom of the bottle, and the reagents then applied to separate portions of the distillate.

The examination of organic mixtures for hydrocyanic acid must be made without delay, as the poison soon begins to decompose, and in a day or two is usually destroyed.

Examination for Phosphorus.

A paste containing phosphorus is commonly employed for destroying vermin. In cases of poisoning the phosphorus is usually in sufficient quantity to be recognized by its characteristic unpleasant smell. A stomach in which it occurs not unfrequently exhibits slight luminosity if opened in a dark room. When the phosphorus is too small in quantity or too much diffused to afford this appearance, a portion of the material is placed in a flask, water acidulated by sulphuric acid added, a long wide glass tube fitted to the neck of the flask by a cork, and the mixture gently boiled. If phosphorus is present (even 1 part in 2,000,000, according to De Vry) the top of the column of steam as it condenses in the tube will appear distinctly phosphorescent when viewed in a dark room. From its liability to oxidation phosphorus cannot be detected after much exposure of an organic mixture to air.

Examination for Strychnia and Morphia.

Strychnia.—If solid or semisolid, digest the matter with water and about 10 per cent. of hydrochloric acid till fluid, filter, evaporate to dryness over a water-bath. If the organic mixture is already liquid, it is simply acidulated with hydrochloric acid and evaporated to dryness. The acid residue is next treated with spirit of wine as long as anything is dissolved, the filtered tincture evaporated to dryness over the water-bath, and the residue digested in water and filtered. This slightly acid aqueous solution must now be rendered alkaline by ammonia, and well shaken in a bottle or long tube with about half an ounce of chloroform, and set by till the chloroform has subsided. The chloroform (which contains the strychnia) is then removed by a pipette, the presence of any aqueous liquid being carefully avoided, and evaporated to dryness in a small basin over a water-bath, the residue moistened with concentrated sulphuric acid, and the basin kept over the water-bath for several hours. (It is highly important that the sulphuric acid used in this operation should be free from nitrous compounds. Test the acid, therefore, by adding powdered sulphate of iron, which becomes pink if nitrous bodies are present. If these are found, the acid should be purified by strongly heating with sulphate of ammonium, seventy or eighty grains to a pint.) The charred material is exhausted with water, filtered, excess of ammonia added, the filtrate shaken with about a quarter of an ounce of chloroform, the mixture set aside for the chloroform to separate, and the chloroform again removed. If on evaporating a small portion of this chloroform solution to dryness, adding a drop of sulphuric acid to the residue, and warming, any darkening in color or charring takes place, the strychnia is not sufficiently pure for chemical detection; in that case the rest of the chloroform must be removed by evaporation, and the residue redigested in warm sulphuric acid for two or three hours. Dilution, neutralization of acid by ammonia, and agitation with chloroform is again practised, and the residue of a small portion of the chloroform solution once more tested with sulphuric acid. If charring still occurs, the treatment must be repeated a third time. Finally a part of the chloroform solution is taken up by a pipette, and drop after drop evaporated on one spot of a porcelain crucible-lid until a fairly distinct dry residue is obtained. A drop of sulphuric acid is placed on the spot, another drop placed near, a minute fragment of red chromate of potassium placed in the second drop, and when the acid has become tinged with the chromate, one drop drawn across the other; the characteristic evanescent purple color is then seen, if strychnia is present. Other tests (*vide* p. 324) may be applied to similar spots.

This is Girwood and Rogers's method for the detection of strychnia when mixed with organic matter. It is tedious but trustworthy, and, though apparently complicated, very simple in principle; thus strychnia is soluble in acidulated water or alcohol, or in chloroform, readily removed from an alkaline liquid by agitation with chloroform, and not charred or otherwise attacked when heated to 212° F. with sulphuric acid: much of the organic matter of the food is insoluble in water; of that soluble in water, much is insoluble in alcohol; and of that soluble in both menstrua, all is charred and destroyed by warm sulphuric acid in a shorter or longer time.

Morphia, and the Meconic Acid with which it is associated in Opium.—To the liquid or the semifluid mixture warmed for some time with a small quantity of acetic acid, filtered, and concentrated if necessary, add solution of acetate of lead until no further precipitate is produced. Filter and examine the *precipitate* for meconic acid, reserving the *filtrate* for the detection of morphia.

The Precipitate.—Wash the *precipitate* (meconate of lead, &c.) with water, place it in a test-tube or test-glass with a small quantity of water, pass hydrosulphuric acid gas through the mixture for a short time, filter, slightly warm in a small basin, well stirring to promote removal of excess of the gas, and add a drop of neutral solution of perchloride of iron; a red color, due to the formation of meconate of iron, is produced if meconic acid is present. This color is not destroyed on boiling the liquid, as is the case with ferric acetate, nor is it bleached by solution of corrosive sublimate, thus distinguishing it from the ferric sulphocyanate. It is discharged by hydrochloric acid.

The Filtrate.—The solution from which meconic acid has been removed by acetate of lead is evaporated to a small bulk over a water-bath, excess of carbonate of potassium added, and evaporation continued to dryness. The residue is then treated with alcohol, which dissolves the morphia. The alcoholic solution evaporated similarly may leave the morphia sufficiently pure for the application of the usual tests (*vide* page 318) to small portions of the residue. If no reaction is obtained, add a drop of sulphuric acid and a little water to the residue and shake with ether, in which the salt of morphia is insoluble. The treatment with ether may be repeated until nothing more is removed, the acid aqueous liquid saturated with carbonate of potassium, the mixture evaporated to dryness, the residue digested in alcohol, filtered, and portions of the alcoholic liquid evaporated to obtain spots of morphia for the application of the ordinary tests.

The examination for morphia must be conducted with great care, and with as large a quantity of material as can be spared; for its isolation from other organic matter is an operation of considerable difficulty, especially when only a minute proportion of alkaloid is present. Fortunately the detection of meconic acid does not include similar difficulties; and as its reactions are quite characteristic, its presence is held to be strong evidence of the existence of opium in an organic mixture.

ANTIDOTES.

Vide "Antidotes" in the Index.

QUESTIONS AND EXERCISES.

849. In examining food and similar matter for poison, why must not the ordinary tests for the poison be at once applied?

850. What preliminary operations should be performed on a vomit in a case of suspected poisoning?

851. How would you proceed in searching for corrosive sublimate in wine?

852. By what series of operations would you satisfy yourself of the presence or absence of arsenic in the contents of a stomach?

853. Describe the treatment to which decoction of coffee should be subjected in testing it for tartar-emetic.

854. State the method by which the occurrence of lead in water is demonstrated.

855. Give a process for the detection of copper in jam.

856. How may the presence of a poisonous quantity of sulphuric acid in gin be proved?

857. In examining ale for free nitric acids what reactions would be selected?

858. Show how you would conclude that a dangerous quantity of hydrochloric acid had been added to cider.

859. Describe the manipulations necessary in testing for hydrocyanic acid in the contents of the stomach.

860. By what method is oxalic acid discovered in infusion of coffee?

861. Give the process by which strychnia is isolated from partially digested food.

862. Mention the experiments by which the presence of laudanum in porter is demonstrated.

863. Name the appropriate antidotes in cases of poisoning by: *a*, alkaloids; *b*, antimonials; *c*, arsenic; *d*, barium salts; *e*, copper compounds; *f*, hydrochloric acid; *g*, hydrocyanic acid; *h*, preparations of lead; *i*, corrosive sublimate; *j*, nitric acid; *k*, oxalic acid; *l*, salts of silver; *m*, oil of vitriol; *n*, tin liquors; *o*, zinc solutions; *p*, carbolic acid.

EXAMINATION OF MORBID URINE AND CALCULI.

The various products of the natural and continuous decay of animal tissue and the refuse matter of food are eliminated from the system chiefly as feces, urine, and expired air. Air exhaled from the lungs carries off from the blood much carbon (about 8 ounces in 24 hours) in the form of carbonic acid gas, and some aqueous vapor—the latter, together with a small amount of oily matter, also escaping by the skin. Directing the breath to a cold surface renders moisture evident; and breathing through a tube into lime-water demonstrates the presence of a considerable quantity of carbonic acid gas. The feces consist mainly of the insoluble *débris* of the system, the soluble matters and water forming the urine. These excretions vary considerably, according to the food and general habits of the individual and external temperature. But in disease the variations become excessive; their detection by the medical practitioner, or by the pharmacist for the medical practitioner, is therefore a matter of importance.

A complete analysis of feces, urine, or expelled air cannot be performed in the present state of our knowledge. Nor can any analysis of feces or air be made with sufficient ease and rapidity to be practically available in medical diagnosis. But with regard to urine, certain abnormal substances and abnormal quantities of normal constituents may be chemically detected in the course of a few minutes by any one having already some knowledge of chemical manipulation.

Healthy Human Urine contains, in 1000 parts, 957 of water, 14 of urea, 1 of uric acid, 15 of other organic matter, and 13 of inorganic salts.

Examination of Morbid Urine for Albumen, Sugar, and excess of Urea; and Urinary Sediment for Urates (or Lithates), Phosphates, Oxalate of Calcium, and Uric Acid.

Albumen.—To detect albumen, acidulate a portion of the clear urine in a test-tube with a few drops of acetic acid (to keep phosphates in solution) and boil; flocks or coagula will separate if albumen be present.

This experiment should first be made on normal urine containing a drop or two of solution of white of egg. A coagulum of pure albumen is white, greenish if bile pigment is present, and brownish-red if the urine contains blood. The influence of acids and alkalies on the precipitation of albumen is noticed on page 366.

The occurrence of albumen in the urine may be temporary and of but little importance; or it may indicate the existence of a serious affection, known as Bright's disease.

Sugar.—To a portion of the clear urine in a test-tube add five or ten drops of solution of sulphate of copper; pour in solution of potash or soda until the precipitate first formed is redissolved; slowly heat the solution to near the boiling-point: a yellow, yellowish-red, or red precipitate (cuprous oxide) is formed if sugar is present.

This experiment should first be made on urine containing a drop or two of solution of grape-sugar (page 338). The hydrate of copper precipitated by the alkali is insoluble in excess of pure potash or soda, but readily dissolves if organic matters, especially sugar, is present. The copper salt must not contain iron.

Other tests may be applied if necessary (*vide* page 338.)

A minute amount of sugar is said to occur in normal urine and a distinct trace is occasionally present. In larger quantities it is a characteristic constituent of the urine of diabetic patients.

Excess of Urea.—Nearly one-half of the solid matter in the urine is urea. Its proportion varies considerably; but $1\frac{1}{2}$ per cent. may be regarded as an average amount. Concentrate urine slightly by evaporation in a small dish, pour the liquid into the test-tube, set the tube aside till cold, or cool it by letting cold water run over the outside, add an equal bulk of strong nitric acid and again set aside; scaly crystals of nitrate of urea are deposited more or less quickly.

With regard to the amount of urea in urine, it is impossible to sharply define excess or deficiency. If nitric acid gives crystals without concentration, excess is certainly present. A rough estimate may be formed by mixing a few drops of the urine and acid on a piece of glass and setting aside; the time which elapses before crystals form is an indication of the quantity in the specimen. The time will vary according to the temperature and state of moisture of the atmosphere; but with care some useful comparative results may in this way be obtained.

Tests.—Urea in solution in water may be detected by the above reaction with nitric acid, and by the readiness with which it yields ammonia on being boiled with alkalies. In putrid urine its conversion into an ammoniacal salt has already been effected.

$$\underset{\text{Urea.}}{CH_4N_2O} + \underset{\text{Water.}}{2H_2O} = \underset{\text{Carb. of ammon.}}{(NH_4)_2CO_3}.$$

Formula of Urea.—The empirical formula of urea is CH_4N_2O. Its rational formula may be thus written:— $\left.\begin{matrix}(CO)''\\H_2\\H_2\end{matrix}\right\} N_2$; that is, it may be regarded as one of the organic bases already referred to, a primary diamine, in which the bivalent radical CO occupies the place of H_2. The other atoms of hydrogen may be displaced by various radicals, and many *compound ureas* be thus obtained.

Artificial Urea.—Urea may be prepared artificially by Williams's modification of Wöhler's method. Cyanide of potassium, of the best commercial quality (containing about 90 per cent. of real cyanide), is fused at a very low red heat in a shallow iron vessel; red lead is added in small quantities at a time, the temperature being kept down by constant stirring. When the red lead ceases to cause further action the mixture (cyanate of potassium and lead) is allowed to cool, the product finely powdered, exhausted with cold water, nitrate of barium added till no more precipitate (carbonate of barium) falls, the mixture filtered and the filtrate treated with nitrate of lead so long as cyanate of lead is thrown down. The latter is thoroughly washed, and dried at a low temperature. Equivalent quantities of cyanate of lead and sulphate of ammonium digested in a small quantity of water at a gentle heat and filtered yield a solution from which urea crystallizes on cooling.

Another process.—Basaroff has found that urea is produced when ordinary carbonate of ammonium is heated in hermetically sealed tubes to about 275° F. for a few hours. The same chemist had previously obtained urea by similarly heating pure carbamate of ammonium, so that the source of the urea in the former case is probably the carbamate of ammonium believed to occur in the carbonate (see page 67).

$$NH_4NH_2CO_2 - H_2O = CH_4N_2O.$$

URINARY SEDIMENTS.

Warm the sediment with the supernatant urine and filter.

<table>
<tr>
<td colspan="3">Insoluble.
Phosphates, oxalate of calcium, and uric acid.
Warm with acetic acid, and filter.</td>
<td rowspan="3">Soluble.
Urates—of ammonium, calcium, or sodium, chiefly the latter.
They are redeposited as the liquid cools, and if sufficient in quantity may be further examined for ammonium, calcium, sodium, and the uric radical by the appropriate tests.</td>
</tr>
<tr>
<td colspan="2">Insoluble.
Oxalate of calcium and uric acid.
Warm with hydrochloric acid, filter.</td>
<td rowspan="2">Soluble.
Phosphates.
Add ammonia, white ppt. = phosphate of calcium, or ammonio-magnesium phosphate, or both.</td>
</tr>
<tr>
<td>Insoluble.
Uric acid.
Apply murexid test (p. 297).</td>
<td>Soluble.
Oxalate of calcium.
May be reprecipitated by ammonia.</td>
</tr>
</table>

Notes.—Urinary deposits are seldom of a complex character: the action of heat and acetic and hydrochloric acids generally at once indicates the character of the deposit, rendering filtration and precipitation unnecessary.

The urates are often of a pink or red color, owing to the presence of a pigment termed *purpurine;* hence the common name of *red gravel* for such deposits. *Purpurine* is soluble in alcohol, and may be removed by digesting a red deposit in that solvent. It is seldom necessary to determine whether the urate be that of ammonium, calcium, or sodium (see also Uric Acid, page 296).

The *phosphate of calcium* and the *ammonio-magnesium phosphate* are usually both present in a phosphatic deposit, the magnesium salt forming the larger proportion. They may, if necessary, and if sufficient in quantity, be separated by collecting on a filter, washing, and boiling with solution of carbonate of sodium. The carbonates of calcium and magnesium thus formed are collected on a filter, washed, dissolved in a drop or two of hydrochloric acid—chloride of ammonium, ammonia, and carbonate of ammonium added, the mixture boiled and filtered; any calcium originally present will then remain insoluble as carbonate of calcium, while any magnesium will be reprecipitated from the filtrate as ammonio-magnesian phosphate on the addition of phosphate of sodium, the mixture being also well stirred.——The chief portion of excreted phosphates is carried off by the fæces, that remaining in the urine being kept in solution by the influence of acid phosphate of sodium, and, frequently, lactic acid.——Occasionally, an hour or two after a hearty meal, the urine becomes sufficiently alkaline for the phosphates to be deposited, and the urine when passed is turbid from their presence.——The ammoniacal constituent of the magnesium salt does not occur normally, but is produced from urea as soon as urine becomes alkaline.

Oxalate of calcium is seldom met with in excessive amounts, but very often in small quantities mixed with phosphates.

Free uric acid is in most cases distinctly crystalline, and nearly always of a yellow, red, or brown color.

Artificial Sediments.—For educational practice, artificial deposits may be obtained as follows: 1. Rub up in a mortar a few grains of serpent's excrement (chiefly urate of ammonium) with an ounce or two of urine; this represents a sediment of urates. 2. Add a few drops of solution of chloride of calcium and of phosphate of sodium to urine; the deposit may be regarded as one of phosphates. 3. To an ounce or two of urine add very small quantities of chloride of calcium and oxalate of ammonium; the precipitate is oxalate of calcium. 4. To urine acidulated by hydrochloric acid add a little serpent's excrement; the sediment is uric acid.

Other deposits than the foregoing are occasionally observed. Thus *hippuric acid* ($HC_9H_8NO_3$), a normal constituent of human urine, and largely contained in the urine of herbivorous animals, is sometimes found associated with uric acid in urinary sediment, especially in that of patients whose medicine contains benzoic acid (p. 279). Its appearance, as observed by aid of the microscope, is characteristic—namely, slender, four-sided prisms, having pointed ends. *Cystin* ($C_3H_7NSO_2$) (from κύστις, *kūstis*, a bladder, in allusion to its origin) rarely occurs as a deposit in urine. It is not soluble in warmed urine or dilute acetic acid, and scarcely in dilute hydrochloric acid, hence would be met with in testing for free uric acid. It is very soluble in ammonia, recrystallizing from a drop of the solution placed on a piece of glass in characteristic microscopic six-sided plates. *Organized sediments* may be due to the corpuscles of pus, mucus, or blood, fat-globules, spermatozoa, cylindrical casts of the tubes of the kidneys, epithelial cells from the walls of the bladder, or foreign matters, such as fibres of wool, cotton, small feathers, dust; these are best recognized by the microscope, as will be seen by the following paragraphs and figures on the microscopic appearances of both crystalline and organized urinary sediments.

Microscopic Examination of Urinary Sediments.

Urine containing insoluble matter is usually more or less opaque. For microscopical examination a few ounces should be set aside in a conical test-glass for an hour or two, the clear supernatant urine poured off from the sediment as far as possible, a small drop of the residue placed on a slip of glass and covered with a piece of thin glass and examined under the microscope with different magnifying-powers.

The respective appearances of the various crystalline and organized matters are given in the following figures, which were drawn from natural specimens (as seen with a two-third inch objective and No. 1 eye piece, *i. e.*, magnified 60 diameters) in the collections of St. Bartholomew's Hospital, H. B. Brady, F. L. S., Dr. Sedgwick, W. W. Stoddart, F. C. S., Mr. Waddington, and the Author.

Uric Acid occurs in many forms, most of which are given in the first two figures. Flat, more or less oval crystals, sometimes attached

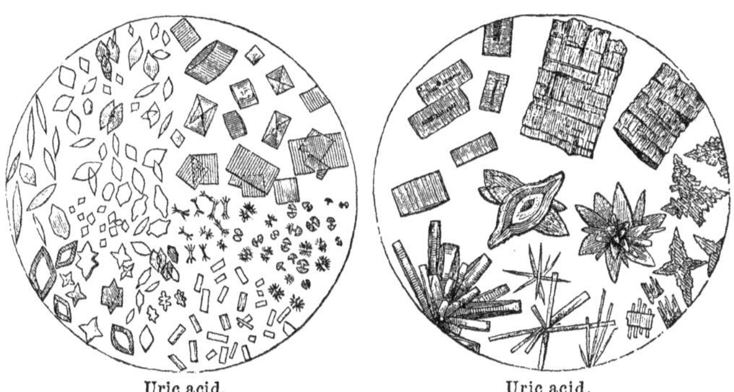

Uric acid. Uric acid.

to each other, their outline then resembling an 8, a cross, or a star, are common. Single and grouped quadratic prisms, aigrettes, spicula, and crystals recalling dumb-bells are met with. From urine acidulated by hydrochloric acid, square crystals, two opposite sides smooth and two jagged, are generally deposited: acidulated by acetic acid more typical forms are obtained. A drop of solution of potash or soda placed on a glass slip will dissolve a deposit of uric acid, a drop of any acid reprecipitating it in minute but characteristic crystals.

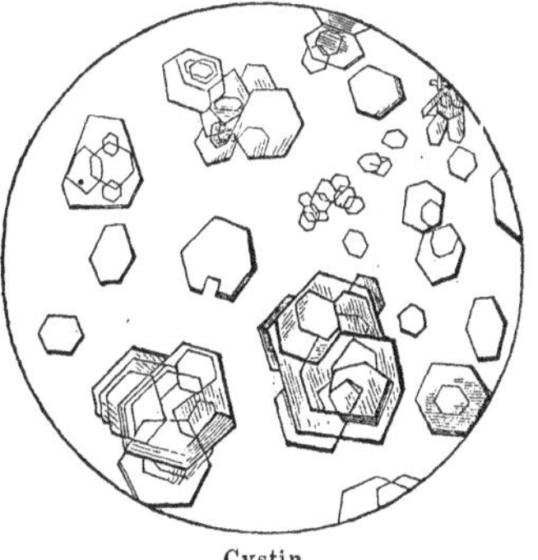

Cystin.

Cystin is very rarely met with as a urinary deposit; that from which the figure was taken was found in the urine of a patient in St. Bartholomew's Hospital. Lamellæ of cystin always assume an hexagonal character; but the angles are sometimes ill defined and the plates superposed: in the latter case, a drop of solution of ammonia placed on the glass at once dissolves the deposit, well-marked six-sided crystals appearing as the drop dries up.

Triple Phosphate (phosphate of magnesium and ammonium) is deposited as soon as urine becomes alkaline, the ammoniacal constituent being furnished by the decomposition of urea. It occurs in large prismatic crystals, forming a beautiful object when viewed by polarized light—sometimes also in ragged stellate or arborescent crystals, resembling those of snow. Both forms may be artificially prepared by adding a small lump of carbonate of ammonium to a few ounces of urine set aside in a test-glass.

Triple Phosphate.

Amorphous deposits are either *earthy phosphates* (a mixture of phosphates of magnesium and calcium) or *urates* (of calcium, magnesium, ammonium, potassium, or sodium—chiefly the latter). They may be distinguished by the action of a drop of acetic acid placed near the sediment on the glass slip, the effect being watched under the microscope; phosphates dissolve, while urates gradually assume characteristic forms of uric acid. Urates redissolve when warmed with the supernatant urine.

Urates of Sodium and Magnesium, though generally amorphous, occasionally take a crystalline form—bundles or tufts of small needles—as shown in the cut.

Oxalate of Calcium commonly occurs in octahedra requiring high magnifying power for their detection. The crystals are easily overlooked if other matters are present, but are more distinctly seen after phosphates have been removed by acetic acid. In certain aspects the smaller crystals look like square plates traversed by a cross. A dumb-bell form of this deposit is also sometimes seen, resembling certain forms of uric acid and the coalescing spherules of a much rarer sediment—carbonate of calcium. Oxalate of calcium is insoluble in acetic but soluble in hydrochloric acid. The octahedra are frequently met with in the urine of persons who have partaken of garden rhubarb; the crystals may often be deposited artificially by dropping a fragment of oxalic acid into several ounces of urine and setting aside for several hours (Waddington).

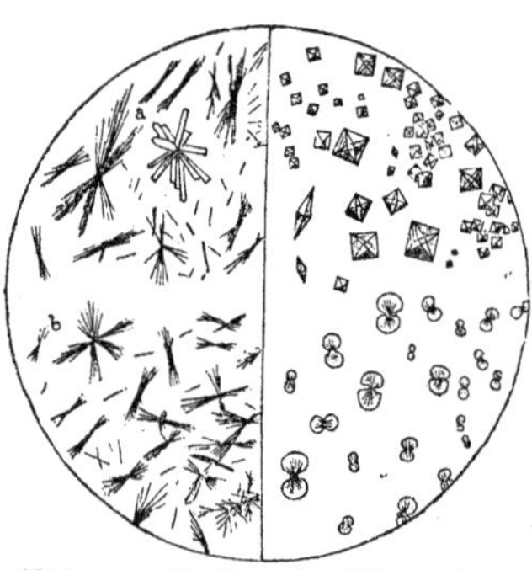

Urates, a, of Sodium, b, of Magnesium.
Oxalate of Calcium.

Carbonate of Calcium is rarely found in the urine of man, but frequently in that of the horse and other herbivorous animals. Human urine containing carbonate of calcium often reddens litmus paper; and it is only after the removal, on standing, of the excess of carbonic acid that the salt is deposited. It consists of minute spherules, varying in size, the smaller ones often in process of coalescence. The dumb-bell form thus produced is easily distinguished from similar groups of uric acid or oxalate of calcium by showing a black cross in each spherule when viewed by polarized light. Acetic acid dissolves carbonate of calcium, liberating carbonic acid gas, with visible effervescence (under the microscope) if the slide has been previously warmed and a group of crystals be attacked.

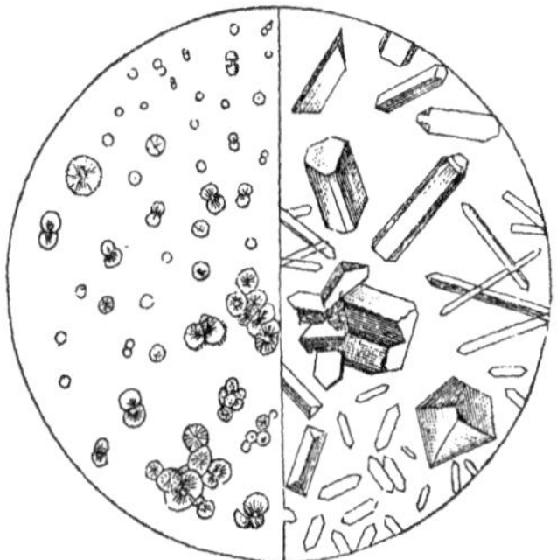

Carbonate of Calcium. Hippuric Acid.

Hippuric Acid.—The pointed rhombic prisms and acicular crystals are characteristic, and easily recognized. The broader crystals may possibly be mistaken for triple phosphate, and the narrower for certain forms of uric acid; but insolubility in acetic acid distinguishes them from the former, and solubility in alcohol from the latter. These tests may be applied while the deposit is under microscopic observation. An alcoholic solution of hippuric acid evaporated to dryness, and the residue treated with water, gives a solution from which characteristic crystalline forms of hippuric acid may be obtained on allowing a drop to dry upon a slip of glass.

The organized deposits in urine entail greater care in their determination, and usually require a higher magnifying power for their proper examination than those of crystalline form. The figures are drawn to 230 diameters. The following notes will assist the observer.

Casts of uriniferous tubuli are fibrinous masses of various forms, and often of considerable length—sometimes delicate and transparent, occasionally granular, and often beset with fat-globules. Epithelial *débris* are frequently present in urine in the form of nucleated cells, regular and oval when full, but angular and unsymmetrical when partially emptied of their contents—sometimes perfect, but more frequently a good deal broken up.

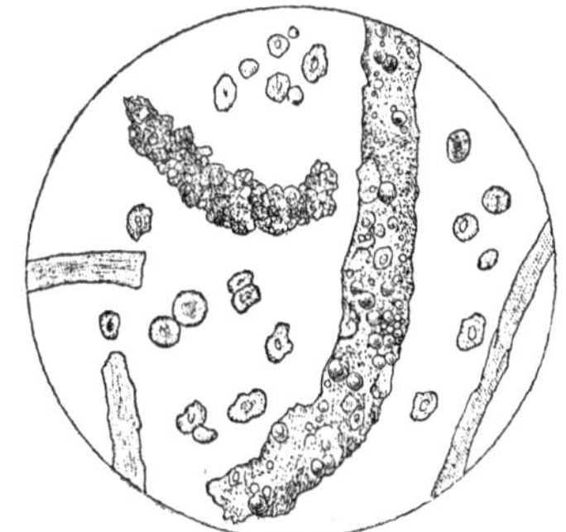

Epithelial Cells and Tubuli.

Blood is easily recognized. Urine containing it is high-colored, and the corpuscles appear under the microscope as reddish circular disks, either single or laid together in strings resembling piles of coin. Their color and somewhat smaller size serve to distinguish them from pus-corpuscles. In doubtful cases a drop of blood from the finger should be diluted with water and used for comparison. After urine containing blood has stood for some time, the corpuscles lose their regular outline and become angular. (See *a* in the figure.) Day, of Geelong, tests for blood in urine, or in stains on clothing, by adding a few drops of a recently prepared alcoholic solution of the inner unoxidized portions of guaiacum resin and then a small quantity of Robbins' aqueous or ethereal solution of peroxide of hydrogen, when a blue color results. If the stain is on a dark-colored fabric, the moistened parts may be pressed with white blotting paper, when blue impressions will be obtained. Contact with many substances causes the blue reaction or oxidation of guaiacum; the peculiarity of blood is that it does not produce this effect unless peroxide of hydrogen or a similar antozonic liquid is present. Bodies such as permanganate of potassium, whose oxygen is, apparently, in the form of ozone, also gives rise to a blue color with guaiacum; peroxide of hydrogen and other compounds whose oxygen is in the opposite, positive, or, according to Schönbein, antagonistic condition, produce no such effect. It would seem as if blood or some other constituent of blood has the power of converting positive into negative oxygen, and thus cause an effect which negative oxygen alone is able to produce; for of all substances which, like blood, do not alone cause guaiacum to become blue, blood is the only one that so affects antozonides (themselves inactive) as to enable them to act as ozonides, that is to oxidize the guaiacum. Both the venous and arterial fluid from any red-blooded animal will produce this blue reaction. Fruit stains are darkened by ammonia, which does not alter the color of blood. Iron stains or iron-mould yield no color to water, whereas the red coloring matter of blood is soluble in water. The peroxide of hydrogen should be free from more than a trace of acid.

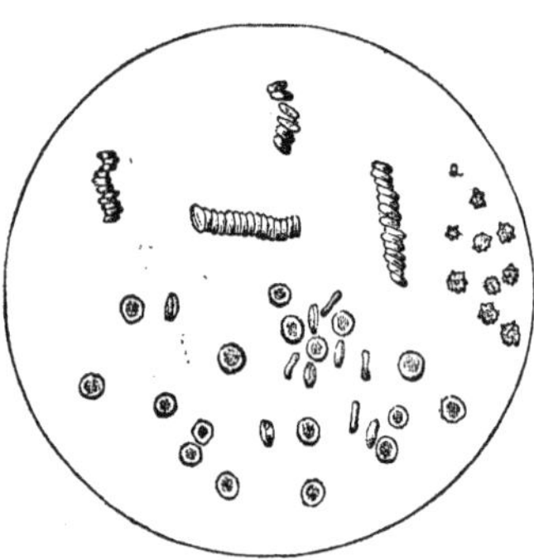

Blood Corpuscles.

Pus and Mucus.—Purulent urine deposits, on standing, a light-colored layer, easily diffused through the liquid by shaking. Acetic acid does not dissolve the sediment; and solution of potash, of official strength, converts it into a gelatinous mass. Under the microscope, pus-corpuscles appear rounded and colorless, rather larger than blood-disks, and somewhat granular on the surface. They generally show minute nuclei, which are more distinctly seen after treatment with acetic acid. (See the portion of the figure marked *a*.) Mucus possesses no definite microscopic characters, but commonly has imbedded in it pus, epithelium, and air-bubbles. Mucus is coagulated in a peculiar and characteristic manner by acetic acid; and this reaction, together with the ropy appearance it imparts to urine, prevents its being confounded with pus. Day's test for pus consists in adding a drop or two of oxidized tincture of guaiacum, to the urine or other liquid, when a clear blue color is produced. It is necessary to moisten dry pus with water before applying the test. The test liquid is made by exposing a saturated alcoholic solution of guaiacum to the air until it has absorbed a sufficient quantity of oxygen to give it the property of turning green when placed in contact with iodide of potassium. Day's test for mucus consists in the application, first, of oxidized tincture of guaiacum, which by itself undergoes no change in the presence of mucus, and then in the addition of carbolic acid or creasote, which quickly changes the color of the guaiacum to a bright blue. Neither carbolic acid nor creasote alone will render guaiacum blue. In testing for mucus on cloths, or when it is mixed with blood, it is necessary to use the carbolic acid pure, but when the mucus is in a liquid state it is better to use carbolic acid diluted with alcohol.

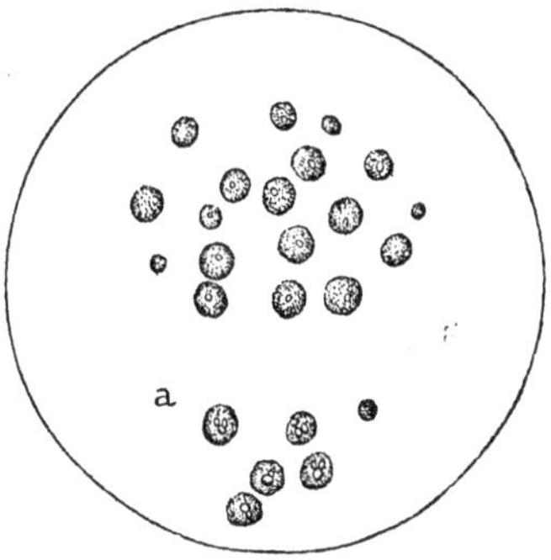

Pus Corpuscles.

Saliva.—Saliva is an aqueous fluid containing less than 1 per cent. of solid matter, of which one-third is an albumenoid substance termed *ptyalin* (from πτύελον, *spittle*), a body that has power of converting starch into dextrin and grape sugar. Alkaline salts, including a trace of sulphocyanide of potassium, and calcareous compounds, are also present.

Day's test for saliva in urine, etc., is similar to that for mucus, with the exception that the blue reaction produced by the oxidized tincture of guaiacum and alcoholic solution of carbolic acid is highly intensified by the addition of Robbins' aqueous or ethereal solution of peroxide of hydrogen.

Fatty matter occurs either as minute globules partially diffused through the urine (as shown at *a*) or in more intimate emulsion (as at *b* in the

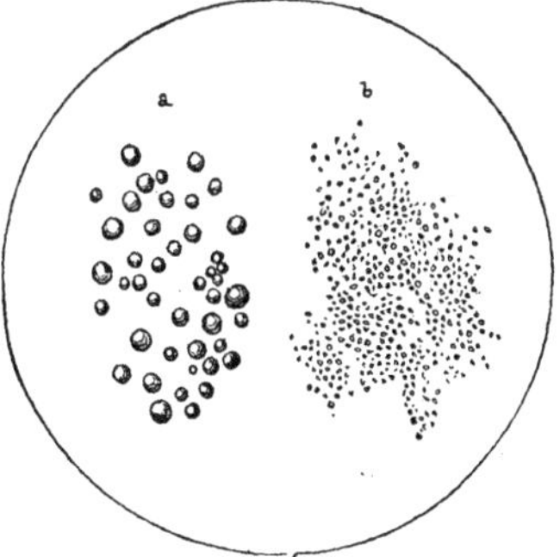

Fat Globules.

figure). When present in larger quantity, it collects as a sort of skim on the surface after standing.

Spermatozoa are liable to escape notice, on account of their small size and extreme transparency. Suspected urine should be allowed to settle some hours in a conical test-glass, and the drop at the bottom examined under a high power. The drawing shows their tadpole-like appearance.

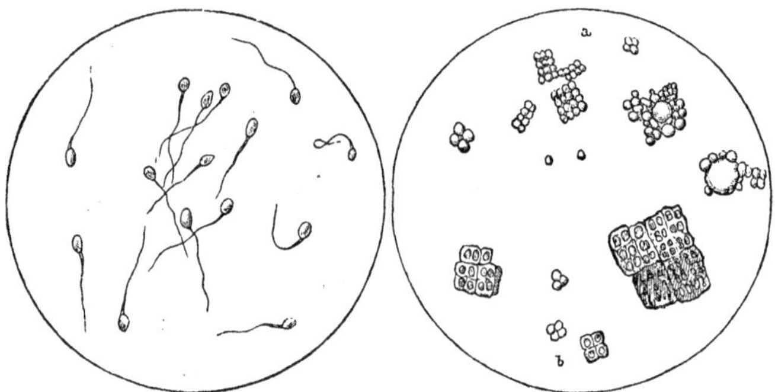

Spermatozoa. Sarcina Ventriculi.

Sarcina ventriculi is an alga of very rare occurrence in urine, though not unfrequent in the matters vomited during certain diseases of the stomach. The upper figures (*a*) are copied from Dr. Thudichum's drawing (from urine); the larger fronds (*b*) are from vomited matter.

Extraneous bodies, such as hair, wool, or fragments of feathers, are often found in urinary deposits; and ludicrous mistakes have been made by observers not on their guard in respect to such casual admixtures.

Examination of Urinary Calculi.

The term *calculus* is the diminutive of *calx*, a lime- or chalk-stone. Knowledge of the composition of a calculus or urinary deposit affords valuable diagnostic aid to the physician; hence the importance of a correct analysis of these substances.

Nature of Calculi.—Urinary calculi have the same composition as unorganized urinary sediments. They consist, in short, of sediments that have been deposited slowly within the bladder, particle on particle, layer on layer, the several substances becoming so compact as to be less easily acted on by reagents than when deposited after the urine has been passed—the urates less readily soluble in warm water, the calcic phosphate insoluble in acetic acid until it has been dissolved in hydrochloric acid and reprecipitated by an alkali.

Preliminary treatment.—If the calculus is whole, saw it in two through the centre, and notice whether it is built up of distinct layers or apparently consists of one substance. If the latter, use about a grain of the sawdust for the analysis; if the former, carefully scrape off portions of each layer, and examine them separately. If the calculus is in fragments, select fair specimens of about half a grain or a grain each, and reduce to a fine powder by placing on a hard surface and crushing under the blade of a knife.

Analysis.—Commence the analysis by heating a portion about the size of a pin's head, on platinum foil, in order to ascertain whether organic matter, inorganic matter, or both, are present. If both, the ash is examined for inorganic substances, and a fresh portion of the calculus for uric acid by the murexid test. (In the absence of uric acid any slight charring may be considered to be due to indefinite animal matter.) If composed of organic matter only, the calculus will in nearly all cases be uric acid, the indication being confirmed by applying the murexid test in a watch-glass to another fragment, half the size of a small pin's head. If organic only, the ash on the platinum foil may be examined for phosphates, and a separate portion of the calculus for oxalates. Even a single drop of liquid obtained in any of these experiments may be filtered by placing it on a filter not larger than a sixpence and previously moistened with water, and adding three or four drops of water one after the other as each passes through the paper. If the calculus is suspected to contain more than one substance, boil about half a grain of the powder in half a test-tubeful of distilled water for a few minutes and pour it on a small filter. Proceed according to the following Table:—

<table>
<tr><td colspan="3">Insoluble.
Phosphates, oxalates of calcium, and free uric acid.
Boil with two or three drops of hydrochloric acid and filter.</td><td rowspan="3">Soluble.
Urates.
These will probably be redeposited as the solution cools. Small quantities may be detected by evaporating the solution to dryness. They are tested for ammonium, sodium, calcium, and the uric radical by the appropriate reagents.</td></tr>
<tr><td rowspan="2">Insoluble.
Uric acid. Apply the murexid test (p. 297).</td><td colspan="2">Soluble.
Phosphates and oxalate of calcium.
Add excess of ammonia, and then excess of acetic acid; filter.</td></tr>
<tr><td>Insoluble.
Oxalate of calcium.</td><td>Soluble.
Phosphates.
They may be reprecipitated by ammonia.</td></tr>
</table>

Varieties of calculi.—Calculi composed entirely of *uric acid* are common; a minute portion heated on platinum foil chars, burns, and leaves scarcely a trace of ash. The phosphates frequently occur together, forming what is known as the *fusible calculus*, from the readiness with which a fragment aggregates, and even fuses to a bead, when heated on a loop of platinum wire in the blowpipe-flame. The phosphates may, if necessary, be further examined by the method described in connection with urinary deposits. Oxalate of calcium often occurs alone, forming a dark-colored calculus having a very rough surface, hence termed the *mulberry calculus.* Smaller calculi of the same substance are called, from their appearance, *hempseed calculi.* Calculi of *cystin* are rarely met with. *Xanthin* (from ξανθὸς, *xanthos*, yellow, in allusion to the color it yields with nitric acid) still less often occurs as a calculus. The earthy concretions, or *chalk-stones*, which frequently form in the joints of gouty persons, are composed chiefly of urates, the sodium salt being that most commonly met with. *Gall-stones*, or *biliary calculi*, occasionally form in the gall-bladder: they contain *cholesterin* (from χολή, *cholē*, bile, and στερεὸς, *stereos*, solid), a fatty substance of alcoholoid constitution, soluble in rectified spirit or ether, and crystallizing from such solutions in well-defined, square, scaly crystals. Calculi of many pounds weight are often found in the stomach and larger intestines of animals.

QUESTIONS AND EXERCISES.

864. In breathing, how much carbon (in the form of carbonic acid gas) is exhaled from the lungs every 24 hours?

865. How may the presence of carbonic acid gas in expired air be demonstrated?

866. Mention an experiment showing the escape of moisture from the lungs during breathing.

867. State the method of testing for albumen in urine.

868. Give the tests for sugar in urine.

869. What is the average composition of healthy urine?

870. Give the tests for urea.

871. Write the rational formulæ of some compound ureas in which methyl or ethyl displace hydrogen.

872. Describe an artificial process for the production of urea, giving equations.

873. Sketch out a plan for the chemical examination of urinary sediments.

874. A deposit is insoluble in the supernatant urine or in acetic acid; of what substances may it consist?

875. Which compounds are indicated when a deposit redissolves on warming it with the supernatant urine?

876. Name the salts insoluble in warmed urine but dissolved on the addition of acetic acid.

877. Mention the chemical characters of cystin. At what stage of analysis would it be recognized?

878. Describe the microscopical appearance of the following urinary deposits:—

Uric Acid.	Tube-casts.
Cystin.	Epithelial *débris*.
Triple phosphate.	Blood.
Earthy phosphates.	Pus.
Urates.	Mucus.
Oxalate of Calcium.	Fat.
Carbonate of Calcium.	Spermatozoa.
Hippuric Acid.	Sarcina.
Extraneous Bodies.	

879. What is the general, physical, and chemical nature of urinary calculi?

880. How are urinary calculi prepared for chemical examination?

881. Draw out a chart for the chemical examination of urinary calculi.

882. Why is the "fusible calculus" so called, and what is its composition?

883. State the characters of "mulberry" and "hempseed" calculi.

884. What are the "chalk-stones" of gout and "gall-stones" or "biliary calculi?"

THE GALENICAL PREPARATIONS OF THE BRITISH PHARMACOPŒIA.

The preparation of Confections, Decoctions, Enemas, Extracts, Glycerines, Infusions, Inhalations, Juices, Liniments, Lozenges, Mixtures, Ointments, Pills, Plasters, Poultices, Powders, Spirits, Suppositories, Syrups, Tinctures, and Wines, includes a number of mechanical rather than chemical operations, and belongs to the domain of pure Pharmacy. The medical or pharmaceutical pupil will have had ample opportunity of practically studying these compounds before working at experimental chemistry, and will probably have prepared many of them according to the directions of the Pharmacopœia; if not, he is referred to the pages of the last edition of that work for details.

Among the extracts of the British Pharmacopœia, however, there are five (namely, those of Aconite, Belladonna, Hemlock, Henbane, and Lettuce) which are not simply evaporated infusions, decoctions, or tinctures, like most others, but are evaporated juices from which vegetable albumen, the supposed source of fermentation and decay, has been removed, and chlorophyll (the green coloring-matter of plant-juice) retained practically unimpaired in tint. In order that attention may be concentrated on the process by which these are prepared, rather than on the extracts themselves, it is advisable to make an extract of some ordinary green vegetable, such as cabbage or turnip-tops. Bruise the green leaves of a good-sized cabbage in a mortar, and press out the juice; heat it gradually to 130°, and remove the green flocks of chlorophyll which separate, by filtration through calico. When the liquor has all passed through the filter, set the chlorophyll aside for a time, heat the strained liquor to 200° to coagulate albumen; remove the latter by filtration and throw away; evaporate the filtrate by a water-bath to the consistence of thin syrup; then add to it the chlorophyll, and, stirring the whole together assiduously, continue the evaporation at a temperature not exceeding 140°, until the extract is of a suitable consistence for forming pills. A higher temperature than that indicated would cause the alteration of the chlorophyll to a dark-brown substance, the extract no longer having the green tint which custom and the British Pharmacopœia demand.

QUESTIONS AND EXERCISES.

885. Enumerate the different classes of official galenical preparations.

886. Describe the general process for the preparation of green extracts:—

Aconite. Hemlock.
Belladonna. Henbane.
Lettuce.

887. Why is vegetable albumen excluded in the preparation of green extracts?

888. How may chlorophyll be removed from vegetable juices, and again be introduced into their evaporated residues, without destroying its color.

889. For what reason is exposure of chlorophyll to heat avoided in the manufacture of green extracts?

THE CHEMICAL PREPARATIONS OF THE PHARMACOPŒIAS.

The process by which every official chemical substance is prepared has already been described, and the strict chemical character of the processes illustrated by experiments and explained by aid of equations. Should the reader, in addition, desire an intimate acquaintance with those details of manipulation on which the successful and economic manufacture of chemical substances depends, he is advised to prepare, if he has not done so already, a few ounces of each of the salts mentioned in the Pharmacopœias or commonly used in Pharmacy. An additional guide in these operations will be the Pharmacopœia itself.

The production of many chemical and galenical substances on a commercial scale can only be successfully carried on in manufacturing-laboratories and with some knowledge of the circumstances of supply and demand, value of raw material, and of by-products. Commercial Chemistry and Pharmacy, however, can best hope for success when founded on the working out of abstract principles. The problem of manufacturing-success is solved with certainty by wisely applied science.

Memorandum.—The next subjects of experimental study will be determined by the nature of the student's future pursuits. In most cases the operations of quantitative analysis will engage attention. These should be of a volumetric and gravimetric character; for details concerning them see the following pages.

QUANTITATIVE ANALYSIS.

INTRODUCTORY REMARKS.

General principles.—The proportions in which chemical substances unite with each other in forming compounds are definite and invariable (page 36). Quantitative analysis is based on this law. When, for example, aqueous solutions of a salt of silver and a chloride are mixed, a white curdy precipitate is produced containing chlorine and silver in atomic proportions, that is, 35.5 parts of chloride to 108 of silver. No matter what the chloride or what the salt of silver, the resulting chloride of silver is invariable in composition. The formula AgCl is a convenient picture of this compound in these proportions. The weight of a definite compound being given, therefore, the proportional amounts of its constituents can be ascertained by simple calculation. Thus, for instance, 8.53 parts of chloride of silver contain 2.11 parts of chlorine and 6.42 of silver; for if 143.5 (the molecular weight) of chloride of silver contain 35.5 (the atomic weight) of chlorine, 8.53 of chloride of silver will be found to contain 2.11 of chlorine:—

```
143.5  :  35.5  ::  8.53 : x
           8.53
          -----
          1.065
          17.75
         284.0
143.5)302.815(2.11
         287.0
         -----
         15.81
         14.35
         -----
          1.465
          1.435              x = 2.11.
```

And if 143.5 of chloride of silver contain 108 of silver, 8.53 of chloride of silver will contain 6.42 of silver. To ascertain, for example, the amount of silver in a substance, containing, say, nitrate of silver, all that is necessary is to take a weighed quantity of the substance, dissolve it, precipitate the whole of the silver by adding hydrochloric acid or other chloride till no more chloride of silver falls, collect the precipitate on a filter, wash, dry, and weigh. The amount of silver in the dried chloride, ascertained by calculation, is the amount of silver in the quantity of substance on which the operation was conducted; a rule-of-three sum gives the quantity per cent.—the form in which the results of quantitative analysis are usually stated. Occasionally a constituent of a substance admits of being isolated and weighed in the uncombined state. Thus the amount of mercury in a substance may be determined by separating and weighing the mercury in the metallic condition; if occurring as calomel (HgCl) or corrosive sublimate ($HgCl_2$), the proportion of chlorine may then be ascertained by calculation (Hg=200; Cl=35.5).

Nature of Gravimetric Quantitative Analysis.—As above stated, a body may be isolated and weighed and its quantity thus ascertained; or it may be separated and weighed in combination with another body whose combining proportion is well known; this is quantitative analysis by the *gravimetric* method.

Nature of Volumetric Quantitative Analysis.—Quantitative analysis by the *volumetric* method consists in noting the volume of a liquid required to be added to the substance under examination before a given effect is produced. Thus, for instance, a solution of nitrate of silver of known strength may be used in experimentally ascertaining an unknown amount of chloride in any substance. The silver solution is added to a solution of a definite quantity of the substance until flocks of chloride of silver cease to be precipitated: every 108 parts of silver added (or 170 of nitrate of silver: Ag=108, N=14, O_3=48; total 170) indicates the presence of 35.5 of chlorine, or an equivalent quantity of any chloride. The preparation of standard solutions, such as that of nitrate of silver, to which allusion is here made, requires considerable care; but when made, certain analyses can be executed with far more rapidity and ease than by gravimetric processes.

Note.—The quantitative analysis of solids and liquids often involves determinations of temperature and specific gravity. These processes will now be explained, after which an outline of volumetric and gravimetric quantitative analysis will be given. The scope of this work precludes any attempt to describe all the little mechanical details observed by quantitative analysts; essential operations, however, are so fully treated that expert manipulators will meet with little difficulty.

Measurement of Atmospheric Pressure.

The Barometer.—The analysis of gases and vapors involves, also, determinations of the varying pressure of the atmosphere as indicated by the *barometer* (from βάρος, *baros*, weight, and μέτρον, *metron*, measure). The ordinary mercurial barometer is a glass tube 33 or 34 inches long, closed at one end, filled with mercury, and inverted in a small cistern or cup of mercury. The mercury remains in the tube owing to the weight or pressure of the atmosphere on the exposed surface of the liquid, the average height of the column being nearly 30 inches. In the popular form of the instrument, the wheel-barometer, the cistern is formed by a recurvature of the tube; on the exposed surface of the mercury a float is placed, from which a thread passes over a pulley and moves an index whenever the column of mercury rises or falls. As supplied to the public these barometers are usually inclosed in ornamental frames with thermometers attached. In the wheel-barometer the glass tube and contained column of mercury are altogether inclosed, the index alone being visible. In the other variety the upper end of the glass tube and mercurial column are exposed and the height of the mercury is ascertained by direct observation.

The aneroid barometer (from ἀ, *a*, *without*, and νηρὸς, *neros*, fluid) consists of a small, shallow, vacuous metal drum, the sides of which approach each other when an increase of atmospheric pressure occurs, their elasticity enabling them to recede toward their former position on a decrease of pressure. This motion is so multiplied and altered in direction by levers, etc., as to act on a hand traversing a plate on which is marked numbers corresponding with those showing the height of the mercurial column of the ordinary barometer by which the aneroid was adjusted. *The Bourdon barometer* (from the name of the inventor) is a modified aneroid containing in the place of the round metal box, a flattened vacuous tube of metal, bent nearly to a circle. These barometers are also useful for measuring the pressure in steam-boilers, etc. Under the name of *pressure-gauges* they are sold to indicate pressures of 500 pounds and upwards per square inch. From their portability (they can be made of 1 to 2 inches in diameter and 1 inch thick) they are excellent companions for travellers wishing to know the heights of hills, mountains, and other elevations.

For further information concerning the influence of pressure on the volume of a gas or vapor see page 430; and for descriptions of the methods of analyzing gases, refer to Ganot's "Physics" (translated by Atkinson), Miller's "Chemical Physics," and "Analysis of Gases" in Watts's "Dictionary of Chemistry."

MEASUREMENT OF TEMPERATURE.

General Principles.—As a rule, all bodies expand on the addition, and contract on the abstraction of heat, the alteration in volume being constant and regular for equal increments or decrements of temperature. The extent of this alteration in a given substance, expressed in parts or degrees, constitutes the usual method of intelligibly stating, with accuracy, precision, and minuteness, a particular condition of warmth or temperature, that is, of sensible heat. The substance commonly employed for this purpose is mercury, the chief advantages of which are that it will bear a high temperature without boiling, a low temperature without freezing, does not adhere to glass to a sufficient extent to "wet" the sides of any tube in which it may be inclosed, and, from its good conducting-power for heat, responds rapidly to changes of temperature. Platinum, earthenware, alcohol, and air are also occasionally used for thermometric purposes.

The Thermometer.—The construction of an accurate thermometer is a matter of great difficulty; but the following are the leading steps in the operation. Select a piece of glass tubing having a fine capillary (*capillus*, a hair) bore, and about a foot long; heat one extremity in the blowpipe-flame until the orifice closes, and the glass is sufficiently soft to admit of a bulb being blown; heat the bulb to expel air, immediately plunging the open extremity of the tube into mercury; the bulb having cooled, and some mercury having entered and taken the place of expelled air, again heat the bulb and tube until the mercury boils and its vapor escapes through the bore of the tube; again plunge the extremity under mercury, which will probably now completely fill the bulb and tube. When cold the bulb is placed in melting ice. The top of the column of mercury in the capillary tube should then be within an inch or two of the bulb; if higher, some of the mercury must be expelled by heat; if lower, more metal must be introduced as before. The tube is now heated near the open end and a portion drawn out, until the diameter is reduced to about one-tenth. The bulb is next warmed until the mercurial column rises above the constricted part of the tube, which is then rapidly fused in the blowpipe-flame, and the extremity of the tube removed.

The instrument is now ready for *graduation.* The bulb is placed in boiling-water (a medium having, *cæteris paribus*, an invariable temperature), and, when the position of the top of the mercurial column is constant, a mark is made on the tube by a scratching diamond or a file. This operation is repeated with melting ice (also a medium having an invariable temperature). The space between these two marks is divided into a certain number of intervals termed *degrees.* Unfortunately this number is not uniform in all countries: in England it is 180, as proposed by Fahrenheit; in France 100, as proposed by Celsius (the Centigrade scale), a number generally adopted by scientific men; in some parts of the Continent the divisions are 80 for the same interval, as suggested by Réaumur. Whichever be the number selected, similar markings should be continued beyond the boiling- and freezing-points as far as the length of the stem admits.

Thermometric Scales.—On the Centigrade and Réaumur scales the freezing-point of water is made zero, and the boiling-point 100 and 80 respectively; on the Fahrenheit scale the zero is placed 32 degrees below the congealing-point of water, the boiling-point of which becomes, consequently, 212. Even on the Fahrenheit system temperatures below the freezing-point of water are often spoken of as "degrees of frost;" thus 19° degrees as marked on the thermometer would be regarded as "13 degrees of frost." It is to be regretted that the freezing-point of water is not universally regarded as the zero-point, and the number of intervals between that and the boiling-point everywhere the same.

The degrees of one scale are easily converted into those of another, if their relations be remembered, namely:—180 (F.), 100 (C.), 80 (R.); or 18, 10, and 8; or, best, 9, 5, and 4.

Formulæ for the conversion of degrees of one thermometric scale into those of another.

F=Fahrenheit. C=Centigrade.
R=Réaumur. D=The observed degree.

If above the freezing-point of water (32° F; 0° C; 0° R),

F into C	. . . .	(D—32)÷9×5.
F " R	. . . .	(D—32)÷9×4.
C " F	. . . .	D÷ 5 ×9+32.
R " F	. . . .	D÷ 4 ×9+32.

35*

If below freezing, but above 0° F (—17°.77 C; —14°.22 R),

F into C . . . .—(32—D)÷9×5.
F " R . . . .—(32—D)÷9×4.
C " F . . . . 32—(D÷5×9).
R " F . . . . 32—(D÷4×9).

If below 0° F (—17°.77 C; —14°.22 R),

F into C . . . .—(D+32)÷9 ×5.
F " R . . . .—(D+32)÷9 ×4.
C " F . . . .—(D÷ 5 ×9)—32.
R " F . . . .—(D÷ 4 ×9)—32.

For all degrees:—

C into R . . . . D÷5×4.
R " C . . . . D÷4×5.

In ascertaining the temperature of a liquid, the bulb of a thermometer is simply inserted and the degree noted. In determining the boiling-point, also, the bulb is inserted in the liquid, if a pure substance. In taking the boiling-point of a liquid which is being distilled from a mixture, the bulb of the thermometer should be near to, but not beneath the surface.

The following are the boiling points of a few substances met with in pharmacy:—

	Centigrade.	Fahrenheit.
Alcohol, absolute	78.3	173
" 84 per cent.	79.5	175
" 49 per cent. (proof spirit)	81.4	178.5
" amylic	132.2	270
Benzol	80.6	177
Bromine	47.2	117
Benzoic acid	239.0	462
Carbolic acid	187.8	370
Chloroform	61	142
Ether (B. P.) (below)	40.5	105
" pure	35	95
Mercury *in vacuo* (as in a thermometer)	304	580
" in air (barom. at 30 inches)	350	662
Water (barom. at 29.92 inches)	100	212
" (" 29.33 ")	99.5	211
" (" 28.74 ")	99	210
Saturated solutions of:—		
Cream of tartar	101	214
Common salt	106.6	224
Sal-ammoniac	113.3	236
Nitrate of sodium	119	246
Acetate of sodium	124.4	256
Chloride of calcium	179.4	355

To determine melting-points of fats.—Heat a fragment of the substance (spermaceti or wax for example) till it liquefies, and then draw up a small portion into a thin glass tube, about the size of a knitting-needle. Immerse the tube in cold water contained in a beaker, and slowly heat the vessel till the thin opaque cylinder of solid fat melts and becomes transparent: a delicate thermometer placed in the water indicates the point of change to the fifth of a degree. Remove the source of heat, and note the congealing-point of the substance; it will be identical with or close to the melting-point.

Pyrometers.—Temperatures above the boiling-point of mercury are determined by ascertaining to what extent a bar of platinum or porcelain has elongated. The bar is inclosed in a cavity of a suitable case, a plug of platinum or porcelain placed at one end of the bar, and the whole exposed in the region whose temperature is to be found. After cooling, the distance to which the bar has forced the plug along the cavity is accurately measured and the corresponding degree of temperature noted. The value of the distance is fixed for low temperatures by comparison with a mercurial thermometer, and the scale carried upwards through intervals of equivalent length. Such thermometers are conventionally distinguished from ordinary instruments by the name *pyrometer* (from πῦρ, *pūr*, fire, and μέτρον, *metron*, measure).

The following melting-points of official substances are given in the British Pharmacopœia:—

	In degrees Centigrade.	In degrees Fahrenheit.
Acetic acid, glacial	8.9	48
" " congeals at	1.1	34
Benzoic acid	120	248
Carbolic acid	35	95
Oil of theobroma	50	122
Phosphorus	43.3	110
Prepared lard . . . (about)	38	100
" suet	39.5	103
Spermaceti	38	100
White wax . . (not under)	65.5	150
Yellow wax	60	140

The order of fusibility of a few of the metals is as follows:—

	In degrees Centigrade.	In degrees Fahrenheit.
Mercury	— 39.4	— 39
Potassium	+ 62.5	+144.5
Sodium	97.6	207.7
Tin	227.8	442
Bismuth	264	507
Lead	325	617
Zinc	411.6	773
Antimony	621	1150
Silver	1023	1873
Copper	1091	1996
Gold	1102	2016
Cast iron	1530	2786

QUESTIONS AND EXERCISES.

890. On what fundamental laws are the operations of quantitative analysis based?

891. What is the general nature of *gravimetric* quantitative analysis?

892. Describe the general principle of *volumetric* quantitative analysis?

893. How are variations in atmospheric pressure quantitatively determined?

894. Explain the construction and mode of action of a mercurial barometer.

895. In what respect does a wheel-barometer differ from an instrument in which the readings are taken from the top of the column of mercury?

896. On what general principles are thermometers constructed?

897. What material is employed in making thermometers?

898. Why is mercury selected as a thermometric indicator?

899. Describe the manufacture of a mercurial thermometer.

900. How are thermometers graduated?

901. Give formulæ for the conversion of the degrees of one thermometric scale into those of another, (*a*) when the temperature is above the freezing-point of water, (*b*) below 32° F. but above 0° F., and (*c*) below 0° F.

902. Name the degree C. equivalent to 60° F.

903. What degree C. is represented by —4° F.?

904. Mention the degree F. indicated by 20° C.

905. Convert 100° R. into degrees C. and F.

906. State the boiling-points of alcohol, chloroform, ether, mercury, and water on either thermometric scale.

907. Describe the details of manipulation in estimating the melting-point of fats.

908. In what respect do pyrometers differ from thermometers?

909. Mention the melting-points of glacial acetic acid, oil of theobroma, lard, suet, and wax.

910. Give the fusing-points of tin, lead, zinc, copper, and cast-iron.

ESTIMATION OF WEIGHT.

DEFINITIONS.

All bodies, celestial and terrestrial, attract each other, the amount of attraction being in direct proportion to the quantity of matter of which they consist, and in inverse proportion to the squares of their distances. This is *gravitation*. When gravitation in certain directions is exactly counterbalanced by gravitation in opposite directions, a body (*e. g.* the earth) remains suspended in space. Such a body, in relation to other bodies, has gravity but not weight. *Weight* is the effect of gravity, being the excess of gravitation in one direction over and above that exerted in the opposite direction. Weight, truly, in any terrestrial substance, is the excess of attraction which it and the earth have for each other over and above the attraction of each in opposite directions by the various heavenly bodies. But, practically, the weight of any terrestrial substance is the effect of the attraction of the earth only. *Specific* weight is the definite or precise weight of a body in relation to its bulk; it is more usually but not quite correctly termed *specific gravity*—gravity belonging to the earth, not to the substance.

QUESTIONS.

911. What is understood by gravitation?
912. State the difference between weight and gravity.
913. Mention a case in which a body has gravity but no apparent weight.
914. Practically, what causes the weight of terrestrial substances?

WEIGHTS AND MEASURES.

The Balance.—The balance used in the quantitative operations of analytical chemistry must be accurate and sensitive. The points of suspension of the beam and pans should be polished steel or agate knife-edges, working on agate planes. It should turn easily and quickly, without too much oscillation, to $\frac{1}{500}$ or $\frac{1}{600}$ of a grain, or $\frac{1}{10}$ of a milligramme, when 1000 grains, or 50 or 60 grammes, are placed in each scale. (Grammes are weights of the metric system, a description of which is given on the next two or three pages.) The beam should be light but strong, capable of supporting a load of 1500 grains or 100 grammes; its oscillations are observed by help of a long index attached to its centre, and continued downwards for some distance in front of the supporting pillar of the balance. The instrument should be provided with screws for purposes of adjustment, a mechanical contrivance for supporting the beam above its bearings when not in use or during the removal or addition of weights, spirit levels to enable the operator to give it a horizontal position, and be inclosed in a glass case to protect from dust. It should be placed in a room the atmosphere of which is not liable to be contaminated by acid fumes, in a situation free from vibration; and a vessel containing lumps of quicklime should be placed in the case to keep the inclosed air dry and prevent the formation of rust on the steel knife-edges or other parts. During weighing, the doors of the balance should be shut, in order that currents of air may not unequally influence the pans.

The Weights.—These should be preserved in a box having a separate compartment for each. They must not be lifted directly with the fingers, but by a small pair of forceps. If grain-weights, they should range from 1000 gr. to $\frac{1}{10}$ gr., a $\frac{1}{10}$ weight being fashioned of gold wire to act as a "rider" on the divided beam, and thus indicate by its position 100ths and 1000ths of a grain. From $\frac{1}{10}$ to 10 grs. the weights may be of platinum; thence upwards to 1000 grs. of brass. The relation of the weights to each other should be decimal. Metric decimal weights may range from 100 grammes to 1 gramme, of brass, and thence downwards to 1 centigramme, of platinum, a gold centigramme rider being employed to indicate milligrammes and tenths of a milligramme.

The Metric System of weights (the word *metric* is from the Greek μέτρον, *metron*, measure) is greatly to be preferred to all others, the relation of the metric weights of all denominations to measures of length, capacity, and surface being so simple as to be within the perfect comprehension of a child; while under the British and American plans, the weights have no such relation, either with each other or with the various measures. Moreover the metric system is in perfect harmony with the universal method of counting; it is a decimal system.

[It is perhaps impossible to realize, much more express, the advantages we enjoy from the fact that in every country of the world the system of numeration is identical. That system is the decimal. Whatever language a man speaks, his method of numbering is decimal; his talk concerning number is decimal; his written or printed signs signifying number are decimal. With the figures 1, 2, 3, 4, 5, 6, 7, 8, 9, 0 he represents all possible variation in number, the position of a figure in reference to its companions alone determining its value, a figure on the left hand of any other figure in an allocation of numeral symbols (for example, 1871) having ten times the value of that figure, while the figure on the right hand of any other has a tenth of the value of that other. When the youngest pupil is asked how many units there are in 1871, he smiles at the simplicity of the question, and says 1871. How many tens? 187, and 1 over. How many hundreds? 18, and 71 over. How many thousands? 1, and 871 over. But if he is asked how many scruples there are in 1871 grains, how many drachms, how many ounces—he first inquires which drachms or which ounces are meant, avoirdupois ounces, troy ounces or wine ounces, and then brings out his slate and pencil. And so with the pints or gallons in 1871 fluidounces, or the feet and yards in 1871 inches, or the pence, shillings, and pounds in 1871 farthings; to say nothing of cross questions, such as the value of 1871 articles at 2 dollars and 20 cents per dozen, or of the perplexity caused by the varying values of several individual weights or of measures of length, capacity, and surface in different parts of the country. What is desired is, that there should be an equally simple decimal relation among weights and measures and coins as already universally exists among numbers. This condition of things having already been introduced into most other countries, there is no good reason why it should not be accomplished in the United States and Great Britain.]

The Metric System of weights and measures is founded on the metre. The engraving represents the tenth part of a metre, divided into 10 centimetres, and each centimetre into 10 millimetres.

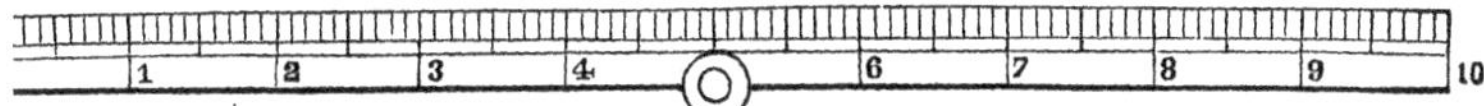

The Decimetre.

The units of the system with their multiples and submultiples are as follows:—

UNITS.

Length.—The *Unit of Length* is the METRE, derived from the measurement of the Quadrant of a Meridian of the Earth. (Practically it is the length of certain carefully preserved bars of metal, from which copies have been taken.)

Surface.—The *Unity of Surface* is the ARE, which is the Square of Ten Metres.

Capacity.—The *Unity of Capacity* is the LITRE, which is the Cube of a Tenth Part of a Metre.

Weight.—The *Unit of Weight* is the GRAM, which is the Weight of that quantity of distilled water, at its maximum density, which fills a Cube of the One-hundredth part of the Metre.

TABLE.

Note.—Multiples are denoted by the Greek words "Deka," "Ten," "Hecto," Hundred, "Kilo," Thousand.
Subdivisions, by the Latin words, "Deci," One-tenth, "Centi," One-hundredth, "Milli," One-thousandth.

Quantities.	Length.	Surface.	Capacity.	Weight.
1000	Kilo-metre	. .	Kilo-litre	Kilo-gram
100	Hecto-metre	Hectare	Hecto-litre	Hecto-gram
10	Deka-metre	. . .	Deka-litre	Deka-gram
1 (Units)	**METRE**	**ARE**	**LITRE**	**GRAM**
.1	Deci-metre	. . .	Deci-litre	Deci-gram
.01	Centi-metre	Centiare	Centi-litre	Centi-gram
.001	Milli-metre	. . .	Milli-litre	Milligram

When the metric method is exclusively adopted these Units and Table, comprising the entire System of Weights and Measures, represent all that will be essential to be learned in lieu of the numerous and complicated Tables hitherto in use. Adopting the style of elementary books on Arithmetic, the Table may be expanded in the following manner:—

10 Milligrams	make	1 centigram.
10 Centigrams	"	1 decigram.
10 Decigrams	"	1 gram.
10 Grams	"	1 dekagram.
10 Dekagrams	"	1 hectogram.
10 Hectograms	"	1 kilogram.

10 Millilitres make 1 centilitre,
&c.

10 Millimetres make 1 centimetre,
&c.

The following approximate equivalents of metrical units should be committed to memory:—

1 Metre	=	3 feet 3 inches and 3 eighths.
1 Are	=	a square whose side is 11 yards.
1 Litre	=	1¾ pint.
1 Gramme	=	15½ grains.

The Metric Ton of 1000 Kilo-grammes = 19 cwt. 2 qrs. 20 lbs. 10 ozs.

The Kilo-gramme = 2 lbs. 3¼ ozs. nearly.

The Hect-are = 2½ acres nearly.

For *exact* equivalents, in many forms, see pages 420 and 421. (The word *gramme* is, in English, usually written *gram.*)

The General Council under whose authority the British Pharmacopœia is issued encourages medical practitioners and pharmacists in the adoption of the metric system, and gives the annexed statement of metric weights and measures.

WEIGHTS AND MEASURES OF THE METRICAL SYSTEM.

(From the British Pharmacopœia, of 1867.)

WEIGHTS.

1 Milligramme	=	the thousandth part of one grm.	or 0.001	grm.
1 Centigramme	=	the hundredth "	0.01	"
1 Decigramme	=	the tenth "	0.1	"
1 Gramme	=	weight of a cubic centimetre of water at 4° C.	1.0	"
1 Decagramme	=	ten grammes	10.0	"
1 Hectogramme	=	one hundred grammes	100.0	"
1 Kilogramme	=	one thousand grammes	1000.0	(1 kilo.).

MEASURES OF CAPACITY.

1 Millilitre	=	1	cub. centim.	or the mea. of	1	gram.	of water.
1 Centilitre	=	10	"	"	10	"	"
1 Decilitre	=	100	"	"	100	"	"
1 Litre	=	1000	"	"	1000	"	(1 kilo.).

MEASURES OF LENGTH.

1 Millimetre	= the thousandth part of one metre or	0.001 metre.
1 Centimetre	= the hundredth "	0.01 metre.
1 Decimetre	= the tenth "	0.1 "
1 Metre	= the ten-millionth part of a quarter of the meridian of the earth.	

The following Tables, from the British Pharmacopœia and the Diary of Messrs. De La Rue, will be found useful for reference :—

WEIGHTS AND MEASURES OF THE BRITISH PHARMACOPŒIA OF 1867.

WEIGHTS.

1 Grain	gr.		
1 Ounce	oz.		= 437.5 grains.
1 Pound	lb.	= 16 ounces	= 7000 "

MEASURES OF CAPACITY.

1 Minim	min.	
1 Fluidrachm	fl. drm.	= 60 minims.
1 Fluidounce	fl. oz.	= 8 fluidrachms.
1 Pint	O.	= 20 fluidounces.
1 Gallon	C.	= 8 pints.

MEASURES OF LENGTH.

1 line = $\frac{1}{12}$ inch.

1 inch = $\frac{1}{39.1393}$ seconds-pendulum.

12 " = 1 foot.

36 " = 3 feet = 1 yard.

Length of pendulum vibrating seconds of mean time in the latitude of London, in a vacuum at the level of the sea. . . . . } 39.1393 inches.

(1 cubic inch of distilled water at 62° F. and 30 inch Barom. =252.458 grains.)

RELATION OF MEASURES TO WEIGHTS.

1 Minim is the measure of		0.91	grain of water.
1 Fluidrachm "		54.68	grains of water.
1 Fluidounce "	1 ounce or	437.5	"
1 Pint "	1.25 pound or	8750.0	"
1 Gallon "	10 pounds or	70,000.0	"

Metrical Measures of Length.

	In English inches.	In English feet = 12 inches.	In English yards = 3 feet.	In Eng. fathoms = 6 feet.	In English miles = 1760 yards.
Millimetre	0.03937	0.003281	0.0010936	0.0005468	0.0000006
Centimetre	0.39371	0.032809	0.0109363	0.0054682	0.0000062
Decimetre	3.93708	0.328090	0.1093633	0.0546816	0.0000621
Metre	**39.37079**	3.280899	1.0936331	0.5468165	0.0006214
Decametre	393.70790	32.808992	10.9363310	5.4681655	0.0062138
Hectometre	3937.07900	328.089920	109.3633100	54.6816550	0.0621382
Kilometre	39370.79000	3280.899200	1093.6331000	546.8165500	0.6213824
Myriometre	393707.90000	32808.992000	10936.3310000	5468.1655000	6.2138244

1 inch = 2.539954 centimetres.
1 foot = 3.0479449 decimetres.
1 yard = 0.9143835 metre.
1 mile = 1.6093149 kilometre.

Metrical Measures of Surface.

	In English square feet.	In Eng. sq. yards = 9 square feet.	In English poles = 272.25 sq. feet.	In English roods = 10890 sq. feet.	In English acres = 43560 sq. feet.
Centiare or square metre	10.764299	1.196033	0.0395383	0.0009885	0.0002471
Are or 100 square metres	1076.429934	119.603326	3.9538290	0.0988457	0.0247114
Hectare or 10,000 square metres	107642.993418	11960.332602	395.3828959	9.8845724	2.4711431

1 square inch = 6.4513669 square centimetres.
1 square foot = 9.2899683 square decimetres.
1 square yard = 0.83609715 square metre or centiare.
1 acre = 0.40467102 hectare.

METRICAL MEASURES OF CAPACITY.

	In cubic inches.	In cubic feet = 1728 cubic inches.	In pints = 34.65923 cubic inches.	In gallons = 8 pints = 277.27384 cubic inches.	In bushels = 8 gallons = 2218.19072 cubic inches.
Millilitre, or cubic centimetre	0.06103	0.000035	0.00176	0.0002201	0.0000275
Centilitre, or 10 cubic centimetres	0.61027	0.000353	0.01761	0.0022010	0.0002751
Decilitre, or 100 cubic centimetres	6.10271	0.003532	0.17608	0.0220097	0.0027512
Litre, or cubic decimetre	61.02705	0.035317	**1.76077**	0.2200967	0.0275121
Decalitre, or centistere	610.27052	0.353166	17.60773	2.2009668	0.2751208
Hectolitre, or decistere	6102.70515	3.531658	176.07734	22.0096677	2.7512085
Kilolitre, or stere, or cubic metre	61027.05152	35.316581	1760.77341	220.0966767	27.5120846
Myriolitre, or decastere	610270.51519	353.165807	17607.73414	2200.9667675	275.1208459

1 cubic inch = 16.386176 cubic centimetres. 1 cubic foot = 28.315312 cubic decimetres. 1 gallon = 4.543358 litres.

METRICAL MEASURES OF WEIGHT.

	In English grains.	In troy ounces = 480 grains.	In avoirdupois lbs. = 7000 grains.	In cwts. = 112 lbs. = 784000 grains.	Tons = 20 cwts. = 15680000 grains.
Milligramme	0.01543	0.000032	0.0000022	0.0000000	0.0000000
Centigramme	0.15432	0.000322	0.0000220	0.0000002	0.0000000
Decigramme	1.54323	0.003215	0.0002205	0.0000020	0.0000001
Gramme	**15.43235**	0.032151	0.0022046	0.0000197	0.0000010
Decagramme	154.32349	0.321507	0.0220462	0.0001968	0.0000098
Hectogramme	1543.23488	3.215073	0.2204621	0.0019684	0.0000984
Kilogramme	15432.34880	32.150727	2.2046213	0.0196841	0.0009842
Myriogramme	154323.48800	321.507267	22.0462126	0.1968412	0.0098421

1 grain = 0.064799 gramme. 1 troy oz. = 31.103496 grams. 1 lb. avd. = 0.453593 kilgr. 1 cwt. = 50.802377 kilogrs.

QUESTIONS AND EXERCISES.

915. Mention some advantages of a decimal system of weights and measures.
916. What is the name of the chief unit of the metric decimal system of weights and measures?
917. Mention the names of the metric units of surface, capacity, and weight, and state how they are derived from the unit of length.
918. How are multiples of metric units indicated?
919. State the designations of submultiples of metric units.
920. How many metres are there in a kilometre?
921. How many millimetres in a metre?
922. How many grams in 5 kilograms?
923. How many milligrams in 13½ grams?
924. In 1869 centigrams how many grams?
925. In a metre measure 5 centimetres wide and 1 centimetre thick how many cubic centimetres?
926. How many litres are contained in a cubic metre of any liquid?
927. State the British equivalent of the metre.
928. How many square yards in an are?
929. How many fluidounces in a litre?
930. How many ounces in a kilogram?
931. Give the relation of a metric ton (1000 kilos.) to a British ton.
932. How many grains are there in 1 ton?
933. How many ounces in 1 ton?
934. How many grains of water in 1 fluidrachm?
935. How many minims in 1 pint?
936. How many grains in 1 pint of water?
937. Whence is the British unit of length derived?

Specific Weight or Specific Gravity.

The *specific* weight of a substance is its weight in comparison with weights of similar bulks of other substances. This comparative heaviness of *solids and liquids* is conventionally expressed in relation to water: they are considered as much lighter or heavier than water. Thus, water being regarded as unity=1, the relative weight, or specific weight, of ether is represented by the figures .720 (it is nearly three-fourths, .750, the weight of water), oil of vitriol by 1.843 (it is nearly twice, 2.000, as heavy as water). The specific weight of substances is, moreover, the weight of similar volumes *at sixty degrees* (60° F.); for the weight of a definite volume of any substance will vary according to temperature, becoming heavier when cooled, and lighter when heated, different bodies (gases excepted) differing in their rate of contraction and expansion. While then, specific weight or conventionally *specific gravity* is truly the comparative weight of equal bulks, the numbers which in Great Britain commonly represent specific gravities, are the comparative weights of equal bulks at 60° F., water being taken as unity.* The standard of comparison for gases was formerly air, but is now usually hydrogen.

Specific Gravity of Liquids.

Procure any small bottle holding from 100 to 1000 grains, and having a narrow neck; counterpoise it in a delicate balance; fill it to about halfway up the neck with pure distilled water having a temperature of 60° F.; ascertain the weight of the water, and, for convenience, add or subtract a drop or two, so that the weight shall be a round number of grains; mark the neck by a diamond or file-point at the part cut by the lower edge of the curved surface of the water. Consecutively fill up the bottle to the neck-mark with several other liquids, cooled or warmed to 60° F., first rinsing out the bottle once or twice with a small quantity of each liquid, and note the weights; the respective figures will represent the relative weights of equal bulks of the liquids. If the capacity of the bottle is 10, 100, or 1000 grains, the resulting weights will, without calculation, show the specific gravities of the liquids; if any other number, a rule-of-three sum must be worked out to ascertain the weight of the liquids as compared with 1 (or 1.000) of water. Bottles conveniently adjusted to contain 250, 500, or 1000 grains, or 100 or 50 grammes of water, when filled to the top of their perforated stopper, and other forms of the instrument, are sold by all chemical apparatus makers.

The following are the stated specific gravities of official liquids:—

Acid, acetic, B. P.	1.044
" " U. S. P.	1.047
" " diluted, B. P. and U. S. P.	1.006
" " glacial	1.065 to 1.066
" carbolic	1.065
" hydriodic, diluted	1.112

* The true weight of the body is its weight in air plus the weight of an equal bulk of air and minus the weight of a bulk of air equal to the bulk of brass or other weights employed; or, in other words, its weight *in vacuo* uninfluenced by the buoyancy of the air; but such a correction of the weight of a body is seldom necessary or, indeed, desirable. *Density* is sometimes improperly regarded as synonymous with *specific gravity*. It is true that the density of a body is in exact proportion to its specific gravity; but the former is more correctly the comparative bulk of equal weights, while specific gravity is the comparative weight of equal bulks.

Acid, hydrochloric, B. P. and U. S. P.	1.160
" " diluted, B. P.	1.052
" " " U. S. P.	1.038
" hydrocyanic, B. P. and U. S. P.	0.997
" lactic, U. S. P.	1.212
" nitric, B. P. and U. S. P.	1.420
" " diluted, B. P.	1.101
" " " U. S. P.	1.068
" nitro-hydrochloric	1.074
" phosphoric diluted, B. P.	1.080
" " " U. S. P.	1.056
" sulphuric, B. P. and U. S. P.	1.843
" " aromatic	0.927
" " diluted, B. P.	1.094
" " U. S. P.	1.082
" sulphurous, solution of, B. P.	1.040
" " " U. S. P.	1.035
Alcohol, U. S. P.	0.835
" absolute	0.795
" (rectified spirit, 84 per cent.)	0.838
" (proof spirit, 49 per cent.)	0.920
" dilutum, U. S. P.	0.941
" fortius, U. S. P.	0.817
" amylic, B. P. and U. S. P.	0.818
Ammonia, aromatic spirit of, B. P.	0.870
" stronger water of, U. S. P.	0.900
" solution of, B. P.	0.959
" strong solution of, B . P.	0.891
Antimony, solution of chloride of, B. P.	1.470
Arsenic, hydrochloric solution of, B. P.	1.009
Arsenical solution (*Liquor Arsenicalis*), B. P. .	1.009
Benzol, B. P.	0.850
Bismuth and ammonia, solution of citrate of, B. P.	1.122
Bromine	2.966
Chlorine solution of, B. P.	1.003
Chloroform, B. P. and U. S. P.	1.490
" spirit of, B. P.	0.871
Cinchona, liquid extract of yellow, B. P. (about) .	1.100
Creasote, U. S. P.	1.046
"	1.071
Ether, B. P.	0.735
" U. S. P.	0.750
" pure, B. P.	0.720
" fortior, U. S. P.	0.728
Glycerine, B. P. and U. S. P.	1.250
Iron, solution of pernitrate of, B. P.	1.107
" " " " " U. S. P.	1.065
" " " persulphate of, B. P.	1.441
" " " " " U. S. P. . . .	1.320
" strong solution of perchloride of, B. P. . . .	1.338
" tincture of perchloride of, B. P. and U. S. P. .	0.992

Lead, solution of subacetate of, B. P.	1.260
" " " " " U. S. P.	1.267
Lime, saccharated solution of, B. P.	1.052
" solution of chlorinated, B. P.	1.035
Mercury (at 0° C.=32° F.)	13.596
" (at 15°.55 C.=60° F.)	13.560
" acid solution of nitrate of	2.246
" " " " " " U. S. P.	2.165
Nitre, sweet spirit of	0.845
" " " " U. S. P.	0.837
Oil of mustard, B. P.	1.015
Potash, solution of, B. P.	1.058
" " " U. S. P.	1.065
Soda, " " B. P.	1.047
" " " U. S. P.	1.071
" " " chlorinated, B. P.	1.103
" " " " U. S. P.	1.045
Squill, oxymel of, B. P.	1.320
Syrup, B. P.	1.330
" U. S. P.	1.317
" of buckthorn, B. P.	1.320
" of ginger, B. P.	
" of hemidesmus, B. P.	1.335
" of iodide of iron, B. P.	1.385
" of lemons, B. P.	1.340
" of mulberries, B. P.	1.330
" of orange-flower, B. P.	1.330
" of " peel, B. P.	
" of phosphate of iron, B. P.	
" of poppies, B. P.	1.320
" of red poppy, B. P.	1.330
" of " roses, B. P.	1.335
" of rhubarb, B. P.	
" of senna, B. P.	1.310
" of squill, B. P.	
" of tolu, B. P.	1.330
Treacle, B. P. (about)	1.400

Hydrometers.—The specific gravity of liquids may be ascertained, without scales and weights, by means of an *hydrometer*—an instrument usually of glass, having a graduated stem and a bulb or bulbs, at the lower part. The specific gravity of a liquid is indicated by the depth to which the hydrometer sinks in the liquid, the zero of the scale marking the depth to which it sinks in pure water. Hydrometers constructed for special purposes are known under the names of saccharometer, galactometer, elæometer, urinometer, alcohometer. Hydrometers require a considerable quantity of liquid to fairly float them, and specific gravities observed with them are less delicate and trustworthy than those obtained by the balance.

Specific Gravity of Solids in Mass.

Weigh a piece (50 to 250 grains) of any solid substance heavier than water in the usual manner. Then weigh it in water, by suspending it from a shortened balance-pan by a fine thread or hair and immersing in a vessel of water. The buoyant properties of the water will cause the solid to apparently lose weight: *this loss in weight is the exact weight of an equal bulk of water.* The weight of the substance and the weight of an equal bulk of water being thus ascertained, a rule-of-three sum shows the proportional weight of the substance to 1.000 of water. To express the same thing by rule, divide the weight in air by the loss of weight in water, the resulting number is the specific gravity in relation to 1 part of water, the conventional standard of comparison.

Verify some of the following specific gravities:—

Aluminium	2.56
Antimony	6.71
Bismuth	9.83
Coins, English, gold	17.69
" " silver	10.30
" " bronze	8.70
Copper	8.95
Gold	19.34
Iron	7.84
Lead	11.36
Magnesium	1.74
Marble	2.70
Phosphorus	1.77
Platinum	21.53
Silver	10.53
Sulphur	2.05
Tin	7.29
Zinc	7.14

Specific gravities of solid substances should be taken in water having a temperature of about 60° F. The body should be immersed about half an inch below the surface of the water; adhering air-bubbles must be carefully removed; the body must be quite insoluble in water.

Specific Gravity of Solids in Powder or Small Fragments.

Weigh the particles; place them in a counterpoised specific-gravity bottle of known capacity, and fill up with water, taking care that the substance is thoroughly wetted;

again weigh. From the combined weights of water and substance subtract the amount due to the substance; the residue is the weight of the water. Subtract this weight of water from the quantity which the bottle normally contains; the residue is the amount of water displaced by the substance. Having thus obtained the weights of equal bulks of water and substance, a rule-of-three sum shows the relation of the weight of the substance to 1 part of water, the specific gravity.

Or, suspend a cup, short glass tube, or bucket from a shortened balance-pan; immerse in water; counterpoise; place the weighed powder in the cup, and proceed as directed for taking the specific gravity of a solid in mass.

This operation may be conducted on fragments of any of the substances the specific gravities of which are given in the foregoing Table, or on the powdered piece of marble the specific gravity of which has been taken in mass. The specific gravity of one piece of glass, first in mass then in powder, may be ascertained; the result should be identical. The specific gravity of shot is about 11.350; sand, 2.600; mercury, 13.56.

Specific Gravity of Solids Soluble in Water.

Weigh a piece of sugar or other substance soluble in water; suspend it from a balance in the usual manner, and weigh it in turpentine, benzol, or petroleum, the specific gravity of which is known or has been previously determined; the loss in weight is the weight of an equal bulk of the turpentine. Ascertain the weight of an equal bulk of water by calculation:—

$$\text{Sp. gr. of turpentine} : \text{sp. gr. of water} :: \text{observed bulk of turp.} : \text{equal bulk of water.}$$

The exact weights of equal bulks of sugar and water being obtained, the weight of a bulk of sugar corresponding to one of water is shown by a rule-of-three sum; in other words, divide the weight of sugar by that of the equal bulk of water, the quotient is the specific gravity of sugar. The specific gravity of sugar ranges from 1.067 to 1.090.

Specific Gravity of Solids Lighter than Water.

This is obtained in a manner similar to that for solids heavier than water; but the light body is sunk by help of a piece of heavy metal, the bulk of water which the latter displaces being deducted from the bulk displaced by both;

the remainder is the weight of a bulk of water equal to the bulk of the light body. For instance, a piece of wood weighing 12 grammes (or grains) is tied to a piece of metal weighing 22 grammes, the loss of weight of the metal in water having been previously found to be 3 grammes. The two, weighing 34 grammes, are now immersed, and the loss in weight found to be 26 grammes. But of this loss 3 grammes have been proved to be due to the buoyant action of the water on the lead; the remaining 23, therefore, represent the same effect on the wood; 23 and 12, therefore, represent the weights of equal bulks of water and wood. As 23 are to 12 so is 1 to .5217. Or, shortly, as before, divide the weight in air by the weight of an equal bulk of water; .5217 is the specific gravity of the wood. Another specimen of wood may be found to be three-fourths (.750) the weight of water, and others heavier. Cork varies from .100 to .300.

Specific Gravity of Gases.

This operation is similar to that for liquids. A globe exhausted of air and holding from 1 to 4 litres (or quarts) is suspended from the arm of a balance, and counterpoised by a similar flask. Gases are introduced in succession and their weights noted. A rule-of-three sum shows their specific gravity in relation to air or hydrogen, whichever be taken as a standard.

Correction of the Volume of Gases for Pressure.—The height of the barometer at the time of manipulation is noted. Remembering the fact that "the bulk of a gas is inversely as the pressure to which it is subjected" (Boyle and Mariotte), a simple calculation shows the volume which the gas would occupy at 760 millimetres (or 29.922 inches), the standard pressure. (30 inches is sometimes adopted as the standard in England.*) Thus, 40 volumes of a gas at 740 millimetres pressure are reduced to 39 when the pressure becomes 760 millimetres (or 90 vols. at 29 ins. barom. become 87 vols. at 30 inches).

Correction of the Volume of Gases for Temperature.—This is done in order to ascertain what volume the gas would occupy at 0° C. (32° F.) or 15°.5 C. (60° F.), according to the standard taken. Gases expand about 0.3665† per cent. ($\frac{1}{273}$) of their volume *at the*

* In France the conventional standard height of the barometer is 760 millimetres at 0° C. (32° F.); in England it is 30 inches, the temperature of the mercurial column being 60° F. 760 millims. is equivalent to 29.922 inches; but the expansion of the metal between 32° F. and 60° F. increases the length of the column to 30.005 inches. The standards are, therefore, almost identical, difference in true length being counterbalanced by the temperature at which the length is observed.

† Corrected for the difference between the mercurial and air thermometers the coefficient of expansion of air is 0.003656 (Miller). Gases vary slightly.

freezing-point of water for every C. degree (0.2036, or $\frac{1}{491}$ for every F. degree) (Regnault). Thus 8 volumes of gas at 0° C. will become 8.293 at 10° C.; for if 100 become 103.665 on being increased in temperature 10° C., 8 will become 8.293 (or if 100 become 102.036 on being increased 10° F., 8 will become 8.1629).

Vapor-density.—Vapors are those gases which condense to liquids at common temperatures. By the density of a vapor is meant its specific gravity. The density of a vapor is the ratio of any given volume to a similar volume of air or hydrogen at the same temperature and pressure. But, for convenience of comparison, this experimental specific gravity is referred, by calculation as just described for permanent gases, to a temperature of 0° C., and 760 millimetres barom. A teaspoonful or so of liquid is placed in a weighed flask of about the capacity of a common tumbler and having a capillary neck; the flask is heated in an oil-bath to a temperature considerably above the boiling-point of the liquid; at the moment vapor ceases to escape, the neck is sealed by a blowpipe-flame, and the temperature of the bath noted; the flask is then removed, cooled, cleaned, and weighed; the height of the barometer is also taken. The neck of the flask is next broken off beneath the surface of water or mercury (which rush in and fill it), and again weighed, by which its capacity in cub. centims. is found. From these data the volume of vapor yielded by a given weight of liquid is ascertained by a few obvious calculations. The capacity of the globe having been ascertained, the weight of an equal bulk of air* is obtained by a rule-of-three sum. This weight of air is deducted from the original weight of the flask, which gives the true weight of the glass. The weight of the glass is next subtracted from the weight of the flask and contained vapor (now condensed), which gives the weight of material used in the experiment. The volume which this weight of material occupied at the time of experiment is next corrected for temperature (to 0° C.) and pressure (760 millimetres) in the manner just described. The weight of a similar volume of hydrogen is next found.† The weights of equal volumes of hydrogen and vapor being thus determined, the amount of vapor corresponding to 1 of hydrogen (the specific gravity or vapor-density) is shown by a short calculation. This process of finding the weight of a given volume of vapor is by Dumas. Gay-Lussac's consists in determining the volume of a given weight.

Experiment shows that the specific gravities of many gases and

*1 cub. centim. of air at 0° C. and 760 millims. weighs 0.001293 gramme.

†1 litre (1000 cub. centims.) of hydrogen at 0° C. and 760 millimetres (the barometer being at 0° C.) weighs 0.8096 gramme—a volume sometimes termed a *crith* (from κριθή, *krithē*, a barley-corn—figuratively, a small weight); thus a litre of oxygen weighs 16 criths, chlorine 35.5 criths, &c. 100 cubic inches of hydrogen at 32° F. weigh 2.265 grains; at 60° F. 2.143 grains (the barometer being 30 ins. at 60° F. in both cases). 100 cubic inches of air at 32° F. weigh 32.698 grains; at 60° F., 30.935 (barom. 30 ins. at 60° F.). 1 cubic inch of water weighs 252.5 (252.458 at 62° F., and 30 in. bar.) grains. 1 gallon of water contains 277¼ (277.274 at 62° F.) cubic inches.

vapors on the hydrogen scale and the proportions in which they combine by weight are identical. Thus, chlorine is 35.5 times as heavy as hydrogen, and 35.5 parts unite with 1 of hydrogen to form hydrochloric acid gas. Hence, if the specific gravity of a gas or vapor is known, its combining proportion may be predicated with reasonable certainty, and *vice versâ*. In applying this rule to gaseous or vaporous compounds, attention must be paid to the extent to which their constituent gases contract at the moment of combination or expand at the moment of decomposition. Thus, steam is found to be composed of two volumes of hydrogen and one of oxygen, the three volumes of constituents condensing to two at the moment of combination. Hence, steam may be expected to be nine times as heavy as hydrogen, which experiment confirms.

These relations may be so expressed as to include both elementary and compound gases and vapors, thus: *molecular weights and specific weights are identical.* Molecular weights represent two volumes of a gas; specific gravity conventionally represents the relative weight of a gas compared with *one* volume of hydrogen or air; hence the specific gravity of a gas or vapor on the H scale is found by calculation on simply dividing the molecular weight by 2; on the air-scale by dividing the hydrogen numbers by 14.44. For example,—

Name.	Molecular formula.	Molecular weight.	Specific gravity. H = 2.	H = 1.	Air = 1.
Hydrogen,	H_2	2	2	1	.069
Chlorine,	Cl_2	71	71	35.5	2.460
Oxygen,	O_2	32	32	16	1.108
Nitrogen,	N_2	28	28	14	.970
Steam,	H_2O	18	18	9	.624
Ammonia gas,	NH_3	17	17	8.5	.589
Carbonic acid gas,	CO_2	44	44	22	1.524
Alcohol (vapor),	C_2H_6O	46	46	23	1.593
Air,	.....	....	28.88	14.44	1.000

These specific gravities closely correspond with those obtained by actual experiment. The specific gravity of any gas or vapor may therefore be calculated if the following data are at hand: (*a*) formula, (*b*) atomic weight of constituent elements; these give the molecular weight, and *the molecular weight divided by* 2 *is the specific gravity* on the hydrogen-scale. Specific gravity on the air-scale is then deducible, if (*c*) the specific gravity of air (14.44) in relation to hydrogen be remembered. The absolute weight of any volume of a gas or vapor on the metric system is then obtainable if (*d*) the weight of a litre of hydrogen (0.0896 gramme) be known, or on the English plan by remembering (*e*) that 100 cubic inches of hydrogen at 60° F. weigh 2.143 grains (100 cubic inches of air at 60° F. weigh 30.935 grains).

In confirmation of these statements regarding the mutual relation of specific gravity and atomic weight, a remarkable fact may be mentioned. Regnault several years ago found the weights of 1 litre of hydrogen and oxygen to be respectively .089578 and 1.429802 gramme. The latter number divided by the former gives 15.96 as the specific gravity of oxygen. Stas, in recent experimental researches on combining-proportion, finds the atomic weight of oxygen to be not 16, but 15.96.

Exceptions to the law occur in a few compounds and in arsenicum and phosphorus, whose vapor-densities are twice that indicated by the rule.

QUESTIONS AND EXERCISES.

938. Define specific weight, or as it is commonly termed, specific gravity.

939. In speaking of light and heavy bodies especially, what standard of comparison is conventionally employed?

940. How are specifie gravities expressed in figures?

941. Why should specific gravities be taken at one constant temperature?

942. How does the buoyancy of air affect the real weight of any material?

943. Describe the difference between density and specific gravity.

944. Give a direct method for the determination of the specific gravity of liquids.

945. A certain bottle holds 150 parts, by weight, of water, or 135.7 of spirit of wine; what is the specific gravity of the latter? *Ans.* 0.9046.

946. Equal volumes of benzol and glycerine weigh 34 and 49 parts respectively, and the sp. gr. of the benzol is 0.850; what is the specific gravity of the glycerine? *Ans.* 1.225.

947. Explain the process employed in taking the specific gravity of solid substances in mass and in powder.

948. State the method by which the specific gravity of a light body, such as cork, is obtained.

949. What modifications of the usual method are necessary in ascertaining the specific gravity of substances soluble in water?

950. How is the specific gravity of gases determined?

951. By what law can the volume of a gas, at any required pressure, be deduced from its observed volume at another pressure?

952. To what extent will 78 volumes of a gas at 29.3 inches barometer alter in bulk when the pressure, as indicated by the barometer, is 30.2 inches?

953. Write a short account of the means by which the volumes of gases are corrected for temperature.

954. At the temperature of 15° C. 40 volumes (litres, pints, ounces, cubic feet, or other quantity) of a gas are measured. To what extent will this amount of gas contract on being cooled to the freezing-point of water (0° C.)?

Answer. As 1 vol. of any gas *at zero* expands or contracts .003665 of a vol. for each rise or fall of 1° C., 1 vol. at 0° C. if heated to 15° C. will become increased by .054975 (that is, .003665) multiplied by 15), 1 vol. will expand to 1.054975. Conversely, 1.054975 vol. will contract to 1 vol. if cooled from 15° C. to 0° C. And if 1.054975 becomes 1 in cooling through 15° C., 40 vols. will (as found by rule-of-three) contract to 37.916.

(The following five problems and solutions are from Williamson's "Chemistry.")

955. 10 litres of oxygen are measured off at 14° F. Required the volume of the gas at 15° C.

Answer. The first operation must be to reduce the temperature quoted in Fahrenheit's degrees to an equivalent value on the Centigrade scale. 14° F. is 18° below 32° F., the freezing-point of water; and a range of 9° on the Fahrenheit's scale is equal to a range of 5° on the Centigrade scale, so that the temperature at which the oxygen is measured off is —10° C. The rise of temperature up to 0° expands the gas in such proportion that its volume at 6° is to its volume at —10° as 1 is to 1—0.03665, *i. e.* as 1 to 0.96335. The further rise of temperature from 0° C. to 15° expands the gas in the proportion of 1 to $1+15\times0.003665$; *i. e.* 1 to 1.054975. The total rise of temperature therefore expands the gas in the proportion of 0.96335 to 1.054975.

$$0.96335 : 1.054975 : : 10 : x;$$

$$\therefore x = \frac{10\times1.054975}{0.06335} = 10.95.$$

956. 230 cubic centimetres of oxygen are measured off at 14° C. and 740 millimetres mercurial pressure. Required the volume of the gas at the normal temperature and pressure (0° C. and 760 millimetres).

Answer. Let the reduction for change of temperature be made first. The proportion

$$1+14\times0.003665 : 1 : : 230 : x$$

gives

$$x = \frac{230}{1.05131} = 218.774.$$

To reduce this volume at 740 millimetres pressure to the volume corresponding to the pressure of 760 millimetres, we have the proportion

$$38 : 37 : : 218.77 : x;$$

whence

$$x = \frac{37\times218.77}{38} = 213.02.$$

957. A litre of oxygen is confined in a glass flask at 10° C. by the atmospheric pressure, added to that of a column of mercury 60 millimetres high. The flask must be heated to 300° C. without any increase of volume taking place in the oxygen. How high must the column of mercury then be which presses on the gas, supposing the atmospheric pressure to remain constant at 760 millimetres?

Answer. The oxygen is given at 10° C. and 820 millimetres pressure. If the pressure remained constant, the rise of temperature from 10° C. to 300° C. would expand the gas in such proportion that 1.03665 volume would expand to 2.0995 volumes. In order to prevent any expansion the pressure must be increased in the same proportion, whence

$$1.03665 : 2.0995 :: 820 : x;$$

$$\therefore x = \frac{820 \times 2.0995}{1.03665} = 1660.6.$$

From this total pressure the atmospheric pressure of 760 millimetres has to be deducted, leaving 900.6 millimetres as the height of the required mercurial column.

958. A litre of oxygen is required of the density of 100 at 0° C. What weight of potassic chlorate must be used for its preparation, and what total pressure must be applied to it?

Answer. The pressure required to compress oxygen from the density of 16 to that of 100 is found by the proportion

$$16 : 100 :: 760 : x;$$

$$\therefore x = \frac{76000}{16} = 4750.$$

At the pressure of 4750 millimetres of mercury the weight of a litre of oxygen (16 grammes measure 11.2 litres at 0° C. and 760 millims. pressure) is found by the proportion

$$760 : 4750 :: \frac{16}{11.2} : x;$$

whence

$$x = \frac{16 \times 4750}{11.2 \times 760} = 8.93 \text{ grammes.}$$

The weight of chlorate required for the evolution of 8.93 grammes of oxygen is found from the proportion

$$48 : 122.5 :: 8.93 : x;$$

$$\therefore x = 22.8 \text{ grammes.}$$

959. What is the volume of 12 grammes of hydrogen at 15° C.?

Answer. One gramme of hydrogen measures 11.2 litres at 0° C., therefore 12 grammes measure $12 \times 11.2 = 134.4$ litres at 0°. To find their volume at 15° C. we have the proportion

$$1 : 1 + 15 \times 0.003665 :: 134.4 : x;$$

whence

$$x = 134.4 \times 1.054975 = 141.788 \text{ litres.}$$

VOLUMETRIC ANALYSIS.

APPARATUS.

The only special vessels necessary in volumetric quantitative operations are : 1. *A litre flask*, which, when filled to a mark on the neck, contains one litre (1000 cubic centimetres, *i. e.* 1000 grammes of water*) ; it serves for preparing solutions in quantities of one litre. 2. A tall cylindrical *graduated litre jar* divided into 100 equal parts; it serves for the measurement and admixture of decimal or centesimal parts of a litre. 3. A graduated tube or *burette*, which, when filled to 0, holds 100 cubic centimetres (a decilitre), and is divided into 100 equal parts; it is used for accurately measuring small volumes of liquids.

The best form of burette is Mohr's (with Erdmann's float). It consists of a glass tube about the width of a little finger and the length of an arm from the elbow, contracted at the lower extremity and graduated. To the contracted portion is fitted a small piece of vulcanized caoutchouc tubing, into the other end of which a small spout made of narrow glass tube is tightly inserted. A strong wire clamp effectually prevents any liquid from passing out of the burette unless the knobs of the clamp are pressed by the finger and thumb of the operator, when a stream or drops flow at will. The accurate reading of the height of a solution in the burette is a matter of great importance. For this purpose a hollow glass float or bulb is used, of such a width that it can move freely in the tube without undue friction, and so adjusted in weight that it shall sink to more than half its length in any ordinary liquid. A fine line is scratched round the centre of the float; this line must be always regarded as marking the height of the fluid in the burette. In charging the burette, a solution is poured in, not until its surface is coincident with 0, but until the mark on the float is coincident with 0.

ESTIMATION OF ALKALIES, ETC.

An equation represents much more than the formation of certain substances from others. Thus

$$\underset{\text{Ammonia.}}{2NH_4HO} + \underset{\text{Crystallized oxalic acid.}}{H_2C_2O_4,2H_2O} = \underset{\text{Oxalate of ammonium.}}{(NH_4)_2C_2O_4,H_2O} + \underset{\text{Water.}}{3H_2O}$$

not only shows that oxalate of ammonium is produced when ammonia and crystallized oxalic acid are mixed together, but among other

* A cubic centimetre is, strictly speaking, the volume occupied by one gramme of distilled water at its point of greatest density, namely, 4° C.; metrical measurements, however, are uniformly taken at 15°.55 C. (60° F.).

facts, that 70 parts of ammonia and 126 of oxalic acid yield 142 of crystallized oxalate of ammonium and 54 of water. For formulæ represent molecules; the weight of a molecule is the sum of the weights of its atoms; and atomic weights are represented by definite invariable numbers (see the Table of atomic weights in the Appendix).

As 126 parts (= 1 molecule) of oxalic acid combine with 70 parts (= 2 molecules) of ammonia, 63 (half of 126) of oxalic acid will unite with 35 (= 1 molecule) of ammonia (NH_4HO); 63 parts of oxalic acid will also unite with 56 of caustic potash ($KHO = 56$), 40 of caustic soda ($NaHO = 40$), 100 of acid carbonate of potassium ($KHCO_3 = 100$), 69 of anhydrous carbonate of potassium ($K_2CO_3 = 138$), 84 of acid carbonate of sodium ($NaHCO_3 = 84$), 53 of anhydrous carbonate of sodium ($Na_2CO_3 = 106$), or 143 of crystallized carbonate of sodium ($Na_2CO_3, 10H_2O = 286$). And if 63 parts of oxalic acid be dissolved in 100 volumes of water, the stated weights of these various salts should be exactly neutralized by such a solution. 143 parts of crystallized carbonate of sodium, for instance, should, if pure, be exactly neutralized by the 100 volumes of the oxalic acid solution; and if a less number of volumes is required, the salt is so much per cent. impure. 143 parts by weight of a commercial sample of carbonate of sodium (common washing-"soda") requiring only 97 of the standard oxalic acid solution is thus shown to contain 97 per cent. of pure carbonate of sodium, the remainder being impurities. Further, the strength of solutions of ammonia, soda, potash, and lime may be accurately determined by adding to any definite quantity of them gradually, from a burette, a solution containing oxalic acid in known quantity, until exact neutralization is effected. If the quantity of oxalic acid required be 63 parts by weight (or 100 volumes of solution of oxalic acid containing 63 parts, by weight, of the crystals), then the quantities of alkaline solutions employed contain, of potash (KHO) 56 parts by weight, of soda ($NaHO$) 40, of ammonia (NH_4HO) 35 parts, of slaked lime ($Ca2HO$) 37, anhydrous lime (CaO) 28, &c. The strength of an alkaline solution, or, in other words, the proportion required to effect neutralization of 100 volumes of the oxalic acid solution, having once been determined and decided by authority (B. P. *e. g.*), that quantity may always be expected to take 100 volumes of the oxalic acid liquid; if less is required, the alkaline liquid is so much per cent. weak.

The exact point of neutralization of acid or alkaline liquids is experimentally ascertained by litmus paper, or, more generally, infusion of litmus, which is turned red by the slightest amount of free acid, and blue by alkali.

Standard Solution of Oxalic Acid.

(Crystallized Oxalic Acid, $H_2C_2O_4, 2H_2O = 126$.)

On account of the bivalent character of the oxalic radical and the univalent character of most of the metals contained in the salts which are estimated by oxalic acid, it is convenient to take half the molecular weight of the acid for experiments, with the whole of the molecular weights of salts of univalent basylous radicals. The oxalic acid must be pure, leaving no ash when a gramme or so is heated to redness in a porcelain or platinum crucible; it must also be quite dry, but not effloresced.

Place 63 grammes of the crystals in a litre flask, add distilled water and shake till dissolved, diluting until the solution, at about 60° F., has an exact volume of 1 litre. Preserve in a stoppered bottle.

100 cubic centimetres of this solution contain $\frac{1}{20}$ of the molecular weight of oxalic acid in grammes, and will neutralize $\frac{1}{20}$ of the molecular weight in grammes of a salt containing one atom of certain bivalent metals (as Ca2HO), or a salt (Na_2CO_3 *e. g.*) containing two atoms of univalent metals, or $\frac{1}{10}$ of the molecular weight in grammes of salts containing one atom of univalent radicals (such as $KHCO_3$).

The following official substances are tested with this solution. In those which are fluid there is commonly a slight variation in strength according as they are made by formulæ of the British or U. S. Pharmacopœia.

	Grammes of substance.		C. c. of vol. sol.
* Ammonia, solution of	17.00	=	100.0
" strong solution of	5.23	=	100.0
Ammonium, carbonate of, B. P. and U. S. P.	5.90	=	100.0
Borax, B. P. and U. S. P.	19.10	=	100.0
Lead, acetate of, B. P. and U. S. P. . . .	9.50	=	50.0
" sol. of subacetate of, B. P. and U. S. P.	51.02	=	100.0
Lime, aqueous solution of, B. P. and U. S. P.	438.00	=	20.0
" saccharated sol. of	45.30	=	25.0
Potash, caustic, B. P. and U. S. P. . . .	5.60	=	90.0 to 100.0
" solution of	48.02	=	50.0
" water, effervescing	292.00	=	10.0
Potassium, bicarbonate of, B. P. and U. S. P.	5.00	=	50.0
" acid tart. of, B. P. and U. S. P.	18.80	=	100.0
" carbonate of, B. P. and U. S. P.	8.30	=	98.0 to 100.0
" citrate of, B. P. and U. S. P. .	10.20	=	100.0
" tartrate of, B. P. and U. S. P. .	11.30	=	100.0
Soda, caustic B. P. and U. S. P.	4.00	=	90.0 to 100.0
" solution of	48.72	=	50.0
" water, effervescing	246.07	=	10.0
Sodium, bicarbonate of, B. P. and U. S. P. .	8.40	=	100.0
" and potassium, tart. of, B.P. and U.S.P.	14.10	=	100.0
" carbonate of, B. P. and U. S. P. .	14.30	=	96.0 to 100.0

* The reading of the Table may be amplified thus: 17 grammes of the official Solution of Ammonia (*Liquor Ammoniæ*, B. P.), carefully weighed, will require, for complete neutralization, if of full strength, 100 cubic centimetres of the official volumetric solution of oxalic acid.

Note 1.—The several substances diluted or dissolved, as described in the following paragraphs, are conveniently placed in a beaker, and the solution of acid run in cautiously from the burette.

Note 2.—A smaller number of c. c. of volumetric solution than 100, and a corresponding amount of substance to be tested, may be employed in any case. But to ascertain percentage of impurity in the substance, the amount corresponding to 100 c. c. of the vol. sol. must be considered to have been used, the number of c. c. then wanting to make up 100 is the percentage of impurity.

The solutions of ammonia require only the addition of solution of litmus, and the acid cautiously added until the last drop turns the liquid red. The amount of acid used previously to the addition to the portion that reddened the litmus indicates the proportional purity of the alkaline liquid. Thus, if only 50 c. c. are required, the solution is only half as strong as it ought to be; if 93 c. c. are needed, the sol. of ammonia is 7 per cent. too weak, and so on. The actual quantity of ammonia (NH_4HO) or ammoniacal gas (NH_3) in the solutions is readily ascertained by calculation, thus: 100 c. c. of the acid solution have been employed; these contain $\frac{1}{20}$ of the molecular weight of oxalic acid in grammes=6.3, and have neutralized $\frac{1}{10}$ of the molecular weight of ammonia in grammes=3.5 (or 1.7 of NH_3); 5.23 parts, by weight, of strong solution of ammonia (the amount employed in the experiment) contain, therefore, 3.5 of ammonia, NH_4HO, or 1.7 of ammoniacal gas NH_3; now if 5.23 parts of a solution contain 3.5 of real ammonia (NH_4HO), 100 parts will contain (by rule-of-three calculation) 67, and if the 5.23 contain 1.7 part of ammonia gas (NH_3), 100 will contain 32.5; hence the Strong Solution of Ammonia, supposed to have been under examination, contains 67 per cent. of the hydrate or 32.5 per cent. of the gas. The formulæ and molecular weights representing this process are as follows:—

$$\underbrace{2NH_4HO}_{70} \quad \underbrace{(\text{or } 2NH_3)}_{34} \quad + \quad \underbrace{H_2C_2O_4,2H_2O}_{126}$$

The carbonate of ammonium should be dissolved in 30 or 40 c. c. of distilled water, infusion of litmus added, the standard oxalic acid solution allowed to flow in until the well-stirred liquid assumes a purple hue (due to the influence of carbonic acid on the litmus), the whole gently warmed to promote evolution of carbonic acid gas, more standard acid then dropped in until the liquid again becomes purple, heat once more applied, and the operation continued until the last drop of acid turns the solution red; the height of the column of liquid in the burette before the last drop escapes represents the true amount of standard solution used, and hence the percentage of real carbonate of ammonium (of official quality) in the specimen on which the experiment was performed. The solution must be heated with care, or ammonia will escape. (Practised analysts usually add excess of the standard acid and thus fix every trace of ammonia; then gently boil to get rid of carbonic acid gas; bring back the liquid to neutrality by an observed volume of standard alkaline solution, and deduct an equivalent volume of acid from the quantity first added.) The formulæ and molecular weights representing the process are as follows:—

$$\underbrace{N_4H_{16}C_3O_8}_{\substack{236 \\ (\textit{vide}\ \text{p. 67})}} \quad + \quad \underbrace{2(H_2C_2O_4,2H_2O)}_{\substack{252 \\ \text{(2 molecules)}}}$$

As 252 parts of oxalic acid neutralize 236 of the so-called carbonate of ammonium, 6.3 of acid (or 100 vols. of its solution) will neutralize 5.9 of carbonate. If 5.9 grammes of carbonate be the quantity employed, and it does *not* require 100 c.c. of the volumetric solution, it is so much per cent. weak. Thus if, say 94 c.c. neutralize the salt, the latter is 6 per cent. weak (some ammonia gas has escaped, and, consequently, an abnormal amount of acid carbonate NH_4HCO_3, is present). Any smaller quantity of salt than 5.9 grammes may be used; in that case a rule-of-three sum must be worked to show how many c.c. of vol. sol. would have been employed if 5.9 grammes had actually been the amount under experiment.

The borax should be dissolved in several ounces of distilled water. The formulæ and molecular weights representing the process are as follows:—

$$\underbrace{2NaBO_2, B_2O_3, 10H_2O}_{382} \quad + \quad \underbrace{H_2C_2O_4, 2H_2O}_{126}$$

The solutions of the acetates of lead in distilled water may be rendered clear by the addition of a few drops of acetic acid. They must be well stirred after each addition of the solution of oxalic acid. The action is complete when the last drop of acid produces no more precipitate (oxalate of lead).

$$\underbrace{Pb2C_2H_3O_2, 3H_2O}_{379} + \underbrace{H_2C_2O_4, 2H_2O}_{126}$$

$$\underbrace{Pb_2O2C_2H_3O_2}_{548} + \underbrace{2(H_2C_2O_4, 2H_2O)}_{252}$$

The solutions of lime require similar treatment.

$$\underbrace{Ca2HO}_{74} \quad \underbrace{(or\ CaO)}_{56} + \underbrace{H_2C_2O_4, 2H_2O}_{126}$$

Solid caustic potash or soda is never met with in a state of chemical purity, but should contain not less than 90 per cent. of the hydrate of potassium or sodium. The standard acid is added to an aqueous solution of the hydrate, the termination of the action between the alkali and acid being observed by aid of litmus.

If carbonic acid be present, the mixture must be gently boiled before a final reading of the amount of acid added is taken.

$$\underbrace{2KHO}_{112} \quad or \quad \underbrace{2NaHO}_{80} + \underbrace{H_2C_2O_4, 2H_2O}_{126}$$

The alkaline carbonates are often moist, and include traces of sulphates, chlorides, and silicates, but are sufficiently pure if containing, in the case of carbonate potassium 98 per cent., and carbonate of sodium 96 per cent., of the respective crystalline salts. The volumetric manipulations with these salts are similar to those for carbonate of ammonium. The strength of soda-ash is often reported in terms of "soda," that is, oxide of sodium ($Na_2O=62$). The old molecular weight of carbonate of sodium, 54 (it should have been 53), derived from that of "soda," 32 (it should have been 31), is still employed by manufacturers in reporting the strength of soda-ash. The true amount of soda equivalent to 54 parts of carbonate is 31.41 parts. A modern analyst having found the true amount of soda in a sample of soda-ash is expected by the manufacturer to report 31.41 parts for every 31, and 54 of carbonate instead of 53, and other quantities in proportion to these figures.

One molecule of tartrate of potassium, or two of the *acid tartrate*, yields one of carbonate when burnt, two molecules of *citrate* yielding three of carbonate under the same circumstances. One molecule of the *tartrate of potassium and sodium* yields one of potassium carbonate and one of sodium carbonate. A volumetric estimation of the amount of carbonate thus produced affords indirect means of quantitatively determining the purity of the original salts.

$$\underbrace{K_2C_4H_4O_6}_{226} \text{ eq. to } \underbrace{H_2C_2O_4, 2H_2O}_{126}$$

$$\underbrace{2KHC_4H_4O_6}_{376} \text{ eq. to } \underbrace{H_2C_2O_4, 2H_2O}_{126}$$

$$\underbrace{2K_3C_6H_5O_7}_{612} \text{ eq. to } \underbrace{3(H_2C_2O_4, 2H_2O}_{378}$$

$$\underbrace{NaKC_4H_4O_6, 4H_2O}_{282} \text{ eq. to } \underbrace{H_2C_2O_4, 2H_2O}_{126}$$

Alkalimetry.—The foregoing processes are often spoken of as those of *alkalimetry* (the measurement of alkalies).

Notes.

Neutral solution of litmus is prepared by digesting the commercial fragments in about fifteen or twenty times their weight of water for a few hours, decanting, dividing into two equal portions, adding acid to one till it is faintly red, then pouring in the other, and mixing. The solution may be kept in a stoppered bottle, but occasionally exposed to the air. It should never be filtered, but gradually allowed to deposit.

Standard sulphuric acid may be used in the place of oxalic acid if the latter cannot readily be obtained in a state of purity, 100 c. c. of the liquid containing $\frac{1}{20}$ of the molecular weight of the pure acid in grammes. It is prepared by diluting oil of vitriol with from three to four times its bulk of distilled water, ascertaining how much of the acid liquid is required to exactly neutralize $\frac{1}{20}$ of the molecular weight of pure carbonate of sodium, taken in grammes (5.3), and adding water until the observed volume of acid is increased to 100 c. c. Pure anhydrous carbonate of sodium (Na_2CO_3) is obtained by heating the pure bicarbonate to dull redness in a platinum or porcelain crucible for about a quarter of an hour. The commercial bicarbonate should be tested for chlorides and sulphates, which are usually present in small quantities. Two or three hundred grammes may be purified by washing first with a saturated solution of bicarbonate of sodium and then cold distilled water until all trace of impurity has disappeared, drying over a water-bath, and then igniting to convert into carbonate.

Other quantities of salts than those stated in the foregoing and following Tables may be employed in volumetric determinations, calculation giving any desired form to the experimental results, an expert analyst thus saving much time and material. In the case of substances which are liable to alter by exposure to air, it is important that a selected quantity should be quickly weighed, rather than selected weights be accurately balanced by material, the former operation occupying much the shorter time.

Salts other than the official may be quantitatively analyzed by the volumetric solutions, slight modifications of manipulation even enabling the processes to be adapted to fresh classes of salts. Ample instructions for extending operations in this manner will be found in Sutton's "Handbook of Volumetric Analysis."

QUESTIONS AND EXERCISES.

960. Describe the various pieces of apparatus used in volumetric determinations.

961. One hundred cubic centimetres of solution of oxalic acid contain 6.3 grammes of the crystallized salt; what weights of bicarbonate of potassium and anhydrous carbonate of sodium will that volume saturate?—*Ans.* 10 grammes and 5.3 grammes.

962. What weight of hydrate of potassium is contained in solution of potash 48.02 grammes of which are saturated by 50 c. c. of the standard solution of oxalic acid?—*Ans.* 5.83 per cent.

963. State the percentage of hydrate of calcium in lime-water 438 grammes of which are neutralized by 20 c. c. of the volumetric solution of oxalic acid.

964. Eight grammes of a sample of Rochelle salt, after appropriate treatment, require 54.3 c. c. of the oxalic acid solution for complete saturation; what is the centesimal proportion of real salt present?—*Ans.* 95.7.

ESTIMATION OF ACIDS.

In the previous experiments a known amount of an acid has been used in determining unknown amounts of alkalies. In those about to be described a known amount of an alkali is employed in estimating unknown amounts of acids. The alkaline salt selected may be a hydrate or a carbonate; but the former is to be preferred; for the carbonic acid, set free when a strong acid is added to a carbonate, interferes to some extent with the indications of alkalinity, acidity, or neutrality afforded by litmus. The alkali most convenient for use is soda, a solution of which has probably already been made the subject of experiment in operations with the standard solution of oxalic acid. It should be kept in a stoppered bottle and exposed to air as little as possible.

Standard Solution of Soda.

(Hydrate of Sodium, $NaHO = 40$.)

100 c. c. of the standard solution of oxalic acid are placed in a beaker with a little litmus, the tube or burette in which the acid was measured rinsed out, and the washings poured into the beaker. A little strong solution of caustic soda is poured through the burette to rinse out water adhering to the tube and float (these rinsings thrown away), and the tube then filled to 0 with more of the alkaline liquid. The solution of soda is cautiously allowed to flow into the beaker until exact neutrality is obtained, the quantity noted, and, to every similar quantity of the whole bulk of the solution of soda, water added until the liquid measures 100 parts. If, for example, 93 c. c. of solution of soda have neutralized the 100 c. c. of acid, then 7 c. c. of distilled water must be added to 93 c. c. of the soda solution, or 70 to 930 to make a litre. A sum of simple proportion will show to what extent any other quantity is to be diluted. Thus, if the bulk of soda solution remaining measures, say, 900 c. c., its volume must be augmented to 967.7 c. c.; for if 93 are to be diluted to 100, 900 must be diluted to 967.7.

100 c. c. of the soda solution contain $\frac{1}{10}$ of the molecular weight (=4.), taken in grammes, of pure hydrate of sodium, and will neutralize an equivalent quantity of any acid. That is, 100 c. c. will neutralize $\frac{1}{10}$ of the molecular weight in grammes of an acid containing one atom of any univalent acidulous radical, $\frac{1}{20}$ of the molecular weight in grammes of an acid containing one atom of any bivalent acidulous radical, or $\frac{1}{30}$ of the molecular weight in grammes of an acid containing one atom of any trivalent acidulous radical.

The following official acids are tested with this solution :—

	Grammes of substance.		C. c. of vol. sol.
Acid, acetic	18.20	=	100.0
" " diluted, B. P. and U. S. P.	70.29	=	50.0
" " glacial	6.00	=	99.0
" citric, B. P. and U. S. P. . . .	7.00	=	100.0
" hydrochloric, B. P. and U. S. P.	11.48	=	100.0
" " diluted	34.50	=	100.0
" nitric, B. P. and U. S. P. . . .	9.00	=	100.0
" " diluted	36.13	=	100.0
" nitro-hydrochloric, diluted . . .	38.30	=	100.0
" sulphuric, B. P. and U. S. P. . .	5.06	=	100.0
" " aromatic	36.65	=	100.0
" " diluted	35.90	=	100.0
" tartaric, B. P. and U. S. P. . .	7.50	=	100.0

Notes.—1. In volumetrically estimating the strength of acids by an alkali, the indicator of neutrality is the same as that used in testing alkalies by an acid, namely, litmus.

2. Pure acetates, citrates, tartrates, and some other organic salts have an alkaline action on litmus, but not to an important extent. If the soda solution be added to acetic, citric, or tartaric acids, containing litmus, until the liquid is fairly blue, the operator will obtain trustworthy results. In delicate experiments turmeric may be used instead of litmus.

3. Six grammes of *pure* glacial acetic acid are neutralized by 100 c. c. of the standard solution of soda. But acid of this degree of purity is extremely difficult to prepare. The commercial acid contains only 1 per cent. of water, and is sufficiently pure for use in medicine.

Acidimetry.—The operations for the quantitative analysis or measurement of acids are often collectively spoken of under the name of *acidimetry.* They admit of considerable extension. (See the work previously cited.)

Percentage strength of Acids.—The percentage strength of the several acids and their official solutions is readily ascertained by calculation in a manner similar to that given for alkalies. Thus the volumetric operation with the liquid commonly termed acetic acid is based on the reaction expressed in the following equation :—

$$\underset{\text{Acetic acid.}}{HC_2H_3O_2} + \underset{\text{Soda.}}{NaHO} = \underset{\text{Acetate of sodium.}}{NaC_2H_3O_2} + \underset{\text{Water.}}{H_2O}.$$

This equation, translated into parts by weight, means that 60 parts (the molecular weight) of true acetic acid are exactly neutralized by 40 parts (the molec. wt.) of soda. Supposing the quantity of "acetic acid" employed in the experiment to have been that recommended in the Table (18.2 grammes), and that to neutralize it 100 c. c. of the soda solution have been used, and remembering that 100 c. c. of the soda solution contain 4 grammes of soda, it follows that the 18.2 grammes of the liquid called acetic acid contain 6 grammes of real acetic acid; for if 40 (the molec. wt.) of soda neutralize 60 (the molec. wt.) of real acetic acid, 4 will neutralize 6. Lastly, if 18.2 contain 6, 100 will contain 33; the so-called acetic acid (really an aqueous solution) contains 33 per cent. of true acetic acid ($HC_2H_3O_2$).

If the 18.2 grammes have taken, say, 93, instead of 100 c. c., the acid liquid is 7 per cent. weak; in other words, it contains only 30.7 per cent. of real acid; for (by rule-of-three) if 100 c. c. added to 18.2 grammes indicate 33 per cent., 93 c. c. added to 18.2 grammes indicate 30.7 per cent.

The remaining acids react with the alkaline salts in the manner and to the extent indicated by the following formulæ and molecular weights:—

$$\underbrace{H_3C_6H_5O_7, H_2O}_{210} + \underbrace{3NaHO}_{120}$$

$$\underbrace{HCl}_{36.5} + \underbrace{NaHO}_{40} \qquad \underbrace{HNO_3}_{63} + \underbrace{NaHO}_{40}$$

$$\underbrace{H_2SO_4}_{98} + \underbrace{2NaHO}_{80} \qquad \underbrace{H_2C_4H_4O_6}_{150} + \underbrace{2NaHO}_{80}$$

QUESTIONS AND EXERCISES.

965. What percentage of real acid is present in diluted sulphuric acid 30 grammes of which are neutralized by 84 c. c. of the official volumetric solution of soda?—*Ans.* 13.72.

966. How much real nitric acid is contained in a solution 36 grammes of which are saturated by 94 c. c. of the standard solution of soda?—*Ans.* 16.45 per cent.

ESTIMATION OF ACIDULOUS RADICALS PRECIPITATED BY NITRATE OF SILVER.

The purity of many salts, and the strength of their solutions may be determined by this process; but at present only three official substances (namely, diluted hydrocyanic acid, bromide of potassium, and arseniate of sodium) are quantitatively analyzed by standard solution of nitrate of silver. The reactions on which the success of the process depends are expressed in the following equations:—

$$\begin{cases} AgNO_3+2NaCy=NaCyAgCy+NaNO_3, \\ NaCyAgCy+AgNO_3=2AgCy+NaNO_3; \end{cases}$$

$$KBr+AgNO_3=AgBr+KNO_3;$$

$$Na_2HAsO_4+3AgNO_3=Ag_3AsO_4+2NaNO_3+HNO_3.$$

Standard Solution of Nitrate of Silver.

(Nitrate of Silver, $AgNO_3 = 170$.)

Dissolve 17 grammes of crystals of pure nitrate of silver in 1 litre of water. 100 c. c. of this solution contain $\frac{1}{100}$ of the molecular weight in grammes of nitrate of silver, and will decompose an equivalent quantity of a salt of any acidulous radical yielding silver compounds insoluble in water.

	Grammes of substance.		C. c. of vol. sol.
Acid, hydrocyanic, diluted, B. P. and U. S. P.	27.00	=	100.0
Potassium, bromide of, B. P. and U. S. P. .	1.19	=	100.0
Sodium, arseniate of (dry)	.62	=	100.0

Diluted hydrocyanic acid is converted into cyanide of sodium by adding caustic soda until, after stirring, litmus shows that the liquid has an alkaline reaction. The nitrate-of-silver solution is then allowed to flow in gradually, until, after thorough agitation, a slight permanent turbidity remains. When this occurs, the quantity of nitrate of silver added represents exactly half the amount of real hydrocyanic acid present in the diluted preparation. Thus the 100 c. c. of standard solution contains $\frac{1}{100}$ of the molecular weight, in grammes, of nitrate of silver (=1.7); this would ordinarily correspond, in a case of complete decomposition, to $\frac{1}{100}$ of the molecular weight in grammes of hydrocyanic acid (=.27); 27 grammes of the diluted acid, the quantity employed in the experiment, apparently contain therefore .27 gramme of real acid, equal to 1 per cent. A glance at the equation shows that at the moment cyanide of silver begins to be precipitated, only half of the cyanogen has been converted into cyanide of silver; the quantity of acid indicated by the amount of nitrate added must therefore be doubled for the correct percentage (=2).

$$\underbrace{2HNC}_{54} \text{ eq. to } \underbrace{AgNO_3}_{170}$$

Bromide of potassium is dissolved in distilled water in a beaker, and the standard solution added until, after agitation of the liquid and subsidence of the bromide of silver, a drop of the solution of nitrate of silver gives no more precipitate.

$$\underbrace{KBr}_{119} + \underbrace{AgNO_3}_{170}$$

Arseniate of sodium ($Na_2HAsO_4,7H_2O$) must be dried at 300° F. before weighing. It is thus reduced to a definite anhydrous salt (Na_2HAsO_4), losing, if pure, 40.38 per cent. of water. The weighed residue is dissolved in distilled water, and treated as described in the previous paragraph.

$$\underbrace{Na_2HAsO_4}_{186} + \underbrace{3AgNO_3}_{510}$$

Spirit of Wine (*Spiritus Rectificatus*, B. P.) may contain traces of amylic alcohol and aldehyd; these may be detected by nitrate of silver, which is reduced by them to the metallic state. Any quantity beyond a mere trace of such bodies renders spirit of wine too impure for use in medicine. "Four fluidounces with thirty grain-measures (about two cub. cent.) of the volumetric solution of nitrate of silver exposed for twenty-four hours to bright light, and then decanted from the black powder which has formed, undergoes no further change when again exposed to light with more of the test."

QUESTIONS AND EXERCISES.

967. Explain the volumetric method of estimating the strength of aqueous solutions of hydrocyanic acid.

968. How much nitrate of silver will indicate, by the official volumetric process, the presence of 1 part of real hydrocyanic acid?

ESTIMATION OF SUBSTANCES READILY OXIDIZED.

Any substance which quickly absorbs a definite amount of oxygen, or is susceptible of any equivalent action, may be quantitatively tested by ascertaining how much of an oxidizing agent of known power must be added to a given quantity before complete oxidation is effected. The oxidizing agents employed for this purpose in the British Pharmacopœia are iodine and the red chromate of potassium; permanganate of potassium is often used for the same purpose. Iodine acts indirectly, by taking hydrogen from water and liberating oxygen; the red chromate of potassium directly, by the facility with which it yields three-sevenths of its oxygen—as indicated by the equations and statements given on pages 451 and 452.

Standard Solution of Iodine.

(Iodine, I=127.)

Prepare pure iodine by mixing the commercial article with about a fourth of its weight of iodide of potassium and subliming. Sublimation may be effected by gently warming the mixture in a beaker, the mouth of which is closed by a funnel; the iodine vapor condenses on the funnel; while fixed impurities are left behind, and any chlorine which the iodine may contain is absorbed by the iodide of potassium, an equivalent quantity of iodine being liberated. Small quantities may be similarly treated between two watch-glasses, placed edge to edge. Any trace of moisture in the resublimed iodine is removed by exposure for a few hours under a glass shade near a vessel containing oil of vitriol.

Place 12.7 grammes of pure iodine and about 18 grammes of pure iodide of potassium (an aqueous solution of which is the best solvent of iodine; the salt plays no other part in these operations) in a litre flask, add a small quantity of water, and agitate until the iodine is dissolved, dilute to 1 litre. 100 c. c. of this solution contain $\frac{1}{100}$ of the atomic weight of free iodine in grammes, and, water being present, will cause the oxidation of $\frac{1}{200}$ of the molecular weight of sulphurous acid (H_2SO_3) in grammes (=.41), or $\frac{1}{200}$ (=.32) of sulphurous acid gas (SO_2) sulphuric acid being formed. 100 c. c. will also oxidize $\frac{1}{200}$ of the molecular weight of arsenious acid (H_3AsO_3) in grammes, or $\frac{1}{400}$ of the molecular weight of common white arsenic (As_2O_3) in grammes (=.495), arsenic acid (H_3AsO_4) being produced. The reactions are expressed in the following equations:—

$$I_2 + H_2O + H_2SO_3 = 2HI + H_2SO_4.$$
$$I_2 + 2H_2O + SO_2 = 2HI + H_2SO_4.$$
$$I_2 + H_2O + H_3AsO_3 = 2HI + H_3AsO_4.$$
$$2I_2 + 5H_2O + As_2O_3 = 4HI + 2H_3AsO_4.$$
$$I_2 + 2(Na_2S_2O_3, 5H_2O) = 2NaI + Na_2S_4O_6 + 10H_2O.$$

The following official substances are tested with the standard solution of iodine:—

	Grammes of substance.		C. c. of vol. sol.
Acid, solution of sulphurous	3.47	=	100
Arsenic, in mass, B. P. and U. S. P. . .	0.495	=	100
" in alkaline sol. (*Liq. Arsenicalis*)	54.64	=	100
" in acid sol. (*Liq. Arsen. Hydrochl.*)	54.64	=	100
Sodium, hyposulphite of	2.48	=	100

The solution of sulphurous acid is diluted with three-fourths of a litre of cold water, and the iodine solution added until a slight permanent brown tint is produced, showing the presence of free iodine. A better indication of the termination of the action is afforded by mucilage of starch, which gives a blue color with the slightest trace of iodine. As already stated, 100 c. c. of this volumetric solution contain an amount of free iodine sufficient to cause the oxidation of $\frac{1}{200}$ of the molecular weight of either sulphurous acid or sulphurous acid gas. Now $\frac{1}{200}$ of the molecular weight of sulphurous acid (H_2SO_3) in grammes is 0.41; if 3.47 grammes of the solution contain 0.41 of the acid, 100 of the solution will be found to contain 11.8. By a similar calculation the official solution may be shown to contain, or, rather, yield 9.22 per cent. of sulphurous acid gas (SO_2).

If the sulphurous acid be diluted to a less degree than .04 or .05 per cent., there will be some risk of the sulphuric acid formed being again reduced to sulphurous acid, with liberation of iodine. In delicate experiments the distilled water used for dilution should previously be freed from air by boiling, to prevent the small amount of oxidizing action which dissolved air would exert.

$$\underbrace{H_2SO_3}_{82} \text{ eq. to } \underbrace{I_2}_{254} \quad \Big| \quad \underbrace{SO_2}_{64} \text{ eq. to } \underbrace{I_2}_{254}$$

The solid arsenic is dissolved in boiling water by help of about two grammes of bicarbonate of sodium. When the liquid is quite cold, mucilage of starch is added, and the iodine solution allowed to flow in until, after well stirring, a permanent blue color is produced.

$$\underbrace{H_3AsO_3}_{126} \text{ eq. to } \underbrace{I_2}_{254} \quad \Big| \quad \underbrace{As_2O_3}_{198} \text{ eq. to } \underbrace{2I_2}_{508}$$

The arsenical solution already containing some carbonate of potassium requires only about one and a half gramme of bicarbonate of sodium for neutralization of the arsenious acid. After boiling and cooling, starch and the iodine solution are added as before.

The solution of arsenic in dilute hydrochloric acid requires about three grammes of acid carbonate of sodium, if 54 or 55 grammes of solution is the quantity employed. After boiling for a few minutes and cooling, the starch and iodine are added.

These arsenical solutions contain .9 per cent. of arsenic.

The *Hyposulphite of sodium* is dissolved in water, starch

mucilage added, and the iodide solution slowly run in, the whole being frequently stirred, until a permanent blue color is produced.

In the previous reactions iodine has acted as an indirect oxidizing agent by uniting with the hydrogen and thus liberating the oxygen of water. In the present case it unites with an analogue of hydrogen, namely, sodium.

QUESTIONS AND EXERCISES.

969. Give equations illustrative of the reactions on which the use of a standard volumetric solution of iodine is based.

970. From what point of view may iodine be regarded as an oxidizing agent?

971. What reagent indicates the termination of the reaction between deoxidizing substances and moist iodine?

972. How much sulphurous acid gas will cause the absorption of 2.54 parts of iodine in the volumetric reaction?

973. What quantity of iodine will be required, under appropriate conditions, to oxidize 5 parts of arsenic?

974. Find by calculation the amount of hyposulphite of sodium equivalent to 13 parts of iodine in volumetric analysis.

Standard Solution of Red Chromate of Potassium.

(Red Chromate of Potassium, K_2CrO_4, CrO_3=295.)

One molecule of red chromate of potassium in presence of an acid, under favorable circumstances, yields four atoms of oxygen to the hydrogen of the acid, leaving three available either for direct oxidation or for combination with the hydrogen of more acid, an equivalent proportion of acidulous radical being liberated for any required purpose.

When used as a volumetric agent, the red chromate always yields the whole of its oxygen to the hydrogen of the accompanying acid, a corresponding quantity of acidulous radical being set free—four-sevenths of this radical immediately combining with the potassium and chromium of the red chromate, three-sevenths becoming available. Ferrous may thus be converted into ferric salts with sufficient rapidity and exactitude to admit of the estimation of an unknown quantity of iron by a known quantity of the red chromate. As one atom of the liberated acidulous radical will convert two molecules of ferrous into one of ferric salt, one molecule of red chromate causes six of ferrous to become three of ferric, as shown in either of the following equations:—

$$K_2CrO_4,\ CrO_3+7H_2SO_4+6FeSO_4=K_2SO_4+Cr_23SO_4+7H_2O$$
$$+3\ (Fe_23SO_4);$$

$$K_2CrO_4,\ CrO_3+14HCl+6FeCl_2=2KCl+Cr_2Cl_6+7H_2O+3Fe_2Cl_6.$$

These equations indicate that, in presence of excess of acid, 295 parts (the molecular weight) of red chromate of potassium will convert 1668 parts of crystallized ferrous sulphate, $6(FeSO_4, 7H_2O = 278)$, or an equivalent quantity of ferrous chloride ($6FeCl_2 = 762$), ferrous carbonate ($6FeCO_3 = 696$), ferrous arseniate ($2Fe_3As_2O_8 = 892$), ferrous phosphate ($2Fe_3P_2O_8 = 716$), or iron itself ($3Fe_2 = 336$), into ferric salt. If these parts be taken in grammes, $\frac{1}{200}$ or less of the stated amounts will be found to be convenient quantities for experiment.

Dissolve 14.75 grammes of red chromate of potassium in one litre of distilled water. 100 c. c. of this solution contain $\frac{1}{200}$ of the molecular weight of the salt in grammes, and will cause the conversion of $\frac{1}{200}$ of the weight of 6 atoms of iron in grammes, or an equivalent quantity of the lower salts of iron, from the ferrous to the ferric state.

The solution is used in determining the strength of the following official ferrous preparations. It is known that the whole of the ferrous has been converted to ferric salt when a small drop of the liquid placed in contact with a drop of a very dilute solution of ferridcyanide of potassium, on a white plate, ceases to strike a blue color.

	Grammes of substance.		C. c of vol. sol.
Iron, arseniate of	2.94	=	25
" magnetic oxide of	2.41	=	10
" phosphate of, B. P. and U. S. P. .	2.00	=	25
" saccharated carbonate of . . .	4.70	=	50

The several compounds are dissolved in excess of hydrochloric acid diluted with water, and the standard solution then dropped in. The ferrous liquid must not be exposed to the air for more than a few seconds after solution has been effected, or oxygen will be absorbed and a corresponding amount of ferric salt formed before the volumetric oxydizing agent is added: in most cases diluted sulphuric acid may be used as a solvent of the ferrous salt, ferrous sulphate absorbing oxygen from the air far less rapidly than ferrous chloride. It will be found that the proportion of carbonate of iron in the saccharated compound, as indicated by the above numbers, is 37 in 100. The theoretical percentage obtainable from the ingredients is 45.5, the quantity that would be present if the compound were anhydrous and unoxidized, conditions never obtained in practice.

The use of these two volumetric solutions in quantitative analysis admits of great extension.

QUESTIONS AND EXERCISES.

975. Write equations explanatory of the oxidizing-power of red chromate of potassium.

976. One hundred cubic centimetres of an aqueous solution of red chromate of potassium contain $\frac{1}{200}$ of the molecular weight of the salt in grammes; what weight of metallic iron, dissolved in hydrochloric acid, will this volume oxidize?—*Ans.* 1.68 gramme.

977. If 8.34 grammes of a specimen of crystallized ferrous sulphate require 93 c. c. of the standard solution of chromate for complete oxidation, what percentage of real salt is present?—*Ans.* 93.

978. How much red chromate of potassium is required for the conversion of 10 parts of ferrous sulphate into ferric salt?

979. What quantity of pure ferrous carbonate is indicated by 1.475 part of red chromate as applied in volumetric analysis?

980. State the amount of official saccharated carbonate of iron equivalent to .7375 part of red chromate in the volumetric reaction.

ESTIMATION OF SUBSTANCES READILY DEOXIDIZED.

Any substance which quickly yields a definite amount of oxygen may be quantitatively tested by ascertaining how much of a deoxidizing agent of known power must be added to a given quantity before complete deoxidation is effected. The chief compounds which may be used as absorbers of oxygen (deoxidizers or reducing agents, as they are commonly termed) are hyposulphite of sodium, sulphurous acid, ferrous sulphate,* oxalic acid, arsenious acid. The first-named is officially employed; it is only used in the estimation of free iodine, and, indirectly, of chlorine and chlorinated compounds. Iodine and chlorine are regarded as oxidizing agents, because their great affinity for hydrogen enables them to become powerful indirect oxidizers in presence of water.

STANDARD SOLUTION OF HYPOSULPHITE OF SODIUM.

(Crystallized Hyposulphite of Sodium, $Na_2S_2O_3,5H_2O=248$.)

Dissolve about 30 grammes of hyposulphite of sodium in a litre or less of water. Fill a burette with this solution, and allow it to flow into a beaker containing exactly 100 c. c. of the volumetric solution of iodine until the brown color of the iodine is just discharged—or, starch being added, until the blue iodide of starch is decolorized.

* "Five grains of Permanganate of Potassium dissolved in water require for decoloration a solution of forty-four grains of granulated sulphate of iron acidulated with two fluidrachms of diluted sulphuric acid."—B. P.

Note the number of c. c. of hyposulphite solution required, and to the bulk of the solution add water, so that 2.48 grammes of hyposulphite of sodium shall be contained in every 100 c. c.

When iodine and hyposulphite of sodium react, two atoms of iodine remove two of sodium from two molecules of the hyposulphite, tetrathionate of sodium being formed, as indicated in the following equation :—

$$I_2 + 2Na_2S_2O_3 = 2NaI + Na_2S_4O_6.$$

As, therefore, 100 c. c. of the iodine solution contain $\frac{1}{100}$ of the atomic weight of iodine in grammes, 100 c. c. of the standard solution of hyposulphite of sodium will contain $\frac{1}{100}$ of the molecular weight of the salt in grammes, and will show the existence of $\frac{1}{100}$ of the atomic weight of iodine in grammes in any quantity of a liquid normally containing free iodine, or iodine liberated by an equivalent quantity of free chlorine.

This solution is employed for quantitatively testing the following substances :—

	Grammes of substance.		C. c. of vol. sol.
Chlorine, solution of	29.26	=	50
Iodine, B. P. and U. S. P.	1.27	=	100
Lime, chlorinated	1.17	=	100
" solution of chlorinated . . .	6.00	=	50
Soda, solution of chlorinated . . .	7.00	=	50

Note.—Owing to the volatility of chlorine and iodine, and the readiness with which they attack the metals of which balances are made, it is not desirable to experiment on stated weights of substances containing these elements. A small stoppered bottle or tube containing the material may be counterpoised, and a convenient quantity removed for analysis, the precise amount taken being ascertained by again weighing the bottle.

The iodine may be dissolved in water containing about a gramme and a half of iodide of potassium, a salt giving no reaction with hyposulphite of sodium.

$$\underbrace{I_2}_{254} \text{ eq. to } \underbrace{2(Na_2S_2O_3, 5H_2O)}_{496}$$

The solution of chlorine is added to water containing excess of iodide of potassium (about a gramme and a third); a quantity of iodine, equivalent to the amount of chlorine present, is thus liberated. The hyposulphite solution is then dropped in.

$$\underbrace{Cl_2}_{71} \text{ eq. to } \underbrace{2(Na_2S_2O_3, 5H_2O)}_{496}$$

The chlorinated lime ("chloride of lime" or "bleaching-powder") is mixed with about a fifth of a litre of water containing excess of iodide of potassium (3.5 grms.) and acidulated with hydrochloric acid. The available oxygen of the chlorinated lime liberates chlorine from an equivalent quantity of hydrochloric acid; and this, with the available chlorine of the chlorinated lime, sets free an equivalent amount of iodine from the iodide of potassium. The hyposulphite and iodine reacting show the direct and indirect oxidizing power of the chlorinated lime; it should correspond to 30 per cent. of chlorine. For example, as 248 (1 molecule) of hyposulphite indicate the presence of 35.5 (1 atom) of chlorine, 2.48 of hyposulphite (the quantity in 100 c. c.) indicate the presence of .355 of chlorine. If 100 c. c. have been used, therefore, .355 of chlorine is obtainable from the quantity of bleaching-powder employed (1.17). And if 1.17 of bleaching-powder yield .355 of chlorine, 100 will yield about 30 ($30\frac{1}{2}$ nearly).

The solution of chlorinated lime is mixed with about a fifth of a litre of water containing a couple of grammes of iodide of potassium, and ten or twelve c. c. of hydrochloric acid. The hyposulphite solution is then added from a burette until the color of the liberated iodine is just discharged. The solution of chlorinated soda is similarly treated.

Note.—1. In these experiments the blue color formed on the addition of mucilage of starch to the liquids will be found to be a more delicate indicator of the termination of reactions than the brown tint of the iodine.

Note.—2. Standard solutions used in volumetric analysis are often described as normal, decinormal, and centinormal. A normal solution (N) contains in every litre the molecular weight of the salt, *taken in grammes;* a decinormal solution is one tenth ($\frac{N}{10}$), and a centinormal ($\frac{N}{100}$) one hundredth the strength of such a normal solution.

QUESTIONS AND EXERCISES.

981. For what purposes is the official volumetric solution of hyposulphite of sodium used?

982. On what reaction is based the quantitative employment of hyposulphite of sodium?

983. How much hyposulphite of sodium is required to show the presence of 10 parts of iodine?

984. To what amount of chlorine is 4.96 parts of hyposulphite of sodium equivalent in volumetric analysis?

985. Describe the operations included in the estimation of the strength of bleaching-powder.

986. By what reagent is the complete absorption of free iodine by hyposulphite of sodium indicated?

MISCELLANEOUS PROBLEMS.

987. How much bicarbonate of potassium is contained in an eight-ounce bottle of medicine, seven fluidrachms of which are saturated by two and a half grains of crystallized oxalic acid?

988. A sample of soda-ash is said to contain 78 per cent. of pure anhydrous carbonate of sodium; if the statement is true, how much of the official volumetric solution of oxalic acid will saturate 5 grammes of the specimen?

989. 2.69 grammes of common brown sulphuric acid are saturated by 43.5 cubic centimetres of the official volumetric solution of soda; how much acid of 96.8 per cent. is present?

990. Four grammes of a litre and a half of concentrated hydrocyanic acid are neutralized by 89 cubic centimetres of volumetric solution of nitrate of silver of official strength; to what volume must the bulk of the acid be diluted for the production of acid of pharmacopœial strength?

991. 3.18 grammes of a powder containing arsenic require for complete reaction 84 cubic centimetres of a volumetric solution of iodine, which is 1.43 weaker than the standard solution of the British Pharmacopœia; what percentage of pure arsenic is contained in the powder?

992. How much pure metal is present in a sample of iron 1.68 gramme of which dissolved in dilute sulphuric acid, is exactly attacked by 95.7 cubic centimetres of a semi-decinormal volumetric solution of red chromate of potassium which is 6 per cent. too strong?

GRAVIMETRIC ANALYSIS.

ESTIMATION OF METALS.

POTASSIUM.

Outline of the Process.—This element is usually estimated in the form of double chloride of potassium and platinum. Qualitative analysis having proved the presence of potassium and other elements in a substance, a small quantity of the material is accurately weighed, dissolved, and the other elements removed by appropriate reagents; the precipitates are well washed, in order that no trace of the potassium salt shall be lost, the resulting liquid concentrated over a water-bath (to avoid loss that would occur mechanically during ebullition), hydrochloric acid added if necessary, solution of perchloride of platinum poured in, and evaporation continued to dryness; excess of the perchloride is then dissolved by adding spirit of wine containing half its bulk of ether (a liquid in which the double chloride is insoluble), the mixture carefully poured on to a tared and dried filter, washed with the spirit till every trace of free perchloride of platinum is removed, the whole dried and weighed; from the resulting amount the proportion of potassium, or equivalent quantity of a salt of potassium, is ascertained by calculation.

Note.—From this short description it will be seen, first, that the chemistry of quantitative is the same as that of qualitative analysis; the second, that the principle of gravimetric is the same as that of volumetric quantitative analysis: the combining-proportions being known, unknown quantities of elements may be ascertained by calculation from known quantities of their compounds.

Apparatus.—In addition to a delicate balance and weights and the common utensils, a few special instruments are used in quantitative manipulation; some of these may be prepared before proceeding with the estimation of potassium.

Filtering-paper should be of the kind known as Swedish, the texture of which is of the requisite degree of closeness, and its ash small in amount. A large number of circular pieces of one size, six to eight centimetres in diameter, should be cut ready for use. In delicate experiments, where a precipitate on a filter has to be heated and the paper consequently burnt, the weight of the ash of the filter must be deducted from the weight of the residue. The ash is estimated by burning ten or twenty of the cut filters. These are folded into a small compass, a portion of a piece of platinum wire twisted a few times round the packet, so as to form a cage, the whole held by the free end of the wire over a weighed porcelain crucible placed in the centre of a sheet of glazed paper, the bundle ignited by a spirit-lamp or smokeless gas-flame, the flame allowed to impinge against the charged mass till it falls into the crucible below, any stray fragments on the sheet carefully shaken into the crucible, the latter placed over a flame till carbon has all burnt off and nothing but ash remains, the whole cooled, weighed, and the weight of the crucible deducted; the weight of the residue divided by the number of pieces used gives the average amount of ash in each filter.

A pair of Weighing-tubes, for holding dried filters during operations at the balance, may be made from two test-tubes, one fitting closely within the other. About five centimetres of the closed end of the outer and seven of the inner are cut off, by leading a crack round the tube with a pencil of incandescent charcoal, and the sharp edges fused in the blowpipe-flame. A filter, after drying, is quickly folded and placed in the narrower tube, the mouth of which is then closed by the wider tube. This presents reabsorption of moisture from the air.

The Washing-bottle, holding the *spirit of wine and ether*, is a common bottle, through the cork of which a short straight tube passes. The outer end of the tube should be sufficiently narrowed to enable it to deliver a very fine stream of the liquid. The bottle being inverted, the warmth of the hand expands the air and vapor to a sufficient extent to force out the liquid.

The Ordinary Washing-bottle for quantitative operations should be formed of a flask in which water may be boiled, fitted up as usual (*vide* p. 81).

A Water-oven is the best form of drying-apparatus. It is a small square copper vessel, jacketed on five sides and having a door on the sixth; water is poured into the space between the inner and outer casing, and the whole placed over a gas-lamp or other source of heat, moist air and steam escaping by appropriate apertures. Desiccation at higher temperatures than the boiling-point of water may be practised by using oil or paraffin instead of water, inserting a thermometer in the fat. The apparatus may be purchased of any maker of chemical instruments.

Pure distilled water must be used in all quantitative determinations.

Note.—In practising the operations of quantitative analysis, experiments should at first be conducted on definite salts of known composition. The accuracy of results may then be tested by calculation.

Estimation of Potassium in the form of double chloride of potassium and platinum.—Select two or three crystals of pure nitrate of potassium, powder them in a clean mortar, dry the powder by gently heating in a porcelain crucible over a flame for a few seconds, place about a couple of decigrammes (0.2 grm.) of the powder in a counterpoised watch-glass, accurately weigh the selected quantity, transfer to a small dish, letting water from a wash-bottle flow over the watch-glass and run into the dish, warm the dish till the nitrate is dissolved, acidulate with hydrochloric acid, add excess of aqueous solution of perchloride of platinum (a quantity containing about 0.4 of solid salt), evaporate to dryness over a water-bath. While evaporation is going on, place a filter and the weighing-tubes in the water-oven, exposing them to a temperature of 212° F. for about half an hour; fold the filter and insert it in the tubes, place them on a plate under a glass shade, and when cold accurately note their weight. Arrange the weighed filter in a funnel over a beaker. Transfer the dried and cooled platinum salt from the dish to the filter by moistening the residue with the mixture of alcohol and ether, and, when the salt is loosened, pouring the contents of the dish into the paper cone. Any salt still adhering may be freed by the finger, which, together with the dish, should be washed in the stream of spirit, the rinsings at once flowing into the filter. The filtrate should have a yellowish-brown color, due to the excess of perchloride of platinum. If it it is colorless, an insufficient amount of perchloride has been added, and the whole operation must be repeated. The washed precipitate and filter are finally dried in the water-oven, folded and placed in the weighing-tubes, the drying continued until the whole, after repeated weighing when cold, ceases to alter; the final weight is noted.

Note.—If filters are not freed from all trace of acid by thorough washing, the paper will be brittle when dry, falling to pieces on being folded.

Analytical memoranda in the note book may have the following form:—

Watch-glass and substance	
Watch-glass	______
Substance . .	______
Weighing-tubes, filter, and Pt salt . .	
Weighing-tubes and filter	______
$PtCl_4, 2KCl$. . .	______

The calculations are simple:—

$$\text{As}\left\{\begin{matrix}PtCl_4, 2KCl\\ =489\end{matrix}\right\}\text{ are equivalent to }\left\{\begin{matrix}2KNO_3\\ =202\end{matrix}\right\}$$

so $\left\{\begin{matrix}\text{the weight of}\\ \text{double chloride}\\ \text{obtained}\end{matrix}\right\}$ are equivalent to x. x will be the amount of *pure* nitrate of potassium in the quantity of substance operated on. x should, in the present instance, be identical with the weight of substance taken, because, for educational purposes, pure nitre is under examination. Only after analyses of pure substances have yielded the operator results identical with those by calculation, can analyses of substances of unknown degree of purity be undertaken with confidence. A table of atomic weights, from which to find molecular weights, is given in the Appendix.

A *Water-bath* for the evaporation of liquids or for drying moist solids at temperatures below 212° F. is an iron, tin, or earthenware pan, the mouth of which can be narrowed by iron or tin diaphragms of various sizes and having orifices adapted to the diameters of evaporating-dishes or plates. In the British Pharmacopœia, "when a *water-bath* is directed to be used, it is to be understood that this term refers to an apparatus by means of which water or its vapor, at a temperature not exceeding 212°, is applied to the outer surface of a vessel containing the substance to be heated, which substance may thus be subjected to a heat near to, but necessarily below, that of 212°. In the *steam-bath* the vapor of water at a temperature above 212°, but not exceeding 230°, is similarly applied."

Platinum residues should be preserved, and the metal recovered from them from time to time (*vide* p. 203).

Hot alcohol sometimes reduces perchloride of platinum, the metal being thrown out of solution in a finely divided form, known as *platinum black;* only aqueous solutions, therefore, of the salt should be used where heat is employed. Hence, also, in washing out excess of perchloride of platinum from the double chloride of platinum and potassium by spirit, the application of heat should be avoided.

Effervescing Potash-Water (*Liquor Potassæ Effervescens*, B.P.) is most easily estimated volumetrically (p. 441). Any adulteration by an equivalent amount of bicarbonate of sodium would, however, by that process be undetected; hence the Pharmacopœia directs that "five fluidounces, evaporated to one-fifth and 12 grains of tartaric acid added, yield a crystalline precipitate, which, when dried, weighs not less than 12 grains." Five fluidounces of this preparation should contain 7.5 grains of bicarbonate, convertible into 14.1 grains of acid tartrate of potassium by 11.25 grains of tartaric acid. The method is somewhat rough, but quite efficient for "potash-water" containing nothing but bicarbonate of potassium.

Proportional weights of equivalent quantities of potassium and its salts.

Metal	K_2	78
Oxide ("Potash")	K_2O	94
Hydrate ("Caustic Potash")	$2KHO$	112
Carbonate (Anhydrous)	K_2CO_3	138
Carbonate (Crystalline)	K_2CO_3+16% aq.	164.285
Bicarbonate	$2KHCO_3$	200
Nitrate	$2KNO_3$	202
Platinum salt	$PtCl_4,2KCl$	489

SODIUM.

Sodium is usually estimated as sulphate. Accurately weigh a porcelain crucible and lid, place within about .3 of pure rock-salt, and again weigh, making a memorandum of the weights in a note-book. Add rather more strong sulphuric acid than may be considered sufficient to convert the chloride into acid sulphate of sodium. Heat the crucible gradually, the flame being first directed against the side of the crucible to avoid violent ebullition, until fumes of sulphuric acid cease to be evolved, towards the end of the operation dropping in one or two fragments of carbonate of ammonium to facilitate complete decomposition. When cold, weigh the crucible and contents. The weight of the crucible having been deducted, the amount of sulphate obtained should be the exact equivalent of the quantity of chloride of sodium employed.

$$\underbrace{2NaCl}_{117} + H_2SO_4 = \underbrace{Na_2SO_4}_{142} + 2HCl.$$

Proportional weights of equivalent quantities of sodium and its salts.

Metal	Na_2	46
Oxide ("soda")	Na_2O	62
Hydrate ("caustic soda")	$2NaHO$	80
Carbonate (anhydrous)	Na_2CO_3	106
Carbonate (crystals)	$Na_2CO_3,10H_2O$	286
Bicarbonate	$2NaHCO_3$	168
Chloride	$2NaCl$	117
Sulphate (anhydrous)	Na_2SO_4	142
Sulphate (crystals)	$Na_2SO_4,10H_2O$	322

AMMONIUM.

Salts of ammonium are, for purposes of quantitative analysis, generally converted into the double chloride of ammonium and platinum ($PtCl_4 2NH_4Cl$), the details of manipulation being the same as those observed in the case of potassium. About 0.15 grm. of pure, white, dry chloride of ammonium may be taken for experiment.

COMPOSITION OF THE PLATINUM SALT.

			In 1 molecule.	In 100 parts.
	Pt	198	198	44.30
	Cl_6	35.5 × 6	213	47.64
	N_2	14.0 × 2	28	6.27
	H_8	1.0 × 8	8	1.79
			447	100.00
or,	$PtCl_4$	340	340	76.06
	$2NH_4Cl$	53.5 × 2	107	23.94
			447	100.00

The proportion of nitrogen, ammonium, or chloride of ammonium in the double chloride may also be ascertained from the weight of platinum left on igniting the double chloride; for this purpose heat must be applied slowly, or platinum will be mechanically carried off with the gaseous products of decomposition.

Proportional weights of equivalent quantities of ammoniacal compounds.

Ammonia (gas)	$2NH_3$	34
Ammonium	$(NH_4)_2$?	36
Chloride of ammonium	$2NH_4Cl$	107
Platinum salt	$PtCl_4,2NH_4Cl$	447
"Carbonate of ammonium"	$(N_4H_{16}C_3O_8) \div 2$	118
Sulphate of ammonium	$(NH_4)_2SO_4$	132

BARIUM.

Barium is estimated in the form of anhydrous sulphate of barium ($BaSO_4$).

Process.—Dissolve 0.3 or 0.4 of pure crystallized and dried chloride or nitrate of barium in about half a litre of water in a beaker, heating to incipient ebullition, and slightly acidulating with hydrochloric or nitric acid. Add diluted sulphuric acid (prepared some days previously, so that sulphate of lead may have deposited) so long as a precipitate forms, keep the mixture hot for some time, set aside for half an hour, pass the supernatant liquid through a filter, gently boil the residue two or three times with more water; finally collect the precipitate on the filter, removing adherent particles from the beaker by the finger, and cleansing by a stream of hot water from the wash-bottle. The precipitate must be washed with hot water until the filtrate ceases to turn litmus paper red, or give any cloudiness when tested with chloride of barium. The filter and sulphate of barium, having thoroughly drained, is dried in a warm place, commonly by supporting the funnel in an inverted bottomless beaker over a sand-bath or hot plate.

The sulphate of barium is now removed from the filter, heated to drive off every trace of moisture, and weighed. This is accomplished by placing a weighed porcelain crucible (and cover) on a sheet of glazed paper, holding the filter over it, and carefully transferring the precipitate; the sides of the filter are then gently rubbed together and detached powder dropped into the crucible, the paper folded, encased in two or three coils of one end of a platinum wire and burnt over the crucible, ash and any particles in the sheet of paper dropped into the sulphate of barium, the open crucible exposed over a flame till its contents are quite white, covered, cooled, and weighed.

	Formulæ.	Molecular weights.
Chloride of barium	$BaCl_2$	208
Nitrate of barium	$Ba2NO_3$	261
Sulphate of barium	$BaSO_4$	233

Composition of Sulphate of Barium.

		In one molecule.	In 100 parts.
Ba	137	137	58.80
S	32	32	13.73
O_4	16×4	64	27.47
		233	100.00

In these experiments it is unnecessary to take filter-ash into account. Faults of manipulation cause far greater errors.

CALCIUM.

Calcium is usually thrown out of solution in the form of oxalate, the precipitate ignited, and the resulting carbonate weighed.

Process.—Dissolve 0.3 or 0.4 of dried colorless crystals of calc-spar in about a third of a litre of water acidulated with hydrochloric acid, heat the solution to near the boiling-point, add excess of solution of oxalate of ammonia, then ammonia until, after stirring, the liquid smells strongly ammoniacal; set aside in a warm place for twelve hours. Carefully pour off the supernatant liquid, passing it through a filter; add hot water to the precipitate, set aside for half an hour, again decant, and, after once more washing, transfer the precipitate to the filter, allowing all contained fluid to pass through before a fresh portion is added. Wash the precipitate with hot water, avoiding a rapid stream, or the precipitate may be driven through the pores of the paper. Dry, transfer to a weighed crucible, and incinerate, as described for sulphate of barium, and slowly heat the precipitate till the bottom of the crucible is just visibly red when seen in the dark. As soon as the residue is white, or only faintly gray, remove the lamp, cool, and weigh.

The resulting carbonate of calcium should have the same weight as the calc-spar from which it was obtained. If loss has occurred, carbonic acid gas has probably escaped. In that case moisten the residue with water, and after a few minutes test the liquid with red litmus or turmeric paper; if an alkaline reaction is noticed, it is due to the presence of caustic lime. Add a small lump of carbonate of ammonium, evaporate to dryness over a water-bath, and again ignite, this time being careful not to go beyond the prescribed temperature. The treatment may, if necessary, be repeated.

Proportional weights of equivalent quantities of calcium salts.

Oxide (quicklime)	CaO	56
Hydrate (slaked) lime	$Ca2HO$	74
Carbonate	$CaCO_3$	100
Sulphate (anhydrous)	$CaSO_4$	136
Sulphate (crystalline or precipit'd)	$CaSO_4, 2HO$	172
Chloride	$CaCl_2$	111
Phosphate (of bone)	$(Ca_3 2PO_4)310 \div 3$	103.3
Superphosphate	$CaH_4 2PO_4$	234

MAGNESIUM.

Process 1.—*The light or heavy carbonate of magnesium* of pharmacy may be estimated by heating a weighed quantity to redness in a porcelain crucible. If it has the composition indicated by the formula given in the British Pharmacopœia ($3MgCO_3, Mg2HO, 4H_2O$), it will yield 42 per cent. of magnesia (MgO). According to that work, the purity of even sulphate of magnesium ($MgSO_4, 7H_2O$) may be determined by boiling a weighed quantity with excess of carbonate of sodium, collecting the precipitate, washing, drying, igniting, and weighing the resulting magnesia (MgO). The crystallized sulphate should afford 16.26 per cent. of oxide. The official solution of carbonate of magnesium in carbonic acid water (*Liquor Magnesia Carbonatis*, B. P.) should yield five grains of pure oxide of magnesium per fluidounce.

Process 2.—*The general form in which magnesium is precipitated* is as phosphate of ammonium and magnesium ($MgNH_4PO_4, 6H_2O$); this, by heat, is converted into pyrophosphate of magnesium ($Mg_2P_2O_7$). Accurately weigh a small quantity (0.4 to 0.5) of pure dry crystals of sulphate of magnesium, dissolve in two or three hundred cubic centimetres of cold water in a beaker, add chloride of ammonium, ammonia, and phosphate of sodium or ammonium, agitate with a glass rod (without touching the sides of the vessel, or crystals will firmly adhere to the rubbed portions), and set aside for twelve hours. Collect on a filter, wash the precipitate with water containing a tenth of its volume of the strongest solution of ammonia, until the filtrate ceases to give a precipitate with an acidulated solution of nitrate silver. Dry, transfer to a crucible, burn the filter in the usual way, heat slowly to redness, cool, and weigh.

Proportional weights of equivalent quantities of magnesium salts.

Pyrophosphate . .	$Mg_2P_2O_7$	222
Sulphate	$2(MgSO_4, 7H_2O)$	492
Oxide	$2(MgO)$	80
Official carbonate .	$(3MgCO_3, Mg2HO, 4H_2O) \div 2$.	191

ZINC.

Zinc is usually estimated as oxide (ZnO), occasionally as sulphide (ZnS).

Process.—Dissolve a weighed quantity (0.5 to 0.6) of sulphate of zinc in about half a litre of water in a beaker, heat to near the boiling-point, add carbonate of sodium in slight excess, boil, set aside for a short time; pass the supernatant liquid through a filter, gently boil the precipitate with more water, again decant; repeat these operations two or three times; collect the precipitate on the filter, wash, dry, transfer to a crucible, incinerate, ignite, cool, and weigh. 287 (=molec. weight) of sulphate should yield 81 (=molec. weight) of oxide.

ALUMINIUM.

Aluminium is always precipitated as hydrate ($Al_2 6HO$) and weighed as oxide (Al_2O_3).

Process.—Dissolve about two grammes of pure dry ammonium-alum in half a litre of water, heat the solution, add chloride of ammonium and a slight excess of ammonia, boil gently till the odor of ammonia has nearly disappeared, set aside for the hydrate to deposit, pass the supernatant liquid through a filter, wash the precipitate three or four times by decantation, transfer to the filter, finish the washing, dry, burn the filter, ignite in a covered crucible, and weigh.

$Al_2 3SO_4$, $(NH_4)_2SO_4$, $24H_2O$	907
Al_2O_3	103
Per cent. of Al_2O_3 yielded by ammonium-alum .	11.356

QUESTIONS AND EXERCISES.

993. Give details of the manipulations observed in gravimetrically estimating salts of potassium or ammonium.

994. What quantity of chloride of sodium is contained in a sample of rock-salt 0.351 gramme of which yields 0.44 of sulphate of sodium?—*Ans.* 100 per cent. (It is absolutely pure.)

995. To what amount of the official alum is 0.894 of a gramme of the double chloride of platinum and ammonium equivalent?—*Ans.* 1.814 gramme.

996. Find the weight of sulphate of barium obtainable from 0.522 of nitrate.—*Ans.* 0.466.

997. Describe the usual method by which salts of calcium are estimated.

998. By what quantitative processes may the official salts of magnesium be analyzed?

999. Calculate the proportion of pure sulphate of zinc in a sample of crystals 0.574 of which yield 0.161 of oxide.—*Ans.* 99.3 per cent.

1000. Ascertain the weight of alumina (Al_2O_3) which should be obtained from 1.814 gramme of ammonium-alum.

IRON.

Iron and its salts are gravimetrically estimated in the form of ferric oxide (Fe_2O_3).

Compounds containing organic acidulous radicals are simply incinerated, and the resulting oxide weighed. Thus 1 gramme of the official citrate of iron and ammonium (*Ferri et Ammoniæ Citras*, B. P.) incinerated, with exposure to air, leaves not less than .27 of ferric oxide. A small quantity of the salt is weighed in a tared covered porcelain crucible, flame cautiously applied until vapors cease to be evolved, the lid then removed, the crucible slightly inclined and exposed to a red heat until all carbonaceous matter has disappeared. The residual ferric oxide is then weighed. The tartrate of potassium and iron (*Ferrum Tartaratum*, B. P.) is treated in the same manner, except that the ash must be washed and again heated before weighing, in order to remove carbonate of potassium produced during incineration; 5 grammes should yield 1.5 gramme of ferric oxide.

From other compounds of iron, soluble in water or acid, the metal is precipitated in the form of hydrate (Fe_26HO) by solution of ammonia, and converted into oxide (Fe_2O_3) by ignition. Dissolve a piece (about 0.2) of the purest iron obtainable (piano wire), accurately weighed, in water acidulated with hydrochloric acid; add a few drops of nitric acid and gently boil; pour in excess of ammonia, stir, set aside till the ferric hydrate has deposited, pass the supernatant liquid through a filter, treat the precipitate three or four times with boiling water; transfer to the filter, wash till the filtrate yields no trace of chlorine (for chloride of ammonium will decompose ignited ferric oxide, with volatilization of ferric chloride), dry and ignite as usual, and weigh. Iron in the official solutions (*Liquor Ferri Perchloridi Fortior*, *Liquor Ferri Pernitratis*, and *Liquor Ferri Persulphatis*) may be estimated by this general process.

The proportion of metallic iron in a mixture of iron and oxides of iron may be determined by digestion in a strong solution of iodine in iodide of potassium, which attacks the metal only. The reduced iron of pharmacy (*Ferrum Redactum*) is in good condition so long as it contains, as shown by this method, half its weight of free metal.

Proportional weights of equivalent quantities of iron and its salts.

Metal	Fe_2	112
Ferric oxide	Fe_2O_3	160
Ferric hydrate	Fe_26HO	214
Ferric chloride	Fe_2Cl_6	325
Ferric sulphate	Fe_23SO_4	400
Ferrous sulphate	$2(FeSO_4, 7H_2O)$	556

ARSENICUM.

Arsenic (As_2O_3) is usually estimated volumetrically (*vide* p. 449). With certain precautions arsenicum may also be precipitated and weighed as sulphide (As_2S_3).

Process.—The pure, white, massive arsenic (about 0.2) is dissolved in a flask in a small quantity of water containing bicarbonate of sodium or potassium, the liquid being heated. A slight excess of hydrochloric acid is then added, and sulphuretted hydrogen gas passed through the solution so long as a precipitate falls, the mouth of the flask being stopped by a plug of cotton-wool (to prevent undue access of air and consequent decomposition of the gas, resulting in precipitation of sulphur). Warm the mixture in the flask and pass carbonic acid gas through it until the odor of sulphuretted hydrogen has nearly disappeared. Collect the precipitate on a tared filter, wash as quickly as possible with hot water containing a little sulphuretted hydrogen, dry in a water-oven and weigh. 198 parts of arsenic should yield 246 of sulphide of arsenicum.

ANTIMONY.

The metal is precipitated in the form of sulphide (Sb_2S_3), with the precautions observed in estimating arsenicum—a small quantity of tartaric acid, as well as hydrochloric, being added, to prevent the precipitation of an oxysalt. The experiment may be performed on about half a gramme of pure tartar-emetic: the salt should yield nearly half its weight (49.56 per cent.) of sulphide. According to Fresenius, the sulphide dried at 100° C. still contains 2 per cent. of water, and must be heated, in a current of carbonic acid gas, until it turns from an orange to a black color, before all moisture is expelled. In the British Pharmacopœia the purity of tartar-emetic (*Antimonium Tartaratum*), and the strength of solution of chloride of antimony (*Liquor Antimonii Chloridi*), are determined by the above process.

COPPER.

Copper is precipitated from its solutions and weighed either (1) as metal (Cu_2), or (2) as oxide (CuO).

Process 1.—Dissolve about half a gramme of dry crystallized sulphate of copper in a small quantity of water, in a tared porcelain crucible or beaker, acidulate with hydrochloric acid, introduce a fragment or two of pure zinc, cover the vessel with a watch-glass, and set aside till evolution of hydrogen has ceased and the still acid liquid is colorless. The copper is then washed with hot water by decantation until no trace of acid remains, the precipitate drained, rinsed with strong spirit of wine, dried in the water-oven, and weighed.

Process 2.—About three-fourths of a gramme of sulphate of copper is accurately weighed, dissolved in half a litre of water, the liquid boiled; dilute solution of potash or soda is then added till no more precipitate falls, ebullition continued for a short time, and the beaker set aside; the supernatant liquid is decanted, the precipitate boiled with water twice or thrice, collected on a filter, washed, dried, transferred to a crucible, the filter incinerated, and its ash moistened with a drop of nitric acid; the whole is finally heated strongly, cooled, and weighed.

249.5 parts of sulphate of copper yield 79.5 of oxide, or 63.5 of metal.

BISMUTH.

Dissolve 0.3 or 0.4 of pure oxycarbonate of bismuth ($2Bi_2O_2CO_3, H_2O$) (*Bismuthi Carbonas*, B. P.) in a small quantity of hydrochloric acid, dilute with water slightly acidulated by hydrochloric acid, pass excess of sulphuretted hydrogen through the liquid, collect the precipitate on a tared filter, wash, dry at 100° C., and weigh. The sulphide must not be exposed too long in the water-oven, or it will increase in weight owing to absorption of oxygen; hence it should be tested in the balance every half-hour during desiccation. 517 of oxycarbonate should yield 512 of sulphide (Bi_2S_3). The strength of the official solution of citrate of bismuth and ammonium (*Liquor Bismuthi et Ammoniæ Citratis*, B. P.) is determined by this process. "Three fluidrachms of the solution, mixed with an ounce of distilled water, and treated with sulphuretted hydrogen in excess, yield a black precipitate, which, collected, washed, and dried, weighs 9.92 grains. One fluidrachm yields three grains of oxide of bismuth." The atomic weight of bismuth is 208.

MERCURY.

This element may be (1) isolated and estimated in the form of metal, or precipitated and weighed as (2) mercurous chloride, or (3) mercuric sulphide.

Process 1.—The process by which the metal itself is separated is one of distillation, into a bulb surrounded by water. About half a metre of the difficultly fusible German glass known as *combustion-tubing* is sealed at one end after the manner of a test-tube; a mixture of bicarbonate of sodium and dry chalk is then dropped into the tube to the height of two or three centimetres, and, next, several small fragments of quicklime so as to occupy another centimetre; a mixture of about a gramme of pure calomel or corrosive sublimate with enough powdered quicklime to occupy 10 or 12 centimetres of the tube is added, then the lime-rinsings of the mixing-mortar, a layer of a few centimetres of powdered quicklime, and finally a plug of *asbestos* (a fibrous mineral unaffected by heat). The whole powder should occupy two-thirds of the length of the tube. The part of the tube just above the asbestos is now softened in the blowpipe-flame and drawn out about a decimetre to the diameter of a narrow quill; it is again drawn out to the same extent at a point about two or three centimetres nearer the mouth, and any excess of tubing cut off. The bulb thus formed may be enlarged by softening and blowing. The tube is next softened at a point close to but anterior to the asbestos, and bent nearly to a right angle; the tube is then softened close to the bulb and slightly bent so that the bulb may be parallel with the large tube; then softened on the other side of the bulb, and the narrow terminal tube bent to a right angle, so that, the tube being held in a horizontal position, the bulb may be sunk in water, and the terminal tube point upwards. The long tube is now laid in the gas-furnace found in most laboratories, a basin so placed that the bulb of the apparatus may be cooled by being surrounded by water, the part of the tube occupied by asbestos heated to redness, and the flame slowly lengthened until the whole tube is red-hot. Under these circumstances the mercurial compound volatilizes, is decomposed by the lime, and its acidulous radical fixed, the mercury carried in vapor to and condensed in the bulb, the carbonic acid gas evolved from the bicarbonate of sodium and chalk washing out the last portions of mercury-vapor from the tube. When the distillation is considered to be complete, the dish of water is removed, the bulb dried, and then detached by help of a file at a point beyond any sublimate of mercury. The bulb is lastly weighed, the mercury shaken, or dissolved out, and the tube again dried and weighed.

Process 2.—The process by which mercury is separated in the form of calomel, consists in adding hydrochloric and phosphorous acids (*vide* p. 289) to an aqueous or even acid solution of a weighed quantity of the mercurial compound, setting the mixture aside for twelve hours, collecting the precipitate on a tared filter, washing, drying at 100° C., and weighing (Rose). The experiment may be tried on half a gramme, to a gramme, of corrosive sublimate.

Process 3.—Two or three decigrammes of corrosive sublimate are dissolved in water, the solution acidulated with hydrochloric acid, excess of sulphuretted hydrogen passed, the precipitate collected on a tared filter, washed with cold water, dried at 100° C., and weighed.

Proportional weights of equivalent quantities of mercury and its salts.

Metal	Hg	200
Mercurous chloride	HgCl	235.5
Mercuric chloride	$HgCl_2$	271
Mercuric sulphide	HgS	232

LEAD.

Lead is generally estimated either as (1) oxide, (2) sulphate, or (3) chromate.

Process 1.—Weigh out one or two grammes of pure

acetate of lead in a covered crucible, previously tared, and heat slowly until no more vapors are evolved. Remove the lid, stir down the carbonaceous mass with a clean iron wire, and keep the crucible in the flame so long as any carbon remains unconsumed. Introduce some fragments of fused nitrate of ammonium, and again ignite until no metallic lead remains, and all excess of the nitrate has been decomposed. Cool and weigh the resulting oxide (PbO).

Process 2.—Dissolve 0.4 or 0.5 of a gramme of acetate of lead in a small quantity of water, drop in diluted sulphuric acid, add to the mixture twice its bulk of methylated spirit of wine, and set aside. Decant the supernatant liquid, collect the sulphate on a filter, wash with spirit, dry, transfer to a porcelain crucible, removing as much of the sulphate as possible from the paper, incinerate on the crucible-lid (not in a platinum coil, for the particles of reduced lead would unite with the platinum by fusion), ignite, cool, and weigh.

Process 3.—About half a gramme of acetate of lead is dissolved in two or three hundred c. c. of water, acetic acid added, and then solution of red chromate of potassium. Collect the precipitate on a tared filter, wash, dry at 100° C., and weigh.

Molecular weights of salts of lead.

Metal . . .	Pb	207
Acetate . .	$Pb2C_2H_3O_2$, $3H_2O$.	379
Oxide . . .	PbO	223
Sulphate . .	$PbSO_4$	303
Chromate . .	$PbCrO_4$	323.5

SILVER.

Compounds of silver which are readily decomposed by heat are estimated in the form of (1) metal, others usually as (2) chloride (AgCl), but sometimes as (3) cyanide (AgNC).

Process 1.—Heat about a gramme of oxide of silver (Ag_2O) in a tared crucible, cool, and weigh. 232 of oxide yield 216 of metal. "29 grains heated to redness yield 27 grains of metallic silver."—*Brit. Pharm.*

Process 2.—Dissolve 0.4 or 0.5 of pure dry crystals of nitrate of silver in water, acidulate with two or three drops of nitric acid, slowly add hydrochloric acid, stirring rapidly, until no more precipitate falls. Pour off the supernatant liquid through a filter, wash the chloride of silver once or twice with hot water, transfer to the filter, complete the washing, and dry. After removing as much as possible of the precipitate from the paper to the crucible, burn the filter, letting its ash fall on the inverted lid of the crucible, moisten with a drop of nitric acid, warm, add a drop of hydrochloric acid, evaporate to dryness, replace the lid on the crucible, ignite the whole until the edges of the mass of chloride begin to fuse; cool, and weigh. 170 of nitrate yield 143.5 of chloride. According to the British Pharmacopœia, 10 parts of nitrate should thus yield 8.44 of chloride, and the filtrate from the chloride evaporated to dryness should leave no residue, indicating absence of nitrates of potassium or sodium and other similar adulterants.

Process 3.—Cyanide of silver may be collected on a tared filter and dried at 100° C. 170 of nitrate yield 134 of cyanide.

Silver and its salts may be volumetrically estimated by a standard solution of chloride of sodium.

Cupellation.—The amount of silver in an alloy may be also determined by a dry method. The metal is folded in a piece of thin sheet lead, placed on a *cupel* (*cupella*, little cup, made of compressed bone-earth) and heated in a furnace, the cupel being protected from the direct action of flame by a muff-shaped, or, rather, oven-shaped case termed a muffle. The metals melt, the baser become oxidized, the oxide of lead fusing and dissolving the other oxides; the fluid oxides are absorbed by the porous cupel, a button of pure silver remaining. An alloy suspected to contain 95 per cent. of silver requires about 3 times its weight of lead for successful cupellation; if 92½ per cent. (English silver coin), between 5 and 6 times as much lead is necessary.

QUESTIONS AND EXERCISES.

1001. Explain the gravimetric process by which the strength of the official solutions of ferric chloride, nitrate, and sulphate are determined.

1002. Mention the various amounts of ferrous and ferric salts equivalent to 100 parts of metal.

1003. State the precautions necessary to be observed in estimating arsenicum or antimony in the form of sulphide.

1004. In what form are the official compounds of bismuth weighed for quantitative purposes?

1005. Give an outline of the process by which mercury may be isolated from its official preparations and weighed in the metallic condition.

1006. Describe three methods for the quantitative analysis of salts of lead; and the weights of the respective precipitates, supposing 0.56 of crystallized acetate to have been operated on in each case.

1007. Describe the processes by which silver is estimated in the forms of metal, chloride, and cyanide.

1008. What proportions of nitrate of silver are indicated, respectively, by 15 of metal, 9.8 of chloride, and 8.1 of cyanide?

1009. Define cupellation.

ESTIMATION OF THE ACIDULOUS RADICALS OF SALTS.

CHLORIDES.

Free chlorine (chlorine-water) and compounds which by action of acids yield free chlorine (Chlorinated Lime, Chlorinated Soda, and their official Solutions) are estimated volumetrically by a standard solution of hyposulphite of sodium (*vide* p. 453). The amount of combined chlorine in pure chlorides (HCl, $NaCl$) may also be determined by volumetric analysis with a standard solution of nitrate of silver (p. 447).

Combined chlorine is gravimetrically estimated in the form of chloride of silver, the operations being identical with that just described for silver salts; 58.5 parts of pure, colorless, crystallized chloride of sodium (rock-salt) yield 143.5 of chloride of silver.

IODIDES.

Free iodine is estimated volumetrically by solution of hyposulphite of sodium (*vide* p. 453).

Combined iodine is determined gravimetrically in the form of iodide of silver, the operations being conducted as with chloride of silver. Iodide of potassium may be used for an experimental determination: $KI=166$ should yield $AgI=235$. Of the official iodide of cadmium (*Cadmii Iodidum*, B. P.) it is stated that "ten grains dissolved in water, and nitrate of silver added in excess, give a precipitate which, when washed with water and afterwards with half an ounce of solution of ammonia, and dried, weighs 12.5 grains."

In presence of chlorides and bromides the iodine in iodides may be precipitated and weighed as iodide of palladium.

BROMIDES.

Free bromine may be estimated by shaking with excess of solution of iodide of potassium, and then determining the equivalent quantity of liberated iodine by a standard solution of hyposulphite of sodium (p. 453).

The bromine in bromides may be precipitated and weighed as bromide of silver, the manipulations being the same as those for chloride of silver: 0.2 to 0.3 of pure bromide of potassium may be used for an experimental analysis.

CYANIDES.

The hydrogen cyanide (hydrocyanic acid) is usually estimated volumetrically (*vide* p. 447).

From all soluble cyanides, cyanogen may be precipitated by nitrate of silver, after acidulating with nitric acid, the cyanide of silver collected on a tared filter, dried at 100° C., and weighed.

Of the official Diluted Hydrocyanic Acid, it is stated that one hundred grains (or 110 minims) precipitated by solution of nitrate of silver yield ten grains of dry cyanide of silver.

Cyanide of Silver.

		In 1 molecule.	In 100 parts.
Silver . .	Ag . .	107.93 . .	80.59
Cyanogen .	CN . .	26.00 . .	19.41
		133.93	100.00

NITRATES.

Nitrate cannot be estimated by direct gravimetric analysis, none of the basylous radicals yielding a definite nitrate insoluble in water. With some difficulty they may be determined by indirect volumetric methods.

Process.—The best method is that by Crum, as modified by Frankland and Armstrong. It consists in agitating with mercury a concentrated solution of the nitrate with a large excess of concentrated sulphuric acid—the whole of the nitrogen being then involved as nitric oxide. From the volume of the latter the weight of nitrate whence obtained is easily calculated. No chlorides must be present. For educational purposes the experiment may be conducted on 3 or 4 c. c. of a solution of one gramme of pure nitrate of potassium in 100 c. c. of distilled water. From 1 to 10 c. c. of such a solution will very well represent the nitrates in half a litre of well-water.

The following is the mode in which this process is applied to the estimation of nitrogen existing as nitrates and nitrites in potable waters. The solid residue from half a litre of water used for determination of total solid constituents* is treated with a small quantity of distilled water, a very slight excess of sulphate of silver is added to convert the chlorides present into sulphates, and the filtered liquid is then concentrated by evaporation in a small beaker until it is reduced in bulk to two or three cubic centimetres. The liquid must now be transferred to a glass tube (about as long as the hand) (see fig.) previously filled with mercury at the mercurial trough, and furnished at its upper extremity with a cup and stopcock, the beaker being rinsed out once or twice with a very small volume of recently boiled distilled water, and finally with pure and concentrated sulphuric acid in somewhat greater volume than that of the concentrated solution and rinsings. (For a method of purifying the acid *vide* p. 392.) By a little dexterity it is easy to introduce successively the concentrated liquid, rinsings, and sulphuric acid by means of the cup and stopcock, without the admission of any trace of air. Should, however, air inadvertently gain admittance, it is readily removed by depressing the tube in the mercury trough, and then momentarily opening the stopcock. If this be done within a minute or two after the introduction of the sulphuric acid, no fear need be entertained of the loss of nitric oxide, as the evolution of this gas does not begin until a minute or so after the violent agitation of the contents of the tube.

The acid mixture being thus introduced, the lower extremity of the tube is to be firmly closed by the thumb, and the contents violently agitated by a simultaneous vertical

* If the water contain nitrates, a separate half litre should be taken for this determination, otherwise there is a risk of loss of nitrogen during evaporation. The nitrites in this half litre of water must be transformed into nitrates by the cautious addition of potassic permanganate to the slightly acidified water before the evaporation is commenced. Immediately after the action of the permanganate the water must be again rendered slightly alkaline.

and lateral movement, in such a manner that there is always an unbroken column of mercury, at least an inch long, at the bottom part of the glass tube. From the description, this manipulation may appear difficult; but in practice it is extremely simple, the acid liquid never coming in contact with the flesh. In about a minute from the commencement of the agitation a strong pressure begins to be felt against the thumb of the operator, and mercury spurts out in minute streams, as nitric oxide gas is evolved. The escape of the metal should be gently resisted, so as to maintain a considerable excess of pressure inside the tube, and thus prevent the possibility of air gaining access to the interior during the shaking. In from three to five minutes the reaction is completed, and the nitric oxide may then be transferred to a suitable measuring-apparatus, where its volume is to be determined over mercury. As half a litre of water is used for the determination, and as nitric oxide occupies exactly double the volume of the nitrogen which it contains, the volume of nitric oxide read off expresses the volume of nitrogen existing as nitrates and nitrites in one litre of the water. From the number so obtained, the weight of nitrogen in these forms in 100,000 parts of water is easily calculated. (1 litre of H weighs .0896, and N is 14 times as heavy as H: 101 of KNO_3 contains 14 of N.)

SULPHIDES.

Process 1.—Soluble sulphides (H_2S, NaHS, *e. g.*) may be determined volumetrically by adding to the aqueous liquid a measured excess of an alkaline solution of arsenic of known strength, neutralizing by hydrochloric acid, diluting to any given volume, filtering off the sulphide of arsenicum precipitated, taking a portion of the filtrate equal to half or a third of the original volume, and, after neutralizing by acid carbonate of sodium, estimating the residual arsenic by the standard iodine solution (*vide* p. 448). The process may be tried on a measured volume of sulphuretted hydrogen (the weight of which is easily calculated; 1 litre of hydrogen = 0.0896 gramme) absorbed by a strong solution of soda or potash.

Process 2.—Sulphur and sulphides may also be quantitatively analyzed by oxidizing to sulphuric acid and precipitating in the form of sulphate of barium. A couple of decigrammes of a pure metallic sulphide may be decomposed by careful deflagration with a mixture of chlorate of potassium and carbonate of sodium, the product dissolved in water, acidulated with hydrochloric acid, solution of chloride of barium added, and the precipitated sulphate of barium purified and collected as described in connection with the estimation of barium (p. 462). Many sulphides may be oxidized in a flask by chlorate of potassium and hydrochloric acid, and then precipitated by chloride of barium. Experimental determinations may also be made on a weighed fragment of sulphur, about 0.1, cautiously fused with a solid caustic alkali, and the product oxidized while hot by the slow addition of powdered nitrate or chlorate of potassium, or, when cold, by treatment with chlorate of potassium and hydrochloric acid, and subsequent precipitation by chloride of barium.

Note.—Fusions performed by help of a gas-lamp must be carefully conducted; for any alkali that may creep over the side of a crucible will certainly absorb sulphurous acid from the products of combustion of the gas, and error result.

Process 3.—Soluble sulphides may also be treated with excess of an alkaline arseniate, arsenious sulphide be then precipitated by the addition of hydrochloric acid, and the precipitate collected and weighed with the usual precautions (*vide* p. 468).

Weights of equivalent quantities of sulphur and its compounds.

Sulphur	S	32
Sulphuretted hydrogen	H_2S	34
Sulphate of barium	$BaSO_4$	233
Arsenious sulphide	$(As_2S_3) \div 3$	82
Iron pyrites	$(FeS_2) \div 2$	60
Galena	PbS	239

SULPHITES.

Sulphites are usually estimated volumetrically by a standard solution of iodine (*vide* p. 448). Sulphites insoluble in water are diffused in that menstruum, hydrochloric acid added, and the iodine solution then dropped in.

If necessary, sulphites may be estimated gravimetrically by oxidation and precipitation in the form of sulphate of barium.

SULPHATES.

These salts are always precipitated and weighed as sulphate of barium, the manipulations being identical with those performed in the determination of barium by means of sulphates (*vide* p. 462). The purity of Sulphate of Sodium (*Sodæ Sulphas*, B. P.), and the presence of not more than a given amount of sulphuric acid in Vinegar (*Acetum*, B. P.), are directed, in the British Pharmacopœia, to be ascertained by this process. Five ounces of vinegar should yield not more than about one-third of a gramme of sulphate of barium.

Proportional weights of equivalent quantities of sulphates.

The sulphuric radical . . .	SO_4	96
Sulphuric acid	H_2SO_4	98
Sulphate of barium	$BaSO_4$	233

CARBONATES.

Carbonates are usually estimated by the loss in weight they undergo on the addition of a strong acid.

Process 1.—A small light flask is selected—of such a size that it can be conveniently weighed in a delicate balance. Two narrow glass tubes are fitted to the flask by a cork; the one straight, extending from about two or three centimetres above the cork to the bottom of the flask; the other cut off close to the cork on the inside and curved outwards so as to carry a thin drying-tube horizontally above the flask. The drying-tube may be a short narrow test-tube, the bottom of which is constricted so as to form a narrow tube open at the end; it is nearly filled with small pieces of chloride of calcium, a plug of cotton-wool preventing escape of any fragments at either end, and is attached by a pierced cork to the free extremity of the curved tube of the flask. A weighed quantity of any pure soluble carbonate is placed in the flask, a little water added, a miniature test-tube containing sulphuric acid lowered into the flask by a thread and supported so that the acid may not flow out, the cork inserted, the outer end of the piece of the straight glass tubing closed by a fragment of cork or wax, and the whole weighed. The apparatus is then inclined so that the oil of vitriol and carbonate may slowly react; carbonic acid gas is evolved and escapes through the horizontal tube, any moisture being retained by the chloride of calcium. When effervescence has ceased, the gas still remaining in the vessel is sucked out; this is accomplished by adapting a piece of India-rubber tubing to the end of the drying-tube, removing the small plug from the straight tube, and aspirating slowly with the mouth for a few minutes. If the heat produced by the action of the oil of vitriol and solution is considered insufficient to expel all the carbonic acid from the liquid, the plug is again inserted in the tube and the contents of the flask gently boiled for some seconds. When the apparatus is cold, more air is again drawn through it, and the whole finally weighed. The loss is due to carbonic acid gas (CO_2), from the weight of which that of any carbonate is ascertained by calculation. Carbonates insoluble in water may be attacked by hydrochloric instead of sulphuric acid; granulated mixtures of carbonates and powdered tartaric or citric acids by inclosing the preparation in the inner tube and placing water in the flask, or *vice versâ*. The apparatus also may be modified in many ways to suit the requirements, convenience, or taste of the operator.

Process 2.—Carbonates from which carbonic acid gas is evolved by heat may be estimated by the loss they experience on ignition.

Process 3.—Free carbonic acid gas may be absorbed by a solid stick of potash or a strong alkaline solution, the loss in volume of the gas or mixture of gases indicating the amount originally present.

Weights of equivalent quantities of carbonic acid gas and certain carbonates.

Carbonic acid gas	CO_2	44
Carbonic acid	H_2CO_3	62
Anhydrous carbonate of sodium	Na_2CO_3	106
Anhydrous carbonate of potassium	K_2CO_3	138
Carbonate of calcium	$CaCO_3$	100

OXALATES.

Process 1.—The oxalic radical is usually precipitated in the form of oxalate of calcium, and weighed as carbonate, the manipulations being identical with those observed in the estimation of calcium (*vide* p. 464). The experiment may be performed on 0.3 or 0.4 of pure crystallized oxalic acid, 126 parts of which should yield 100 of carbonate of calcium.

Process 2.—Oxalates may also be determined by conversion of their acidulous radical into carbonic acid gas, and observation of the weight of the latter. The oxalate, water, and excess of black oxide of manganese are placed in the carbonic acid apparatus, a tube full of oil of vitriol lowered into the flask, the whole weighed, and the operation completed as for carbonates. From the following equation it will be seen that every 88 parts of carbonic acid gas evolved indicate the presence of 126 parts of crystallized oxalic acid or an equivalent quantity of other oxalate:—

$$Na_2C_2O_4 + MnO_2 + 2H_2SO_4 = MnSO_4 + Na_2SO_4 + 2H_2O + 2CO_2.$$

The black oxide of manganese used in this experiment must be free from carbonates. The amount of materials employed is regulated by the size of the vessels.

PHOSPHATES.

Process 1.—*From phosphates dissolved in water*, the phosphoric radical may be precipitated and weighed in the form of pyrophosphate of magnesium, the details of manipulation being similar to those observed in estimating magnesium (*vide* p. 465). Half a gramme or rather more of pure dry crystallized phosphate of sodium may be employed in experimental determinations. The official phosphate of ammonium (*Ammoniæ Phosphas*, B. P.) is quantitatively analyzed by this method. "If twenty grains of this salt be dissolved in water, and solution of ammonio-sulphate of magnesia added, a crystalline precipitate falls, which, when well washed upon a filter with solution of ammonia diluted with an equal volume of water, dried, and heated to redness, leaves 16.8 grains." Half a gramme or less is a more convenient quantity, if the operations be conducted with care. Solution of ammonio-sulphate of magnesium (B. P.) is prepared by dissolving 2 parts of sulphate of magnesium, 1 of chloride of ammonium, and 1 of solution of ammonia (20.6 per cent. NH_4HO) in 18 or 20 of distilled water; such a solution is of considerable use if several phosphoric determinations are about to be made.

Process 2.—*Free phosphoric acid* is most readily deter-

41

mined as phosphate of lead (Pb_32PO_4). Of the official solution of phosphoric acid it is stated that "355 grains by weight poured upon 180 grains of oxide of lead in fine powder leave, by evaporation, a residue (principally phosphate of lead) which, after it has been heated to dull redness, weighs 215.5 grains." One-tenth of these quantities may be used for experimental purposes; one to two grammes will give good results. The oxide of lead must be quite pure; it should be prepared by digesting red lead in warm dilute nitric acid, washing, drying, and heating the resulting puce-colored plumbic oxide in a covered porcelain crucible. The increase in weight obtained on evaporating a given amount of solution of phosphoric acid with a known weight of perfectly pure oxide of lead (PbO) may be regarded as entirely due to phosphoric anhydride (P_2O_5),

$$3PbO + P_2O_5 = Pb_32PO_4,$$

the actual reaction being,

$$3PbO + 2H_3PO_4 = Pb_32PO_4 + 3H_2O.$$

From these equations, and the table of atomic weights (*vide* Appendix), the percentage of phosphoric acid (H_3PO_4) in any specimen of its solution may be easily calculated.

Process 3.—*The strength of pure solution of phosphoric acid* may be ascertained by taking its specific gravity at 15°.5 C. (*Vide* Appendix.)

Process 4.—Bone-earth, "superphosphate," the *Calcis Phosphas* of pharmacy, and other forms of phosphate of calcium known to be tolerably free from iron or aluminium, may be estimated by treating about half a gramme with hydrochloric acid somewhat diluted, filtering if necessary, warming, precipitating with excess of ammonia, collecting the precipitate (Ca_32PO_4), washing, drying, igniting, and weighing. "*Calcis phosphas*," if pure, will, in this process, lose no weight.

Process 5.—*Insoluble phosphates* in ashes, manures, etc., are treated as follows: a weighed quantity of the material (1.0 to 10.0) is digested in hydrochloric acid diluted with three or four times its bulk of water; filtered (the precipitate and filter being thoroughly exhausted by water); ammonia added to the filtrate and washings until, after stirring, a faint cloudy precipitate is perceptible; solution of oxalic acid dropped in until, after agitation for a few minutes, the opalescence is removed; oxalate of ammonium next added, the whole warmed, oxalate of calcium removed by filtration, and the filtrate concentrated if very dilute; the liquid treated with citric acid in such quantity that ammonia when added in excess gives a clear *lemon-yellow* solution (Warington), magnesian mixture poured in (as in Process 1), and the precipitate of ammonio-magnesian phosphate collected, washed, dried, and weighed as already described in connection with the estimation of magnesium.

Relative weights of equivalent quantities of phosphoric compounds.

Phosphoric acid	H_3PO_4	98
Pyrophosphate of magnesium	$(Mg_2P_2O_7=222)\div 2=$	111
Phosphate of lead	$(Pb_32PO_4=811)\div 2=$	405.5
Phosphoric anhydride . . .	$(P_2O_5=142)\quad\div 2=$	71
Phosphate of calcium . . .	$(Ca_32PO_4=310)\div 2=$	155
Superphosphate of calcium	$(CaH_42PO_4=234)\div 2=$	117

QUESTIONS AND EXERCISES.

1010. What quantity of pure rock-salt is equivalent to 4.2 parts of chloride of silver?—*Ans.* 1.712.

1011. State the percentage of real iodide of potassium contained in a sample of which 8 parts yield 10.9 of iodide of silver.—*Ans.* 96.25.

1012. What is the strength of a solution of hydrocyanic acid 10 parts of which, by weight, yield .9 of cyanide of silver?—*Ans.* 1.81 per cent.

1013. How are nitrates quantitatively estimated?

1014. By what processes may the strength of sulphides be determined?

1015. How much real sulphate of sodium is contained in a specimen 10 parts of which yield 14.2 of sulphate of barium?—*Ans.* 86.34 per cent.

1016. Give details of the operations performed in the quantitative analysis of carbonates.

1017. What amount of carbonic acid gas should be obtained from 10 parts of acid carbonate (or bicarbonate) of potassium?—*Ans.* 4.4 parts.

1018. To what operation and what quantities of materials does the following equation refer?

$$Na_2C_2O_4 + MnO_2 + 2H_2SO_4 = MnSO_4 + Na_2SO_4 + 2H_2O + 2CO_2.$$

1019. Explain the lead process for the estimation of phosphoric acid in the official solution.

1020. State the amount of superphosphate of calcium equivalent to 7.6 parts of pyrophosphate of magnesium.—*Ans.* 8.01 parts.

SILICATES.

Silica (SiO_2) may be separated from alkaline silicates, or from silicates decomposable by hydrochloric acid, by digesting the substance in hydrochloric acid at a temperature of 70° or 80° C., until completely disintegrated, evaporating to dryness, heating in an air-bath, again moistening with acid, diluting with hot water, filtering, washing, drying, igniting, and weighing.

ESTIMATION OF WATER.

Water, being readily volatilized, is most usually estimated by the loss in weight which a substance undergoes on being heated to a proper temperature. Thus, in the British Pharmacopœia, crystalline gallic acid ($H_3C_7H_3O_5$, H_2O) is stated to lose 9.5 per cent. of its weight at a temperature of 100° C., oxalate of cerium (CeC_2O_4, $3H_2O$) 52 per cent. on incineration, carbonate of potassium about 16 per cent. on exposure to a red heat, sulphate of quinine ($2C_{20}H_{24}N_2O_2$, H_2SO_4, $7H_2O$) 14.4 per cent. at 100° C., arseniate of sodium (Na_2HAsO_4, $7H_2O$) 40.38 per cent. at 149° C., carbonate of sodium (Na_2CO_3, $10H_2O$) 63 per cent., phosphate of sodium (Na_2HPO_4, $12H_2O$) 63 per cent., and sulphate of sodium (Na_2SO_4, $10H_2O$) 55.9 per cent. at a low red heat.

Process.—One or two grammes of substance is sufficient in experiments on desiccation, the material being placed in a watch-glass, covered or uncovered porcelain crucible, or other vessel, according to the temperature to which it is to be exposed. Rapid desiccation at an exact temperature may be effected by introducing the substance into a tube having somewhat the shape of the letter U, sinking the lower part of the tube into a liquid kept at a definite temperature by aid of a thermometer, and drawing or forcing a current of dry air slowly through the apparatus. Substances liable to oxidation may be desiccated in a current of dried carbonic acid gas. The weights of the U-tube before and after the introduction of the salt, and after desiccation, give the amount of water sought. In all cases the material must be heated until it ceases to lose weight. Occasionally it is desirable to estimate water directly by conveying its vapor in a current of air through a weighed tube containing chloride of calcium and re-weighing the tube at the close of the operation; the increase shows the amount of water.

Note.—Highly dried substances rapidly absorb moisture from the air; they must therefore be weighed quickly, inclosed, if possible, in tubes (p. 458), a pair of clamped watch-glasses, or a crucible having a tightly fitting lid.

CARBON, HYDROGEN, OXYGEN, NITROGEN.

The quantitative analysis of animal and vegetable substances is either *proximate* or *ultimate*. Proximate analysis includes the estimation of water, oil, albumen, starch, cellulose, gum, resin, alkaloids, acids, glucosides, ash. It requires the application of much theoretical knowledge and manipulative skill, and cannot well be studied except under the guidance of a tutor. The best published work on the subject is by Rochleder, a translation of whose monograph will be found in the Pharmaceutical Journal, vol. i. 2d ser. pp. 562, 610; vol. ii. 2d ser. pp. 24, 129, 160, 215, 274, 420, 478.

Ultimate organic analysis can only be successfully accomplished with the appliances of a well-appointed laboratory—a good balance, a gas-furnace giving a smokeless flame (7 or 8 centimetres wide and 70 or 80 centimetres long), special forms of glass apparatus, &c. *The theory of the operation* is simple: a weighed quantity of a substance is burnt to carbonic acid gas (CO_2=44) and water (H_2O=18), and these products collected and weighed; 12 parts in every 44 of carbonic acid gas ($=\frac{3}{11}$) are carbon, 2 in every 18 of water ($=\frac{1}{9}$) are hydrogen; nitrogen if present escapes as gas. If nitrogen be a constituent, more of the substance is strongly heated with a mixture of the hydrates of sodium and calcium; these bodies then split up into oxides, oxygen, and hydrogen; the oxygen burns the carbon of the substance to carbonic acid gas, its hydrogen and nitrogen appearing as water and ammonia respectively; the carbonic acid and water are disregarded, the ammonia collected and weighed in the form of a double chloride of platinum and ammonium ($PtCl_4 2NH_4Cl$ =447), of which 28 parts in every 447 ($=\frac{1}{16}$) are nitrogen. The difference between the sum of the weights of hydrogen and carbon, and the weight of substance taken, is the proportion of oxygen in the body, supposing nitrogen to be absent. If nitrogen is present, the difference between the sum of the percentages of carbon, hydrogen, and nitrogen and 100, is the percentage of oxygen. Shortly, carbon is estimated in the form of carbonic acid gas, hydrogen as water, nitrogen as ammonia, and oxygen by loss.

The following is the outline of the necessary manipulations. The source of the oxygen for the combustion of carbon and hydrogen is black oxide of copper in coarse powder. 200 or 300 grammes of this material are heated in a crucible to low redness for a short time to expel every trace of moisture; then transferred to tubes (store-tubes) resembling test-tubes, half a metre long, and having a slightly narrowed mouth, the tube being held in a cloth to protect the hand while the hot oxide is being directly introduced into the mouth of the tube by a scooping motion. As soon as the well-corked tube is cool, the oxide is poured, portion by portion, into a similar tube (the combustion-tube), somewhat longer, drawn out to a quill (bent upwards nearly to a right-angle) at one end, not constricted at the mouth, and containing a few decigrammes of fused chlorate of potassium. After ten or fifteen centimetres of oxide have been poured in, about a decigramme of the substance to be analyzed is dropped down the tube, then a few grammes of oxide, then another decigramme of substance, then more oxide, until three or four decigrammes of the body under examination have been added. The fifteen or twenty centimetres of alternate layers are next thoroughly mixed by a long copper wire having a short helix, more oxide is introduced, the wire cleansed by twisting the helix about in the pure oxide, and a plug of asbestos finally placed on the top of the oxide at about five centimetres from the mouth of the tube; the tube is then securely corked and set aside. The substance operated on may be pure white sugar, powdered and dried; the tube in which it is contained is weighed before and after the removal of a portion for combustion, the loss is the quantity employed in the experiment. If the combustion-furnace is powerful, or the combustion-tube not of the hardest glass, the tube should be inclosed in wire gauze the elasticity of which has been destroyed by heating to redness. In the combustion of substances containing nitrogen, the plug of asbestos must be displaced by one of copper turnings, which serve to reduce any oxides of nitrogen, and thus insure the escape of nitrogen itself. The *water* produced when the prepared tube is heated, is collected in a small U-tube containing pieces of chloride of calcium, or pumice-stone moistened with sulphuric acid; the *carbonic acid gas* in a series of bulbs containing solution of potash (sp. gr. about 1.27). These bulbs may be purchased at any apparatus-shop. The chloride-of-calcium tube is fitted by a good cork to a combustion-tube, the potash-bulbs by a short piece of India-rubber tubing to the chloride-of-calcium tube. The potash-bulbs may carry a short light tube containing a rod of caustic potash three or four centimetres long; this serves to arrest any moisture that might be carried away from the solution of potash by the dried expanded air which escapes during the operation. The combustion-tube having been placed in the furnace, and the drying-tube and potash bulbs weighed and attached, the gas is lit under the asbestos, and, when the tube is red-hot, the flame slowly extended until nearly the whole tube is at the same temperature, the operation being conducted at such a rate that bubbles of gas escape through the bulbs at about the rate of one per second. When no more gas passes, the extremity of the tube containing the chlorate of potassium is gently heated until oxygen ceases to be evolved; the quilled extremity of the combustion-tube is then broken, and air drawn slowly through the apparatus by suction through an India-rubber tube fixed on the free end of the potash-bulbs, perfect combustion of carbon and removal of all carbonic acid gas is thus insured. The drying-tube and bulbs are disconnected and weighed; the increase in weight due to carbonic acid gas and water respectively noted, and the percentages of carbon, hydrogen, and (by loss) oxygen calculated. This method is that of Liebig, with modifications by Bunsen; one of the best combustion-furnaces is that known as Hofmann's.

The general manipulations for substances containing nitrogen resemble the foregoing so far as the use of a combustion-tube and furnace and collection of the ammoniacal gas are concerned. The combustion-tube must be quilled at one end, and about a third of a metre long. The soda-lime is made by slaking quicklime with a solution of soda, of such a strength that about two parts of quicklime shall be mixed with one of hydrate of sodium, drying the product, heating to bright redness, and finely powdering; it should be preserved in a well-closed bottle. Some of the soda-lime is introduced into the tube, then layers of substance and soda-lime, mixture effected by a wire, more soda-lime added, and lastly a plug of asbestos. Bulbs, known as those of Will and Varrentrapp (the originators of the method), containing hydrochloric acid of about 25 per cent., are then fitted by a cork, and the tube heated in the furnace. When gas ceases to pass, the quill is broken, and aspiration continued slowly until ammoniacal gas may be considered to have been all removed. The bulbs are disconnected, their contents and rinsings poured into a small dish, solution of perchloride of platinum added, and the operation completed as in the estimation of ammonium and potassium salts (*vide* pages 515 and 459).

Liquids are analyzed by a similar method to that adopted for solids, volatile liquids being inclosed in small bulbs having a long quill. These are weighed previously to and after the introduction of the liquid; just before being dropped into the combustion-tube the quill is broken.

Formulæ.—From the percentage composition of an organic substance an empirical formula may be deduced by dividing the weight of each constituent by its atomic weight, and converting the product into the simplest whole numbers; a rational formula by ascertaining the proportion in which the substance unites with a body having a known combining proportion (*vide* p. 348).

Chlorine, *bromine*, or *iodine* contained in an organic substance is usually estimated by heating to redness a given weight of the material with ten times as much pure lime in a combustion-tube. Chloride, bromide, or iodide of calcium is thus produced. While still hot the tube is plunged into water, the mixture of broken glass and powder treated with diluted nitric acid in very slight excesses; the filtered liquid precipitated by nitrate of silver, and the chloride, bromide, or iodide of silver collected, washed, dried, and weighed.

Sulphur, *phosphorus*, and *arsenicum* in organic salts may be estimated by gradually heating in a combustion-tube 1 part of the substance with a mixture of 10 parts nitre, 2 dried carbonate of sodium, and 30 chloride of sodium (in order to moderate deflagration). The product is dissolved in water acidulated by nitric acid, the sulphuric radical precipitated and estimated as sulphate of barium, the phosphoric and arsenic radicals as ammonio-magnesian phosphate or arseniate.

QUINIA.

The following process for the estimation of the quality of yellow cinchona-bark is from the pages of the British Pharmacopœia:—

Boil 100 grains (or 6 to 7 grammes) of the bark reduced to very fine powder for a quarter of an hour in a fluid-ounce of distilled water acidulated with ten minims of hydrochloric acid, and allow it to macerate for twenty-four hours. Transfer the whole to a small percolator, and, after the fluid has ceased to drop, add at intervals about an ounce and a half of similarly acidulated water, or until the fluid which passes through is free from color. Add to the percolated fluid solution of subacetate of lead, until nearly the whole of the coloring-matter has been removed, taking care that the fluid remains acid in reaction. Filter and wash with a little distilled water. To the filtrate add about thirty-five grains of caustic potash, or as much as will cause the precipitate which is at first formed to be nearly redissolved, and afterwards six fluidrachms of pure ether. Then shake briskly, and, having removed the ether, repeat the process twice with three fluidrachms of ether, or until a drop of the ether employed leaves on evaporation scarcely any perceptible residue. Lastly, evaporate the mixed ethereal solutions in a capsule. The residue, which consists of nearly pure quinia, when dry, should weigh not less than 2 grains (2 per cent.), and should be readily soluble in diluted sulphuric acid. (The sulphate—sometimes termed the acid sulphate—of quinia is freely soluble in water, the corresponding salt of quinidia only sparingly soluble. The oxalate of quinia, on the contrary, is almost insoluble in water, the oxalate of quinidia being readily soluble.) 200 grains of pale cinchona-bark treated in the same manner, with the substitution of chloroform for ether, should yield not less than 1 grain of alkaloids, and 100 of red cinchona-bark 1.5 grain of alkaloids.

A quantitative determination of the purity of commercial sulphate of quinia may be made by De Vry's process. 2 grammes of the salt are dissolved in 12 c. c. of distilled water and 1.6 c. c. of diluted sulphuric acid (B. P.). 8 c. c. of solution of hydrate of sodium (1 to 12) and 30 c. c. of pure dry ether are added, the whole well shaken and laid aside for twelve hours. The ethereal solution decanted and evaporated gives the quinia. The aqueous solution carefully neutralized by acetic acid and strong solution of iodide of potassium (1 in 4) added, gives a white precipitate of hydriodate of quinidia, the mother-liquor containing any cinchonia and cinchonidia that may be present. The precipitate is collected on a tared filter, washed, dried, and weighed; it contains 71.68 per cent. of pure quinidia. The filtrate and washings are rendered alkaline by solution of soda; cinchonia and cinchonidia are precipitated, and may be collected, washed, dried, and weighed.

Note.—If the quinia in drying assumes a resinoid character, it should be redissolved in ether, and the solution when concentrated allowed to finally evaporate very slowly or spontaneously.

Of the Citrate of Iron and Quinia (*Ferri et Quiniæ Citras*, B. P.) it is officially stated that "fifty grains dissolved in a fluidounce of water and treated with a slight excess of ammonia give a white precipitate which, when collected on a filter and dried, weighs eight grains. The precipitate is almost entirely soluble in two or three fluidrachms of pure ether," and the ethereal solution set aside for twelve hours in a small well-corked bottle yields no crystalline deposit (of quinidia).

MORPHIA.

The official process for the estimation of this alkaloid in opium is conducted in the following manner:—

Take of opium 100 grains, slaked lime 100 grains, distilled water 4 ounces. Break down the opium, and steep it in an ounce of the water for twenty-four hours, stirring the mixture frequently. Transfer it to a displacement-apparatus, and pour on the remainder of the water in successive portions, so as to exhaust the opium by percolation. To the infusion thus obtained, placed in a flask, add the lime, boil for ten minutes, place the undissolved matter on a filter, and wash it with an ounce of boiling water. Acidulate the filtered fluid slightly with diluted hydrochloric acid, evaporate it to the bulk of half an ounce, and let it cool. Neutralize cautiously with solution of ammonia, carefully avoiding an excess; remove by filtration the brown matter which separates, wash it with an ounce of hot water, mix the washings with the filtrate, concentrate the whole to the bulk of half an ounce, and add now solution of ammonia in slight excess. After twenty-four hours collect the precipitated morphia on a weighed filter, wash it with cold water, and dry it at 212° F. It ought to weigh at least from six to eight grains.

Of Hydrochlorate of Morphia it is stated that "twenty grains of the salt dissolved in half an ounce of warm water, with ammonia added in the slightest possible excess, give on cooling a crystalline precipitate which, when washed with a little cold water and dried by exposure to the air, weighs 15.18 grains."

Testing Opium.—Professor Schneider has proposed, in the 6th revised edition of the Pharmacopœia Austriaca, the following method for testing the quality of opium. Ten grammes of previously dried and powdered opium are treated with a mixture of 150 grammes of distilled water, to which 20 grammes of pure hydrochloric acid, sp. gr. 1.12, are added; the residue, after extraction, should not exceed 4.5 grammes weight; to the acid fluid 20 grammes of common salt are added, and the precipitate thereby caused is collected, after twenty-four hours, on a filter, and the latter washed with a solution of common salt; to the filtrate ammonia is added, and the fluid left standing again for twenty-four hours; the crystals which have separated are collected, redissolved in acetic acid, and precipitated with ammonia; the precipitate so obtained is washed, dried, and weighed; its weight should not be less than 1 gramme.

SUGAR.

The qualitative test for sugar, by means of an alkaline copper solution (*vide* p. 336), may be applied in the estimation of sugar in sacchariferous substances.

Process.—34.64 grammes of pure dry crystals of ordinary sulphate of copper are dissolved in about 250 c. c. of distilled water, 173 grammes of pure crystals of the double tartrate of potassium and sodium are dissolved in 480 c. c. of solution of caustic soda of sp. gr. 1.14. The solutions are mixed and water added to one litre. 100 c. c. of this solution represent 3.464 grammes of sulphate of copper, and correspond to 0.5 of a gramme of pure anhydrous grape-sugar, 0.475 of cane-sugar, or 0.45 of starch. It must be preserved in a well-stoppered bottle to prevent absorption of carbonic acid, and be kept in a dark place. If it give a precipitate on boiling, a little solution of soda may be added in making experiments.

Dissolve 0.475 of pure dry powdered cane-sugar in about 50 c. c. of water, convert into grape-sugar by acidulating with sulphuric acid, and boiling for an hour or two, neutralize with carbonate of sodium, and dilute to 100 c. c. Place 10 c. c. of the copper solution in a small flask, dilute with three or four times its bulk of water, and gently boil. Into the boiling liquid drop the solution of sugar from a burette, one cubic centimetre, or less, at a time, until, after standing for the precipitate to subside, the supernatant liquid has just lost its blue color; 10 c. c. of the solution of the sugar should be required to produce this effect, = 0.475 of cane-sugar or 0.5 of grape-sugar. Experiments on pure cane-sugar must be practised until accuracy is attained; syrups, diabetic urine, and saccharated substances containing unknown quantities of sugar may then be analyzed.

Starch is converted into grape-sugar by gentle ebullition with dilute acid for eight or ten hours, the solution being finally diluted so that one part of starch, or rather sugar, shall be contained in about 150 of water.

Saccharimetry.—A generic term for certain volumetric operations undertaken with the view of ascertaining the quantity of sugar present in any matter in which it may be contained.

Saccharimetry is frequently performed upon common syrup (*Syrupus*, B. P.) and solutions which are known to contain nothing but cane- (ordinary) sugar, the object being merely to ascertain the amount present. In such a case it is only necessary to take the specific gravity of the liquid at 60° F., and then refer to a previously prepared Table of densities and percentages.

Specific gravity.	Sugar per cent.	Specific gravity.	Sugar per cent.	Specific gravity.	Sugar. per cent.
1.007 . .	1.8	1.100 . .	23.7	1.210 . .	46.2
1.014 . .	3.5	1.108 . .	25.6	1.221 . .	48.1
1.022 . .	5.2	1.116 . .	·27.6	1.231 . .	50.0
1.029 . .	7.0	1.125 . .	29.4	1.242 . .	52.1
1.036 . .	8.7	1.134 . .	31.5	1.252 . .	54.1
1.044 . .	10.4	1.043 . .	33.4	1.261 . .	56.0
1.052 . .	12.4	1.152 . .	35.2	1.275 . .	58.0
1.060 . .	14.4	1.161 . .	37.0	1.286 . .	60.1
1.067 . .	16.3	1.171 . .	38.8	1.298 . .	62.2
1.075 . .	18.2	1.180 . .	40.6	1.309 . .	64.4
1.083 . .	20.0	1.190 . .	42.4	1.321 . .	66.6 ?
1.091 . .	21.8	1.199 . .	44.3	1.330 (B.P.)	66.6 ?

The sp. gr. may be taken by an hydrometer, technically termed a *saccharometer*. (The above spec. gravs. = 1° to 35° Baumé.)

If a liquid contains other substances besides cane-sugar, the test of specific gravity is of little or no value. Advantage may then be taken of the fact that syrup causes right-handed twisting of a ray of plane polarized light to an extent exactly proportionate to the amount of sugar in solution. The saccharine fluid is placed in a long tube having opaque sides and transparent ends; and a ray of homogeneous light, polarized by reflection from a black-glass mirror or otherwise, is sent through the liquid and optically examined by a plate of tourmaline, Nicol's prism, or other polarizing eyepiece. Attached to the eyepiece is a short arm which traverses a circle divided into degrees. The eyepiece and arm are previously so adjusted that when the ray is no longer visible the arm points to the zero of the scale of degrees. The saccharine solution, however, so twists the ray as to again render it visible; and the number of degrees which the eyepiece has to be rotated before the ray is once more invisible is exactly proportionate to the strength of the solution. The value of the degrees having been ascertained by direct experiment and the results tabulated, a reference to the Table at once indicates the percentage of sugar in the liquid under examination. Grape-sugar also possesses the property of dextro-rotation, but less powerfully than cane-sugar; moreover the former variety does not, like cane-sugar, suffer inversion of the direction of rotation on the addition of hydrochloric acid to its solution—an operation that furnishes data for ascertaining the amounts of cane- and of grape-sugar, or of crystallizable and non-crystallizable sugar, present in a mixture. In using the polariscope-saccharometer, it is convenient to employ tubes of uniform size, and always to operate at the same temperature.

ALCOHOL.

Mulder's process for the determination of the amount of alcohol in wines, beer, tinctures, and other alcoholic liquids containing vegetable matter is as follows: Take the specific gravity and temperature of the liquid, and measure off a certain quantity (100 cubic centimetres); evaporate to one-half or less, avoiding ebullition in order that particles of the material may not be carried away by the steam. Dilute with water to the original bulk, and take the specific gravity at the same temperature as before. Of the figures representing this latter specific gravity, all over 1.000 show to what extent dissolved solid matter affected the original specific gravity of the liquid. Thus, the specific gravity of a sample of wine at 15°.5 C. is 0.9951; evaporated till all alcohol is removed and diluted with water to the original bulk, the specific gravity at 15°.5 C. is 1.0081: 0.0081 represents the gravitating effect of dissolved solid matter in 0.9951 parts of original wine. 0.0081 subtracted from 0.9951 leaves 0.987, which is the specific gravity of the water and alcohol of the wine. On referring to a Table of the strengths of diluted alcohol of different specific gravities (p. 506), 0.987 at 15°.5 C. is found to indicate a spirit containing 8 per cent. of real alcohol. If the foregoing operation be conducted in a retort, the liquid being boiled and the steam carefully condensed, the distillate, diluted with water to the original bulk of wine operated on, will still more accurately represent the amount of water and alcohol in the wine—its specific gravity showing the percentage of real alcohol present.

DIALYSIS.

Dialysis (from διὰ, *dia*, through, and λύσις, *lusis*, a loosing or resolving) is a term applied by Graham to a process of analysis by diffusion through a septum. The apparatus used in the process is called a *dialyzer*, and is constructed and employed in the following manner. The most convenient septum is the commercial article known as *parchment paper*, made by immersing unsized paper for a short time in sulphuric acid; it is sold by most dealers in chemical apparatus. A piece of this material is stretched over a gutta-percha hoop, and secured by a second external hoop. Dialyzers of useful size are one or two inches deep and five to ten inches wide. Liquids to be dialyzed are poured into the dialyzer, which is then floated in a flat dish containing distilled water.

The practical value of dialysis depends upon the fact that certain substances will diffuse through a given septum far more rapidly than others. Uncrystallizable bodies diffuse very slowly. Of such matters as starch, gum, albumen, and gelatine, the last named is perhaps least diffusive; hence substances of this class are termed *colloids*, or bodies like *collin*, which is the soluble form of gelatine. Substances which diffuse rapidly are mostly crystalline; hence bodies of this class are termed *crystalloids*.

Solutions of two parts of the following named substances in 100 parts of distilled water were dialyzed by Graham for twenty-four hours. The amounts of each substance which passed through the septum bore the following relations to one another:—

Chloride of sodium	1000
Ammonia	847
Theine	703
Salicin	503
Cane-sugar	472
Amygdalin	311
Extract of logwood	168
Catechu	159
Extract of cochineal	51
Gallo-tannic acid	30
Extract of litmus	19
Purified caramel	5

Ten-per-cent. solutions, under similar circumstances, gave the following results:—

Gum Arabic	4
Starch-sugar	266
Cane-sugar	214
Glycerine	440
Alcohol	476
Chloride of sodium	1000

The phenomena of dialysis show that crystalloids are superior to colloids in affinity for water. If a solution of chloride of sodium be placed at the bottom of a jar, and covered by a hot solution of gelatine of sufficient strength to solidify on cooling, the chloride of sodium will diffuse up into the solid jelly, because the water of the solid jelly has a greater affinity for the salt than it has for the gelatine. The solid jelly may obviously be reduced in thickness, and saline liquids placed above it; indeed the conditions would then be still more favorable for diffusion. Replace the stratum of jelly by a permanent colloid, such as parchment paper; the result is the same, but the permanent character of the septum admits of its practical application.

Further researches on dialysis will probably throw much light on several important points in connection with physiological chemistry; for there is little doubt that alimentary matter passes through the cell-walls of animals and plants by this process.

QUESTIONS AND EXERCISES.

1021. Carbonate of potassium is said to lose 16 per cent. of water on exposure to a red heat; give the details of manipulation observed in verifying this statement.

1022. Write a few paragraphs descriptive of the process of ultimate organic analysis.

1023. In what forms are carbon, hydrogen, and nitrogen weighed in quantitative analysis?

1024. In the combustion of .41 of a gramme of sugar, what weights of products will be obtained?—*Ans.* .632 of carbonic acid gas (CO_2) and .237 of water (H_2O).

1025. Describe De Vry's process for the assay of commercial quinia.

1026. Give the official method for the estimation of morphia in opium.

1027. Mention the operations necessary for the estimation of the proportion of sugar in saccharated carbonate of iron, or in a specimen of diabetic urine.

1028. What is understood by *saccharimetry?*

1029. Give two processes for the estimation of the percentage of alcohol in tinctures, wines, or beer.

1030. Define dialysis.

CONCLUSION.

Detailed instructions for the quantitative analysis of potable water, articles of food, general technical products, special minerals, soils, manures, air, illuminating agents (including solid fats, oils, spirits, petroleum, and gas), dyes, and tanning-materials, would scarcely be in place in this volume.

The course through which the reader has been conducted will, it is hoped, have taught the principles of the science of chemistry, and given special knowledge concerning the applications of that science to medicine and pharmacy, as well as have imparted sufficient manipulative skill to meet the requirements of manufacture or analysis. The author would venture to suggest that this knowledge be utilized, not only in the way of personal advantage, but in experimental researches on chemical subjects connected with therapeutics and pharmacy. The discovery and publication of a new truth, great or small, is the best means whereby to aid in advancing the calling in which we may be engaged, benefit our fellow creatures, and glorify the Creator of all things.

APPENDIX.

TABLE OF OFFICIAL TESTS FOR IMPURITIES IN PHARMACOPŒIAL PREPARATIONS.*

Name of Preparation.	Impurities.	Test.	Page.
Acaciæ Gummi	Starch	Iodine	226
Acetum	More than one-thousandth of Sulphuric acid	Quantitative analysis	479
Acidum Aceticum	Traces of Lead or Copper	Sulphuretted Hydrogen	179
	Sulphuric acid	Chloride or Nitrate of Barium	256
	Hydrochloric acid	Nitrate of Silver	222
	Sulphurous acid	Nascent Hydrogen	253
Acid. Acetic. Glaciale	Sulphurous acid	Nascent Hydrogen	253
Acidum Boracicum	Alkaline salts	Insolubility in Alcohol	274
Acidum Citricum	Traces of Copper or Lead	Sulphuretted Hydrogen	179
	Tartaric acid	Acetate of Potassium	266
	Tartaric acid	Excess of Lime-water	270
	Sulphuric acid	Chloride or Nitrate of Barium	256
	Mineral matter	Incineration	74
Acidum Gallicum	Tannic acid	(Isinglass) Gelatine	294
Acidum Hydrochloricum	Sulphuric acid	Chloride or Nitrate of Barium	256
	Arsenic	Sulphuretted Hydrogen, Copper	133
	Sulphurous acid	Nascent Hydrogen	253
Acidum Hydrocyanicum Dilutum	Sulphuric acid	Chloride or Nitrate of Barium	256
	Hydrochloric acid	Ppt. by Nitr. silver, insol. in nitric acid	222
Acidum Nitricum	Mineral matter	Evaporation and ignition	74
	Sulphuric acid	Chloride or Nitrate of Barium	256
	Hydrochloric acid	Nitrate of Silver	222
Acidum Oxalicum	Mineral matter	Incineration	74
Acidum Phosphoricum Dilutum	Lead or Platinum	Sulphuretted Hydrogen	211
	Sulphuric acid	Chloride or Nitrate of Barium	256
	Hydrochloric acid	Nitrate of Silver and Nitric acid	322
	Metaphosphoric acid	Albumen	222
	Nitric acid	Ferrous Sulphate and Sulphuric acid	237
	Phosphorous acid	Corrosive sublimate	290

* The manipulations necessary to be observed in testing for impurities will be found described in the paragraphs treating of those substances. The Table also includes references to processes for ascertaining deficiency in strength of official articles.

The other "characters and tests" of pharmacopœial compounds have been given in connection with the respective synthetical and analytical reactions.

Name of Preparation.	Impurities.	Test.	Page.
Acidum Sulphuricum	Mineral matter	Evaporation and ignition	74
	Nitric acid	Ferrous Sulphate	327
	Arsenic or Lead	Sulphuretted Hydrogen	179
Acidum Sulphurosum	Sulphuric acid	Chloride or Nitrate of Barium	256
Acidum Tannicum	Mineral matter	Incineration	74
Acidum Tartaricum	Metallic matter, as Lead	Sulphuretted Hydrogen	179
	Oxalic acid	Sulphate of Calcium	262
	Calcium (tartrate or sulphate).	Oxalate of Ammonium	86
	Mineral matter	Incineration	74
Aconitia	Mineral matter	Incineration	74
Adeps præparatus	Chloride (of sodium)	Nitrate of Silver	222
	Starch (flour)	Iodine	226
Æther	Alcohol	Boiling point, sp. gravity.	352
Æther Purus	Alcohol, Water	Specific gravity	352
Alcohol	Resin or oil	Opalescence on dilution	349
	Water	Anhydrous Sulphate of Copper	349
Alcohol Amylicum	Other spirituous matter	Boiling point, sp. gravity.	362
Alum	Iron (sulphate)	Yellow or red prussiate	121
Ammoniæ Benzoas	Fixed salts	Non-volatility	72
Ammoniæ Carbonas	Fixed salts	Non-volatility	72
	Sulphate (of Ammonium).	Chloride or Nitrate of Barium	256
	Chloride (of Ammonium).	Nitrate of Silver	222
Ammonii Chloridum	Fixed salts	Non-volatility	72
Amylum	Alkaline matter	Red Litmus	71
	Acid matter	Blue Litmus	71
Antimonium Nigrum	Silica	Insolubility in HCl	292
Antimonii Oxidum	Higher oxides of antimony	Insolubility in sol. of acid tartrate of potassium	140
Antimonium Tartaratum.	General	Quantitative analysis	468
Aqua Aurantii Floris	Metallic matter (Pb, Cu, Sn)	Sulphuretted Hydrogen	211
Aqua Destillata	Fixed salts	Evaporation and ignition.	74
	Tin, Lead, or Copper	Sulphuretted Hydrogen	211
	Calcium salts	Oxalate of Ammonium	86
	Chlorides	Nitrate of Silver	222
	Sulphates	Chloride or Nitrate of Barium	256
	Carbonates	Lime-water	260
Argenti Nitras	Other nitrates, &c.	Quantitative analysis, &c.	471
Argenti Oxidum	Metallic silver	Effervescence with Nitric acid	174
	General	Quantitative analysis	471
Argentum Purificatum	Copper	Ammonia to the Nitric solution	152
Atropia	Mineral matter	Incineration	74
Atropiæ Sulphas	Mineral matter	Incineration	74
Balsamum Peruvianum	Fixed oil	Immiscibility with Alcohol	372
	Alcohol	Non-diminution of volume when mixed with water	348
Beberiæ Sulphas	Mineral matter	Incineration	74
Bismuthi Carbonas	Nitrates (of Bismuth or Ammonium).	Sulphate of Indigo	238
	Lead (carbonate)	Diluted Sulphuric acid	172
	Chloride (oxychloride of bismuth).	Nitrate of Silver	222
Bismuthi Subnitras	Lead (oxynitrate)	Diluted Sulphuric acid	172
	Chlorides (oxychloride of bismuth).	Nitrate of Silver	222
Bismuthum Purificatum.	Copper	Ammonia to Nitric solut'n	152
Borax	General	Quantitative analysis	438
Bromum	General	Specific gravity (465) and boiling point	414
	Iodine	Starch	226

Name of Preparation.	Impurities.	Test.	Page.
Cadmii Iodidum	Zinc (iodide)	Potash in excess, then Sulphydrate of Ammonium	204
	General	Quantitative analysis	474
Calcii Chloridum	Hypochlorite of Calcium	Hydrochloric acid	241
	Carbonic acid	Lime-water	260
Calcis Carbonas Præcipitata	Alumina, Oxide of Iron, and Phosphates.	Sacc. solution of lime to sol. in nitric acid	80
	Chlorides	Nitrate of Silver	222
Calcis Phosphas.	Carbonates (of Calcium)	Effervescence with acids	259
	Alumina	Solution of potash	104
	Sand	Insolubility in acid	292
Calx	Carbonate of Calcium	Effervescence with acids	259
	Alumina, Oxide of Iron, &c.	Sacc. sol. of lime, to sol. in acids	80
Calx Chlorata	General	Quantitative analysis	455
Cambogia	Starch	Iodine (Green)	226
Camphora	Fixed salts	Non-volatility	71
Carbo Animalis Purificatus.	Earthy salts	Incineration (by help of red ox. of mercury)	74
Carbo Ligni	More than 2 per ct. of ash	Incineration	74
Catechu Pallidum	Starch	Iodine	226
Cera Alba	Soft Fats	Melting-point	415
Cera Flava	Soft Fats	Melting-point	415
	Resin	Solubility in Alcohol	379
	Flour	Insolubility in Turpentine, Iodine	226
Cerii Oxalas	Carbonates and other oxalates.	Ash sol. in acids with effervescence	259
	Alumina	Insolubility of Hydrate in Ammonia	185
	General	More or less than 48 per cent. of ash	185
Cetaceum	Soft Fats	Melting-point	415
Chloroform	General	Specific gravity	424
	Hydrocarbons	Sulphuric acid	361
	Non-volatile matter	Residue on evaporation	74
Copaiba	Wood-oil	Gelatinization at 270° F.	381
		Incomplete solubility in Benzol	381
Creasotum	Carbolic acid	Oxidation	364
		Non-volatility at 212° F.	363
		Dextro-rotation of polarized ray	363
		Crystallization on cooling	363
Cupri Sulphas	Iron (ferrous sulphate)	Nitric acid and ammonia	122
Elaterium	Carbonates (chalk)	Effervescence with acids	259
	General	Quantitative analysis	343
Fel Bovinum Purificatum.	Mucus, crude bile	Incomplete solubility in spirit	371
Ferri Arsenias	Sulphate of (sodium)	Chloride or Nitrate of Barium	256
	General	Quantitative analysis	452
Ferri Carbonas Saccharata	Sulphate (of ammonium)	Chloride or Nitrate of Barium	256
	General	Quantitative analysis	452
Ferri et Ammoniæ Citras	Tartrate (of iron and ammonium)	Ebullition with potash and saturation with Acetic acid (=$KHC_4H_4O_6$)	48
	General	Quantitative analysis	467
	Potassium or Sodium, salts	Alkalinity of ash	71
Ferri et Quiniæ Citras	Potassium or Sodium, salts	Alkalinity of ash	71
	General	Quantitative analysis	467
	Alkaloids other than Quinia.	Insolubility of pptd. alkaloid in ether	321
Ferri Oxidum Magneticum	Metallic iron	Effervescence with acids	119
	General	Quantitative analysis	452

Name of Preparation.	Impurities.	Test.	Page.
Ferri Peroxidum Humidum	Ferrous hydrate	Red prussiate to acid solution	121
	Ferric oxyhydrate	Insolubility in cold dil. Hydrochloric acid	138
Ferri Phosphas	Arsenicum (ferri arsenias)	Slip of Copper in acid solution	133
	General	Quantitative analysis	452
Ferri Sulphas; Ferri Sulphas Granulata	Ferric oxysulphate	Insolubility in Water	107
	Ferric compounds	Ppt. of S in aqueous sol. by H_2S	124
	Copper, &c.	Sulphuretted Hydrogen	211
Ferrum Redactum	Less than 50 per cent.	Quantitative analysis	458
Ferrum Tartaratum	Ferrous compounds	Red prussiate to acid solution	121
	Ammoniacal salts	Soda	70
	General	Quantitative analysis	467
Glycerinum	General	Specific gravity	365
Hydrargyri Iodidum Rubrum.	Fixed salts	Non-volatility	168
Hydrargyri Iodidum Viride.	Red Iodide	Insolubility in ether	155
Hydrargyri Oxidum Rubrum	Fixed Salts	Non-volatility	168
	Nitrates (of mercury)	Orange vapor on heating in a tube	161
Hydrargyri Subchloridum	Corrosive Sublimate	Treatment with ether	160
	Fixed salts	Non-volatility	168
Hydrargyri Sulphas	Fixed salts	Non-volatility	168
Hydrargyrum	Fixed metals (Pb, Sn, Zn, Bi, Cu).	Non-volatility	168
Hydrargyrum Ammoniatum.	Fixed salts	Non-volatility	168
Hydrargyrum cum Creta.	Mercuric oxide	Stannous chloride to sol. in HCl	168
Iodum	Fixed salts	Non-volatility	225
	Cyanide of Iodine	Physical characters	225
	General	Quantitative analysis	454
Jalapæ Resina	Resin	Solubility in Turpentine	314
Limonis Succus	Deficiency of Citric acid	Quantitative analysis	268
Liquor Ammoniæ	General	Specific gravity	426
		Quantitative analysis	439
Liquor Ammoniæ Fortior	General impurity or deficiency.	Specific gravity (449) and Quantitative analysis	439
	Carbonate of Ammonium.	Lime-water	260
	Calcium salts (chloride &c.)	Oxalate of Ammonium	86
	Iron salts (ferrous hydrate).	Sulphydrate of Ammonium	121
	Sulphur salts (AmHS)	Ammonio-sulphate of Copper	252
	Chloride of Ammonium	Nitrate of Silver to acidified sol.	222
	Sulphate of Ammonium	Chloride of Barium to acidified sol.	256
Liq. Antimonii Chloridi	. . . .	. . . .	449
Liq. Arsenicalis			468
Liq. Arsenici Hydrochloricus	General impurity or deficiency	Specific gravity; Quantitative analysis	449
Liq. Bismuthi et Ammoniæ Cit.	. . . .	. . . .	470
Liq. Calcis	Deficiency in strength	Quantitative analysis	438
Liq. Calcis Chloratæ	General impurity or deficiency	Specific gravity	449
Liq. Calcis Saccharatus		Quantitative analysis (507)	438
Liquor Chlori	General quality	Specific gravity	449
	Fixed matter	Residue on evaporation	80
	Deficiency in strength	Quantitative analysis	455

Name of Preparation.	Impurities.	Test.	Page.
Liq. Ferri Perchloridi Fort. Liq. Ferri Pernitratis. Liq. Ferri Persulphatis	Ferrous salts	Red Prussiate	122
	General impurity or deficiency	Specific gravity	427
		Quantitative analysis	467
Liq. Hydrargyri Nit. Acid	Deficiency in strength	Specific gravity	427
	Mercurous salts (nitrate)	Hydrochloric acid	165
Liq. Lithiæ Effervescens	General impurity or deficiency.	Quantitative analysis, &c.	183
Liq. Magnesiæ Carbonatis	Other magnesian salts	Bitter taste ($MgCl_2MgSO_4$).	88
	General impurity or deficiency.	Quantitative analysis	465
Liq. Plumbi Subacetatis	General impurity or deficiency	Specific gravity	427
		Quantitative analysis	438
Liquor Potassæ	General impurity or deficiency	Specific gravity	427
		Quantitative analysis	438
	Carbonate (of potassium)	Effervescence with acids	259
		Lime-water	260
	Calcium salts	Oxalate of Ammonium.	86
	More than traces of Silica	Insol. in acid after evap. &c	292
	More than traces of Sulphates	Chloride of Barium to acid sol.	256
	More than traces of Chlorides	Nitrate of silver to acid sol.	222
	More than traces of Alumina	Ammonia to acid sol.	104
Liq. Potassæ Effervescens	Deficiency in strength	Quantitative analysis	438
	Bicarbonate of sodium	Tartaric acid, &c.	460
Liquor Sodæ	General impurity or deficiency	Specific gravity	427
		Quantitative analysis	438
	Calcium salts	Oxalate of Ammonium	86
	Carbonate (of sodium)	Effervescence with acids	259
		Lime-water	260
	More than traces of Silica	Insol. in acids after evap &c	292
	More than traces of Sulphates	$BaCl_2$ to acid sol.	256
	More than traces of Chlorides	$AgNO_3$ to acid sol.	222
	More than traces of Alumina	Ammonia to acid sol.	104
Liquor Sodæ Chloratæ	Salts of Potassium or Ammonium.	Perchloride of Platinum to acid sol. (54)	71
	General impurity or deficiency.	Quantitative analysis	454
	Calcium salts	Oxalate of Ammonium	86
Liq. Sodæ Effervescens	Deficiency in strength	Quantitative analysis	438
Lithiæ Carbonas	General impurity or deficiency.	Quantitative analysis	194
	Calcium salts	Oxalate of Ammonium &c.	183
	Alumina	Lime-water, &c.	183
Lithiæ Citras	Deficiency in strength	Quantitative analysis	183
Magnesia. Magnesia Levis	Carbonate (of magnesium)	Effervescence with acids	87
	Calcium (hydrate or carbonate).	Oxalate of Ammonium to acet. sol.	86
	Sulphates (of magnesium or sodium).	Chloride of Barium to acid sol.	256
Magnesiæ Carbonas. Magnesiæ Carb. Levis.	Alumina	Ammonia to acid sol.	104
	Sulphates (of magnesium or sodium).	Chloride of Barium to acid solution	256
	Calcium (carbonate)	Oxalic acid to Ammoniacal solution	86
	Iron, Lead, &c.	Sulph. hydrogen to sol. in acid + excess of Ammon.	211
	General impurity or deficiency.	Quantitative analysis	465
Magnesiæ Sulphas	Calcium (sulphate)	Oxalate of Ammonium	86
	Iron (sulphate)	Chlorinated Lime or Soda	87
	General impurities	Quantitative analysis	465
Manna	Deficiency of mannite	Quantitative analysis	339
Mel	Starch (flour)	Iodine	226
Morphiæ Hydrochloras	General impurities	Quantitative analysis	490

Name of Preparation.	Impurities.	Test.	Page.
Olea Destillata	Fixed oil	Permanent greasy stain on paper	..
	Alcohol	Loss in volume on shaking with water	..
Opium	Deficiency in morphia	Quantitative analysis	490
Plumbi Acetas	General	Quantitative analysis	438
Plumbi Carbonas	Sulphate of Lead or Barium or Silicates.	Insolubility in Acetic acid [(172, 76)	292
	Calcium (chalk)	Oxal. Ammonium after removing Lead	86
Plumbi Oxidum	Carbonates	Effervescence with acids	259
	Copper (oxide)	Ammonia to acid solution	152
Potassa Caustica	More than traces of Chloride	Nitrate of silver to acid solution	222
	More than traces of Sulphate	Chloride of Barium to acid sol.	256
	General impurities (water &c.).	Quantitative analysis	438
Potassa Sulphurata	Excess of Carbonate or Sulphate.	More than 25 per cent. insol. in spirit	46
Potassæ Acetas	Iron and other metallic impurities.	Sulphydrate of Ammonium	211
	Carbonate of Potassium	Effervescence with acids; alkalinity; insolubility in spirit	259 47
Potassæ Bicarbonas	General	Quantitative analysis	438
Potassæ Carbonas	More than traces of Silicate	Insol. in acids after evap. &c.	292
	More than traces of Sulphate	Chloride of Barium to acid sol.	256
	More than traces of Chloride	Nitr. of Silver to acid sol.	222
	General	Quantitative analysis	438
Potassæ Chloras	Chloride (of potassium)	Nitrate of Silver	222
	Calcium (chloride)	Oxalate of Ammonium	86
Potassæ Citras	General	Quantitative analysis	441
Potassæ Nitras	Sulphate (of potassium)	Chloride of Barium	256
	Chloride (of potassium)	Nitrate of Silver	222
Potassæ Permanganas	General	Quantitative analysis	453
Potassæ Sulphas	Acid Sulph. of Potassium	Test-paper	71
	Calcium (sulphate)	Oxalate of Ammonium.	86
Potassæ Tartras Potassæ Tartr. Acida	General	Quantitative analysis	441
Potassii Bromidum	Free bromine	Odor	223
	Iodide (of potassium)	Chlorine-water and starch	226
	General	Quantitative analysis (446)	475
Potassii Ferridcyanidum.	Ferrocyanide (of potassium).	Ferric salt	280
Potassii Iodidum	Iodate (of potassium)	Tartaric acid and starch	52
	Chloride (of potassium)	Nitrate of Silver, &c.	222
	Carbonate (of potassium).	Sacc. solution of Lime	260
Quiniæ Sulphas	Salicin	Sulphuric acid	345
	General	Quantitative analysis	489
Rhei Radix	Turmeric	Boracic acid	275
Santoninum	Mineral matter	Incineration	74
	Earthy soaps, &c.	Insolubility in spirit	371
Sapo Durus	Oil	Oily stain to paper..	371
	Potassium compounds	Deliquescence of ash	371
Sapo Mollis	Earthy soaps, &c.	Insolubility in spirit	371
	Oil	Oily stain to paper	371
Scammoniæ Resina	Resin of guaiacum	Inner surface of Potato-paring	359
	Resin of Jalap	Insolubility in ether	359
Scammonium	Carbonate (of calcium and magnesium).	Effervescence with acids	259
	Starch (flour)	Solution of Iodine	226
Sinapis	Starch (flour)	Solution of Iodine	226

Name of Preparation.	Impurities.	Test.	Page.
Soda Caustica	More than traces of Chloride	Nitr. of Silver to acid sol.	222
	More than traces of Sulphate	Chloride of Barium to acid sol.	256
	General impurities (water &c.).	Quantitative analysis	438
Soda Tartarata	General	Quantitative analysis	441
Sodæ Acetas	Acid or alkaline matter	Test-paper	71
	Sulphates (sodium or calcium).	Chloride of Barium to acid sol.	256
	Chlorides (sodium or calcium).	Nitrate of Silver to acid sol.	222
Sodæ Arsenias	Excess or deficiency of water of crystallization.	Quantitative analysis	448
	General	Quantitative analysis	447
Sodæ Bicarbonas	Neutral Carbonate (of sodium).	Mercuric chloride	166
	More than traces of Chlorides	Nitr. of Silver to acid sol.	222
	More than traces of Sulphates	Chloride of Barium to acid sol.	256
	General	Quantitative analysis	438
Sodæ Carbonas	Excess or deficiency of water of cryst. &c.	Quantitative analysis	484
	More than traces of Chlorides	Nitr. of Silver to acid sol.	222
	More than traces of Sulphates	Chloride of Barium to acid sol.	256
Sodæ Hyposulphis	General	Quantitative analysis	449
Sodæ Nitras	Chloride (of sodium)	Nitrate of Silver	222
	Sulphate (of sodium)	Chloride or Nitrate of Barium	256
Sodæ Phosphas	More than trace of Sulphate.	Chloride or Nitrate of Barium to acid sol.	256
	Deficiency or excess of water of cryst.	Quantitative analysis	484
Sodæ Sulphas	Ammonium salts	Solut'n of potash heated	70
	Ferric salts	Solut'n of potash heated	123
	General	Quantitative analysis	479
	Excess or deficiency of water of cryst.	Quantitative analysis	484
Sodæ Valerianas	Free soda or carbonate	Test-papers	79
		Insolubility in spirit	322
Spiritus Ætheris Nitrosi	General	Specific gravity	427
	More than trace of acid	Effervescence with bicarbonate of sodium	259
	Free acid	More than "feeble" effervescence with bicarbonate of sodium	259
	Deficiency of nitrite of ethyl.	Quantitative analysis	354
Spiritus Ammonio-Aromat.; Spiritus Chloroformi	General	Specific gravity	426
Spiritus Rectificatus	General (excess of water)	Specific gravity	426
	Resin or oil	Opalescence on dilution	349
	More than traces of fusil oil, &c.	Nitrate of Silver	448
Spiritus Tenuior	General (excess of water).	Specific gravity	347
Strychnia	Brucia	Nitric acid	324
	Mineral matter	Incineration	74
Sulphur Præcipitatum	Sulphate of calcium	Appearance under microscope	251
		Residue on ignition	251
Sulphur Sublimatum	Earthy matter	Incineration	74
	Trace of Acid (H_2SO_4 or H_2SO_3).	Litmus-paper	71
	Sulphide of Arsenicum	Ammonia	136
Sulphuris Iodidum	Deficiency of Iodine	Quantitative analysis	226
Syrupi	Deficiency of Sugar	Specific gravity	427
Tamarindus	Traces of Copper	Iron	151
Veratria	Mineral matter	Incineration	74

Name of Preparation.	Impurities.	Test.	Page.
Zinci Acetas . . .	Sulphates	Chloride or Nitrate of Barium	256
	Chlorides	Nitrate of Silver	222
	Metals (As, Cd, Cu, Pb) .	Sulphuretted Hydrogen .	211
	Iron (acetate)	Nitric Acid: Ammonia .	124
	Copper (acetate)	Ammonia	152
Zinci Carbonas . .	Sulphates	Chloride or Nitrate of Barium to acid sol. . . .	256
	Chlorides	Nitr. of Silver to acid sol.	222
	Copper (carbonate) . . .	Ammonia to acid solution	152
Zinci Chloridum . .	Metals (As,Cd,Cu,Pb) . .	Sulphuretted Hydrogen .	211
	Sulphates	Chloride or Nitrate of Barium	256
	Calcium (chloride) . . .	Oxalate of Ammonium .	86
	Ferrous salts (chloride) .	Ferridcyanide of Potass'm	121
	Ferric salts (chloride) . .	Ferrocyanide of Potass'm	121
	Carbonate (of zinc) . . .	Effervescence with acids .	259
Zinci Oxidum . .	Sulphates (sodium or zinc)	Chloride or Nitrate of Barium to acid sol. . . .	256
	Chlorides	Nitr. of Silver to acid sol.	222
	Copper (oxide)	Ammonia to acid solution	152
Zinci Sulphas . .	Metals (As,Cd,Cu,Pb) . .	Sulphuretted hydrogen .	211
	Iron (sulphate)	Tincture of galls	394
		Nitric acid: Ammonia .	124
	Copper (sulphate) . . .	Ammonia	152
Zinci Valerianas .	Sulphate (of zinc) . . .	Chloride or Nitrate of Barium	256
	Butyrate (of zinc) . . .	Acetate of Copper, &c. . .	322

43

Equivalent weights of Citric Acid, Tartaric Acid, Carbonate of Potassium, Bicarbonate of Potassium, Carbonate of Sodium, Bicarbonate of Sodium, Carbonate of Ammonium, and Carbonate of Magnesium; repeated (in **black**) for 20 parts of each, and incidentally (in roman) for other proportions. (Exact to two places of decimals.)

Citric Acid ($H_3C_6H_5O_7$, H_2O) $\div 3 \times 2 = 140$ . . .	**20.00**	18.66	**16.96**	**14.00**	**9.78**	**16.66**	**23.72**	**29.31**
Tartaric Acid $H_2C_4H_4O_6 = 150$	21.43	**20.00**	**18.26**	**15.00**	**10.49**	**17.85**	**25.42**	**31.41**
Carbonate of Potassium $K_2CO_3 + 16$ % $Aq = 164.285$	**23.47**	**21.90**	**20.00**	16.43	11.48	19.52	27.87	34.40
Bicarbonate of Potassium $2(KHCO_3) = 200$	**28.57**	**26.66**	24.34	**20.00**	13.98	23.81	33.89	41.90
Carbonate of Sodium Na_2CO_3, $10H_2O = 286$	**40.08**	**38.13**	34.81	28.60	**20.00**	34.04	48.47	59.98
Bicarbonate of Sodium $2(NaHCO_3) = 168$	**24.00**	**22.40**	20.45	16.80	11.74	**20.00**	28.47	35.18
Carbonate of Ammonium $(N_4H_{16}C_3O_8) \div 2 = 118$ . .	**16.85**	**15.73**	14.36	11.80	8.25	14.04	**20.00**	24.71
Carb. of Magnes. $((MgCO_3)_3$, $Mg2HO,4H_2O) \div 4 = 95.5$	**13.64**	**12.73**	11.62	9.55	6.68	11.37	16.18	**20.00**

The amount of acid given in any column will saturate the amount of carbonate in the same column, and *vice versa*.

The amounts of carbonate in any column are equal to each other in chemical power.

Lemon-Juice (sp. gr. 1039) contains, on an average, 7 per cent. by weight of citric acid.

The same Table in round numbers, for purposes of prescribing and dispensing.

(The old names in Latin.)

Citric Acid	**20**	19	**17**	**14**	**10**	**17**	**24**	**30**
Tartaric Acid	22	**20**	**18**	**15**	**11**	**18**	**26**	**32**
Carbonate of Potassium (Potassæ Carbonas)	**24**	**22**	**20**	16	12	20	28	35
Bicarbonate of Potassium (Potassæ Bicarbonas) . .	**29**	**27**	24	**20**	14	24	34	42
Carbonate of Sodium (cryst.) (Sodæ Carbonas) . . .	**40**	**38**	35	28	**20**	34	49	60
Bicarbonate of Sodium (Sodæ Bicarbonas)	**24**	**22**	20	17	12	**20**	29	36
Carbonate of Ammonium (Ammoniæ Carbonas) . .	**17**	**16**	14	12	8	14	**20**	25
Carbonate of Magnesium (Magnesiæ Carbonas) . . .	**13**	**13**	11	9	7	11	16	**20**

The Table is read thus: 20 grains of Citric Acid will saturate 29 grains of Bicarbonate of Potassium; 20 grains of Bicarbonate of Sodium will saturate, or be saturated by, 18 grains of Tartaric Acid; 11 grains of Tartaric Acid = 8 grains of Carbonate of Ammonium; 20 grains of Bicarbonate of Sodium are equivalent to, or will do as much work as, 34 grains of Carbonate of Sodium; 14 grains of Citric Acid are as strong as 15 of Tartaric Acid. It is occasionally convenient to double the numbers, halve them, or take some other proportion; also to employ them in weights other than grains.

Lemon-Juice contains, on an average, $32\frac{1}{2}$ grains of Citric Acid in 1 fluidounce, or 4 grains per fluidrachm.

THE PROPORTION BY WEIGHT OF ABSOLUTE OR PLAIN ALCOHOL (C_2H_5HO) IN 100 PARTS OF REAL SPIRITS OF DIFFERENT SPECIFIC GRAVITIES (FOWNES).

Sp. gr. at 60° (15°.5 C.).	Per-centage of real alcohol.	Sp. gr. at 60° (15°.5 C.).	Per-centage of real alcohol.	Sp. gr. at 60° (15°.5 C.).	Per-centage of real alcohol.
0.9991	0.5	0.9511	34	0.8769	68
0.9981	1	0.9490	35	0.8745	69
0.9965	2	0.9470	36	0.8721	70
0.9947	3	0.9452	37	0.8696	71
0.9930	4	0.9434	38	0.8672	72
0.9914	5	0.9416	39	0.8649	73
0.9898	6	0.9396	40	0.8625	74
0.9884	7	0.9376	41	0.8603	75
0.9869	8	0.9356	42	0.8581	76
0.9855	9.	0.9335	43	0.8557	77
0.9841	10	0.9314	44	0.8533	78
0.9828	11	0.9292	45	0.8508	79
0.9815	12	0.9270	46	0.8483	80
0.9802	13	0.9249	47	0.8459	81
0.9789	14	0.9228	48	0.8434	82
0.9778	15	0.9206	49	0.8408	83
0.9766	16	0.9184	50	0.8382	84
0.9753	17	0.9160	51	0.8357	85
0.9741	18	0.9135	52	0.8331	86
0.9728	19	0.9113	53	0.8305	87
0.9716	20	0.9090	54	0.8279	88
0.9704	21	0.9069	55	0.8254	89
0.9691	22	0.9047	56	0.8228	90
0.9678	23	0.9025	57	0.8199	91
0.9665	24	0.9001	58	0.8172	92
0.9652	25	0.8979	59	0.8145	93
0.9638	26	0.8956	60	0.8118	94
0.9623	27	0.8932	61	0.8089	95
0.9609	28	0.8908	62	0.8061	96
0.9593	29	0.8886	63	0.8031	97
0.9578	30	0.8863	64	0.8001	98
0.9560	31	0.8840	65	0.7969	99
0.9544	32	0.8816	66	0.7938	100
0.9528	33	0.8793	67		

THE ELEMENTS.

	Symbol and atomic value.	Atomic weight.
Aluminium (Al_2^{VI})	Al^{IV}	27.5
Antimony (Sb^{III})	Sb^{V}	122
Arsenicum (As^{III})	As^{V}	75
Barium	Ba^{II}	137
Beryllium (Glucinum)	Be^{II}	9.5
Bismuth (Bi^{III})	Bi^{V}	210
Boron	B^{III}	11
Bromine (79.75, Stas)	Br^{I}	80
Cadmium	Cd^{II}	112
Cæsium	Cs^{I}	133
Calcium	Ca^{II}	40
Carbon (C^{II})	C^{IV}	12
Cerium (Ce^{II})	Ce^{VI}	92
Chlorine (35.368, Stas)	Cl^{I}	35.5
Chromium (Cr_2^{VI})	Cr^{VI}	52.5
Cobalt (Co^{II})	Co^{VI}	58.8
Copper	Cu^{II}	63.5
Didymium	D^{II}	96
Erbium?	Eb^{II}	112.6
Fluorine	F^{I}	19
Glucinum. *See* Beryllium.		
Gold	Au^{III}	196.7
Hydrogen	H^{I}	1
Indium	In^{VI}	75.6
Iodine (126.533, Stas)	I^{I}	127
Iridium	Ir^{IV}	197
Iron (Fe^{II} & Fe_2^{VI})	Fe^{VI}	56
Lanthanium	L^{II}	92
Lead ($^{II}Pb^{II}$)	Pb^{IV}	207
Lithium (7.004, Stas)	Li^{I}	7
Magnesium	Mg^{II}	24
Manganese (Mn^{II} & Mn^{IV})	Mn^{VI}	55
Mercury	Hg^{II}	200
Molybdenum	Mo^{VI}	96
Nickel (Ni^{II})	Ni^{VI}	58.8
Niobium	Nb^{V}	97.6
Nitrogen (N^{I} & N^{III}) (14.009, Stas)	N^{V}	14
Osmium	Os^{IV}	199
Oxygen (15.96, Stas)	O^{II}	16
Palladium	Pd^{IV}	106.5
Phosphorus (P^{III})	P^{V}	31

	Symbol and atomic value.	Atomic weight.
Platinum (197.88, Andrews)	Pt^{IV}	198
Potassium (39.04, Stas)	K^{I}	39
Rhodium	Rh^{IV}	104
Rubidium	Rb^{I}	85.5
Ruthenium	Ru^{IV}	104
Selenium	Se^{VI}	79
Silicon	Si^{IV}	28
Silver (107.66, Stas)	Ag^{I}	108
Sodium (22.98, Stas)	Na^{I}	23
Strontium	Sr^{II}	87.5
Sulphur (S^{II} & S^{IV})	S^{VI}	32
Tantalum	Ta^{V}	137.5
Tellurium	Te^{VI}	129
Thallium (203, Crookes)	Tl^{III}	204
Thorinum or Thorium	Th^{II}	115.7
Tin (Sn^{II})	Sn^{IV}	118
Titanium	Ti^{IV}	50
Tungsten	W^{VI}	184
Uranium	U^{VI}	120
Vanadium	V^{V}	51.3
Yttrium	Y^{II}	68
Zinc	Zn^{II}	65
Zirconium	Zi^{IV}	90
Total	63	

The quantivalence or atomic value of some elements is, apparently, variable; in the above Table the full coefficients are given in the column of symbols, other common values in brackets.

Atomic weights are sometimes obscurely termed *equivalents*.

INDEX.

CATALOGUE OF BOOKS

PUBLISHED BY

HENRY C. LEA,

(LATE LEA & BLANCHARD.)

The books in the annexed list will be sent by mail, post-paid, to any Post Office in the United States, on receipt of the printed prices. No risks of the mail, however, are assumed, either on money or books. Gentlemen will therefore, in most cases, find it more convenient to deal with the nearest bookseller.

Detailed catalogues furnished or sent free by mail on application. An illustrated catalogue of 64 octavo pages, handsomely printed, mailed on receipt of 10 cents. Address,

HENRY C. LEA,
Nos. 706 and 708 Sansom Street, Philadelphia.

AMERICAN JOURNAL OF THE MEDICAL SCIENCES. Edited by Isaac Hays, M.D., published quarterly, about 1100 large 8vo. pages per annum,
MEDICAL NEWS AND LIBRARY, monthly, 384 large 8vo. pages per annum, } For five Dollars per annum in advance.

OR,

AMERICAN JOURNAL OF THE MEDICAL SCIENCES, Quarterly,
MEDICAL NEWS AND LIBRARY, monthly,
RANKING'S HALF-YEARLY ABSTRACT OF THE MEDICAL SCIENCES. 2 vols. a year, of about 300 pages each.
In all, over 2000 large 8vo. pages per annum, } For six Dollars per annum in advance.

ABSTRACT, RANKING'S HALF-YEARLY, per volume, $1 50; per annum, $2 50.

ALLEN (J. M.) THE PRACTICAL ANATOMIST; or, THE STUDENT'S GUIDE IN THE DISSECTING ROOM. With 266 illustrations. 1 vol royal 12mo., over 600 pages, cloth, $2.

ASHTON (T. J.) ON THE DISEASES, INJURIES, AND MALFORMATIONS OF THE RECTUM AND ANUS. With remarks on Habitual Constipation. Second American from the fourth London edition, with illustrations. 1 vol. 8vo. of about 300 pp., cloth, $3 25.

ARNOTT (NEIL). ELEMENTS OF PHYSICS; or, NATURAL PHILOSOPHY, GENERAL AND MEDICAL. 1 vol. 8vo., with illustrations, cloth, $2 25.

ASHWELL (SAMUEL). A PRACTICAL TREATISE ON THE DISEASES OF WOMEN. Third American from the third London edition. In one 8vo. vol. of 528 pages, cloth, $3 50.

ASHHURST (JOHN Jr.) THE PRINCIPLES AND PRACTICE OF SURGERY FOR THE USE OF STUDENTS AND PRACTITIONERS. (*Preparing.*)

ATTFIELD'S CHEMISTRY—GENERAL, MEDICAL, AND THERAPEUTICAL. In 1 vol. 12mo. (*Nearly ready.*)

BRINTON (WILLIAM). LECTURES ON THE DISEASES OF THE STOMACH; with an introduction on its Anatomy and Physiology. From the second London edition, with illustrations. 1 vol. 8vo. of about 300 pages, cloth, $3 25.

BRANDE (WM. T.), AND ALFRED S. TAYLOR. CHEMISTRY. Second American edition, thoroughly revised by Dr. Taylor. In one large and handsome octavo volume, extra cloth, $5 ; leather, $6.

BIGELOW (HENRY J.) ON DISLOCATION AND FRACTURE OF THE HIP, with the Reduction of the Dislocations by the Flexion Method. In one 8vo. vol. of 150 pp., with illustrations, ext. cloth, $2 50.

BASHAM (W. R.) RENAL DISEASES; A CLINICAL GUIDE TO THEIR DIAGNOSIS AND TREATMENT. With Illustrations. 1 vol. 12mo., extra cloth, $2 00. (*Just issued.*)

BUMSTEAD (F. J.) THE PATHOLOGY AND TREATMENT OF VENEREAL DISEASES. Including the results of recent investigations upon the subject. A new and revised edition, with illustrations. 1 vol. 8vo., of 640 pages, cloth, $5.

——**AND CULLERIER'S** ATLAS OF VENEREAL. See 'CULLERIER.'

BARCLAY (A. W.) A MANUAL OF MEDICAL DIAGNOSIS; being an Analysis of the Signs and Symptoms of Disease. Third American from the second revised London edition. 1 vol. 8vo., of 451 pages, cloth, $3 50.

BARLOW (GEORGE H.) A MANUAL OF THE PRACTICE OF MEDICINE. With additions by D. F. Condie, M.D. 1 vol. 8vo., of over 600 pages, cloth, $2 50.

BAIRD (ROBERT). IMPRESSIONS AND EXPERIENCES OF THE WEST INDIES AND UNITED STATES. 1 vol. royal 12mo., cloth, 75 cents.

BUCKLER (THOMAS H.) ON FIBRO-BRONCHITIS AND RHEUMATIC PNEUMONIA. 1 vol. 8vo., of 150 pages, cloth, $1 25.

BARNES (ROBERT.) A PRACTICAL TREATISE ON THE DISEASES OF WOMEN. In one handsome 8vo. vol. (*Preparing.*)

BRYANT (THOMAS.) THE PRACTICE OF SURGERY. In one handsome volume, with many illustrations. (*Preparing.*)

BLANDFORD (G. FIELDING.) INSANITY AND ITS TREATMENT. In one handsome 8vo. vol. (*Just ready.*)

BOWMAN (JOHN E.) A PRACTICAL HAND-BOOK OF MEDICAL CHEMISTRY. Edited by C. L. Bloxam. Fifth American, from the fourth and revised London edition. With numerous illustrations. 1 vol. royal 12mo. of 350 pages, cloth, $2 25.

—— INTRODUCTION TO PRACTICAL CHEMISTRY, INCLUDING ANALYSIS. Edited by C. L. Bloxam. Fifth American, from the fifth and revised London edition, with numerous illustrations. 1 vol. royal 12mo. of 350 pages, cloth, $2 25.

BRODIE (SIR BENJAMIN). CLINICAL LECTURES ON SURGERY. 1 vol. 8vo., of 350 pages, cloth, $1 25.

CHAMBERS (T. K.) THE INDIGESTIONS; OR, DISEASES OF THE DIGESTIVE ORGANS FUNCTIONALLY TREATED. Third American Edition, thoroughly revised by the author. 1 vol. 8vo., of over 300 pages, cloth, $3 00. (*Lately issued.*)

COLOMBAT DE L'ISERE. THE DISEASES OF FEMALES. Translated by Charles D. Meigs, M.D. Second edition, with numerous illustrations. 1 vol. 8vo., of 720 pages, cloth, $3 75.

CARPENTER (WM. B.) PRINCIPLES OF HUMAN PHYSIOLOGY, WITH THEIR CHIEF APPLICATIONS TO PSYCHOLOGY, PATHOLOGY, THERAPEUTICS, HYGIENE, AND FORENSIC MEDICINE. A new American edition edited by Francis G. Smith, M.D. With nearly 300 illustrations. In one large vol. 8vo., of nearly 900 closely printed pages, cloth, $5 50; leather, raised bands, $6 50.

CARPENTER (WM. B.) PRINCIPLES OF COMPARATIVE PHYSIOLOGY. New American, from the fourth and revised London edition. With over 300 beautiful illustrations. 1 vol. 8vo., of 752 pages, cloth, $5 00.

——— PRIZE ESSAY ON THE USE OF ALCOHOLIC LIQUORS IN HEALTH AND DISEASE. New edition, with a Preface by D. F. Condie, M.D. 1 vol. 12mo. of 178 pages, cloth, 60 cents.

CARSON (JOSEPH). A SYNOPSIS OF THE COURSE OF LECTURES ON MATERIA MEDICA AND PHARMACY, delivered in the University of Pennsylvania. Fourth and revised edition. 1 vol. 8vo., extra cloth, $3 00.

CHRISTISON (ROBERT.) DISPENSATORY OR COMMENTARY ON THE PHARMACOPŒIAS OF GREAT BRITAIN AND THE UNITED STATES. With a Supplement by R. E. Griffith. In one 8vo. vol. of over 1000 pages, containing 213 illustrations, extra cloth, $4 00.

CHURCHILL (FLEETWOOD). ON THE THEORY AND PRACTICE OF MIDWIFERY. A new American from the fourth revised London edition. With notes and additions by D. Francis Condie, M.D. With about 200 illustrations. In one handsome 8vo. vol. of nearly 700 pages, extra cloth, $4 00; leather, $5 00.

——— ESSAYS ON THE PUERPERAL FEVER, AND OTHER DISEASES PECULIAR TO WOMEN. In one neat octavo vol. of about 450 pages, extra cloth, $2 50.

CONDIE (D. FRANCIS). A PRACTICAL TREATISE ON THE DISEASES OF CHILDREN. Sixth edition, revised and enlarged. In one large octavo volume of nearly 800 pages, extra cloth, $5 25; leather, $6 25.

COOPER (B. B.) LECTURES ON THE PRINCIPLES AND PRACTICE OF SURGERY. In one large 8vo. vol. of 750 pages, extra cloth, $2 00.

CULLERIER (A.) AN ATLAS OF VENEREAL DISEASES. Translated and edited by FREEMAN J. BUMSTEAD, M.D. A large imperial quarto volume, with 26 plates containing about 150 figures, beautifully colored, many of them the size of life. In one vol., strongly bound in extra cloth, $17. (*Lately published.*)

———Same work, in five parts, paper covers, for mailing, $3 per part.

CYCLOPEDIA OF PRACTICAL MEDICINE. By Dunglison, Forbes, Tweedie, and Conolly. In four large super royal octavo volumes, of 3254 double-columned pages, leather, raised bands, $15; extra cloth, $11.

CAMPBELL'S LIVES OF LORDS KENYON, ELLENBOROUGH, AND TENTERDEN. Being the third volume of "Campbell's Lives of the Chief Justices of England." In one crown octavo vol., cloth, $2.

DALTON (J. C.) A TREATISE ON HUMAN PHYSIOLOGY. Fourth edition, revised, with nearly 300 illustrations on wood. In one very handsome octavo volume of about 700 pages, extra cloth, $5 25; leather, $6 25.

DE JONGH, ON THE THREE KINDS OF COD-LIVER OIL. 1 small 12mo. vol., 75 cents.

DON QUIXOTE DE LA MANCHA. Translated by Chas. Jarvis, Esq., with illustrations by Tony Johannot. In two handsome vols. crown 8vo., fancy cloth, $3; plain cloth, $2 50; library sheep, $3 20; half morocco, $3 70.

DEWEES (W. P.) A TREATISE ON THE DISEASES OF FEMALES. With illustrations. In one 8vo. vol. of 536 pages, extra cloth, $3.

——— A COMPREHENSIVE SYSTEM OF MIDWIFERY. In one octavo volume of 600 pages, with plates, extra cloth, $3 50.

DEWEES (W. P.) A TREATISE ON THE PHYSICAL AND MEDICAL TREATMENT OF CHILDREN. In one octavo volume of 548 pages, extra cloth, $2 80.

DICKSON (S. H.) ELEMENTS OF MEDICINE. Second edition, revised. 1 vol. 8vo., of 750 pages, extra cloth, $4.

DRUITT (ROBERT). THE PRINCIPLES AND PRACTICE OF MODERN SURGERY. A revised American, from the eighth London edition. Illustrated with 432 wood engravings. In one handsome 8vo. vol. of nearly 700 large and closely printed pages, extra cloth, $4; leather, $5.

DUNGLISON (ROBLEY). MEDICAL LEXICON; a Dictionary of Medical Science. Containing a concise explanation of the various subjects and terms of Anatomy, Physiology, Pathology, Hygiene, Therapeutics, Pharmacology, Pharmacy, Surgery, Obstetrics, Medical Jurisprudence, and Dentistry. Notices of Climate and of Mineral Waters; Formulæ for Officinal, Empirical, and Dietetic Preparations, with the accentuation and Etymology of the Terms, and the French and other Synonymes; so as to constitute a French as well as English Medical Lexicon. In one very large royal 8vo. vol. of 1048 double columned pages, in small type; strongly bound in cloth, $6; leather, raised bands, $6 75.

——— HUMAN PHYSIOLOGY. Eighth edition, thoroughly revised. In two large 8vo. vols. of about 1500 pages, with 532 illustrations, extra cloth, $7.

——— NEW REMEDIES, WITH FORMULÆ FOR THEIR PREPARATION AND ADMINISTRATION. Seventh edition. In one very large 8vo. vol. of 770 pages, extra cloth, $4.

DE LA BECHE'S GEOLOGICAL OBSERVER. In one large 8vo. vol. of 700 pages, with 300 illustrations, cloth, $4.

DANA (JAMES D.) THE STRUCTURE AND CLASSIFICATION OF ZOOPHYTES. With illustrations on wood. In one imperial 4to. vol., cloth, $4 00.

ELLIS (BENJAMIN). THE MEDICAL FORMULARY. Being a collection of prescriptions derived from the writings and practice of the most eminent physicians of America and Europe. Twelfth edition, carefully revised by A. H. Smith, M. D. In one 8vo. volume of 374 pages, extra cloth, $3.

ERICHSEN (JOHN). THE SCIENCE AND ART OF SURGERY. A new and improved American, from the fifth enlarged and revised London edition. Illustrated with over 630 engravings on wood. In one large imperial 8vo. vol. of 1228 closely printed pages, extra cloth, $7 50; leather, raised bands, $8 50.

——— ON RAILWAY AND OTHER INJURIES OF THE NERVOUS SYSTEM. In one small 8vo. vol., extra cloth, $1.

ENCYCLOPÆDIA AMERICANA. Complete in 14 large 8vo. vols Containing nearly 9000 double columned pages, cloth, $22.

ENCYCLOPÆDIA OF GEOGRAPHY. In three large 8vo. vols. Illustrated with 83 maps and about 1100 wood-cuts, cloth, $5.

FISKE FUND PRIZE ESSAYS ON TUBERCULOUS DISEASE. In one small 8vo. vol., cloth, $1.

FLETCHER'S NOTES FROM NINEVEH, AND TRAVELS IN MESOPOTAMIA, ASSYRIA, AND SYRIA. In one 12mo. vol., cloth, 75 cts.

FLINT (AUSTIN). A TREATISE ON THE PRINCIPLES AND PRACTICE OF MEDICINE. Third edition, thoroughly revised and enlarged. In one large 8vo. volume of 1002 pages, extra cloth, $6; leather, raised bands, $7.

FLINT (AUSTIN). A PRACTICAL TREATISE, ON THE PHYSICAL EXPLORATION OF THE CHEST, AND THE DIAGNOSIS OF DISEASES AFFECTING THE RESPIRATORY ORGANS. Second and revised edition. One 8vo. vol. of 595 pages, cloth, $4 50.

——— A PRACTICAL TREATISE ON THE DIAGNOSIS AND TREATMENT OF DISEASES OF THE HEART. Second edition, enlarged. In one neat 8vo. vol. of over 500 pages, $4 00. (*Just issued.*)

FOWNE (GEORGE). A MANUAL OF ELEMENTARY CHEMISTRY. From the tenth enlarged English edition. In one royal 12mo. vol. of 857 pages, with 197 illustrations, extra cloth, $2 75; leather, $3 25.

FULLER (HENRY). ON DISEASES OF THE LUNGS AND AIR PASSAGES. Their Pathology, Physical Diagnosis, Symptoms and Treatment. From the second English edition. In one 8vo. vol. of about 500 pages, extra cloth, $3 50.

GLUGE (GOTTLIEB). ATLAS OF PATHOLOGICAL HISTOLOGY. Translated by Joseph Leidy, M.D., Professor of Anatomy in the University of Pennsylvania, &c. In one vol. imperial quarto, with 320 copper plate figures, plain and colored, extra cloth, $4.

GRAHAM (THOMAS). THE ELEMENTS OF INORGANIC CHEMISTRY, INCLUDING THE APPLICATION OF THE SCIENCE IN THE ARTS. A new and enlarged edition by H. Watts and Robert Bridges, M.D. In one 8vo. vol., of over 800 pages, with 232 woodcuts, extra cloth, $5 50.

GIBSON'S INSTITUTES AND PRACTICE OF SURGERY. In two 8vo. vols. of about 1000 pages, leather, $6 50.

GRAY (HENRY). ANATOMY, DESCRIPTIVE AND SURGICAL. A new American, from the fifth and enlarged London edition. In one large imperial 8vo. vol. of about 900 pages, with over 400 large and elaborate engravings on wood. Cloth, $6; leather, $7. (*Just issued.*)

GRIFFITH (ROBERT E.) A UNIVERSAL FORMULARY, CONTAINING THE METHODS OF PREPARING AND ADMINISTERING OFFICINAL AND OTHER MEDICINES. In one large 8vo. vol. of 650 pages, double columns, extra cloth, $4; leather, $5.

GUIZOT'S HISTORY OF OLIVER CROMWELL. In two royal 12mo. vols. Containing 900 pages. cloth, $2.

GROSS (SAMUEL D.) A SYSTEM OF SURGERY, PATHOLOGICAL, DIAGNOSTIC, THERAPEUTIC, AND OPERATIVE. Illustrated by over 1300 engravings. Fourth edition, revised and improved. In two large roya 18vo. vols. of 2200 pages, strongly bound in leather, raised bands. $15.

——— A PRACTICAL TREATISE ON FOREIGN BODIES IN THE AIR PASSAGES. In one 8vo. vol. of 468 pages. Extra cloth, $2 75.

——— ELEMENTS OF PATHOLOGICAL ANATOMY. Third edition. In one large 8vo. vol. of nearly 800 pages, with about 350 illustrations, extra cloth, $4.

GUERSANT (P.) SURGICAL DISEASES OF INFANTS AND CHILDREN. Translated by R. J. Dunglison, M. D. (*Publishing in the Med. News and Library for* 1871.)

HUDSON (A.) LECTURES ON THE STUDY OF FEVER. 1 vol. 8vo., 316 pages, cloth, $2 50.

HEATH (CHRISTOPHER). PRACTICAL ANATOMY; A MANUAL OF DISSECTIONS. With additions, by W. W. Keen, M. D. In 1 volume; with 247 illustrations. Cloth, $3 50; leather, $4. (*Now ready.*)

HARTSHORNE (HENRY). ESSENTIALS OF THE PRINCIPLES AND PRACTICE OF MEDICINE. Second and revised edition. In one 12mo. vol. of about 450 pages, cloth, $2 38; half bound, $2 63 (*Just issued.*)

—— CONSPECTUS OF THE MEDICAL SCIENCES. Comprising Manuals of Anatomy, Physiology, Chemistry, Materia Medica, Practice of Medicine, Surgery, and Obstetrics. In one royal 12mo. volume of over 1000 pages, with about 300 illustrations. Strongly bound in leather, $5 25; extra cloth, $4 50.

——MANUAL OF ANATOMY AND PHYSIOLOGY. One volume royal 12mo., cloth, $1 75.

HAMILTON (FRANK H.) A PRACTICAL TREATISE ON FRACTURES AND DISLOCATIONS. Third edition, revised. In one handsome 8vo. vol. of 777 pages, with 294 illustrations, extra cloth, $5 75.

HARRISON'S ESSAY TOWARD A CORRECT THEORY OF THE NERVOUS SYSTEM. In one vol. 8vo. of 292 pages, cloth, $1 50.

HOBLYN (RICHARD D.) A DICTIONARY OF THE TERMS USED IN MEDICINE AND THE COLLATERAL SCIENCES. In one 12mo. vol. of over 500 double columned pages, cloth, $1 50; leather, $2.

HODGE (HUGH L.) ON DISEASES PECULIAR TO WOMEN, INCLUDING DISPLACEMENTS OF THE UTERUS. Second and revised edition. In one 8vo. volume, cloth, $4 50.

—— THE PRINCIPLES AND PRACTICE OF OBSTETRICS. Illustrated with large lithographic plates containing 159 figures from original photographs, and with numerous wood-cuts. In one large quarto vol. of 550 double-columned pages. Strongly bound in extra cloth, $14.

HOLLAND (SIR HENRY). MEDICAL NOTES AND REFLECTIONS. From the third English edition. In one 8vo. vol. of about 500 pages, extra cloth, $3 50.

HODGES (RICHARD M.) PRACTICAL DISSECTIONS. Second edition. In one neat royal 12mo. vol., half bound, $2.

HUGHES' SCRIPTURE GEOGRAPHY AND HISTORY, with 12 colored maps. In 1 vol. 12mo., cloth, $1.

HORNER (WILLIAM E.). SPECIAL ANATOMY AND HISTOLOGY. Eighth edition, revised and modified. In two large 8vo. vols. of over 1000 pages, containing 300 wood-cuts, extra cloth, $6.

HILL (BERKELEY). SYPHILIS AND LOCAL CONTAGIOUS DISORDERS. In one 8vo. volume of 467 pages, extra cloth, $3 25.

HILLIER (THOMAS). HAND-BOOK OF SKIN DISEASES. Second Edition. In one neat royal 12mo. volume, about 300 pp., with two plates, cloth, $2 25.

HALL (MRS. M.) LIVES OF THE QUEENS OF ENGLAND BEFORE THE NORMAN CONQUEST. In one handsome 8vo. vol., cloth, $2 25; crimson cloth, $2 50; half morocco, $3.

JONES (C. HANDFIELD), AND SIEVEKING (E. D. H.) A MANUAL OF PATHOLOGICAL ANATOMY. In one large 8vo. vol. of nearly 750 pages, with 397 illustrations, extra cloth, $3 50.

JONES (C. HANDFIELD). CLINICAL OBSERVATIONS ON FUNCTIONAL NERVOUS DISORDERS. Second American Edition. In one 8vo. vol. of 348 pages, extra cloth, $3 25.

KIRKES (WILLIAM SENHOUSE). A MANUAL OF PHYSIOLOGY. From the third London edition, with 200 illustrations. In one large 12mo. vol. of 586 pages, cloth, $2 25; leather, $2 75.

KNAPP (F.) TECHNOLOGY; OR CHEMISTRY APPLIED TO THE ARTS AND TO MANUFACTURES, with American additions, by Prof. Walter R. Johnson. In two 8vo. vols., with 500 illustrations, cloth, $6.

KENNEDY'S MEMOIRS OF THE LIFE OF WILLIAM WIRT. In two vols. 12mo., cloth, $2.

LEA (HENRY C.) SUPERSTITION AND FORCE; ESSAYS ON THE WAGER OF LAW, THE WAGER OF BATTLE, THE ORDEAL, AND TORTURE. Second edition, revised. In one handsome royal 12mo. vol., $2 75. (*Lately issued.*)

——— STUDIES IN CHURCH HISTORY. The Rise of the Temporal Power—Benefit of Clergy—Excommunication. In one handsome 12mo. vol. of 515 pp., extra cloth, $2 75. (*Lately issued.*)

LALLEMAND (M.) AND WILSON (MARRIS). A PRACTICAL TREATISE ON THE CAUSES, SYMPTOMS, AND TREATMENT OF SPERMATORRHŒA. Translated and edited by Henry J. McDougall. Fifth American edition. To which is added———ON DISEASES OF THE VESICULÆ SEMINALES. With special reference to the Morbid Secretions of the Prostatic and Urethral Mucous Membrane. By Marris Wilson, M. D. In one neat octavo volume, of about 400 pages, extra cloth, $2 75.

LA ROCHE (R.) YELLOW FEVER IN ITS HISTORICAL, PATHOLOGICAL, ETIOLOGICAL, AND THERAPEUTICAL RELATIONS. In two 8vo. vols. of nearly 1500 pages, extra cloth, $7.

——— PNEUMONIA, ITS SUPPOSED CONNECTION, PATHOLOGICAL AND ETIOLOGICAL, WITH AUTUMNAL FEVERS. In one 8vo. vol. of 500 pages, extra cloth, $3.

LAURENCE (J. Z.) AND MOON (ROBERT C.) A HANDY-BOOK OF OPHTHALMIC SURGERY. Second edition, revised by Mr. Laurence. With numerous illustrations. In one 8vo. vol., extra cloth, $2 75.

LEHMANN (C. G.) PHYSIOLOGICAL CHEMISTRY. Translated by George F. Day, M. D., and edited by R. E. Rogers, M. D., Prof. of Chemistry, in the University of Pennsylvania. With plates, and nearly 200 illustrations. In two large 8vo. vols., containing 1200 pages, extra cloth, $6.

——— A MANUAL OF CHEMICAL PHYSIOLOGY. Translated with notes and additions, by J. Cheston Morris, M. D. With an Introductory Essay on Vital Force, by Prof. Samuel Jackson. In one very handsome 8vo. vol. of 336 pages, extra cloth, $2 25.

LAWSON (GEORGE). INJURIES OF THE EYE, ORBIT, AND EYELIDS, with about 100 illustrations. From the last English edition. In one handsome 8vo. vol., extra cloth, $3 50.

LUDLOW (J. L.) A MANUAL OF EXAMINATIONS UPON ANATOMY, PHYSIOLOGY, SURGERY, PRACTICE OF MEDICINE, OBSTETRICS, MATERIA MEDICA, CHEMISTRY, PHARMACY, AND THERAPEUTICS. To which is added a Medical Formulary. Third edition. In one royal 12mo. vol. of over 800 pages, extra cloth, $3 25; leather, $3 75.

LAYCOCK (THOMAS). LECTURES ON THE PRINCIPLES AND METHODS OF MEDICAL OBSERVATION AND RESEARCH. In one 12mo. vol., extra cloth, $1.

LYNCH (W. F.) A NARRATIVE OF THE UNITED STATES EXPEDITION TO THE DEAD SEA AND RIVER JORDAN. In one large and handsome octavo vol., with 28 beautiful plates and two maps, cloth, $3.

——— Same Work, condensed edition. One volume royal 12mo., extra cloth, $1.

LYONS (ROBERT D.) A TREATISE ON FEVER. In one neat 8vo. vol. of 362 pages, extra cloth, $2 25.

MARSHALL (JOHN). OUTLINES OF PHYSIOLOGY, HUMAN AND COMPARATIVE. With Additions by FRANCIS G. SMITH. M. D., Professor of the Institutes of Medicine in the University of Pennsylvania. In one 8vo. volume of 1026 pages, with 122 illustrations. Strongly bound in leather, raised bands, $7 50; extra cloth, $6 50.

MACLISE (JOSEPH). SURGICAL ANATOMY. In one large imperial quarto vol., with 68 splendid plates, beautifully colored; containing 190 figures, many of them life size, extra cloth, $14.

MACKENZIE (W.) A PRACTICAL TREATISE ON DISEASES AND INJURIES OF THE EYE. In one handsome 8vo. vol. of 1027 pages, with plates and numerous wood-cuts, extra cloth, $6 50.

MEIGS (CHAS. D.) OBSTETRICS, THE SCIENCE AND THE ART. Fifth edition, revised, with 130 illustrations. In one beautifully printed 8vo. vol. of 760 pages, extra cloth, $5 50; leather, $6 50.

——— WOMAN: HER DISEASES AND THEIR REMEDIES. Fourth and improved edition. In one large 8vo. vol. of over 700 pages, extra cloth, $5; leather, $6.

——— ON THE NATURE, SIGNS, AND TREATMENT OF CHILD-BED FEVER. In one 8vo. vol. of 365 pages, extra cloth, $2.

MILLER (JAMES). PRINCIPLES OF SURGERY. Fourth American, from the third Edinburgh edition. In one large 8vo. vol. of 700 pages, with 240 illustrations, extra cloth, $3 75.

——— THE PRACTICE OF SURGERY. Fourth American, from the last Edinburgh edition. In one large 8vo. vol. of 700 pages, with 364 illustrations, extra cloth, $3 75.

MONTGOMERY (W. F.) AN EXPOSITION OF THE SIGNS AND SYMPTOMS OF PREGNANCY. From the second English edition. In one handsome 8vo. vol. of nearly 600 pages, extra cloth, $3 75.

MORLAND (W. W.) DISEASES OF THE URINARY ORGANS. With illustrations. In one handsome 8vo. vol. of about 600 pages, extra cloth, $3 50.

MORLAND (W. W.) ON THE RETENTION IN THE BLOOD OF THE ELEMENTS OF THE URINARY SECRETION. In one vol. 8vo., extra cloth, 75 cents.

MULLER (J.) PRINCIPLES OF PHYSICS AND METEOROLOGY. In one large 8vo. vol. with 550 wood-cuts, and two colored plates, cloth, $4 50.

MIRABEAU; A LIFE HISTORY. In one royal 12mo. vol., cloth, 75 cents.

MACFARLAND'S TURKEY AND ITS DESTINY. In 2 vols. royal 12mo., cloth, $2.

MARSH (MRS.) A HISTORY OF THE PROTESTANT REFORMATION IN FRANCE. In 2 vols. royal 12mo., extra cloth, $2.

NEILL (JOHN) AND SMITH (FRANCIS G.) COMPENDIUM OF THE VARIOUS BRANCHES OF MEDICAL SCIENCE. In one handsome 12mo. vol. of about 1000 pages, with 374 wood-cuts, extra cloth, $4; leather, raised bands, $4 75.

NELIGAN (J. MOORE). A PRACTICAL TREATISE ON DISEASES OF THE SKIN. Fifth American, from the second Dublin edition. In one neat royal 12mo. vol. of 462 pages, extra cloth, $2 25.

——— AN ATLAS OF CUTANEOUS DISEASES. In one handsome quarto vol. with beautifully colored plates, &c., extra cloth, $5 50.

NIEBUHR (B. G.) LECTURES ON ANCIENT HISTORY; comprising the history of the Asiatic Nations, the Egyptians, Greeks, Macedonians, and Carthagenians. Translated by Dr. L. Schmitz. In three neat volumes, crown octavo, cloth, $5 00.

ODLING (WILLIAM). A COURSE OF PRACTICAL CHEMISTRY FOR THE USE OF MEDICAL STUDENTS. From the fourth revised London edition. In one 12mo. vol. of 261 pp., with 75 illustrations, extra cloth, $2. (*Lately issued.*)

PAVY (F. W.) A TREATISE ON THE FUNCTION OF DIGESTION: ITS DISORDERS AND THEIR TREATMENT. From the second London Ed. In one 8vo. vol. of 246 pp., ext. cl., $2. (*Lately issued.*)

PARRISH (EDWARD). A TREATISE ON PHARMACY. With many Formulæ and Prescriptions. Third edition. In one handsome 8vo. vol. of 850 pages, with several hundred illustrations, extra cloth, $5.

PIRRIE (WILLIAM). THE PRINCIPLES AND PRACTICE OF SURGERY. In one handsome octavo volume of 780 pages, with 316 illustrations, extra cloth, $3 75.

PEREIRA (JONATHAN). MATERIA MEDICA AND THERAPEUTICS. An abridged edition. With numerous additions and references to the United States Pharmacopœia. By Horatio C. Wood, M. D. In one large octavo volume, of 1040 pages, with 236 illustrations, extra cloth $7 00; leather, raised bands, $8 00.

PULSZKY'S MEMOIRS OF AN HUNGARIAN LADY. In one neat royal 12mo. vol., extra cloth, $1.

PAGET'S HUNGARY AND TRANSYLVANIA. In two royal 12mo. vols., cloth, $2.

ROBERTS (WILLIAM). A PRACTICAL TREATISE ON URINARY AND RENAL DISEASES. With numerous illustrations. In one very handsome 8vo. vol. (*New edition preparing.*)

RAMSBOTHAM (FRANCIS H.) THE PRINCIPLES AND PRACTICE OF OBSTETRIC MEDICINE AND SURGERY. In one imperial 8vo. vol. of 650 pages, with 64 plates, besides numerous woodcuts in the text. Strongly bound in leather $7.

RIGBY (EDWARD). THE CONSTITUTIONAL TREATMENT OF FEMALE DISEASES. In one neat royal 12mo. vol. of about 250 pp., extra cloth, $1.

——— A SYSTEM OF MIDWIFERY. Second American edition. In one handsome 8vo. vol. of 422 pages, extra cloth, $2 50.

RANKE'S HISTORY OF THE TURKISH AND SPANISH EMPIRES in the 16th and beginning of 17th Century. In one 8vo. volume, paper, 25 cts.

——— HISTORY OF THE REFORMATION IN GERMANY. Parts I. II. III. In one vol., extra cloth, $1.

ROYLE (J. FORBES). MATERIA MEDICA AND THERAPEUTICS. Edited by Jos. Carson, M. D. In one large 8vo. vol. of about 700 pages, with 98 illustrations, extra cloth, $3.

RADCLIFFE, AINSTIE, AND OTHERS. ON DISEASES OF THE SPINAL COLUMN AND OF THE NERVES. 1 vol. 8vo., extra cloth. $1 50. (*Just issued.*)

SMITH (EUSTACE). ON THE WASTING DISEASES OF CHILDREN. Second American edition, enlarged. In one 8vo. vol., extra cloth. $2 50. (*Just issued.*)

SARGENT (F. W.) ON BANDAGING AND OTHER OPERATIONS OF MINOR SURGERY. New edition, with an additional chapter on Military Surgery. In one handsome royal 12mo. vol. of nearly 400 pages, with 184 wood-cuts, extra cloth, $1 75.

SMITH (LEWIS J.) A TREATISE ON THE DISEASES OF INFANCY AND CHILDHOOD. A New Work, now ready. In one large 8vo. volume of 620 pages, strongly bound in leather, $5 75; extra cloth, $4 75.

SHARPEY (WILLIAM) AND QUAIN (JONES AND RICHARD). HUMAN ANATOMY. With notes and additions by Jos. Leidy, M. D., Prof. of Anatomy in the University of Pennsylvania. In two large 8vo. vols. of about 1300 pages, with 511 illustrations, extra cl. $6.

SIMPSON (SIR JAMES Y.) CLINICAL LECTURES ON THE DISEASES OF WOMEN. (A new edition preparing.)

SIMON'S GENERAL PATHOLOGY. In one 8vo. vol. of 212 pages extra cloth, $1 25.

SKEY (FREDERIC C.) OPERATIVE SURGERY. In one 8vo. vol. of over 650 pages, with about 100 wood-cuts, cloth, $3 25.

SLADE (D. D.) DIPHTHERIA; ITS NATURE AND TREATMENT. Second edition. In one neat royal 12mo. vol., extra cloth, $1 25.

SMITH (HENRY H.) AND HORNER (WILLIAM E.) ANATOMICAL ATLAS. Illustrative of the structure of the Human Body. In one large imperial 8vo. vol., with about 650 beautiful figures, extra cloth, $4 50.

SMITH (EDWARD). CONSUMPTION; ITS EARLY AND REMEDIABLE STAGES. In one 8vo. vol. of 254 pp., extra cloth, $2 25.

SOLLY (SAMUEL). THE HUMAN BRAIN; ITS STRUCTURE, PHYSIOLOGY, AND DISEASES. In one neat 8vo. vol. of 500 pp. with 120 wood-cuts, extra cloth, $2 50.

STILLE (ALFRED). THERAPEUTICS AND MATERIA MEDICA. Third edition, revised and enlarged. In two large and handsome 8vo. vols., extra cloth, $10; leather, $12.

SALTER (H. H.) ASTHMA; ITS PATHOLOGY, CAUSES, CONSEQUENCES, AND TREATMENT. In one volume 8vo., extra cloth, $2 50.

SWAYNE (JOSEPH GRIFFITHS). OBSTETRIC APHORISMS. From the fourth revised English edition. With additions by E. R. Hutchins, M. D. In one small 12mo. vol. of 177 pp., with illustrations, extra cloth, $1 25. (*Lately issued.*)

SCHOEDLER (FREDERICK) AND MEDLOCK (HENRY). WONDERS OF NATURE. An elementary introduction to the Sciences of Physics, Astronomy, Chemistry, Mineralogy, Geology, Botany, Zoology, and Physiology. Translated from the German by H. Medlock. In one neat 8vo. vol., with 679 illustrations, extra cloth, $3.

SMALL BOOKS ON GREAT SUBJECTS. Twelve works; each one 15 cents, sewed, forming a neat and cheap series; or done up in 3 vols., extra cloth, $1 50.

STRICKLAND (AGNES). LIVES OF THE QUEENS OF HENRY THE VIII. AND OF HIS MOTHER. In one crown octavo vol., extra cloth, $1; black cloth, 90 cents.

——MEMOIRS OF ELIZABETH, SECOND QUEEN REGNANT OF ENGLAND AND IRELAND. In one crown octavo vol., extra cloth, $1 40; black cloth, $1 30.

SCHMITZ AND ZUMPT'S CLASSICAL SERIES. In royal 18mo.
CORNELII NEPOTIS LIBER DE EXCELLENTIBUS DUCIBUS EXTERARUM GENTIUM, CUM VITIS CATONIS ET ATTICI. With notes, &c. Price in extra cloth, 60 cents; half bound, 70 cts.

C. I. CÆSARIS COMMENTARII DE BELLO GALLICO. With notes, map, and other illustrations. Price in extra cloth, 60 cents; half bound, 70 cents.

C. C. SALLUSTII DE BELLO CATILINARIO ET JUGURTHINO. With notes, map, &c. Price in extra cloth, 60 cents; half bound, 70 cents.

Q. CURTII RUFII DE GESTIS ALEXANDRI MAGNI LIBRI VIII. With notes, map, &c. Price in extra cloth, 80 cents; half bound, 90 cents.

P. VIRGILII MARONIS CARMINA OMNIA. Price in extra cloth, 85 cents; half bound, $1.

M. T. CICERONIS ORATIONES SELECTÆ XII. With notes, &c. Price in extra cloth, 70 cents; half bound, 80 cents.

ECLOGÆ EX Q. HORATII FLACCI POEMATIBUS. With notes, &c. Price in extra cloth, 70 cents; half bound, 80 cents.

ADVANCED LATIN EXERCISES, WITH SELECTIONS FOR READING. Revised, with additions. Extra cloth, price 60 cents; half bound, 70 cents.

TANNER (THOMAS HAWKES). A MANUAL OF CLINICAL MEDICINE AND PHYSICAL DIAGNOSIS. Third American from the second revised English edition. Edited by Tilbury Fox, M. D. In one handsome 12mo. vol. of 366 pp., cloth, $1 50. (*Lately published.*)

——— ON THE SIGNS AND DISEASES OF PREGNANCY. First American from the second English edition. With four colored plates and numerous illustrations on wood. In one vol. 8vo. of about 500 pages, extra cloth, $4 25.

TAYLOR (ALFRED S.) MEDICAL JURISPRUDENCE. Sixth American from the eighth London edition. With notes and references to American Decisions, by C. B. Penrose of the Philadelphia Bar. In one large 8vo. vol. of 776 pages, extra cloth, $4 50; leather, $5 50.

THOMAS (T. GAILLARD). A COMPLETE PRACTICAL TREATISE ON THE DISEASES OF FEMALES. Second and revised edition. In one large and handsome octavo volume of about 650 pages, with illustrations, extra cloth, $5; leather, $6. (*Lately published.*)

TODD (ROBERT B.) AND BOWMAN (W.) PHYSIOLOGICAL ANATOMY AND PHYSIOLOGY OF MAN. In one large 8vo. vol. of about 950 pages, with 300 illustrations on wood, extra cloth, $4 75.

TODD (ROBERT BENTLEY). CLINICAL LECTURES ON CERTAIN ACUTE DISEASES. In one vol. 8vo. of 320 pp., extra cloth, $2 50.

TOYNBEE (JOSEPH). THE DISEASES OF THE EAR: Their nature, Diagnosis, and Treatment. Second American edition. In one handsome 8vo. vol. of 440 pp., with 100 illustrations, extra cloth, $4.

THOMPSON (SIR HENRY). CLINICAL LECTURES ON DISEASES OF THE URINARY ORGANS. In one 8vo. volume of 204 pages, with illustrations, extra cloth, $2 25. (*Lately issued.*)

——— THE PATHOLOGY AND TREATMENT OF STRICTURE OF THE URETHRA AND URINARY FISTULÆ. From the third English edition. In one 8vo. vol. of 359 pp., with illustrations, extra cloth, $3 50. (*Lately issued.*)

WALSHE (W. H.) PRACTICAL TREATISE ON THE DISEASES OF THE HEART AND GREAT VESSELS. Third American from the third revised London edition. In one 8vo. vol. of 420 pages, extra cloth, $3.

WALES (PHILIP S.) MECHANICAL THERAPEUTICS: A Practical Treatise on Surgical Apparatus, Appliances, and Elementary Operations; embracing Minor Surgery, Bandaging, Orthopraxy, and Treatment of Fractures and Dislocations. In one large 8vo. vol. of about 700 pages, with 642 illustrations on wood, extra cloth, $5 75; leather, $6 75.

WELLS (J. SOELBERG). A TREATISE ON THE DISEASES OF THE EYE. Edited with additions by I. Minis Hays, M. D. In one large and handsome octavo vol. of 736 pp., with 6 colored plates and 216 wood-cuts, also selections from the test-types of Jaeger and Snellen, extra cloth, $5; leather, $6. (*Lately issued.*)

WHAT TO OBSERVE AT THE BEDSIDE AND AFTER DEATH IN MEDICAL CASES. In one royal 12mo. vol., extra cloth, $1.

WATSON (THOMAS). LECTURES ON THE PRINCIPLES AND PRACTICE OF PHYSIC. A new American from the last revised English edition, with additions by D. Francis Condie. With 185 illustrations on wood. In one very large volume imperial 8vo. of over 1200 pages, in small type, extra cloth, $6 50; strongly bound in leather, raised bands, $7 50.

WEST (CHARLES). LECTURES ON THE DISEASES PECULIAR TO WOMEN. Third American from the Third English edition. In one octavo volume of 550 pages, extra cloth, $3 75; leather, $4 75. (Now ready.)

—— LECTURES ON THE DISEASES OF INFANCY AND CHILDHOOD. Fourth American from the fifth revised English edition. In one large 8vo. vol. of 656 closely printed pages, extra cloth, $4 50; leather, $5 50.

—— AN ENQUIRY INTO THE PATHOLOGICAL IMPORTANCE OF ULCERATION OF THE OS UTERI. In one vol. 8vo., extra cloth, $1 25.

WILLIAMS (CHARLES J. B.) PRINCIPLES OF MEDICINE. A new American from the third revised London edition. In one 8vo. vol. of about 500 pages, extra cloth, $3 50.

WILSON (ERASMUS). A SYSTEM OF HUMAN ANATOMY. A new and revised American from the last English edition. Illustrated with 397 engravings on wood. In one handsome 8vo. vol. of over 600 pages, extra cloth, $4; leather, $5.

—— ON DISEASES OF THE SKIN. The seventh American from the last English edition. In one large 8vo. vol. of over 800 pages, extra cloth, $5.

Also A SERIES OF PLATES, illustrating "Wilson on Diseases of the Skin," consisting of 20 plates, thirteen of which are beautifully colored, representing about one hundred varieties of Disease. $5 50.

Also, the TEXT AND PLATES, bound in one volume, extra cloth, $10.

—— THE STUDENT'S BOOK OF CUTANEOUS MEDICINE. In one handsome royal 12mo. vol., extra cloth, $3 50.

WINSLOW (FORBES). ON OBSCURE DISEASES OF THE BRAIN AND DISORDERS OF THE MIND. In one handsome 8vo. vol. of nearly 600 pages, extra cloth, $4 25.